ANALYSIS OF FINANCIAL STATEMENTS: FINANCIAL ACCOUNTING AND THE CAPITAL MARKET

AMERICAN ACCOUNTING ASSOCIATION

The By-Laws of the American Accounting Association state that the first purpose of the Association shall be "to initiate, encourage, and sponsor research in accounting and to publish or aid in the publication of the results of research." In harmony with this objective, the publication of the Studies in Accounting Research is aimed at encouraging and publishing research. This series is an outgrowth of the research program initiated by the Association in 1965. Under this program research projects and authors are selected by the Director of Research, who is assisted by a Research Advisory Committee.

When the project is commissioned, the author is allowed maximum freedom in conducting research. The author is solely responsible for the procedures followed and the research conclusions.

This project was commissioned by Eugene E. Comiskey during his term as Director of Research. It was completed when Shyam Sunder was Director of Research. The Research Advisory Committee for this project consisted of:

Werner G. Frank	University of Wisconsin
Thomas L. Stober	University of Michigan
Mark Wolfson	Stanford University

ANALYSIS OF FINANCIAL STATEMENTS: FINANCIAL ACCOUNTING AND THE CAPITAL MARKET

by

Nicholas J. Gonedes
University of Pennsylvania

and

Nicholas Dopuch
Washington University

AMERICAN ACCOUNTING ASSOCIATION

1988

Library of Congress Catalog Card Number 88-082963
ISBN 0-86539-069-X
Printed in the United States of America

TABLE OF CONTENTS

ACKNOWLEDGEMENTS

We thank all those who wish to be thanked for helping us improve this monograph. A very special note of indebtedness is due to Tom Stober (University of Michigan) for his many remarks and suggestions.

CHAPTER ONE

Introduction and Overview of Issues

1.1 Preliminary Remarks

Why should anyone be interested in "financial statement analysis"? More generally, (1) why should anyone be interested in the kinds of inferences that can be made conditionally on sample evidence consisting of accounting numbers (perhaps among other things), and (2) what sort of inferences can be made via financial statement analysis? These are among the major questions considered in this monograph. In the end, we (hope to) provide a conceptual framework for financial statement analysis. This framework incorporates ideas from available analytical work (e.g., portfolio theory and asset-pricing theory) and insights based on available empirical work (primarily that dealing with accounting numbers). During the development of our framework, we shall use various perspectives, such as the perspective of a firm's management or its securityholders. For present purposes, we choose to use the perspective of firms' securityholders. For convenience, we stick to a single-period scenario. In the remainder of this introductory chapter, we shall identify some of the major topics that we consider.

1.2 Financial Statement Analysis and Information Production

In general, a security issued by a firm entitles the holder of that security to a future payoff (e.g., future value plus a dividend, if any, in the case of equity). The value of that payoff is now uncertain. That is, the value of that payoff can, in general, be described only in terms of its probability distribution (or characteristics thereof, such as its mean or variance). In order to make an optimal (or simply a "good") decision about a security's inclusion in or exclusion from one's portfolio, one implicity or explicity assesses the probability distribution of the security's payoff. This distribution is usually not a "given." Nor is it usually known with certainty. It is something about which inferences (forecasts) must be made. These inferences provide a foundation for making inferences about some determinants of expected utility—such as "risk" and "return" (however defined), and thus for making portfolio decisions. Various types of sample evidence might be used to make these inferences. Of particular interest to us is sample evidence consisting of observed values of accounting numbers.

Such inferential activities are costly—eg., they are time-consuming. Hence, in a general sense, such activities, and thus financial statement analysis, involve resource allocation decisions. They constitute one aspect of the more general process of "information production." As such, they involve the usual (and some novel) issues of costs and benefits. All of this is embedded in the task of making (or recommending) optimal portfolio decisions. In view of this, we begin our monograph, in Chapter Two, with a formal analysis of the role of information in an individual's consumption-investment problem (or his "portfolio" problem).

Of course, the costs and benefits of financial statement anaylsis are affected by the nature of the market for information. For example, the structure of the market for information determines, among other things, whether returns in excess of competitive returns can be expected on investments in information-production activities. Also relevant to financial statement analysis is the nature of the capital market, because the latter affects the manner in which securities' equilibrium values are established. And one aspect of financial statement analysis involves making inferences about securities' future values. In view of this, Chapter Three provides a discussion of relevant features of both the capital market and the market for information. As will be seen, the assumptions that one makes about these markets can have a critical effect on the theoretical benchmarks that are appropriate for financial statement analysis.

1.3 The Relevance of Accounting Numbers

Financial statement analysis involves, among other things, making inferences about the distribution functions of securities' future payoffs. In general, the distribution function of a security's payoff depends on the issuing firm's economic environment (broadly defined) and the decisions (actions) selected by the firm's management. But many attributes of both a firm's environment and its management's decisions are not directly observable. For example, we often cannot *separately* identify the effects of management's actions and the effects of exogenous ("environmental") variables on the observable outcomes (e.g., the quantity of output sold) experienced by a firm. In general, we usually use observables that are presumed to be influenced by a firm's environment and its management's actions in order to make inferences about the unobservables that are of ultimate interest (e.g., the distribution function of a firm's future value). Observed values of accounting numbers are among the observables that can be used for this purpose.

Accounting numbers are, because of their definitions, taken to be random variables whose probability distributions depend on a firm's economic environment and its management's decisions. Thus, observed values of accounting numbers are potentially informative vis-à-vis making inferences about the characteristics of a management's decisions. Such inferences provide, in turn, (1) bases for making inferences about the distribution function of a security's payoff and, thus, (2) relevant information for setting a security's current equilibrium value.

Chapters Four and Five develop some basic ideas about tools that can be used to produce implications about (and thus assess) probability distributions of securities' payoffs. In those chapters we exploit a theoretical model of asset pricing in order to provide a framework for the use of accounting numbers in making inferences about securities' payoffs.

1.4 Role of Asset-Pricing Models

Our motivation for casting our framework's details in terms of a specific asset pricing model is easily explained. Setting the equilibrium values of securities in a world of uncertainty involves more than assessing probability distributions of those securities' payoffs. It involves, in addition, specifying the attributes of those distributions (e.g., means, variances, medians, etc.) that are determinants of securities' equilibrium values. An asset pricing model constitutes such a specification and, therefore, provides substantial structure for making inferences conditionally on observed values of accounting numbers. Without such a model, one would not be able to directly link (1) assessed probability distributions of securities' payoffs and (2) securities' current equilibrium prices.

1.5 Remarks on Accounting Methods

We shall be concerned with accounting numbers because they can serve as informative sources of sample evidence, within the context of financial statement analysis. As would be the case with any other type of sample evidence that one considers using, we shall, therefore, be interested in the empirical properties of accounting numbers. This leads immediately to an interest in the effects of alternative accounting methods.

Ideally, we should like to make a direct inferential link between the inferred probability models of accounting numbers and the attributes of management's decisions, conditional on the economic environment. Inferences about the latter attributes could then be used to make inferences about the probability distributions of securities' payoffs.

But this sort of reasoning does not recognize that accounting procedures are also determinants of accounting numbers' probability models, along with the attributes of managerial decisions and the economic environment. Thus, before we can make an inferential link connecting probability models of accounting numbers to attributes of management's decisions, it seems necessary to account for the effects (if any) of accounting procedures. In order to do this, we shall consider the potential effects of different procedures on different firms' numbers as of a given time (cross-sectional effects) and the effects of different procedures on a given firm's numbers over time (time-series effects). Moreover, for reasons best explained later, we shall also have to say something about the effects of potential interactions between managements' decisions and accounting procedures. We shall attempt to make relevant statements about the direct and indirect effects of accounting procedures by exploiting empirical evidence pertinent to this issue along with whatever theoretical statements seem relevant. This is done in Chapter Six.

1.6 Relevance of Accounting Numbers' Empirical Properties

The inferential slant of our framework leads to a concern with the empirical properties of accounting numbers. As indicated earlier, we end up treating observed values of accounting numbers as a type of sample evidence. Making inferences based on such evidence involves applications of appropriate statistical tools (and various aspects of economic theory). But the appropriateness of alternative statistical tools depends on what one assumes or knows about the probability model that generated one's sample evidence. Inferences about this model can be based on the observed empirical properties of accounting numbers. By pursuing such inferences, one can reduce the likelihood of experiencing the adverse effects of gross model misspecification errors.

In Chapter Seven we focus directly on the empirical properties of accounting numbers. We deal with both available empirical results and statistical tools. This chapter emphasizes time-series analysis mainly for two reasons. First, the problems and tools associated with time-series analysis are likely to be less familiar to most readers—relative to the tools associated with cross-sectional analyses (e.g., running regressions on data for different firms as of a particular time period, such as a year). Second, results from some type of time-series analysis are likely to be among the most useful and frequently encountered in work on financial statement analysis.

1.7 Signaling Issues

The final chapter, Chapter Eight, deals with managements' influence on accounting numbers' observed values and some implications of this influence for financial statement analysis.

It is well known that firm's managements have some (and, often, substantial) latitude of choice regarding their firm's accounting techniques and disclosure rules. Thus, if managements perceive that investors use the properties of accounting numbers as bases for inferring distributions of securities' payoffs and, thus, as bases for setting securities values, then management may be motivated to behave as if they use accounting techniques and disclosure rules to alter firm's equilibrium values. And these alterations may or may not be justified by the substantive economic aspects of those firms activities. This sort of scenario leads to a so-called signaling perspective of external accounting, which explicitly recognizes that investors' inferential activities may affect managements' incentives regarding selections of accounting techniques and disclosure rules.

Chapter Eight gives a development of the signaling perspective, examines some of its implications for financial statement analysis, and reviews some available statistical tools and empirical evidence pertaining to this topic.

CHAPTER TWO

Optimal Consumption-Investment Decisions for an Individual and the Role of Information

2.1 Review of Salient Points

Earlier, we indicated that any security issued by a firm entitles the holder of that security to participate in a gamble, viz., the probability distribution of returns to the type of security held. In order to make an optimal (or simply a "good") decision about investing in a security, one must—implicity or explicity—assess the probability distribution of returns to the security. That assessed distribution provides a basis for making optimal consumption-investment decisions.

The indicated assessment process will have to recognize, in one way or another, that the probability distribution of returns to the holders of a firm's securities is dependent upon the firm's production/investment (or "operating") decisions and its financing decisions.[1] And, in general, one's assessed distribution of returns is dependent upon available information about those decisions.

The remainder of this chapter provides a formal statement of the role of information in the consumption-investment problem of an individual. There are at least three reasons for providing this perspective. The first, and most obvious, is that such a framework provides a basis for understanding and interpreting issues related to financial statement analysis, which is one type of information-production activity. Second, such a framework allows one to pinpoint the importance of the nature of the capital market to financial statement analysis. Third, the same framework permits identification of the importance of the market for information to financial statement analysis.

The emphasis of this section is on individual behavior. Issues pertaining to market equilibrium will be tackled in a later section.

Some of the material in Sections 2.2–2.4 is somewhat technical in nature. An informal discussion of the major points made in these sections is provided in Section 2.5. The reader who has difficulty with the technical material in Sections 2.2–2.4 should skim through those sections—in order to gain familiarity with our key assumptions and main lines of development—and then place greater emphasis on the informal discussion of Section 2.5.

We begin by providing a characterization of the market setting and agents' consumption-investment problem. This characterization incorporates assumptions about the capital market, among other things. At a later point in the chapter, we shall discuss the importance of some of these assumptions.

2.2 The Market Setting and Consumption-Investment Decisions

The capital market is assumed to be perfect, in that each agent can acquire as much of any asset that he wants without affecting its price; all assets are infinitely divisible; and there are no transactions costs or taxes. Also, any information that is currently in the public domain is costlessly available to everybody.

---

[1] As indicated earlier, this does not imply that the *total* value of the firm (or returns to the firm) is affected by financing decisions. Nor does it imply that an investor's total wealth is affected by those decisions.

Goods and services are produced by "firms." Firms purchase and pay for the services of their inputs at the beginning of each period, t. They use these services to produce goods and services that will be sold at the beginnings of future periods. At the beginning of period t, firms sell shares at their period $t + 1$ market value (which is a random variable at the beginning of period t) in order to finance their outlays at the beginning of period t. The shares sold by firms are the investment assets that consumers hold. Maximization of the current market value of the shares held by its current shareholders is the firm's goal. This is the so-called market value rule.

For the most part, we assume that each firm has only one kind of outstanding security (e.g., common stock). This does not affect the major points made here.

Consumer-investors are assumed to maximize the expected utility of lifetime consumption, $\underset{\sim}{c}_T = (c_0, c_1, \ldots, c_t, \ldots, c_T)$, where c_i, $i = 0, 1, \ldots, T$ denotes consumption at the beginning of period i, measured via some numeraire. For simplicity, we assume that the consumer-investor dies, with probability 1, at the beginning of period T; thus c_T is his bequest. The consumer-investor's preferences for lifetime consumption can be represented by a function $(V_T(\underset{\sim}{c}_T)$ that is nondecreasing and strictly concave in each component of $\underset{\sim}{c}_T$. Some additional notation is defined below. For brevity, the phrases "at period t" or "at time t" will often be used instead of the phrase "at the beginning of period t."

$\tilde{\Gamma}_\tau$ = the state of the world prevailing at time τ. (Throughout, tilde denotes a random variable.)

$R_j(\Gamma_\tau)$ = the rate of return on security j over the period $\tau - 1$ to τ when the state at time τ is Γ_τ.

$x_{j\tau}$ = the proportion of the consumer-investor's portfolio invested in security j at time τ; $\Sigma x_{j\tau} = 1$, for each τ.

$F(\Gamma_{\tau+1}|\Gamma_\tau)$ = the distribution function of ${}^j\tilde{\Gamma}_{\tau+1}$ conditional on $\tilde{\Gamma}_\tau = \Gamma_\tau$.

w_τ = the consumer-investor's wealth at time τ.

$\underset{\sim}{c}_\tau = (c_0, c_1, \ldots, c_t, \ldots, c_\tau)$.

M_τ = the number of securities available in the capital market at time τ.

Suppose that the beginning of period $t > 0$ is the "present." The consumer-investor's wealth at time $t + 1$ is given by:

$$\tilde{w}_{t+1} = \sum_{j=1}^{M_t} x_{jt}(w_t - c_t)(1 + R_j(\tilde{\Gamma}_{t+1})).$$

Using the backward-optimization approach of dynamic programming (see Bellman [1957, pp. 81–86]), the consumer-investor's problem at time t may be expressed as:

$$V_t(\underset{\sim}{c}_{t-1}, w_t|\Gamma_t) = \underset{\{c_t, \underset{\sim}{x}_t\}}{\underline{\max}} \int_{\Gamma_{t+1}} V_{t+1}(\underset{\sim}{c}_t, w_{t+1}|\Gamma_{t+1})dF(\Gamma_{t+1}|\Gamma_t)$$

$$\underline{\text{Subject to}}\ w_t \geq c_t \geq 0 \text{ and } \sum_j x_{jt} = 1,$$

for $t \leq T - 1$, where $\underset{\sim}{x}_{1t} = (\underset{\sim}{x}_{1t}, x_{2t}, \ldots, x_{M_t}t)$. $V_t(\underset{\sim}{c}_{t-1}, w_t|\Gamma_t)$, for $t \leq T$, is the consumer-investor's maximum expected utility of lifetime consumption conditional on the state, Γ_t, the consumer-investor's wealth, w_t, both at time t, the past consumption expenditures,

$\underset{\sim}{c}_{t-1}$. Note that $V_t(\underset{\sim}{c}_{t-1}, w_t|\Gamma_t)$, for $t < T$, is derived from $V_T(\underset{\sim}{c}_T)$, the consumer-investor's utility function defined on lifetime consumption. At time t, $\underset{\sim}{c}_{t-1}$ is known. Thus, for the given $\underset{\sim}{c}_{t-1}$, we may write:

$$U_t(c_t, w_{t+1}|\Gamma_{t+1}) = V_{t+1}(\underset{\sim}{c}_{t-1}, c_t, w_{t+1}|\Gamma_{t+1}).$$

Consequently, the consumer-investor's problem at time t may be re-expressed as:

$$\underline{\max}\ E\{U_t(c_t, \tilde{w}_{t+1}|\tilde{\Gamma}_{t+1})\}$$

$$\underline{\text{Subject to}}\ w_t \geq c_t \geq 0, \sum_j x_{jt} = 1,$$

where the maximization is with respect to $(c_t, \underset{\sim}{x}_t)$. In short, even though we are dealing with a multiperiod problem, the consumer-investor's preferences at the beginning of any period, say, period t, may be represented by the induced "one-period" utility function $U_t(c_t, w_{t+1}|\Gamma_{t+1})$. It can be shown that, given the properties of $V_T(\cdot)$, $U_t(\cdot)$ is nondecreasing and strictly concave in c_t and w_{t+1}; see Fama [1970]. In the remainder of this monograph, the consumer-investor's problem at the beginning of period t will be represented by the induced utility function $U_t(c_t, w_{t+1}|\Gamma_{t+1})$. Also, for added simplicity, we assume that preferences are not "state dependent." Thus, we consider the simplified induced utility function $U_t(c_t, w_{t+1})$. Remarks on state-dependent utility functions are provided by Fama [1970].

It is important for what follows to note that $E\{U_t, (c_t, \tilde{w}_{t+1})\}$ is conditional upon assessed distribution functions for returns in each period τ such that $T \geq \tau \geq t$. That is, as of t and for every firm j, the consumer-investor must assess a distribution function for the *vector* random variable $\tilde{\underset{\sim}{\pi}}_j = (\tilde{\pi}_{jt}, \tilde{\pi}_{jt+1}, \ldots, \tilde{\pi}_{jT})$, where $\pi_{j\tau}$, $\tau = t, t + 1, \ldots, T$, is the value of firm j at time τ. Given the current value of the firm, which is determined by the current price for each of the firm's shares, the assessed distribution function of $\tilde{\underset{\sim}{\pi}}_j$ can be used to derive an assessed distribution function for the vector of one-period rates of return $\tilde{\underset{\sim}{R}}_j = (\tilde{R}_{jt}, \tilde{R}_{jt+1}, \ldots, \tilde{R}_{jT})$.[2]

The behavior of consumers may now be summarized as follows. Consumers come to the market (at the beginning of each period t) with portfolios of assets (acquired in previous periods) and resources (e.g., labor, services) that may be sold to firms. The consumer needs to select a level of current consumption and a portfolio of assets whose value at the beginning of period $t + 1$ is the value of $\tilde{w}_{t+1}$. Consumers are assumed to behave in accordance with the rule of maximizing expected utility.

2.3 Representations of Information and Information-Production Opportunities

The major objective of this section is to present a precise analytical framework for representing the notion of "information" and the "production" of information conditional on parts of the market setting described in Section 2.2. An informal discussion covering the material in this section is provided in Section 2.5.

Consider the consumer-investor's problem at time t. In order to select an optimal

---

[2] If the firm has more than one type of security (e.g., bonds and stocks) outstanding, then the consumer-investor would have to assess the distribution function of returns to each type of security. This situation adds some complications—most of them notational—but it does not affect the points to be made here.

portfolio of investment assets at time t and an optimal level of period t consumption, c_t, the consumer-investor needs to assess the distribution function of $\tilde{\underline{R}}_j = (\tilde{R}_{jt}, \tilde{R}_{jt+1}, \ldots, \tilde{R}_{jT})$ for each firm j whose ownership shares are traded in the capital market at time t. Of course, each consumer-investor wants his assessed distribution functions to be identical to the "underlying" or "true" distributions of returns, since realized returns will be drawn from the latter distributions.[3] But we shall not assume that this identity holds. Instead, we permit differences between assessed and "true" distributions of returns and use these differences in characterizing the information-production process.[4] Unless otherwise indicated, the following discussion applies to any one capital market agent. This enables us to avoid excessive use of subscripting to distinguish among capital market agents. The same approach is used in the next section.

The production of new information will be envisaged as an interaction with Nature. Information produced will be treated as a completely reliable signal from Nature pertaining to the "true" or "underlying" distribution functions of returns on assets traded in the capital market. That is, for any given firm, information produced is about the distribution function of returns to holders of that firm's securities.

As with the production of other goods and services, the production of information to be used at time $\tau + 1$, for any τ, must be initiated at time τ. For our purposes, it will be sufficient to consider the production of information to be used at the beginning of one period, $t + 1$ will not be permitted.

At time $t + 1$, two sets of information are available to capital market agents: (1) newly produced signals associated with information-production decisions made at time t, and (2) all information that is available to capital market agents when they come to the market at $t + 1$ but which is not associated with agents' periods t information-production decisions. We often refer to the second type as the initially available information. This kind of information may be associated, for example, with information-production decisions made prior to time t.

---

[3]In other words, this identity never leads to lower maximum expected utility, if attaining the identity is costless. Consider the following example. Suppose that only one kind of asset is traded in the capital market and that we are dealing with a one-period model. Further suppose that some investor is convinced that the distribution function to be used by Nature will be either F_1, F_2, or F_3. From this investor's perspective, Nature will first pick a distribution function and then draw a rate of return from this distribution function. If the investor must make his consumption-investment decision before the distribution function selected by Nature is revealed, then his consumption-investment decision is constrained to be identical for F_1, F_2, and F_3. If, however, he can arrange (at no cost) to receive the realization of a completely reliable signal, say $\tilde{\Theta}$, such that (a) $\tilde{\Theta} = 1$ if Nature chooses either F_1 or F_2 and $\tilde{\Theta} = 0$ if Nature chooses F_3, and (b) the realization of $\tilde{\Theta}$ will be available *before* he must make his consumption-investment decision, then his consumption-investment problem will be *less constrained*. This is because his decision, in the latter situation, is constrained to be the same for F_1 and F_2, but not for F_3. Consequently, maximum expected utility in the second situation is no less than that in the first ("no information") situation. In short, so long as the cost of doing so is zero, the investor will be motivated to develop schemes for determining Nature's (i.e., the "true") distribution function of returns.

[4]The notion of a "true" distribution is, of course, an analytical device. It is simply a label for the distribution that will ultimately be used by Nature in determining the realized rates of return on assets. Capital market agents need not agree on these distributions.

The essence of the signal received from Nature can be explained as follows. We represent attributes of the economic environment by scalar random variables. The information-production process will involve selecting (1) an attribute and (2) the system which determines what aspects of that attribute will be made known to an agent by Nature. That which is made known to the agent constitutes the *signal* from Nature. Different signals will pertain to different attributes of the economic environment. Signals pertaining to combinations of attributes will also be considered.

Suppose, for example, that the scalar random variable $\tilde{\Theta}$ denotes some attribute of the economic environment. A tilde appears above Θ because before the information-production process is completed, the attribute's value, which will be selected by Nature, is a random variable. Let Ω_i, $i = 1, 2, \ldots, N$ be a partitioning of the possible values of $\tilde{\Theta}$ into N mutually exclusive and exhaustive sets. Suppose that the signal from Nature is $\tilde{\Theta} \in \Omega_i$, for some i. In this case, it is assumed that for any firm j, $j = 1, 2, \ldots, f$, the implied distribution function for the vector of rates of return, $\tilde{\underline{R}}_j$, on the jth firm's shares is $F_j(\underline{R}_j|\Omega_i)$. (The implied distribution for different firms' shares are not assumed to be identical.) The initially available information is that $\tilde{\Theta} \in \Omega_0 = \cup_{i=1}^{N} \Omega_i$. Thus, if the signal from Nature is $\tilde{\Theta} \in \Omega_0$, then this information is not "new," in the sense that it does not have implications different from those implied by the information available when agents first come to the market.

Suppose (for simplicity) that $\tilde{\Theta}$ is a discrete random variable. Then the distribution function of $\tilde{\underline{R}}_j$ would be the marginal distribution function $F_j(\underline{R}_j|\Omega_0) = \Sigma_{i=1}^{N} F_j(\underline{R}_j|\Omega_j)Pr(\tilde{\Theta} \in \Omega_i)$, if no signal from Nature were received. Note that $F_j(\underline{R}_j|\Omega_i) = \Sigma_{\Theta \in \Omega_i} F_j(\underline{R}_j|\Theta)Pr(\tilde{\Theta} = \Theta|\tilde{\Theta} \in \Omega_i)$, for $i = 0, 1, 2, \ldots, N$. Thus, if the completely reliable signal from Nature were the scalar-valued realization, say, $\tilde{\Theta} = \Theta$, then one would know the exact distribution from which the realization of $\tilde{\underline{R}}_j$ will be drawn. When the signal from Nature is the set-realization, say, $\tilde{\Theta} \in \Omega_i$, then (in general) one only knows that the value of $\tilde{\underline{R}}_j$ will be drawn from one member of the set of distributions, $F_j(\underline{R}_j|\Theta)$ for $\Theta \in \Omega_i$.

Signals pertaining to combinations of attributes are easily handled by considering vectors $\tilde{\underline{\Theta}} = (\tilde{\Theta}_1, \tilde{\Theta}_2, \ldots, \tilde{\Theta}_\ell)$ where $\tilde{\Theta}_i$ denotes the ith attribute. Let $\underline{\Omega}^k = (\Omega_1^k, \Omega_2^k, \ldots, \Omega_{\bar{N}}^k)$ be the partition for the kth attribute; for each k, Ω_i^k, $i = 1, 2, \ldots, \bar{N}$, are mutually exclusive and $Pr(\tilde{\Theta}_k \in \cup_i \Omega_i^k) = 1$. For simplicity, we assume that the same value of $\bar{N}$ applies to all attributes. The sample space for all ℓ attributes is $X_{k=1}^{\ell} \underline{\Omega}^k$, where X denotes Cartesian product. The initially available information on the kth attribute is that $\tilde{\Theta}_k \in \Omega_0^k = \cup_{i=1}^{\bar{N}} \Omega_i^k$. We assume that there exist producers of signals pertaining to any combination of the ℓ economic attributes. Thus, consumer-investors may contemplate purchasing observations pertaining to any of 2^ℓ vectors $\tilde{\underline{\Theta}}_j$, $j = 1, 2, \ldots, 2^\ell$, where $\tilde{\underline{\Theta}}_j$ denotes the jth combination of attributes.[5] We assume that the possible realizations of $\tilde{\underline{\Theta}}_j$, for each j, may be partitioned into N exhaustive and mutually exclusive subsets, $\underline{S}_1^j, \underline{S}_2^j, \ldots, \underline{S}_N^j$. If the signal received is $\tilde{\underline{\Theta}}_j \in \underline{S}_i^j$, for some i, then the implied distribution of returns on the mth firm's shares is $F_m(\underline{R}_m|\underline{S}_i^j)$. For each i, the dimensionality of $\underline{S}_i^j$ equals j, for all $j = 1, 2, \ldots, 2^\ell$. The initially available information on the jth combination of attributes is that $\tilde{\underline{\Theta}}_j \in \underline{S}_0^j = \cup_{i=1}^{N} \underline{S}_i^j$.

The information conveyed by the realization $\tilde{\underline{\Theta}}_j \in \underline{S}_i^j$, for some j and $i \neq 0$, is said

---

[5]Note that an individual may be both a producer of information and a consumer-investor.

to have an *effect* if, for some firm s, $F_s(\underset{\sim}{R}_s|\underset{\sim}{S}^j_i) \neq F_s(\underset{\sim}{R}_s|\underset{\sim}{S}^j_0)$. That is, new information has an effect if it induces a change in an agent's assessed distribution functions.

Note that we made no assumptions on the agreement among agent's assessments. In particular, we did not (and will not) assume that agents agree on the distributions of returns implied by a realization of any signal. Finally, note that an opportunity to invest in a signal on a specific combination of attributes using a specified partition defines one opportunity to produce information.

The production function of each producer of information (viewed from the perspective of an individual consumer-investor) still needs to be characterized. We assume that the (known) production function of one who produces information is such that different levels of production costs induce different sample-space partitions defining the signal produced. In effect, each partition represents a different experiment; the signal from Nature is the outcome of the experiment.

We assume that each producer of a signal pertaining to a given combination of attributes $\tilde{\underset{\sim}{\Theta}}_j$, $j = 1, 2, \ldots, 2^\ell$, can produce any of a finite number of partitions, $\{\underset{\sim}{S}^j_{ik}; i = 1, 2, \ldots, N_k\}$, $k = 1, 2, \ldots, n_j$, for the jth attribute, where n_j is the total number of alternative partitions that can be produced for attribute j.

2.4 Gains from Information-Production

The major objective of this section is to provide details on the way in which opportunities to purchase information affect maximum expected utility of lifetime consumption. The framework given here leads to a precise analytical representation for the *gains* to be had from purchasing information. The characterizations provided in this section are conditional on the setting described in Section 2.2 and the representations given in Section 2.3. An informal discussion covering the material provided in this section is provided in Section 2.5.

Recall from the derivation of $U_t(c_t, w_{t+1})$, the consumer's induced one-period utility function, that $U_t(c_t, w_{t+1}) \equiv V_{t+1}(\underset{\sim}{c}_{t-1}, c_t, w_{t+1})$. Thus:

$$U_t(c_t, w_{t+1}) = \max_{\{c_{t+1}, \underset{\sim}{x}_{t+1}\}} \int_{\Gamma_{t+2}} V_{t+2}(\underset{\sim}{c}_{t+1}, w_{t+2}) dF(\Gamma_{t+2}|\Gamma_{t+1}) \tag{2.1}$$

where $\tilde{w}_{t+2} = \Sigma_j x_{jt+1}(w_{t+1} - c_{t+1})(1 + R_j(\tilde{\Gamma}_{t+2}))$. Thus $U_t(c_t, w_{t+1})$ is the value of maximum expected utility at the beginning of $t+1$, conditional on c_t and the realization $\tilde{w}_{t+1} = w_{t+1}$. As indicated earlier, the decisions made by any consumer-investor at the beginning of any period are also conditional upon the initially available information at the beginning of that period. Let $\underset{\sim}{S}^I$ denote the information that is publicly available at the beginning of period $t + 1$. Note that $\underset{\sim}{S}^I = \{\underset{\sim}{S}^j_{ok}; k = 1, 2, \ldots, n_j; j = 1, 2, \ldots, 2^\ell\}$. That is, if for any attribute j and partition k one observes $\tilde{\underset{\sim}{\Theta}}_j \in \underset{\sim}{S}^j_{ok}$, then this realization provides no new information at time $t + 1$.

The dependence of $U_t(c_t, w_{t+1})$ on $\underset{\sim}{S}^I$, $\underset{\sim}{x}_{t+1}$, and w_{t+1} will be recognized by writing:

$$U_t(c_t, w_{t+1}) = E[U_{t+1}(c^o_{t+1}, \tilde{w}_{t+2})|\underset{\sim}{x}^o_{t+1}, \underset{\sim}{S}^I, w_{t+1}],$$

where $(c^o_{t+1}, \underset{\sim}{x}^o_{t+1})$ is the optimal value of $(c_{t+1}, \underset{\sim}{x}_{t+1})$ at the beginning of period $t + 1$.

Suppose that the consumer-investor receives, at time $t + 1$, a costless drawing based on the kth partition, $\{\underset{\sim}{S}^j_{ik}; i = 1, 2, \ldots, N_k\}$ for some j. If the realization is $\tilde{\underset{\sim}{\Theta}}_j \in \underset{\sim}{S}^j_{ik}$, for specified i, then the maximum expected utility that can be had by using this information is:

$$E\{U_{t+1}\,(c^{jk}_{it+1},\,\tilde{w}_{t+2})|w_{t+1},\,\underset{\sim}{x}^{jk}_{it+1},\,\underset{\sim}{S}^{j}_{ik},\,\underset{\sim}{S}^{l}\},$$

where $(c^{jk}_{it+1}, \underset{\sim}{x}^{jk}_{it+1})$ is the optimal consumption-investment decision conditional on the signal $\underset{\sim}{\tilde{\Theta}}_j \in \underset{\sim}{S}^j_{ik}$. Since (by assumption) this signal is a completely reliable message "from Nature" about the actual distribution functions of $\underset{\sim}{\tilde{R}}_h$, for all h:

$$E\{U_{t+1}\,(c^{jk}_{it+1},\,\tilde{w}_{t+2})|w_{t+1},\,\underset{\sim}{x}^{jk}_{it+1},\,\underset{\sim}{S}^{j}_{ik},\,\underset{\sim}{S}^{l}\} \geq E\{U_{t+1}\,(c^{o}_{t+1},\,\tilde{w}_{t+2})|\underset{\sim}{x}^{o}_{t+1},\,w_{t+1},\,\underset{\sim}{S}^{l}\}.$$

Next, consider the case where information is not costless. Suppose that the consumer must pay an amount at $t + 1$ equal to K for a signal on $\underset{\sim}{\tilde{\Theta}}_j$; using partition k. Let:

$$\phi_{t+1}\,(K,\,\underset{\sim}{S}^j_{ik}) = \max_{\{c_{t+1},\underset{\sim}{x}_{t+1}\}} E\{U_{t+1}\,(c_{t+1},\,\tilde{w}_{t+2})|w_{t+1} - K,\,\underset{\sim}{x}_{t+1},\,\underset{\sim}{S}^j_{ik},\,\underset{\sim}{S}^l\} \tag{2.2}$$

and:

$$W_{t+1}\,(\underset{\sim}{S}^j_{ik},\,\underset{\sim}{S}^l) = E\{U_{t+1}\,(c^o_{t+1},\,\tilde{w}_{t+2})|w_{t+1},\,\underset{\sim}{x}^o_{t+1},\,\underset{\sim}{S}^j_{ik},\,\underset{\sim}{S}^l\}. \tag{2.3}$$

Consider $E\{\tilde{W}_{t+1}\,(\underset{\sim}{S}^j_{ik}, \underset{\sim}{S}^l)\}$, where the expectation is taken with respect to the distribution function of the signal on $\underset{\sim}{\tilde{\Theta}}_j$ using partition k. From the definition of $(c^o_{t+1}, \underset{\sim}{x}^o_{t+1})$, $E\{\tilde{W}(\underset{\sim}{S}^j_{ik}, \underset{\sim}{S}^l)\} = E\{U_{t+1}(c^o_{t+1}, \tilde{w}_{t+2})|w_{t+1}, \underset{\sim}{x}^o_{t+1}, \underset{\sim}{S}^l\}$, the maximum expected utility when no signal on any attribute is purchased before the consumer must make his optimal consumption-investment decision at the beginning of period $t + 1$. Thus, $\phi_{t+1}(0, \underset{\sim}{S}^l) = E\{\tilde{W}(\underset{\sim}{S}^j_{ik}, \underset{\sim}{S}^l)\}$.

Before the signal about $\underset{\sim}{\tilde{\Theta}}_j$ is observed, the consumer-investor simply owns a gamble on the signal. The outcome of this gamble will be available at $t + 1$ before the process of making optimal consumption-investment decisions at $t + 1$ ends. Letting $\pi^j_{ik} = Pr(\underset{\sim}{\tilde{\Theta}}_j, \in \underset{\sim}{S}^j_{ik})$, for $i = 1, 2, \ldots, N_k$, for given k and j, the maximum expected utility of this gamble at $t + 1$ for $K = 0$ is:

$$E\{\tilde{\phi}_{t+1}(0,\,\underset{\sim}{S}^j_{ik})\} = \sum_i \left[\max_{\{c_{t+1},\underset{\sim}{x}_{t+1}\}} E\{U_{t+1}(c_{t+1},\,\tilde{w}_{t+2})|w_{t+1},\,\underset{\sim}{x}_{t+1},\,\underset{\sim}{S}^j_{ik},\,\underset{\sim}{S}^l\}\right]\pi^j_{ik}. \tag{2.4}$$

If no signal (and thus no gamble) is purchased, the maximum expected utility outcome is $\phi_{t+1}(0, \underset{\sim}{S}^l)$.

It can be shown that $\phi_{t+1}(K, \underset{\sim}{S}^j_{ik})$ is a nonincreasing concave function of K.[6] This implies that $E\{\tilde{\phi}_{t+1}\,(K, \underset{\sim}{S}^j_{ik})\}$ is a nonincreasing concave function of K. Thus, there exists a value $K'' \geq 0$ such that $E\{\phi_{t+1}(K'', \underset{\sim}{S}^j_{ik})\} = \tilde{\phi}_{t+1}\,(0, \underset{\sim}{S}^l)$ and $E\tilde{\phi}_{t+1}(K, \underset{\sim}{S}^j_{ik})\} \geq \phi_{t+1}\,(0, \underset{\sim}{S}^l)$ for $K \leq K''$. All of this says that the consumer-investor gains nothing in terms of maximum expected utility if the cost of the gamble on the signal about $\underset{\sim}{\tilde{\Theta}}_j$ is K''; he gains (loses) if this cost is less (greater) than K''. This suggests that one may measure the consumer-investor's *gain* (or net payoff), at time $t + 1$, from purchasing information by the difference between K'' and the amount that he must actually pay for the gamble on the signal about $\underset{\sim}{\tilde{\Theta}}_j$, for any j.

An information-production opportunity is said to be more *desirable* than another if the gain from the first opportunity exceeds that from the second. "Indifference" and "less desirable" can be expressed in terms of these gains in obvious ways.

---

[6]See Luenberger [1969, p. 261]. This result may be more visible if the consumer-investor's maximization problem is formulated in terms of the amounts invested in different securities rather than the proportions of his portfolio invested in each security.

In the above, we assumed that the realized value of the purchased signal is available and is used at the beginning of period $t + 1$ and that payment for the opportunity to receive and use a realization of any signal is made at the beginning of $t + 1$. It is a small matter, however, to consider the same setting but with the payment (for the signal) being made at the beginning of period t.

If payment for the signal (the realization of which is still available for use at $t + 1$) is made at time t, then the induced one-period utility function applicable at the beginning of period t is $U_t(c_t, w_{t+1}) = E\{\tilde{\phi}_{t+1}(0, \underset{\sim}{S}^j_{ik})\}$, for the purchase of a signal on attribute j using partition k. Suppose that an amount equal to L must be paid at time t for this drawing. Then at time t, the consumer-investor's problem is:

$$\underset{\{c_t, \underset{\sim}{x}_t\}}{\underline{\max}}\ E\{U_t\,(c_t, \tilde{w}_{t+1})\} \tag{2.5}$$

$$\underline{\text{subject to}}\ (w_t - L) \geq c_t \geq 0$$

$$\sum_j x_{jt} = 1$$

where $\tilde{w}_{t+1} = \Sigma_j\ x_{jt}\ (w_t - L - c_t)(1 + \tilde{R}_{jt})$. Just as $E\{\tilde{\phi}_{t+1}\ (K, \underset{\sim}{S}^j_{ik})\}$ is a nonincreasing concave function of K, $\underline{\max}_{\{c_t, \underset{\sim}{x}_t\}}\ E\{U_t\ (c_t, \tilde{w}_{t+1})\}$ is a nonincreasing concave function of L. This result follows from the fact that the payment of $L > 0$ at time t reduces every possible realization of $\tilde{w}_{t+1}$. The payment of $K > 0$ at time $t + 1$ also reduced the value of whatever realization of $\tilde{w}_{t+1}$ happened to be observed at time $t + 1$. Since both payments have the same effect on the ultimate realization of $\tilde{w}_{t+1}$, they affect maximum expected utility at time $t + 1$ in the same way. And since $E\{U_t(c_t, \tilde{w}_{t+1})\}$ is a positive linear combination of maximum expected utility at time $t + 1$, it is affected in the same way by K and L.

It will be helpful, for what follows, to have an alternative way of characterizing the effects of purchasing information (i.e., drawings on signals). The alternative provided here is expressed in terms of *simple* and *compound* lotteries. (Such lotteries or "gambles" are discussed in, e.g., Luce and Raiffa [1957, p. 26] and LaValle [1970, pp. 401–3].)

Suppose that the consumer-investor is now at the beginning of period t and that he decides not to purchase drawings on any signals. When the consumer-investor solves his multiperiod consumption-investment problem, he ends up with an optimal decision rule that defines the optimal consumption-investment decision for each period conditional upon the realization of wealth in the predecessor period and the predecessor period's consumption decision. At the beginning of period t, the investor can derive his conditional distribution function of wealth for any period $\tau > t$. The conditioning arguments of this distribution function are the optimal decision rule, $\underset{\sim}{c}_{t-1}$, w_t, and the investor's assessed distribution functions of rates of return of firms' ownership shares. Consider the derived conditional distribution function of $\tilde{w}_{t+2}$, denoted by $G(w_{t+2})$; for simplicity, the aforementioned conditioning arguments will be left as implicit arguments of $G(\cdot)$.

Now suppose that the investor purchase the right to receive a signal on attribute j from partition k. This drawing will be available for use at the beginning of period $t + 1$ (as in our earlier analysis). Also suppose that the investor must pay an amount equal to L for this drawing, and the payment must be made at the beginning of period t. As indicated earlier, when the consumer-investor purchases such a right, his optimal decision at time $t + 1$ is conditional on the realization of the signal and L, as well as past realizations of wealth and past consumption. That is, the investor's decision rule for $t + 1$ now has two additional arguments: the value of the payment L and the realization of the signal. Note that the value of L affects the realized value of $\tilde{w}_{t+1}$, which is an argument of the optimal decision rule in the no-information case. Once again, for each realization of the signal about $\tilde{\Theta}_j$ and for the stated value of L, the investor can derive, at time t, the distribution function of $\tilde{w}_{t+2}$ conditional on c_{t-1}, w_t, L, the realization of the signal about $\tilde{\Theta}_j$, and his associated optimal decision rule. Consider the case of $\tilde{\Theta}_j \in S^j_{ik}$, for some value of i. Denote the corresponding conditional distribution function of $\tilde{w}_{t+2}$, constructed at time t, by $F(w_{t+2}|S^j_{ik}, L)$. As of time t, however, this is not the distribution of $\tilde{w}_{t+2}$ that the investor faces. Since there is one such conditional distribution for each value of i, the distribution that the investor will ultimately face at $t + 1$ will be determined by a random selection device. Thus, at time t, the conditional distribution of $\tilde{w}_{t+2}$ faced by the investor is:

$$F^*(w_{t+2}|L) = E[\tilde{F}(w_{t+2}|S^j_{ik}, L)] = \sum_i F(w_{t+2}|S^j_{ik}, L)Pr(\tilde{\Theta}_j \in S^j_{ik}).$$

In short, relative to the no-purchase-of-information case, the consumer-investor is now dealing with a compound gamble. The first part of the gamble involves a signal about $\tilde{\Theta}_j$ from partition k. The second part of the gamble involves a drawing on $\tilde{w}_{t+2}$, with distribution function $F(w_{t+2}|S^j_{ik}, L)$ if $\tilde{\Theta}_j \in S^j_{ik}$. The ultimate outcome of this compound gamble can be described, as of the beginning of period t, by the distribution function $F^*(w_{t+2}|L)$. Thus, the consumer-investor will decide to purchase, at t, the signal about j from partition k (where the observed signal becomes available at $t + 1$) if, at time t, the distribution function $F^*(w_{t+2}|L)$ induces higher expected utility than the distribution function $G(w_{t+2})$. In the special case where, for a given value of L, $F^*(w_{t+2}|L)$ and $G(w_{t+2})$ are identical distribution functions, the consumer-investor would be indifferent toward purchasing or not purchasing a signal about $\tilde{\Theta}_j$ from partition k.

The value of L, for a given consumer-investor, will be referred to as the *price* paid by that consumer-investor for the results of information production.

At this point, the procedure to be followed by a consumer-investor in optimally selecting an information-production opportunity should be clear. Given the values of L for the various information-production opportunities, the consumer-investor selects the composite gamble that induces maximum expected utility of lifetime consumption. This is equivalent to solving the problem in (2.5) for each combination of attributes, $\tilde{\Theta}_j$, $j = 1, 2, \ldots, 2^\ell$, and each partition applicable to that combination of attributes. In the constraints of problem 2.5, there will, in general, be a different value of L for each attribute/partition pair. The repeated solving of (2.5) leads to a value of maximum expected utility for each attribute/partition pair. The attribute/partition pair that is associated with the highest value of those maxima defines the optimal information-production decision. That is, that attribute/production pair induces highest expected utility of lifetime consumption when one's decision variables pertain to portfolio proportions, consumption expenditures, and information-production opportunities.

2.5 Informal Discussion of Information, Information-Production, and the Gains from Information-Production

Perhaps the key to understanding the role of information in making consumption-investment decisions is to recognize that, in our world, the consumer-investor is selecting gambles that define the consumer-investor's distribution function of wealth for each future period. In the absence of opportunities to produce or purchase information, the consumer-investor can select from among the gambles defined by the assessed distribution functions of returns. The outcome of this gamble at, say, period t determines the consumer-investor's wealth at period t. The consumer's wealth at period t defines his budget constraint at period t. Thus, the consumer's wealth at period t is a determinant of his period t consumption expenditures and the amount of wealth that can be used to purchase gambles whose outcomes will be known in future periods. The objective pursued by the consumer in selecting consumption expenditures and gambles at any point in time is to arrange for the "best" pattern of lifetime consumption expenditures. Here the "best" pattern is the one that maximizes the consumer's expected utility of lifetime consumption. At any point in time, the consumer-investor must pay a price for any gamble that he might want. Insofar as the securities issued by firms are concerned, the price of any such gamble is the prevailing market price of the security that defines the gamble. In short, there is no free lunch. If the consumer-investor wants to acquire the right to participate in a gamble—because doing so induces the maximum expected utility of lifetime consumption—then he must pay for that right, given the assumed nature of the capital market.

Information-production opportunities, as characterized here, simply represent additional types of gambles. The outcomes of these additional gambles pertain to (i.e., "say something about") the distributions of returns corresponding to the elementary gambles represented by firm's outstanding securities. In our framework, these outcomes are treated as—in picturesque terms—completely reliable signals from Nature about the "true" or "underlying" distribution functions of returns on assets traded in the capital market. Since each consumer-investor's expected utility is increased by new information (conveyed via the signals) about "true" distributions of securities' returns, rights to receive and use such information are valuable. But acquiring or producing those rights requires payment, in the framework provided above. There is, again, no free lunch. Moreover, the outcome of an investment in information-production is uncertain, as in the outcome of any other production activity. At the time resources are committed to information-production, one does not know what the signal (i.e., the outcome) will be. At that time, one can only describe the results of information-production in terms of the distribution function of outcomes. Thus, the opportunity to produce (or purchase) information is really another kind of gamble.

We assume that the results of information-production activities initiated at time t will be available for use when consumption-investment decisions are made at time $t + 1$. This assumption applies to all values of t. Since the results of information-production will be available when optimal consumption-investment decisions have to be made, those decisions can be conditioned upon the results of information-production. The scenario is as follows. Optimal consumption-investment decisions depend on the assessed distribution functions of returns on shares and the consumer-investor's wealth. If, at time $t + 1$, the consumer-investor expects to use the results of information-production initiated at time t, then the assessed distribution to be used at time $t + 1$ is a random variable. That is, there is a different assessed distribution for each outcome of information-production. And the outcome of information-production is, at time t, a random variable. Thus, at time t, when the consumer-investor is looking forward to time $t + 1$, he must design a strategy (i.e., a plan of action for time $t + 1$) that incorporates a different consumption-investment decision for each outcome of information-production. For each such decision, there is a distribution of future wealth (for time periods beyond $t + 1$), and that distribution is conditional on the same information-production outcome upon which the decision is conditional. These conditional distributions can be used at time t to derive the marginal distribution of future wealth; this derivation is based on the distribution function of the information-production outcomes and the conditional distributions of future wealth mentioned above. The resulting marginal distribution is a distribution of future wealth associated with a composite gamble. It is a composite gamble (relative to the case of no information-production) because it encompasses two kinds of elementary gambles: (1) the gambles represented by firms' shares and (2) the gambles represented by information-production opportunities. The cost of the composite gamble, as of any time period t, equals the sum of the total costs of the two kinds of gambles. Thus, the total cost of the composite gamble is determined by the prevailing prices of firms' shares and the prevailing prices of rights to receive and use produced information.

But note that the consumer-investor has a choice about whether he purchases composite gambles or just the elementary gambles represented by firms' shares. If the amounts that must be paid for the gambles represented by information-production opportunities were equal to zero, every consumer-investor would opt for the composite gambles. This is because each individual is not harmed by, and there is a nonzero probability of his benefiting from, having the right to receive and use a completely reliable signal from Nature about true distributions of returns of firms' shares. But if the prices of gambles represented by information-production opportunities are positive, then trade-offs must be made. And these trade-offs are made in the usual way—by adopting the strategy that maximizes the expected utility of lifetime consumption.

Throughout, we have assumed that the rights to receive and use the results of information-production can be treated as if they were private property rights. That assumption implies that there is exclusion of non-purchasers: those who do not purchase such rights do not get to receive and use the results of information-production. At a later point we shall consider the theoretical appropriateness of that assumption. To do so now would simply obscure some more important issues.

2.6 The Importance of the Nature of the Capital Market and the Market for Information

In Section 1.2, it was argued that the nature of both the capital market and the market for information is important in a study of financial statement analysis or, more generally, a study of the economics of information and consumption-investment decisions. The underpinnings of that argument can be clarified by using the framework introduced above. We begin by considering the nature of the capital market.

In the framework given above, it was assumed that each agent (or "consumer-investor") can acquire as much of any asset that he wants without affecting its price. All assets were assumed to be infinitely divisible, and we assumed that there were no transactions costs or taxes. In short, each agent was assumed to be a price-taker in a frictionless market.

Some of the implications of these assumptions can be seen by examining our setup for an agent's consumption-investment problem. Recall that we imposed the constraint $\Sigma_j x_j = 1$ on the portfolio proportions, x_j, $j = 1, 2, \ldots, N$, of each agent. But we did not impose any other constraints (e.g., nonnegativity constraints, upper bound constraints, etc.) on the portfolio proportions. The implication of this is that the agent can purchase as much of the jth firm's shares (for every j) as he wants (subject only to his budget constraint) and issue gambles identical to those represented by the jth firm's shares on the same terms (i.e., at the same price). He can issue such gambles by, for example, "short selling" the jth firm's shares.[7] A short sale is a transaction in which (at the time of sale) the short-seller borrows units of the assets sold in exchange for a promise to repay the lender of the shares the market value of the shares at some future date.[8] Insofar as the lender of the shares is concerned, the distribution function of his future wealth is unchanged. Indeed, from his point of view, the only change is that a security issued by an individual (i.e., the latter's promise) is substituted for the firm's shares. And, of course, the buyer of the shares sold short is (given his decision to buy) unaffected by the short sale.

The preceding remarks point to a fundamental consequence of our perfect market assumption: equivalent gambles are perfect substitutes no matter who issues the gambles. This also applies to "degenerate" gambles (or "risk-free" assets), for which there is only one outcome. In short, the same terms of trade face all agents. This implies, in turn, that no agent can affect the kinds of assets that are available in the capital market because of, e.g., a monopolistic position with respect to a type of asset.

As indicated, all agents are assumed to be price-takers in a frictionless capital market. We also assumed that any information that is currently in the public domain is costlessly available to everybody. These two assumptions imply that, for each agent, there are neither barriers to the use of publicly available information in assessing distributions of returns to firms' shares nor barriers to transaction in order to make consumption-investment decisions that are optimal, relative to the currently assessed distribution functions. Thus, at any time period t, the implications of all publicly available information as of t should be fully impounded in the consumption-investment decisions made by each agent at time t.[9] Similarly, the implications of any information (i.e., signals) available to an agent at time t because of his private information-production activities (initiated prior to t) should be fully impounded in that agent's period t consumption-investment decisions.

At this point, it should be clear that the nature of the capital market setting is an important determinant of the opportunities that confront each consumer-investor. Thus, it is a determinant of the constraints under which agents make optimal consumption-investment decisions. This implies, in turn, that the nature of the capital market setting is a determinant of the maximum expected utility attainable by each agent as a result of consumption-investment decisions. From the discussion of Section 3.2 (especially expression 2.2), it can be seen that each consumer-investor's evaluation of information-production opportunities will also be affected by the constraints dictated by the nature of the capital market setting.

The nature of the market for information also plays an important role in our framework. We assumed that all consumer-investors face the same information-production opportunities. And we assumed that all information-producers face the same opportunities to produce information. This implies that the nature of an information-production opportunity is not affected by the actions of any individual producer or any individual consumer-investor. In short, we have (once again) a setting in which there are no discriminatory terms of trade facing consumer-investors or information-producers in the market for information.

---

[7]A short sale of asset j is identified by $x_j < 0$ and a purchase by $x_j > 0$.

[8]In reality, a short sale involves more than this.

[9]Of course, agents may not be in agreement about the implications of publicly available information.

The nature of the market for information is a determinant of the constraints under which information-production decisions must be made, just as the nature of the capital market is a determinant of the constraints under which portfolio decisions must be made. The reasoning is the same as that used above with respect to the capital market.

Suppose, for example, that some individual's resources (e.g., human capital) are not available—on the same terms of trade—to others. Then that individual is a monopolist in the market for information. And, as a result, he can expect to earn "economic rent" (or "monopolistic returns") on his information-production activities. This, of course, affects the prices that other agents must pay for rights to receive and use produced information. Thus, it affects the prices that must be paid for the composite gambles consisting of (1) the gambles represented by firms' shares and (2) the gambles represented by information-production opportunities. Looked at from a different perspective, the monopolistic position of the indicated individual imposes a constraint on other agents. If they choose to purchase rights to receive and use the information associated with that individual's special opportunity, they are constrained to transacting with that individual. They cannot go to some other information-producer.

We should repeat a point made earlier: we have been treating rights to receive and use the results of information-production as if they were private property rights. This approach implies that there is exclusion of nonpurchasers: those who do not purchase such rights do not get to receive and use the result of information-production. The theoretical appropriateness of this approach will be considered at a late point.

It is also well to note that we have been discussing matters from the perspective of an individual agent. We have not yet provided an explicit and formal characterization of equilibrium in either the capital market or the market for information. We shall do so in a subsequent chapter.

CHAPTER THREE

Capital Market Equilibrium and Equilibrium in the Market for Information

3.1 Preliminary Remarks

In Chapter 2, we discussed information-production and consumption/portfolio decisions from the perspective of an individual, conditional upon a specific market setting. We did not provide an explicit characterization of equilibrium in either the market for information or the capital market. These are among the things that we try to do in this section. There are several reasons for being interested in the equilibrium properties of both the capital market and the market for information. Consider the capital market first.

In Chapter 2, we employed several assumptions about the capital market. We assumed that this market is perfect in the sense that each agent can acquire as much of any asset that he wants without affecting its price. All assets are assumed to be infinitely divisible. Transactions costs and taxes are assumed to be zero. In short, every agent is assumed to be a price-taker in a frictionless market.

This characterization of the capital market has some important implications for the opportunities that confront each consumer and for each consumer's evaluation of information-production opportunities, as was indicated in Chapter 2. It seems important to ask, therefore, whether this characterization is descriptively adequate, in the sense that its testable implications are consistent with available data. One way to attack this issue, at least on some fronts, is to consider our characterizations' implications for equilibrium price in the capital market. If the testable features of those implications are consistent with the available evidence on price behavior, then one can claim that our characterization has some—and perhaps substantial—descriptive validity.

On the other hand, if the testable implications of our characterization are not consistent with available evidence, then perhaps we can get more accurate (i.e., more descriptively valid) insights into the nature of the capital market, which is one of the determinants of consumers' investment opportunities and of their evaluations of information-production opportunities. So, even negative findings can be helpful; and one should expect some negative results. Few frameworks are completely and unambiguously consistent with available evidence. But that is more or less irrelevant. The important issue is the extent to which a theoretical framework provides a relatively good description of the major features of the setting that an individual faces—relative, that is, to the alternative frameworks available. As always, one must be prepared to revise one's perspective in accordance with new theoretical or empirical developments.

By considering the perspective of a manager contemplating a change in his firm's accounting procedures (used for external reporting), one can get another reason for our interest in the nature of the capital market and the market for information. The effect of such a change on accounting income is often alleged to play a critical role in decisions about changes in accounting methods. This role is ascribed to the perceived influence of a firm's earnings number on the equilibrium value established for the firm, a value determined via the capital market mechanism. But this says something about investors' alternative sources of information and about their rules for evaluating assets. It says, for example, that accounting earnings numbers are the only information random variables used to set assets' equilibrium values. This is, of course, tantamount to saying that there are no competing bases for making the inferences upon which such values are conditioned. And this, in turn, means that the market for information is a monopolistic setting. Aside from this, the alleged role of accounting earnings presumes that the rules used to set equilibrium values imply a somewhat mechanical relationship between firms' earnings numbers and the equilibrium values of their securities. This perspective implys, therefore, that a firm can change its equilibrium value by changing its accounting procedures, even though the firm experiences no substantive economic changes. The descriptive adequacy of this perspective can be assessed if one has descriptively adequate models of the capital and information markets. With the joint implications of such models in hand, one can assess the extent to which assets' equilibrium values are directly affected by accounting earnings numbers—however much those numbers' behavior is affected by accounting acrobatics devoid of substantive economic implications.

The perspective just ascribed to management is not unlike that adopted by many in the accounting profession. Thus, it may motivate a variety of unnecessary accounting rules and conventions. A glance at some official pronouncements (e.g., Opinions of the Accounting Principles Board, Discussion Memoranda of the Financial Accounting Standard Boards, and Accounting Series Releases of the Securities and Exchange Commission) suggests that it has been one motivating factor behind some of the policy decisions made by the accounting profession and the S.E.C. But if the indicated perspective is not descriptively valid, then perhaps attention and resources are being diverted from more important considerations, and ones that might enhance the information content of accounting numbers. Once again, we can get some insights into this issue by examining aspects of the capital market and the market for information.

In Chapter 2, we assumed that there is no discrimination regarding opportunities for or the costs of information-production. Among other things, this implies that we should not observe any phenomena suggestive of monopolistic access to information-production opportunities. That, in turn, rules out a variety of phenomena usually associated with both the notion of "inside information" and of "special" (or "superior") analytical skills not available to all agents—such as the skills that might lead to "superior" portfolio performance. The extent to which these implications are descriptively valid is another issue that we shall consider.

Finally, it is well to recall that, throughout Chapter 2, we treated rights to receive and use the results of information-production as if they were private property rights. That implied exclusion of nonpurchasers—that is, those who do not purchase such rights do not get to receive or use any results of information-production. The extent to which that characterization is appropriate will also be considered, primarily at a theoretical level.

We begin with an examination of capital market equilibrium. The first part of this examination entails a discussion of capital market efficiency, a notion that has had a profound impact on both theoretical and empirical work on the capital market.

3.2 Capital Market Efficiency Conditions

The strongest and most conventional definition of an efficient capital market is: an efficient capital market is one wherein prices fully reflect all available information and, thus, one wherein prices adjust rapidly and unbiasedly to new information.[1] While this

---

[1]A review of theory and evidence pertaining to this notion of capital market efficiency is provided by Fama [1970]. See also Fama [1976].

definition conveys some of what is involved, it is not very concrete. So, a more concrete characterization will be stated. Unless otherwise indicated, a conventional "homogeneous expectations" assumption will be used. Specifically, all capital market agents having the same information are assumed to agree on the assessed distribution functions of returns on assets. This assumption may seem overly restrictive. It does not, however, affect the major points made below, particularly those in Sections 3.4 and 3.6. Some other conventional assumptions used throughout are as follows. (1) All agents act as price-takers in a frictionless capital market, and (2) equilibrium in the capital market is established via a process of tâtonnement with recontracting. Another assumption made in this section but relaxed at a later point is that all available information is costlessly available to each agent. For convenience, the standard one-period framework is used; this is not something that affects the major points made below.

Let I_t denote the set of all information available at time t.[2] Since information available at time t is also available at time $t + 1$, I_t is a never-decreasing set with respect to time. That is, $I_{t-s} \subset I_{t-s+1} \subset \ldots \subset I_t$, for all $s > 0$. In short, I_t contains all available information on the present and past structure of the system. Thus, I_t includes realizations of random variables (e.g., firms' earnings and returns on firms' shares for periods $\tau \leq t$) as well as all identifiable relationships among such variables (e.g., joint distribution functions).[3]

Next, Let I_t^m denote the set of information used by the capital market (i.e., each agent) as time t in establishing equilibrium prices. The precise relationship between I_t^m and the equilibrium prices of assets will depend on whatever model of equilibrium prices is appropriate. The two-parameter asset-pricing model is one such model. The appropriate equilibrium model is not, however, an issue that needs to be considered now. Finally, let $\tilde{\pi}_{jt+1}$ denote the value of asset j at time $t + 1$, where tilde ($\tilde{\ }$) denotes random variable.

By definition, an efficient capital market is one wherein:

$$I_t^m = I_t, \text{ for all } t. \tag{3.1}$$

That is, in an efficient capital market, agents act as if they use all of the information available at time t in establishing equilibrium prices at time t, for all t. Condition (3.1) implies that an efficient capital market is one wherein, for all j and t:

$$F_m(\pi_{jt+1}|I_t^m) = F(\pi_{jt+1}|I_t), \tag{3.2}$$

where F_m is a generic symbol for a distribution function assessed by the market, conditional on the information that it uses, and F is a generic symbol for the corresponding correct distribution function, conditional on I_t. Taken together, (3.1) and (3.2) say (1) that the market acts as if it uses all of the information available at time t in setting equilibrium prices at time t and (2) that the market acts as if it uses that information correctly, in the sense that its assessed distribution functions of assets' values are precisely those implied by I_t.[4] When viewed in this light, expressions (3.1) and (3.2) formalize what is usually meant when it is said that an efficient capital market "fully reflects" all available information. And, of course, if the capital market is to fully reflect all available information,

---

[2]The descriptions "at time t" and "at the beginning of time period t" will be used interchangeably.

[3]Alternatively, we can treat I_t as the set of implications induced by the available values of informative random variables. For present purposes, either treatment will suffice.

[4]Given homogeneous expectations, there is no disagreement over what is implied by I_t.

it must adjust instantaneously to new information (i.e., changes in I_t). Moreover, these adjustments must be unbiased in the sense that condition (3.2) underlies the resulting equilibrium prices.

$F(\pi_{jt+1}|I_t)$ was referred to as the "correctly assessed" distribution function of $\tilde{\pi}_{jt+1}$, conditional on I_t. The perspective underlying this characterization is as follows. I_t is taken to be the set of all available information available at time t and it is assumed that, conditional on I_t, there is a "true" or "underlying" distribution function of π_{jt+1}, a function that is an element of I_t.[5] The statement that the market "correctly" assesses the distribution function of $\tilde{\pi}_{jt+1}$, for each j, simply means that the market fully understands the implications of I_t. That implies that the market's assessed distribution function for $\tilde{\pi}_{jt+1}$, conditional on I_t, is none other than the "true" one, given I_t. If this were not the case, there would be a detectable difference between $F_m(\pi_{jt+1}|I_t^m)$ and $F(\pi_{jt+1}|I_t)$, for some j. Any such difference would imply either that $I_t^m \neq I_t$ or that the market does not fully understand the implications of I_t—conditions that contradict our assumptions.

The above characterization can, of course, be easily recast in terms of one-period rates of return, $\tilde{R}_{jt+1} = (\tilde{\pi}_{jt+1}/\pi_{jt}) - 1$, for all j. Given the "perfect market" assumption, no agent affects current prices. Thus, given a set of prices at time t for all assets and given condition (3.2), all agents face the same distribution functions of one-period rates of return. That is, the same gambles are confronted by each agent.

It might seem that the above characterization deals only with the capital market. Nothing was said about, for example, the nature (perfect vs. imperfect) of any market for goods or services. Upon closer examination, one should recognize, however, that our characterization of the capital market incorporates some strong assumptions about a different market, *viz.*, the market for information. We shall pursue this issue in substantial detail in Section 3.4. But before getting to that, it seems appropriate to attack a different issue raised above—the relationship between available information and assets' equilibrium prices. As indicated earlier, this relationship depends on whatever model of asset pricing is appropriate. The implications of one such model are developed below. This provides insights on the role of asset-pricing models in theoretical work. It also provides a foundation for dealing with the testable implications of central market efficiency.

3.3 Capital Market Efficiency: Modeling Prices and Getting Testable Propositions

3.3.1 The Role of Models of Equilibrium Prices

The conditions for capital market efficiency deal with the information used by the market in establishing equilibrium prices and the set of distribution functions assessed by the market conditional on that information. But neither of these things is observable. Thus, the conditions for efficiency are, as they stand, untestable. In order to get testable propositions, we must say something about the relationship between available information, assessed distribution functions, and equilibrium prices. In short, we must make some assumptions about the aspects of the assessed distribution functions that are determinants of equilibrium, prices which are presumed to be the same as observed prices at each t. Note that tests of propositions based on such assumptions are not only tests of capital market

[5]Recall that I_t contains specifications of all identifiable relationships (e.g., distribution functions) pertinent to describing the economic system.

efficiency. They are tests of both capital market efficiency and the specified pricing model. Thus, if any evidence is inconsistent with the propositions, we shall not know whether the inconsistency should be ascribed to capital market inefficiency or to an inadequate model for equilibrium prices. There appears to be no way out of this situation. We shall see later that several other hypotheses are also members of the set of hypotheses jointly tested in most available studies.

Several explicit and implicit models of market equilibrium underlie the available evidence on capital market efficiency.[6] In this section, we shall deal primarily with one model that is sufficiently general to cover tests on both individual securities and several securities (e.g., portfolios). Specifically, we concentrate on a version of the two-parameter asset-pricing model.

3.3.2 A Version of the Two-Parameter Asset-Pricing Model

Assume the following:

(A.1) The capital market is perfect. In particular, all agents behave as price-takers in a frictionless capital market.

(A.2) All investors are risk-averse.[7]

(A.3) There is unrestricted short selling of every asset.

(A.4) In each time period, each agent behaves as if the joint distribution of assets' future values is a nonsingular multivariate normal distribution.[8] (The nonsingularity assumption means that no pair of returns exhibits perfect correlation and no individual asset's value has a zero variance.) Conditional on the prevailing prices of assets, this assumption implies that the joint distribution of assets' one-period rates of return is multivariate normal.

(A.5) Agents having the same information end up making the same inferences. Conditional on the conventional notion of capital market efficiency, this implies that investors are in agreement regarding the assessed joint distribution function of assets' future values. (Recall that the conventional efficiency notion states that every agent has unrestricted access to all information available at time t.)

We begin by considering assets' one-period rates of return. For convenience—and with no loss of substance—we ignore dividends and other interim payments. That is, the only source of return on an asset is the asset's future value. If $\tilde{\pi}_{jt+1}$ denotes the value of asset j at time $t + 1$ and if we are now at time t, then asset j's one-period rate of return, conditional on its prevailing price, π_{jt}, is $\tilde{R}_{jt+1} = (\tilde{\pi}_{jt+1}/\pi_{jt}) - 1.0$.

For convenience, we shall omit time subscripts from rates of return, with the understanding that all one-period rates of return are from time t to $t + 1$. Thus, $\tilde{R}_i$ denotes the rate of return on asset i from time t to time $t + 1$.

A double subscript will be used to denote the rate of return on a given asset included

---

[6]An extensive review of evidence available as of 1970 is provided in Fama [1970]. Additional relevant material is provided in Bicksler [1979] and Fama [1976].

[7]Loosely stated, this means that risk is not, by itself, a desired item; an individual must receive positive compensation (in the form of some desired item) in order to willingly bear risk.

[8]Discussions of multivariate distributions can be found in most enconometrics and advanced statistics texts; see, for example, Anderson [1976], Goldberger [1964], and Theil [1971]. For a discussion related directly to portfolio theory, see Fama [1976].

in a specific portfolio, e.g., the portfolio held by agent e. In particular, $\tilde{R}_{je}$ denotes the one-period rate of return on the jth asset included in the portfolio held by agent e. Note that the subscript e identifies both an agent and the portfolio held by that agent. So we can—and often will—refer to $\tilde{R}_{je}$ as the rate of return on the jth asset in portfolio e.

Under assumptions (A.1)–(A.4), it can be shown that, in equilibrium, every agent will hold an efficient portfolio. Thus, in equilibrium, portfolio e must be efficient.[9] A portfolio is efficient if there is no other portfolio with the same or higher expected rate of return and a lower standard deviation of return. It can also be shown that the expected value of $\tilde{R}_{je}$, the return on the jth security in the efficient portfolio of agent e, must satisfy the following condition at the beginning of period t:

$$E(\tilde{R}_{je}|E(\tilde{R}_{ze}), E(\tilde{R}_e), \beta_{je}) = E(\tilde{R}_{ze}) + [E(\tilde{R}_e) - E(\tilde{R}_{ze})]\beta_{je} \tag{3.3}$$

where $\tilde{R}_e$ is the one-period rate of return on portfolio e; $\beta_{je} = \text{Cov}(\tilde{R}_j,\tilde{R}_e)/\text{Var}(\tilde{R}_e)$ is the relative risk of asset j in portfolio e; and $\tilde{R}_{ze}$ is the rate of return on an asset, z, with $\beta_{ze} = 0$.

Note that $\tilde{R}_e = \Sigma_j x_{je}\tilde{R}_j$, where x_{je} is the proportion of portfolio e's value allocated to asset j, $\Sigma_j x_{je} = 1$. Thus, $E(\tilde{R}_e)$, β_{je}, and $E(\tilde{R}_{ze})$ are, in general, functions of the portfolio proportions, the x_{je}'s, that define agent e's efficient portfolio. Looked at in this light, condition (3.3) is simply a condition that must be satisfied by the portfolio proportions of an efficient portfolio. And since agents' optimal portfolios are efficient portfolios, condition (3.3) is an optimality or equilibrium condition from the view of each agent e.

This optimality or equilibrium feature of condition (3.3) is worth emphasizing. In general, no agent begins with condition (3.3). This follows from at least two aspects of consumption-investment problems. First, the parameter values that appear in (3.3) must be assessed by each agent, using, for example, the results of information-production decisions made at time t. These assessed values are, in general, not exogenous to an agent's inferential activities. Second, an agent must use his inferences to select the optimal values of his portfolio proportions—the values of the x_{je}'s for agent e. For values other than the optimal values, condition (3.3) need not hold. In general, the optimal values of an investor's portfolio proportions depend on his probability beliefs, his wealth endowments, and his utility function. Thus, the specific portfolio that is optimal for one investor need not be optimal for another. (This is a general result; there are specialized assumptions that separate the optimality of a portfolio, or aspects thereof, from the individualistic aspects of an investor's portfolio selection problem.)

These remarks may seem like a digression. But they are really aimed at the way results such as (3.3) are often presented vis-à-vis issues pertinent to financial statement analyses. It is often argued that conditions such as (3.3) make such analyses unnecessary because conditions "solve" an investor's optimal portfolio problem. What is not recognized is that conditions such as (3.3) characterize the solution to an investor's portfolio problem after the inferential inputs and optimal values of portfolio proportions are obtained. Thus, condition (3.3) is certainly no substitute for financial statement analysis activities. (More on this later.)

---

[9]The term efficiency as used here does not mean the same things as it does when discussing capital market efficiency. One word—efficiency—is being used for two different purposes. This is regrettable but standard.

Our ultimate interest is in getting an equilibrium condition that applies to the market as a whole. That is, we want an equilibrium condition that is relevant for all capital market agents. This is where assumption (A.5) enters. It can be shown that when (A.5) is invoked along with (A.1)–(A.4), then the market portfolio is an efficient portfolio for every capital market agent. Conditions (A.1)–(A.5) are sufficient, not necessary, conditions for this result.

The proportion of the market portfolio invested in security i, $i = 1, 2, \ldots, N$, is defined by:

$$x_{im} = \frac{\text{Value of all outstanding units of asset } i}{\text{Value of all outstanding units of all assets}} \tag{3.4}$$

Since the market portfolio is an efficient portfolio and since condition (3.3) applies to every efficient portfolio, we have, for all i:

$$E(\tilde{R}_{im}|E(\tilde{R}_{zm}), E(\tilde{R}_m), \beta_{im}) = E(\tilde{R}_{zm}) + [E(\tilde{R}_m) - E(\tilde{R}_{zm})]\beta_{im}, \tag{3.5}$$

where all notation is as defined above, except that we now use portfolio m (i.e., the portfolio "held by the market") rather than portfolio e (i.e., an efficient portfolio for agent e).[10]

Condition (3.5) is an equilibrium condition for every agent, because portfolio m is an efficient portfolio for every agent. Thus, condition (3.5) is a condition that must be satisfied when the capital market as a whole is in equilibrium. This condition says that when the market is in equilibrium, the expected rate of return on asset i, for all i, is linearly related to β_{im}, the risk of asset i in the market portfolio.

For convenience, we did not include I_t—the set of all available information—in the arguments provided above. We do so now. Recall that capital market efficiency[11] implies that the capital market uses I_t in setting equilibrium prices and that those prices are based on correct assessments of return distributions, conditional on I_t. In the above two-parameter approach, the distribution assessed by each capital market agent is a multivariate normal distribution. This is the assessed joint distribution function of returns on all assets. Given our homogeneous expectations assumption (see (A.5)), all agents' assessed joint distributions are identical. So, we can talk about *the* assessed joint distribution of returns.[12] Capital market efficiency implies that this assessed distribution is the correct assessment conditional on I_t.

The parameters of the market's assessed distribution define the quantities $E(\tilde{R}_{im})$, $E(\tilde{R}_{zm})$, $E(\tilde{R}_m)$, and β_{im}. Thus, I_t is—strictly speaking—a conditioning argument of these quantities. Upon explicitly recognizing this, condition (3.5) can be rewritten as:

$$E(\tilde{R}_{im}|E(\tilde{R}_{zm}|I_t), E(\tilde{R}_m|I_t), \beta_{im}(I_t), I_t) = E(\tilde{R}_{zm}|I_t) + [E(\tilde{R}_m|I_t) - E(\tilde{R}_{zm}|I_t)]\beta_{im}(I_t). \tag{3.6}$$

---

[10]Note that one investor will, in general, have many efficient portfolios. An optimal portfolio for this investor is one of these efficient portfolios.

[11]See footnote 9 for remarks on the two uses of the word "efficient."

[12]The "homogeneous expectations" assumption often seems to be too strong to lead to a descriptively adequate model. It is well to re-emphasize, therefore, that this assumption provides a sufficient condition, not a necessary one. Similar results have been obtained under "heterogeneous expectations," using restrictions on the nature of the heterogenity. See, e.g., Gonedes [1976] and Lintner [1969].

Condition (3.6) states that the information used by the market in establishing equilibrium expected returns is identical to I_t, and the assessed means and relative risk that appear on the right-hand side of (3.6), for each i, are the correct values conditional on I_t.

At this point, it should be clear that the importance (and thus the role) of assumptions (A.1)–(A.5) revolves around their implications for the way in which the market's assessed joint distribution of returns is used in establishing equilibrium prices. The end result is a specific statement about equilibrium conditions for the capital market. With such a statement in hand, one can discuss testable propositions about capital market efficiency in a meaningful way. That will be done in Section 3.3.4, below. But before we get to that, it seems appropriate to translate (3.6)—which deals with equilibrium expected returns—into a statement about equilibrium prices. For notational convenience, we omit explicit recognition of the conditioning arguments in (3.6).

Let P_i be the equilibrium value of all units of asset i outstanding at time t and let $\tilde{V}_i$ be the aggregate value of these same units at time $t + 1$. Clearly, $\tilde{V}_i = (1 + \tilde{R}_i)P_i$, where $\tilde{R}_i$ is the rate of return on asset i from t to $t + 1$. In addition, let $P_m = \Sigma_{i=1}^{N} P_i$ and $\tilde{V}_m = \Sigma_{i=1}^{N} \tilde{V}_i = (1 + \Sigma_{i=1}^{N} x_{im}\tilde{R}_i)P_m = (1 + \tilde{R}_m)P_m$. P_m is simply the equilibrium value of all units of all assets at time t, and $\tilde{V}_m$ is the aggregate value of those assets at time $t + 1$. $\tilde{R}_m = \Sigma_{i=1}^{N} x_{im}\tilde{R}_i$ is the rate of return on the period t market portfolio, whose current equilibrium value is P_m.

The equilibrium expected rate of return on asset i from t to $t + 1$ can be written as $(E(\tilde{V}_i)/P_i) - 1$. Combining this with expression (3.6) yields:

$$\frac{E(\tilde{V}_i)}{P_i} = E(\tilde{R}_i) + 1, \tag{3.7}$$

where $E(\tilde{R}_i)$ is the equilibrium expected rate of return on asset i given by (3.6). From (3.6) and (3.7), we have:

$$\begin{aligned} \frac{E(\tilde{V}_i)}{P_i} &= 1 + E(\tilde{R}_{zm}) + [E(\tilde{R}_m) - E(\tilde{R}_{zm})]\beta_{im} \\ &= 1 + E(\tilde{R}_{zm}) + \lambda_m \frac{\text{Cov}(\tilde{R}_i,\tilde{R}_m)}{\text{Var}(\tilde{R}_m)}, \end{aligned} \tag{3.8}$$

where $\lambda_m \equiv [E(\tilde{R}_m) - E(\tilde{R}_{zm})]$.

Our next step is to express $\text{Cov}(\tilde{R}_i,\tilde{R}_m)/\text{Var}(\tilde{R}_m)$ in terms of current and future dollar values (i.e., P_i, P_m, $\tilde{V}_i$, and $\tilde{V}_m$). Since $\tilde{R}_i = (\tilde{V}_i/P_i) - 1$ and $\tilde{R}_m = (\tilde{V}_m/P_m) - 1$, we have:

$$\begin{aligned} \text{Cov}(\tilde{R}_i,\tilde{R}_m) &= \text{Cov}\,[(\tilde{V}_i/P_i) - 1, (\tilde{V}_m/P_m) - 1] \\ &= \text{Cov}[(\tilde{V}_i/P_i),(\tilde{V}_m/P_m)] - \text{Cov}[(\tilde{V}_i/P_i),1] \\ &\quad - \text{Cov}[1, (\tilde{V}_m/P_m)] + \text{Cov}[1,1]. \end{aligned} \tag{3.9}$$

But all the covariances involving constants are equal to zero. Hence:

$$\text{Cov}(\tilde{R}_i,\tilde{R}_m) = \text{Cov}[(\tilde{V}_i/P_i),(\tilde{V}_m/P_m)] = (P_iP_m)^{-1}\text{Cov}(\tilde{V}_i,\tilde{V}_m). \tag{3.10}$$

Next, note that $\text{Var}(\tilde{R}_m) = \text{Cov}(\tilde{R}_m,\tilde{R}_m)$. Thus, from (3.10), we have:

$$\text{Var}(\tilde{R}_m) = (P_m)^{-2}\text{Var}\,(\tilde{V}_m). \tag{3.11}$$

Using (3.10) and (3.11), we can express our measure of relative risk of asset i as follows:

$$\beta_{im} = \frac{\text{Cov}(\tilde{R}_i,\tilde{R}_m)}{\text{Var}(\tilde{R}_m)} = \frac{(P_iP_m)^{-1}\text{Cov}(\tilde{V}_i,\tilde{V}_m)}{(P_m)^{-2}\text{Var}(\tilde{V}_m)} = \frac{P_m}{P_i}\frac{\text{Cov}(\tilde{V}_i,\tilde{V}_m)}{\text{Var}(\tilde{V}_m)}. \quad (3.12)$$

Now, rewrite λ_m in terms of dollar returns. In particular, let λ_m^* be as follows:

$$\begin{aligned}\lambda_m^* &= \lambda_m P_m \\ &= [E(\tilde{R}_m) - E(\tilde{R}_{zm})]P_m \\ &= [(E(\tilde{R}_m) + 1) - (1 + E(\tilde{R}_{zm}))]P_m \\ &= [E(\tilde{V}_m) - (1 + E(\tilde{R}_{zm}))P_m]. \end{aligned} \quad (3.13)$$

Note that $(1 + E(\tilde{R}_{zm}))P_m$ is the expected dollar value of the investment of P_m dollars in the "risk-free" asset, z, which has an equilibrium expected return equal to $E(\tilde{R}_{zm})$. Asset z is risk-free in the sense that $\beta_{zm} = 0$. That is, asset z does not contribute anything to the risk of portfolio m. The difference $\lambda_m^* = E(\tilde{V}_m) - (1 + E(\tilde{R}_{zm}))P_m$ is the dollar compensation per unit of risk borne, where risk is here expressed in terms of future dollar values, i.e., $\text{Cov}(\tilde{V}_i,\tilde{V}_m)/\text{Var}(\tilde{V}_m)$.

Upon combining (3.8), (3.12), and (3.13), one gets:

$$\frac{E(\tilde{V}_i)}{P_i} = 1 + E(\tilde{R}_{zm}) + \lambda_m^* P_i - 1 \frac{\text{Cov}(\tilde{V}_i,\tilde{V}_m)}{\text{Var}(\tilde{V}_m)} \quad (3.14)$$

Multiplication of both sides of (3.14) by P_i gives:

$$E(\tilde{V}_i) = (1 + E(\tilde{R}_{zm}))P_i + \lambda_m^* \frac{\text{Cov}(\tilde{V}_i,\tilde{V}_m)}{\text{Var}(\tilde{V}_m)}. \quad (3.15)$$

This expression implies:

$$P_i = (1 + E(\tilde{R}_{zm}))^{-1}\left[E(\tilde{V}_i) - \lambda_m^* \frac{\text{Cov}(\tilde{V}_i,\tilde{V}_m)}{\text{Var}(\tilde{V}_m)}\right]. \quad (3.16)$$

The expression in brackets is, in effect, a certainty equivalent for the gamble represented by $\tilde{V}_i$. That is, an individual would be indifferent between a security with a certain dollar return equal to $E(\tilde{V}_i) - \lambda_m^*\text{Cov}(\tilde{V}_i\tilde{V}_m)/\text{Var}(\tilde{V}_m)$ and a security with the random (or stochastic) return given by $\tilde{V}_i$. Viewed in this way, expression (3.16) says that the current equilibrium price, P_i, of asset i equals the discounted value of the certainty equilvalent corresponding to asset i's random dollar return. The discount factor is equal to the reciprocal of one plus the riskless rate of return, which seems—at an intuitive level—appropriate because the quantity being discounted is a deterministic amount.

There is another way to interpret (3.16). The factor $(1 + E(\tilde{R}_{zm}))^{-1}$ can be interpreted as the current price per unit of expected dollar return. And the factor $-\lambda_m^*(1 + E(\tilde{R}_{zm}))^{-1}$ can be interpreted as the current price per unit of dollar risk. The price P_i of the security can be viewed as the price of a composite commodity—a commodity consisting of some amount of expected dollar return and some amount of dollar risk. The value of the composite (evaluated using the current equilibrium price) is equal to the value of the composite's ingredients, each evaluated at its current equilibrium price.

Note that the equilibrium price of risk is negative.[13] This simply means that when all agents are risk-averse, risk is "undesirable" in the sense that an agent must be compensated to bear risk. On the other hand, the price of expected dollar return is positive, implying that an agent must pay for units of expected dollar return.

It is well to note that both the price of expected dollar return, $(1 + E(\tilde{R}_{zm}))^{-1}$, and the price of risk, $-\lambda_m^*(1 + E(\tilde{R}_{zm}))^{-1}$, are the same for all firms (indexed by i in expression (3.16)). The implication of this is that one firm's expected dollar return and dollar risk are perfect substitutes for another firm's expected dollar return and dollar risk, respectively. In short, no firm's securities encompass any unique features, insofar as the determinants of equilibrium prices are concerned. (Of course, the *number* of *units* of expected dollar return and of dollar risk may vary across securities.)

As indicated earlier, all of the conditioning arguments that appear in (3.6) were omitted in the derivation of (3.16) for notational convenience. In particular, the conditioning argument I_t—the set of all available information at time t—does not appear explicitly as a conditioning argument of the parameters in (3.16). These parameters are $E(\tilde{R}_{zm})$, $E(\tilde{V}_i)$, $E(\tilde{V}_m)$, and $\text{Cov}(\tilde{V}_i,\tilde{V}_m)/\text{Var}(\tilde{V}_m)$. When I_t is recognized explicitly as a conditioning argument, we write $E(\tilde{R}_{zm}|I_t)$, $E(\tilde{V}_i|I_t)$, $E(\tilde{V}_m|I_t)$, and $\text{Cov}(\tilde{V}_i,\tilde{V}_m|I_t)/\text{Var}(\tilde{V}_m|I_t)$. When this is done, one sees that (3.16) is simply an expression indicating the relationship between the market's assessed distribution of returns conditional on I_t and the equilibrium prices of assets at time t. In particular, (3.16) identifies both the attributes of the latter distribution that are important in the determination of equilibrium prices and the way in which those attributes affect equilibrium prices. And, as noted above, this kind of result is needed to formulate testable propositions about capital market efficiency, whether those propositions are expressed in terms of rates of return or prices. Such testable propositions are considered in the next subsection.

The next subsection continues to use the conventional notion of capital market efficiency, as developed in Section 3.2. As was indicated there, this conventional notion actually incorporates some rather strong assumptions about the market for information. The implications of this will be discussed in detail later. Before breaking new ground, however, we continue with our overview of the existing literature on capital market efficiency. Specifically, we describe some of the testable propositions that have spawned a sizable body of empirical work—as well as much controversy. This description will clearly indicate the role of asset pricing models in work on capital market efficiency.

3.3.3 Testable Propositions About Capital Market Efficiency

In this section, we combine the conventionally defined notion of capital market efficiency with the market equilibrium conditions implied by the two-parameter model developed above. This is done to indicate some testable propositions on capital market efficiency. Our discussion will serve to emphasize that tests of these propositions are actually tests of a joint hypothesis consisting of the market efficiency hypothesis and the two-parameter pricing hypothesis, among other things. As a result, any inconsistency between available evidence and the testable implications of market efficiency may be due to an inefficiency in the capital market or to our using a descriptively inadequate model of equilibrium prices. As was hinted at earlier, hypotheses about the market for information

---

[13]If all investors are risk-averse, then $[E(\tilde{R}_m) - E(\tilde{R}_{zm})] > 0$ and, thus, $\lambda_m^* < 0$.

are also components of the joint hypothesis tested in empirical work on capital market efficiency. (More on this later.)

According to the conventionally defined notion of capital market efficiency, the capital market (i.e., each investor) will act as if all available information is used correctly when assessing the joint probability distribution of assets' future values. Given this assessed joint distribution, one can derive the marginal probability distribution for any particular asset of interest or the joint distribution for a subset of assets. And, of course, if the market's assessment of the joint distribution of future values is correct, then the implied assessment of the joint distribution of rates of return is correct (conditional on assets' prevailing prices).

The two-parameter model encompasses a description of capital market equilibrium in terms of the market's assessed distribution function of the vector of one-period returns. Given multivariate normality of this vector, risk aversion, unrestricted short selling, homogeneous expectations, and a perfect capital market (as defined earlier), equilibrium prices must be such that the expected return on asset i, for all i, is given by:

$$E(\tilde{R}_{im}|E(\tilde{R}_{zm}|I_t), E(\tilde{R}_m|I_t), \beta_{im}(I_t), I_t) = E(\tilde{R}_{zm}|I_t) + [E(\tilde{R}_m|I_t) - E(\tilde{R}_{zm}|I_t)]\beta_{im}(I_t). \quad (3.17)$$

Given capital market efficiency, the expected return given in (3.17) is the correct expected return conditional on I_t. Moreover, expression (3.17) represents a characterization of equilibrium for the market as a whole, given the two-parameter model. Henceforth, the left-hand side of (3.17) will be written as $E(\tilde{R}_{im}|I_t)$ for notational convenience.

The statement that $E(\tilde{R}_{im}|I_t)$ is the correct equilibrium expected return, conditional on prevailing prices and I_t, means that no matter how I_t is used, no agent will be able to assess a more accurate expected return on asset i. We can illustrate the import of this by focusing on a subset of I_t, namely, observed past returns.

In order to avoid cluttered notation, we omit the subscript m from asset i's return. But we shall have to add back the subscript t for reasons that will be obvious. In short, we shall write $\tilde{R}_{it}$ for the rate of return on asset i from t to $t + 1$.

Clearly, at time t the observations $R_{it-1}, R_{it-2}, \ldots, R_{it-n}, \ldots$ are components of I_t. Consider the conditional expected value of $\tilde{R}_{it} - E(\tilde{R}_{it}|I_t)$ given by:

$$E[(\tilde{R}_{it} - E(\tilde{R}_{it}|I_t))|R_{i,t-1}, R_{i,t-2}, \ldots, R_{i,t-n}]. \quad (3.18)$$

If this expected value is nonzero, then the observed past returns provide information on the difference between the expected value of $\tilde{R}_{it}$ and $E(\tilde{R}_{it}|I_t)$. But those past observations are components of I_t. Given capital market efficiency, $E(\tilde{R}_{it}|I_t)$ is the correct expected value of $\tilde{R}_{it}$ conditional on I_t and, therefore, conditional on every component of I_t. Therefore, we must have:

$$E\{(\tilde{R}_{it} - E(\tilde{R}_{it}|I_t))|R_{i,t-1}, R_{i,t-2}, \ldots\} = 0.0. \quad (3.19)$$

There is a slightly different way of getting to the same result. Consider the serial correlation coefficient:

$$\rho(\tilde{\epsilon}_{it},\tilde{\epsilon}_{i,t-s}) = \frac{\mathrm{Cov}(\tilde{\epsilon}_{it},\tilde{\epsilon}_{i,t-s})}{\sqrt{\mathrm{Var}(\tilde{\epsilon}_{it})\mathrm{Var}(\tilde{\epsilon}_{i,t-s})}}, \quad (3.20)$$

where $\tilde{\epsilon}_{it} = \tilde{R}_{it} - E(\tilde{R}_{it}|I_t)$.[14] Since the variances that appear in the denominator of this expression are positive, the sign of $\rho(\tilde{\epsilon}_{it},\tilde{\epsilon}_{i,t-s})$ depends on the sign of $\text{Cov}(\tilde{\epsilon}_{it},\tilde{\epsilon}_{i,t-s})$, for which I_t is an implicit conditioning argument.[15] Since $E(\epsilon_{it}|I_t) = 0$, we have:

$$\begin{aligned}\text{Cov}(\tilde{\epsilon}_{it},\tilde{\epsilon}_{i,t-s}) &= \int_{\epsilon_{it}}\int_{\epsilon_{i,t-s}} \epsilon_{it}\epsilon_{i,t-s}dF(\epsilon_{it},\epsilon_{i,t-s}|I_t) \\ &= \int_{\epsilon_{it}}\int_{\epsilon_{i,t-s}} \epsilon_{it}\epsilon_{i,t-s}dF(\epsilon_{it}|\epsilon_{i,t-s},I_t)dF(\epsilon_{i,t-s}|I_t). \end{aligned} \tag{3.21}$$

But $\epsilon_{i,t-s}$ is a component of I_t; so, we can write:

$$\begin{aligned}\text{Cov}(\tilde{\epsilon}_{it},\tilde{\epsilon}_{i,t-s}) &= \int_{\epsilon_{it}}\int_{\epsilon_{i,t-s}} \epsilon_{it}\epsilon_{i,t-s}dF(\epsilon_{it}|I_t)dF(\epsilon_{i,t-s}|I_t) \\ &= \int_{\epsilon_{i,t-s}} \epsilon_{i,t-s}\left[\int_{\epsilon_{it}} \epsilon_{it}dF(\epsilon_{it}|I_t)\right]dF(\epsilon_{i,t-s}|I_t) \\ &= \int_{\epsilon_{i,t-s}} \epsilon_{i,t-s}[E(\tilde{\epsilon}_{it}|I_t)]dF(\epsilon_{it-s}|I_t) \\ &= \int_{\epsilon_{i,t-s}} \epsilon_{i,t-s}[0.0]dF(\epsilon_{it-s}|I_t) \\ &= 0.0. \end{aligned} \tag{3.22}$$

This result also holds for an arbitrary number of past differences between realized returns and the corresponding equilibrium expected returns. That is, using mechanics similar to those used in (3.22), one can show that:

$$E[\tilde{\epsilon}_{it}|\epsilon_{i,t-1},\epsilon_{i,t-2},\ldots,\epsilon_{i,t-s},\ldots] = 0.0. \tag{3.23}$$

In short, realizations of $\tilde{\epsilon}_{i,t-s}$, $s = 1, 2, \ldots$, convey no information about the equilibrium expected return that is not already impounded in $E(\tilde{R}_{it}|I_t)$. Thus, $\tilde{\epsilon}_{it}$, $t = 1, 2, \ldots$, is a sequence of uncorrelated random variables.

Note that the above propositions—summarized in expressions (3.19) and (3.23)—are testable in the sense that they are conditions on random variables for which observations can be obtained (directly or indirectly via estimation procedures). Since those propositions are implications of capital market efficiency—when combined with the two-parameter model—an inconsistency between empirical results and those conditions would represent evidence against capital market efficiency, when the two-parameter model is used to characterize equilibrium conditions. Correspondingly, if the evidence is consistent with those

---

[14]Given our immediate objectives, a first-order serial correlation coefficient—such as that in (3.20)—may be treated as a first-order correlation coefficient between any pair of random variables. It is simply the case that the "pair" of interest here is a random variable observed at different dates.
[15]It is also an implicit conditioning argument of both $\text{Var}(\tilde{\epsilon}_{it})$ and $\text{Var}(\tilde{\epsilon}_{i,t-s})$.

conditions, then that evidence provides no grounds for rejecting capital market efficiency.[16]

An implication of capital market efficiency is that new information (i.e., a change in the set of all available information, I_t, will be immediately impounded in market prices. And the equilibrating price adjustments will be correct in the sense that they are based on a correct reassessment of the joint distribution function of future prices. Such adjustments are often referred to as being "unbiased," conditional on I_t and the new information (i.e., the change in I_t). Of course, in stating that the market will respond immediately and correctly to a change in I_t, we are assuming that the change is pertinent to assessing the distribution function of future prices. Clearly, in an efficient market, one does not expect equilibrium prices to change in response to information having no implications for the distribution functions of future prices.

The preceding remarks suggest another testable proposition about efficiency and another problem in formulating such propositions. Suppose that equilibrium is established at time t, and after that, say, at time $t + e$, $e > 0$, a new piece of information arrives. Consider the properties of market equilibrium established at time $t + e$ after the new information is available. Let ΔI_t denote the new information.[17] Given capital market efficiency, one should observe that:

$$E[\tilde{\epsilon}_{i,t+e}|I_t,\Delta I_t] = 0.0, \tag{3.24}$$

where $\tilde{\epsilon}_{i,t+e} = \tilde{R}_{i,t+e} - E(\tilde{R}_{i,t+e}|I_t,\Delta I_t)$ and $\tilde{R}_{i,t+e}$ is the one-period rate of return on asset i from $t + e$ to $t + e + 1$. Moreover, one should observe that, for any t:

$$E\{\tilde{\epsilon}_{it+e}|\Delta I_t,\Delta I_{t-1},\Delta I_{t-2},\ldots\} = 0.0. \tag{3.25}$$

That is, given an efficient capital market, equilibrium expected returns should adjust in a manner that correctly accounts for the implications of any new available information. After that information is available, it is not possible to learn anything about the expected value of the difference between any successor rate of return and its corresponding equilibrium expected return. In short, the market adjusts immediately and correctly in response to new information.

If tests of the conditions summarized by (3.24) and (3.25) are to be meaningful and interesting, it seems necessary to conduct such tests using new information having implications for distribution functions of future prices. The efficiency conditions, (3.1) and (3.2), state that the market will use all available information and it will use it correctly. For some changes in I_t, a correct interpretation of that change's implications may lead to no adjustment in equilibrium prices. Presumably, one is also (more?) interested in tests conducted on new information that does have implications for distributions of future prices. In the latter case, one can at least formulate interesting alternatives to (3.24) and (3.25), such as $E[\tilde{\epsilon}_{i,t+e}|I_t,\Delta I_t] \neq 0$ or $E[\tilde{\epsilon}_{i,t+e}|I_t] > 0$ or $E[\tilde{\epsilon}_{i,t+e}|I_t,\Delta I_t] > 0$. The specific alternative chosen will depend, of course, on the nature of the new information being examined. All

[16]Observe that we did not say consistent evidence provides grounds for accepting efficiency. The evidence can be consistent with conditions (3.19) and (3.23) as well as many other conflicting conditions.

[17]Note that $\Delta I_t = I_{t+e} - I_t$, the difference between the sets of information available at times $t + e$ and t.

of this leads to a problem encountered before—namely, that formulating testable propositions about capital market efficiency usually involves adding assumptions to the market efficiency conditions. As a result, any inconsistencies between the propositions and the evidence may be due either to sources of market inefficiency or to inadequacies of the additional assumptions, or to both. This situation first arose when we invoked the two-parameter asset-pricing model, which involved adding assumptions to the market efficiency conditions in order to derive testable propositions. It seems that we face a similar problem when considering tests of (3.24) and (3.25). Specifically, we must be prepared to state whether new information of some kind (e.g., announcements of dividend policy changes, announcements of accounting income numbers, and announcements of changes in accounting procedures) is pertinent to assessing distribution functions of future prices.[18]

3.3.3.1 Alternative Models Used in Empirical Work

The two-parameter model's implications for asset pricing are not the only ones used in empirical work on capital market efficiency. For example, in some studies it is simply assumed (implicitly or explicitly) that a correct interpretation of I_t leads to $E(\tilde{R}_{it}|I_t) = \mu_i$, for all t and i. No further elaboration on capital market agents' choice behavior is provided. In other words, this condition is not derived from some formal theory of asset pricing.

The condition $E(\tilde{R}_{it}|I_t) = \mu_i$, for all i and t, simply means that whatever the characteristics of agents' behavior, the market's assessed distributions of future prices and the equilibrium prices of assets always imply constant expected rates of return. Using this condition instead of the two-parameter model's implications for expected returns has no major effect on the testable propositions presented above. Indeed, the only modification needed is a redefinition of $E(\tilde{R}_{it}|I_t)$.

Some studies (e.g., Fama and Blume [1970]) invoke another condition on the implications of correctly interpreting I_t. Specifically, it is assumed that $E(\tilde{R}_{it}|I_t) > 0$. This assumption does not imply any specific magnitudes for expected returns. It simply says that a correct interpretation of I_t implies positive expected rates of return. The testable propositions that evolve from this statement are a little different from those discussed above. Specifically, the assumption that $E(\tilde{R}_{it}|I_t) > 0$, for all i and t, and the capital market efficiency conditions imply that no strategy using I_t in order to move from cash to securities to cash can earn an expected (nominal) rate of return higher than that provided by a "buy and hold" strategy. That is, since cash earns a zero nominal return and since $E(\tilde{R}_{it}|I_t)$—the expected nominal return on asset i given I_t—is positive, a buy and hold strategy will have higher expected return than a strategy which attempts to use I_t in order to determine when cash should be held and when it should be invested in other assets. This would not be the case if assessing positive expected returns for all assets represented an incorrect interpretation of I_t.

3.3.3.2 Additional Remarks

The above discussion points to some important testable propositions on capital market efficiency. In actual tests of those propositions, it is often necessary to invoke additional assumptions, usually for statistical reasons. One of these assumptions is that the distri-

---

[18] In Bayesian terms, this involves assessing prior pdf's on competing hypotheses, e.g., the existence or nonexistence of information content.

bution function $F(\underline{R}_t|I_t)$ is stationary over time, where $\tilde{\underline{R}}_t$ denotes the vector of assets' one-period rates of return. This implies that $F(\underline{R}_t|I_t) = F(\underline{R}_t)$, independent of t. In some cases, this condition is assumed to hold for the entire time interval covered by a study (e.g., the entire post-World War II period). In others, it is assumed to apply only to subperiods (e.g., successive five-year periods).

Observe that the condition $F(\underline{R}_t|I_t) = F(\underline{R}_t)$, for all t, is not the same as the condition $E(\tilde{R}_{it}) = \mu_i$, for all i and t. It is true that the former condition implies the latter; but it also implies much more. Specifically, it implies that all moments (e.g., means, variances, and covariances) are constant over time. Also observe that $F(\underline{R}_t|I_t) = F(\underline{R}_t)$ is not an implication of capital market efficiency. It is simply another assumption added to the efficiency conditions in order to develop propositions that can be tested using real-world data and existing statistical tools.

Relative to other hypotheses in economics, the efficient capital market hypothesis has undergone a substantial amount of testing. An extensive and detailed review of the available evidence is provided by Fama (1970; 1976, chap. 5). For the most part, the available empirical studies deal with subsets of I_t that are obviously publicly available. Such elements of I_t include past returns (Fama [1965], Roll [1970], and Hagerman and Richmond [1973]), annual accounting numbers (Ball and Brown [1968] and Gonedes [1974; 1975]), announced changes in dividend policy (Watts [1973] and Scholes and Spangler [1973]), changes in accounting techniques (Sunder [1973], Ball [1972], and Kaplan and Roll [1972]), stock-split announcements (Fama, Fisher, Jensen, and Roll [1969]), changes in the Federal Reserve Board's Discount Rate (Waud [1970]), and a variety of seemingly important world events (Niederhoffer [1972]), among other things. On balance, the results reported in these studies can be interpreted as being consistent with the capital market efficiency conditions. Not unexpectedly, there are departures from those conditions. But the economic significance of the departures does not appear to be major.

Note that the efficiency conditions are conventionally expressed in terms of all available information, and not only information that is obviously publicly available. As will be indicated below, this aspect of the conventional capital market efficiency conditions actually involves assumptions about the market for information. The next few sections consider aspects of that market. We then consider the implications for our formulation of the capital market efficiency conditions.

3.4 The Market for Information: Issues and Implications

For the most part, we have said little about the characteristics of the market for information. This is not the same, however, as making no assumptions about that market. Consider conditions (3.1) and (3.2). Condition (3.1) and—under our homogeneous expectations assumption—condition (3.2) must hold for every investor. Thus, every investor must have unrestricted access to all information available at time t. This implies that each investor has unrestricted access to all of the "initially available" public information (i.e., the information available to each agent when investors first come to the market at time t) as well as all results of information production decisions initiated by every agent on *personal account*. And for both sources of information the terms of trade facing every agent are assumed to be identical, namely, costless access. In short, the conventional specification of the capital market efficiency conditions implicitly assumes that there is no discrimination with respect to the costs of or the opportunities for information-production.

The fact that information costs are assumed to be zero for each agent guarantees that all agents will fully exploit all available information-production opportunities. But this assumption does more; it discourages explicit recognition of collusion in the market for information. As indicated below in Section 3.4.1, the public good attribute of information provides incentives for collusion in the production of costly information.

It should be clear, therefore, that the conventional notion of capital market efficiency—as developed earlier—really deals with both the capital market and the market for information.[19] Thus if one finds, for example, inconsistencies between available evidence and the capital market efficiency conditions, it is possible that the true source of the inconsistencies turns on the information market's nature rather than the capital market's nature. Of course, inconsistencies between available evidence and these efficiency conditions can be due to an inadequacy of any of the jointly tested hypotheses used in empirical work on capital market efficiency (e.g., the hypothesis about the appropriate equilibrium model, the implicit assumptions about the information market, and the efficiency conditions themselves). It is often impossible to determine, within a given study, which members of the joint hypothesis are descriptively invalid. Yet, it is important to recognize precisely what the components of that hypothesis are—to provide a basis for both future theoretical and future empirical work and to provide a basis for identifying the possible (and most likely) sources of observed inconsistencies between evidence and theory. We are now identifying an overlooked component of that jointly tested hypothesis—one that can alter interpretations of empirical results.

Moreover, by not giving explicit attention to the market for information, some important theoretical issues may be overlooked. For example, discrimination in the market for information can induce a capital market setting characterized by problems of "adverse selection"—of the kind discussed by Akerloff [1970]—and by problems associated with "signaling" behavior—of the kind discussed by Spence [1974]; see, for example, Gonedes, Dopuch, and Penman [1975].[20] It is with these possibilities in mind that we provide a brief discussion of the market for information in Section 3.4.1. Then, in the remaining sections, we consider some implications obtained by explicitly considering the market for information rather than implicitly imposing conditions on it via a characterization of the capital market (as was done in Section 3.2).

3.4.1. Issues Specific to the Market for Information

3.4.1.1 Preliminaries

Some remarks on the mechanism through which resource allocation is affected by produced information are in order. The game-theoretic mechanism introduced by Gonedes [1975a] is used as a starting point. It can be loosely described as follows. The market for inputs (e.g., labor and capital) used by information-producers and the capital market are

---

[19]One might have expected recognition of this issue to have been induced by the popular trichotomizing of the efficient capital market notion into the so-called weak, semistrong, and strong forms; see Fama [1970]. It seems, however, that this trichotomy has been used to characterize the capital market and the results of tests dealing with that market. It has not shifted attention from the capital market to the market for information. Hence, the importance of the latter market's structure is not exposed via the trichotomy.

[20]A framework that allows for these problems permits a natural identification of the kinds of issues considered by Jensen and Meckling [1975].

assumed to be perfect in the sense that all participants in these markets act as price-takers in frictionless markets. The production and dissemination of information are permitted to be handled via the unrestricted contracting and recontracting of groups or "coalitions."

In order to make optimal portfolio decisions, agents assess the distributions of returns on assets. Newly produced information permits the use of distributions conditional upon completely reliable signals (from Nature) on the exact distributions of returns. Thus, produced information affects the distributions used by investors in making optimal portfolio decisions and, consequently, it affects the equilibrium prices of firms' shares. Given firms' adherence to the "market value rule," such information affects firms' production-investment decisions, or the allocation of real resources. In short, information produced for investors' use on personal account affects firms' production-investment decisions via the information's effects on the prices of firms' shares. Details are provided in Gonedes [1975a].

3.4.1.2 Remarks on Produced Information

One of the basic problems faced in considering the market for the results of information-production is that, unlike "private" goods, one person's use of produced information does not reduce the "amount," or affect the attributes, of produced information that is available for other users. Suppose, for example, that returns on assets can be characterized by the familiar two-parameter model. This model implies that the equilibrium expected return on an asset is linearly related to that asset's relative risk, which is conditional upon the portfolio held by an agent in equilibrium. Next, suppose that one provides a completely reliable signal pertaining to the true value of an asset's relative risk. That signal can be used by that person in assessing the equilibrium expected return on the asset. But the same signal can be used by any agent who wishes to assess the equilibrium expected return on the asset. And the first person's use or nonuse of the signal does not affect the information content of the signal insofar as any other agent's assessments of equilibrium expected returns are concerned. In short, produced information is a "public good."

The fact that information is a public good does not imply that the market mechanism cannot be used for information-production. It does imply that special care is needed in specifying the kind of market setting that can be used. Two plausible specifications are discussed by Gonedes and Dopuch [1974, sec. 5]. One is based on the game-theoretic perspective used by Gonedes [1975a]. The other involves a setting discussed by Demsetz [1970] regarding the private production of public goods. Using either specification, one gets a setting for information-production that leads to a competitive pricing mechanism for the results of information-production. The equilibrium induced by this mechanism will consist of a Pareto optimal set of information-production decisions. In equilibrium, no information used solely for "trading" purposes—such as that considered by Fama and Laffer [1971], Hirshleifer [1971], Marshall [1974], and Ng [1975]—is produced if doing so requires the use of real resources. This does not imply, however, that there will be no wealth transfers, since side-payments may be needed to prevent information-production that requires the use of real resources and that simply induces wealth redistributions.

Note that the distinction between a public good and a private good—and the reason for our classifying information as a public good—turns on what is technically feasible. Insofar as consumer issues are concerned, "public goods" are those for which collective consumption (of the real goods or services) is technically feasible. That is, the technical characteristics of the good or service are such that one person's consumption of it does not preclude consumption of it by another person. Insofar as factors of production are concerned, "public goods" are those for which collective use (of the real goods or services) is technically feasible. The distinction between a private good and a public one does not turn on whether nonpurchasers are, in fact, excluded. Whether or not they are—and the devices ultimately used for exclusion—depends on the prevailing structure of property rights and the available technology for metering use and enforcing claims. Nor does the distinction depend on whether making the goods available leads to wealth redistributions (or "trading gains") in favor of those who organize production or those who supply the factors used in making the goods available. A new police protection program may induce a variety of wealth redistributions—in favor of, say, producers of guns and uniforms—but that does not imply that it is technically infeasible to have collective consumption or use of police protection. Nor does it imply, by itself, that the available means and costs of excluding nonpurchasers are consistent with attaining economic efficiency. Similarly, a new good can qualify, on technical grounds, as a private good even though its initial production is not associated with any wealth redistributions. This may result because the new good replaces an existing good and the new good's production and distribution fully utilize all the factors that were previously utilized for the old good. Consider another example—"inside information." At first glance, this may seem to be a private good, since one person (the insider) benefits from it (by getting trading gains) and nonpurchasers do not get to use it. But this is an illusion induced by a failure to disentangle various aspects of (1) technically feasible uses, (2) exclusion technology, and (3) wealth redistribution. The insider's information is a public good because collective use is *technically feasible*.

The public good characteristic of information raises another interesting issue—the potential for a difference between what is privately optimal and socially optimal regarding uses of real resources. For example, a costly information-production activity that can only lead to a wealth redistribution may be privately optimal (for the person who stands to gain wealth) even though it is not socially optimal (because real resources are used up in an activity that has no chance of creating real resources for society). In this case, society is better off (as far as resource conservation is concerned) when the potential information producer is given more wealth (in the form of a side-payment) in exchange for his promising not to engage in information-production activities.

Divergences between private and public benefits (and costs) have received considerable attention in the literature on the economic aspects of externalities. They have also received considerable attention in the literature on information and information-production activities. A detailed consideration of this literature is beyond the scope of our analysis. For our purposes, it suffices to acknowledge that these divergences may exist under certain conditions. The reader interested in this topic should consult the above-cited papers by Fama and Laffer, Hirshleifer, Marshall, and Ng as well as Murota [1976], Moussa and Murota [1978], and Hakansson, Kunkel, and Ohlson [1979].

3.4.2 Observations and Implications

There are several noteworthy features of the scenario of information-production sketched above. First, there are obvious incentives for collusion—collusion that might involve the managements of different firms, the holders of different classes of securities (or the same class), managements and securities analysts, or managements and "institutional investors." Basically, these incentives exist because of the public good attribute of produced information and a setting wherein mutually acceptable arrangements for group action are feasible and enforceable.

Second, the scenario indicates that one cannot reject on theoretical grounds the characterization of the market for information implicit in the conventional notion of capital market efficiency (see Section 3.2). This holds even though there may be collusive actions among agents in the market for information and even though different agents may pay different prices for the same property rights in the information market.[21]

Third, and most important, the information-market conditions leading to the above scenario's results identify a variety of potential inconsistencies between (1) the nature of the market for information and (2) the nature of that market impicitly assumed in the conventional characterization of capital market efficiency. Consider, for example, the "exclusion of nonpurchasers" rule, which plays a critical role in the mechanisms that induce a Pareto optimal competitive equilibrium in the market for information.

Suppose that the existing technology or the existing property rights system does not sustain enforcement of the exclusion of nonpurchasers rule. This may lead to a "failure" in the market for information. If it does, then the information-production results implied by the conventional notion of capital market efficiency may not be attained. To be sure, contemporary disclosure laws may alleviate the effects of this "market failure," but there are a variety of reasons for not expecting them to do so (see Gonedes, Dopuch, and Penman [1975, sec. 3]). Moreover, disclosure laws are not intended to deal with all forms of information-production activities. For the most part, they deal with a firm's production of information about itself.

The issue of excluding nonpurchasers is related to an arrangement that has been discussed frequently—the bundling of services of market institutions. A bundling of the results of information-production activities and the results of other activities (e.g. portfolio management activities, safekeeping activities, and trade-execution activities) is equivalent to creating a so-called tying arrangement, which has been widely discussed in the industrial organization literature. On the one hand, this kind of tying-in can be viewed as a practice that imposes restrictions on agents' latitude of choice and one whose elimination would induce an increase in agents' welfare. Mann [1975, p.315] seems to adopt this perspective. On the other hand, such a tie-in arrangement can be viewed as an attempt to enforce the exclusion of nonpurchasers rule for a particular public good, viz., the results of information-production activities. Purchases of the tied good(s) or service(s)—e.g., portfolio management activities—may serve as an effective metering device for measuring usage of that public good. Charging a price for the tied good in excess of the tied good's marginal cost would then be consistent with practicing price discrimination vis-à-vis sales of the

---

[21]The existence of different equilibrium prices for different agents is not inconsistent with competitive equilibrium and Pareto optimality when one is dealing with a public good; see, e.g., Samuelson [1954; 1955] and Demsetz [1970].

public good.[22] That is not inconsistent with attaining Pareto optimal results for the problem at hand (see footnote 21).

In the tying-in situation, forced unbundling of services may not increase agents' welfare. It will not do so if the tying arrangements are the most efficient means of enforcing exclusion of nonpurchasers vis-à-vis information-production activities. In the latter case, untying may lead to no change in information-production activities but to the use of more resources in the enforcement of property rights. Or, if other means of enforcement are less effective, it may lead to changes in the composition and/or scale of information-production activities.[23]

Other kinds of inconsistencies can arise when there are discriminatory terms of trade in the market for information, due to differential costs of or opportunities for information-production. One kind of discriminatory setting arises when a firm (i.e., a firm's management) is a "monopolist" in the market for information about itself. Situations involving "inside" information are essentially of this type.

Another kind of discriminatory setting arises when some agent has a monopolistic position vis-à-vis some kind of human capital. Recognition of this possibility enables one to assess the forcefulness of some arguments dealing with, for example, portfolio management activities. It has often been suggested that economic rents on such activities attributable to special skills (e.g., data-analysis skills) are not to be expected in an efficient capital market. This suggestion often leads to a recommendation of "passive portfolio management."[24] But the situation of interest here pertains to the market for information not the capital market. Specifically, skills such as data-analysis skills (due, for example, to accounting, legal, or economic expertise) constitute a productive resource with respect to information-production, just as management skills constitute a productive resource with respect to producing, say, hand calculators or medical products.[25] To say that one has "special" skills presumably means that one has a monopoly over some kind of human

---

[22]See e.g., Bowman [1973], Burstein [1960], and Singer [1968, chap. 16]. For a given quantity of the tied good, the aggregate of the "excess charges" equals the price of the public good charged to the consumer of that quantity. Consumers of different quantities of the tied good pay different prices for the public good.

Of course, the possibility of reselling information may weaken the metering power of the tied good, insofar as the original producers are concerned. Presumably, they recognize this possibility and attempt to make appropriate adjustments in their prices, contractual terms, selections of customers, etc. One can also presume that potential purchasers recognize these possibilities and bid accordingly. Note that related issues arise in, e.g., analyses of markets for new and used durable goods; see Benjamin and Kormendi [1974].

[23]Note that we are here dealing with tying arrangements per se, not the now defunct "fixed commission" regime usually associated with the bundling of services by members of organized national securities exchanges.

[24]This notion is discussed by Black [1971].

[25]Note that the nature of human capital affects what one can do with the information-production technology perceived to exist as well as one's perception of what the existing technology is relative to the economy as a whole (i.e., at least one agent). For example, agents with special legal or accounting skills may, at given point in time, be aware of opportunities unknown to agents without such skills.

capital at a particular point in time. One does not have to resort to mysterious arguments about capital market agents' "errors" or to challenge the descriptive validity of capital market efficiency conditions in order to explain the potential existence of such a position.[26] Indeed, such arguments fail to deal with the relevant market, vis., the market for information.

Whether or not the kind of monopolistic position described above can be preserved (i.e., whether or not it can support systematic economic rents) depends on the structure of the market for information (e.g., entry possibilities). Capital market efficiency is, in general, not sufficient to undo such a position. Specifically, the oft-heard argument that no "superior" type of portfolio management system can be superior for very long "because of capital market efficiency" is a seemingly misguided argument. The latter argument attempts to state the consequences of entry conditions in the capital market for results in the information market. Entry conditions in one of these markets need not, however, be the same as in the other. More generally, the structure of one of these markets need not have any implications on results in the other market. A recent paper in which this is ignored is Boudreaux [1975]. He correctly notes that the notion of capital market efficiency deals with the rapidity and unbiasedness of the capital market's reaction to new available information. He then proceeds to use these (and other) features of an efficient capital market to make statements about information-production activities, such as statements about the equilibrium allocation of real resources to information-production. Alas, this involves confusing two different markets. It is just as misleading as using the structure of the capital market to make statements about the structure of the input markets in which factors of production are sold to firms whose shares are traded in the capital market.

The kinds of inconsistencies mentioned above may lead to important inconsistencies between (1) available evidence and (2) the conditions and implications of the conventional notion of capital market efficiency. Such violations may be observed even though each agent is correctly using all of the information available to that agent (which is not necessarily the same as all the available information). When such departures are observed, it seems best to ascribe them to an aspect of the market for information rather than to an aspect of the capital market, even though the effects of the departures show up in attributes of the capital market.[27]

In short, it appears that the conventional capital market efficiency conditions encompass conditions on capital market agents' behavior, the nature of the capital market (e.g., whether it is frictionless or not), and the nature of the market for information. If one is primarily interested in the descriptive validity of the conditions vis-à-vis the capital market, then it appears appropriate to restrict the efficiency conditions to situations for which one is willing to adopt (on a priori and/or empirical grounds) the maintained hypothesis of nondiscriminatory opportunities for information-production at zero cost. Situations involving readily available public data and announcements that are specified (on a priori

---

[26]See, e.g., Treynor [1974] and Bernstein [1975] for discussions that resort to these kinds of arguments.

[27]As indicated earlier, it may not always be possible to determine the precise reason for a departure from the market efficiency conditions. In such cases, pending additional work, all that one can do is recognize the possibility of the information market's structure having induced the departure.

and/or empirical grounds) to have known implications are examples of such situations.[28]

At first glance, it might seem that the suggested restriction is important only for empirical work. We would argue that this is not the case. The theory of capital market efficiency is, presumably, supposed to provide insights into the allocation of resources and the effects of the capital market's structure on that allocation. If, however, the role of the market for information is not recognized, then it seems unlikely that a complete understanding (at least at a theoretical level) of resource allocation under uncertainty will be obtained. In a world of uncertainty, information and the opportunities for information-production play important roles in the allocation of resources. This has not gone unrecognized, as is indicated by the burgeoning literature on information economics; see, for example, the recent survey article by Hirshleifer [1973] and the overview paper by Arrow [1974].

The above discussion points to a variety of areas for research on the information market, such as the kinds of collusive arrangements (if any) used, the extent to which there are discriminatory costs of or opportunities for information-production, entry conditions and opportunities, etc. The work by Herman and Safanda [1973] on allocating "investment information," the work by Stillson [1974] on financial institutions' information services, and the work by Maisel [1975] on information and the regulation of financial institutions essentially deal with some issues of this sort.

The above discussion also provides a new perspective for interpreting empirical results on the "abnormal returns" earned by various types of market agents. This topic is the subject of the next section.

3.5 Discrimination in the Market for Information: Another Look at Some Existing Evidence

3.5.1 Preliminaries

Suppose we identify groups of agents who might have special information-production opportunities. And suppose their produced information is used for allocating resources to securities. If, in fact, those groups do have special information-production opportunities, then one expects to observe that they earn, on average, economic rents or "abnormal returns." If no such rents are, on average, observed for the groups deemed most likely to have special information-production opportunities, then we shall have evidence inconsistent with the existence or at least the persistence of rent-producing discriminatory opportunities for information-production.[29] In this regard, several types of agents come immediately to mind, such as mutual funds, corporate insiders, and specialists on the New York and American Stock Exchanges. Empirical evidence pertaining to the first two groups is

---

[28]If the implications of such data and announcements are not presumed to be known by all market agents, then one must say something about the opportunities for and costs of ferreting out those implications. In this regard, one would have to consider, for example, the extent to which there is restricted access to forms of human capital (e.g., accounting, legal, or economic expertise) that are useful in ferreting out those implications.

[29]Forces acting against the persistence of such opportunities are discussed below. If there is free entry and exit with respect to information-production and exclusion of nonpurchasers (or some alternative means of metering and exacting payment for use), then information producers will earn "normal" profits on information-production.

provided by Jensen [1969], Scholes [1972], and Jaffe [1974], among others. A brief review of their work is given in Section 3.5.2. A variety of observations and implications are given in Section 3.5.3, where the issues discussed in Section 3.4 are recognized.

As with many other aspects of capital market efficiency, dealing with the issue of special information-production opportunities requires some statements about the relationship between information and asset prices, and thus a characterization of capital market equilibrium. One such statement is provided by the equilibrium expected return/risk relationship implied by the two-parameter asset-pricing model reviewed in Section 3.3.2. That relationship provides a specification of equilibrium expected returns conditional on available information. If the special groups considered here do have and use special information-production opportunities, then their expected returns, before information-production costs are deducted, should differ systematically from the equilibrium expected returns conditional on readily available public information presumed to have known implications. In short, the two-parameter model provides a norm or benchmark that can be used in testing for agents' access to special information-production opportunities. A review of theory and evidence pertaining to this model is provided by Jensen [1972].

3.5.2 A Brief Review of Some Evidence[30]

The norm provided by the two-parameter framework was used by Jensen [1969] in his examination of 115 mutual funds. The returns on the 115 mutual funds shares were compared to the expected returns implied by the two-parameter model, holding portfolio risk constant.

Jensen assessed the funds' performance at several levels of analysis. He considered, for example, shareholders' returns net of management fees, loading charges, and other avoidable expenses and shareholders' returns measured gross of loading charges and all other identifiable expenses (conditional on the information disclosed by the funds). The crux of his results is that, on average, the funds' performance was not superior to the two-parameter model's predictions. In general, Jensen's results seem to provide no support for the funds' having had persistent special information-production opportunities.[31]

The two-parameter model was also used by Jaffe [1974] in his examination of insider trading. The extent to which insiders earn systematic abnormal profits was assesed by estimating the differences between returns on insiders' transactions and the predictions of the two-parameter model.[32] His estimation results are consistent with the claim that insiders have special information-production opportunities. After transactions costs are recognized, only the results for his "intensive trading" samples are consistent with this claim. Jaffe's results are essentially consistent with results provided by Penman [1980].

Additional evidence on the extent to which insiders and other groups have special

---

[30]Some familiarity with the studies reviewed here is assumed. A lengthy review of these and related studies is provided by Fama [1970].

[31]One might argue that some of Jensen's results are consistent with the existence of special information-production opportunities and the subsequent dissipation of rents via costly rent-seeking behavior, which affects the funds' expenses. Yet, his results based on ignoring all identifiable expenses seem inconsistent with that argument. In any event, this alternative interpretation does not affect our major points. It does, however, lead to implications not considered here. See, e.g., Posner [1975] and Krueger [1974].

[32]Jaffe's technique is more complicated than this statement suggests; but his method boils down to the indicated kind of comparison.

information-production opportunities is provided by Scholes [1972]. His analysis deals with the expected value of a departure from the two-parameter model's equilibrium expected rate of return. These expected values were estimated for the day of and several days surrounding those large-block sales called secondary distributions. On balance, his results are consistent with the "information hypothesis." This hypothesis states that a large block sale will affect a security's price if there is information implicit in the fact that some capital market agent is trying to sell a large block of shares. Shortly after the day of the secondary offering (on average, one to five days), there appeared to be no further price adjustments. The extent of the price adjustment appeared to depend on the initiator of the sale, with the largest adjustment observed for corporations or corporate officers and the second largest observed for investment companies and mutual funds (see Scholes [1972, table 6]).

Scholes's results are consistent with the following. Up to the time of a secondary offering, the source of the distribution had special information and this information is "received" by the market via the selling activity (given the source) rather than before that activity (when the source of the distribution acquired the information). In short, one can view Scholes's results as being consistent with some agents'—in particular, corporations' and corporate officers'—having special information-production opportunities.

Scholes's results, which are based on returns measured gross of all expenses, seem to be somewhat consistent with investment companies' and mutual funds' occasionally having special information-production opportunities. This finding appears to be somewhat inconsistent with Jensen's [1969] results for returns measured gross of all expenses. Note, however, that Scholes' analyses deal with selected transactions (i.e., large-block secondary distributions) of funds rather than their overall performance. We shall return to this issue in the next section.

The evidence provided by Lloyd-Davies and Canes [1978] concerns the effects of stock analysts' recommendations on capital market equilibrium. They deal with recommendations published in the *Wall Street Journal's* "Heard on the Street" column. If these recommendations do lead to revisions of equilibrium prices, one can infer that they provide information beyond that already available to capital market agents. But this implies, in turn, that the stock analysts who supplied the recommendations acquired or produced information not already available to the capital market. In short, these analysts had access to special information-production opportunities, on at least a transient basis.[33]

On balance, Lloyd-Davies' and Canes' results are consistent with analysts' recommendations' having information content. They also infer, however, that once the analysts' recommendations are made public (in the *Wall Street Journal*), one cannot, on average, earn abnormal returns (net of transactions costs).

The results provided by Stickel [1985] also deal with the existence of special information-production opportunities. He examined the effects of the Value Line Investment Survey's rank changes on capital market equilibrium.[34] The basic issues examined by Stickel are similar to those considered by Lloyd-Davies and Canes. The major difference is that

---

[33]Lloyd-Davies and Canes did not provide results on the recommendations of specific analysts, due to the unavailability of appropriate data. Their results deal with analysts as a group. Hence, we cannot make any inferences about the permanence or transience of any analyst's special information-production opportunities.

[34]Value Line ranks common stocks on a scale of 1 through 5, with a rank of 1 being given to securities expected to have the best relative price performance over the next 12 months.

Stickel focuses on the Value Line Investment Survey—which is one type of information-producer—instead of on stock analysts.

Stickel's results are largely consistent with Value Line's rank-changes' having information content.[35] Thus, they are consistent with Value Line's having some comparative advantage in the market for information.

3.5.3 Some Interpretations and Observations

Taken at face value, the evidence discussed above seems to be consistent with the statement that some groups of agents have access to special information-production opportunities. That is, there seems to be an inconsistency between this evidence and the conventional statement of capital market efficiency (see Section 3.2). In terms of the perspective adopted here (see Section 3.4), this inconsistency is something that can be ascribed, at least in part, to the nature of the market for information rather that the capital market—if the inconsistency really exists.

For example, the previously discussed results regarding Value Line and stock analysts may be attributable to these agents' having restricted access to factors used in the production of information. Human capital pertinent in information-production is an obvious possibility. Presumably the fees and wages received by these agents are such that they are the ones who expropriate the gains induced by their restricted access.

But not all of the results discussed above clearly point to any inconsistency to be ascribed to the market for information. Consider, in particular, results on the abnormal returns that accrued to selected groups, e.g., corporate insiders and mutual funds. With one exception, these abnormal returns were measured before costs of information-production, both explicit and implicit. The one exception is Jensen's study of mutual funds, wherein the effects of the funds' explicit expenses were (to the extent possible) recognized. It is quite possible that all of these apparent cases of abnormal returns would vanish if all explicit and implicit costs of information-production were recognized. Indeed, this cost factor may explain the weak inconsistency (see above) between Jensen's and Scholes's results on the extent to which mutual funds have access to special information-production opportunities. Scholes's results effectively assume zero information-production costs. Jensen's results conditional on ignoring identifiable expenses are the most comparable to Scholes's results. But, as Jensen himself indicated, his adjustments were not very precise because of deficiencies in the data disclosed by funds.[36] And, of course, implicit costs (opportunity costs) would not be easy to compute even if there were no disclosure problems. In any event, if Jensen's adjustments were more precise—or if Scholes has made some adjustments for non-zero information-production costs—the evidence on mutual funds from these two studies might have been more consistent, insofar as their implications for the information market are concerned.[37]

---

[35]The effects of the rank changes do not, however, appear to be identical across types of changes (e.g., a change from rank 2 to rank 1 versus a change from rank 5 to rank 4).

[36]Adjusting returns for brokerage commissions was one of his important problems; see Jensen [1969, p. 228, n. 89).

[37]Scholes's estimated value of the information impounded in funds' distributions is substantially reduced, but still nonnegative, after adjusting by his assumed commission rate of 1 percent; see his table 6. The estimated value implied by Jensen's results for returns measured gross of all costs is essentially zero; adjusting for commissions leads to negative estimates. Thus, the slight inconsistency between Scholes's and Jensen's results exists even after recognizing the transactions costs that would be induced by attempts to exploit information.

If studies such as Jensen's and Scholes's are viewed as attempts to test for the existence of discrimination in the market for information, then the inadequate adjustments for the resources consumed by information-production activities appear to severely restrict the studies' implications. Such adjustments seem to be important for making inferences about the opportunities available to the indicated groups but not to other agents. In addition, they seem to be important in testing for differences in the opportunities available to subgroups of the identified special groups. Both types of differences (if they exist) can provide insights into the market for information.

In this regard, note that to adjust results completely for information-production costs may involve adjusting the returns on benchmark portfolios. Suppose, for example, that the version of the two-parameter model used to provide benchmark results implies that agents must make inferences about various parameters' values (e.g., the values of assets' expected returns and risks) in order to select optimal portfolios.[38] This implies that selecting optimal portfolios involves at least estimation costs, which are types of information-production costs.[39] If the returns on those portfolios are used to establish benchmarks and if those returns are not adjusted for information-productions costs, then one's results will be biased against detecting special information-production opportunities. This is obviously important when there is high probability of discrimination with respect to the costs of, but not necessarily the technology for, information-production.

Adjusting for the costs of information-production activities involves, of course, a variety of heady problems in data collection. This is illustrated by the problems encountered by Jensen [1969], because of inadequate disclosures regarding expenditures. But the problems encompass more than disclosures of explicit expenditures. Some transactions in the market for information may be barter transactions involving swaps of produced information. Others may involve tie-in sales or similar arrangements designed to enforce exclusion of nonpurchasers. It is not clear that any "real-world" data are available for attacking these problems—not a very cheery thought for those interested in empirical work.

Finally, note that the various alleged forms of collusion among groups such as those identified above (e.g., collusion among analysts and managements) are not indications of "failure" in the market for information.[40] As indicated earlier (see Section 3.4.2), there are reasons for expecting collusion in a well-functioning market for information. Thus, taken by themselves, collusive acts in the market for information do not imply that some agents face obstacles not confronted by or induced by other agents. Dealing with this issue requires an analysis of the extent to which the opportunities for collusion are discriminatory.

3.6 External Accounting: Issues and Implications

3.6.1 Preliminaries

As indicated in Section 3.1, some of the theoretical underpinnings that can be exploited in work on external accounting and disclosure laws arise from the connection be-

[38]Several versions of the two-parameter model are reviewed by Jensen [1972]; but the review in Section 3.3.2 should suffice.

[39]A detailed serious treatment of estimation problems pertinent to asset pricing is provided by Bawa, Brown, and Klein [1979].

[40]An illustrative allegation is provided in the SEC's recent proposal on forecast disclosures; see Securities and Exchange Commission [1975, p. 3] and the analysis in Gonedes, Dopuch, and Penman [1975].

tween information-production activities and capital market equilibrium. In this section, we consider some implications of our previous analysis of those activities and the capital market. Implications based on the conventional definition of capital market efficiency are considered. Also, implications of the altered perspective developed in Section 3.4 are considered. We begin with a discussion of some issues that motivate some investigations of external accounting and capital market equilibrium. The illustrative issues that we consider are among those frequently encountered in works dealing with financial statement analysis. But our list of issues is certainly not exhaustive. We shall consider others in later sections of this monograph.

Earlier, we used the notions of "signals" and "sets of implications" in our discussion of information-production activities. Given mappings from signals to sets of implications and from sets of implications to probability assessments, one can always construct a corresponding direct mapping from signals to probability assessments. This is implicit in our use of a set of information (which includes signals) as the conditioning argument of a probability assessment in our discussion of capital market efficiency. In the remainder of this section, we shall shift back to our use of signals and implications in order to avoid confusion when we consider competitors vis-à-vis accounting numbers.

3.6.2 Illustrative Issues

Consider a change in the accounting procedures used by some firm for external accounting (e.g., a switch from FIFO to LIFO for external reporting that perhaps was induced by making that change for tax reporting). It is often alleged that the effect of any such change on a reported earnings number (i.e., the value of a potentially informative random variable) plays a critical role in managements' decisions about effecting such a change.[41] This role is ascribed to the perceived influence of earnings numbers' values on firms' equilibrium values. This perspective seems to involve an important assumption about the determination of firms' equilibrium values. Specifically, it seems to assume a somewhat mechanical relationship between the values of earnings numbers and firms' equilibrium values. As it stands, this perspective imples, therefore, that a firm can change its equilibrium value by changing its accounting techniques, even though the firm undergoes no substantive economic changes.

The perspective just ascribed to some managements is not too different from that adopted by many in the accounting profession.[42] Thus, in addition to affecting some managements' decisions it may motivate a variety of accounting rules and regulations. A glance at some official pronouncements—e.g., Opinions of the Accounting Principles Board, Statements of the Financial Accounting Standards Board, and the SEC's Accounting Series Releases—will probably suffice to indicate that it has motivated some policy decisions made by the accounting profession and the SEC. Announcements and proposals on the following topics are among those for which support or opposition involves this perspective to some extent: (1) accounting for leases (see FASB [1975] and Hawkins [1975]), (2) income accounting for insurance companies (see Foster [1975]), (3) accounting for extraordinary items (see Gonedes [1975b]), and (4) the inclusion of interim results in footnotes to annual reports (see Coopers and Lybrand [1975]). If the indicated perspective is not descriptively valid, then perhaps attention and resources are being diverted from more

[41]See, for example, Wallich and Wallich [1974], which deals with changes from FIFO to LIFO.
[42]See, for example, Spacek [1959] and Chambers [1974].

important issues—ones that might enhance the information content of accounting numbers.

Issues such as the above are among those motivating work on external accounting, financial statement analyses, and capital market equilibrium.[43] The notion of capital market efficiency plays a critical role in this work—in the design of empirical studies and in the development of relevant theoretical propositions. Some of these propositions are considered below. We shall take two passes at them. On the first pass, we shall use the conventional notion of capital market efficiency, a notion that implicitly imposes conditions on the market for information. Our second-pass treatment of these propositions explicitly recognizes the role of the information market's nature.

3.6.3 Implications for External Accounting: First Pass

We begin by considering some of the alternative bases (or "conditioning arguments") for making inferences and revising current assessments. In general, the values of all random variables whose behavior is determined by or associated with events or states pertinent to setting equilibrium values can serve as signals that affect inferences. These are the random variables of interest to us.

Accounting numbers are in this group of random variables because the determinants of accounting numbers' values include (among other things) events that impinged on firms' operations and thus affected the substantive characteristics of their performance. Such events include (1) those that occur within the factor-input markets in which a firm transacts and (2) those that occur within a firm's output markets. These events may be specific to a particular industry or they may be economy-wide events. Also, some of these events may be specific to a given firm's operations. In any event, a connection between such events and accounting numbers' values means that these values can be used to make inferences about firms' operations. In other words, these values can alter the sets of implications underlying investors' assessments (see chapter 3).

But there are other observables connected to these events. They are provided by industrial production reports, reports on industrial prices, reports on stabilization policies (e.g., the policies of the Federal Reserve Board), and forecasts issued by trade associations, among other things. Since these other observables are also affected by (or just associated with) events pertinent to the substantive features of firms' operations, they too can be used in making inferences relevant to setting firms' values. Whether these other sources of potentially informative random variables are ultimately used along with or in place of accounting numbers is irrelevant. What is relevant is that there exists a set of potentially competing bases for making inferences and revising assessments.

Still other bases are provided by statements made by corporate officials regarding their firms' operations, releases issued by brokerage firms, releases issued by market newsletter services, the contents of filings with the SEC (which do not include only values of accounting numbers), and, more generally, all the results of information-production activities undertaken personally by investors and analysts. For the latter types of activities, an individual's human capital is a critical input with regard to the production of signals pertinent to setting firms' equilibrium values. In any event, the inferences ultimately made depend on the joint implications of a wide variety of signal-sources, both human and nonhuman.

---

[43]A detailed review of this kind of work is provided in Gonedes and Dopuch [1974].

In general, if any random variable (i.e., any source of signals) reflects something that is, *ex ante*, pertinent to evaluating a firm, then the information content of this random variable will, in a conventionally defined efficient capital market, be fully reflected in assets' equilibrium prices.

Asserting that the inferences ultimately used by investors depend on the joint implications of a variety of inputs (human and nonhuman) and that these inputs are available to all agents on the same terms implies something about the market for information. Specifically, it implies that inferences are not, in general, mechanically related to any one input and that all the inferences that can be made by any investor can also be made by every other investor (i.e., the inputs available to any investor are equally available to every other investor). As in any other market, the existence of producers (in our case, information-producers) who can serve as perfect substitutes for each other and the characteristics of free entry and free exit mean that there is no potential for a monopoly in the market for information.

One implication of the preceding remarks is that—in a conventionally defined capital market—investors will not blindly and mechanically use accounting numbers' values in setting firms' equilibrium values. If any information-production activity induces any one agent (perhaps an accountant) to infer that accounting numbers are "deficient" sources of information vis-à-vis the setting of equilibrium values, all other agents will have access to the same inferential bases. Thus, the capital market will approporiately take into account the informational deficiencies of accounting numbers—which may mean ignoring them entirely. Ignoring them completely may be optimal when the available informative random varables are such that there are perfect substitutes vis-à-vis whatever information is reflected in accounting numbers after adjustments for the latters' deficiencies. In any event, in a conventionally defined efficient capital market, accounting numbers will affect equilibrium prices (i.e., they will be used as bases for inferences) only to the extent that they actually convey substantive information pertinent to assessing firms' values.

3.6.4 Implications for External Accounting: Second Pass to Take Into Account the Information Markets' Structure

The above "first pass" discussion is conditional on the conventional notion of capital market efficiency, as given in expressions (3.1) and (3.2). But we have argued that those conditions incorporate fundamental conditions on the market for information as well as on the capital market. With an explicit treatment of the market for information, one can easily defend various plausible counterarguments vis-à-vis our previous conclusions. Not unexpectedly, these counterarguments turn on some sort of friction or imperfection in the market for information.

One might argue, for example, that (1) accounting numbers are deficient sources of information for assessing firms values and (2) only a restricted group of persons (e.g., those trained in accounting, firms' managements, etc.) has the opportunities for detecting such deficiencies. The deficiences may exist because of outright attempts to produce "distorted" information or simply because of the accepted rules and regulations of external accounting.[44] In effect, this situation involves discriminatory opportunities for information-

---

[44]Some incentives for producing distorted information—capital market efficiency notwithstanding—are discussed in Gonedes, Dopuch, and Penman [1975].

production. It is one in which some agents do not have access to opportunities actually available to other agents or to perfect substitutes for those opportunities. Depending on the structure of the *market for information*, such situations may arise. And they cannot be undone because of *capital market* efficiency (see Section 3.4).

It is important to recognize, however, that monopolistic situations such as the above cannot persist. If they are to persist, then the select groups(s) of persons who have opportunities to identify accounting numbers' deficiencies must be able to *retain* a monopoly position in the market for information. This implies that there will never be opportunities to gain access to the restricted groups' opportunities or to develop perfect substitutes for those opportunities via actions taken on personal account or via public regulatory actions. In short, the persistence of such situations seems to require an extreme form of monopoly in the market for information. Indeed, this appears to be one of the implicit assumptions made in some arguments about the effects of accounting numbers. For example, Chambers (1974, p. 49) stated:

> An efficent market, in the fullest sense, would, by the prices established in it, secure the support of enterprises or projects of companies which have demonstrated earning capacity superior to that of other companies. But if earnings reports are differentially distorted by the asset valuation and the income calculation rules adopted by different companies . . . the stock market cannot discriminate between the more and the less efficient companies.

Clearly, this argument assumes that there is no unrestricted access to information-production activities that can identify the alledged informational deficiences of accounting numbers. Chambers may have envisaged a situation wherein only firms' managements have access to such activities.

When viewed in this light, it is easy to suggest factors acting against the existence or at least the persistence of such a situation. First, for example, the implications of the alternative inferential bases discussed earlier may work against any distorting influences of accounting numbers. Second, if training in accounting is really the critical issue, then there will be incentives for investors to acquire the requisite human capital—which is an input for information-production opportunities for which restricted access now induces a monopoly in the market for information. This too works against the persistence of a monopoly in the market for information. Third, the "nonmonopolists" may themselves engage in collusive acts, on private account or via governmental bodies, that weaken or destroy monopolistic positions. Illustrations of this are provided by the proposals for more disclosures about banks' portfolios (see SEC [1974] and Coldwell [1975]) and about the financial affairs of municipalities that make public offerings. These illustrations pertain to actions taken via governmental bodies to reduce or eliminate restrictions on access to information-production activities. In short, the existence of a monopoly leads to economic rents. Therefore, it induces rent-seeking behavior, which works against preservation of a monopolistic position and, thus toward the dissipation of rents.[45]

Another counterargument challenging our original conclusions turns on the extent to

---

[45]Recent analyses of rent-seeking behavior, including its implications for private and social costs, are provided by Krueger [1974] and Posner [1975].

which investors are conditioned vis-à-vis their uses of accounting numbers as inferential bases. A concise statement of this argument was provided by Sterling [1970, p. 453]:

> Accounting reports have been issued for a long time, and their issuance has been accompanied by a rather impressive ceremony performed by the managers and accountants who issue them. The receivers are likely to have gained the impression that they ought to react, and have noted that others react, and thereby have become conditioned to react.

Clearly, if this argument is to make any sense, there must be at least one individual (perhaps an accountant) who can recognize that some other agents are conditioned. If so, then at least one individual has information-production opportunities not available—on the same terms of trade—to other agents. That is, it implies the existence of a monopoly in the market for information. But as it stands, this second counterargument is also inadequate because it does not recognize the effects of countervailing forces in the market for information—forces set into motion by the very monopoly that it implies. That is, the argument fails to explain how a monopolistic position can be preserved. Indeed, it does not even explain how such a position can ever arise. Some agents' inferences are alleged to be affected (i.e., those agents react because they observe or somehow conclude that other agents' inferences are affected by values of accounting numbers). The counterargument never explains how those other agents' inferences came to be affected in the first place.

The point of the above discussion is twofold and simple: (1) an efficient *capital* market will not suffice to eliminate discriminatory costs of or opportunities for information-production (because such phenomena are attributes of the market for information not the capital market), and (2) asserting that such instances of discrimination do arise is, by itself, inadequate because it ignores all the forces that work against the existence or preservation of that discrimination. Such forces may entail exploitation of the joint implications of signals other than values of accounting numbers. Or they may entail the development of new techniques for information-production, based on new uses of either human or nonhuman inputs. In any event, it appears that a complete understanding of the connection between external accounting and capital market equilibrium requires theoretical and empirical analyses dealing with both the capital market and the market for information, rather than with only the former. In this regard, a substantial amount of work remains to be done.

3.7 Summary

This chapter has explored several aspects of information-production and capital market equilibrium that seem to have been ignored in the available literature. It was argued that the prevalent use of a definition of capital market efficiency imposing strong conditions on the information market seems to have disguised the importance of explicitly analyzing the market for information. One consequence is that many assertions about what capital market efficiency implies—about, e.g., "superior" portfolio performance and the allocation of resources to information-production—appear to be misleading, because they do not deal with the relevant market. Moreover, it is usually not recognized that some evidence interpreted as being inconsistent with capital efficiency is best viewed as pertaining to the market for information rather than the capital market. More generally, failure to consider explicitly the market for information may induce unwarranted inferences about the capital market. Finally, it was argued that, in general, the notion of capital market efficiency does not, taken by itself, provide a basis for understanding fully the connection between external accounting and capital market equilibrium, or any other potential source of information and capital market equilibrium.

CHAPTER FOUR

Inferences About Firms' Production-Investment and Financing Decisions

4.1 Preliminaries

Observed values of accounting numbers constitute a type of sample evidence on which inferences about the attributes of firms' decisions may be based. Pursuit of such inferences is motivated by the objective of assessing distribution functions (or "probability models") of the returns of firms' securities, such as their bonds and common stock. The essential line of reasoning leading to this perspective is as follows: the characteristics of the distribution functions of returns on firms' securities are dependent on the characteristics of firms' production-investment and financing decisions.[1] Those distribution functions are, in general, among the ultimate objects of analysis in making optimal consumption-investment decisions. This provides incentives for making inferences about those distributions, which are not directly observable.

The characteristics of accounting numbers are also determined (in part) by the attributes of firms' decisions.[2] Thus, observed values of accounting numbers can be viewed as a form of sample evidence that can be used to make inferences about those attributes. The latter inferences can, in turn, provide a basis for inferring the characteristics of distribution functions of securities' future values. Alternatively, sample evidence consisting of accounting numbers' values can be used to directly infer the characteristics of those return distributions.

But this line of reasoning says nothing concrete about the attributes of firms' decisions that are pertinent to evaluating firms' securities. Thus, as it stands, it provides no concrete guidance for selecting characteristics of accounting numbers. Indeed, it does not even identify the sorts of accounting numbers that are likely to reflect information pertinent to inferring the attributes of firms' decisions. In order to get such guidance, we must, it appears, impose more structure on the problem at hand.

Identifying the attributes of firms' decisions that are relevant to inferring return distributions and the equilibrium values of firms' securities requires some sort of valuation model—in order to identify what is "priced out" when firms' securities are evaluated and in order to indicate the attributes of firms' securities are evaluated and in order to indicate the attributes of firms' decisions that affect what is "priced out." That is, one cannot make concrete meaningful statements about the "relevance" of the attributes of firms' decisions (in the context of security evaluation) without a theoretical framework for the determination of equilibrium prices of securities—equilibrium for a given agent and equilibrium for the capital market as a whole. Such a model can be used to identify the characteristics of firms' decisions—and, thus, the attributes of return distributions—that are relevant to

[1]The environment of a firm (consisting of economic, political, and other factors) is a determinant of the characteristics of a firm's decisions. Thus, our framework does not rule out factors that affect those characteristics but which are not under the direct control of the firm.

[2]The characteristics of accounting numbers are also affected by accounting techniques. We shall say more about this issue in Chapter 6.

evaluating securities, in the sense that variations in those characteristics induce variations in one's evaluations, in general. Given the characteristics identified via this route, one can attempt to identify the accounting numbers and the characteristics of those numbers that are likely to reflect information pertinent to evaluating securities—because of connections between the identified characteristics of firms' decisions and the identified characteristics of the selected accounting numbers. With this in mind, we shall deal with inferences about the attributes and implications of firms' decisions by using the two-parameter asset-pricing framework, which underlies much of the theoretical and empirical literature of financial economics.

We begin with a review of our characterization of firms and consumer-investors, which was first presented in Chapter 2. Until otherwise indicated, a no-tax single-period framework is used. This will facilitate the identification key points without introducing unnecessary complications. Taxes and multiperiod isues will be considered later.

The following discussion deals with operating decisions, financing decisions, and risk. At first, our discussion of determinants of risk assumes that the probability of bankruptcy is zero. Then, in Section 4.6, we allow for a nonzero probability of bankruptcy. The relevance of debt claims' indenture provisions to assessments of risk is also discussed.

We provide both derivations of some basic theoretical relationships and discussions of some uses of these relationships in making inferences. In line with this, part of this chapter deals with sources of data and some basic disclosure regulations imposed by, for example, the Securities and Exchange Commission (SEC) and the Financial Accounting Standards Board (FASB). There have been recent changes in the disclosure regulations pertinent to our discussion, and many more changes are likely to occur. Thus, the kinds of details disclosed by a given firm may vary over time. Anyone using data from a lengthy period of time must keep in mind that what is disclosed in one period may not be disclosed in another, or it may not be disclosed in the same way.

Parts of our discussion are somewhat technical. But the reader should not be "put off" by the technicalities. The mathematically wary reader should at least skim over the technical material—in order to gain familiarity with the main lines of development—and then rely heavily on the verbal explanations.

4.2 The Market Setting, Firms, and Consumer-Investors

Goods and services are produced by "firms." Firms purchase and pay for the services of their inputs at the beginning of period 1. They use these services to produce goods and services that will be sold at the end of period 1 or the beginning of period 2.[3] At period 1, firms sell shares in their period 2 market values, which are random variables, in order to finance their period 1 outlays. The shares sold by firms are the investment assets that consumers hold. Maximization of the current market value of the shares held by its current shareholders is taken to be each firm's goal. This is the so-called market value rule.

Consumer-investors are assumed to maximize the expected utility of consumption at periods 1 and 2—c_1 and $\tilde{c}_2$, respectively. In our single-period framework, $\tilde{c}_2$ equals the consumer's wealth, $\tilde{w}_2$, at period 2. Consumers come to the market at period 1 with portfolios of assets acquired at previous periods and resources (e.g., labor services) that may

---

[3]Throughout, we use the phrase "at period t" rather than the lengthier but precise statement "at the beginning of period t." The phrases "at period t" and "at time t" will be used interchangeably.

be sold to firms. A consumer's problem is to select a level of current consumption, c_1, and a portfolio of assets whose value at period 2 is the value of $\tilde{w}_2$.

In this setting, the single-period two-parameter asset-pricing framework gives a characterization of equilibrium when the following assumptions are made:[4]

(A.1) The capital market is perfect. In particular, all agents behave as price-takers in a frictionless capital market.

(A.2) All investors are risk-averse.

(A.3) There is unrestricted short-selling of every asset.

(A.4) Each agent behaves as if the joint distribution of assets' values is a nonsingular multivariate normal distribution.[5]

(A.5) Agents having the same information end up making the same inferences.

As indicated in Chapter 3 the above assumptions are sufficient for the result that, in equilibrium:

$$E(\tilde{R}_i) = E(\tilde{R}_z) + [E(\tilde{R}_m) - E(\tilde{R}_z)]\beta_{im},$$

where $\tilde{R}_i$ is the rate of return on asset i from time 1 to time 2; $\tilde{R}_m$ is the one-period rate of return on the market portfolio, m; $\beta_{im} = \text{Cov}(\tilde{R}_i, \tilde{R}_m)/\text{Var}(\tilde{R}_m)$ is the relative risk of asset i in the market portfolio; and $\tilde{R}_z$ is the one-period rate of return on an asset z such that $\beta_{zm} = 0$.

Let V_{i1} and $\tilde{V}_{i2}$ denote the values of firm i at periods 1 and 2, respectively. The definition $1 + \tilde{R}_i = \tilde{V}_{i2}/V_{i1}$ and the above expression for the equilibrium value of $E(\tilde{R}_i)$ imply that, in equilibrium:

$$V_{i1} = (1 + E(\tilde{R}_z))^{-1}\left[E(\tilde{V}_{i2}) - \lambda_m \frac{\text{Cov}(\tilde{V}_{i2}, \tilde{V}_{m2})}{\text{Var}(\tilde{V}_{m2})}\right],$$

where $\tilde{V}_{m2} = \Sigma_i\tilde{V}_{i2}$, $\lambda_m = E(\tilde{V}_{m2}) - (1 + E(\tilde{R}_z))V_{m1}$, and $V_{m1} = \Sigma_i V_{i1}$.[6]

As indicated in Chapter 3, the above expression for the equilibrium value of V_{i1} can be interpreted as saying that the current value, V_{i1}, of firm i is the value of a composite commodity—specifically, a commodity consisting of some amount, $E(\tilde{V}_{i2})$, of expected dollar return and some amount, $\text{Cov}(\tilde{V}_{i2}, \tilde{V}_{m2})/\text{Var}(\tilde{V}_{m2})$, of dollar risk. The equilibrium prices of expected dollar return and dollar risk are $(1 + E(\tilde{R}_z))^{-1}$ and $\lambda_m(1 - E(\tilde{R}_z))^{-1}$, respectively. In a world of risk-averse investors, $\lambda_m > 0$.

Note that the above expression for the equilibrium expected rate of return and the

---

[4]These assumptions provide sufficient conditions. Not all of them are necessary for the results reviewed below.

[5]The normality assumption cannot, of course, be literally correct because the future values of assets are nonnegative random variables. It may still be the case, however, that the normal distribution provides an adequate description of the correct distribution—in terms of its shape and its behavior as a function of first- and second-order moments. Thus, theoretical and empirical work based on the normality assumption can still provide accurate insights. Finally, prior empirical work is consistent with the normal distribution providing an adequate descriptive probability model for returns on a variety of assets. See Blattberg and Gonedes [1974], Fama [1976, chap. 1], and the references cited therein.

[6]Observe that $\text{Cov}(\tilde{V}_{i2}, \tilde{V}_{m2}) = V_{il}V_{ml}\text{Cov}(\tilde{R}_i, \tilde{R}_m)$ and $\text{Var}(\tilde{V}_{m2}) = V^2_{m1}\text{Var}(\tilde{R}_m)$. As a result, $\text{Cov}(\tilde{V}_{i2}, \tilde{V}_{m2})/\text{Var}(\tilde{V}_{m2}) = (V_{il}/V_{ml})\beta_{im}$.

above expression for the equilibrium value of V_{i1} are *end* results of the capital market's "pricing out" process at time 1. They simply identify relationships that must hold in equilibrium, given assumptions (A.1)–(A.5). These relationships are conditional on investors' assessed distributions of firms' future values. Except for describing equilibrium conditions for a given set of assessments, they cannot, taken as they stand, provide a basis for making inferences about the distribution functions of firms' future values. Rather, they *result from investors' assessments of those distributions*. But by identifying the distributional attributes that will ultimately determine equilibrium values—for a given agent or, when (A.5) holds, for the market as a whole—they do identify the things that are "priced out" in attaining capital market equilibrium. That is, they do identify the features of assessed probability distributions that are relevant vis-à-vis asset pricing. During this pricing process, the values of the prices $\lambda_m(1 + E(\tilde{R}_z))^{-1}$ and $(1 + E(\tilde{R}_z))^{-1}$—and, thus, the value of V_{i1} for each i—are established, conditional on the supplies of and demands of expected dollar returns—$E(\tilde{V}_{i2})$ for each i—and risks of dollar returns—$\text{Cov}(\tilde{V}_{i2}, \tilde{V}_{m2}/\text{Var}(\tilde{V}_{m2})$ for each i. And the latter are, as stated, features of investors' assessed distributions of firms' future values—assessments that are necessarily made before the ultimate equilibrium state is attained.

A related point pertaining to *rates* of return should be emphasized. At time 1, attaining equilibrium involves setting equilibrium prices of securities or, what is equivalent, setting the current equilibrium values of firms. These prices and values are, however, the denominators used to define the rates of return from time 1 to time 2. Thus, in general, the distribution functions of *rates* of return that correspond to equilibrium at time 1 are also determined by the market's "pricing out" process. They are not, in general, assessed distributions brought to the market by investors in order to "price out" securities (i.e., in order to establish equilibrium). In other words, the distributions of rates of return are endogenous. In our single-period framework, the assessments that can, in general, be "brought to" the market are the assessed distributions of firms' future values, $\tilde{V}_{i2}$ $i = 1, 2, \ldots, N$, where N denotes the number of firms.

This does not mean that one cannot assess distribution functions of rates of return prior to the attainment of equilibrium. Such distributions can be defined in terms of one's assessed distributions of future values and the current proposed prices of securities (e.g., "asking" prices). But until our fictional "tatonnement process with recontracting" reaches its end, these distributions of rates of return need not be consistent with all implications of the two-parameter asset-pricing model. They should be consistent with those implications when the distributions of rates of return are defined in terms of the results of our fictional recontracting process—i.e., in terms of prices consistent with market clearing. All of this is consistent with the fact that the implications of the single-period two-parameter model—which is a static model—constitute conditions that must be satisfied when a state of the economy is an equilibrium state. They need not be satisfied in states that prevail at time 1 prior to the market's being cleared at time 1; i.e., they need not be satisfied when nonequilibrium prices are used to define distributions of rates of return. Moreover, they are conditional on (not conditioning arguments of) investors' assessed distributions of future values of securities. Thus, taken by themselves, the two-parameter model's implications do not imply that information-production activities are, in general, unnecessary. They do, however, provide guidance for conducting those activities by identifying the things that are "priced out" in the capital market.

When using the single-period model in a multiperiod setting (see Chapter 5), one can, of course, decide to assume that the distribution function of every security's rate of return (conditional on equilibrium prices) repeats itself over time. This and the assumption that all transactions' prices ultimately observed are equilibrium prices imply that all observed periodic rates of return are drawings from the same distribution and that this distribution corresponds to each period's equilibrium. These are the sorts of conditions that usually underlie statistical work based on historical rates of return. There is nothing inherently "wrong" with this approach; not recognizing its underlying assumptions is the larger problem.

A basic point of the above remarks is that the conditions given by the two-parameter asset-pricing framework do not "solve" an investor's inferential problems. Inferring distribution functions is still an issue to be addressed. Not unexpectedly, it can be attacked in a variety of ways, using many different sorts of sample evidence. In what follows, we emphasize one of those sources, *viz.*, accounting numbers. We consider theoretical connections between firms' production-investment and financing decisions and the distributional attributes "priced out" by the capital market—namely, $E(\tilde{V}_{i2})$ and $\text{Cov}(\tilde{V}_{i2}, \tilde{V}_{m2})/\text{Var}(\tilde{V}_{m2})$, $i = 1, 2, \ldots, N$. We consider various uses of these connections as guides for financial statement analysis, which is one type of information-production activity. And we consider the availability and limitations of data that could be used to implement these guides.

4.3 Operating Decisions and Relative Risk

4.3.1 Preliminaries

In this section we deal with the operating decisions of a firm in a single-period setting. In order to abstract from financing-decision issues, we assume that each firm issues only one type of security—namely, "common stock"—in order to finance its activities. This implies that all agents who provide resources (e.g., labor services, raw materials) to a firm at period 1 are viewed as holders of that firm's equity if payment for the resources is made at period 2. The value of their equity holdings at time 1 equals the time 1 aggregate value of the resources provided. In other words, instead of getting equity shares in exchange for cash, they get equity shares in exchange for goods and services. The ultimate value of the payment for these goods and services is the total value of the equity interests as of time 2.

We assume that each firm faces two sources of uncertainty about the results of its operating (or "production-investment") decisions. First, the prices of its outputs and the amounts to be paid for its inputs are uncertain. Second is the firm's output quantities. For a given operating decision, only the joint probability distribution of output prices, input prices, and output quantities can be specified, conditional on given quantities of inputs.

There is a theoretical condition that must be recognized when the prices of commodities are random variables. In our statement of the single-period consumption-investment problem, each consumer-investor is assumed to maximize the expected value of $U(c_1, \tilde{c}_2)$, where c_1 denotes dollars of consumption (optimally allocated to goods and services) at period 1 and $\tilde{c}_2$ denotes dollars optimally spent on consumption goods and services at period 2. In the single-period model, $\tilde{c}_2 = \tilde{w}_2$, the consumer-investor's wealth at period 2. But dollars of consumption are assumed to provide utility only because of the quantities of goods and services that can be consumed with those dollars. Thus, in general, the utility of dollars of consumption depends on the prices of goods and services available at periods 1 and 2. But our characterization of the single-period consumption-investment problem seems to recognize no dependency of maximum expected utility on the prices of goods and services. This really reflects some hitherto implicit assumptions about the relationship between the returns on securities from period 1 to period 2 and the relative prices of goods and services at period 2.

First, note that our ultimate interest is in real, rather than nominal, returns. This is justified by our viewing the consumer-investor as deriving utility from dollars of consumption because of the quantities of goods and services that can be purchased with those dollars. Second, and perhaps more obvious, we are concerned with relative prices, stated in terms of "dollars," not the absolute level of prices.

It turns out that our not giving explicit recognition to the influence of relative prices on expected utility can be justified in several ways. For example, it can be justified when the prices of goods and services prevailing at period 2 are, in fact, fixed and known at period 1. In this case, formal recognition of the influence of prices on expected utility is not needed because there is only one possible set of prices at period 2. Thus, nothing substantive is added to our framework by formally recognizing the role of relative prices. But we are allowing prices to be random variables; so, this approach will not suffice.

An alternative way of justifying our not giving formal recognition to the influence of prices on expected utility is to assume that real returns from period 1 to period 2 are stochastically independent of the prices of goods and services prevailing at time 2. This is the perspective that we adopt. Under this assumption, one can proceed as if the consumption-investment decision (of any consumer) at period 1 is based on maximizing the expected value of $U(c_1, \tilde{c}_2)$, a utility function wherein the role of relative prices is not explicitly recognized. The technical details of the argument leading to this conclusion are provided elsewhere.[7]

There is another aspect of the probability distribution of prices that must be recognized. Throughout, we shall assume that all markets are perfectly competitive. This implies that the probability distribution of prices facing any agent—a firm or a consumer—is independent of that agent's actions.[8] Thus, for example, the distribution of the price for any of a firm's outputs is, in a competitive market, independent of the quantity of output produced by the firm.

Before we proceed, it is well to note that this independence condition is a "substantive attribute" of a firm's production-investment decisions. After all, firms decide what market conditions to face when they slect their outputs and inputs, which are aspects of their production-investment decisions.[9] In any event, this is one area where accounting numbers (e.g., sales numbers) may provide useful inferential bases. Such numbers have been used to examine market structure issues by students of industrial organization. (See Weiss [1971] for a review of empirical work.) There is no obvious reason financial analysts cannot form insights from such pursuits.

---

[7]See Fama and MacBeth [1974]. Also relevant is the material in Fama [1977].

[8]In a world of perfect markets and perfect certainty, the value of every price is assumed to be unaffected by any industrial agent's actions. In a world of uncertainty about prices, one must deal with a probability distribution of prices. Our assumption about this distribution and an individual agent's actions is the appropriate analogue of the situation assumed in perfect certainty models, condition on market perfection.

[9]So-called anticompetitive practices are decisions about altering or preserving the market conditions themselves.

4.3.2 The Relationship Between Operating Decisions and Relative Risk

In this section, the following notation will be used:

$\tilde{V}_{i2}$ = the total real value at period 2 of the ith firm's outstanding shares as of period 1.
V_{i1} = the total real value at period 1 of the ith firm's outstanding shares as of period 1.
$\tilde{P}_j$ = the price, at period 2, of one unit of the jth commodity or service (e.g., the jth factor of production or the jth output).
$\tilde{q}_{ij}$ = the quantity, at period 2, of output j produced by firm i.
y_{ik} = the quantity of input k used by firm i as a result of its operating decisions. The value of this variable is established at period 1 when operating decisions are made.
f_i = total fixed costs of firm i.
$\tilde{R}_i$ = the real rate of return on firm i, from period 1 to period 2.
$\tilde{R}_m$ = the real rate of return on the market portfolio, from period 1 to period 2.
β_{im} = the relative risk of firm i
$= \text{Cov}(\tilde{R}_i, \tilde{R}_m)/\text{Var}(\tilde{R}_m) = (V_{mi}/V_{i1})\text{Cov}(\tilde{V}_{i2}, \tilde{V}_{m2})/\text{Var}(\tilde{V}_{m2})$.
$\rho(\tilde{q}_{ij}, \tilde{R}_m) = \rho(\tilde{q}_{ij}, \tilde{V}_{m2})$ = the coefficient of correlation between $\tilde{q}_{ij}$ and $\tilde{R}_m$.
= the coefficient of correlation between $\tilde{q}_{ij}$ and $\tilde{V}_{m2}$.

Typically, variables such as $\tilde{V}_{i2}$, V_{i1}, and F_i would be expressed in terms of "dollars." However, since we shall be interested in real rates of return, we assume that these variables are expressed in real terms. That is, we assume that they are expressed in terms of the number of units of a relevant commodity basket that can be acquired at time 2 using all of firm i's time 2 resources, the number of units that can be acquired at time 1 using the time 1 resources of firm i, and the number of units that could have been acquired in exchange for the goods and services corresponding to firm i's fixed factors at time 1, respectively. Selecting the composition of such a relevant commodity basket is, of course, a long-standing issue in economics.[10] We bypass a discussion of that issue here.

In line with our present single-period framework, all "fixed" assets carried over from period 1 to period 2 are assumed to have a zero salvage value at period 2. Thus, the value of any firm at period 2 is equal to the firm's net cash proceeds, expressed in real terms, resulting from sales of its produced goods.[11]

Given our assumptions, the value of firm i at period 2 is:

$$\tilde{V}_{i2} = \text{Revenue} - \text{Costs}$$

$$= \sum_j \tilde{p}_j \tilde{q}_{ij} - \sum_k \tilde{p}_k y_{ik} - F_i, \tag{4.1}$$

where $\tilde{q}_{ij} = h_{ij}(y_{i1}, y_{i2}, \ldots, y_{ik}|\tilde{\theta}_{ij})$. The function $h_{ij}(\ldots|\tilde{\theta}_{ij})$ is the production function for

---

[10]Relevant discussions of this issue are provided in Fisher Shell [1972].

[11]Alternatively, one can think of all "fixed" assets carried over from period 1 to period 2 as being produced goods sold for consumption purposes at period 2.

product j. The first summation (4.1) represents the firm's revenues. The second summation represents the firm's "variable" costs.[12]

The production function given above is not quite the same as that usually encountered in microeconomics under certainty, because our function is randomly selected in accordance with Nature's choice of a value for $\tilde{\theta}_{ij}$. Under certainty, a firm's production function is defined to be a function that specifies the maximum quantity of output for a firm's given inputs. Alternatively, for a prespecified value of the jth output, say, q_{ij}, and for prespecified values of all inputs except one, say $y_{i\ell}$, $1 \leq \ell \leq K$, a production function, as conventionally defined, specifies the minimum value of $y_{i\ell}$ needed to attain the prespecified value of output, q_{ij}.

Since we are allowing for a source of uncertainty in the quantity of output, $\tilde{q}_{ij}$, corresponding to prespecified quantities of inputs, the indicated maximization (or minimization) aspects of the conventionally defined production function do not apply here. Since there is a source of uncertainty in the production function, the indicated notions of maximization and minimization are not, in general, uniquely defined. The maximum quantity of output for a given set of inputs and a given value, say, $\tilde{\theta}_{ij} = \theta'_{ij}$, may not be the maximum quantity for the same set of inputs and a different value, say $\tilde{\theta}_{ij} = \theta''_{ij}$. And since a firm must, in our scenario, select its inputs at time 1, it cannot specify its inputs as a function of $\tilde{\theta}_{ij}$—the value of which will not be known until time 2.

In the end, we must define the function $h_{ij}(y_{i1}, Y_{i2}, \ldots, y_{iK}|\theta_{ij})$ to be the quantity of output j actually achieved by firm i at time 2 when its input factors are specified, at time 1, to be y_{ik}, $k = 1, 2, \ldots, K$, and when the value of $\tilde{\theta}_{ij}$ is revealed to be θ_{ij} at time 2. Of course, the input decisions made by the ith firm at time 1 will be made in accordance with the "market value rule."

For convenience, we shall assume that the functional form of our production function, for given i and j, does not depend on the value of $\tilde{\theta}_{ij}$. Thus, for example, if this function is concave for one value of $\tilde{\theta}_{ij}$, it is concave for all of them. This assumption allows us to consider issues such as returns-to-scale and factor substitution possibilities in a fairly uncomplicated way.

Our explicit recognition of the role of production functions (and hence the technology facing a firm) is by no means intended to appear profound. But it does single out a substantive economic phenomenon that is often treated cavalierly or simply ignored in much of the literature on financial statement analysis and corporation finance. One major exception is the recent paper by Thomadakis [1976]. We shall have more to say about this later. Suffice it to note here that the attributes of the distribution of $h_{ij}(\ldots|\tilde{\theta}_{ij})$, for each j, can affect the distribution of firm i's future value. They are, therefore, among the attributes about which one might want to make explicit inferences when assessing the distributions of firms' future values.

Finally, note that taking the ith firms' production-investment decisions as given involves taking all of the following as having been fixed: (a) the production functions, $h_{ij}(\ldots|\tilde{\theta}_{ij})$, for each value of $\tilde{\theta}_{ij}$, for all j; (b) the types of goods and services that will be produced, *viz.*, the $\tilde{q}_{ij}$'s with which firm i will be concerned; and (c) the values of the production inputs y_{ik}, for all k. Once these decisions are given, the ultimate value of $\tilde{q}_{ij}$, for each j, is entirely determined by the value of $\tilde{\theta}_{ij}$, for the corresponding value of j. Of course, the

---

[12] Tax factors will be considered in a later subsection.

fact that these decisions are given does not mean that their characteristics are known to all "outsiders"—or even to all of firm i's "insiders."

Using expression (4.1), one can examine the connection between the attributes of firm i's production-investment decisions and the risk of returns on firm i's securities. This exercise can be pursued for gross dollar returns, $\tilde{V}_{2i}$, or gross rates of return, $1 + \tilde{R}_i$—where the distributional properties of $\tilde{R}_i$ are defined in terms of the prevailing tentative prices of firm i's securities. (See the discussion of rates of return in Section 4.2 above.) We shall deal with rates of return in order to illustrate conveniently some of the mechanics involved in moving from dollar returns to rates of return.

By definition, the one-period real rate of return on the ith firm's shares is given by:

$$\tilde{R}_i = (\tilde{V}_{i2}/V_{i1}) - 1. \tag{4.2}$$

Therefore:

$$\begin{aligned}\text{Cov}(\tilde{R}_i, \tilde{R}_m) &= \text{Cov}[(\tilde{V}_{i2}/V_{i1}) - 1, \tilde{R}_m] \\ &= \text{Cov}[(\tilde{V}_{i2}/V_{i1}), \tilde{R}_m] - \text{Cov}[1, \tilde{R}_m] \\ &= V_{i1}^{-1}\,\text{Cov}(\tilde{V}_{i2}, \tilde{R}_m) - 0.0 \\ &= V_{i1}^{-1}\,\text{Cov}(\tilde{V}_{i2}, \tilde{R}_m).\end{aligned} \tag{4.3}$$

Use of (4.1) in (4.3) leads to:

$$\begin{aligned}\text{Cov}(\tilde{R}_i, \tilde{R}_m) &= V_{i1}^{-1}\,\text{Cov}\left(\sum_j \tilde{p}_j\tilde{q}_{ij} - \sum_k \tilde{p}_k y_{ik} - F_i, \tilde{R}_m\right) \\ &= V_{i1}^{-1}\,\text{Cov}\left(\sum_j \tilde{p}_j\tilde{q}_{ij}, \tilde{R}_m\right) \\ &\quad - V_{i1}^{-1}\left[\text{Cov}\left(\sum_k \tilde{p}_k y_{ik}, \tilde{R}_m\right) - \text{Cov}(F_i, \tilde{R}_m)\right] \\ &= V_{i1}^{-1}\sum_j \text{Cov}(\tilde{p}_j\tilde{q}_{ij}, \tilde{R}_m) \\ &\quad - V_{i1}^{-1}\sum_k \text{Cov}(\tilde{p}_k y_{ik}, \tilde{R}_m) - 0.0.\end{aligned} \tag{4.4}$$

We now proceed to analyze each summand appearing ont he right-hand side (RHS) of (4.4). Consider, for example, any summand, say the kth, of the second summation, *viz.*, $\text{Cov}(\tilde{p}_k y_{ik}, \tilde{R}_m)$. Since y_{ik} is not a random variable, we can write:

$$\text{Cov}(\tilde{p}_k y_{ik}, \tilde{R}_m) = y_{ik}\,\text{Cov}(\tilde{p}_k, \tilde{R}_m). \tag{4.5}$$

Now, recall our assumption on the relationship between real rates of return and prices. We assumed that real rates of return are stochastically independent of the prices of goods and services. (This does not imply that securities' future values are independent of these prices.) But that implies that real rates of return and prices are uncorrelated. Thus, for any k, $\text{Cov}(\tilde{p}_k, \tilde{R}_m) = 0.0$. In short, we have, for any firm i:

$$\mathrm{Cov}(\tilde{p}_k y_{ik}, \tilde{R}_m) = 0.0, \quad \text{for all } k. \tag{4.6}$$

Dealing with a particular summand of the first summation on the RHS of (4.5) is a little more difficult. We shall find, however, that our assumptions have unambiguous implications about any such summand.

The following analysis may seem (and it may be) overly complicated. In any event, the reader is encouraged at least to skim through it and attempt to follow the main lines of development.

From the definition of a covariance, we know that:

$$\mathrm{Cov}(\tilde{p}_j\tilde{q}_{ij}, \tilde{R}_m) = E\{(\tilde{p}_j\tilde{q}_{ij} - E(\tilde{p}_j\tilde{q}_{ij}))(\tilde{R}_m - E(\tilde{R}_m))\}. \tag{4.7}$$

Note that the expectation operator, E, on the RHS of (4.7) applies to the joint distribution of $\tilde{p}_j\tilde{q}_{ij}$ and $\tilde{R}_m$. That is:

$$E\{(\tilde{p}_j\tilde{q}_{ij} - E(\tilde{p}_j\tilde{q}_{ij}))(\tilde{R}_m - E(\tilde{R}_m))\}$$

$$= \int_{p_jq_{ij}}\int_{R_m} (p_jq_{ij} - E(\tilde{p}_j\tilde{q}_{ij}))(R_m - E(\tilde{R}_m))\, dF(p_jq_{ij}, R_m), \tag{4.8}$$

where $F(p_jq_{ij}, R_m)$ is the joint (cumulative) distribution function of $(\tilde{p}_j\tilde{q}_{ij})$ and $\tilde{R}_m$.

From (4.7) one gets the alternative expression:

$$\mathrm{Cov}(\tilde{p}_j\tilde{q}_{ij}, \tilde{R}_m) = E\{(\tilde{p}_j\tilde{q}_{ij})(\tilde{R}_m)\} - E(\tilde{p}_j\tilde{q}_{ij})\, E(\tilde{R}_m). \tag{4.9}$$

The expression in (4.9) can also be obtained from the general rule for taking the expected value of the product of any two random variables, say $\tilde{v}$ and $\tilde{w}$. Specifically, $E(\tilde{v}\tilde{w}) = E(\tilde{v})\, E(\tilde{w}) + \mathrm{Cov}(\tilde{v}, \tilde{w})$.

By definition:

$$E[(\tilde{p}_j\tilde{q}_{ij})(\tilde{R}_m)] = E[E\{\tilde{p}_j|\tilde{q}_{ij}, \tilde{R}_m\}\, (\tilde{q}_{ij}\tilde{R}_m)], \tag{4.10}$$

where the outer expectation applies to the joint distribution of $\tilde{q}_{ij}$ and $\tilde{R}_m$.

Since $\tilde{p}_j$ is independent of $\tilde{q}_{ij}$ (because of market perfection) and since $\tilde{p}_j$ is independent of $\tilde{R}_m$ (by assumption, see Section 4.3.1), we get $E\{\tilde{p}_j|q_{ij}, R_m\} = E(\tilde{p}_j)$ for all values of $\tilde{q}_{ij}$ and $\tilde{R}_m$. Thus, (4.10) can be rewritten as:

$$E(\tilde{p}_j\tilde{q}_{ij}\tilde{R}_m) = E(p_j)\, E(\tilde{q}_{ij}\tilde{R}_m). \tag{4.11}$$

And we can also write:

$$E(\tilde{p}_j\tilde{q}_{ij}) = E(\tilde{p}_j)\, E(\tilde{q}_{ij}), \tag{4.12}$$

because $\tilde{p}_j$ is independent of $\tilde{q}_{ij}$.

Using (4.11) and (4.12) in the RHS of (4.9) leads to:

$$\mathrm{Cov}(\tilde{p}_j\tilde{q}_{ij}, \tilde{R}_m) = E(\tilde{p}_j)\, E(\tilde{q}_{ij}\tilde{R}_m) - E(\tilde{p}_j)\, E(\tilde{q}_{ij})\, E(\tilde{R}_m)$$

$$= E(\tilde{p}_j)\, [E(\tilde{q}_{ij}\tilde{R}_m) - E(\tilde{q}_{ij})\, E(\tilde{R}_m)]. \tag{4.13}$$

By definition, $E(\tilde{q}_{ij}\tilde{R}_m) = E(\tilde{q}_{ij})\, E(\tilde{R}_m) + \mathrm{Cov}(\tilde{q}_{ij}, \tilde{R}_m)$ (see the paragraph preceding (4.10)). Thus, the bracketed expression on the RHS of (4.13) equals $\mathrm{Cov}(\tilde{q}_{ij}, \tilde{R}_m)$. Thus, (4.13) can be rewritten as:

$$\mathrm{Cov}(\tilde{p}_j\tilde{q}_{ij}, \tilde{R}_m) = E(\tilde{p}_j)\, \mathrm{Cov}(\tilde{q}_{ij}, \tilde{R}_m). \tag{4.14}$$

In short, we find that the properties of a covariance and the implications of our assumptions about market perfection and about the stochastic relationship between prices of goods and services and rates of return on the market portfolio lead to the simple result that $\text{Cov}(\tilde{p}_j\tilde{q}_{ij}, \tilde{R}_m) = E(\tilde{p}_j)\,\text{Cov}(\tilde{q}_{ij}, \tilde{R}_m)$. This result and the result given by (4.6) allow us to rewrite (4.4) as:

$$\text{Cov}(\tilde{R}_i, \tilde{R}_m) = V_{i1}^{-1} \sum_j E(\tilde{p}_j)\,\text{Cov}(\tilde{q}_{ij}, \tilde{R}_m). \tag{4.15}$$

At the risk of losing the reader's interest, a few more restatements will be made. Their major objective is to obtain an expression for $\text{Cov}(\tilde{R}_i, \tilde{R}_m)$ that can be interpreted with greater ease than (4.15). First, note that the covariance between $\tilde{q}_{ij}$ and $\tilde{R}_m$ and the coefficient of correlation, $\rho(\tilde{q}_{ij}, \tilde{R}_m)$, between $\tilde{q}_{ij}$ and $\tilde{R}_m$ are related by the following equality:

$$\text{Cov}(\tilde{q}_{ij}, \tilde{R}_m) = \rho(\tilde{q}_{ij}, \tilde{R}_m)\sigma(\tilde{q}_{ij})\sigma(\tilde{R}_m), \tag{4.16}$$

where, in general, $\sigma(\tilde{x}) \equiv \sqrt{\text{Var}(\tilde{x})}$ for any random variable $\tilde{x}$.

As with the coefficient of correlation between any two random variables, the value of $[\rho(\tilde{q}_{ij}, \tilde{R}_m)]^2$ can be interpreted as the proportion of the total variance of $\tilde{q}_{ij}$ that can be accounted for ("explained") by the linear relationship between $\tilde{q}_{ij}$ and $\tilde{R}_m$. Recall that $\tilde{R}_m$ is a real rate of return, expressed in terms of units of a relevant bundle of goods and services. In this sense, $1 + \tilde{R}_m$ represents the (cross-sectional) average gross aggregate output of all firms at time 2 per unit of real resource input at time 1. Similarly, $\tilde{q}_{ij}/V_{i1}$, where V_{i1} is also measured in real terms, represents the average real output of product j by firm i per unit of firm i's total real resources as of time 1. Since $\rho((\tilde{q}_{ij}/V_{i1}), \tilde{R}_m) = \rho(\tilde{q}_{ij}, \tilde{R}_m)$, the latter is a measure of association between aggregate average real output and firm i's average real output of project j.

Thus, using (4.15), (4.16), and the definition of β_{im}, we get:

$$\beta_{im} = \text{Cov}(\tilde{R}_i, \tilde{R}_m)/\sigma^2(\tilde{R}_m) = V_{i1}^{-1} \sum_j E(\tilde{p}_j)\rho(\tilde{q}_{ij}, \tilde{R}_m)\frac{\sigma(\tilde{q}_{ij})}{\sigma(R_m)}. \tag{4.17}$$

Expression (4.17) simply indicates the attributes of a firm's operations that are important in determining the firm's relative risk, β_{im}, in the market portfolio, conditional on the prevailing value of V_{i1}. Using the RHS of (4.17), one sees that the risk of firm i in the market portfolio is affected by (1) the expected value of each output's price, (2) the "sensitivity" of each output quantity to general economic factors, where this "sensitivity" is measured by $\rho(\tilde{q}_{ij}, \tilde{R}_m)$ for each j, and (3) the dispersion of the probability distribution of each output quantity—as measured by $\sigma(\tilde{q}_{ij})$, for each j—relative to the dispersion of general economic factors, as measured by $\sigma(\tilde{R}_m)$. Recall that $\tilde{p}_j$ is a *relative* price variable. It represents the number of units of our standard bundle of goods and services (i.e., our numeraire good) that can be converted into one unit of product j. The relative price of the bundle itself is, of course, always unity. Thus, all components of the RHS of (4.17) are expressed in terms of a common unit.

Expression (4.17) can provide some structure to financial statement analysis because it directs one's attention to some specific factors that affect relative risk, β_{im}, conditional on the value of V_{i1}. Before we get more specific about all this, it seems worthwhile to provide formal recognition to the "output mix," or "lines of business," of firm i in the expression for β_{im}.

Let δ_{ij} be the proportion of the ith firm's total time 1 real resources, V_{i1}, invested in the production of product j. Of course, $\Sigma_j \delta_{ij} = 1$ for each i. At equilibrium, and in the absence of "synergy," $\delta_{ij} V_{i1}$ is the period 1 equilibrium value of a firm that specializes in the production of output j. Thus, the equilibrium of firm i at time 1 may be viewed as the sum of the (implicit) equilibrium values of its various "lines of business," where each line corresponds to a particular type of output.[13] For an arbitrary set of prevailing prices, $\delta_{ij} V_{i1}$ need not, in general, equal the value of a firm specializing in the production of output j. But it still represents the real resources committed to that activity by firm i, conditional on the tentatively prevailing prices.

Multiply and divide the jth summand of (4.17) by δ_{ij} and move V_{i1}^{-1} inside the summation. The result is:

$$\beta_{im} = \sum_j \left(\frac{\delta_{ij}}{V_{i1}\delta_{ij}}\right) E(\tilde{p}_j)\rho(\tilde{q}_{ij}, \tilde{R}_m)\left(\frac{\sigma(\tilde{q}_{ij})}{\sigma(\tilde{R}_m)}\right). \tag{4.18}$$

Next, recognize, using the properties of a variance, that:

$$\sigma^2(\tilde{q}_{ij}/\delta_{ij} V_{i1}) = \left(\frac{1}{\delta_{ij} V_{i1}}\right)^2 \sigma^2(\tilde{q}_{ij}) \tag{4.19}$$

and, therefore:

$$\sigma(\tilde{q}_{ij}/\delta_{ij} V_{i1}) = \left(\frac{1}{\delta i_j V_{i1}}\right) \sigma(\tilde{q}_{ij}). \tag{4.20}$$

Use of (4.20) in (4.18) leads to:

$$\beta_{im} = \sum_j \delta_{ij} E(\tilde{p}_j)\sigma(\tilde{q}_{ij}, \tilde{R}_m)\left(\frac{\sigma(\tilde{q}_{ij}/\delta_{ij} V_{i1})}{\sigma(\tilde{R}_m)}\right). \tag{4.21}$$

The parameter $\sigma(\tilde{q}_{ij}/\delta_{ij} V_{i1})$ may be interpreted as a measure of uncertainty of firm i's output of product j per unit of real resources invested in the jth line of business. (Note that $(\tilde{q}_{ij}/\delta_{ij} V_{i1})$ is simply unity plus the real rate of return on firm i's j^{th} line of business.) If, for example, an increase in the scale of activities dealing with the production of j leads to greater dispersion in the quantity of output, $\tilde{q}_{ij}$, per unit of real resource input, then—other things being equal—one's inferred value of the ith firm's relative risk, β_{im}, will increase.

Of course, there may be a variety of reasons—both behavioral and technological—for not expecting "other things" to remain unchanged. For example, an inferred change in the scale of the jth line of business may have been induced by a change in the value of $E(\tilde{p}_j)$—a change that might also be inferred upon closer study of available evidence (if it was not already inferred). Moreover, an inferred change in the value of $E(\tilde{p}_j)$ may imply entry or exit by other firms (depending on the reasons for the change in the value of $E(\tilde{p}_j)$); this can affect the ultimate attributes of firm i's j^{th} line of business. Finally, internal consistency of one's analysis may demand examination of the prices of outputs that are either substitutes or complements vis-à-vis product j. And this analysis may lead to additional inferences about the expected values of the prices of firm i's outputs and the scale of its

[13]A technical derivation of this result is provided in Fama and Miller [1972, pp. 304–7].

investment in each available line of business. In short, a variety of general equilibrium issues surrounds any particular inferred change in the determinants of a firm's risk. And, of course, one's ultimate inferences about firm i's risk conditional on having explored these issues may be quite different from what would be concluded on the basis of an inferred change in only one of those determinants, along the lines of a partial equilibrium analysis. The types of data that might be used for conducting such an exploration are discussed below.

Expression (4.21) applies to the risk of firm i's rate of return. A parallel expression for the gross dollar return, $\tilde{V}_{i2}$, is, however, easily obtained. Recall (from fn. 6) that:

$$\mathrm{Cov}(\tilde{V}_{i2}, \tilde{V}_{m2})/\mathrm{Var}(\tilde{V}_{m2}) = (V_{i1}/V_{m1})\beta_{im}. \tag{4.22}$$

Thus, after multiplying both sides of (4.21) by (V_{i1}/V_{m1}), one gets:

$$\begin{aligned}
\frac{\mathrm{Cov}(\tilde{V}_{i2}, \tilde{V}_{m2})}{\mathrm{Var}(\tilde{V}_{m2})} &= \sum_j \delta_{ij}\, E(\tilde{p}_j)\, \rho(\tilde{q}_{ij}, \tilde{R}_m)\left(\frac{V_{i1}}{V_{m1}}\right)\left(\frac{\sigma(\tilde{q}_{ij}/\delta_{ij}V_{i1})}{\sigma(\tilde{R}_m)}\right) \\
&= \sum_j \delta_{ij}\, E(\tilde{p}_j)\, \rho(\tilde{q}_{ij}, \tilde{R}_m)\left(\frac{V_{i1}}{V_{m1}}\right)\left(\frac{1}{\delta_{ij}V_{i1}}\right)\left(\frac{\sigma(\tilde{q}_{ij})}{\sigma(\tilde{R}_m)}\right) \\
&= \sum_j E(\tilde{p}_j)\, \rho(\tilde{q}_{ij}, \tilde{R}_m)\left(\frac{\sigma(\tilde{q}_{ij})}{\sigma(\tilde{V}_{m2})}\right) \\
&= \sum_j E(\tilde{p}_j)\, \rho(\tilde{q}_{ij}, \tilde{V}_{m2})\left(\frac{\sigma(\tilde{q}_{ij})}{\sigma(\tilde{V}_{m2})}\right).
\end{aligned} \tag{4.23}$$

In deriving the next to the last equality, we used the fact that $V_{m1}\,\sigma(\tilde{R}_m) = V_{m1}\,\sigma(1 + \tilde{R}_m) = \sigma(\tilde{V}_{m2})$. For the last equality, we used the fact that $\rho(\tilde{q}_{ij}, \tilde{R}_m) = \rho(\tilde{q}_{ij}, 1 + \tilde{R}_m) = \rho(\tilde{q}_{ij}, V_{m1}(1 + \tilde{R}_m)) = \rho(\tilde{q}_{ij}, \tilde{V}_{m2})$. All random variables that appear in (4.23) were discussed earlier. Suffice it to note here that $\tilde{V}_{m2}$ denotes aggregate real output at time 2; $\tilde{q}_{ij}$ denotes the ith firm's total real output of product j.

4.3.3 Operating Decisions and Risk Assessments

Expression (4.23) provides one characterization of the relationship between the relative risk of firm i's dollar returns and the stochastic attributes of firm i's operating activities. By doing so, it indicates some of the inferences that are useful in assessing the relative risk of dollar returns. Expression (4.21) fulfills the same objective regarding rates of return, conditional on prevailing prices of securities and on investors' assessments of the distribution functions of firms' future values. In what follows, we shall assume that observed rates of return are, in fact, drawings from the rate-of-return distributions corresponding to market equilibria; this assumption was discussed in Section 4.2.

The discussion that follows applies to assessments of both dollar risk and rate-of-return risk. It is couched in terms of assessments of β_{im}, which is (in our framework) the relevant measure rate-of-return risk.

Suppose that one is trying to assess the risk of the ith firm. On the one hand, one might use an estimate of β_{im} based only on observed values of $\tilde{R}_i$ and $\tilde{R}_m$ for past periods (e.g., months). But this approach assumes that the characteristics of the firm's operating decisions were unchanged over the time period from which observations are taken (e.g., the post-World War II period). If that is not the case, then—strictly speaking—no one value of β_{im} prevailed over that time period. Thus, an estimate of β_{im} based on pooling the observations on $\tilde{R}_i$ and $\tilde{R}_m$ would be an estimate of some kind of "average" of the values of β_{im} that prevailed over the observation period. In some cases, this kind of estimate has some desirable statistical properties. Whether it does or not depends, however, on the precise way in which the value of β_{im} changes.[14]

Second, if, in fact, the characteristics of the firm's operating decisions were, and are expected to continue, changing, then the risk of the firm during (at least) the forthcoming future period may be very different from the past value (or values) of its risk. Thus, an estimate of risk based only on past data—such as an estimate produced by Ordinary Least Squares—may not be very informative with respect to the firm's risk over the future (or even a past) period for which a risk assessment is desired. The discussion that immediately follows expression (4.21) points to some of the forces that can induce risk changes. In short, one can conceive of many plausible settings in which estimating risk may require more than using only observed rates of return in a way that assumes a fixed value of risk.

A variety of empirical studies have provided results on the stability of individual securities' relative risks. Most of them focused, in particular, on common stocks. Thus, for reasons given later, these results reflect the joint effects of firms' production-investment and financing decisions on relative risks. The crux of their results is that the relative risks of common stock rates of return are not, in general, stationary over time (see, e.g., Blume [1971], Fisher and Kamin [1975], Gonedes [1973], Levy [1971], Rosenberg and McKibben [1973], Rosenberg and Marathe [1975], Rosenberg and Guy [1975], and Sunder [1976]). A critique of statistical methods used for some of these results and additional empirical results are provided by Kon and Lau [1977], who also infer nonstationarity of common stocks' relative risks.

Of course, it is quite possible to have $\mathrm{Cov}(\tilde{V}_{i2}, \tilde{V}_{m2})/\mathrm{Var}(\tilde{V}_{m2})$ stationary and $\mathrm{Cov}(\tilde{R}_i, \tilde{R}_m)/\mathrm{Var}(\tilde{R}_m) = \beta_{im}$ nonstationary. Since $\beta_{im} = (V_{m1}/V_{i1})\,\mathrm{Cov}(\tilde{V}_{i2}, \tilde{V}_{m2})/\mathrm{Var}(\tilde{V}_{m2})$, the nonstationarity in β_{im} could be due to temporal variation in the ratio (V_{i1}/V_{m1}), which is simply the proportion of the market portfolio's time 1 value accounted for by firm i. Also, as indicated above, the cited empirical results deal with returns on common stocks (a subset of firms' securities) rather than firms' total returns. Yet, this evidence and a priori considerations pertinent to the determinants of the risks of firms' future values motivate one at least to entertain the possibility of risk changes when distributions of firms' future values are being assessed. This position seems no less palatable than the more dogmatic position that does not even allow for the possibility of risk changes.

Expressions (4.21) and (4.23) are specifications of some determinants of relative risks of rates of return and dollar returns, respectively. Given these statements, one can attack the issue of risk changes by making inferences about the changes (if any) in those determinants' values and then inferences about the implied changes in risk. Some possible routes toward this end are discussed next.

Suppose, for example, that one can associate each of a firm's products with a well-defined industry and suppose that accounting numbers on the attributes of the industry associated with product j, for each j, are available. Such data can often be obtained from

---

[14]For details, see Swamy [1971].

various publications of the U.S. government or trade associations, among other sources.[15] In this case, one can attempt to use such data in order to make inferences about $\rho(\tilde{q}_{ij}, \tilde{R}_m)$ and $\sigma(\tilde{q}_{ij}/\delta_{ij}, V_{i1})$, on the assumption that aggregate industry data are representative of the product-j attributes for any firm producing that product.

Using industry data to make inferences about the attributes of individual firms' operations can be justified on theoretical grounds. In general, the major attributes of firms' decisions in a market economy are induced by demand conditions and cost conditions, or the market(s), for firms' outputs and firms' factors of production, respectively. In theory, one expects the decisions of firms facing the same demand and cost conditions (i.e., firms operating in the same markets) to have similar attributes due to the forces leading to equilibrium in those markets. That is, those forces lead to an interdependence among the operations of different firms participating in the same markets and, therefore, to similarity among the attributes of those firms' operations. Using industry data to make inferences about the attributes of a member firm's decisions reflects an attempt to exploit those similarities.[16]

In principle, one would like industry data to be based on groupings of firms' activities that are consistent with the theoretical notion of an industry. Specifically, the groupings should pertain to firms or parts of firms facing essentially the same demand and cost conditions. Whether the industry groupings that underlie available data satisfy this criterion is not something about which we are prepared to generalize. If seemingly relevant data (e.g., observed industry sales of product j) based on several industrial classification schemes are available, it might be advisable to make inferences conditional on each set and to assess the consistency of those inferences. This is simply a form of "sensitivity analysis."

As indicated earlier, the random variables considered here are in "real" terms. Thus, available industry data expressed in terms of "dollars" (i.e., in nominal terms) would, in principle, have to be adjusted for price level changes. This is avoidable, of course, when corresponding series expressed in real terms are available—as is often the case with the data provided by, e.g., the Department of Commerce in its *Survey of Current Business* (see fn. 15). When such corresponding series are not available, the nominal data may have to be adjusted for purchasing power changes. A variety of seemingly useful approximations have been developed for this task (see, e.g., Young [1975; 1986*a*; 1986*b*], Shoven and Bulow [1975; 1976], Largay and Livingstone [1976], Davidson, Stickney, and Weil [1976], Parker [1977], Winn [1975, appendix D], and Tideman and Tucker [1976]). More recently, the FASB [1979] has required certain large firms to disclose price-level-adjusted

---

[15]Two especially useful U.S. government publications are (1) the Department of Commerce's *Survey of Current Business* (published monthly) along with the various supplementary publications that provide additional details and data on the economic series covered in the *Survey* and (2) the Internal Revenue Service's *Statistics of Income, Corporation Income Tax Returns,* which provides a variety of balance sheet and income statement data for industry groups. (The IRS does not make individual firms' data available.) Another useful source of data on industry groupings is Robert Morris Associates' *Annual Statement Studies,* which has been published annually for more than 50 years. This publication supplies values of numerous ratios, balance sheet numbers, and income statement numbers. Finally, a seemingly important source of data on firms' activities is the line-of-business data disclosed by firms in their filings with the Securities and Exchange Commission (SEC) and in their published annual reports. This source is discussed below.

[16]Some empirical results pertinent to this approach are provided in: Gonedes and Twombly [1981].

accounting numbers, which reduces the estimation task for these firms. In any event, if one can make inferences about $\rho(\tilde{q}_{ij}, \tilde{R}_m)$ and $\sigma(\tilde{q}_{ij}/\delta_{ij}V_{i1})$ when dealing with real rates of return, or $\rho(\tilde{q}_{ij}, \tilde{V}_{m2})$ and $\sigma(\tilde{q}_{ij})$ when dealing with dollar returns (in terms of "constant" dollars), then one can make tentative inferences about the kinds of risk changes that a firm is likely to experience, holding the values of other parameters constant. Final inferences will, of course, depend on the inferred values of those other parameters and the sorts of general equilibrium issues mentioned earlier.

Inferences about $\rho(\tilde{q}_{ij}, \tilde{R}_m)$ and $\sigma(\tilde{q}_{ij}/\delta_{ij}V_{i1})$ need not be based only on aggregate industry data. Indeed, when one cannot (or choses not to) associate a given product of a firm with a well-defined industry, such data may not be helpful. An alternative source of potentially useful data is the firm-by-firm "line of business" (or "business segment") disclosures that are now publicly available. The line of business data provided by a given firm can be used to make inferences about the attributes of that firm's decisions. In addition, the line-of-business data supplied by all firms providing such data can be used to construct aggregate line-of-business data for groups of firms formed by the data analyst. The latter data can be used for the same purposes (and under the same assumptions) for which other sorts of industry data can be used. A discussion of line-of-business reporting requirements follows.

There have been several changes in line-of-business disclosure requirements over the years; so the kinds of details disclosed by a particular firm will vary over time. Moreover, the firms which fall under the requirements to make line-of-business disclosures have changed over time. In order to provide some insights into what one will encounter when using disclosures provided over, say, a 10- or 20-year period, we describe some key aspects of past disclosure rules and key aspects of the currently effective rules.[17]

For most firms, detailed line-of-business reporting began in 1969, when the SEC adopted a new requirement for such reporting.[18] This requirement applied to registration statements filed on or after August 14, 1969. It dealt with material disclosed in the narrative sections of three documents filed in conjunction with registrations: Forms S-1, S-7, and 10. It did not require disclosures in other filings with the SEC. This requirement led to the disclosure—by some publicly owned firms engaged in more than one line of business—of sales, revenues, and pretax earnings for each principal component of a firm's business. The text of the SEC's 1969 line-of-business reporting requirement is as follows:[19]

> *Information as to lines of business.* If the registrant and its subsidiaries are engaged in more than one line of business, state, for each of the registrant's last five fiscal years, or for each fiscal year ending after December 31, 1966, or for each fiscal year the registrant had been engaged in business, whichever period is less, the approximate amount or percentage of (i) total sales and revenues, and (ii) income (or loss) before income taxes and extraordinary items, attributable to each line of business which during either of the last two fiscal years accounted for—
>
> (A) 10 percent or more of the total of sales and revenues,

---

[17]For additional details, see Twombly [1980].

[18]Securities and Exchange Commission, Release No. 4988 (Securities Act of 1933) and Release No. 8650 (Securities Exchange Act of 1934), July 14, 1969.

[19]See the SEC Releases cited in fn. 18 or Rappaport [1972, pp. 23.15–23.23].

(B) 10 percent or more of income before income taxes and extraordinary items computed without deduction of loss resulting from operations of any line of business, or

(C) a loss which equalled or exceeded 10 percent of the amount of income specified in (B) above;

provided, that if total sales and revenues did not exceed $50,000,000 during either of the last two fiscal years, the percentages specified in (A), (B), and (C) above shall be 15 percent, instead of 10 percent.

If it is impractical to state the contribution to income (or loss) before income taxes and extraordinary items for any line of business, state the contribution thereof to the results of operations most closely approaching such income, together with a brief explanation of the reasons why it is not practicable to state the contribution to any such income or loss.

Instructions. 1. If the number of lines of business for which information is required exceeds ten, the registrant may, at its option, furnish the required information for only the ten lines of business deemed most important to an understanding of the business. In such event, a statement to that effect shall be set forth.

2. In grouping products or services as lines of business, appropriate consideration shall be given to all relevant factors, including rates of profitability of operations, degrees of risk and opportunity for growth. The basis for grouping such products or services and any material changes between periods in such groupings shall be briefly described.

3. Where material amounts of products or services are transferred from one line of business to another, the receiving and transferring lines may be considered a single line of business for the purpose of reporting the operating results thereof.

4. If the method of pricing intra-company transfers of products or services or the method of allocation of common or corporate costs materially affects the reported contribution to income of a line of business, such methods and any material changes between periods in such methods and the effect thereof shall be described briefly.

5. Information regarding sales or revenues or income (or loss) from different classes of products or services in operations regulated by Federal, State or municipal authorities may be limited to those classes of products or services required by any uniform system of accounts prescribed by such authorities.

In October 1970 the SEC extended its line-of-business disclosure requirements to filings on Form 10-K, which is filed annually by registrants. This extension applied to 10-K filings for fiscal years ending on or after December 31, 1970.[20]

Observe that the above requirements are among those that apply to "filings" with the SEC. In general, annual reports to stockholders are not deemed to be filings with the SEC. Thus, some data included in, for example, a firm's form 10-K filing with the SEC may

---

[20]This extension was part of a revision of Form 10-K. See Securities and Exchange Commission, Release No. 9000 (Securities Exchange Act of 1934), October 21, 1970.

not appear in that firm's annual report to stockholders.[21] The SEC often stipulates, however, that parts of all of its disclosure requirements do apply to annual reports to stockholders.[22]

In 1974, the SEC extended its line-of-business disclosure requirements to financial statements sent to stockholders.[23] That extension required disclosures in the latter that are at least as comprehensive as those required in 10-K filings (starting with fiscal years ending on or after December 20, 1974).

The disclosure requirements for filings with the SEC were reconsidered because of the requirements adopted by the FASB in its *Statement No. 14: Financial Reporting for Segments of a Business Enterprise* (December). On May 10, 1977, the SEC released proposed rule changes that were designed to coordinate its own line-of-business disclosure requirements with the FASB's new requirements and to modify the FASB's requirements for purposes of SEC filings.

Briefly, FASB *Statement No. 14* requires firms doing business in more than one industry to disclose revenue, income, and assets for each significant "industry segment." In addition, firms are required to report data on their foreign operations, export sales, and their dependence on one or a few major customers.

Firms' definitions of "industry segments" are supposed to recognize the nature of their products, production processes, and their markets and marketing methods. Available coding systems—such as the Standard Industrial Classification Code—are identified as sources of guidelines. It is indicated, however, that no single classification scheme should be viewed as universally applicable and that considerable management judgment will be required in defining industry segments.

In general, *Statement No. 14* requires segment disclosures for any segment whose revenue, operating profit or loss, or "identifiable" assets are 10 percent or more of the corresponding totals for the firm as a whole. If each individual segment accounts for less than 10 percent of all of these company totals, segment reprots will have to be provided for segments that account, in the aggregate, for at least 75 percent of the indicated firm-wide total amounts. If a firm has one dominant segment—defined as one that accounts for at least 90 percent of the indicated firm-wide total amounts—then no segment data are required.

The minimal disclosures for domestic segments and foreign operations (assuming the 10 percent materiality criterion is satisfied) are revenue, operating profit or loss, and "identifiable" assets. In computing segment operating profit or loss, the following items are supposed to be excluded from consideration: revenue not derived from operations, general corporate expenses, interest expense, income taxes, and extraordinary items, among other things.

Statement No. 14 notes that disaggregating some or all of a firm's foreign operations

---

[21] Such differences seem destined to disappear or become less prevalent due to radical changes adopted in 1980. See, e.g., *The SEC's Integrated Disclosure System* (Commerce Clearing House, 1980).

[22] See, e.g., A. A. Somer, Jr. (Commissioner, Securities and Exchange Commission), "The American Experience with Accounting Principles," an address delivered at a conference on International Business: Finance, Tax, and Accounting Problems, London, England, December 11, 1974, p. 14.

[23] Securities and Exchange Commission, Release No. 34-11079, October 31, 1974.

along industry lines may be exceedingly difficult, conditional on its notion of an industry segment. In such cases, these foreign operations may be treated as one industry segment.

This *Statement* also requires some disclosures even when the above information on industry segments is not required. These include disclosures pertaining to export sales, sales to a single customer (or group of customers under common control), and sales to domestic government agencies or foreign governments, if such sales exceed 10 percent of consolidated net sales.

Statement No. 14 applies to annual financial statements issued for fiscal years beginning after December 15, 1976 and for interim periods within those years for which "complete financial statements" are presented, if those interim reports are described as having been prepared in accordance with GAAP. Statements for earlier periods presented for comparative purposes need not be provided in accordance with *Statement No. 14*.

When results for fiscal years beginning after December 15, 1976 are presented as "prior period" results, for comparative purposes, those results are supposd to be restated when (1) all results for the current period are restated (e.g., to account for a pooling of interest), (2) the groupings of products and services into industry segments are changed, or (3) the groupings of foreign operations into geographic areas are changed.

The above overview of *Statement No. 14* is sufficient for our purposes. Additional details can be obtained from the statement itself. Exhibit 1(a) provides a comparative summary of line-of-business reporting requirements under *FASB Statement No. 14*, the SEC's existing rules, and a disclosure program initiated by the Federal Trade Commission (FTC). The FTC's program covers selected large firms. The data received by the FTC from individual firms are not intended to be publicly available. However, the FTC does plan to publish aggregate data on, e.g., various industries and lines of business. These data are, therefore, among the aggregate data that one might use in making inferences about a particular firm's risk determinants, along the lines suggested earlier.

Exhibit 1(b) provides a comparative summary of FASB *Statement No. 14* and the SEC's *proposed* line-of-business reporting requirements, which were made in May 1977.

We should point out that some data on product lines, or lines of business, were available (at least in SEC filings) long before the SEC's 1969 line-of-business reporting requirements were adopted. The general picture before that adoption was as follows (Rappaport [1972, pp. 23.1–23.2]):

> . . . it had been a rule of long standing that companies registering under the Securities Acts had to disclose the relative importance of each product or service, or class of similar products or services, that contributed 15% or more of the total gross volume of business. This disclosure was required in the narrative or text portion of a registration statement—not in the financial statements. . . . In addition, if income was derived from the sale of products as well as revenues for services, Regulation S-X called for a separate reporting in the formal income statement of such sales and revenues if either item was more than 10% of the combined total. The regulation also calls for a separate showing of cost of goods sold and operating expenses where sales and revenues are shown separately, but there was no requirement for a breakdown of new income by product lines or services.

Requirements for line-of-business disclosures in registration statements (in particular, Form S-1) can be traced back to at least 1947. The instructions for Form S-1 effective as

EXHIBIT 1(a)

Requirements	Line of Business/Segment Reporting Programs		
	FASB	Present SEC Rules /1/	FTC
Does the program apply to all companies issuing financial statements based upon GAAP?	Yes (For all business enterprises)	No (Registrants only)	No (Selected larger manufacturing companies only)
Are world-wide operations to be reported?	Yes /2/	Yes	No (Domestic activities only)
Is there a formal list of categories which must be used in developing industry segments?	No	No	Yes (Aggregated SIC Codes)
Is there a limit to the number of reportable segments?	Suggests no more than ten	Suggestes no more than ten	No
How often must the information be reported?	Included in any GAAP financial statements	Annually (Form 10K) and specified filings	As ordered, generally on an annual basis
Test to determine if a segment is significant and reportable?	Essentially 10% of enterprise revenues, identifiable assets, or profits /3/	Segment equal to 10% or more of consolidated revenues or profits /3/, /4/	Segment revenues over $10 million
Is the following information required by segment:			
Operating revenues?	Yes	Yes	Yes
Operating profit?	Yes	No /5/	Yes
Pretax earnings?	No	Yes /5/	No
Allocation of indirect expenses?	Yes (If necessary to determine operating profit)	No /5/	Yes
Assets?	Yes	No	Yes
Depreciation, depletion, and amortization expense?	Yes	No	Yes
Capital expenditures?	Yes	No	No
Effect of change in accounting principle?	Yes	Not explicitly	No
Industry and geographic area of equity investments?	Yes	No	No
Is information required on a geographic basis as well as industry segmentation?	Yes	No /6/	No

EXHIBIT 1(a) Cont.

Requirements	Line of Business/Segment Reporting Programs		
	FASB	Present SEC Rules /1/	FTC
Are major customers disclosed?	Yes	Yes /7/	No
Are export sales disclosed?	Yes	No	No

/1/ The SEC has proposed to conform its present line of business rules to Statement No. 14.
/2/ Except where disaggregation of foreign operations is not practical.
/3/Although the SEC and FASB significance rules are similar, there are some differences in determining measurable revenues and profits which *may* result in differences between reportable segments.
/4/ 15% for companies with less than $50 million in sales.
/5/ SEC rules require disclosure of "income (or loss) before income taxes and extraordinary items" except where it is "impractical" to state. If this is the case, the registrant should disclose results of operations most closely approaching income. Because of these differences, a company may report different levels of profitability for FASB, SEC, and FTC purposes.
/6/SEC rules provide for disclosure of the volume of foreign sales where they are material.
/7/ SEC rules require a textual description of the registrant's business including the identity of major customers. (Statement No. 14 does not require disclosure of the major customers' identity.)
Source: Ernst & Ernst [1977*c*, pp. 8–9].

EXHIBIT 1(b)

Requirement	Disclosures Required?	
	FASB Statement No. 14	Proposed SEC Rules
Applicability to annual statements	Years beginning after December 15, 1976.	Most recent five years. Comments requested on application to years beginning prior to December 15, 1976.
Applicability to interim statements	Complete statements "expressly described" as in conformity with GAAP.	Complete interim period statements.
Industry segment data:		
Revenue	Yes	Yes
Operating profit	Yes	Yes
Identifiable assets	Yes	Yes
Depreciation expense	Yes	Yes
Capital expenditures	Yes	Yes
Equity in unconsolidated investments	Yes	/4/
Reconciliation of segment data to consolidated amounts	Yes	Yes
Revenue by class of product	No	Disclose revenue by major (10 percent of total sales; 15 percent for smaller companies) class of products.
Foreign and domestic operations:		
Revenue	Yes	Yes

EXHIBIT 1(b) Cont.

Requirement	Disclosures Required? FASB Statement No. 14	Proposed SEC Rules
Operating profit, net profit or other	Yes	Yes
Identifiable assets	Yes	Yes
Reconciliation of area data to consolidated amounts	Yes	Yes
Export sales	Yes	Yes
Major customers:		
Applicability	Disclose if amounts are at least 10 percent of total revenue.	Disclose if a material part of the industry segment.*
Disclosures	Amount and segment.	Customer name, relationship and material facts.*
Intersegment or interarea transfers:		
Revenue by segment or area	Yes	Yes
Purchases by segment or area	No	Yes
Comparative pricing data	No	Yes
Other disclosures:		
Description of segment accounting policies	Identify major policies.	No
Description of segment products and services	Briefly identify	Lengthy description of major business factors.*
Effect, by segment or area, of change in accounting method or allocation method	Amount and nature of change	No
Unusual or infrequently occurring items by segment	Amount and nature	No

*Not required by proxy rules regulating annual reports to shareholders but would be required in Form 10-K and other SEC filing forms.
Source: Ernst & Ernst [1977*b*, pp. 8–9].

of January 1947 called for such disclosures (in somewhat general terms) in the narrative material pertaining to "Description of Business."

The availability of line-of-business data means that one can attempt to make inferences about parameters such as $\rho(\tilde{q}_{ij}, \tilde{R}_m)$ and $\sigma(\tilde{q}_{ij}/\delta_{ij}V_{i1})$ using data on firm i's operations rather than aggregate data. Alternatively, one can make such inferences using both aggregate data and data specific to the firm under investigation.

Another potentially useful pursuit is to make inferences about the relative importance of each of a firm's lines of business. In expression (4.21), the relative importance of line j for firm i is indicated by the value of δ_{ij}, where $\Sigma_j\delta_{ij} = 1$. In principle, the value of δ_{ij} is given by the ratio of (1) the real resources committed to line j by firm i to (2) firm i's total real resources. In practice, data on neither the real resources nor the nominal resources committed to a firm's line of business are likely to be readily available over extended periods of time. As indicated above, the current disclosure requirements embodied in FASB *Statement No. 14* call for disclosures of "identifiable assets" by segments of a firm. But these data may not correspond to the lines of business that are of interest to an analyst. Moreover, such data may not be provided for many past time periods. (*Statement No. 14* does not require disclosures of these past data.) Thus, it seems that proxies for δ_{ij}, as defined earlier, will often have to suffice. As before, aggregate industry data may reflect information pertinent to a particular firm in the identified industry grouping. The relative sales or operating income contribution computed using the firm's own line-of-business disclosures may also reflect such information. Additional bases for making inferences about the kinds of activities in which a firm is involved, the relative importance of each activity, and changes in the types and relative importance of a firm's lines include announcements (in, e.g., press releases) about new products, merger and divestiture activities, capital expenditure plans (indicating, e.g., whether the firm is increasing or decreasing the real resources devoted to each of its lines or whether it is entering new lines), and announcements about changes in management or the firm's internal (organizational) structure, among other things. Changes in management or organizational structure may signal—or even be "advertised" as motivated by—intentions to alter the nature and emphasis of the firm's activities. For example, such intentions may motivate replacing an "operations-oriented" chief executive officer with a "marketing-oriented" one.

As of any point in time, announcements provided by and data on a particular firm are not the only potential sources of useful information about the attributes of that firm's production-investment decisions. As indicated earlier, a variety of general equilibrium issues are pertinent to assessing those attributes. Thus, announcements by other firms constitute potential sources of information for making inferences about those attributes. Moreover, data on, say, industry or activity j constitute a potentially useful source of information for making inferences about industry or activity k, $j \neq k$. For example, new entry into, say, the aluminum products industry may lead to lower (relative) prices of aluminum-content cans. That, in turn, may induce (relative) price decreases for steel-content cans—which are substitutes for aluminum cans—and perhaps an outflow of real resources (i.e., exit) from the steel products industry, in general, and the steel cans line of business, in particular. And all of this may alter one's inferences about the characteristics of a given steel firm's production-investment decisions—depending on the firm's involvement in the steel cans line of business. Inferences about such things might be based, in part, on estimated cross-elasticities of demand and estimates of scale elasticities—both of which can be obtained by using available data or by using estimates provided in published reports.[24] (See, for example, Bridge [1971], Douglas [1975], Desai [1976] Philips [1974], Bishop [1952], and Scherer [1970] for discussions, numerous references, and remarks on available empirical studies.)

In addition, and related to the previous example, one might attempt to use directly available theory and evidence on the effects of entry and exit on market structure and the implied effects on the attributes of a particular firm's production-investment decisions. Suppose, for example, that one is attempting to make an inference about the "market share" of a particular firm with respect to one of its lines of business—perhaps on the assumption that the relative importance of that line (for the given firm) will vary directly

[24]For any output, the scale elasticity is defined by the percentage change in the quantity of output corresponding to an equi-proportional change in all inputs. The cross-elasticity of demand for products j and k is defined by the percentage change in the quantity of j demanded corresponding to a given percentage change in the price of product k, holding all other prices constant.

with this market share. And suppose that one forecasts new entry into that market by firms not now involved in that market. What are the likely effects on the given firm's market share if it is now a "dominant" firm relative to that market? One might predict, on theoretical grounds, that sufficient new entry will probably lead to a less dominant position. On the other hand, this kind of result might depend on the kinds of firms that seem likely to be the new entrants. If they are "small"—relative to the resources devoted to this market by the firm under analysis—reduced dominance may be unlikely. If the new entrants are relatively large, reduced dominance might be ascribed a higher probability.[25] These are the kinds of market structure/market peformance issues considered in the literature on industrial organization.[26] It should be clear that theory and evidence on those issues are, in general, relevant to making inferences about the attributes of firms' production-investment decisions within the context of financial statement analysis.

Of course, the activities of competing firms and potential competitors are not the only ones that might have implications for the nature and relative importance of a given firm's lines of business. The antitrust activities of the U.S. government—and perhaps even state governments—might be equally important. Such activities may, for example, lead to forced divestitures and, thus, less involvement in certain lines of business. Or the fear of antitrust actions may induce a firm to forego entry into or expansion in certain lines. In any event, announcements by, e.g., the U.S. Department of Justice and the U.S. Federal Trade Commission about their actions and objectives constitute other potentially useful sources of information about a firm's production-investment decisions—even though these announcements are not among those made by the firm itself.[27]

When making inferences about $\tilde{q}_{ij}$, for any j, the role of the firm's production function for line j can be exploited. Recall (from Section 4.3.2) that, in general, $\tilde{q}_{ij} = h_{ij}(y_{i1}, y_{i2}, \ldots, y_{ik}|\tilde{\theta}_{ij})$, where y_{ie}, $e = 1, 2, \ldots, k$, are the inputs and $\tilde{\theta}_{ij}$ represents the source(s) of uncertainty about the quantity of output j that can be obtained from given quantities of the inputs. In general, the characteristics of the production functions, $h_{ij}(\cdot|\tilde{\theta}_{ij})$, are determined by the existing technology to which the *ith* firm has access. Any changes in that technology—due to the firm's or others' efforts—are potential inducements to alter the production function characterizing line j's operations, for any j. And such a change may alter the stochastic characteristics of $\tilde{q}_{ij} = h_{ij}(y_{i1}, y_{i2}, \ldots, y_{ik}|\tilde{\theta}_{ij})$. In addition, changes in the attributes of the source(s) of uncertainty affecting output quantities may have this effect. For example, the nature of the firm's system of internal control may change, and that change may lead to changes in the rewards and penalties affecting production workers' behavior. The latter changes may, in turn, alter the distribution of output corresponding to given quantities of inputs, because they constitute a change in the distribution of $\tilde{\theta}_{ij}$, for any j. Changes in weather conditions, repair and maintenance policies, and the qualities of factors of production (e.g., raw materials) may have similar effects.

The characteristics of the production function $h_{ij}(\cdot|\tilde{\theta}_{ij})$, for any j, can also be exploited

---

[25]Evidence bearing directly on this issue is provided in Berry [1975, chap. 6].

[26]See, e.g., Scherer [1970].

[27]More generally, announcements by and actions of all regulatory agencies, governmental and nongovernmental, are potentially useful sources of information. Trade associations that pursue what are, in effect, regulatory actions—such as enforcing advertising and product standards—are among the relevant nongovernmental agencies. In this regard, see, e.g., Hemenway [1975].

when attempting to make inferences by using evidence on relationships among values of accounting (or other) numbers—as is done in ratio analysis. Conditional on the distribution function of $\tilde{\theta}_{ij}$, the production function $h_{ij}(\cdot|\tilde{\theta}_{ij})$ and the market value rule imply economically efficient *combinations* of inputs (e.g., direct labor, materials, and supervision) corresponding to the distribution function of $\tilde{q}_{ij}$. Thus, this production function provides a basis for interpreting inferred relationships among numbers pertaining to input/output relationships (e.g., the cost of labor relative to sales and the stock of fixed assets relative to output). Inferring important shifts in the systematic characteristics of these relationships may lead one to infer production-function changes. The latter inference may, in turn, lead one to infer changes in the stochastic characteristics of $\tilde{q}_{ij}$, for any j. Alternatively, inferring shifts in the attributes of these relationships may lead to inferring changes in the firm's policies but no production-function changes. Such policy changes may be induced by changes in managements' expectations about relative prices (e.g., the expected price of labor relative to that of capital services or the expected price of highly trained new workers relative to that of workers with few skills). Comparisons of different firms' production-function characteristics may also provide useful insights. For example, inferred systematic differences between the production functions characterizing one firm's operations and those characterizing the operations of another firm that supplies the same outputs might lead to important insights regarding "cost advantages" and "technological advantages." Or they may lead to inferred departures from the "market value rule." In any event, production functions' implications for combinations of inputs and relationships among accounting numbers can supply guidelines for pursuits such as ratio analyses and analyses based on related tools.

Another term that appears as a determinant of risk is $E(\tilde{p}_j)$, one for each j. As with the other parameters of (4.21) or (4.23), inferences about $E(\tilde{p}_j)$, which is the expected value of a relative price, can be made using publicly available data. For example, if product j can be associated with a particular industry, then publicly available price-index data can be used as sources of sample evidence.[28] Also, if product j is one of those commodities for which there is trading in futures contracts, then available price data on futures contracts might be used—along with some theory of pricing in futures markets—to make inferences about $E(\tilde{p}_j)$.[29] In addition, the characteristics of prevailing governmental policies (e.g., macroeconomic policies, subsidy legislation, antitrust activities, price-support legislation, etc.) can be used in making inferences about the expected values of relative prices for different products. Announcements (by the firm under analysis or its competitors) about new products—particularly products that are substitutes for or complementary to product j—and information available from trade associations can also be used in making such inferences.[30] Finally, the implications of the various general equilibrium issues discussed above might be exploited in making inferences about expected values of relative prices.

---

[28]These kinds of data are published by the Department of Labor and the Department of Commerce. A useful guide to such data is Namias [1969]. Various data of this sort can also be found in the Department of Commerce's monthly publication, the *Survey of Current Business*.

[29]See, e.g., Labys and Granger [1970] and the many references cited therein.

[30]Any information on the prices of existing complementary and substitute goods' prices can be useful here.

4.3.4 An Alternative Analysis of Operating Decisions and Risk Assessments

Expressions (4.21) and (4.23) are not the only means of characterizing the connections between operating decisions and risk. By adopting different assumptions about functional forms and stochastic processes, one can derive alternative (albeit theoretically consistent) characterizations. This is what we do in this section. One of our major objectives is to emphasize the numerous connections between the risks of firms' securities and substantive microeconomic factors, such as the nature of a firm's production function. These connections help to identify, in turn, the sorts of accounting data (and other sample evidence) that are likely to be relevant to risk assessments.

For simplicity, we assume that each firm is engaged in the same single "line of business." This does not affect the crux of our results. As before, the price of a firm's output is a random variable as of time 1; the realized value of this random variable will be known at time 2. The prices of firms' "variable" factors of production (e.g., labor, raw material, etc.) are also assumed to be random variables as of time 1. Unlike our previous analysis, however, we now assume that the actual quantity of output at time 2 is known at time 1—which is when the firm must select its factors of production. The firm's output and input markets are assumed to be perfectly competitive.

In our previous analysis we assumed that each relative price of a commodity or service is uncorrelated with every asset's rate of return. We made this assumption in order to satisfy one of the *sufficient* conditions for applicability of the two-parameter asset-pricing model in a world of uncertain prices. Now we just make the direct assumption that this pricing model characterizes the setting of assets' equilibrium prices. This is equivalent to presuming that, at least, all *necessary* conditions for the two-parameter model's applicability are satisfied. (For a discussion of relevant technical issues in a multiperiod setting, see Stapleton and Subrahamanyam [1979].) In any event, under the assumptions made now, we do not rule out nonzero correlations between contemporaneous relative prices and assets' rates of return.

The inverse demand function facing firm j is identical to that facing every other producer. This function is presumed to be given by:

$$\tilde{p}(q_j) = \bar{p}(q_j)(1 + \tilde{e}), \tag{4.24}$$

where the quantity of firm j's output is denoted by q_j; $E(\tilde{e}) = 0.0$; and Var $(\tilde{e}) = \sigma_e^2$.

Note that the random variable $\tilde{e}$ is the same for every firm. Also note that under conditions of perfect competition, the probability distribution of $\tilde{p}(q_j)$ is independent of q_j, the value of which is selected at time 1. Thus, $E(\tilde{p}(q_j)|q_j) = \bar{p}$, a constant. And Var $(\tilde{p}(q_j)|q_j) = \text{Var}\,(1 + \tilde{e})\,\bar{p}^2 = \bar{p}^2\sigma_e^2$, another constant. Moreover, the value of each constant is the same for every firm.

Production by each firm is assumed to require two homogeneous factors of production—labor and capital. The price per unit of capital is assumed to be known at time 1. Since only relative prices matter, we specify this price to equal unity.

The price per unit of labor, which is a random variable as of time 1, is denoted $\tilde{w}$. The distribution of this price, which is the same for all firms, is governed by:

$$\tilde{w}(\ell_j) = \bar{w}(\ell_j)(1 + \tilde{v}), \tag{4.25}$$

where ℓ_j denotes the number of units of labor demanded by firm j; $E(\tilde{v}) = 0.0$; and Var $(\tilde{v}) = \sigma_v^2$. The labor requirements of firm j, ℓ_j, are dictated by the firm's production function, $q_j = h_j(\ell_j, k_j)$, where k_j denotes the units of capital employed by j. Since both q_j and k_j are set at time 1, ℓ_j must also be set at time 1—even though the price per unit of labor is not known until time 2. Only the probability distribution of $\tilde{w}$ is known at time 1.

Since all input markets are perfectively competitive, no individual firm alters the probability distribution of $\tilde{w}$. Thus, $E(\tilde{w}(\ell_j)|\ell_j) = \bar{w}$ and Var $(\tilde{w}(\ell_j)|\ell_j) = \bar{w}^2\sigma_v^2$ both constants.

Given our single-period setting, the value of firm j at time 2, $\tilde{V}_{j2}$, is equal to the value of its net cash flow at time 2, *viz*.:[31]

$$\tilde{V}_{j2} = \tilde{F}_j = \tilde{p}q_j - \tilde{w}\ell_j. \tag{4.26}$$

The "entry" cost of setting up the jth firm at time 1 is equal to the total outlay for fixed capital, k_j.

Conditional on the version of the two-parameter model used here (see Section 4.2), the equilibrium value of the firm at time 1 is given by:

$$V_{j1} = (1 + E(\tilde{R}_z))^{-1}[E(\tilde{V}_{j2}) - \lambda_m^* \operatorname{Cov}(\tilde{V}_{j2}, \tilde{V}_{m2})], \tag{4.27}$$

where, in terms of our earlier notation:

$$\lambda_m^* = \frac{E(\tilde{V}_{m2}) - (1 + E(\tilde{R}_z))V_{m1}}{\operatorname{Var}(\tilde{V}_{m2})}$$

$$\tilde{V}_{m2} = \sum_{j=1}^{N} \tilde{V}_{j2},$$

and:

$$V_{m1} = \sum_{j=1}^{N} V_{j1},$$

where the N is the total number of firms.

A more detailed expression for V_{j1} can be obtained by incorporating (4.24)–(4.26) into (5.27), after noting that $\tilde{V}_{m2} = \Sigma_j\tilde{V}_{j2} = \Sigma_j\tilde{F}_j = \Sigma_j(\tilde{p}q_j - \tilde{w}\ell_j) = \tilde{F}_m$, where $\tilde{F}_m$ denotes aggregate cash flow, and that:

$$\begin{aligned}\operatorname{Cov}(\tilde{V}_{j2}, \tilde{V}_{m2}) &= \operatorname{Cov}(\tilde{F}_j, \tilde{F}_m)\\ &= \operatorname{Cov}\left(\tilde{F}_j, \sum_i \tilde{\mathrm{F}}_\mathrm{i}\right)\\ &= \sum_i \operatorname{Cov}(\tilde{F}_j, \tilde{F}_i)\end{aligned} \tag{4.28}$$

Using (4.24)–(4.26), a typical summand of (4.28) can be expressed as

$$\begin{aligned}\operatorname{Cov}(\tilde{F}_j, \tilde{F}_i) &= \operatorname{Cov}(\tilde{p}q_j - \tilde{w}\ell_j, \tilde{p}q_i - \tilde{w}\ell l_i)\\ &= q_iq_j \operatorname{Var}(\tilde{p}) - \ell_jq_i \operatorname{Cov}(\tilde{p}, \tilde{w}) - q_j\ell_i \operatorname{Cov}(\tilde{p}, \tilde{w}) + \ell_j\ell_i \operatorname{Var}(\tilde{w}).\end{aligned} \tag{4.29}$$

---

[31]We assume that units of capital stock acquired at time 1 have a zero salvage value at time 2. As an alternative, one can treat units of capital stock sold at time 2 as another output and then incorporate a nonzero salvage value into the firm's net cash flow.

Given (4.24) and (4.25), Cov $(\tilde{p}, \tilde{w}) = \bar{p}\bar{w}\sigma_{ev}$, where σ_{ev} = Cov $(\tilde{e}, \tilde{v})$. Thus:

$$\text{Cov}\,(\tilde{F}_j, \tilde{F}_i) = q_i q_j \bar{p}^2 \sigma_e^2 - \bar{p}\bar{w}\sigma_{ev}(\ell_j q_i + q_j \ell_i) + \bar{w}^2 \ell_j \ell_i \sigma_v^2 \tag{4.30}$$

and:

$$\begin{aligned}\text{Cov}\left(\tilde{F}_j, \sum_i \tilde{F}_i\right) &= \bar{p}q_j\left(\sum_i \bar{p}q_i\right)\sigma_e^2 - \sigma_{ev}\left[\left(\bar{w}\ell_j \sum_i \bar{p}q_i\right)\right.\\ &\quad \left. + \left(\bar{p}q_j \sum_i \bar{w}\ell_i\right)\right] + \left(\bar{w}\ell_j \sum_i \bar{w}\ell_i\right)\sigma_v^2 \\ &= \bar{p}q_j\bar{R}\sigma_e^2 + \bar{w}\ell_j\bar{C}\sigma_v^2 - \sigma_{ev}[\bar{w}\ell_j\bar{R} + \bar{p}q_j\bar{C}],\end{aligned} \tag{4.31}$$

where $\bar{R} \equiv \Sigma_i \bar{p}q_i$ and $\bar{C} \equiv \Sigma_i \bar{w}\ell_i$ denote aggregate revenues and aggregate payments to labor, respectively.

Moreover, since Var $(\tilde{V}_{m2}) = \Sigma_j$ Cov $(\tilde{V}_{j2}, \tilde{V}_{m2}) = \Sigma_j$ Cov $(\tilde{F}_j, \tilde{F}_m)$, we get:

$$\begin{aligned}\text{Var}\,(\tilde{V}_{m2}) &= \sum_j \left[\bar{p}q_j\bar{R}\sigma_e^2 + \bar{w}\ell_j\bar{C}\sigma_v^2 - \sigma_{ev}(\bar{w}\ell_j\bar{R} + \bar{p}q_j\bar{C})\right] \\ &= \bar{R}^2\sigma_e^2 + \bar{C}^2\sigma_v^2 - 2\,\bar{C}\bar{R}\sigma_{ev}.\end{aligned} \tag{4.32}$$

Expressions (4.31) and (4.32) can be used for a recharacterization of firm j's relative risk, β_j. Recall that $\beta_j \equiv$ Cov $(\tilde{R}_j, \tilde{R}_m)/$Var $(\tilde{R}_m)$, where $\tilde{R}_j \equiv (\tilde{F}_j/V_{j1}) - 1.0$ and $\tilde{R}_m \equiv (\tilde{F}_m/V_{m1}) - 1.0$ are single-period rates of return. Using these definitions, we can write:

$$\begin{aligned}\beta_j &= \frac{\text{Cov}\left(\dfrac{\tilde{F}_j}{V_{j1}}, \dfrac{\tilde{F}_m}{V_{m1}}\right)}{\text{Var}\,(\tilde{F}_m/V_{m1})} \\ &= \frac{\dfrac{1}{V_{j1}}\dfrac{1}{V_{m1}}\,\text{Cov}\,(\tilde{F}_j, \tilde{F}_m)}{\left(\dfrac{1}{V_{m1}}\right)^2 \text{Var}\,(\tilde{F}_m)} \\ &= \frac{V_{m1}}{\text{Var}\,(\tilde{F}_m)}\,\frac{\bar{p}q_j\bar{R}\sigma_e^2 + \bar{w}\ell_j\bar{C}\sigma_v^2 - \sigma_{ev}[\bar{w}\ell_j\bar{R} + \bar{p}q_j\bar{C}]}{V_{j1}}.\end{aligned} \tag{4.33}$$

Our motivation for expressing relative risk in this fashion will become clearer after we consider the implications of our results for the operating decisions of a value-maximizing firm. We turn to this task now.

As before, we assume that firm j's management makes production-investment decisions so as to maximize the value of firm j's currently outstanding securities. (Since we are abstracting from financing decisions, all securities constitute equity.) It is easily shown that this result is attained by selecting a feasible combination of ℓ_j, k_j, and q_j (in accordance with production function $q_j = h_j(\ell_j, k_j)$) so that the "certainty equivalent" value of marginal revenue equals the "certainty equivalent" value of average total cost. Conditional on the two-parameter model, the certainty equivalent value of marginal revenue is obtained by adjusting the expected value of marginal revenue so as to account for its contribution to aggregate risk, Var $(\tilde{V}_{m2})$ = Var $(\tilde{F}_m)$. Under perfect competition, marginal revenue equals price per unit of output and is independent of the level of an individual firm's output. Thus, the contribution of marginal revenue to aggregate risk can be obtained from (4.31) by specifying $\ell_j = 0.0$ and by dividing the resulting expession by q_j. This gives:

$$\begin{aligned} \text{Cov}\,(\tilde{p}, \tilde{F}_m) &= \text{Cov}\,(\bar{p}(1 + \tilde{e}), \tilde{F}_m) \\ &= \bar{p}\bar{R}\sigma_e^2 - \sigma_{ev}\bar{p}\bar{C} \\ &= \bar{p}(\bar{R}\sigma_e^2 - \sigma_{ev}\bar{C}). \end{aligned} \tag{4.34}$$

Conditional on the two-parameter model, the certainty equivalent value of marginal revenue is, therefore:

$$\begin{aligned} \text{CEQ}\,(\tilde{p}) &= E(\tilde{p}) - \lambda_m^*\,\text{Cov}\,(\tilde{p}, \tilde{F}_m) \\ &= \bar{p} - \lambda_m^*[\bar{p}(\bar{R}\sigma_e^2 - \sigma_{ev}\bar{C})] \\ &= \bar{p}[1 - \lambda_m^*(\bar{R}\sigma_e^2 - \sigma_{ev}\bar{C})], \end{aligned} \tag{4.35}$$

where CEQ $(\tilde{x})$ denotes the certainty equivalent of $\tilde{x}$. Nóte that the relative risk of marginal revenue depends on the covariation of $\tilde{p}$ with aggregate revenues as well as its covariation with aggregate costs. In other words, the characteristics of both output and input markets are relevant to assessing the risk of each firm's marginal revenue.

The CEQ of average total cost can be derived in a similar fashion. Total costs includes the cost of capital units acquired, k_j, and the cost of labor units. The outlay k_j equals the equityholders' investment in firm j. (Recall that the price per unit of capital equals unity.) The certainty equivalent value of this outlay at time 2 is equal to $(1 + E(\tilde{R}_z))k_j$. Thus, the certainty equivalent value of average total cost is given by:

$$\frac{\text{CEQ}(\tilde{w}\ell_j)}{q_j} + \frac{[1 + E(\tilde{R}_z)]k_j}{q_j}. \tag{4.36}$$

To get CEQ$(\tilde{w}\ell_j)$, we must compute the contribution of $\tilde{w}\ell_j$ to aggregate risk. We have:

$$\begin{aligned} \text{Cov}\,(\tilde{w}\ell_j, \tilde{F}_m) &= -\bar{w}\ell_j\bar{C}\sigma_v^2 + \sigma_{ev}\bar{w}\ell_j\bar{R} \\ &= -\bar{w}\ell_j(\bar{C}\sigma_v^2 - \bar{R}\sigma_{ev}). \end{aligned} \tag{4.37}$$

A negative sign appears here because the aggregate wage payment incorporated into $\tilde{F}_m$ appears as a deduction from aggregate revenue. Using (4.37) and the two-parameter model, one finds that:

$$\begin{aligned} \text{CEQ}(\tilde{w}\ell_j) &= E(\tilde{w}\ell_j) + \lambda_m^*\bar{w}\ell_j(\bar{C}\sigma_v^2 - \bar{R}\sigma_{ev}) \\ &= \bar{w}\ell_j[1 + \lambda_m^*(\bar{C}\sigma_v^2 - \bar{R}\sigma_{ev})]. \end{aligned} \tag{4.38}$$

Thus, the CEQ average total cost of firm j, $\tilde{A}C_j$, is:

$$\text{CEQ}(\tilde{\text{A}}\text{C}_j) = \frac{\bar{w}\ell_j[1 + \lambda_m^*(\bar{C}\sigma_v^2 - \bar{R}\sigma_{ev})] + (1 + E(\tilde{R}_z))k_j}{q_j}. \tag{4.39}$$

Our maximizing firm will select a combination of values of k_j, ℓ_j, and q_j such that CEQ($\bar{p}$) = CEQ($\tilde{AC}_j$), or:

$$\bar{p}[1 - \lambda_m^*(\bar{R}\sigma_e^2 - \sigma_{ev}\bar{C})] = \frac{\bar{w}\ell_j[1 + \lambda_m^*(\bar{C}\sigma_v^2 - \bar{R}\sigma_{ev})] + [1 + E(\tilde{R}_z)]k_j}{q_j}. \quad (4.40)$$

When this equality is incorporated into our expression for the equilibrium value of V_{i1}—see (4.27)—one gets a familiar result for our perfectly competitive value-maximizing firm, *viz.*, the net present value of the firm is equal to zero. This is equivalent to saying that, in equilibrium, the investment of k_j in firm j earns a competitive rate of return—conditional on the risk of firm j. The mechanics behind this result provide some insights on the connection between operating decisions and risk. So, we supply them below.

Recall our expression for the equilibrium value of V_{j1}:

$$\begin{aligned} V_{j1} &= (1 + E(\tilde{R}_z))^{-1}[E(\tilde{V}_{j2}) - \lambda_m^* \operatorname{Cov}(\tilde{V}_{j2}, \tilde{V}_{m2})] \\ &= (1 + E(\tilde{R}_z))^{-1}[E(\tilde{F}_j) - \lambda_m^* \operatorname{Cov}(\tilde{F}_j, \tilde{F}_m)]. \end{aligned} \quad (4.41)$$

From (4.26), we have

$$E(\tilde{F}_j) = \bar{p}q_j - \bar{w}\ell_j \quad (4.42)$$

and from (4.31) we have:

$$\operatorname{Cov}(\tilde{F}_j, \tilde{F}_m) = \bar{p}q_j\bar{R}\sigma_e^2 + w\ell_j\bar{C}\sigma_v^2 - \sigma_{ev}[w\ell_j\bar{R} + \bar{p}q_jC]. \quad (4.43)$$

Thus, the expression in the square brackets of (4.41) can be restated as:

$$\begin{aligned} &[\bar{p}q_j - \bar{w}\ell_j] - \lambda_m^*[\bar{p}q_j\bar{R}\sigma_e^2 + \bar{w}\ell_j\bar{C}\sigma_v^2 - \sigma_{ev}(\bar{w}\ell_j\bar{R} + \bar{p}q_j\bar{C}] \\ &\qquad = q_j\left[\bar{p}\{1 - \lambda_m^*(\bar{R}\sigma_e^2 - \sigma_{ev}\bar{C})\} - \bar{w}\frac{\ell_j}{q_j}\{1 + \lambda_m^*(\bar{C}\sigma_v^2 - \sigma_{ev}\bar{R})\}\right]. \end{aligned} \quad (4.44)$$

Given (4.40), the expression in the square brackets of the right-hand side (RHS) of (4.44) is equal to $(1 + E(\tilde{R}_z))\, k_j/q_j$. This result can be incorporated into (4.41) to get the equilibrium result:

$$V_{j1} = k_j. \quad (4.45)$$

That is, the net present value, $V_{j1} - k_j$, of firm j equals zero.

The characteristics of value-maximizing firms' optimal decisions have direct implications for the determinants of firms' relative risks. We consider this issue now.

From (4.40) we have:

$$\bar{p}q_j = \frac{\bar{w}\ell_j[1 + \lambda_m^*(\bar{C}\sigma_v^2 - \bar{R}\sigma_{ev})] + [1 + E(R_z)]\, k_j}{[1 - \lambda_m^*(\bar{R}\sigma_e^2 - \sigma_{ev}\bar{C})]}. \quad (4.46)$$

Thus:

$$\bar{p}q_j(\bar{R}\sigma_e^2 - \sigma_{ev}\bar{C}) = G_1[\bar{w}\ell_j 1 + \lambda_m^*(\bar{C}\sigma_v^2 - \bar{R}\sigma_{ev})\}] + k_j[1 + E(\tilde{R}_z)], \quad (4.47)$$

where $G_1 \equiv (\bar{R}\sigma_e^2 - \sigma_{ev}\bar{C})/[1 - \lambda_m^*(\bar{R}\sigma_e^2 - \sigma_{ev}\bar{C})]$. Also:

$$\bar{p}q_j(\bar{R}\sigma_e^2 - \sigma_{ev}\bar{C}) = \bar{w}\ell_j(\bar{C}\sigma_v^2 - \bar{R}\sigma_{ev})$$
$$= G_1[\bar{w}\ell_j + k_j(1 + E(\tilde{R}_z)] + G_1\bar{w}\ell_j\lambda_m^*(\bar{C}\sigma_v^2 - \bar{R}\sigma_{ev})$$
$$+ \bar{w}\ell_j(\bar{C}\sigma_v^2 - \bar{R}\sigma_{ev}). \tag{4.48}$$

Therefore:

$$\frac{\bar{p}q_j(\bar{R}\sigma_e^2 - \sigma_{ev}\bar{C}) + \bar{w}\ell_j(\bar{C}\sigma_v^2 - \bar{R}\sigma_{ev})}{k_j} = G_1(1 + E(\tilde{R}_z))$$
$$+ G_1\left(\frac{\ell_j}{k_j}\right)[\bar{w} + \bar{w}\lambda_m^*(\bar{C}\sigma_v^2$$
$$- \bar{R}\sigma_{ev}) + \bar{w}(\bar{C}\sigma_v^2 - \bar{R}\sigma_{ev})]$$
$$= H_1 + H_2(\ell_j/k_j), \tag{4.49}$$

where:

$$H_1 \equiv G_1(1 + E(\tilde{R}_z))$$
$$H_2 \equiv G_1\bar{w}[1 + (1 + \lambda_m^*)(\bar{C}\sigma_v^2 - \bar{R}\sigma_{ev})].$$

Using (4.43), we can see that:

$$\text{Cov}(\tilde{F}_j, \tilde{F}_m) = k_jH_1 + \ell_jH_2. \tag{4.50}$$

This result and the fact that $V_{j1} = k_j$ in equilibrium allow us to write:

$$\beta_j = \frac{V_{m1}}{\text{Var}(\tilde{F}_m)}[H_1 + H_2(\ell_j/k_j)]. \tag{4.51}$$

Neither the value of H_1 nor that of H_2 is specific to firm j. Hence:

$$\text{Var}(\tilde{F}_m) = \sum_j \text{Cov}(\tilde{F}_j, \tilde{F}_m)$$
$$= H_1\left(\sum_j k_j\right) + H_2\left(\sum_j \ell_j\right)$$
$$= H_1k_m + H_2\ell_m, \tag{4.52}$$

where k_m denotes the aggregate capital stock, $\Sigma_j k_j$, and ℓ_m denotes the aggregate labor input, $\Sigma_j \ell_j$. Moreover, since $V_{m1} = \Sigma_j V_{j1}$, we have $V_{m1} = k_m$. We can therefore write:

$$\frac{V_{m1}}{\text{Var}(\tilde{V}_{m2})} = \frac{V_{m1}}{\text{Var}(\tilde{F}_m)} = \frac{k_m}{\text{Var}(\tilde{F}_m)} = H_1 + H_2\left(\frac{\ell_m}{k_m}\right). \tag{4.53}$$

Substituting this result into (4.51) leads to:

$$\beta_j = \frac{H_1 + H_2(\ell_j/k_j)}{H_1 + H_2(\ell_m/k_m)}. \tag{4.54}$$

That is, in equilibrium, the relative risk of firm j is linearly related to its optimal labor–capital ratio, which is an attribute of its optimal production-investment decisions.[32]

Expression (4.54) has some basic implications for the sorts of accounting numbers that might be informative with respect to relative risk. Suppose, for example, that all of firm j's "variable" costs are strictly determined by its labor input (ℓ_j) and that all "fixed" costs can be traced to its capital input (k_j). Then a ratio analysis dealing with the firm's cost structure (e.g., an analysis based on "common size" statements) can shed some light on the relative importance of units of labor and of capital in the firm's selected production decisions and thus on the value of the ratio ℓ_j/k_j that appears in (4.54).

The result in (4.54) re-emphasizes the connection between a firm's production function and its relative risk. That function specifies the feasible combinations of capital and labor for any given quantity of output. (The optimal combination is determined by both the feasible combinations and the relative prices of outputs and inputs.) Insights on what is feasible for a firm seem to be relevant to inferences about a firm's decisions because they identify what a firm cannot do—and thus each decision to which one should assign a probability equal to zero. Such insights seem, therefore, to be relevant to assessments of relative risk that are supposed to be conditional on available information about firms' production-investment decisions.

Inferences about the implications of a firm's production functions can also be useful in assessing the effects of technological change on a firm's optimal decisions, and thus on its relative risk. If the consequences of predicted technological change can be tied to the firm's production function and then to its value-maximizing ratio ℓ_j/k_j, then assessments of relative risk can be made conditionally on the predicted consequences of technological change. This approach may be helpful even though an exact specification of the firm's production function is not made. For some types of change (e.g., a change that affects the marginal productivity of every factor of production by the same scalar multiple), knowing the general form of the production function (e.g., whether it belongs to the family of Constant Elasticity of Substitution [CES] production functions) may suffice. Or just having "qualitative" information (e.g., on increasing versus decreasing returns to scale) may be adequate. Extended analyses pertaining to the substantive implications of different functional forms and qualitative characteristics can be found in, e.g., Ferguson [1969], Shephard [1970], Brown [1968], and Fuss and McFadden [1978]. In any event, it seems clear that seemingly mundane tools, such as those of conventional "cost analysis" (see, e.g., Dopüch, Birnberg, and Demski [1982], and Johnston [1960]), can have major inferential payoffs—to the extent that they provide insights on a firm's production function and identify sample evidence useful for inferring shifts in that function.

As indicated, the optimal value of ℓ_j/k_j is, in general, determined by both the jth firm's

---

[32]The development given here for the case of perfect competition is based on the analysis in Subrahamanyam and Thomadakis [1980], where an analysis is presented for a case of imperfect competition too. But the latter analysis is based on a simplifying assumption that seems to have induced a logical inconsistency. The authors assume that a given firm's output decision determines the equilibrium price per unit of output received by that firm. Specifically, each firm is presumed to face a downward-sloping demand curve. But no firm's output decision is allowed to affect aggregate output, from the perspective of an individual firm. On the surface, this seems inconsistent with the assumption of a downward-sloping demand curve for an individual firm.

production function and the relative prices of inputs and outputs that it faces. (For a given quantity of output, only the relative prices of inputs are pertinent.) Thus, inferences about changes in relative prices may also have implications for a firm's relative risk. For example, if a firm's expansion path[33] does not dictate a constant value of ℓ_j/k_j, then inferences about changes in the prices of outputs relative to inputs may have such risk implications, since such changes imply, in general, output level changes. If the firm's expansion path is linear, then the same value of ℓ_j/k_j is optimal for every level of output.

It is important to note that the characteristics of a firm's output and input markets are determinants of the connection between relative risk and the values of q_j, k_j, and ℓ_j. The specific expression given in (4.54) applies to conditions of perfectly competitive input and output markets. Under different market conditions (e.g., elements of monopoly, monopsony, or both), the appropriate expression may be very different. By itself, this seems to imply that financial statement analysis should go beyond analyses of a specific firm's accounting numbers. In other words, since the constraints and opportunities facing a given firm are, in general, affected by the market setting within which it makes decisions, the nature of that market mechanism is relevant when making inferences about the attributes of a firm's decisions and about the implications of those decisions for equilibrium prices. This provides a concrete justification for what is often called "industry analyses" by financial analysts.

Indeed, the more we think about the inferential directions given by expression (4.54), the more we think that many tools of conventional "financial statement analysis" can be used profitably even though the capital market is fully efficient (see Section 3) and even though the two-parameter model is fully correct—contrary to what one might infer from debates over the implications of market efficiency or the two-parameter model for accounting.[34] A major problem with available expositions of these tools is that their uses and objectives are not tied to the implications of any specific asset-pricing model or, more generally, to any explicit model of resource allocation under uncertainty. Without some such model, the purposes to be served by using alternative types of sample evidence (e.g., values of accounting numbers) and alternative inferential tools (e.g., statistical cost analysis, ratio analysis, etc.) can hardly be identified. In any event, it seems clear that neither the two-parameter model nor any other model of equilibrium prices, by itself, makes financial statement analysis "irrelevant" or of questionable value. Rather, such a model provides guidance and structure for the conduct of such an analysis.

4.3.5 Additional Remarks

As is the case with any inferential task, inferences about the parameters on the RHS of (4.21) or (4.23) can be made in a variety of ways using a variety of types of data. Our

---

[33]The expansion path is defined to be the locus of input combinations for which the input price ratio equals the marginal rate of technical substitution. It shows, therefore, how factor proportions change as the level of input changes.

[34]An illustrative statement regarding the "implications" of the efficient capital market hypothesis is as follows: "You don't have to go very far in the company of proponents of the [efficient market] hypothesis to find someone who will assert that the market is so quick to absorb developments that accounting determinations and, therefore, the entire financial reporting process is superfluous as far as investors are concerned. To the accountant, concerned primarily with reporting to investors, these are fighting words" (Young [1978, p. 3]).

analytical result on the determinants of risk does not—and was not intended to—identify any one approach as being "best." It is supposed to identify the attributes of firms' operating decisions that are relevant to assessments of risk and, therefore, equilibrium expected returns. By doing so, it provides a framework for an important aspect of financial statement analysis.

This framework is useful in identifying sources of information that can be used in making inferences about various parameters, such as the expected values of the prices of a firm's outputs. In some cases, these inferences might be based on the results of applying formal estimation methods to available data. Our framework does not, however, point to the types of estimation methods that might be used. Nor was it intended to do so. The appropriateness of applying a given estimation method to a given source of sample evidence—such as observed values of accounting numbers—depends on the stochastic properties of the source (e.g., whether the underlying random variables are normally distributed). Thus, in order to evaluate the quality of results obtainable from a given method, one has to be able to specify such properties. For the most part, this is an empirical issue. A detailed treatment of some basic aspects of this issue is provided in Chapter 7.

The framework provided above is based on a structural approach for making inferences. Rather than using the common approach of regressing firms' observed returns on returns of a market portfolio to estimate the two-parameter asset-pricing model, it proposes an approach based on the determinants of firms' relative risks. In the above discussion, these microeconomic determinants consisted of aspects of firms' production-investment decisions. This approach permits one to explain, on theoretical grounds, differences across firms regarding values of relative risks. It also identifies some forces that can cause relative risk changes over time.

The "empirical payoff" from using this approach is nicely illustrated in the recent study by Kupiec [1985]. Using an approach similar to that presented above, Kupiec developed a microeconomic model of relative risk, conditional on both competitive and noncompetitive market conditions regarding firms' outputs. His model allows for uncertainty with respect to wages, output prices, and output. He uses his model to characterize a firm's optimal production-investment decisions and to specify the determinants of firms' relative risks conditional on these decisions. His empirical work deals with a comparison of (1) the descriptive adequacy of his structural model and (2) the commonly used approach of directly regressing a firm's observed returns on the return of a market portfolio to estimate a firm's relative risk. On balance, his results favor the structural approach.

Kupiec's work encompasses determinants of risk not discussed above, *viz,* firms' financing decisions. These decisions can affect the risks borne by some class of a firm's securityholders. We shall examine the implications of firms' financing decisions in the next two subsections.

4.4 Financing Decisions and Relative Risk

4.4.1 Preliminaries

Another class of decisions made by firms consists of so-called financing decisions. The production-investment decisions proposed by a firm at period 1 determine the probability distribution of the firm's period 2 total market value. In order to implement its proposed production-investment decisions, the firm must acquire resources at period 1. The firm obtains the funds needed for these acquisitions by selling claims against its period

2 total market value. Such claims might be a right to receive some specified fraction of whatever the firm's value actually turns out to be. Or they might be a right to receive the lesser of some prespecified amount or the realized value of the firm. Decisions about the types of claims to be issued at period 1 constitute the firm's financing decisions. In effect, these decisions deal with the risk-sharing arrangements offered to those who supply real resources to the firm so that it can implement its production-investment decisions.

In a perfect capital market, the firm's financing decisions have no effect on the total equilibrium value of the firm at period 1 or on the period 1 wealth of any holder of any claim issued by the firm prior to period 1.[35] But a firm's financing decisions can affect the risks of—and thus the equilibrium expected returns on—the different types of claims issued by a firm. This is the aspect of financing decisions considered below.

The single-period framework used in Section 4.3 is used here as well. In addition, it is assumed that each firm issues either or both of only two types of claims against its period 2 market value. One type of claim, called a "bond," represents a right to received a prespecified payment at period 2 or a prespecified fraction of the period 2 value of the firm, whichever is less. If the total period 2 value of the firm is less than the total value of the promised payments to the bondholders, bankruptcy is said to have occurred. In this section, the probability of bankruptcy is assuméd to be zero. Section 4.6 deals with cases where that probability is nonzero.

The other type of claim that a firm can issue, called "common stock" or an "equity claim," represents a right to receive a portion of the value of the firm *minus* the total amount promised the bondholders. In the event of bankruptcy, the common stockholders receive nothing. Nor do they lose anything in excess of their original investment. That is, the common stockholders are protected by the rule of "limited liability."

Of course, many other types of claims can be issued by "real world" firms. Some of these may be truly "unique"; others may be equivalent to combinations of claims that are already outstanding. For our purposes, an analysis based on our pure "equity" and "debt" claims will suffice. Discussions of more complicated claims can be found in, e.g., Copeland and Weston [1979] and Brealey and Myers [1984].

4.4.2 The Relationship Between Financing Decisions and Relative Risk

Most of the notation used in Section 4.3 is used below. In addition, the following notation will be used:

B_{i2} = the total period 2 promised payments to the bondholders of firm i. This amount includes both interest and principal, expressed in real terms.

B_{i1} = the period 1 value of all the outstanding bonds of firm i as of period 1.

S_{i1} = the period 1 value of all the outstanding common stock of firm i as of period 1.

$\tilde{R}^*_{i1}$ = the real rate of return on firm i's common stock, from period 1 to period 2.

---

[35]By definition, a perfect capital market is one in which (1) all assets are infinitely divisible, (2) there are no transactions costs or taxes, (3) all agents pay the same price for a given asset, and (4) no firm can affect the investment opportunities facing capital market agents. Many of these conditions (e.g., the ones dealing with transaction costs and taxes) can be dropped or relaxed without invalidating any major results based on the perfect market assumption. Many authors add assumptions about the availability and costs of information to the assumptions above. The material in Chapter 4 deals with that issue. As indicated earlier, tax issues will be considered in a later section.

As before, we can focus on dollar returns or rates of return. We choose to deal first with rates of return.

By definition, the one-period expected real rates of return for the ith firm and the ith firm's common stock are, respectively:

$$E(\tilde{R}_i) = (E(\tilde{V}_{i2}) - V_{i1})/V_{i1}, \text{ and} \tag{4.55}$$

$$E(\tilde{R}_i^*) = (E(\tilde{V}_{i2}) - B_{i2} - S_{i1})/S_{i1}. \tag{4.56}$$

Since the probability of bankruptcy is assumed to be zero, the one-period rate of return on the ith firm's bonds must equal the riskless real rate of return; i.e.:[36]

$$R_f = (B_{i2} - B_{i1})/B_{i1}. \tag{4.57}$$

Using (4.55) and (4.57), one can write $E(\tilde{V}_{i2}) = V_{i1}(1 + E(\tilde{R}_i))$ and $B_{i2} = B_{i1}(1 + R_f)$. Insertion of the latter expressions into (4.54) leads to:

$$E(\tilde{R}_i^*) = \frac{V_{i1}(1 + E(\tilde{R}_i)) - B_{i1}(1 + R_f) - S_{i1}}{S_{i1}}. \tag{4.58}$$

Since $V_{i1} = B_{i1} + S_{i1}$, by definition, (4.58) can be rewritten as:

$$\begin{aligned} E(\tilde{R}_i^*) &= \frac{[B_{i1} + S_{i1}](1 + E(\tilde{R}_i)) - B_{i1}(1 + R_f) - S_{i1}}{S_{i1}} \\ &= \frac{B_{i1}(1 + E(\tilde{R}_i)) + S_{i1}(1 + E(\tilde{R}_i)) - (1 + R_f)B_{i1} - S_{i1}}{S_{i1}} \\ &= (1 + E(\tilde{R}_i))\frac{B_{i1}}{S_{i1}} + (1 + E(\tilde{R}_i)) - (1 + R_f)\frac{B_{i1}}{S_{i1}} - 1 \\ &= E(\tilde{R}_i) + [E(\tilde{R}_i) - R_f]\frac{B_{i1}}{S_{i1}}. \end{aligned} \tag{4.59}$$

Next, consider the expression for $E(\tilde{R}_i^*)$ given by the Sharpe/Lintner version of the two-parameter pricing model—a version which assumes the existence of riskless (i.e., zero-variance) borrowing and lending opportunities. According to that version of the two-parameter model, the equilibrium expected rate of return on the ith firm's outstanding equity claims is:

$$E(\tilde{R}_i^*) = R_f + [E(\tilde{R}_m) - R_f]\beta_{im}^*, \tag{4.60}$$

where $\tilde{R}_m$ is the one-period rate of return on the market portfolio and $\beta_{im}^* = \text{Cov}(\tilde{R}_i^*, \tilde{R}_m)/\text{Var}(\tilde{R}_m)$ is the risk of the ith firm's common stock in the market portfolio.

Since holding all of the ith firm's bonds and common stocks is equivalent to holding a portfolio with return $\tilde{R}_i$ and since the two-parameter model is (under our assumptions) applicable to all individual assets and portfolios, one can write:

---

[36]We are dealing with real rates of return; nominal returns to those holding debt securities are assumed to be "indexed," so as to eliminate purchasing power uncertainty.

$$E(\tilde{R}_i) = R_f + [E(\tilde{R}_m) - R_f]\beta_{im}, \tag{4.61}$$

where $\beta_{im} = \text{Cov}(\tilde{R}_i, \tilde{R}_m)/\text{Var}(\tilde{R}_m)$ is the relative risk of firm i.

After inserting expression (4.61) into (4.59), one gets:

$$\begin{aligned} E(\tilde{R}_i^*) &= R_f + [E(\tilde{R}_m) - R_f]\beta_{im} + [E(\tilde{R}_m) - R_f]\beta_{im}(B_{i1}/S_{i1}) \\ &= R_f + [E(\tilde{R}_m) - R_f]\beta_{im}\left(1 + \frac{B_{i1}}{S_{i1}}\right). \end{aligned} \tag{4.62}$$

Upon comparing (4.62) with (4.60), one finds that:

$$\beta_{im}^* = \beta_{im}\left(1 + \frac{B_{i1}}{S_{i1}}\right) = \beta_{im}\left(\frac{V_{i1}}{S_{i1}}\right), \tag{4.63}$$

since $V_{i1} = B_{i1} + S_{i1}$.

Note that the value of β_{im}, the risk of firm i's rate of return, is determined by the ith firm's production-investment decisions, along the lines described in Section 4.3, which dealt with a firm financed only by common stock. Thus, expression (4.63) says that, conditional on a firm's production-investment (or "operating") decisions (and thus conditional on the value of β_{im}), the risk of its common stock's rate of return is determined by the firm's financing decisions, in particular its debt/equity ratio, B_{i1}/S_{i1}. In a world of risk-averse investors, $[E(\tilde{R}_m) - R_f] > 0$. Consequently, the equilibrium expected return, $E(\tilde{R}_i^*)$, on the ith firm's equity is an increasing linear function of β_{im}. That implies, in turn, that $E(\tilde{R}_i^*)$ is an increasing linear function of the ith firm's debt/equity ratio, B_{i1}/S_{i1}.

Expression (4.63) identifies what is important about financing decisions insofar as the risk of equity is concerned. Specifically, it indicates that the relevant aspect of financing decisions is the resultant ratio of the market value of all outstanding debt to the market value of all outstanding equity. This seems like a pretty simple result. But when one considers using it as a basis for structuring inferential tasks, one discovers that the simplicity is deceptive—even in a single-period model. Before we get into this issue, it seems worthwhile to review the motivation for deriving a result such as (4.63). Unless otherwise indicated, we assume that firms' production-investment decisions are fixed. That is, the value of β_{im} in (4.63) is treated as given. It should be clear, however, that changes in this value constitute another potential cause of nonstationarity in the risk, β_{im}^*, of the rate of return on the ith firm's equity shares.

Clearly, if a firm's financing policy does not change, in the sense that the value of B_{i1}/S_{i1} is fixed, if enough observations on $(\tilde{R}_i, \tilde{R}_m)$ are available, and if it is assumed that these observations are drawings from the equilibrium joint distribution function of $(\tilde{R}_i, \tilde{R}_m)$, then one might use only observed returns to estimate (i.e., make inferences about) the value of β_{im}^*. Suppose, however, that a firm's financing policy is not fixed over the period for which observed returns are available. In that case, an estimate of β_{im}^* based only on past returns is an estimate of some kind of average of the "true values" of β_{im}^* experienced by the firm. Such an estimate, taken by itself, may not be very informative with respect to the value of β_{im}^* that is now appropriate. Moreover, even if a firm's financing policy was fixed in the past, there may be little reason to believe that it will remain fixed and, thus, that the current value of β_{im}^* is the same as the value that prevailed in the past. In short, even when it seems that enough observed returns are available, other kinds of data may be useful in making inferences about risk, conditional on firms' production-investment decisions. Specifically, it appears that data dealing directly with a firm's financing policy may be useful. Of course, such data may support only qualitative statements about, for example, changes in risk. But that is still a useful kind of argument.

Note that a fixed value of the ratio B_{i1}/S_{i1} may require just as much "active intervention" by management as does a change in the ith firm's financing policy. After each period, uncontrollable changes in the market values of debt and equity may lead to changes in a firm's debt/equity ratio, and thus a change in its financial structure. In order to maintain a fixed financial policy—in the sense of a fixed debt/equity ratio—some financing action by firm i's management is required in this case. If one infers that no such action is forthcoming, then (assuming no other information) it is appropriate to infer that a change in financial structure was permitted.

4.4.3 Financing Decisions and Assessments of Risk, Conditional on Production-Investment Decisions

What kinds of data can be used in making inferences about the implications of financing decisions for risk? First, note that the ratio B_{i1}/S_{i1} is a ratio of market values. Thus, one possible source of data for making inferences about the behavior of B_{i1}/S_{i1} consists of observed values of B_{i1}/S_{i1}, stated in terms of market values, conditional on assuming that these values represent equilibrium values. An alternative source of data consists of observed values of B_{i1}/S_{i1} stated in terms of reported accounting numbers, i.e., "book values." To be sure, the book value of B_{i1} (S_{i1}) may differ from the market value of B_{i1} (S_{i1}). That does not imply, however, that the *ratio* of book values conveys no information about the behavior of B_{i1}/S_{i1} stated in terms of market values. And, as was the case with inferences about operating decisions, one can consider exploiting both aggregate (e.g., industry) and individual firms' data in making inferences about financing decisions.

But there is a more pressing problem than the book value vs. market value issue. It can be recognized by noting the definition of B_{i1}, stated in terms of either market or book value. B_{i1} pertains to all of the ith firm's outstanding debt, not just the debt claims explicitly recognized on a firm's published balance sheet. Unfortunately, not all things that are essentially debt claims are disclosed on a firm's balance sheet. Moreover, not all of a firm's debt claims, even if disclosed, are traded in the capital market. So, there is a problem of "missing numbers." This problem can apply to data on equity claims too, especially contingent claims such as "stock appreciation rights" and other forms of "management stock options." (Such claims, if they are parts of an executive compensation system, are justifiably viewed as payments for labor services.) In any event, the "missing numbers" problem affects inferences based on both market values and book values. What kinds of numbers might be missing? What can be done to alleviate this problem? These are among the questions considered in the next few subsections. Note, however, that we do not deal with every type of liability that does not explicitly appear in a firm's formal financial statements. Some types not discussed or mentioned just briefly here pertain to so-called unasserted claims (see, e.g., Shoenthal [1976] and Benson [1977]), to the various explicit and implicit warranties issued by a firm with respect to its products (or by another firm whose products are composed of one or more parts produced by the firm under review), or to the firm's status as an explicit guarantor of debt formally issued by another equity—such as an Employee Stock Option Plan established by the firm for its employees. We shall confine most of our attention to three types that have received substantial attention: leases, pension plans, and project-financing devices.

4.4.3.1 Leasing

Perhaps the best-known instrument that is appropriately viewed as being equivalent to debt is the fixed noncancellable lease, usually called a "financial lease." Under this kind of contract, the lessor receives rights to a stream of payments extending over the life of the contract. The lessee receives rights to the services of the leased item, such as a truck or computer hardware. Insofar as an outside observer is concerned, this arrangement differs little, if at all, from a buy/borrow arrangement.[37]

Until the early 1970s, the available data on firms' financial lease obligations were, in general, quite skimpy—and in some cases nonexistent. In almost all cases, financial lease obligations were not recognized as types of debt in firms' published financial statements. It seems clear, however, that one will prefer such data on lease obligations when expression (4.63) is being used as a framework for inferences about risk—unless there are reasons for believing that those obligations are relatively unimportant.

The disclosure rules pertaining to leases are generally covered now by FASB *Statement No. 13: Accounting for Leases* (November 1976), effective for leases entered in or revised after December 1981 and subsequent statements. Before the issuance of *Statement No. 13,* disclosures about leases were regulated by Accounting Principles Board *Opinion No. 31* (which took effect for fiscal periods ending on or after December 31, 1973) and by the SEC's *Accounting Series Release No. 147* (which took effect for annual shareholders' reports and filings with the SEC issued after November 1973). The latter *ASR* was rescinded following the issuance of *Statement No. 13.*

In order to provide some perspective on the types of past disclosures that one will encounter when using data for past time periods and how those data might differ following *Statement No. 13,* we briefly consider the provisions of *APB No. 31, ASR No. 147,* and *Statement No. 13.*

APB Opinion No. 31 required disclosure of various information on the yearly expenses associated with all noncapitalized lease commitments for either real or personal property. Lease agreements pertaining to natural resources (e.g., oil, gas, timber, and mineral rights) were not covered by the *Opinion*'s provisions. In brief, this opinion required the following disclosures:

> *Rental Expense.* For each income statement presented, there must be separate disclosure of: (1) total rental expense and (2) contingent rentals (e.g., those based upon sales or usage of leased assets). Rental payments under short-term leases covering one month or less need not be included in these disclosures.
>
> *Future Lease Commitments.* For all leases with initial or remaining noncancellable terms of more than one year, there must be separate disclosure, as of the latest balance sheet presented, of the minimum rental commitments for: (1) each of the five succeeding fiscal years, (2) each of the next three five-year periods, and (3) the remainder as a single amount. These data are supposed to be provided on an aggregate basis and for each major category of property. For purposes of this provision, a "noncancellable lease" is defined as one that has an initial life of more than one year and is noncancellable, or is cancellable only upon the occurrence of some remote contingency or upon the payment of a substantial penalty.

[37]An empirical investigation of this issue—with a good historical overview of disclosure rules—is given in Basu [1981].

Observe that *APB Opinion No. 31* did not require disclosure of capitalized values, i.e., the present values of payments associated with lease obligations. In short, it did not require disclosure of the approximate "debt equivalent" of outstanding lease obligations. In this regard, the *Opinion* merely noted that some kinds of present value information "may be helpful," and it provided a list of items that should have been disclosed if present value data were reported.

The SEC's *Accounting Series Release No. 147* required disclosures similar to those under *APB No. 31*. In addition, and more important, it required disclosure of present value information for financing leases and information about the effects on net income induced by treating those present values as capitalized amounts. In short, these disclosures were supposed to provide numbers approximating those that would have been disclosed if buy/borrow arrangements equivalent to the leasing arrangements were used instead of the latter. Any contractual commitment having the economic characteristics of a financing lease is to be treated as a financing lease for purposes of satisfying *ASR No. 147*. Leases covering oil and gas production rights and mineral and timber rights were excluded from the *Release*'s scope. For purposes of applying *ASR No. 147,* a financing lease was defined as:

> . . . a lease, which during the noncancellable lease period, either (i) covers 75 percent or more of the economic life of the property or (ii) has terms which assure the lessor a full recovery of the fair market value (which would normally be represented by his investment) of the property at the inception of the lease plus a reasonable return on the use of the assets invested subject only to limited risk in the realization of the residual interest in the property and the credit risks generally associated with secured loans. [*ASR No. 147,* pp. 4–5.]

For all noncapitalized financial leases, the present value disclosures required by *ASR No. 147* are described as follows:

> (i) The present values of the minimum lease commitments in the aggregate and by major categories of properties, such as real estate, aircraft, truck fleets and other equipment. Present values shall be computed by discounting net lease payments (after subtracting, if practicable, estimated, or actual amounts, if any, applicable to the taxes, insurance, maintenance and other operating expenses) at the interest rate implicit in the terms of each lease at the time of entering into the lease. Such disclosure shall be made as of the date of any balance sheet presented. If the present value of the minimum lease commitments is less than five percent of the sum of long term debt, stockholders' equity and the present value of the minimum lease commitments, and if the impact on net income required to be disclosed under (iv) below is less that three percent of the average net income for the most recent three years, this disclosure is not required.
>
> (ii) Either the weighted average interest rate (based on present value) and range of rates or specific interest rates for all lease commitments included in the amount disclosed under (i) above.
>
> (iii) The present value of rentals to be received from existing noncancellable subleases of property included under (i) above based on the interest rates implicit in the terms of the subleases at the times of entering into the subleases.

(iv) The impact upon net income for each period for which an income statement is presented if all noncapitalized financing leases were capitalized, related assets were amortized on a straight-line basis and interest costs was accrued on the basis of the outstanding lease liability. The amount of amortization and interest costs included in the computation shall be separately identified. If the impact on net income is less than three percent of the average net income for the most recent three years, that fact may be stated in lieu of this disclosure. [*ASR No. 147*, pp. 5–6.]

Finally, *ASR No. 147* stated that provisions of renewal options should not be used in determining the life of a lease and the associated minimum rentals unless the probability of exercising the option is extremely high. It suggested that the latter probability might be high because of the terms of the option or because of the nature and useful life of lessee-provided improvements to the leased property.

FASB *Statement No. 13* specifies accounting rules for both lessees and lessors. Only the rules for lessee accounting are considered here.

Statement No. 13 is similar in spirit to *ASR No. 147,* and often with respect to details as well. According to its rules, leases are to be capitalized and asset/liability accounting procedures used if leases meet *any one* of four conditions which serve to define "capital" leases. If a lease does not meet any one condition, it should be classified as an "operating" lease. The four conditions are:

(1) The present value of the minimum lease payments is 90% or more of the "fair value" of the property to the lessor.

(2) The term of the lease is 75% or more of the leased property's estimated economic life.

(3) The lease contains a "bargain purchase" option (i.e., an option to purchase at less than "fair value"—which is defined to be the selling price in an arm's-length transaction between unrelated parties).

(4) Ownership is transferred to the lessee by the end of the lease term.

If the term of a lease begins with the last 25 percent of the leased asset's total estimated economic life, then conditions (1) and (2) are supposed to be ignored when classifying that lease.

The capitalized values of leases are supposed to be computed using the minimum payments stipulated by the lease and, with one exception, the lessee's "incremental borrowing rate." The exceptional case occurs when the interest rate implicit in the lease is known and is lower that this "incremental" rate. In this case, the implicit rate is to be used.

The assets corresponding to the capitalized leases are supposed to be accounted for using established depreciation procedures applied to the lease term—or to the corresponding assets economic lives when condition (3) or (4) is satisfied.

A summary of the disclosures required by *Statement No. 13,* for both capital and operating leases, is provided in Exhibit 1(c). As can be seen, many of the disclosures required under *ASR No. 147* (described earlier) are also required under *Statement No. 13,*

EXHIBIT 1(c)

Disclosure	Disclosure Applicable To: Capital Leases	Disclosure Applicable To: Non-Cancelable Operating Leases of More Than One Year	Disclosure Applicable To: All Operating Leases	Disclosure Required For: Each Balance Sheet Presented	Disclosure Required For: Latest Balance Sheet Presented	Disclosure Required For: Each Income Statement Presented
1. General description of lessee's leasing activities including:						
a. Basis for determining contingent rentals.	X	X	X			
b. Existence and terms of renewal or purchase options and escalation clauses.	X	X	X			
c. Dividend or other restrictions.	X	X	X			
2. Gross amount of assets by major property categories.	X			X		
3. Total accumulated amortization.	X			X		
4. Separate disclosure of amortization unless it is included in depreciation expense and that fact disclosed.	X					X
5. Current and long-term portions of obligations.	X			X		
6. Minimum future lease payments in the aggregate and for each of the five succeeding fiscal years.	X	X			X	
7. Amount of aggregate future minimum lease payments representing:						
a. Executory costs, including any profit.	X				X	
b. Imputed interest to reduce to present value.	X				X	
8. Total minimum future rentals due from noncancelable subleases.	X	X			X	
9. Total contingent rentals actually incurred.	X					X
10. Rental expense, with separate amounts for minimum and contingent rentals and sublease rental income.*		X	X			X

*Amounts for leases with terms of one month or less that are not renewed need not be included.

Source: Ernest & Ernest [1977*a*].

which initially applied to leases entered into on or after January 1, 1977.[38] Retroactive application of *Statement No. 13* to all leases is required in years ending after December 1981. In short, following the release of this *Statement,* what was previously "off balance sheet" financing is now required to be reported as assets and liabilities—just as when buy/borrow arrangements are used.

The kinds of disclosures encountered in financial statements issued before the effective dates of *Statement No. 13* will, of course, be those made under the joint influence of *APB No. 31* and the SEC's *ASR No. 147*. Exhibit 1(d) provides illustrative details on these disclosures, which are from Federated Department Stores' Annual Report for the 52-week fiscal year ending February 2, 1974.

As an exercise, the reader might examine the material in Exhibit 1(d) carefully and pinpoint the disclosures induced by each aspect of the pre-1977 disclosure rules discussed above and the kinds of new or altered disclosures that are expected under *Statement No. 13*'s rules.

4.4.3.2 Debt Claims Associated with Pension Plans

Another type of claim that seems to be essentially a debt obligation arises because of pension plans. In order to clarify the issues involved here, it seems necessary to understand three cost concepts associated with pension plans: (1) "current" or "normal" costs, (2) past service costs, and (3) prior service costs.

The past service cost is the cost of giving employees credit toward pension plan benefits for work performed before the inception of the pension plan. For any period after the plan's inception, the current cost for that period is the cost of giving benefits in exchange for work performed during that period.

There are often changes in the benefit provisions of a pension plan. These may involve changes in the benefits provided for work performed prior to amending the plan and, therefore, in the benefits provided for work already performed. These costs are classified as prior service costs; they are costs that arise under a plan for work already performed. In general, all costs ascribed to work provided in prior periods constitute "prior service" costs. Therefore, past service costs are a component of prior service costs, as are the costs induced by changed benefit provisions that are retroactively applied to periods after the plan's inception. Nevertheless, "past service costs" and "prior service costs" are often used interchangeably to refer to costs of all labor services already received.

Another important concept related to pension plans is "funding." If a firm's pension plan is "funded," the firm actually makes payments to some funding agency, which may be an organization or an individual (e.g., a specific corporate or individual trustee or an insurance company). The funding agency provides for an accumulation of assets—via portfolio management activities—for the payment of benefits in acccordance with the pension plan's provisions. The process of making payments to a funding agency is called *funding*. Note that an employer may establish a special fund for paying benefits under a

---

[38]*ASR No. 147* and *Statement No. 13* are not, however, identical in all respects. For example, *ASR No. 147* requires that the present values of leases be computed using the interest rate implicit in the lease rather than the lessee's "incremental borrowing rate." *Statement No. 13* requires that the latter rate be used except when the rate implicit in the lease is known *and* is lower than this "incremental" rate.

EXHIBIT 1(d)

FOOTNOTE NO. 11 FROM FEDERATED DEPARTMENT STORES' ANNUAL REPORT FOR THE 52-WEEK FISCAL YEAR ENDING FEBRUARY 2, 1974

	Rent Expense consists of: 52 Weeks Ended February 2, 1974	53 Weeks Ended February 3, 1973
Real estate rent expense (principally from noncapitalized financing leases):		
Base Rent	$23,358,226	$21,675,482
Computed as percentages of sales	2,064,928	2,078,707
Total	$25,423,154	$23,754,191
Personal property rent expense (included in "Cost of goods sold and expenses")	$ 7,268,541	$ 5,833,086
Income from subleases (included in "Rental revenues")	$ 1,766,537	$ 2,018,649

	Gross Commitments	Deduct Commitments Under Sub-Leases	Net Commitments
Minimum rental commitments under noncancellable leases as of February 2, 1974			
Years ending January:			
1975	$21,872,000	$1,237,000	$20,635,000
1976	21,145,000	1,096,000	20,049,000
1977	19,805,000	963,000	18,842,000
1978	18,902,000	859,000	18,043,000
1979	17,676,000	716,000	16,960,000
Five years ending January:			
1984	77,530,000	1,990,000	75,540,000
1989	58,215,000	764,000	57,451,000
1994	35,272,000	129,000	35,143,000
Subsequent to January 1994	51,393,000	—	51,393,000

Most leases require the Company to pay taxes (recorded as taxes) and other expenses; some call for additional amounts based on percentages of sales; and some contain purchase options.

At February 2, 1974 the present value of minimum rental commitments under noncapitalized financing leases (excluding taxes and other expenses assumed by lessors) was $163,400,000 for real estate and $800,000 for personal property. The weighted average interest rate used in these computations was 5.5%. The present value of noncancellable subleases at February 2, 1974 was $5,600,000.

If noncapitalized financing leases had been capitalized, net income would have been reduced $610,000 for the year ended February 2, 1974 and $583,000 for the prior year, which amounts are not material.

pension plan. But if that fund is under the employer's control, it would be designated as unfunded.

The concept of *vesting* is also important. An employee's right to receive a present or future pension benefit "vests" when his right to eventually receive the benefit is no longer conditional on his remaining in the employer's service. Generally, such rights provide for payment upon retirement, and not necessarily when the employee leaves a firm providing vested benefits. Of course, inadequacy of a pension fund may preclude the employee's receiving the value of his vested benefits.

At least on the surface, a firm's obligations under a pension plan's provisions seem little different from obligations that arise under conventional borrowing arrangements. It is just as if the firm paid an amount of cash to its employees, in exchange for their services, and then immediately sold bonds to them in exchange for some or all of that cash. In the end, the employees end up with cash and creditors' rights—which were acquired in exchange for labor services. There are, of course, various contingencies impounded in pension plan obligations. Thus, these acquired creditors' rights may be quite complex. But similar complexities arise under other sorts of securities sold by firms. Moreover, complexity hardly seems to be a basis for recognizing or not recognizing obligations that arise as a result of exchanges—such as those involving exchanges of labor services for claims on the joint probability distribution of a firm's future values.

If the above perspective of pension plan obligations is adopted, then "funding" can be viewed as being analogous to making payments of principal plus interest on outstanding debt—whose total value is determined via actuarial methods.[39] And "unfunded prior service costs" as of a point in time would be viewed as the remaining total liability as of that time, conditional on the actuarial methods used. (Given the role of actuarial methods, that total is, strictly speaking, a specification of the *expected* present value of the amounts that a firm would have to pay in order to satisfy all of its pension plan obligations.) But this view is not fully reflected in contemporary disclosure rules. Moreover, this characterization does not incorporate the implications of the 1974 Pension Reform Act. We consider disclosure rules first.

Insofar as financial statements to stockholders are concerned, the major disclosure rules for pension plans at the time of this writing are still in *Accounting Principles Board Opinion No. 8*.[40] However, the FASB has an exposure draft under consideration which will alter these rules. But since prior disclosures will have been governed by *APB No. 8*, we discuss its provisions in some detail. *APB No. 8* deals with current and prior costs. Current costs are recognized as expenses as they are incurred (i.e., as the covered employees provide labor services to the firm). In order for such costs to be tax deductible, they must be *funded immediately*.

The major problems arise, however, in accounting for prior service costs. If these costs were viewed as inducing a liability, and thus treated as amounts that will probably be paid, they would have to be charged to income, perhaps over the remaining employment periods of the covered employees. If they are not viewed in this way, no such expense and liability would be recognized. *Opinion No. 8* did not adopt an ambiguous stand on this issue. That is, it provided for a set of alternative accounting methods by specifying maximum and minimum pension plan expenses that can be charged to income. Charges within the maximum and minimum amounts are, it appears, also permitted—provided that they are computed according to an "acceptable" actuarial cost method applied consistently from year to year.

---

[39] A variety of assumptions must be invoked in order to compute an "actuarial value" of pension plan obligations. For example, assumptions must be made (perhaps on the basis of historical data) about the probability that a worker will remain with a firm until retirement age, the rate of mortality among both active and retired plan participants, salary scale, early retirements, and employee disability (when disability benefits are to be provided), among other things.

[40] Since the SEC requires that filings with the SEC be consistent with "Generally Accepted Accounting Principles" as well as its own specific disclosure rules, *Opinion No. 8* also affects financial statements (e.g., Form 10-K reports) filed with the SEC.

These minimum and maximum amounts are defined as follows:[41]

> The defined minimum is the total of normal cost, interest equivalents on unfunded prior service costs, and possible additional provisions for vested benefits; the defined maximum is the total of normal cost, 10% of past service cost until fully amortized, 10% of any increases or decreases in prior service cost upon amendments of an existing plan until fully amortized, and interest equivalents on the difference between cumulative amounts expensed and cumulative amounts funded.

Note that the major difference between the maximum and minimum amounts turns on prior service costs. And, of course, the pension expense number depends on a firm's funding arrangements, since the latter determine what is "unfunded," among other things.

Insofar as accounting numbers on a firm's liabilities (in an economic sense) are concerned, the important numbers that have been missing pertain to prior service costs.[42] That is, these costs generally have not appeared (in whole or in part) as a liability, even though the firm made a commitment similar to the kind that is made when a conventional debt claim is issued, along the lines described above. In general, unfunded prior service costs have not been recognized as sources of expenses and, thus, have not appeared as a liability. This practice may have been encouraged by the income tax laws, which do not permit deduction (for purposes of tax reporting) of pension costs unless they are funded or otherwise paid out when the expense is recognized—which seems equivalent to requiring cash-basis rather than accrual accounting in such cases.[43]

Opinion No. 8 did require disclosure of the extent to which *vested* benefits were unfunded. But it did not require disclosure of either the total amount of unfunded prior service costs or the vesting terms of a firm's pension plan. The amounts of unfunded prior service costs have, nevertheless, often been disclosed in footnotes. Disclosure of vesting terms has been less common.

One reason for the oft-observed footnote disclosure of the total amount of unfunded prior service cost was the prior set of disclosure rules for filings with the SEC.[44] One of those rules required that the total amount of unfunded prior service costs be disclosed. Specifically, the rule stated, in part: "If a plan has not been fully funded or otherwise

---

[41]See Nurnberg, [1974, p. 170]. Various issues pertaining to additional provisions for vested benefits and plan revisions' implications for prior service costs are deliberately ignored here.

[42]As indicated earlier, the value of prior service costs may be viewed as the value of a claim on the firm's value that was given to its employees in lieu of an immediate cash payment of equal value. It is as if the cash payment were made and all covered employees immediately purchased claims on the firm's future values.

[43]In general, assuming a pension plan is not overfunded, the maximum deduction permitted in any year for a contribution to a so-called qualified plan is equal to the greater of: (i) 5% of total compensation paid or accrued for covered employees, or (ii) the plan's "normal" cost for the year *plus* 10% of past service cost until fully funded *plus* 10% of any increase in prior service cost upon amendment of the plan until fully funded *minus* actuarial gains. For additional details, see Owen and Werner [1967].

[44]See Rule 3-16(g) of Regulation S-X. That regulation and the SEC's *Accounting Series Releases* set forth the requirements of form and content of financial statements filed in compliance with the Securities Act of 1933, the Securities and Exchange Act of 1934, the Public Utility Holding Company Act of 1935, and the Investment Company Act of 1940.

provided for, the estimated amount that would be necessary to fund or otherwise provide for the past [i.e., "prior"] service cost of the plan shall be disclosed as of the date most recently determined." This rule represented an important difference between the SEC's required disclosures and the provisions of *Opinion No. 8*. FASB *Statement No. 36* (1980) specifies disclosure requirements which are more consistent with the SEC's interest.

The 1974 Pension Reform Act seems to provide formal recognition of the liability status of unfunded prior service costs. The act decrees, in effect, that prior service costs will probably be paid and, thus, that these costs must be funded. This act's funding standards may be summarized as follows:[45]

> All covered pension plans must make annual minimum contributions equal to normal cost plus amortization over 30 years (for single employer plans) or 40 years (for multi-employer plans) of unfunded accrued liabilities for all plan benefits. Plans may amortize existing liabilities on the effective date over 40 years. Experience gains and losses are to be amortized over no more than 15 years for single employer plans and 20 years for multi-employer plans. An alternative way of meeting the minimum funding standard is provided for certain plans which use accelerated funding methods that ordinarily lead to a high degree of benefit security for participants.
>
> The amortization periods noted above may be extended by the Secretary of Labor if certain conditions are met. The IRS may also waive the funding requirements on a year-by-year basis (up to 5 waivers in a 15-year period) if hardship can be demonstrated.
>
> A failure to meet the minimum funding requirements may result in a 5% excise tax being levied on the employer. An additional 10% excise tax may be imposed for failure to correct funding deficiencies after notification by the IRS.
>
> The new funding requirements provide only minimum standards for funding a pension plan. An employer may contribute an amount in excess of the minimum funding requirements and still be entitled to a deduction for the entire contribution. Provisions which are independent of the minimum funding requirements are used to determine whether pension contributions are tax deductible.

Note that "amortization" in the Act's rules refers to funding, as defined earlier. On balance, this Act speeds up funding and vesting relative to the arrangements that prevailed prior to its passage (more on this later).

In response to this legislation, the Financial Accounting Standards Board (FASB), successor to the APB, issued its *Interpretation No. 3*. There, the FASB argued that, in general, the Pension Reform Act does *not* create a legal obligation for unfunded prior service costs. Hence, with two exceptions, unfunded prior service costs still will not induce recognition of a liability. The FASB's position was as follows:[46]

> Based on an analysis of information presently available, the Board does not believe that the Act creates a legal obligation for unfunded pension costs that war-

---

[45]*The 1974 Pension Reform Act* (Chicago: Ernst & Ernst, 1974), p. 10.

[46]See FASB [1974, p. 2]. For an update on current developments in this area, see Norby [1981, pp. 22 ff.].

> rants accounting recognition as a liability pursuant to paragraph 18 of *APB Opinion No. 8* except in the following two respects. First, an enterprise with a plan subject to the Act must fund a minimum amount annually unless a waiver is obtained from the Secretary of the Treasury. If a waiver is not obtained, the amount currently required to be funded shall be recognized as a liability by a charge to pension expense for the period, by a deferred charge, or by a combination of both, whatever is appropriate under *APB Opinion No. 8*. Second, in the event of the termination of a pension plan, the act imposes a liability on an enterprise. When there is convincing evidence that a pension plan will be terminated, evidenced perhaps by a formal commitment by management to terminate the plan, and the liability on termination will exceed fund assets and related prior accruals, the excess liability shall be accrued. If the amount of the excess liability cannot be reasonably determined, disclosure of the circumstances shall be made in the notes to the financial statements, including an estimate of the possible range of the liability.

At this point, it is appropriate to provide some data on the importance of unfunded prior service costs as estimated for the 1970s. These unfunded costs apparently motivated the vesting and funding rules incorporated in the 1974 Pension Reform Act and much of the rhetoric in the financial analysis literature on the "enormity" of unfunded pension costs as of that era.

Our immediate interest in pension plans is the extent to which they were source of "missing liability numbers." This would be a minor nuisance if past disclosure rules induced the regular disclosure of data sufficient for computing those numbers' values, assuming they are desired. But, in general, that was not the case. Moreover, there were no studies—based on, say, firm-specific data not routinely disclosed to "outsiders"—that could be used for this purpose when attempting to assess the risk characteristics of individual firms. For the most part, each available study consisted of disclosures for one or a few selected years—later ones provided disclosures for small groups of firms. Moreover, most provided aggregated rather than firm-specific values of accounting numbers. This sort of data seems to fall short of what one will normally desire for formal analyses.

Results from several surveys of selected years' data are given in Exhibits 2–8. Exhibit 2 is from a U.S. Senate report (identified in the exhibit) prepared in conjunction with the hearings that led to the 1974 Pension Reform Act—more precisely, the Employee Retirement Income Security Act (ERISA). Exhibits 3, 4, and 5 are based on survey results obtained by Treynor and Regan—some of which were first provided in reports written by Regan and issued by Merrill Lynch Pierce Fenner and Smith. All of these results are based on the sample of 40 firms identified in Exhibit 5. The 1974 results were later provided in a book by Treynor, Regan, and Priest [1976]. Exhibits 6 and 7 are from reports that appeared in *Business Week,* which were based on reports prepared by Investors Management Sciences, Inc., a division of Standard and Poor's Corporation. The 1974 results in Exhibit 6 are for 25 firms included in a report on 200 firms. They were not randomly selected from the group of 200 firms but were selected for presentation because they had "relatively high" ratios of "amortized unfunded prior service costs" to an average of annual pretax accounting earnings, based on observed annual earnings from the 5-year period 1969–1973. The values for amortized costs were computed by dividing total unfunded prior service costs by 40, on the assumption of a 40-year funding period. The 1976 results

EXHIBIT 2

ASSETS AT MARKET VALUE AS A PERCENT OF PRESENT VALUE OF TOTAL ACCRUED RETIREMENT BENEFITS, 1972 DATA

Assets as Percent of Accrued Benefits	By Plan		By Participant	
	Number	Percent	Number	Percent
25% or less	33	7	541,801	8
26–50%	118	25	1,798,945	25
51–75%	104	22	2,134,601	30
76–100%	117	25	1,211,298	17
101–125%	55	12	949,975	13
126–150%	20	4	134,252	2
151–175%	8	2	52,498	1
Over 175%	14	3	276,835	4
Total	469	100	7,100,205	100

Source: U.S. Congress, Senate, Committee on Labor and Public Welfare, *Retirement Security for Employees Act of 1972*, No. 92-1150, 92nd Congress, 2nd session, September 18, 1972, page 97. As reported in Ture [1976, p. 90].

in Exhibit 7 pertain to 83 firms selected from a survey described as having covered "1,644 of the largest U.S. industrial and service companies." The 83 firms were those "whose unfunded pension liability was $100 million or greater" (see *Business Week* [July 18, 1977]: 86). More will be said about this obvious selection bias later. The results in Exhibit 8 are based on compilations prepared by Professor Sidney Davidson of the University of Chicago: the firms he used were the 30 firms underlying the Dow Jones Industrial index of stock prices.

EXHIBIT 3

UNFUNDED VESTED BENEFITS AND TOTAL UNFUNDED PENSION LIABILITIES AS A PERCENT OF NEW WORTH, 1973

Percent Range	Unfunded Vested Benefits as a Percent of Net Worth		Total Unfunded Liability as a Percent of Net Worth	
	No. of Firms	Percent of Firms	No. of Firms	Percent of Firms
Not available	1	2.5	10	25.0
None	20	50.0	2	5.0
0–5	2	5.0	6	15.0
5–10	7.5	3	4	10.0
10–15	4	10.0	2	5.0
15–20	0	0.0	3	7.5
20–25	5	12.5	1	2.5
25–40	3	7.5	5	12.5
Over 40	2	5.0	7	17.5
	40	100.0	40	100.0
Median	None		15	

Source: Merrill Lynch, Pierce, Fenner & Smith, Inc., *Pension Costs and Unfunded Liabilities* (October 2, 1974) p. 9. As reported by Swimmer and Malca [1976, p. 22].

EXHIBIT 4

UNFUNDED VESTED BENEFITS AND UNFUNDED PAST-SERVICE COSTS AS A PERCENT OF NET WORTH (SAMPLE OF 40 LARGE COMPANIES, BASED ON 1974 AND FISCAL 1975 FIGURES)

	Unfunded vested benefits as a percent of net worth		Unfunded past-service costs as a percent of net worth	
Range	No. of firms	Percent of firms	No. of firms	Percent of firms
Not available	1	2.5	7	17.5
None	10	25.0	2	5.0
0% to 5%	9	22.5	6	15.0
5% to 10%	5	12.5	3	7.5
10% to 20%	2	5.0	7	17.5
20% to 30%	7	17.5	2	5.0
30% to 50%	4	10.0	8	20.0
50% and over	2	5.0	5	12.5
	40	100.0	40	100.0
Median unfunded liability as a percent of net worth	5%		19%	

Source: Treynor, Regan, and Priest [1976, p. 31].

Not unexpectedly, each survey emphasized the magnitudes of firms' unfunded costs. The indicated values of these numbers are roughly those that would formally appear among the values of firms' other liabilities. It is evident that some pension-plan-induced obligations were sizable relative to, say, a firm's common equity. During the 1980s, this ratio has switched to 80 percent overfunded and 20 percent underfunded.

Note also that roughly 80 percent of the survey firms had "underfunded" pension plans, according to Exhibit 2. The other side of this coin, of course, is that approximately 20 percent of the survey firm had "overfunded" plans. Whether the extent or frequency of underfunding was, for firms in general, "enormous"—as was inferred by, e.g., Swimmer and Malca [1976], among many others—is not too clear. Keep in mind that there was a strong selectivity bias in some of the data used in the surveys underlying these Exhibits. Specifically, selection criteria underlying some surveys and the criteria used by some authors in choosing firms for discussion purposes could have led to the selection of firms whose pension plans had particular characteristics—such as seemingly large unfunded costs. (See, e.g., our earlier remarks on the *Business Week* surveys.)

Moreover, these sorts of surveys, by themselves, provided no clearcut insights on the seemingly most critical issue: how were pension-plan participants' incentives affected by firms' funding practices? There may have been little effect if the risk characteristics of pension plans were offset by portfolio transactions made on personal account—when doing so is consistent with portfolio optimality. In addition, there may have been efficiency gains associated with the risk-sharing arrangements implied by firms' funding practices (see Ture [1976] for some perspective on this issue).

It also seems important to recognize the limitations put on firms' pension plan liabilities by the Pension Benefit Guaranty Corporation (PBGC), which was established as

EXHIBIT 5

CAPITAL STRUCTURE AND DEBT-TO-EQUITY RATIOS, AFTER ADJUSTMENT FOR UNFUNDED VESTED PENSION LIABILITIES (40 COMPANY SAMPLE, 1974 DATA)

Company	Debt-to-equity ratio		Adjusted capital structure		
	Before UVB	After UVB	UVB	LTD	SE
Lockheed	31.38	45.39*	1%	97%	2%
Western Union	1.16	2.09*	14	54	32
Uniroyal	.77	1.53*	17	44	39
Babcock & Wilcox	.73	1.44	17	42	41
B. F. Goodrich	.66	1.13	13	40	47
Chrysler	.37	.96*	22	27	51
Caterpillar Tractor	.45	.90	17	31	52
Goodyear	.53	.89	12	35	53
Westinghouse	.44	.87	16	30	54
Dow Chemical	.66	.81	5	40	55
Bethlehem Steel	.26	.80*	24	21	55
Republic Steel	.22	.74*	25	18	58
Ford	.24	.62	19	19	62
Xerox	.59	.59	0	37	63
Firestone	.44	.56	6	30	64
American Motors	.21	.52	17	17	66
F. W. Woolworth	.44	.52	4	30	66
Honeywell	.46	.52	2	32	66
Borden	.42	.48	3	29	68
General Motors	.07	.47	25	7	68
General Electric	.32	.46	7	24	69
Armco Steel	.24	.45	11	20	69
U.S. Steel	.30	.43	7	23	70
Sperry Rand	.43	.43	0	30	70
Monsanto	.33	.39	3	25	72
Union Carbide	.36	.39	2	26	72
Beatrice Foods	.32	.33	1	24	75
Kraftco	.28	.31	2	22	76
Combustion Engineering	.30	n.a.	n.a.	23	77
Pfizer	.30	.30	0	23	77
General Foods	.29	.29	0	22	78
J. C. Penny	.26	.26	0	21	79
Sears	.21	.24	2	17	81
Kresge	.21	.21	0	17	83
DuPont	.21	.21	0	17	83
Warner Lambert	.11	.11	0	10	90
Eastman Kodak	.03	.07	4	3	93
IBM	.03	.05	2	3	95
Johnson & Johnson	.04	.04	0	3	97
American Home Products	No LTD or UVB		0	0	100
Average	.30	.47	9	23	68

UVB—unfunded vested pension liability.
LTD—long-term debt.
SE—adjusted stockholders' equity, or stockholders' equity minus UVB.
n.a.—not available.
*UVB is limited to 30 percent of net worth.
Source: Treynor, Regan, and Priest [1976, p. 35].

EXHIBIT 6

CORPORATE PENSION COSTS, 1974 DATA

	Unfunded Prior Service Costs (UPSC) (millions of dollars)	UPSC as percent of Common Equity	Unfunded Vested Benefits (UVB) (millions of dollars)	UVB as percent of UPSC	Amortized UPSC as percent of Five-Year Average Pretax Income*
Pan American World Airways	106	27	34	32	NM
Trans World Airways	98	27	64	66	114
Chrysler	1,821	68	1,201	66	27
LTV	545	193	341	63	26
Western Union	291	55	233	80	26
American Motors	190	50	80	42	23
Crane	278	126	172	62	20
Revere Copper & Brass	73	43	44	60	20
Uniroyal	525	92	492	94	19
Budd	122	65	91	75	18
Lykes-Youngstown	234	60	64	27	13
Reynolds Metals	283	40	245	85	11
Republic Steel	447	36	422	94	11
U.S. Steel	1,600	36	400	225	10
Bethlehem Steel	1,169	47	1,029	88	10
Interlake	114	47	56	49	9
Allegheny Ludium	138	75	70	51	9
Babcock & Wilcox	124	36	99	80	8
Aluminum Co. of America	510	34	195	38	8
Caterpillar	880	60	350	40	7
American Can	344	48	59	17	7
SCM	54	20	0	0	6
Staley (A.E.)	39	32	14	36	6
Owens-Illinois	273	39	123	45	6
Ford Motor	2,700	43	1,465	54	5
200-Company Average	146	16	80	41	3

*Unfunded Prior Service Cost amortized over 40 years.
NM: not meaningful because of pretax loss.
Source: *Business Week* (June 16, 1975): p. 81.

a part of the 1974 pension legislation. Much of the motivation for the 1974 Pension Reform Act came from pension plans' assets not being sufficient to cover, and firms not being held fully liable for, benefits granted under existing plans. In general, pension plan beneficiaries had no rights to firms' assets; only assets formally assigned to firms' pension plans could be used to satisfy pension plans' promised benefits. This, of course, put a limit on firms' liabilities. Since the 1974 Act was intended to provide plans' beneficiaries with greater "security"—a goal motivated by observed magnitudes of "underfunding"—one might have expected the Act to make all corporate assets available for satisfaction of pension plan obligations, along with other liabilities (e.g., bonds, accounts payable, etc.). But the creation of the PBGC also reinforced the limitations on firms' liabilities.

In an attempt to avert beneficiary losses, the Act requires pension plans to obtain

EXHIBIT 7

CORPORATE PENSION PLAN COSTS, 1976 DATA

COMPANY	FY end	Unfunded past/ prior service costs $ mil.	UPSC as % 3-yr. avg. pretax profit	Unfunded vested benefits $ mil.	UVB as % net worth	1976 pens. & ret. exp. $ mil.	P & RE as % 1975 labor exp.
Allegheny Ludium Industries	12	206.0	355	99.0	32	25.7	2
Allied Chemical	12	281.0	138	51.5	5	42.3	7
Aluminum Co. of America	12	770.0	403	416.0	25	94.7	10
American Airlines	12	117.0	467	NR	NR	59.5	7
American Brands	12	200.5	68	134.9	12	38.0	NR
American Can	12	356.5	209	82.8	9	77.0	9
American Motors	9	360.0	NEG	185.0	59	37.0	6
American Telephone & Telegraph	11	NR	NR	684.2	2	1843.0	15
Armco Steel	12	574.0	268	NR	NR	82.9	9
Babcock & Wilcox	12	205.6	254	45.7	11	33.4	NR
Bendix	9	405.3	256	192.6	25	55.5	6
Bethlehem Steel	12	1137.0	312	1284.0	48	261.2	11
Boeing	12	NR	NR	107.0	10	84.8	7
Boise Cascade	12	194.0	138	76.0	0	21.1	5
Borg-Warner	12	129.0	132	99.0	13	30.2	NR
Budd	12	220.0	825	147.0	87	33.0	9
CPC International	12	113.1	55	53.1	7	25.6	5
Caterpillar Tractor	12	750.0	138	270.0	13	100.3	6
Champion Spark Plug	12	122.0	127	72.0	23	16.7	9
Chrysler	12	2045.0	2741	1095.0	39	277.1	8
Colt Industries	12	NR	NR	121.0	29	35.2	NR
Combustion Engineering	12	127.9	146	32.4	8	26.1	NR
Continental Group	12	367.0	183	208.0	22	73.7	NA
Crane	12	NR	NR	120.0	42	35.4	NR
Crown Zeflerbach	12	NR	NR	101.0	12	49.2	8
Cyclops	12	125.9	1131	109.4	75	15.7	9
Dana	8	245.7	184	103.6	21	33.4	8
Deere	10	329.0	102	231.0	17	82.0	8
Du Pont	12	959.7	147	443.9	11	212.8	8
Eston	12	294.0	194	181.0	27	38.0	NR
Esmark	10	101.0	74	90.0	13	30.0	NR
FLIC	12	120.0	82	0.0	0	25.3	NR
Ford Motor	12	3300.0	363	870.0	14	506.0	8
Fruehauf	12	137.0	254	64.5	17	22.8	7
General Electric	12	781.0	65	568.0	11	240.1	4
General Motors	12	7300.0	230	3000.0	21	1071.0	7
General Telephone & Electronics	12	435.0	51	0.0	0	177.0	NR
General Tire & Rubber	11	122.0	92	65.7	8	21.5	NR
Goodyear Tire & Rubber	12	638.2	215	384.0	21	87.7	6

EXHIBIT 7 Cont.

COMPANY	FY end	Unfunded past/ prior service costs $ mil.	UPSC as % 3-yr. avg. pretax profit	Unfunded vested benefits $ mil.	UVB as % net worth	1976 pens. & ret. exp. $ mil.	P & RE as % 1975 labor exp.
Gulf Oil	12	310.0	10	0.0	0	136.0	12
Honeywell	12	192.0	135	40.0	4	50.2	NR
Interflake	12	151.0	224	78.0	26	19.0	9
International Business Machines	12	727.0	19	161.0	1	590.0	NR
International Paper	12	189.0	47	76.0	4	57.0	6
International Telephone & Telegraph	12	240.0	30	54.0	1	133.0	NR
Kaiser Aluminum	12	220.0	167	91.0	11	33.1	NR
Kaiser Industries	12	140.4	144	79.0	12	27.3	NR
Kaiser Steel	12	116.5	143	54.5	11	25.0	NR
Kennecon Copper	12	231.1	331	92.8	7	25.1	NR
Keystone Consolidated Industries	6	724.0	742	61.0	32	11.7	NR
Kroger	12	115.5	151	47.5	10	42.7	NR
LTV	12	738.0	990	417.0	108	86.3	NR
Lockheed	12	NR	NR	276.0	166	96.0	7
Lykes	12	205.0	245	72.0	10	52.1	11
Martin Marietta	12	114.0	25	59.0	9	36.0	MR
McDonnell Douglas	12	NR	NR	123.0	14	115.7	11
NCR	12	175.2	112	94.1	11	44.5	NR
National Steel	12	NR	NR	468.0	37	77.0	9
PPG Industries	12	257.0	136	61.0	6	42.0	7
Pan American World Airways	12	228.0	NEG	209.5	59	45.9	7
Phelps Dodge	12	162.5	212	66.0	7	19.4	NR
Raytheon	12	111.6	89	63.7	12	27.7	4
Republic Steel	12	837.0	583	497.0	38	83.8	9
Reynolds (R.J.) Industries	12	167.0	22	25.0	1	40.0	NR
Reynolds Metals	12	443.0	365	225.0	25	53.0	7
Sears Roebuck	1	227.7	26	53.5	1	32.8	NA
Shell Oil	12	164.4	16	NR	NR	120.9	15
Signet	12	184.5	175	NR	NR	46.3	NR
Standard Oil Co. of California	12	325.0	21	0.0	0	72.2	8
TRW	12	306.0	150	141.0	17	83.3	NR
Tenneco	12	140.0	23	60.0	2	49.0	NA
Textron	12	161.0	83	NA	NA	37.0	4
Timken	12	287.7	256	83.0	15	33.3	NR
Trans World Airlines	12	185.5	NEG	75.0	20	38.0	NR
UAL	12	330.0	401	80.0	10	120.2	11
Union Carbide	12	830.0	103	195.0	6	130.3	NR
Uniroyal	12	687.0	1250	560.0	89	79.4	10
United Brands	12	135.0	NEG	30.5	6	11.7	NR
U.S. Steel	12	1200.0	151	400.0	8	221.0	6

EXHIBIT 7 Cont.

COMPANY	FY end	Unfunded past/ prior service costs $ mil.	UPSC as % 3-yr. avg. pretax profit	Unfunded vested benefits $ mil.	UVB as % net worth	1976 pens. & ret. exp. $ mil.	P & RE as % 1975 labor exp.
Westinghouse Electric	12	817.0	291	751.0	35	108.5	NR
Weyerhauser	12	159.0	42	NR	NR	33.6	4
Wheeling-Pittsburgh Steel	12	299.4	838	273.5	75	48.5	13
White Consolidated Industries	12	NR	NR	110.5	32	25.5	NR
COMPOSITE		36206.5	274	18236.8	23	8265.4	8

Source: *Business Week* (July 18, 1977): 86–87.
Note: The following definitions and notes were provided by the source.

Notes and Definitions

FY end

Month in which company's fiscal year ends.

Unfunded prior and/or past service costs

The unfunded portion of a company's pension plan related to employee service before the plan was started, adjusted for changes in actuarial assumptions, changes in plan benefits, and changes in market values. The unfunded prior and/or past service costs include benefits that are vested and are expected to become vested. The liability for these costs will be greater than the unfunded vested benefits when the pension assets are valued on the same basis (market or actuarial cost). In a few instances, unfunded vested benefits are larger than prior and/or past service costs due to the use of different valuation methods or dates.

Prior service costs represent the portion of the total pension cost identified with all periods prior to the date of an actuarial valuation of the plan. Past service costs represent the portion identified with periods prior to adoption of the plan.

Unfunded prior and/or past service costs as a % of a company's three-year average pretax profit

Pretax profit is income (operating and nonoperating) before provision for income taxes and minority interest.

Unfunded vested benefits

The amount of vested benefits in a company's pension plan that are not funded; benefits exceed fund assets.

Vested benefits are those claims under particular benefit plans and, since ERISA, under law that cannot be taken away from employees.

Unfunded vested benefits as a % of net worth

Net worth equals the sum of preferred stock, common stock, capital surplus, and retained earnings.

Pension and retirement expense

The cost of all pension plans and profit-sharing retirement plans of the company and consolidated subsidiaries included as an expense on the income statement for fiscal 1976.

Pension and retirement expense as a % of a company's reported labor expense for fiscal 1976

Labor expense is the total amount of employee wages and benefits for the company's consolidated operations, including salaries, pension costs, profit-sharing, incentive compensation, payroll taxes, and other employee benefits.

NR = not reported.
NA = not available.
NEG = earnings deficit.

termination insurance, which is supposed to insure beneficiaries against losses due to inadequate pension plan assets.[47] The PBGC is supposed to administer this aspect of the Act. In essence, the PBGC guarantees payment of all nonforfeitable basic benefits (except for those benefits that become fully vested because of plan termination) in the form of a monthly benefit, which is subject to various limitations.[48] In the event of plan termination, the employer—if solvent—is liable for reimbursement of the PBGC for the latter's payments to plan beneficiaries.

But an employer's liability is, in general, limited to 30 percent of the employer's net worth. And the PBGC is supposed to establish a program for employers to purchase insurance against this contingent liability—which arises, of course, only in the event that pension plan assets (which the PBGC first uses to discharge its obligations) are inadequate to satisfy pension plan obligations. The employer is liable for 100 percent of the underfunding, but in no case can this liability exceed 30 percent of the firm's net worth. In short, when unfunded pension costs exceed 30 percent of net worth, the appropriate value of the "missing liability number" may not be the value of unfunded costs but, rather, the value of 30 percent of net worth. It appears that the provisions surrounding the PBGC's programs established formal limitations on employers' liabilities under pension plans, all of which seems unusual in view of the alleged motivation for the 1974 Act. Additional valuable perspective on this issue is provided by Treynor, Regan, and Priest [1976]. Suffice it to say that "unfunded pension costs" may substantially overstate a firm's liability under its pension plans.[49]

Note also that the Pension Reform Act of 1974—and rulings and regulations under that Act—could have induced modifications in some firms' pension plans (e.g., in the actuarial assumptions and vesting terms of the plans). Historical data on pension plans should be interpreted with this in mind when such data are being used to make inferences about future conditions. This is particularly important with respect to multiemployer plans. At this point, the liabilities of the different employers involved in such a plan still have not been unambiguously defined. A given employer may, under certain conditions, find that he will be held liable for the effects of some other employers' funding decisions.[50] In effect, each employer may be treated as a guarantor of the other employers' obligations. As noted earlier, the prevalence of overfunding in the 1980s has seemed to attract critics of U.S. firms' pension plans and the alleged problem of unrecognized liabilities.[51]

---

[47] A plan may be terminated for any of several reasons. It may be terminated by the plan administrator in accordance with plan termination procedures. Also, the PBGC may institute proceedings to terminate a plan whenever it determines that (1) minimum funding standards have not been met, (2) the plan is unable to pay benefits when due, (3) a distribution of $10,000 or more is made to an owner employee in any 24-month period—if not paid by reason of death and if this payment leaves unfunded vested liabilities, or (4) the plan's long-term liability to the PBGC may reasonably be expected to increase substantially if the plan is not terminated. See Ernst & Ernst [1974, p. 19].

[48] See Ernst & Ernst [1974, p. 11].

[49] We may be making too much of this. Presumably, if firms abused the limitations established by the PBGC program, there would be moves to effect "corrective" legislative changes designed to avert further abuses.

[50] For additional remarks on this issue, see Diamond [1975, pp. 74–79].

[51] See, e.g., *The Wall Street Journal* (March 6, 1986).

EXHIBIT 8

EFFECTS OF UNFUNDED PENSION LIABILITIES ON DEBT RATIOS CONSOLIDATED, EQUITY SUBSIDIARIES EXCLUDED, 1976 DATA.

Dow Jones Industries	(1) Long-term Debt ($)	(2) Equity ($)	(3) Debt-Equity Ratio (1) ÷ (2)	(4) Unfunded Vested ($)	(5) Unfunded Vested + Long-term Debt ($) (1) + (4)	(6) New DE Ratio (5) ÷ (2)	(7) Unfunded Prior Service Cost ($)	(8) Nw Long-term Debt ($) (1) + (7)	(9) New Debt-Equity Ratio (8) ÷ (2)
Allied Chemical	1,118,345	1,114,288	1.004	51,474	1,169,819	1.050	280,991	1,399,336	1.256
Alcoa	1,178,600	1,689,100	.698	416,000	1,594,600	.944	770,000	1,948,600	1.154
American Brands	502,222	1,171,584	.429	134,900	637,122	.544	200,500	702,722	.560
American Can	364,200	870,100	.419	82,600	446,800	.514	356,500	720,700	.828
American Telephone & Telegraph	32,524,826	36,319,538	.896	684,150	33,208,976	.914	684,150[1]	33,208,976	.914
Bethlehem Steel	1,163,900	2,692,600	.432	1,284,000	2,447,900	.909	1,137,000	2,300,900	.855
Chrysler	1,047,700	2,815,300	.372	1,105,000	2,142,700	.761	1,095,000[1]	2,142,700	.761
Du Pont	1,334,000	4,039,200	.330	443,900	1,777,900	.440	959,700	2,293,700	.568
Eastman Kodak	139,040	4,026,299	.035	0	139,040	.035	520,000	659,040	.164
Esmark	401,134	710,588	.565	90,000	491,134	.691	101,000	502,134	.707
Exxon	4,343,466	18,470,352	.235	0	4,343,466	.235	790,000	5,133,466	.277
General Electric	2,072,900	5,252,900	.395	642,000[3]	2,714,900	.517	781,000[3]	2,853,900	.543
General Foods[4]	278,709	1,084,962	.257	0	278,709	.257	125,000	403,709	.372

General Motors	1,661,800	14,385,200	.116	3,000,000	4,661,800	.324	7,300,000	8,961,800	.623
Goodyear	981,235[2]	1,861,911	.527	384,000	1,365,235	.733	638,177	1,619,412	.870
Inco	849,569	1,562,365	.544	0	849,569	.544	140,000	989,569	.633
International Harvester	922,883	1,580,781	.584	676,000	1,598,883	1.011	920,000	1,842,883	1.166
International Paper	1,054,300	1,826,500	.577	76,000	1,130,300	.619	189,000	1,243,300	.681
Johns-Manville	218,892	672,015	.326	0	218,892	.326	0	218,892	.326
Minnesota Mining & Mfg.	475,469	2,045,754	.232	0	475,469	.232	0	475,469	.232
Owens-Illinois	551,793	1,007,534	.548	130,000	681,793	.677	342,000	893,793	.887
Proctor & Gamble	575,963	2,357,470	.244	0	575,963	.244	0	575,963	.244
Sears Roebuck	1,563,512	5,936,924	.263	55,533	1,619,045	.273	227,689	1,791,201	.302
Standard Oil of California	1,571,016	7,007,013	.224	0	1,571,016	.224	325,000	1,806,016	.271
Texaco	2,835,462	9,002,077	.315	0	2,835,462	.315	0	2,835,462	.315
Union Carbide	1,574,100	3,055,100	.515	195,000	1,769,100	.579	830,000	2,404,100	.787
U.S. Steel	1,959,900	5,129,000	.382	40,000	2,359,900	.460	1,200,000	3,159,900	.616
United Technologies	444,023	1,244,633	.357	0	444,023	.357	70,056	514,079	.413
Westinghouse Electric	543,164	2,138,435	.254	751,000	1,294,164	.605	817,000	1,360,164	.636
Woolworth	453,800	1,076,800	.421	43,200	497,000	.461	48,400	502,200	.466

—All dollar amounts in thousands

—Long-term Debt = Long-term Liability not including those relating to taxes and minority interest.

Source: Davidson [1977].

[1]Figure in column 4 is unfunded vested obligations.

[2]Long-term debt includes $125,705,000 of indebtedness to consolidated subsidiaries.

[3]Includes $74 million of unamortized liabilities for supplementary pension plan.

[4]Figures reported are for fiscal year 1976 (for the 53 weeks ended April 3, 1976).

4.4.3.3 Project Financing Devices

Debt claims associated with financial leases and pension plan have been important sources of "missing numbers" vis-à-vis firms' reported liabilities; but they have not been the only ones. Other sources of missing numbers—which have been quite important in the oil and energy related industries—are various forms of "off-balance sheet" project-funding devices. These have included so-called take-or-pay contracts, throughput and deficiency agreements, and bareboat charters. The first two types of devices were often used for off-shore oil and pipeline projects. The bareboat charter contract has often been used to finance the provision of fuel carrier services. Loosely speaking, each of these arrangements involves the issuance of debt by an entity on the basis of the financial strength of specified "customers" of the entity rather than directly on the strength of the issuing entity. Those "customers" are often the founders of the issuing entity. The crux of this story can be seen by considering the take-or-pay contract.[52]

Under a take-or-pay contract, a "taker" (i.e., a specified consumer of goods and/or services) promises to pay a producer of goods and/or services a specified amount for a specified quantity of output. The total promised payments of all takers are supposed to be sufficient to service the debt claims issued by the producer to finance the production project's activities. Moreover, the takers agree to make their promised payments even if delivery of the project's output is interrupted, so that the debt issued directly by the legally recognized producer can be serviced independently of the producer's output.

Observe that the debt issued to finance this kind of project appears on the financial statements of the legally recognized producer, not on the takers' financial statements. Yet, it seems—at least on the surface—that such an arrangement involves essentially an issuance of debt claims by the takers.

The details and importance of such project-financing arrangements have varied across industries. Thus, even though the amount of debt issued under such arrangements may have been small in the aggregate, relative to lease and pension plan liabilities, it may have been quite large for firms in specific industries.

To a large extent, arrangements such as "take-or-pay" contracts are similar to prevailing arrangements for financing firms' operations via municipalities' issuances of debt. They too involve, in effect, the issuance of debt by an entity (the municipality) on the basis of a specified "customer's" financial strength. One typical arrangement involves (1) the issuance of debt by a municipality to finance the construction of some facility, in which the municipality has ownership rights, (2) the leasing of the facility to some private entity, (3) securing the municipality's debt by the lease payments to be made by the lessee, and (4) the lessee's serving as guarantor of the municipality's debt. As such, this set of arrangements seems essentially equivalent to having the private entity directly issue tax-exempt bonds, rather than having it do so indirectly through the governmental body in whose domain the facility of interest is constructed. And this view is reinforced by the contents of the Official Statements that accompany such issuances of municipal debt, wherein the lessee's financial condition, the lessee's serving as guarantor, and the lessee's lease payment's serving as the security for debt servicing are all given great emphasis. This source of reinforcement is illustrated by the following excerpts from the Introduction to

---

[52]A lengthier discussion of the uses of project funding devices is provided in Kelly [1974, pp. 30–42.

the recent City of Valdez, Alaska, Official Statement for their Marine Terminal Revenue Bonds (Exxon Pipeline Company Project), dated May 3, 1977.[53]

> This Official Statement is provided to furnish information regarding the Marine Terminal Revenue Bonds (Exxon Pipeline Company Project) Series A (the "Bonds") to be issued in an aggregate principal amount not exceeding $250,000,000 by the City of Valdez, Alaska.
>
> The Bonds are being issued to provide funds for the acquisition, construction and equipping of certain docks, wharves and facilities directly related thereto and real property and interests therein constituting a portion of the Trans Alaska Pipeline System Marine Terminal (the "TAPS Marine Terminal") being constructed in Port Valdez in the City of Valdez, Alaska, The City will acquire a leasehold interest in the undivided interest of Exxon Pipeline Company (the "Company") in the TAPS Marine Terminal (the "Project") pursuant to a Lease, dated as of May 1, 1977 (the "Lease"), between the City and the Company. The City will sublease the Project to the Company pursuant to a Sublease Agreement, dated as of May 1, 1977 (the "Sublease"), between the City and the Company.
>
> The Bonds are being issued pursuant to an Indenture of Trust, dated as of May 1, 1977 (the "Indenture"), between the City and the Bank of New York, as Trustee (the "Trustee"). The bonds will be secured by the subrents derived under the Sublease, which subrents will be sufficient to pay the principal of, premium, if any, and interest on the Bonds. In addition, pursuant to a Guarantee Agreement, dated as of May 1, 1977 (the "Guarantee Agreement), Exxon Corporation (the "Guarantor") has guaranteed to the Trustee, for the benefit of the holders of the Bonds and of the coupons appertaining thereto, the payment of the principal of, premium, if any, and interest on the Bonds.

In short, it appears that these sorts of indirect financing constitute additional sources of "missing liability numbers." Other potential sources include Pollution Control Bonds (whose features are similar to those of Industrial Revenue Bonds) and Employee Stock Ownership Plans (often used by firms to indirectly finance their operations), among other things.[54] As in the case of "take-or-pay" contracts, the importance of these sources may vary across industries.

---

[53]Official Statements are supposed to serve purposes analogous to those served by the prospectuses that accompany firms' debt offerings.

[54]Employee Stock Ownership Plans (ESOPs) are the subject of a Statement of Position (SOP) issued by the AICPA in December 1976: "Accounting Practices for Certain Employee Stock Ownership Plans." This pronouncement states that a firm should account for its ESOPs' debt as if it were its own (and thus record a liability) when it has either guaranteed the debt or committed future contributions sufficient to meet the debt service requirements. When a liability is recorded, the offset would be a reduction of shareholders' equity. Both amounts would be reduced as principal payments are made. (The involvement of equity arises because ESOPs typically acquire equity shares with the funds that they acquire via debt issues.) Technically, SOPs are not established standards enforceable under the AICPA's code of ethics. Formally, they are guidelines to be followed unless the FASB takes a position. Thus, a firm's departing from the SOP's prescriptions may not induce a qualified auditor's opinion on that firm's financial statements.

4.4.4 Additional Remarks

The preceding sections point to several important types of liabilities that may not have been completely recognized in firms' formal financial statements and/or in data on the market values of firms' liabilities. And they point to some disclosure rules that have affected the availability of data on individual firms' liabilities. The upshot of the discussion is that the kinds of data called for by expression (4.63) may not be completely available or, if available, may not appear where one might expect to find them. Clearly, some amount of detective work and approximation may have to be used. Moreover, it is well to note that data on individual firms are not the only kinds of data that are potentially useful. There are a variety of data sources dealing with particular industries and the economy as a whole.[55] If one is willing to assume that a firm under analysis is "typical"—vis-à-vis its industry or the economy—then such aggregate data may be useful in making inferences about that firm.

The data problems surrounding use of expression (4.63) are not unique to that result. They characterize all analytical results. Also, as with any inferential task, inferences based on (4.63) can be made in a variety of ways using a variety of types of data. In general, no one approach or source of data can be declared "best." All that our analytical result can do is identify the attributes of a firm's financing decisions that are relevant to assessments of risk and, thus, equilibrium returns, conditional on the firm's production-investment decisions. By doing this, it provides additional structure and interpretive tools for financial statement analysis.

Finally, note that expression (4.63) pertains to the joint distribution function of assets' *rates* of return. The role of financing decisions in determining the riskiness of returns is different if one focuses on the joint distribution of dollar returns. From expression (4.22), we have: $\text{Cov}(\tilde{V}_{i2}, \tilde{V}_{m2})/\text{Var}(\tilde{V}_{m2}) = \beta_{im}(V_{i1}/V_{m1})$. Similarly, $\text{Cov}(\tilde{S}_{i2}, \tilde{V}_{m2}) = \beta^*_{im}(S_{i1}/V_{m1})$. But, assuming a zero probability of bankruptcy and perfect markets, $\tilde{S}_{i2} = \tilde{V}_{i2} - B_{i2}$, where, as before, B_{i2} is a constant. Thus, $\text{Cov}(\tilde{S}_{i2}, \tilde{V}_{m2}) = \text{Cov}(\tilde{V}_{i2} - B_{i2}, \tilde{V}_{m2}) = \text{Cov}(\tilde{V}_{i2}, \tilde{V}_{m2})$. Therefore, $\text{Cov}(\tilde{S}_{i2}, V_{m2})/\text{Var}(\tilde{V}_{m2}) = \beta^*_{im}(S_{i1}/V_{m1}) = \beta_{im}(V_{i1}/V_{m1}) = \text{Cov}(V_{i2}, \tilde{V}_{m2})/\text{Var}(\tilde{V}_{m2})$, the value of which is unaffected by financing decisions. In short, under the assumptions of perfect markets and zero probability of bankruptcy, the sole source of uncertainty in the dollar returns to equityholders, $\tilde{S}_{i2}$, is the uncertainty in the dollar returns to the firm as a whole, $\tilde{V}_{i2}$—which is entirely determined by the characteristics of the firm's production-investment decisions. As will be seen, a very different picture emerges when the probability of bankruptcy is nonzero. But before getting to that, we consider some factors intimately related to bankruptcy, namely, the indenture provisions of debt claims. In general, these provisions establish constraints on firms' production-investment and financing decisions and they define the "acts of default" that can lead to bankruptcy.

4.5 Additional Aspects of Financing Decisions: Indenture Provisions

The availability of pertinent data on firms' financing decisions was discussed in Section 4.4. The point of gathering such data is to provide an empirical basis for making inferences about the risks of claims issued by a firm against its future market values.

---

[55]Such as the publications of trade associations (e.g., the American Association of Equipment Lessors), economic research organizations (e.g., the Brookings Institution and the National Bureau of Economic Research), private information producers (e.g., Dun and Bradstreet and Robert Morris Associates), and governmental agencies (e.g., the Department of Commerce). A useful compendium of data sources on liabilities and characteristics of creditors is Fiedler [1971].

One type of information not discussed in Section 4.4, but which may be useful in making inferences about risk, is information about the constraints on a firm's decisions imposed by prior financing decisions. These constraints may deal with financing decisions or production-investment decisions. Specifically, the provisions of the indenture of existing claims may indicate the kinds of decisions that a firm is not supposed to make if it wants to avoid violating the contractual provisions of outstanding claims.[56]

As indicated earlier, the securities issued by a firm represent claims against the firm's period 2 total market value. Each type of claim carries with it a set of property rights indicating the extent to which it shares in the realized value of the firm at period 2. But claimholders also want to ensure that they do not experience any uncompensated expropriations of their wealth. The crux of this issue is best explained via an example.

Suppose that a firm now has one type of outstanding debt claim. Assume that the firm issues another type of debt with an equal amount of total promised payments and the same priority as the old debt. In short, the firm simply doubles the amount of outstanding debt. Assume that the proceeds of the new issuance are used to reduce the number of outstanding equity claims. That is, the firm is simply altering its financial structure. Its production-investment decisions are given. Since the latter decisions are given, the distribution function of $\tilde{V}_{i2}$ is unchanged.

Before the new debt issue, the old debtholders, in the aggregate, had rights to receive the lesser of (1) the payment promised to them (interest plus principal) or (2) the value of the firm. If the value of the firm is the lesser amount, the firm is, by definition, bankrupt.

After the new bonds are issued, the holders of the old bonds are entitled to receive the lesser of (1) their promised payment or (2) one-half of the value of the firm. That is, in the event of bankruptcy, the old bondholders must share the value of the firm with the new bondholders. Moreover, the probability of bankruptcy is higher after the new bonds are issued. This too alters the probability distribution of payoffs to the old bondholders.[57] But the resulting claim is not the kind of claim for which the old bondholders paid. Thus, the firm's issuance of debt, with the rights described above, induces a transfer of wealth away from the old bondholders, because it reduces their expected payoff conditional on bankruptcy. And the old bondholders are not compensated for that wealth transfer. The holders of the firm's equity are the ones who gain from this financing shift, because the firm is able to sell debt claims on more favorable terms than would otherwise be the case by giving the new bondholders some of the rights previously held by the old bondholders and, thus, the firm effectively transfers the value of those rights to the equityholders. (This is analogous to selling the same thing twice, even though ownership was supposed to have

---

[56]Such violations may trigger declarations of insolvency or attempts to renegotiate the terms of outstanding claims.
Note that indenture provisions are not the only sources of constraints for all firms. For example, firms in regulated industries (e.g., insurance companies, banks, savings and loan associations, and bank holding companies) are subject to a variety of constraints imposed by law or regulatory commissions' rulings. An extensive treatment of indenture provisions is provided by Kennedy and Landau [1975].

[57]Note that we are assuming that bankruptcy costs for a firm are zero. Such costs might include administrative and legal costs. Also, they might include the costs of changes in the attributes of firms' operating decisions induced by bankruptcy—such as losses of customers and creditor-enforced restrictions against pursuing seemingly profitable operating decisions.

been transferred after the first sale.) If the old bondholders were able to prevent this, the equityholders would have to give the new bondholders higher promised payments for the given amount to be raised by the new debt issue. This would mean that smaller "residual" amounts for the existing equityholders would remain after deducting the promised payments to both the old and the new bondholders from the firm's future values. (Consequently, the value of the firm's remaining equity would be lower that it is conditional on the uncompensated expropriation.) When the old bondholders cannot prevent this, the aggregate value of their wealth decreases because the probability distibution of their future payoffs is the one that is adversely affected. The old bondholders lose property rights, but they receive no compensation for this loss. The loss occurs because there are states for which the old bondholders' payoffs are lower than they were before the new debt was issued—and thus lower than those (implicitly or explicitly) incorporated into their original contractual agreement.

The data in Exhibit 9 serve to illustrate the above scenario. Assume that the total payments *promised* to the old bondholders of firm i, B_{i2}, equals \$10 in each of five equally likely states of the world and that the possible values of the firm at time 2, $\tilde{V}_{i2}$, are \$0.0, \$10.00, \$15.00, \$20.00, and \$25.00. The probability of a given value equals the probability of the state on which it is conditional; thus the probability of each value is equal to 0.20. Before the new bonds are issued, the old bondholders face the probability distribution of payoffs defined by the equally probable state-contingent actual payoffs indicated in Part I of Exhibit 9. The actual payoff for any given state is the value of min $(\tilde{V}_{i2}, B_{i2})$ for each state. The residual amount max $[0, \tilde{V}_{i2} - \min(\tilde{V}_{i2}, B_{i2})]$ for each state defines the payoff to the equityholders for that state. Thus, as indicated in Part I of Exhibit 9, the payoffs to equity are \$0.0, \$0.0, \$5.0, \$10.0, and \$15.0 for states 1, 2, 3, 4, and 5 respectively. These payoffs to equity also define the *maximum* payoffs that can be made to new securityholders if the payoffs to the old bondholders are to be fully protected. In this case, "full protection" means that their actual payoffs remain as indicated in Part I of Exhibit 9 or, if they do not, that the old bondholders receive the value, as of time 1, of all payoff-changes—so that the old bondholders' wealths are unchanged.

Recall that we are dealing with a pure financing decision under perfect market conditions. Thus, the distribution function of $\tilde{V}_{i2}$ is unaffected by the issuance of the new bonds, which are assumed to have exactly the same terms as the old bonds. In effect, the firm's debt is simply doubled. The state-contingent payoff distributions that prevail after the new debt is issued are given in Part II of Exhibit 9. Focus on the actual state-contingent payoffs promised to the new bondholders. In all states except 3, 4, and 5, the latter payoffs exceed the firm's "maximum debt capacity" as defined earlier. Specifically, they exceed the state-contingent payoffs that would have been received by the equityholders prior to the new debt's issuance. Somehow, the equityholders sold state-contingent payoffs (via their issuance of the new debt) that they did not own. The way that they accomplished this feat is clear from the new specification of the old bondholders' state-contingent claims. Note that their new state-contingent payoffs in the first two states are lower than what they were before, by precisely the amounts by which the state-contingent payoffs to the new bondholders exceed the firm's previously defined "maximum debt capacity," *viz.*, \$5.0 and \$2.5 in states 1 and 2, respectively. In effect, the equityholders re-sold some of the state-contingent payoffs originally sold to the old bondholders, thereby allowing an issuance of debt in excess of that implied by the firm's "maximum debt capacity." And

EXHIBIT 9

Part I: Before New Bonds Issued

Random Variable	Dollar Values of Payoffs for possible States, Each Having Probability Equal to 0.20				
	States				
	(1)	(2)	(3)	(4)	(5)
Value of Firm ($\tilde{V}_{i2}$)	0	10	15	20	25
Total Payment Promised to Old Bondholders (B_{i2})	10	10	10	10	10
Actual Payment to Old Bondholders ($\text{Min}(\tilde{V}_{i2}, B_{i2})$)	0	10	10	10	10
Actual Payment to Equity	0	0	5	10	15

Part II: After New Bonds Issued

Random Variable	Dollar Values of Payoffs for Possible States, Each Having Probability Equal to 0.20				
	States				
	(1)	(2)	(3)	(4)	(5)
Value of Firm ($\tilde{V}_{i2}$)	0	10	15	20	25
Total Payment Promised to Old and New Bondholders ($2\ B_{i2}$)	20	20	20	20	20
Actual Payment to Old and New Bondholders ($\text{Min}(\tilde{V}_{i2}, 2\ B_{i2})$)	0	10	15	20	20
Actual Payment to Old Bondholders ($1/2\ \text{Min}(\tilde{V}_{i2}, 2\ B_{i2})$)	0	5	7-1/2	10	10
Actual Payment to New Bondholders ($1/2\ \text{Min}(\tilde{V}_{i2}, B_{i2})$)	0	5	7-1/2	10	10
Actual Payment to Equity	0	0	0	0	5

the old bondholders received no compensation for this re-sale of these payoffs. Thus, the old bondholders experienced an uncompensated expropriation of their wealth.

In order to prevent the above kind of uncompensated expropriation of wealth, the contractual provisions of debt claims usually preclude the issuance of new debt with priority equal to or greater than the priority of existing claims, in the absence of some (explicit or implicit) payment to the holders of the existing claims. Such payments might be effected by renegotiating the terms of the existing debt claims. Provisions for renegotiated terms are usually included in debt agreements. In any event, the contractual provisions of debt claims are constraints on the types of financing decisions that a firm can make.

But that is only one of the provisions that claimholders can impose on a firm in order to preclude deliberate alterations of the rights that they purchased. Other kinds of provisions may deal with a firm's liquidity position (via restrictions based on a firm's current ratio, quick ratio, etc.) and the structure of a firm's assets. The provisions dealing with asset structure represent attempts to prevent a firm from deliberately making operating decisions that alter the probability distribution of the firm's future value in a way that is known to have adverse effects on a class of claims issued against that distribution—unless compensation for those effects is provided. Such an adverse effect could arise if, for example, the firm plans to make operating decisions that alter the probability of bankruptcy or the probability distribution of the firm's value conditional on bankruptcy and if all of this is not anticipated by the holders of the affected claims when the claims are purchased (see Section 4.6).

Clearly, such contractual provisions are potentially useful sources of information for making inferences about the kinds of decisions that a firm will make. Using that kind of information, one might infer, for example, that certain kinds of decisions will have to be made in order to avoid violating some contractual provisions. In addition, one might infer that some kinds of decisions will not be made because they increase the probability of a violation.

Insofar as publicly offered debt claims are concerned, the best sources of data on indenture provisions are the indentures filed with the trustees of the claims. The trustee of a debt claim is supposed to monitor the issuing firm's actions and results so as to assure compliance with the provisions of the claim. In this regard, the role of the Trust Indenture Act of 1939 should be noted. This Act stipulates that bonds, debentures, and (with some exceptions) other forms of debt may not be offered for public sale unless they are issued under a trust indenture approved by the SEC. This law's provisions are implemented via a registration device. The required registration form demands an analysis of an issue's indenture provisions plus other information on the basis of which the SEC is supposed to rule on the eligibility of the trustee. Annual reports are required of the trustee and they may be required of the issuer of the securities as well. The statements filed under this Act are, of course, an important source of information on indenture provisions.

Another source of information is the formal registration statement filed with the SEC under the Securities Act of 1933 when a debt claim is offered to the public.[58] The information filed with the SEC when debt claims are registered under the 1933 Act is governed by the following requirement:[59]

> If debt securities are to be registered, outline briefly such of the following as are relevant:
>
> (a) Provisions with respect to interest, conversion, maturity, redemption, amortization, sinking fund or retirement.
>
> (b) Provisions with respect to the kind and priority of any lien securing the issue, together with a brief identification of the principal properties subject to such lien.
>
> (c) Provision with respect to the subordination of the rights of holders of the securities registered to other security holders or creditors of the registrant.
>
> (d) Provisions restricting the declaration of dividends or requiring the maintenance of any ratio of assets, the creation or maintenance of reserves or the maintenance of properties.
>
> (e) Provisions permitting or restricting the issuance of additional securities, the withdrawal of cash deposited against such issuance, the incurring of additional debt, the release or substitution of assets securing the issue, the modification of the terms of the security, and similar provisions.

---

[58]The registration provisions of the Securities Act of 1933 apply to securities sold in interstate commerce, foreign commerce, and through the mails. Securities sold within a given state are covered, in addition or exclusively, by that state's laws.

[59]Securities Act of 1933, Form S-7, Item 8: Debt Securities to be Registered.

> *Instructions*. 1. In the case of secured debt, there should be stated (i) the approximate amount of unbonded bondable property available for use against the issuance of bonds, as of the most recent practicable date, and (ii) whether the securities being registered are to be issued against such property, against the deposit of cash, or otherwise.
>
> 2. Provisions permitting the release of assets upon the deposit of equivalent funds or the pledge of equivalent property, the release of property no longer required in the business, obsolete property or property taken by eminent domain, the application of insurance moneys, and similar provisions, need not be described.
>
> (f) The name of the trustee and the nature of any material relationship with the registrant or any of its affiliates; the percentage of securities of the class necessary to require the trustee to take action, and what indemnification the trustee may require before proceeding to enforce the lien.
>
> (g) The general type of event which constitutes a default and whether or not any periodic evidence is required to be furnished as to the absence of default or as to compliance with the terms of the indenture.

Firms' published financial statements are additional sources of information on the contractual provisions of outstanding debt claims. The kinds of details provided in this source vary from one firm to another. According to Generally Accepted Accounting Principles, the stipulations of an indenture should be described in a firm's published balance sheet, or the notes to it, "whenever these stipulations are significant to an adequate interpretation of the financial statements issued by the firm."[60] That this guideline is ambiguous should be obvious. A more specific disclosure rule is imposed by the SEC's Regulation S-X, which applies to the financial statements filed with the SEC, such as a firm's Form 10-K report. As indicated earlier, some of the disclosures made in those filings are also made in firms' published financial statements, perhaps in their footnotes.

According to Rule 3-16 of Regulation S-X, the general notes to financial statements filed with the SEC must include specified information on indenture restrictions which limit the availability of retained earnings for dividend purposes. Specifically, a firm must "describe the most restrictive of such restrictions . . . indicating briefly its source, its pertinent provisions and, where appropriate and determinable, the amount of retained earnings (i) so restricted or (ii) free of such restrictions."[61]

The various articles of Regulation S-X specify additional disclosures that are required. For example, the balance sheets filed by "Commercial and Industrial Companies" must, according to Article 5 of Regulation S-X, be consistent with the following provision regarding the contents of the balance sheet section dealing with long-term debt:[62]

> BONDS, MORTGAGES AND SIMILAR DEBT. (a) State separately here, or in a note referred to herein, each issue or type of obligation and such information as will indicate (see Rule 3-13) (1) the general character of each type of debt

---

[60]See Grady [1965, p. 285].

[61]Regulation S-X, Rule 3-16(h).

[62]Rule 5-02, Item 29, of Article 5 (Commercial and Industrial Companies) of Regulation S-X.

including the rate of interest; (2) the date of maturity, or if maturing serially, a brief indication of the serial maturities, such as "maturing serially from 1980 to 1990"; (3) if the payment of principal or interest is contingent, an appropriate indication of such contingency; (4) a brief indication of priority; (5) if convertible, the basis; and (6) the combined aggregate amount of maturities and sinking fund requirements for all issues, each year for the five years following the date of the balance sheet. For amounts owed to affiliates, state separately in the registrant's balance sheet the amounts which in the related consolidated balance sheet are (i) eliminated and (ii) not eliminated.

(b) The amount and terms (including commitment fees and the conditions under which commitments may be withdrawn) of unused commitments for long-term financing arrangements that would be disclosed under this rule if used shall be disclosed in the notes to the financial statements if significant.

The disclosures made by firms in their annual reports to stockholders often lack some of the detailed disclosures provided in filings with the SEC.[63] In general, those annual reports' disclosures tend to be more condensed, the exact extent to which varies across firms. But those annual reports can still be a useful source of information on the contractual provisions of debt claims.

The restrictions described in annual reports typically involve constraints on both financing decisions and production-investment decisions. For example, restrictions dealing with net current assets and net tangible assets are examples of restrictions that affect production-investment decisions because they impose constraints on the firm's asset structure.

The important point to recognize is the debt-covenant constraints generally imply that certain decisions must not be made if a firm wants to avoid violating its existing contractual obligations. Consequently, they are potentially useful sources of information in making inferences about a firm's decisions.

4.6 Financing Decisions, Operating Decisions, and the Probability of Bankruptcy

4.6.1 Introduction

Thus far, we have assumed that the probability of bankruptcy is zero. Consequently, the effects of this event on expected return and risk have not yet been examined. Nor have we considered the way in which financing and operating decisions can affect the probability of bankruptcy. These are among the issues addressed in this section.

The probability of bankruptcy has been the subject of numerous empirical investigations, dealing with firms in general, specific industries, and specific bankruptcy cases (e.g., the Penn Central case). A central concern in many of these works is assessing the probability of bankruptcy—often using statistical models applied to values of accounting numbers and other sources of sample evidence. One frequent inference is that, for firms in general, sample evidence consisting of observed accounting numbers is helpful in the sense that models based on such evidence can lead to improved predictions of bankruptcy status (i.e., bankrupt vs. nonbankrupt), relative to some benchmark prediction-error rate. The benchmark rate often used is 50 percent, which is supposed to represent the results

---

[63]The extent to which financial statement data filed with the SEC are the same as those in reports to stockholders will increase under the SEC's "Integrated Disclosure System" adopted in 1980.

of a naive model. Thus, if ones statistical model led to a misclassifications, on average, of fewer than 50 percent of the firms classified, one would—according to this approach—declare an improvement in forecasting performance.

However, the actual failure rate for firms in general in the U.S. is often 1–2 percent, and in some years less than that.[64] In short, bankruptcy is, in general, a "rare event." And this puts the results from available empirical studies into better focus. Specifically, inferences about being able to attain rates of prediction success in excess of the commonly adopted benchmark rate of 50 percent now seem much less impressive. A super-naive model (i.e., always predict "no bankruptcy") can surpass that, for firms in general.

But a "rare event" is, of course, not necessarily an unimportant event. That is, the losses induced by bankruptcy may be quite sizable.[65] As a result, the overall effect of bankruptcy on, say, the expected dollar returns and the risk of dollar returns to various classes of securityholders may be quite important. This provides a motivation for examining the relationship between the probability of bankruptcy, the attributes of firms' production-investment and financing decisions, and the risks of the returns on firms' securities. Making assessments on the basis of these relationships is equivalent to using conditional (rather than marginal) probability distributions.

The single-period framework used earlier will be used here. The production-investment decisions proposed by a firm at period 1 determine the probability distribution of the firm's period 2 market value. In order to implement its proposed production-investment decisions, the firm acquires resources at period 1. The funds for acquiring resources are obtained by selling claims against the firm's period 2 market value. Two types of claims can be sold—equity claims ("common stocks") and debt claims ("bonds"). All bonds are assumed to be pure discount bonds. Finally, all markets are assumed to be perfect.

4.6.2 Preliminaries on Bankruptcy and Financing Decisions

As before, let $\tilde{V}_{i2}$ be the value of firm i at period 2 and let B_{i2} be the value of the total payments (interest plus principal) promised to the bondholders. The attributes of the distributions of dollar returns to the firm's bondholders and to its stockholders are depicted in Figure 1.

The "bell-shaped" curve in Figure 1 represents the probability density function of $\tilde{V}_{i2}$. The shape of this function is implied by our assuming $\tilde{V}_{i2}$ to be normally distributed. The vertical line at the value $\tilde{V}_{i2} = B_{i2}$ defines the range of values for $\tilde{V}_{i2}$ against which the stockholders and bondholders hold claims. When $\tilde{V}_{i2} > B_{i2}$, the bondholders get only B_{i2}; the stockholders get the difference $\tilde{V}_{i2} - B_{i2}$, whatever its value happens to be. When $\tilde{V}_{i2} \leq B_{i2}$, each stockholder gets nothing. In this case, assuming bankruptcy costs equal zero, the bondholders get $\tilde{V}_{i2}$, whatever its value is. The lower bound of zero on the payment to each stockholder is due, of course, to the rule of limited liability: the common stockholders are not liable to the bondholders for amounts in excess of the value of what they invested in the firm.

In this section, the state called "bankruptcy" is defined by the event $\tilde{V}_{i2} < B_{i2}$. In

---

[64]Data pertaining to this issue can be obtained from Dun & Bradstreet's *Business Failure Record* or the U.S. Department of Commerce's *Survey of Current Business*.

[65]Moreover, the losses induced by classifying a bankrupt firm as nonbankrupt may be much larger—or at least more visible—than the losses induced by classifying a nonbankrupt firm as bankrupt.

FIGURE 1

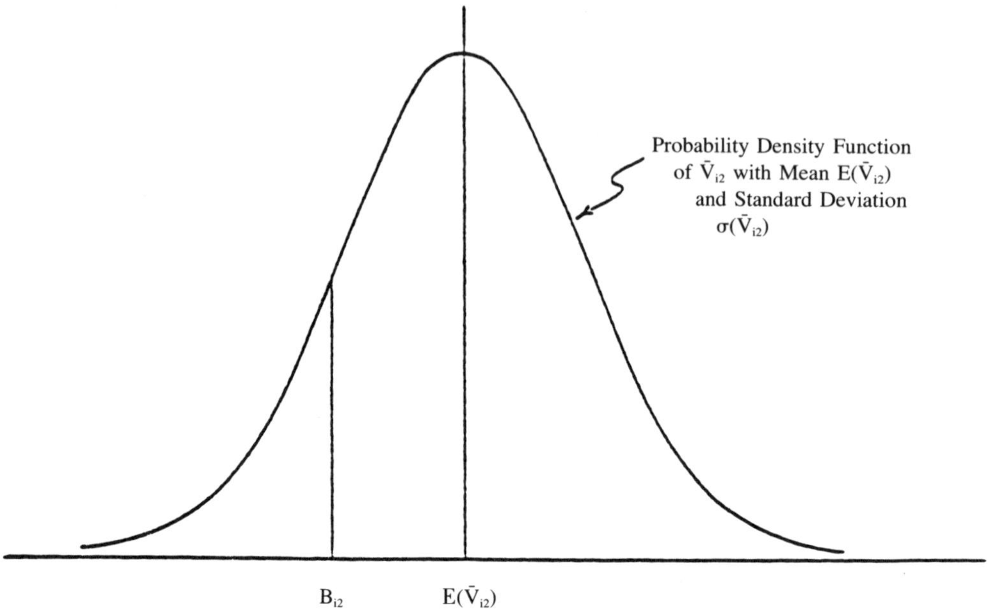

short, the firm is bankrupt when it cannot make the payments promised to holders of its debt claims.

Given the firm's production-investment decisions—and thus the probability distribution of $\tilde{V}_{i2}$—the probability of bankruptcy is determined by the firm's financing decisions. Specifically, it is determined by the value of the fixed claims (i.e., "promised payments") issued against the probability distribution of $\tilde{V}_{i2}$. This can be seen in Figure 1. As the value of the total promised payments to the bondholders increases for the given operating decisions, the probability distribution function of $\tilde{V}_{i2}$ remains the same but the value of B_{i2} increases. As a result, the probability of observing $\tilde{V}_{i2} \leq B_{i2}$, i.e., $\Pr(\tilde{V}_{i2} \leq B_{i2})$, increases.

It is important to note that, given perfect markets and no bankruptcy costs, the probability distribution of $\tilde{V}_{i2}$ is not affected by any changes in the probability of bankruptcy (i.e., changes in the value of B_{i2}). In short, under our assumptions, the total value of the firm is unaffected by the firm's financing decisions, given its production-investment decisions.[66]

Defining bankruptcy and assessing the probability of bankruptcy is, of course, more

---

[66]This is a case where the Modigliani-Miller Theorem on the "irrelevance" of financing decisions applies even though the probability of bankruptcy is nonzero. A proof can be found in Stiglitz [1969]. In short, financing decisions, taken by themselves, affect neither the total equilibrium value of the firm nor the wealths of the firm's securityholders.

complicated in a multiperiod framework. But the above single-period framework and the associated definition of bankruptcy will suffice for the present discussion.

The way that financing decisions affect the probability of bankruptcy was specified above. The theoretical implications of alternative production-investment decisions, which are discussed below, are slightly more difficult to specify.

4.6.3 Operating Decisions, the Probability of Bankruptcy, and Expected Dollar Returns

Since $\tilde{V}_{i2}$ is, by assumption, normally distributed, the probability distribution of $\tilde{V}_{i2}$ is completely defined by its mean, $E(\tilde{V}_{i2})$, and its standard deviation, $\sigma(\tilde{V}_{i2})$. Thus, in general, any aspect of the firm's operating decisions that affects the value of either $E(\tilde{V}_{i2})$ or $\sigma(\tilde{V}_{i2})$ will, other things being equal, affect the probability of bankruptcy. The implications of such effects for the expected dollar returns of the bondholders and stockholders are examined below.

To sum up, the basic scenario that we have in mind is as follows. The attributes of the ith firm's production-investment decisions establish the values of $E(\tilde{V}_{i2})$ and $\sigma(\tilde{V}_{i2})$. Thus, they establish the probability of bankruptcy, $\Pr(\tilde{V}_{i2} < B_{i2})$. Since the latter probability is one aspect of the complete probability distribution of returns to each class of the firm's securityholders, it is something directly or indirectly assessed when agents make inferences about distribution functions of returns on securities. Thus, making those assessments is one of the objectives of making inferences about the characteristics of the ith firm's production-investment decisions and the implications of those characteristics for return distributions, such as the distribution function of returns to the firm's bondholders. We begin our formal analysis by examining the effects of changes in $\sigma(\tilde{V}_{i2})$ on the bondholders' expected dollar returns.

Let $\tilde{D}_{i2}$, a random variable, denote the aggregate dollar payments to the bondholders of firm i at period 2. The value of these payments is a random variable because the probability of bankruptcy is not set equal to zero.

When $\tilde{V}_i \geq B_{i2}$, the bondholders' conditional expected dollar return is $E[\tilde{D}_{i2}|\tilde{V}_{i2} \geq B_{i2}] = B_{i2}$, the value of the promised payments. This outcome's probability equals $\Pr(\tilde{V}_{i2} \geq B_{i2})$. When $\tilde{V}_{i2} < B_{i2}$, the bondholders' conditional expected dollar return is $E[\tilde{D}_{i2}|\tilde{V}_{i2} < B_{i2}] = E[\tilde{V}_{i2}|\tilde{V}_{i2} < B_{i2}]$, because $\tilde{D}_{i2} = \tilde{V}_{i2}$ when bankruptcy occurs, i.e., when $\tilde{V}_{i2} < B_{i2}$. This outcome's probability equals $\Pr(\tilde{V}_{i2} < B_{i2})$. Consequently, the total dollar returns to the bondholders have an unconditional expected value equal to:

$$\begin{aligned} E(\tilde{D}_{i2}) &= E[\tilde{D}_{i2}|\tilde{V}_{i2} \geq B_{i2}] \cdot \Pr(\tilde{V}_{i2} \geq B_{i2}) \\ &\quad + E[D_{i2}|\tilde{V}_{i2} < B_{i2}] \cdot \Pr(\tilde{V}_{i2} < B_{i2}) \\ &= B_{i2} \cdot \Pr(\tilde{V}_{i2} \geq B_{i2}) \\ &\quad + E[\tilde{V}_{i2}|\tilde{V}_{i2} < B_{i2}] \cdot \Pr(\tilde{V}_{i2} < B_{i2}). \end{aligned} \tag{4.64}$$

The implications of changes in the value of $\sigma(\tilde{V}_{i2})$—holding other things constant—are easiest to specify when the various parts of (4.64) are analyzed.

It can be shown that:

$$E[\tilde{V}_{i2}|\tilde{V}_{i2} < B_{i2}] = E(\tilde{V}_{i2}) - \left[\frac{f(z_B)}{F(z_B)}\right]\sigma(\tilde{V}_{i2}), \tag{4.65}$$

where $f(\cdot)$ is the probability density function of a standardized normal random variable (i.e., one with mean equal to zero and standard deviation equal to unity); $F(\cdot)$ is the (cumulative distribution) function of a standardized normal random variable; and $z_B \equiv (B_{i2} - E(\tilde{V}_{i2}))/\sigma(\tilde{V}_{i2})$.[67] Since $\Pr(\tilde{V}_{i2} < B_{i2}) = F(z_B)$, one can write, using (4.65):

$$E[\tilde{V}_{i2}|\tilde{V}_{i2} < B_{i2}] \cdot \Pr(\tilde{V}_{i2} < B_{i2}) = E(\tilde{V}_{i2}) \cdot F(z_B) - f(z_B)\sigma(\tilde{V}_{i2}). \tag{4.66}$$

It can be shown, using (4.66), that:[68]

$$\frac{\partial[E(\tilde{V}_{i2}|\tilde{V}_{i2} < B_{i2}) \cdot \Pr(\tilde{V}_{i2} < B_{i2})]}{\partial\sigma(\tilde{V}_{i2})} = -f(z_B)\left[\frac{E(\tilde{V}_{i2})z_B}{\sigma(\tilde{V}_{i2})} + 1 + z_B^2\right] \tag{4.67}$$

and:

$$\frac{\partial \Pr(\tilde{V}_{i2} \geq B_{i2})}{\partial\sigma(\tilde{V}_{i2})} = f(z_B)z_B/\sigma(V_{i2}). \tag{4.68}$$

Using (4.67) and (4.68), one gets:[69]

$$\frac{\partial E(\tilde{D}_{i2})}{\partial\sigma(\tilde{V}_{i2})} = -f(z_B). \tag{4.69}$$

For the standardized normal random variable, the probability density function, $f(\cdot)$, is strictly positive. Thus, $\partial E(\tilde{D}_{i2})/\partial\sigma(\tilde{V}_{i2}) < 0$ for all values of $\tilde{B}_{i2}$.

An intuitive grasp of the relationship between $E(\tilde{D}_{i2})$ and $\sigma(\tilde{V}_{i2})$ can be obtained with the aid of Figure 2, where it is assumed that $B_{i2} < E(\tilde{V}_{i2})$. If the standard deviation of a normally distributed random variable is increased while holding the value of its mean constant, the probability density function of that variable "flattens out." The density function's values around the mean are reduced. At the extreme values of $\tilde{V}_{i2}$, the density function's values increase. These changes are illustrated in Figure 2, where it is assumed that $\sigma_2(\tilde{V}_{i2}) > \sigma_1(\tilde{V}_{i2})$.

For the case where $B_{i2} < E(\tilde{V}_{i2})$, the total area underneath the density function and to the left of B_{i2} is increased by the increase in the standard deviation from $\sigma_1(\tilde{V}_{i2})$ to $\sigma_2(\tilde{V}_{i2})$. This is what is indicated by expression (4.68), where $z_B \equiv (B_{i2} - E(\tilde{V}_{i2}))/\sigma(\tilde{V}_{i2})$. In short, an increase in the standard deviation leads to a decrease in the probability of solvency, $\Pr(\tilde{V}_{i2} \geq B_{i2})$, and thus to an increase in the probability of bankruptcy, $\Pr(\tilde{V}_{i2} < B_{i2})$, when the total payments promised to the bondholders, B_{i2}, are less than the expected value of

---

[67] The result in (4.65) is a consequence of the properties of a truncated normal random variable; see Johnson and Kotz [1970, pp. 81–83].
Recall that:

$$f(z) = (2\pi)^{-1/2}e^{-1/2z^2}$$

and:

$$F(z^*) = \int_{-\infty}^{z^*} f(z)dz = Pr(\tilde{z} \leq z^*),$$

where z^* is a possible value of $\tilde{z}$, $-\infty < z^* < \infty$.

[68] See Appendix I.

[69] See Appendix I.

FIGURE 2

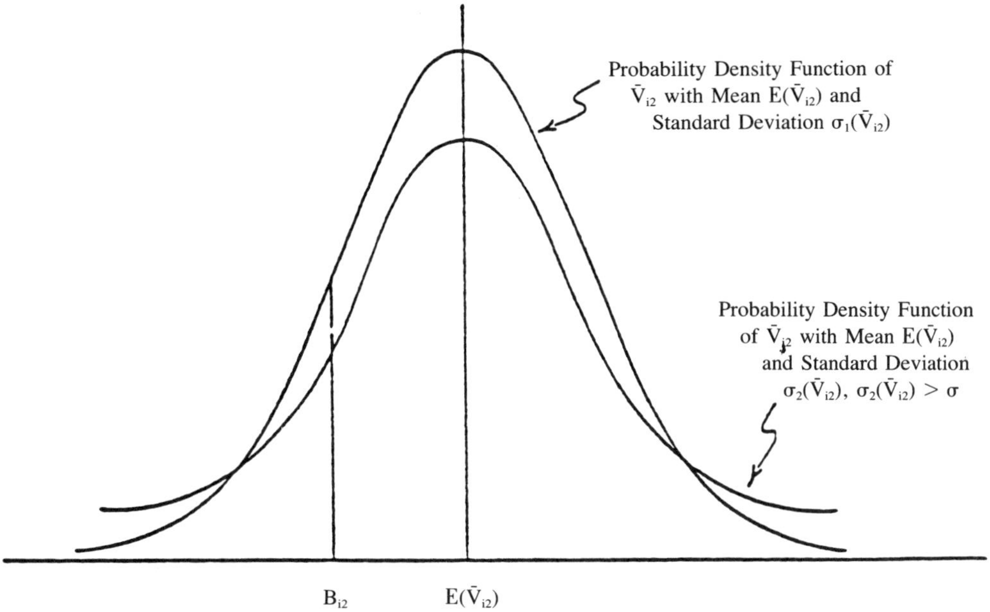

the entire firm, $E(\tilde{V}_{i2})$. By itself, the direction of the change in $E(\tilde{V}_{i2}|\tilde{V}_{i2} < B_{i2})$ depends on the value of z_B. We have, using (4.65):

$$\frac{\partial E[\tilde{V}_{i2}|\tilde{V}_{i2} < B_{i2}]}{\partial \sigma(\tilde{V}_{i2})} = -\left[\frac{\partial h}{\partial \sigma}\sigma + h\right], \tag{4.70}$$

where $h = h(z) \equiv f(z)/F(z)$ and $\sigma \equiv \sigma(\tilde{V}_{i2})$, and:

$$\frac{\partial h}{\partial \sigma} = \frac{\partial f(z_B)}{\partial \sigma}(F(z_B))^{-1} + (-1)(F(z_B))^{-2}\frac{\partial F(z_B)}{\partial z}\frac{\partial z}{\partial \sigma}(f)$$

$$= \frac{\partial f}{\partial \sigma}(F)^{-1} - (F)^{-2}(f^2)((-1)(B_{i2} - E(\tilde{V}_{i2}))\sigma^{-2})$$

$$= \left[\frac{\partial f}{\partial \sigma}F + (z/\sigma)f^2\right]\Big/F^2. \tag{4.71}$$

Moreover, from expression (a5) in Appendix I:

$$\frac{\partial f}{\partial z} = (-f)(z). \tag{4.72}$$

Therefore:

$$\frac{\partial f}{\partial \sigma} = \frac{\partial f}{\partial z}\frac{\partial z}{\partial \sigma} = (-f)(z)(-z/\sigma) = (f)(z^2/\sigma). \tag{4.73}$$

Using (4.73) in (4.71) gives:

$$\frac{\partial h}{\partial \sigma} = [(f)(z^2/\sigma)F + (f^2)(z/\sigma)]/F^2$$

$$= (f)(z/\sigma)\left[\frac{zF + f}{F^2}\right]. \tag{4.74}$$

And using (4.74) in (4.70) gives:

$$\frac{\partial E[\tilde{V}_{i2}|\tilde{V}_{i2} < B_{i2}]}{\partial \sigma(\tilde{V}_{i2})} = -\left[zf\left(\frac{zF + f}{F^2}\right) + \frac{f}{F}\right]$$

$$= -\left[\frac{z^2(f)(F) + zf^2 + fF}{F^2}\right]$$

$$= -(f/F^2)[F + zf + Z^2]. \tag{4.75}$$

If $|z| < 1$, then $|z^2| < |z|$, and thus if $z < 0$ and $|z| < f$, then $(z^2 + zf) < 0$ because $0 < f < 1$ for the standard normal density f. Thus, since $F(z) > 0$ for finite values of z, there is a critical value, $z' < 0$, of z such that $z'f + (z')^2 + F = 0$, and $zf + z^2 + F > 0$ for $z < z'$. And, therefore, when $z \leq (>)\ z'$, we have $\partial E[\tilde{V}_{i2}|\tilde{V}_{i2} < B_{i2}]/\partial\sigma(\tilde{V}_{i2}) \leq (>)\ 0$.

In short, if the total payment promised to the bondholders is less than $E(\tilde{V}_{i2})$—i.e., if $z_B < 0$ for $E(\tilde{V}_{i2}) > 0$ and $B_{i2} > 0$—then some changes in the standard deviation of $\tilde{V}_{i2}$ will induce increases in the expected dollar returns to bondholders *conditional* on bankruptcy. If B_{i2} is sufficiently far below $E(\tilde{V}_{i2})$, then the expected dollar returns conditional on bankruptcy will be reduced by an increase in $\sigma(\tilde{V}_{i2})$. But, as indicated in (4.69), no matter what the value of $(B_{i2} - E(\tilde{V}_{i2}))$ is, an increase in $\sigma(\tilde{V}_{i2})$ will always lead to a decrease in the *unconditional* expected dollar returns to the bondholders.

Note that the value of B_{i2} is not affected by the changed value of $\sigma(\tilde{V}_{i2})$. It is assumed that the payments promised to the firm's bondholders were established before the change in $\sigma(\tilde{V}_{i2})$ and that those payments are not renegotiated.

What is the effect of the change in $\sigma(\tilde{V}_{i2})$ on the expected dollar returns to the equityholders? By definition, $\tilde{V}_{i2} = \tilde{S}_{i2} + \tilde{D}_{i2}$, where $\tilde{S}_{i2}$ denotes the total dollar returns to the common stockholders. If $\tilde{V}_{i2} \leq \tilde{B}_{i2}$, then $\tilde{S}_{i2} = 0$. If $\tilde{V}_{i2} > B_{i2}$, then $\tilde{S}_{i2} = \tilde{V}_{i2} - B_{i2}$. We are considering the effect of a change in $\sigma(\tilde{V}_{i2})$ for a given value of $E(\tilde{V}_{i2})$. This effect is represented by:

$$\frac{\partial E(\tilde{S}_{i2})}{\partial \sigma(\tilde{V}_{i2})} = \frac{\partial E(\tilde{V}_{i2})}{\partial \sigma(\tilde{V}_{i2})} - \frac{\partial E(\tilde{D}_{i2})}{\partial \sigma(\tilde{V}_{i2})} = 0.0 - \frac{\partial E(\tilde{D}_{i2})}{\partial \sigma(\tilde{V}_{i2})}.$$

In short, a change in the standard deviation, $\sigma(\tilde{V}_{i2})$, has a redistributive effect, insofar as expected dollar returns are concerned. The amount by which $E(\tilde{D}_{i2})$ is, say, reduced when $\sigma(\tilde{V}_{i2})$ increases is equal to the amount by which $E(\tilde{S}_{i2})$ is increased. Thus, whereas the stockholders would gain from an unanticipated increase in $\sigma(\tilde{V}_{i2})$, the bondholders would lose. The opposite situation occurs when $\sigma(\tilde{V}_{i2})$ is unexpectedly reduced. Of course, this potential source of wealth redistribution can be an important source of internal conflict between the bondholders and stockholders. Thus, it supplies some of the motivation for the use of indenture provisions by bondholders in order to protect themselves against uncompensated expropriations of their wealth induced by deliberate and unanticipated changes in $\sigma(\tilde{V}_{i2})$. The role of indenture provisions was discussed in Section 4.5. For additional details and insights, see Smith and Warner [1979].

Unexpected changes in the value of $\sigma(\tilde{V}_{i2})$ can occur because of unexpected changes in the nature of firm i's production-investment decisions. This can be seen in greater detail by using the model of production-investment decisions introduced in Section 4.3. Recall that $\tilde{V}_{i2} = \Sigma_j \tilde{P}_j \tilde{q}_{ij} - \Sigma_k \tilde{p}_k y_{ik} - F_i$, where $\tilde{p}_j$ is the price of commodity or service j at period 2, $\tilde{q}_{ij}$ is the output quantity of commodity or service j, y_{ik} is the quantity of input factor k, and F_i denotes total fixed costs. Thus, $\tilde{G}_{i2} \equiv \Sigma_j \tilde{p}_j \tilde{q}_{ij}$ equals total revenues and $\tilde{C}_{i2} \equiv \Sigma_k \tilde{p}_k y_{ik}$ equals total variable costs. We have, therefore:

$$\begin{aligned} \operatorname{Var}(\tilde{V}_{i2}) &= (\sigma(\tilde{V}_{i2}))^2 \\ &= \operatorname{Var}(\tilde{G}_{i2}) + \operatorname{Var}(\tilde{C}_{i2}) - 2\operatorname{Cov}(\tilde{G}_{i2}, \tilde{C}_{i2}). \end{aligned} \tag{4.76}$$

In short, the value of $\sigma(\tilde{V}_{i2})$ can be altered by any change in production-investment decisions that alters the dispersion of the firm's flow variables, $\operatorname{Var}(\tilde{G}_{i2})$ and $\operatorname{Var}(\tilde{C}_{i2})$, or the magnitude of the linear association between revenues and variable costs, as measured by $\operatorname{Cov}(\tilde{G}_{i2}, \tilde{C}_{i2})$. Such changes might be induced by, for example, (1) changes in production technology, (2) changes in the firm's product mix (or "lines of business"), (3) changes in the structure of commodity markets (e.g., increased competition), or (4) changes in macroeconomic factors (e.g., stabilization policies), etc. To the extent that the implications of such changes are anticipated, they will, of course, be taken into account when the terms and equilibrium prices of debt and equity claims are established.

The other important parameter of the distribution of $\tilde{V}_{i2}$ is $E(\tilde{V}_{i2})$, the value of which is also affected by firm i's production-investment decisions. The implications of a change in $E(\tilde{V}_{i2})$ for the value of $E(\tilde{D}_{i2})$ can be identified with the apparatus used above.

It can be shown that:

$$\frac{\partial[E(\tilde{V}_{i2}|\tilde{V}_{i2} < B_{i2}) \cdot \Pr(\tilde{V}_{i2} < B_{i2})]}{\partial E(\tilde{V}_{i2})} = F(z_B) - \left(\frac{E(\tilde{V}_{i2}) f(z_B)}{\sigma(\tilde{V}_{i2})}\right) - f(z_B) z_B \tag{4.77}$$

and:

$$\frac{\partial[B_{i2} \cdot \Pr(\tilde{V}_{i2} \geq B_{i2})]}{\partial E(\tilde{V}_{i2})} = \frac{B_{i2} f(z_B)}{\sigma(\tilde{V}_{i2})}, \tag{4.78}$$

where $f(\cdot)$, $F(\cdot)$, and z_B are as defined earlier.[70] Addition of (4.77) and (4.78) and rearrangement of terms gives:

$$\frac{\partial E(\tilde{D}_{i2})}{\partial E(\tilde{V}_{i2})} = F(z_B). \tag{4.79}$$

Since the value of the distribution function, $F(\cdot)$, is always positive, it is always the

---

[70] See Appendix I.

case that $\partial E(\tilde{D}_{i2})/\partial E(\tilde{V}_{i2}) > 0$. That is, the bondholders' expected dollar returns are always increased (decreased) by changes in production-investment decisions that increase (decrease) the value of $E(\tilde{V}_{i2})$.

Since $E(\tilde{S}_{i2}) = E(\tilde{V}_{i2}) - E(\tilde{D}_{i2})$, we have:

$$\frac{\partial E(\tilde{S}_{i2})}{\partial E(\tilde{V}_{i2})} = 1 - \frac{\partial E(\tilde{D}_{i2})}{\partial E(\tilde{V}_{i2})}$$

$$= 1 - F(z_B). \tag{4.80}$$

Since $0 < F(z_B) < 1$ for $-\infty < z_B < \infty$, $\partial E(\tilde{S}_{i2})/\partial E(\tilde{V}_{i2}) > 0$. Just as the bondholders' expected dollar returns are increased (decreased) by an increase (decrease) in $E(\tilde{V}_{i2})$, the stockholders' expected dollar returns increase (decrease) when $E(\tilde{V}_{i2})$ increases (decreases). Thus, unlike the effects of changes in $\sigma(\tilde{V}_{i2})$, changes in $E(\tilde{V}_{i2})$ do not induce redistributions of expected dollar returns. Both the equityholders and the debtholders gain (lose) when the value of $E(\tilde{V}_{i2})$ is increased (decreased) by changes in production-investment decisions.

An intuitive grasp of the effects of changing $E(\tilde{V}_{i2})$ can be obtained with the aid of Figure 3. A change in the value of $E(\tilde{V}_{i2})$—holding the value of $\sigma(\tilde{V}_{i2})$ constant—leads to a "sideward" movement of the density function of $\tilde{V}_{i2}$, with no change in any other aspect of the distribution. The distribution moves to the left (right) when $E(\tilde{V}_{i2})$ is decreased (increased). As can be seen in Figure 3, when the value of $E(\tilde{V}_{i2})$ increases from $E(\tilde{V}_{i2})^*$ to $E(\tilde{V}_{i2})^{**}$, the value of $\Pr(\tilde{V}_{i2} < B_{i2})$ is decreased. And if $B_{i2} < E(\tilde{V}_{i2})$, then the value of $E[\tilde{V}_{i2}|\tilde{V}_{i2} < B_{i2}]$ decreases when the value of $E(\tilde{V}_{i2})$ increases. The net result is an increase in the value of $E(\tilde{D}_{i2})$, which is defined by expression (4.64).

The payoff to equityholders is zero if $\tilde{V}_{i2} < B_{i2}$ and it is $\tilde{V}_{i2} - B_{i2}$ if $\tilde{V}_{i2} \geq B_{i2}$. Since $\Pr(\tilde{V}_{i2} \geq B_{i2}) = 1.0 - \Pr(\tilde{V}_{i2} < B_{i2})$ increases as $E(\tilde{V}_{i2})$ increases, the expected dollar return to the equityholders also increases.[71] The opposite effect on expected dollar returns—for both equity and debt claims—occurs when the value of $E(\tilde{V}_{i2})$ is decreased.

The attributes of firm i's production-investment decisions that affect $E(\tilde{V}_{i2})$ are easily identified. Since $\tilde{V}_{i2} = \Sigma_j \tilde{P}_j \tilde{q}_{ij} - \Sigma_k \tilde{p}_k y_{ik} - F_i$:

$$E(\tilde{V}_{i2}) = \sum_j E(\tilde{p}_j \tilde{q}_{ij}) - \sum_k E(\tilde{p}_k) y_{ik} - F_i. \tag{4.81}$$

And since, under our assumptions, $\tilde{p}_j$ and $\tilde{q}_{ij}$ are stochastically independent (see Section 4.3.1), expression (4.81) can be rewritten as:

$$E(\tilde{V}_{i2}) = \sum_j E(\tilde{p}_j) E(\tilde{q}_{ij}) - \sum_k E(\tilde{p}_k) y_{ik} - F_i. \tag{4.82}$$

As can be seen, the determinants of $E(\tilde{V}_{i2})$ include fixed costs, the expected values of output and input prices, the quantities of variable factors of production, and the expected

---

71

$$\frac{\partial F(z)}{\partial E(\tilde{V}_{i2})} = \frac{\partial F(z)}{\partial z} \frac{\partial z}{\partial E(\tilde{V}_{i2})} = f(z)(-1/\sigma). \text{ Thus:}$$

$$\frac{\partial [1 - F(z)]}{\partial E(\tilde{V}_{i2})} = - \frac{\partial F(z)}{\partial E(\tilde{V}_{i2})} = [f(z/\sigma] > 0.$$

FIGURE 3

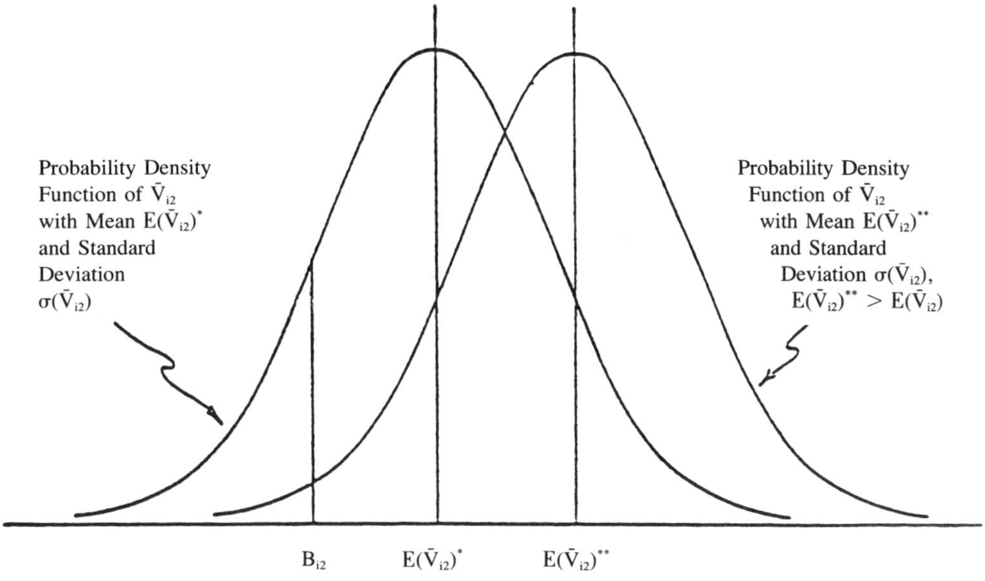

values of output quantities. The kinds of economic events that can alter the value of $E(\tilde{V}_{i2})$ include those that can alter the value of $\sigma(\tilde{V}_{i2})$. Examples of these events were given above (see the discussion below expression (4.76)).

The above analysis indicates the effects of changes in the probability of bankruptcy on the expected dollar returns of classes of claimholders. And it points to the attributes of production-investment decisions that affect the probability of bankruptcy. Making inferences about these attributes was discussed in Section 4.3, where several important sources of data for making inferences were also discussed. That discussion will not be repeated here. Our next task is to examine the relationship between the probability of bankruptcy and relative risk.

4.6.4 Risk and the Probability of Bankruptcy

4.6.4.1 General Results

The results provided above deal with expected values of dollar returns. In this section, we focus on the risks of dollar returns. Conditional on evaluations consistent with the two-parameter asset-pricing model, the appropriate measure of risk for a particular security is that security's contribution to portfolio risk—which is given by a covariance expression. Specifically, for the distribution of returns to the ith firm as a whole, $\tilde{V}_{i2}$, the relevant measure of risk is $\text{Cov}(\tilde{V}_{i2}, \tilde{V}_{m2})/\sigma^2(\tilde{V}_{m2})$ (see Section 4.2). Here, as before, $\tilde{V}_{i2}$ denotes the value of the ith firm at time 2 and $\tilde{V}_{m2}$ denotes the value of the market portfolio at time 2, where $\Sigma_i \tilde{V}_{i2} = \tilde{V}_{m2}$. For the distribution of returns to the common equity of firm i, $\tilde{S}_{i2}$, the appropriate measure of risk is $\text{Cov}(\tilde{S}_{i2}, \tilde{V}_{m2})/\sigma^2(\tilde{V}_{m2})$. We begin by considering the latter risk. Then we consider the risk of the total dollar returns to the ith firm's bondholders, $\tilde{D}_{i2}$. Since $\sigma^2(\tilde{V}_{m2})$, also denoted $\text{Var}(\tilde{V}_{m2})$, is independent of the production-investment and financing decisions of firm i—both of which influence the ith firm's probability of bankruptcy—we focus on the numerator of our measure of risk, namely, $\text{Cov}(\tilde{S}_{i2}, \tilde{V}_{m2})$.[72]

Recall that, by assumption, $\tilde{V}_{i2}$ is normally distributed. Thus, in the absence of the "limited liability" (LL) rule, $\tilde{S}_{i2} = \tilde{V}_{i2} - B_{i2}$ is also normally distributed, with $E(\tilde{S}_{i2}) = E(\tilde{V}_{i2}) - B_{i2}$, $\text{Var}(\tilde{S}_{i2}) = \text{Var}(\tilde{V}_{i2})$, and $\text{Cov}(\tilde{S}_{i2}, \tilde{V}_{m2}) = \text{Cov}(\tilde{V}_{i2} - \tilde{B}_{i2}, \tilde{V}_{m2}) = \text{Cov}(\tilde{V}_{i2}, \tilde{V}_{m2})$. But the rule of LL puts a lower bound of zero on the returns to the ith firm's equityholders. Thus, conditional on LL, the specification on $\tilde{S}_{i2}$ is:

$$\tilde{S}_{i2} = \begin{cases} \tilde{V}_{i2} - B_{i2}, & \text{if } \tilde{V}_{i2} > B_{i2} \\ 0, & \text{if } \tilde{V}_{i2} \leq B_{i2}. \end{cases} \tag{4.83}$$

In short, given LL, $\tilde{S}_{i2}$ has a truncated (from below) normal distribution. In order to emphasize the role of LL, the *marginal* (with respect to bankruptcy) distribution of $\tilde{S}_{i2}$ will be denoted $F(\tilde{S}_{i2}|\text{LL})$. The *marginal* moments of $\tilde{S}_{i2}$ will be written with the same conditioning argument. Thus, for example, when dealing with the expected value of $\tilde{S}_{i2}$ taken marginally with respect to bankruptcy, we shall write $E(\tilde{S}_{i2}|\text{LL})$ rather than $E(\tilde{S}_{i2})$.

An expression for $\text{Cov}(\tilde{S}_{i2}, \tilde{V}_{m2}|\text{LL})$ can be obtained by exploiting the properties of the bivariate truncated normal distribution, which is the joint distribution of $\tilde{S}_{i2}$ and $\tilde{V}_{i2}$ where the values of $\tilde{S}_{i2}$ are restricted to the interval $\tilde{S}_{i2} \geq 0$. The same distribution was used earlier to derive the expected value of $\tilde{S}_{i2}$ conditional on $\tilde{S}_{i2} \geq 0$ (see Section 4.6.3).

From the properties of the truncated normal distribution, we get:[73]

$$E(\tilde{S}_{i2}|\tilde{S}_{i2} > 0, \text{LL}) = [E(\tilde{V}_{i2}) - B_{i2}] + \left(\frac{f(z_B)}{1 - F(z_B)}\right)\text{Var}(\tilde{V}_{i2}), \tag{4.84}$$

where, as before, $z_B = (B_{i2} - E(\tilde{V}_{i2}))/(\text{Var}(\tilde{V}_{i2}))^{1/2}$. In more compact form:

$$E(\tilde{S}_{i2}|\tilde{S}_{i2} > 0, \text{LL}) = [E(\tilde{V}) - B_{i2}] + r(z_B)\text{Var}(\tilde{V}_{i2}), \tag{4.85}$$

where $r(z_B) \equiv f(z_B)[1 - F(z_B)]^{-1}$. As before, $f(z_B)$ and $F(z_B)$ are the density function and the distribution function, respectively, of a standardized normal random variable. The function $r(z_B)$ is known as the "hazard function" for the standardized normal distribution.[74] (A similarly defined function can be specified for any distribution.)

It can also be shown that:

$$\text{Var}(\tilde{S}_{i2}|\tilde{S}_{i2} > 0, \text{LL}) = \text{Var}(V_{i2})g(z_B), \tag{4.86}$$

where $g(z_B) \equiv 1 + z_B r(z_B) - (r(z_B))^2$, and:

$$\text{Cov}(\tilde{S}_{i2}, \tilde{V}_{m2}|\tilde{S}_{i2} > 0, \text{LL}) = \text{Var}(\tilde{S}_{i2}|\tilde{S}_{i2} > 0, \text{LL}) \left(\frac{\text{Cov}(\tilde{V}_{i2}, \tilde{V}_{m2})}{\text{Var}(\tilde{V}_{i2})}\right). \tag{4.87}$$

Using (4.86) in (4.87), we get:

---

[72]Given perfect markets, the distribution function of $\tilde{V}_{m2}$ and, thus, the values of $E(\tilde{V}_{m2})$ and $\text{Var}(\tilde{V}_{m2})$ are independent of the attributes of the distribution of $\tilde{V}_{i2}$ from the view of firm i.

[73]See Johnson and Kotz [1970, pp. 81–83; 1972, pp. 112–113.

[74]See, e.g., Barlow, Proschen, and Hunter [1965, esp. chap. 2] for a variety of details relevant to hazard functions.

$$\begin{aligned}\text{Cov}(\tilde{S}_{i2}, \tilde{V}_{m2}|\tilde{S}_{i2} > 0, \text{LL}) &= \left(\frac{\text{Cov}(\tilde{V}_{i2}, \tilde{V}_{m2})}{\text{Var}(\tilde{V}_{m2})}\right)g(z_B)\text{Var}(\tilde{V}_{i2}) \\ &= \text{Cov}(\tilde{V}_{i2}, \tilde{V}_{m2})g(z_B) \\ &= \text{Cov}(\tilde{V}_{i2}, \tilde{V}_{m2}|\tilde{V}_{i2} > B_{i2}),\end{aligned} \tag{4.88}$$

where the last equality follows from the equivalence of the conditions $\tilde{S}_{i2} > 0$ and $\tilde{V}_{i2} > B_{i2}$.

Note that, ex ante, the ith firm's equityholders face a gamble defined, in general, by both a nonzero probability of $\tilde{S}_{i2} > 0$ and a nonzero probability of $\tilde{S}_{i2} = 0$ (i.e., $\tilde{V}_{i2} \leq B_{i2}$). Thus, in general, the risk conditional on $\tilde{S}_{i2} > 0$—which is given by expression (4.88)—is not the ex ante (or "before the facts are in") risk facing any equityholder. The risk that the equityholders face is defined by the joint distribution of $\tilde{S}_{i2}$ and $\tilde{V}_{m2}$ conditional only upon LL. This risk is marginal with respect to the events $\tilde{V}_{i2} > B_{i2}$ and $\tilde{V}_{i2} \leq B_{i2}$ and, therefore, it depends on the probabilities of each of these events.

In general, it can be shown that:

$$\text{Cov}(\tilde{x}, \tilde{y}) = E_{\tilde{H}}[\text{Cov}(\tilde{x}, \tilde{y}|\tilde{H})] + \text{Cov}_{\tilde{H}}[E(\tilde{x}|\tilde{H}), E(\tilde{y}|\tilde{H})], \tag{4.89}$$

where $\tilde{x}$ and $\tilde{y}$ are any two random variables, $\tilde{H}$ is some conditioning random variable, and $E_{\tilde{H}}(\cdot)$ and $\text{Cov}_{\tilde{H}}(\cdot, \cdot)$ are the expectation and covariance operators, respectively, applied with respect to the distribution function of $\tilde{H}$ (see Raj [1968, p. 14] for a derivation of (5.89)). Applying this result to the problem at hand, one finds that:

$$\begin{aligned}\text{Cov}(\tilde{S}_{i2}, \tilde{V}_{m2}|\text{LL}) &= E_{\tilde{I}}[\text{Cov}(\tilde{S}_{i2}, \tilde{V}_{m2}|\tilde{I}, \text{LL})] \\ &\quad + \text{Cov}_{\tilde{I}}[E(\tilde{S}_{i2}|\tilde{I}, \text{LL}), E(\tilde{V}_{m2}|\tilde{I}, \text{LL})],\end{aligned} \tag{4.90}$$

where $\tilde{I}$ is an indicator random variable defined as follows:

$$\tilde{I} = \begin{cases} 1, & \text{if } \tilde{V}_{i2} > B_{i2} \\ 0, & \text{if } \tilde{V}_{i2} \leq B_{i2}. \end{cases} \tag{4.91}$$

Thus, $\Pr(\tilde{I} = 1) = \Pr(\tilde{V}_{i2} > B_{i2})$ and $\Pr(\tilde{I} = 0) = \Pr(\tilde{V}_{i2} \leq B_{i2})$.

Given our perfect markets assumption, the distribution function of $\tilde{V}_{m2}$ is independent of the attributes of $\tilde{V}_{i2}$. Thus, $E(\tilde{V}_{m2}|\text{LL}, \tilde{I}) = E(\tilde{V}_{m2}|\text{LL})$ for all values of $\tilde{I}$. *Therefore,* $Cov_{\tilde{I}}[E(\tilde{S}_{i2}|\tilde{I}, \text{LL}), E(\tilde{V}_{m2}|\tilde{I}, \text{LL})] = 0$ and, as a result:

$$\text{Cov}(\tilde{S}_{i2}, \tilde{V}_{m2}|\text{LL}) = E_{I}[\text{Cov}(\tilde{S}_{i2}, \tilde{V}_{m2}|\tilde{I}, \text{LL})]. \tag{4.92}$$

But $\tilde{S}_{i2} = 0$ for all values of $\tilde{V}_{m2}$ when $\tilde{I} = 0$. Consequently, from (4.88):

$$\text{Cov}(\tilde{S}_{i2}, \tilde{V}_{m2}|\text{LL}) = \text{Cov}(\tilde{V}_{i2}, \tilde{V}_{m2})g(z_B)\Pr(\tilde{V}_{i2} > B_{i2}). \tag{4.93}$$

Alternatively, using the definition of a first-order coefficient of correlation:

$$\text{Cov}(\tilde{S}_{i2}, \tilde{V}_{m2}|\text{LL}) = (\rho_{im})[\text{Var}(\tilde{V}_{i2})\text{Var}(\tilde{V}_{m2})]^{1/2}g(z_B)\Pr(\tilde{z} > z_B), \tag{4.94}$$

where, by definition, $\tilde{z} = (\tilde{V}_{i2} - E(\tilde{V}_{i2}))/(\text{Var}(V_{i2}))^{1/2}$ and $z_B = (B_{i2} - E(\tilde{V}_{i2}))/(\text{Var}(V_{i2}))^{1/2}$.

The implications of various financing decisions for the risk of firm i's equity, conditional on the firm's production-investment decisions, can be assessed by examining the changes in $\text{Cov}(\tilde{S}_{i2}, \tilde{V}_{m2}|\text{LL})$ induced by changes in B_{i2}, conditional on the distribution function of $\tilde{V}_{i2}$. Similarly, the implications of changes in production-investment decisions can be assessed by examining the changes in $\text{Cov}(\tilde{S}_{i2}, \tilde{V}_{m2}|\text{LL})$ induced by changes in the distribution of $\tilde{V}_{i2}$—in particular, changes in $E(\tilde{V}_{i2})$ and $\text{Var}(\tilde{V}_{i2})$. Changes in the values of the latter parameters induce changes in the value of z_B. The next subsection considers changes in financing decisions. Then we focus on production-investment decisions.

4.6.4.2 Changes in Financing Decisions

Suppose that firm i changes the amount of debt used to finance its given production-investment decisions. Since the latter decisions are fixed, the probability distribution of $\tilde{V}_{i2}$ and, therefore, the values of $E(\tilde{V}_{i2})$, $\text{Var}(\tilde{V}_{i2})$, and $\text{Cov}(\tilde{V}_{i2}, \tilde{V}_{m2})$ are fixed.

Let $B_{i2} = \lambda E(\tilde{V}_{i2})$, where λ is defined to be the total promised payment to the bondholders per dollar of firm i's expected future value. In terms of Figure 1, changes in the value of λ correspond to movements of B_{i2} for a fixed distribution function of $\tilde{V}_{i2}$ and, thus, fixed values of $E(\tilde{V}_{i2})$ and $\sigma(\tilde{V}_{i2})$ in Figure 1. We assume that $E(\tilde{V}_{i2}) \geq 0$ and $\lambda E(\tilde{V}_{i2}) \geq 0$, or $\lambda \geq 0$. By definition, $E(\tilde{S}_{i2}|\tilde{V}_{i2} > B_{i2}, \text{LL}) = (1 - \lambda)E(\tilde{V}_{i2})$. When $0 \leq B_{i2} \leq E(\tilde{V}_{i2})$, then $0 \leq \lambda \leq 1$.

In the above setup, changes in financing decisions are represented by changes in the value of λ. Such changes induce changes in the value of z_B, since $z_B = (B_{i2} - E(\tilde{V}_{i2}))/\sigma(\tilde{V}_{i2}) = (\lambda - 1)E(\tilde{V}_{i2})/\sigma(\tilde{V}_{i2})$, where $\sigma(\tilde{V}_{i2}) = \sqrt{\text{Var}(\tilde{V}_{i2})}$.

Using (4.94) one gets:

$$\frac{\partial\,\text{Cov}(\tilde{S}_{i2}, \tilde{V}_{m2}|\text{LL})}{\partial\lambda} = (\rho_{im})\sigma(\tilde{V}_{i2})\sigma(\tilde{V}_{m2}) \times \left[\frac{\partial g(z_B)}{\partial z_B}\frac{\partial z_B}{\partial\lambda}(1 - F(z_B)) + g(z_B)\frac{\partial[1 - F(z_B)]}{z_B}\frac{\partial z_B}{\partial\lambda}\right]. \tag{4.95}$$

Since:

$$\partial z_B/\partial\lambda = E(\tilde{V}_{i2})/\sigma(\tilde{V}_{i2}), \tag{4.96}$$

and:

$$\partial[1 - F(z_B)]/\partial z_B = -f(z_B), \tag{4.97}$$

expression (4.95) can be restated as:

$$\frac{\partial\,\text{Cov}(\tilde{S}_{i2}, \tilde{V}_{m2}|\text{LL})}{\partial\lambda} \propto \left[\frac{\partial g(z_B)}{\partial z_B}(1 - F(z_B)) - g(z_B)f(z_B)\right], \tag{4.98}$$

where $\propto$ denotes "proportional to" and the factor of proportionality for (4.98) is $(\rho_{im})\sigma(\tilde{V}_{m2})\sigma(\tilde{v}_{i2})(E(\tilde{V}_{im})/\sigma(\tilde{V}_{i2})) = \rho_{im}E(\tilde{V}_{i2})\sigma(\tilde{V}_{m2})$.

It can be shown, using the properties of the "hazard function" for a normal distribution, that $0 \leq g(z_B) \leq 1$ and $\partial g(z_B)/\partial z_B < 0$ (see Heckman [1977, p. 14]). Thus, the bracketed term on the right-hand side of (4.98) is less than or equal to zero. The sign of $\partial\,\text{Cov}\,(\tilde{S}_{i2}, \tilde{V}_{m2}|\text{LL})/\partial\lambda$ depends, therefore, on the sign of the factor of proportionality associated with (4.98). Hence, for $E(\tilde{V}_{i2}) > 0$, we find that when $\rho_{im} \geq 0$ (<0), $\partial\text{Cov}\,(\tilde{S}_{i2}, \tilde{V}_{m2}|\text{LL})/\partial\lambda \leq 0$ (> 0). In short, when the ith firm's equity contributes positively to portfolio risk (i.e., $\rho_{im} > 0$), then the risk of its equity's dollar returns decreases as the firm increases the extent to which it uses debt, for given production-investment decisions.

This behavior of $\text{Cov}(\tilde{S}_{i2}, \tilde{V}_{m2}|\text{LL})$ seems to "make sense." As λ increases, the probability of bankruptcy increases and, therefore, the probability associated with the outcome $\tilde{S}_{i2} = 0$—for all values of $\tilde{V}_{m2}$—increases. Thus, as λ increases, the constant (zero) payoff part of the distribution of the dollar returns to equity receives a greater probability weight in the determination of $\text{Cov}(\tilde{S}_{i2}, \tilde{V}_{m2}|\text{LL})$ and the only potentially nonzero contributor to the latter's value—$\text{Cov}(\tilde{V}_{i2}, \tilde{V}_{m2})g(z_B)$—receives a lower weight, which is given by the value of $\Pr(\tilde{V}_{i2} > B_{i2})$ (see expression (4.93)). The net result is a decrease (increase) in the value of $\text{Cov}(\tilde{S}_{i2}, \tilde{V}_{m2}|\text{LL})$ when $\rho_{im} \geq 0$ (< 0), assuming $E(\tilde{V}_{i2}) > 0$. Of course, this covariance value converges to zero as λ becomes arbitrarily large, i.e., as the constant payoff outcome $\tilde{S}_{i2} = 0$ becomes more and more certain and the debt becomes more and more like equity.

The fact that the risk $\text{Cov}(\tilde{S}_{i2}, \tilde{V}_{m2}|\text{LL})$ decreases as λ increases, when $\rho_{im} > 0$, does not imply that, in equilibrium, the ith firm's equity shares are more or less "attractive" than before λ is changed. At time 1, the equilibrium price per unit of equity will be set so as to reflect the risk of the ith firm's equity. Therefore, the equilibrium expected rate of return on the ith firm's equity will have a value consistent with that risk. Finally, it is well to note, from (4.85) and the specification $z_B = (\lambda - 1)E(\tilde{V}_{i2})/\sigma(\tilde{V}_{i2})$, that changes in λ induce changes in the equityholders' expected dollar returns. The value of the equilibrium expected rate of return on the ith firm's equity—which depends on the equilibrium value of the equity set at time 1—will reflect both the change in the risk of and the change in the expected value of the equity's dollar returns.

4.6.4.3 Changes in Production-Investment Decisions

If the marginal probability distribution of $\tilde{V}_{m2}$ is not affected by the attributes of firm i's decisions, then, in general, the unconditional coefficient of correlation $\rho_{im} = \text{Cov}(\tilde{V}_{i2}, \tilde{V}_{m2})/\sigma(\tilde{V}_{i2})\sigma(\tilde{V}_{m2})$ is not independent of changes in firm i's production-investment decisions.[75] Such changes can alter the value of either $\text{Cov}(\tilde{V}_{i2}, \tilde{V}_{m2})$ or $\sigma(\tilde{V}_{i2})$. For the most part, the potential for changes in either of these parameters increases the mechanical burdens of evaluating the implications of changes in production-investment decisions for risk. Indeed, the major burden is one of notation and of overly lengthy mathematical expressions. The basic assessment route is, however, the same when both parameters are affected as it is when only one is affected.

We begin by considering the implications of changes in production-investment decisions that end up altering z_B by altering $E(\tilde{V}_{i2})$. For simplicity, $\sigma(\tilde{V}_{i2})$ and $\text{Cov}(\tilde{V}_{i2}, \tilde{V}_{m2})$ are assumed to be unchanged.[76] Moreover, the ith firm's financing decisions are held fixed.

Recall that:

$$\text{Cov}(\tilde{S}_{i2}, \tilde{V}_{m2}|\text{LL}) = \text{Cov}(\tilde{V}_{i2}, \tilde{V}_{m2})g(z_B)(1 - F(z_B)). \tag{4.99}$$

---

[75]The independence between the distribution of $\tilde{V}_{i2}$ and $\tilde{V}_{m2}$ means that changes in the attributes of one of these random variable's distribution do not induce offsetting changes in the other's, thus leaving ρ_{im} unchanged.

[76]Since the marginal distribution function of $\tilde{V}_{m2}$ is not affected by firm i's decisions, $\text{Var}(\tilde{V}_{m2})$ is not affected. Since $\text{Cov}(\tilde{V}_{i2}, \tilde{V}_{m2})$ is also assumed to be unaffected, the risk of firm i's *dollar* return, $\text{Cov}(\tilde{V}_{i2}, \tilde{V}_{m2})/\text{Var}(\tilde{V}_{m2})$ is unchanged. This does not imply, however, that the risk of the rate of return on firm i as a whole is unchanged. Indeed, as will be explained in our section on multiperiod valuation, a sufficient condition for changing this risk is a change in the value of the ratio $\text{Cov}(\tilde{V}_{i2}, \tilde{V}_{m2})/E(\tilde{V}_{i2})$.

Thus:

$$\frac{\partial\, \mathrm{Cov}(\tilde{S}_{i2}, \tilde{V}_{m2}|\mathrm{LL})}{\partial E(\tilde{V}_{i2})} = \mathrm{Cov}(\tilde{V}_{i2}, \tilde{V}_{m2})$$

$$\times \left[\frac{\partial g}{\partial z_B}(1 - F(z_B)) + \frac{\partial(1 - F(z_B))}{\partial z_B} g(z_B)\right] \times \left(\frac{\partial z_B}{\partial E(\tilde{V}_{i2})}\right)$$

$$= \mathrm{Cov}(\tilde{V}_{i2}, \tilde{V}_{m2})\left[\frac{\partial g}{\partial z_B}(1 - F(z_B)) - f(z_B)g(z_B)\right] \times \left(-\frac{1}{\sigma(\tilde{V}_{i2})}\right)$$

$$= \frac{\mathrm{Cov}(\tilde{V}_{i2}, \tilde{V}_{m2})}{\sigma(\tilde{V}_{i2})}\left[\frac{\partial g(z_B)}{\partial z_B}(F(z_B) - 1) + f(z_B)g(z_B)\right]. \tag{4.100}$$

As indicated earlier, $g(z_B) > 0$ and $\partial g(z_B)/\partial z_B < 0$. Thus, since $F(z_B) - 1 < 0$ and $f(z_B) > 0$, the bracketed term on the right-hand side of the last line of (4.100) is positive. The sign of $\partial\, \mathrm{Cov}(\tilde{S}_{i2}, \tilde{V}_{m2}|\mathrm{LL})/\partial E(\tilde{V}_{i2})$ is, therefore, the same as the sign of $\mathrm{Cov}(\tilde{V}_{i2}, \tilde{V}_{m2})$. In short, if the ith firm's equity contributes positively to portfolio risk before changes in production-investment decisions that increase (decrease) $E(\tilde{V}_{i2})$, then those changes will, other things being equal, increase (decrease) the risk of firm i's equity. This sort of change corresponds to an increase in the "scale" of the ith firm's activities.

The implications of changes in $\sigma(\tilde{V}_{i2})$ can be evaluated along similar lines. But since $\rho_{im}\epsilon[-1, 1]$, it should be clear that, in general, $\mathrm{Cov}(\tilde{V}_{i2}, \tilde{V}_{m2})$ cannot, as indicated earlier, always be unaffected by such changes if $\mathrm{Var}(\tilde{V}_{m2})$ is unchanged. We shall assume that $\mathrm{Cov}(\tilde{V}_{i2}, \tilde{V}_{m2})$ is a fixed multiple of $\sigma(\tilde{V}_{i2})$ for all production-investment decisions—and thus for all values of $\sigma(\tilde{V}_{i2})$. This implies that $\partial\rho_{im}/\partial\sigma(\tilde{V}_{i2}) = 0$.

From (4.94), we have:

$$\mathrm{Cov}(\tilde{S}_{i2}, \tilde{V}_{m2}|\mathrm{LL}) = \rho_{im}\sigma(\tilde{V}_{im})\sigma(\tilde{V}_{m2})g(z_B)(1 - F(z_B)). \tag{4.101}$$

Thus:

$$\frac{\partial\, \mathrm{Cov}(\tilde{S}_{i2}, \tilde{V}_{m2}|\mathrm{LL})}{\partial\sigma(\tilde{V}_{i2})} = \rho_{im}\sigma(\tilde{V}_{m2})g(z_B)(1 - F(z_B))$$

$$+ [\rho_{im}\sigma(\tilde{V}_{i2})\sigma(\tilde{V}_{m2})]\left[\frac{\partial g(z_B)}{\partial z_B}(1 - F(z_B))\right.$$

$$\left. + g(z_B)\frac{\partial(1 - F(z_B))}{\partial z_B}\right]\left(\frac{\partial z_B}{\partial\sigma(\tilde{V}_{i2})}\right)$$

$$= \rho_{im}\sigma(\tilde{V}_{m2})g(z_B)(1 - F(z_B))$$

$$+ \rho_{im}\sigma(\tilde{V}_{m2})\left(\frac{E(\tilde{V}_{i2}) - B_{i2}}{\mathrm{Var}(\tilde{V}_{i2})}\right)$$

$$\times \left[\frac{\partial g(z_B)}{\partial z_B}(1 - F(z_B)) - g(z_B)f(z_B)\right]. \tag{4.102}$$

Since $\partial g(z_B)/\partial z_B < 0$ and $g(z_B) > 0$, the bracketed term in the last line is positive.

Thus, the sign of the risk change depends on the signs of ρ_{im} and $(E(\tilde{V}_{i2}) - B_{i2})$. For our assumed condition $E(\tilde{V}_{i2}) > B_{i2}$, the sign of the risk change is the same as the sign of ρ_{im}. In short, the value of $\mathrm{Cov}(\tilde{S}_{i2}, \tilde{V}_{m2}|\mathrm{LL})$ increases (decreases) as the value of $\sigma(\tilde{V}_{i2})$ increases (decreases) when the fixed value of ρ_{im} is positive (negative).

4.6.4.4 Remarks

It should be clear that the behavior of the risk of equity, $\mathrm{Cov}(\tilde{S}_{i2}, \tilde{V}_{m2}|\mathrm{LL})$, is a more complicated function of its determinants when the probability of bankruptcy is positive than when it is zero. Yet, the major point now is the same as before: there are a variety of factors than can alter the risk of a firm's common equity, whether or not the risk of the firm is unchanged. The preceding discussion simply deals with another of them, namely, the probability of bankruptcy. By doing so, it identifies additional things about which inferences might be made when assessing distributions of returns. And this points to additional potential uses of sample evidence consisting of observed values of accounting numbers—for specific firms or for aggregates of firms (e.g., an industry).

4.6.4.5 The Risk of Debt

Of course, the same kinds of factors that affect the risk of the returns to firm i's equity claims can affect the risk of the returns to its debt claims. By definition:

$$\begin{aligned}\mathrm{Cov}(\tilde{V}_{i2}, \tilde{V}_{m2}|\mathrm{LL}) &= \mathrm{Cov}(\tilde{S}_{i2} + \tilde{d}_{i2}, \tilde{V}_{m2}|\mathrm{LL}) \\ &= \mathrm{Cov}(\tilde{S}_{i2}, \tilde{V}_{m2}|\mathrm{LL}) + \mathrm{Cov}(\tilde{d}_{i2}, \tilde{V}_{m2}|\mathrm{LL}), \qquad (4.103)\end{aligned}$$

where, as before, $\tilde{d}_{i2}$ is the total dollar return to the holders of the ith firm's debt. Thus, since $\mathrm{Cov}(\tilde{V}_{i2}, \tilde{V}_{m2}|\mathrm{LL}) = \mathrm{Cov}(\tilde{V}_{i2}, \tilde{V}_{m2})$, we have, using (4.94) and (4.103):

$$\begin{aligned}\mathrm{Cov}(\tilde{d}_{i2}, \tilde{V}_{m2}|\mathrm{LL}) &= \mathrm{Cov}(\tilde{V}_{i2}, \tilde{V}_{m2}) - \mathrm{Cov}(\tilde{V}_{i2}, \tilde{V}_{m2})g(z_B)(1 - F(z_B)) \\ &= \mathrm{Cov}(\tilde{V}_{i2}, \tilde{V}_{m2})[1 - g(z_B)(1 - F(z_B))]. \qquad (4.104)\end{aligned}$$

In short, just as the decisions that affect the characteristics of the distribution of $\tilde{V}_{i2}$ or the probability of bankruptcy affect the risk of firm i's equity, so too do they affect the risk of its debt. Of course, when the probability of bankruptcy is zero, then $g(z_B) = 1$ and $\Pr(\tilde{z} \geq z_B) = (1 - F(z_B)) = 1$, in which case $\mathrm{Cov}(\tilde{d}_{i2}, \tilde{V}_{m2}|\mathrm{LL}) = 0$. This is why the behavior of $\mathrm{Cov}(\tilde{d}_{i2}, \tilde{V}_{m2}|\mathrm{LL})$ was not discussed in Section 4.4, where the probability of bankruptcy was assumed to be zero.

4.7 Taxes and Production-Investment Decisions: A Brief Look

4.7.1 Preliminaries

The analysis given above, with respect to both operating and financing decisions, abstracts from the effects of taxes—most importantly, income taxes. If all effective tax rates were equal and strictly proportional to net present value (and changes thereof), this abstraction would be unimportant—because a given firm's value-maximizing decisions would be unaffected by such tax rates. The same can be said for the effects of lump-sum taxes on the operating decisions of existing firms. Interesting issues arise, however, when different types of income (e.g., corporate versus noncorporate) are taxed at different rates and when there are differences in the deductibility provisions pertaining to different types of costs. These are the sorts of things that can make a tax system nonneutral, in the sense that optimal decisions are altered by the system's existence.

When the tax system is not neutral, a change in any feature of the tax system may alter optimizing decisions and the relationships between these decisions and a firm's relative risk. Thus, the expressions given earlier to characterize the connections between risk and decisions may no longer apply. The purpose of this section is to provide an analysis that illustrates the types of changes that can be induced in these characterizations.

Our analysis will be quite restrictive and (therefore) substantially incomplete. There is an ongoing debate over the actual incidence of taxes.[77] Thus, there are many unanswered questions about the types of taxes actually borne by firms and about firms' effective tax rates. Our results are based on one perspective of these issues. Moreover, we shall be providing a partial equilibrium analysis. That is, we take as fixed several variables that would, in general, change as a result of the aggregate effects of all firms' decisions. For the most part, we focus on the decisions of one firm. Since our major goal is to convey some qualitative impressions regarding the issues raised by taxation, this approach seems adequate. But it is well to remember that we certainly do not provide a full-fledged analysis of the ultimate (general equilibrium) effects of taxes.[78]

As before, we restrict attention to a single-period model, value-maximizing firms, and perfect markets. The variant of the two-parameter model used in Section 4.4 will be used again. But now we allow for a positive income tax rate, applied to income defined by "historical cost" accounting methods. Specifically, the deductible "fixed capital" cost, for tax purposes, is based on "historical" (or acquisition) cost. The only "variable" cost in our model is labor cost. Since the wage rate is a random variable whose value is not known until time 2 (i.e., the end of our single period), "historical" cost of labor is equal to the "current" cost at the time of payment.

Initially, we abstract from financing decisions by assuming that firms only use equity securities to finance their operating activities. Some connections between taxes and financing decisions will be discussed later. Additional material on this topic is provided by Hite [1977].

We previously gave no special treatment to the resale (or "salvage") value of the units of capital on hand at time 2. We simply assumed that the terminal value of the units acquired at time 1, k_j, for firm j, equals zero at time 2 or that the resale value (if nonzero) is incorporated into the jth firm's net cash flow. This approach will not suffice for an analysis of an income tax system similar to the prevailing U.S. system, because of the latter's extensive use of historical cost accounting methods for the computation of deductible costs, in particular, "depreciation." This is one of the tax factors that will make income taxes not strictly proportional to net operating earnings and, thus, not strictly proportional to a capital-using firm's net present value.[79]

Finally, we note the (perhaps) most critical assumptions of our analysis. We shall assume, first, that there is both a taxed corporate sector and an otherwise equivalent un-

---

[77]See, e.g., Aaron and Pechman [1981].

[78]Indeed, a general equilibrium analysis would have to deal with more than firms' tax payments or the "inflow" side of governmental budgets. It would also have to deal with the expenditure (or "outflow") side of these budgets.

[79]And we assume that every active producer is a captial-using firm in the sense that $q_j > 0$ implies $k_j > 0$ for each firm j.

taxed noncorporate sector. Second, we shall assume that the government's budget is balanced and "distributionally neutral," in the sense defined by McClure and Thirsk [1975]. The major implication of this second assumption is that the value of the aggregate market portfolio at time 2 will equal whatever it would have equaled in our no-tax world, *viz.*, $\tilde{F}_m$. Consistent with these two assumptions, and our partial equilibrium approach, the price per unit of expected dollar return and the price per unit of risk are taken to be the values established in the untaxed sector. And these, in turn, are assumed to equal the values that prevailed in our no-tax world, *viz.*, $(1 + E(\tilde{R}_z))^{-1}$ and $\lambda_m^*(1 + E(\tilde{R}_z))^{-1}$, respectively. In addition, all other "before tax" exogenous variables (e.g., products' and factors' prices) for the corporate sector have values equal to those prevailing in the noncorporate sector, and thus to their counterparts in our no-tax setting.

We now proceed to consider the implications of taxation for a firm in the taxed corporate sector.

4.7.2 More Details

Under our new assumptions, the after-tax net operating cash flow for corporation j, $\tilde{F}_j^a$, is given by:

$$\begin{aligned}\tilde{F}_j^a &= \tilde{p}q_j^a - \tilde{w}\ell_j^a - \tau(\tilde{p}q_j^a - \tilde{w}\ell_j^a - \delta k_j^a)\\ &= (1 - \tau)(\tilde{p}q_j^a - \tilde{w}\ell_j^a) + \tau\delta k_j^a, \qquad (4.105)\end{aligned}$$

where τ denotes the corporate income tax rate, δ denotes the fraction of the original outlay for capital that is recognized as "depreciation expense," and q_j^a, k_j^a, ℓ_j^a are the optimal values of the firm's decision variables conditional on taxation.[80] As before, the proceeds (= market value) from liquidation of the firm's capital stock at time 2 is assumed to be zero.[81] Using mechanics similar to those used in Section 4.4, we can proceed directly to the implications of $\tau > 0$ for a firm's operating decisions.

In the following analysis, F_j^o denotes the net cash flow that would be received by firm j if $\tau = 0$ *and* if it makes the decisions k_j^a, ℓ_j^a, and q_j^a. And V_{j1}^o denotes the current equilibrium value of the net cash flow $\tilde{F}_j^o$.

First, note that $\tilde{F}_j^a$, for each j, differs from F_j^o because of the scalar multiple $(1 - \tau)$ and the additive factor $\tau\delta k_j^a$, both of which are nonrandom. Therefore:

$$\text{Cov}(\tilde{F}_j^a, \tilde{F}_m) = (1 - \tau)\text{Cov}(\tilde{F}_j^o, \tilde{F}_m) \qquad (4.106)$$

and:

$$E(\tilde{F}_j^a) = (1 - \tau)E(\tilde{F}_j^o) + \tau\delta k_j^a. \qquad (4.107)$$

Using the above, along with our assumptions about $(1 + E(\tilde{R}_z))$ and λ_m^*, we find that the current equilibrium value of firm j in our tax world, V_{j1}^a, is:

---

[80]Recall that the price per unit of capital is set equal to unity. Thus the outlay for k_j^a units of capital equals k_j^a dollars.

[81]Alternatively, one can assume that the net proceeds are incorporated into the operating cash flow, in which case they are assumed to be taxed as the "ordinary" income rate, τ (and not, e.g., at a special "capital gains" rate).

$$\begin{aligned} V_{j1}^a &= (1 + E(\tilde{R}_z))^{-1} [E(\tilde{F}_j^a) - \lambda_m^* \operatorname{Cov}(\tilde{F}_j^a, \tilde{F}_m)] \\ &= (1 + E(\tilde{R}_z))^{-1}[(1 - \tau)E(\tilde{F}_j^o) + \tau\delta k_j^a \\ &\quad - \lambda_m^*(1 - \tau) \operatorname{Cov}(\tilde{F}_j^o, \tilde{F}_m)] \\ &= (1 - \tau)V_{j1}^o + (1 + E(\tilde{R}_z))^{-1}\tau\delta k_j^a. \end{aligned} \tag{4.108}$$

Note that V_{j1}^o differs from what the value would be conditional on optimizing behavior in a no-tax world because V_{j1}^o is conditional on k_j^a, q_j^a, and ℓ_j^a, rather than the decisions that are *optimal* in a no-tax world.

By itself, δ does not affect any of the determinants of V_j^o. Thus, as can be seen from (4.108), δ will be set equal to its maximum allowable value by a value-maximizing firm. This applies to all values of $\tau > 0$ and $k_j^a > 0$. Since we are assuming that some amount of capital, however small, is required to get $q_j^a > 0$, this will automatically be the result for each active producer.

The implications of $\tau > 0$ for the optimal value of k_j are slightly less obvious because k_j is a determinant of V_{j1}^o via the production function $q_j = h_j(\ell_j, k_j)$. That is, changes in k_j^a alter the distribution function of $\tilde{F}_j^o$. For each level of output, q_j, a change in the value of k_j will induce a change in the corresponding optimal value of l_j. This will lead, in turn, to changes in the relative-risk determinants associated with the firm's total labor inputs. And, of course, any changes in k_j will affect the determinants of relative risk associated with total output. The full implications of these direct and indirect changes can be highlighted by using mechanics similar to those used for our no-tax world.

As before, a value-maximizing firm will select a feasible combination of l_j,k_j, and q_j such that the certainty equivalent value of marginal revenue equals the certainty equivalent value of average total cost. Now, however, both marginal revenue and average total cost are affected by taxes.

Marginal revenue after taxes is:

$$(1 - \tau)\tilde{p} = (1 - \tau)\bar{p}(1 + \tilde{e}). \tag{4.109}$$

Thus, the contribution of a given firm's marginal revenue to aggregate risk is:

$$\operatorname{Cov}((1 - \tau)\tilde{p}, \tilde{F}_m) = (1 - \tau) \operatorname{Cov}(\tilde{p}, \tilde{F}_m) = (1 - \tau)[\bar{p}(\bar{R}\sigma_e^2 - \sigma_{ev}\bar{C})]. \tag{4.110}$$

And the certainty equivalent value of after-tax marginal revenue is:

$$\begin{aligned} \mathrm{CEQ}((1 - \tau)\tilde{p}) &= (1 - \tau)E(\tilde{p}) - \lambda_m^*(1 - \tau) \operatorname{Cov}(\tilde{p}, \tilde{F}_m) \\ &= (1 - \tau)\bar{p}[1 - \lambda_m^*(\bar{R}\sigma_e^2 - \sigma_{ev}\bar{C})]. \end{aligned} \tag{4.111}$$

The after-tax cost of labor is given by:

$$(1 - \tau)\tilde{w}\ell_j^a = (1 - \tau)\bar{w}(1 + \tilde{v})\ell_j^a. \tag{4.112}$$

Thus, the contribution of this random payoff to aggregate risk is:

$$\begin{aligned} \operatorname{Cov}((1 - \tau)\tilde{w}\ell_j^a, F_m) &= (1 - \tau) \operatorname{Cov}(\tilde{w}\ell_j^a, \tilde{F}_m) \\ &= -(1 - \tau)\bar{w}\ell_j^a(\bar{C}\sigma_v^2 - \bar{R}\sigma_{ev}). \end{aligned} \tag{4.113}$$

And:

$$CEQ((1 - \tau)\tilde{w}\ell_j^a) = (1 - \tau)\bar{w}\ell_j^a[1 + \lambda_m^*(\bar{C}\sigma_v^2 - \bar{R}\sigma_{ev})]. \tag{4.114}$$

Under our assumptions, the certainty equivalent value at time 2 of the equityholders' initial outlay, k_j^a, is $(1 + E(\tilde{R}_z))k_j^a$. But the depreciation deduction allowed for tax purposes reduces total costs. Recognition of these two results, along with (4.114), leads to the following expression for the certainty equivalent value of average after-tax total cost, $\tilde{AC}_j^a$:

$$\text{CEQ}(\tilde{AC}_j^a) = \frac{(1 - \tau)\bar{w}\ell_j^a[1 + \lambda_m^*(\bar{C}\sigma_v^2 - \bar{R}\sigma_{ev})] + k_j^a[1 + E(\tilde{R}_z) - \tau\delta]}{q_j^a}. \qquad (4.115)$$

Consistent with our assumptions, all before-tax prices have values equal to those that prevail in our no-tax world. Thus, we cannot have $\text{CEQ}((1 - \tau)\tilde{p}) = \text{CEQ}(\tilde{AC}_j^a)$. Rather we have:

$$\text{CEQ}(\tilde{p}) - \text{CEQ}(\tilde{AC}_j) = 0, \qquad (4.116)$$

where $\tilde{AC}_j$ equals average cost conditional on optimal decisions for $\tau = 0$. This implies:

$$(1 - \tau)[\text{CEQ}(\tilde{p}) - \text{CEQ}(\tilde{AC}_j)] = 0 \qquad (4.117)$$

for the no-tax world optimal decisions q_j^1, ℓ_j^1, k_j^1. This implies, in turn, that:

$$\begin{aligned}\text{CEQ}((1 - \tau)\tilde{p}) &= \frac{(1 - \tau)\bar{w}\ell_j^1[1 + \lambda_m^*(\bar{C}\sigma_v^2 - \bar{R}\sigma_{ev})] + (1 - \tau)k_j^1(1 + E(\tilde{\text{R}}_{\text{j}}))}{q_j^1} \\ &= \frac{(1 - \tau)\bar{w}\ell_j^1[1 + \lambda_m^*(\bar{C}\sigma_v^2 - \bar{R}\sigma_{ev})] + k_j^1]1 + E(\tilde{R}_z) - \tau(1 + E(\tilde{R}_z)}{q_j^1} \\ &< \frac{(1 - \tau)\bar{w}\ell_j^a[1 + \lambda_m^*(\bar{C}\sigma_v^2 - \bar{R}\sigma_{ev})] + k_j^a[1 + E(\tilde{R}_z) - \tau\delta]}{q_j^1},\end{aligned} \qquad (4.118)$$

if $\delta < 1 + E(\tilde{R}_z)$. When the latter inequality holds, the values of the decision variables that are optimal for $\tau = 0$ are not optimal for $\tau \neq 0$ because the optimal values for $\tau = 0$ do not satisfy the optimality condition requiring equality between marginal revenue and average cost when $\tau \neq 0$ and $\delta < 1 + E(\tilde{R}_z)$. In other words, as indicated earlier, the optimal values of q_j, ℓ_j, and k_j are not unaltered by taxation if taxes are not strictly proportional to "economic" income, which means that the deduction for the cost of units of capital must be $1 + E(\tilde{R}_z)$ per unit of capital. If average cost is an increasing function of output, then optimizing decisions conditional on $\tau \neq 0$ and $\delta < 1 + E(\tilde{R}_z)$ will involve $q_j^a < q_j^1$ and a different capital-labor ratio.

An alternative, and revealing, means of establishing insights on the capital-labor ratio can be developed by considering the corporate firm's cost minimization problem for a given level of output. Total after-tax cost for a given level of output, q_j, is defined by:

$$(1 - \tau)\bar{w}\ell_j[1 + \lambda_m^*(\bar{C}\sigma_v^2 - \bar{R}\sigma_{ev})] + [1 + E(\tilde{R}_z) - \tau\delta]k_j, \qquad (4.119)$$

where the values selected for ℓ_j and q_j are consistent with the production function $q_j = h_j(\ell_j, k_j)$. For each output level, a value-maximizing firm wants to minimize costs. Thus, it will select values of ℓ_j and k_j that satisfy its production function constraint and the first-order condition:

$$\frac{\partial h_j/\partial k_j}{\partial h_j/\partial \ell_j} = \frac{1 + E(\tilde{R}_z) - \tau\delta}{(1 - \tau)\bar{w}[1 + \lambda_m^*(\bar{C}\sigma_v^2 - \bar{R}\sigma_{ev})]}. \qquad (4.120)$$

This is the familiar condition stating that the marginal rate of technical substitution of labor for capital must be equal to the input price ratio—the price of capital divided by the price of labor. In certainty equivalent form, the effective price ratio is the ratio on the right-hand side of (4.120).

Note that this input price ratio would be unaffected by $\tau > 0$ if $\delta = 1 + E(\tilde{R}_z)$, which is the effective before-tax opportunity cost of capital. In this case, the optimal labor-capital ratio for each level of output in our world with corporate taxes would be identical to the optimal ratio in the absence of taxes. On the other hand, if $\delta < 1 + E(\tilde{R}_z)$, then $(1 + E(\tilde{R}_z))(1 - \tau) < 1 + E(\tilde{R}_z) - \tau\delta$, in which case the cost per unit of capital relative to the cost per unit of labor is higher than it would have been if $\tau = 0$ or if $\delta = 1 + E(\tilde{R}_z)$. This implies, in turn, that the labor-capital ratio, ℓ_j/k_j, will be higher, for each q_j, than it would otherwise be.

This does not mean, however, that the optimal level of labor input will be higher. From the discussion below (4.118), we know that $q_j^a < q_j^1$. If labor and capital are "normal" inputs, this inequality implies that $k_j^a < k_j^1$ and $\ell_j^a < \ell_j^1$.[82] In other words, the reduced optimal output leads to both a reduced capital input and a reduced level of labor input. The details of these induced changes will depend, of course, on the details of the firm's production function. This is another testimonial to the importance of this function in financial statement analysis. In any event, it should be clear that these tax-induced changes in k_j, ℓ_j, and q_j may lead, in general, to changes in a firm's relative risk and, therefore, to changes in the equilibrium expected returns on its securities.

The above remarks are cast in terms of a comparison between a tax world and a no-tax world. But they also provide guidance for inferring the effects of *changes* in the tax rate τ, on a firm's relative risk. This is probably more important insofar as contemporary financial statement analysis is concerned.

The analysis provided here, its restrictiveness notwithstanding, indicates that it is not enough simply to infer that a change in τ will alter a firm's profits. Since a change in τ will, in general, induce a firm to alter its operating decisions, it may have a variety of substantive implications for the attributes of a firm's operating decisions. The distribution function of net earnings (which pertains to "profitability") is only one of these attributes. The firm's cost structure and relative risk are others.

4.8 Summary

Assessing the distribution function of returns on the claims (e.g., "bonds" and "common stocks") issued by firms involves using available information to make inferences about firms' production-investment and financing decisions. An important part of this task is identification of the attributes of those decisions that are relevant when making inferences about return distributions. This requires the use of some valuation model that characterizes the equilibrium values of firms' claims. The two-parameter asset-pricing model was used for that purpose in this section.

This section identified the attributes of firms' decisions that are relevant for making inferences about the risks of the claims issued by any firm, and thus for the equilibrium

---

[82] A factor of production is defined here to be a "normal" factor if the scale of its use varies directly with the scale of its output. Alternatively stated, if an input is normal, then a decrease in its utilization implies a decrease in the level of output.

expected returns on those claims. The resulting theoretical relationships between those attributes and the risk of a claim provide structures for financial statement analysis by identifying the relevant objects of analysis. Those structures also provide a framework for indicating what kinds of data are potentially useful. In our discussion of these issues, we considered the implications of various disclosure regulations for the kinds of data available for financial statement analysis. Various sources of "indirect" data (e.g., industry data) were also discussed. And, not unexpectedly, we identified areas where pertinent data are not readily available.

We did not, however, consider the types of estimation methods and inferential tools that might be used when assessing distributions of returns. As was argued earlier, the appropriateness of applying a given method or tool to a given source of sample evidence, such as observations on accounting numbers, depends on the stochastic properties of the source. Thus, in general, evaluating the quality of results obtainable from applying a given method involves specifying such properties. This gets to so-called empirical issues. A detailed treatment of some basic issues relevant to this aspect of assessing distributions of returns is provided in Chapter 7.

APPENDIX I

Suppose that the random variable $\tilde{V}$ is normally distributed with mean equal to μ and variance equal to σ^2. Then the expectation of $\tilde{V}$ conditional on the outcome $L \leq \tilde{V} \leq U$—where L and U are, respectively, lower and upper bounds—is given by:[83]

$$E[\tilde{V} | L \leq \tilde{V} \leq U] = \mu + \frac{f(z_L) - f(z_U)}{F(z_U) - F(z_L)} \sigma, \tag{a1}$$

where $f(\cdot)$ is the density function of a standardized normal random variable (i.e., one with mean equal to zero and variance equal to unity); $F(\cdot)$ is the (cumulative) distribution function of a standardized normal random variable; $z_L \equiv (L - \mu)/\sigma$; and $z_U \equiv (U - \mu)/\sigma$.

The definitions of $f(\cdot)$ and $F(\cdot)$ are as follows:

$$f(z) = (2\pi)^{-1/2} e^{-1/2z^2} \tag{a2}$$

and:

$$F(z^*) = Pr(\tilde{z} \leq z^*) = \int_{-\infty}^{z^*} f(z)dz = 1 - Pr(\tilde{z} > z^*), \tag{a3}$$

where z^* is a possible value of $\tilde{z}$, $-\infty < \tilde{z} < +\infty$.

If $L = -\infty$, then $f(z_L) \equiv 0$, $F(z_L) \equiv 0$, and—in this case—$E[\tilde{V} | L \leq \tilde{V} \leq U] = E[\tilde{V} | \tilde{V} \leq U]$, where, from (al):

$$E[\tilde{V} | \tilde{V} \leq U] = \mu - \frac{f(z_U)}{F(z_U)} \sigma. \tag{a4}$$

[83]See Johnson and Kotz [1970, pp. 81–83].

The following two results are useful in deriving the results given in the text:

$$\frac{\partial f(z)}{\partial z} = (2\pi)^{-1/2} \frac{\partial(e^{-1/2z^2})}{\partial z}$$

$$= (2\pi)^{-1/2} e^{-1/2z^2}(-1)z$$

$$= -f(z)z, \tag{a5}$$

and:

$$\frac{\partial F(z^*)}{\partial z^*} = f(z^*). \tag{a6}$$

Let $\tilde{z} \equiv (\tilde{V} - \mu)/\sigma$. Then, using the chain rule for differentiation and expressions (a5) and (a6), one finds the following:

$$\frac{\partial f(z)}{\partial \mu} = \frac{\partial f(z)}{\partial z} \frac{\partial z}{\partial \mu}$$

$$= [-f(z)z]\left[-\frac{1}{\sigma}\right]$$

$$= f(z)\frac{z}{\sigma}, \tag{a7}$$

$$\frac{\partial f(z)}{\partial \sigma} = \frac{\partial f(z)}{\partial z} \frac{\partial z}{\partial \sigma}$$

$$= [-f(z)z][(-1)(V - \mu)\sigma^{-2}]$$

$$= f(z)\frac{z^2}{\sigma}, \tag{a8}$$

$$\frac{\partial F(z^*)}{\partial \mu} = \frac{\partial F(z^*)}{\partial z^*} \frac{\partial z^*}{\partial \mu}$$

$$= [f(z^*)]\left[-\frac{1}{\sigma}\right], \tag{a9}$$

$$\frac{\partial F(z^*)}{\partial \sigma} = \frac{\partial F(z^*)}{\partial z^*} \frac{\partial z^*}{\partial \sigma}$$

$$= [f(z^*)][(-1)(V^* - \mu)\sigma^{-2}]$$

$$= -f(z^*)\frac{z^*}{\sigma}, \tag{a10}$$

and:

$$\frac{\partial[1 - F(z^*)]}{\partial \sigma} = -\frac{\partial F(z^*)}{\partial \sigma} = f(z^*)\frac{z^*}{\sigma}, \tag{a11}$$

where $1 - F(z^*) = Pr(\tilde{z} \geq z^*)$.

The first result given in the text is in expression (4.67). The derivation is given below. This derivation uses the fact that $Pr(\tilde{V}_{i2} < B_{i2}) = Pr(\tilde{V}_{i2} - E(\tilde{V}_{i2}) < B_{i2} - E(\tilde{V}_{i2})) = Pr[(\tilde{V}_{i2} - E(\tilde{V}_{i2}))/\sigma(\tilde{V}_{i2}) < (B_{i2} - E(\tilde{V}_{i2}))/\sigma(\tilde{V}_{i2})] = Pr(\tilde{z} < z_B) = F(z_B)$, where all notation is as defined in the text.

The result given in expression (4.66) of the text is:

$$E[\tilde{V}_{i2} \mid \tilde{V}_{i2} < B_{i2}] \cdot Pr(\tilde{V}_{i2} < B_{i2}) = E(\tilde{V}_{i2}) \cdot F(z_B) - f(z_B)\sigma(\tilde{V}_{i2}). \tag{a12}$$

The derivative of this expression with respect to $\sigma(\tilde{V}_{i2})$ is:

$$E(\tilde{V}_{i2}) \frac{\partial F(z_B)}{\partial \sigma(\tilde{V}_{i2})} - \left[\frac{\partial f(z_B)}{\partial \sigma(\tilde{V}_{i2})} \sigma(\tilde{V}_{i2}) + f(z_B) \frac{\partial \sigma(\tilde{V}_{i2})}{\partial \sigma(\tilde{V}_{i2})} \right]. \tag{a13}$$

Using the results given in (a8) and (a10), one finds that (a13) can be written as:

$$\begin{aligned} & E(\tilde{V}_{i2})\left[-f(z_B) \frac{z_B}{\sigma(\tilde{V}_{i2})} \right] - \left[f(z_B) \frac{z_B^2}{\sigma(\tilde{V}_{i2})} \right] \sigma(\tilde{V}_{i2}) - f(z_B) \\ & = -f(z_B)\left[\frac{E(\tilde{V}_{i2})z_B}{\sigma(\tilde{V}_{i2})} + z_B^2 + 1 \right], \end{aligned} \tag{a14}$$

which is the result given in expression (4.68) of the text.

The result in expression (4.68) is given in (all). Expression (4.69) is obtained by differentiating (4.64) with respect to $\sigma(\tilde{V}_{i2})$, using the results given in (4.67) and (4.68). Expression (4.64) is:

$$E(\tilde{D}_{i2}) = B_{i2} \cdot Pr(\tilde{V}_{i2} \geq B_{i2}) + E(\tilde{V}_{i2} \mid \tilde{V}_{i2} < B_{i2}] \cdot Pr(\tilde{V}_{i2} < B_{i2}). \tag{a15}$$

Therefore:

$$\frac{\partial E(\tilde{D}_{i2})}{\partial \sigma(\tilde{V}_{i2})} = B_{i2} \frac{\partial Pr(\tilde{V}_{i2} \geq B_{i2})}{\partial \sigma(\tilde{V}_{i2})} + \frac{\partial [E(\tilde{V}_{i2} \mid \tilde{V}_{i2} < B_{i2}) \cdot Pr(\tilde{V}_{i2} < B_{i2})]}{\partial \sigma(\tilde{V}_{i2})}. \tag{a16}$$

Using (a11) and (a14), (a16) can be written as:

$$\begin{aligned} \frac{\partial E(\tilde{D}_{i2})}{\partial \sigma(\tilde{V}_{i2})} & = B_{i2}\left[f(z_B) \frac{z_B}{\sigma(\tilde{V}_{i2})} \right] - f(z_B)\left[\frac{E(\tilde{V}_{i2})z_B}{\sigma(\tilde{V}_{i2})} + z_B^2 + 1 \right] \\ & = (B_{i2} - E(\tilde{V}_{i2})) \frac{f(z_B)z_B}{\sigma(\tilde{V}_{i2})} - f(z_B)z_B^2 - f(z_B) \\ & = f(z_B)z_B^2 - f(z_B)z_B^2 - f(z_B) \\ & = -f(z_B), \end{aligned} \tag{a17}$$

which is the result given in expression (4.69).

The result given in expression (5.77) of the text is obtained by differentiating (a12) with respect to $E(\tilde{V}_{i2})$. The resulting derivative is:

$$\frac{\partial E(\tilde{V}_{i2})}{\partial E(\tilde{V}_{i2})} F(z_B) + E(\tilde{V}_{i2}) \frac{\partial F(z_B)}{\partial E(\tilde{V}_{i2})} - \left[\frac{\partial f(z_B)}{\partial E(\tilde{V}_{i2})} \sigma(\tilde{V}_{i2}) + f(z_B) \frac{\partial \sigma(\tilde{V}_{i2})}{\partial E(\tilde{V}_{i2})} \right]. \tag{a18}$$

After using the results in (a7) and (a9) and recognizing that $\partial\sigma(\tilde{V}_{i2})/\partial E(\tilde{V}_{i2}) = 0$, one can rewrite (a18) as:

$$F(z_B) - E(\tilde{V}_{i2})\frac{f(z_B)}{\sigma(\tilde{V}_{i2})} - f(z_B)z_B, \tag{a19}$$

which is the result given in (4.77). The result given in (4.78) is obtained by using the result in (a9) and the fact that:

$$\frac{\partial Pr(\tilde{V}_{i2} \geq B_{i2})}{\partial E(\tilde{V}_{i2})} = \frac{\partial[1 - F(z_B)]}{\partial E(\tilde{V}_{i2})}$$

$$= -\frac{\partial F(z_B)}{\partial E(\tilde{V}_{i2})}. \tag{a20}$$

Upon using (a19) and (a20), one finds that:

$$\begin{aligned}\frac{\partial E(\tilde{D}_{i2})}{\partial E(\tilde{V}_{i2})} &= B_{i2} - \frac{\partial Pr(\tilde{V}_{i2} \geq B_{i2})}{\partial E(\tilde{V}_{i2})} \\ &\quad + \frac{\partial[E[\tilde{V}_{i2} \,|\, \tilde{V}_{i2} < B_{i2}] \cdot Pr(\tilde{V}_{i2} < B_{i2})]}{\partial E(\tilde{V}_{i2})} \\ &= B_{i2}\left[\frac{f(z_B)}{\sigma(\tilde{V}_{i2})}\right] + F(z_B) - E(\tilde{V}_{i2})\left[\frac{f(z_B)}{\sigma(\tilde{V}_{i2})}\right] - f(z_B)z_B \\ &= (B_{i2} - E(\tilde{V}_{i2}))\left[\frac{f(z_B)}{\sigma(\tilde{V}_{i2})}\right] + F(z_B) - f(z_B)z_B \\ &= z_B f(z_B) + F(z_B) - f(z_B)z_B \\ &= F(z_B),\end{aligned} \tag{a21}$$

which is the result given in expression (4.79) of the text.

CHAPTER FIVE

Multiperiod Valuation

5.1 Preliminaries

Thus far, our analytical results have been based on a single-period asset-pricing model. For some problems, this may be an acceptable approximation. In other cases, it may be more appropriate to give some explicit representation for multiperiod issues. This may occur when, for example, one is considering the implications of long-range strategies newly announced by firms. Or it may be appropriate when attempting to evaluate the implications of income tax changes for firms' operations. Coping with these tasks requires a framework for multiperiod evaluation. The objective of this chapter is to supply that framework by extending our two-parameter asset-pricing framework.

We begin by discussing additional assumptions and technical details pertinent to two-parameter asset pricing in a multiperiod setting. This leads to a statement of equilibrium conditions. We then provide a general discussion of inferential tasks pertinent to a multiperiod setting. As will be indicated, some of these tasks are identical to ones encountered in our single-period setting (see Ch. 4); others are unique to our multiperiod scenario.

It will be clear that resolving many theoretical and empirical problems encountered when applying our model depends critically on the details of the problem at hand. In order to provide insights on aspects of our multiperiod model, as well as to provide an exercise in model application, we shall use our model to evaluate the effects of a firm's choice with respect to Last-In-First-Out (LIFO) vs. First-In-First-Out (FIFO) inventory accounting for tax reporting. Since this choice affects a firm's cash flows over many periods, it is appropriately examined via a multiperiod model. As a by-product of what was intended to be an "illustrative exercise," we shall obtain some insights on substantive issues that have, in fact, been of considerable concern to accounting researchers.

5.2 Basic Results

5.2.1 Theoretical Issues

The easiest way to begin is to consider the valuation of a firm (or a project) that has one future net cash flow at, say, time $t = T$. Suppose that the firm ceases to exist after time T. Assuming, as before, that no assets with nonzero salvage values are still on hand at time T, the (before-tax) value of the firm at time T is equal to its (before-tax) net cash flow at time T:

$$\tilde{V}_T = \tilde{Y}_T = \tilde{S}_T - \tilde{C}_T, \tag{5.1}$$

where $\tilde{V}_T$ denotes the value of the firm at time T, $\tilde{Y}_T$ denotes the net cash inflow, $\tilde{S}_T$ denotes gross cash inflow, and $\tilde{C}_T$ denotes gross cash outflow. Unless otherwise indicated, we shall assume a no-tax world. This does not affect the crux of our analysis.

Conditional on the Sharpe/Lintner version of the single-period two-parameter model, the equilibrium value of the firm at time $T - 1$, V_{T-1}, is equal to:

$$V_{T-1} = (1 + R_{fT})^{-1} E_{T-1} (\tilde{V}_T) - \lambda_T \frac{\text{Cov}_{T-1} (\tilde{V}_T, \tilde{V}_{mT})}{\sigma_{T-1} (\tilde{V}_{mT})}, \tag{5.2}$$

where $E_{T-1}(\cdot)$, $\sigma_{T-1}(\cdot)$, and $\text{Cov}_{T-1}(\cdot,\cdot)$ denote, respectively, the expectation, standard deviation, and covariance operators applied at time $t - 1$ (using information available at that time); R_{fT} is the value of the equilibrium zero variance ("risk-free") rate of return for the period $T - 1$ to T; $\tilde{V}_{mT}$ is the value of the "market portfolio" (or aggregate wealth) at time T; $(1 + R_{fT})^{-1}$ is the time $T - 1$ equilibrium price per unit of expected dollar return (where this return will be observed at time T); and $(1 + R_{fT})^{-1}\lambda_T$ is the price per unit of dollar risk.

Strictly speaking, we should add a second subscript to V to indicate the time at which the evaluated cash inflow will be received (time T in our present example). For the moment, however, we shall omit this, with the understanding that we are evaluating just one net cash inflow—the one that will be realized at the end of our firm's life (time T).

Expression (5.2) can be rewritten as:

$$
\begin{aligned}
V_{T-1} &= (1 + R_{fT})^{-1}E_{T-1}(\tilde{V}_T)\left[1 - \lambda_T \frac{\text{Cov}_{T-1}(\tilde{V}_T, \tilde{V}_{mT})/E_{T-1}(\tilde{V}_T)}{\sigma_{T-1}(\tilde{V}_{mT})}\right] \\
&= E_{T-1}(\tilde{V}_T)\left[\frac{1 - \lambda_T^* \text{Cov}_{T-1}(\tilde{V}_T, \tilde{R}_{mT})/E_{T-1}(\tilde{V}_T)}{1 + R_{fT}}\right] \\
&= E_{T-1}(\tilde{Y}_T)\left[\frac{1 - \lambda_T^* \text{Cov}_{T-1}(\tilde{Y}_T, \tilde{R}_{mT})/E_{T-1}(\tilde{V}_T)}{1 + R_{fT}}\right], \qquad (5.3)
\end{aligned}
$$

where $\lambda_T^* \equiv \lambda_T/\sigma(\tilde{R}_{mT})$ and $\tilde{R}_{mT}$ is the rate of return on the market portfolio from $T - 1$ to T. Here we use the assumption that the standard deviation of $\tilde{R}_{mT}$ is constant over time (hence the time subscript on this parameter is omitted) and the definition $\tilde{V}_{mT} = (1 + \tilde{R}_{mT})V_{mT-1}$.

We know that:

$$V_{T-1}(1 + E_{T-1}(\tilde{R}_T)) = E_{T-1}(\tilde{V}_T) = E_{T-1}(\tilde{Y}_T). \qquad (5.4)$$

Thus, (5.3) and (5.4) imply:

$$1 + E_{T-1}(\tilde{R}_T)^{-1} = \left[\frac{1 - \lambda_T^* \text{Cov}_{T-1}(\tilde{Y}_T, \tilde{R}_{mT})/E_{T-1}(\tilde{Y}_T)}{1 + R_{fT}}\right]. \qquad (5.5)$$

Note that the only firm-specific parameter on the right-hand side of (5.5) is:

$$
\begin{aligned}
\frac{\text{Cov}_{T-1}(\tilde{Y}_T, \tilde{R}_{mT})}{E(\tilde{Y}_T)} &= \text{Cov}_{T-1}\left(\frac{\tilde{Y}_T}{E_{T-1}(\tilde{Y}_T)}, \tilde{R}_{mT}\right) \\
&= \text{Cov}_{T-1}\left(\frac{\tilde{E}_T(\tilde{Y}_T)}{E_{T-1}(\tilde{Y}_T)}, \tilde{R}_{mT}\right), \qquad (5.6)
\end{aligned}
$$

where $\tilde{E}_T(\tilde{Y}_T) = \tilde{Y}_T$, from the calculus of probability. Thus, at time $T - 1$, the only source of cross-sectional variation in the equilibrium expected rate of return, $E_{T-1}(\tilde{R}_T)$, is the extent to which the percentage change in the *expected* cash payoff covaries with the percentage change in aggregate wealth, $\tilde{R}_{mT}$. The values of λ_T^* and R_{fT} affect the investment opportunity set facing investors at time $T - 1$. But these values do not vary across assets.

Expression (5.3) results from applying the Sharpe/Lintner model to a single-period setting—the period from time $T - 1$ to time T. In order to apply this single-period model to a multiperiod evaluation problem—which seems quite relevant for financial statement analysis—we shall impose restrictions on the behavior of opportunity sets facing investors at different points in time. In the end, we shall obtain expressions for V_S for all $S \leq T - 1$.

The conditions that we impose are those discussed by Fama [1977]. As indicated there, a *sufficient* condition for the applicability of the single-period Sharpe/Lintner model to a multiperiod world is that the opportunity set facing investors at a given future point in time be known at all preceding points within the multiperiod horizon. Thus, since equilibrium expected rates of return from $t - 1$ to t, for any t, are components of the opportunity set at time $t - 1$, this condition implies that these expected values must be known at all times $S \leq t - 1$. For the case at hand, $E_{T-1}(\tilde{R}_T)$ in (5.5) must be known at all times $S \leq T - 1$. From the right-hand side of (5.5), one can see that this implies that, in general, λ_T^*, R_{fT}, and $\text{Cov}_{T-1}(\tilde{Y}_T, \tilde{R}_{mT})/E_{T-1}(\tilde{Y}_T)$ are nonstochastic variables.

This has an immediate implication for establishing the equilibrium value of $\tilde{V}_{T-1}$ at time $T - 2$—which is also the equilibrium value of $\tilde{Y}_T$ at time $T - 2$. Using (5.3) and (5.5), one sees that the only admissible source of uncertainty about the value of $\tilde{V}_{T-1}$ is uncertainty about the value of $\tilde{E}_{T-1}(Y_T)$—which is an expectation whose value is set at time $T - 1$ on the basis of information available at that time; i.e., the value of this expectation at time $S < T - 1$ is, in general, a random variable. In addition, the calculus of probability implies that this expectation must evolve over time according to a martingale model (see Doob [1953, pp. 91–94]). That is, the stochastic process $\tilde{E}_S(\tilde{Y}_T)$ for $S < T - 1$ is a martingale process.

One model consistent with martingale behavior and convenient for our treatment of financial statement analysis is:

$$\tilde{E}_S(\tilde{Y}_T) = E_{S-1}(\tilde{Y}_T)(1 + \tilde{\eta}_{ST}), \tag{5.7}$$

where $E_{S-1}(\tilde{\eta}_{ST}) = 0.0$. By definition, $\tilde{\eta}_{ST}$ is the percentage change from time $S - 1$ to S in the *expected value* of $\tilde{Y}_T$.

As of time $T - 2$, the next period payoff for the asset with cash flow $\tilde{Y}_T$ at time T is given by:

$$\tilde{V}_{T-1} = \tilde{E}_{T-1}(\tilde{Y}_T)\,[1 + E_{T-1}(\tilde{R}_T)]^{-1}, \tag{5.8}$$

which follows from (5.3) and (5.5). Incorporating (5.7) into (5.8) gives:

$$\tilde{V}_{T-1} = [E_{T-2}(\tilde{Y}_T)(1 + \tilde{\eta}_{T-1,T})][1 + E_{T-1}(\tilde{R}_T)]^{-1}. \tag{5.9}$$

And upon applying the Sharpe/Lintner model to get the equilibrium value of $\tilde{V}_{T-1}$ as of time $T - 2$, one gets:

$$\begin{aligned} V_{T-2} &= (1 + R_{F,T-1})^{-1}\,[E_{T-2}(\tilde{V}_{T-1}) - \lambda_{T-1}^*\text{Cov}_{T-2}(\tilde{V}_{T-1}, \tilde{R}_{mT-1})] \\ &= E_{T-2}(\tilde{V}_{T-1})\left[\frac{1 - \lambda_{T-1}^*\text{Cov}_{T-2}(\tilde{V}_{T-1}, \tilde{R}_{mT-1})/E_{T-2}(\tilde{V}_{T-1})}{1 + R_{fT-1}}\right], \end{aligned} \tag{5.10}$$

where, from (5.9):

$$E_{T-2}(\tilde{V}_{T-1}) = E_{T-2}(\tilde{Y}_T)\,[1 + E_{T-1}(\tilde{R}_T)]^{-1} \tag{5.11}$$

$$\text{Cov}_{T-2}(\tilde{V}_{T-1}, \tilde{R}_{mT-1}) = E_{T-2}(\tilde{Y}_T)\,[1 + E_{T-1}(\tilde{R}_T)]^{-1}\text{Cov}_{T-2}(\tilde{\eta}_{T-1,T}, \tilde{R}_{mT-1}). \tag{5.12}$$

Taking the ratio of (5.12) to (5.11) gives:

$$\frac{\text{Cov}_{T-2}(\tilde{V}_{T-1},\tilde{R}_{mT-1})}{E_{T-1}(\tilde{V}_{T-1})} = \text{Cov}_{T-2}(\tilde{\eta}_{T-1,T}, \tilde{R}_{mT-1}). \tag{5.13}$$

But from (5.7) applied to time $S = T - 1$:

$$\text{Cov}_{T-2}(\tilde{\eta}_{T-1,T}, \tilde{R}_{mT-1}) = \text{Cov}_{T-2}\left(\frac{\tilde{E}_{T-1}(\tilde{Y}_T)}{E_{T-2}(\tilde{Y}_T)}, \tilde{R}_{mT-1}\right). \tag{5.14}$$

In short, the admissible risk affecting the equilibrium value of V_{T-2} pertains to the covariation of percentage changes in aggregate wealth at time $T - 1$, $\tilde{R}_{mT-1}$, and percentage changes in *expected values* (or forecasts) of the terminal cash flow from time $T - 2$ to time $T - 1$, $\tilde{E}_{T-1}(\tilde{Y}_T)/E_{T-2}(\tilde{Y}_T)$.

Ultimately, one finds that as of time $T - 2$:

$$V_{T-2} = E_{T-2}(\tilde{Y}_T)\,[1 + E_{T-2}(\tilde{R}_{T-1})]^{-1}\,[1 + E_{T-1}(\tilde{R}_T)]^{-1} \tag{5.15}$$

and as of $t = 0$:

$$V_0 = E_0(\tilde{Y}_T) \prod_{i=0}^{T-1} [1 + E_i(\tilde{R}_{i+1,T})]^{-1}. \tag{5.16}$$

The above results apply to the equilibrium value of the single net cash flow $\tilde{Y}_T$ as of each point in time $S < T$. If the same mechanics are applied to an asset with cash flows at multiple points in time, say, time t, $t = 1, 2, \ldots, T - 1$, one finds that the equilibrium value, as of time $t = 0$, of such a multiple cash flow project is given by the sum of the distinct cash flows' equilibrium values, where each one is assessed as of time $t = 0$. To represent this result, we now resort to double subscripts. Let V_{Si} denote the equilibrium value as of time S of a cash flow that will occur at time $i \geq S$. Using this notation, expression (5.16) represents the value of V_{0T}. Also, let P_0 denote the value of a "project" (e.g., a firm) for which there will be a net cash flow at each time i, $i = 1, 2, \ldots, T$. Then our previous mechanics imply that:

$$\begin{aligned} P_0 &= \sum_{i=1}^{T} V_{0i} \\ &= \sum_{i=1}^{T} \left\{ E_o(\tilde{Y}_i) \prod_{s=0}^{i=1} [1 + E_s(\tilde{R}_{s+1,i})]^{-1} \right\}. \end{aligned} \tag{5.17}$$

Observe that the "discount factors" applied to a given expected cash flow—$E_0(\tilde{Y}_i)$ for a fixed i—can vary over time. And the sequence of discount factors used for a given period's expected cash flow (e.g., the sequence $1 + E_S(\tilde{R}_{S+1,i})$ for a given i and $S = 1, 2, \ldots, i = 1$) may differ, in whole or in part, from the sequence used for a different period's expected cash flow. From our previous analysis of V_{0T}—now applied to V_{0i} for each i—one can see that the temporal differences for a given period's expected cash flow will depend on the temporal variation in the risk of *that period's* cash flow. Also, quite naturally, the contemporaneous discount-factor differences across different period's cash flows will depend on the risk variations across these cash flows, which may be induced by temporal changes in the economic characteristics of a firm's production investment decisions. (More on this later.) Before getting to these issues, we briefly consider "beta coefficients" or, more precisely, relative risks.

The relative risk, as of $S = T - 1$, of a cash flow to be realized at time T is given by $\mathrm{Cov}_{T-1}(\tilde{Y}_T, \tilde{V}_{mT})/\sigma^2(\tilde{V}_{mT})$. And the relative risk of the dollar return on a portfolio is equal to the sum of the relative risks of the portfolio's component assets. A special type of portfolio is one consisting of assets, each of which has a cash flow at one point in time, where the time of receipt for one component asset differs from that of each other asset. This type of portfolio is equivalent to one multiple cash-flow project. Thus, the relative risk of such a project is the sum of the relative risks of its different cash flows. That is:

$$\beta_p = \sum_{i=1}^{T} \beta_i, \tag{5.18}$$

where β_p is the time $t = 0$ relative risk of the project with equilibrium value P_0 and β_i is the time $t = 0$ relative risk of the single cash flow with equilibrium value V_{0i} (see (5.17)).

5.2.2 Inferential Tasks and Opportunities

Most of the tasks facing a financial analyst attempting to use our multiperiod framework are the same as those pertinent to our single-period setting. It is still the case, for example, that the market structure facing a firm (for both inputs and outputs) is relevant to an assessment of its value, because that structure has implications for the prices received and paid by the firm. And as before, the characteristics of the firm's production function, which influences its output quantities and quantities of inputs, are relevant to an assessment of the firm's value. The characteristics of the firm's production function, along with the stochastic properties of its input prices, also determine the extent to which a firm's value is affected by supply function uncertainty.

This does not imply, however, that nothing changes when we go from a single-period to a multiperiod world. It is now the case that the intertemporal behavior of, for example, market structure and production functions is relevant. This introduces a variety of dynamical issues into the scope of financial statement analysis. Now, for example, technological changes, market growth, investments in human capital, entry and exit of firms, and new product development play particularly important roles—because each is a determinant of the intertemporal characteristics of a firm's production-investment decisions.

Dealing with these issues presents special problems for financial statement analysis because pertinent sample evidence may be largely unavailable. Clearly, if one is dealing with the implications of new products or new production methods—i.e., products (methods) not yet offered (used) by a firm—then available data may not be informative because they pertain to different structural conditions. That is, the underlying stochastic process consistent with the new developments may differ from the one that prevailed in the past. The random variables whose values will be observed later will, therefore, have probability models different from those that applied in the past. This is simply an instance of what econometricians typically call "structural change." If the structural changes themselves do not progress in some systematic fashion, then available sample evidence may not be useful in modeling the changes' behavior either.

This seems to be one setting where profitable use can be made of non-databased prior probability assessments, along the lines of so-called Bayesian statistics. Using this route involves a heavy reliance on an analyst's theoretical insights on the economics of each firm or industry of interest and an analyst's expertise in applying these insights. We make no pretense of being able to specify the appropriate steps to pursue. At best, we can, as we did above, specify a theoretically appropriate model of multiperiod evaluation—and thus a specification of the ultimate objects of an analyst's inferential task.

An additional aspect of this task which is not present in a single-period setting is worth mentioning. Consider the cash flow to be observed at, say, time T. From our previous results, we know that the stochastic behavior of expectations assessed as of each point in time $S \leq T$ is relevant to the setting of this cash flow's value as of time $t = 0$. And this sequence of (random) expected values is for a cash flow whose value will be observed at time $T \geq S$. Thus, the economic implications of $\tilde{R}_{mS}$ for *subsequent* events are relevant in evaluating the covariance terms incorporated into the values of $E_S(\tilde{R}_{S+1,T})$, $S = 0, 1, \ldots, T - 1$, in expression (5.17) for V_{0T}. If events subsequent to, say, time $S = S^*$ do not affect the attributes of the production-investment decisions pertinent to the time T cash flow, then there should be no correlation between $\tilde{R}_{mS*}$ and the time $S = S^*$ expectation of $\tilde{Y}_T$. In other words, when an analyst is assessing this correlation, he must consider the connections between the events reflected in the value of $\tilde{R}_{mS}{}^*$ and the determinants of his time $t = S^*$ *forecast* of $\tilde{Y}_T$, $T \geq S^*$. The nature of these connections may be affected by substantive economic aspects of the firm or attributes of the analyst's forecasting methods.

The multiperiod valuation model developed above can be used for a variety of tasks. It can be used as a framework for valuing an entire firm, viewed as one (complicated) project, or for valuing one of a firm's projects, such as a particular long-lived asset. Or it can be used to identify the valuation consequences of a general policy or procedure that will affect a firm's net cash flows for several future periods. A firm's accounting techniques, especially those used for tax reporting, constitute cash-flow determinants of the latter type. The next section provides an illustration of our multiperiod model by considering the valuation consequences of inventory accounting methods.

5.3 An Application to the Effects of Alternative Accounting Methods

Analysts often consider the implications of alternative accounting methods for a firm's equilibrium value, particularly when these methods will be used for tax reporting and thus when they can have direct effects on a firm's net cash flows. This seems quite natural. But there may also be a connection between a firm's accounting methods and its equilibrium value when the methods of interest are not used for tax reporting. This may be due, for example, to the variety of contractual agreements that are expressed in terms of accounting numbers used for financial (but not tax) reports—such as convenants of bond indentures or sharing rules of management compensation plans.[1] In addition, an analyst may perceive a connection between accounting techniques and the substantive attributes of a firm's decisions when the analyst believes that these techniques are being used for "signaling" purposes (see, e.g., Gonedes and Dopuch [1978]). In any event, if an analyst concludes that such a connection exists, then what might otherwise seem to be "mere bookkeeping" issues in financial statement analysis may actually correspond to substantive economic issues. When examining several firms, these sorts of issues may imply different equilibrium values of firms.

---

[1]See Fogelson [1978] for a discussion of techniques and restrictive covenants in credit agreements and indentures.

Such substantive economic issues may show up in actual interfirm data analyses as, for example, industry or risk differences among firms using different accounting techniques or making different changes in accounting methods. This sort of phenomenon obviously can complicate an analyst's empirical task of inferring the effects of accounting techniques on firms' values—whether the effects turn on the techniques' implications for accounting numbers' information content or on the information content of the techniques themselves (due to any perceived signaling implications of accounting method choices). Moreover, it can complicate an analyst's attempts to "explain" firms' selections of accounting techniques: assertions about cosmetic "income smoothing" and "earnings management" designed to affect firms' values by, say, "fooling" investors will no longer suffice once one allows for a connection between accounting techniques and the substantive attributes of firms' decisions. There is nothing cosmetic about a change in techniques associated with a change in these substantive attributes.

In the following analysis, we shall use our multiperiod evaluation model to analyze the selection and effects of accounting techniques that have substantive economic implications—such as the inventory costing techniques used for tax reporting. For specificity we shall restrict our attention to the LIFO/FIFO decision with respect to tax reporting. It should be clear, however, that our approach applies to other tax-reporting issues as well. Indeed, the only key features of the LIFO/FIFO decision that we exploit are that firms have some latitude of choice in their selection of tax-reporting methods and that the alternative methods have effects on the probability distributions of firms' net after-tax cash flows—and thus, in general, on firms' equilibrium values. Our analysis is suppposed to illustrate one use of our multiperiod models. Thus, we shall invoke substantial simplifications of the tax-reporting problem facing any "real world" firm.[2] Nevertheless, our investigation will capture the seemingly major distinguishing features of the LIFO/FIFO problem. In the end, we shall provide a basis for identifying some of the key theoretical determinants of firms' optimal inventory costing methods and some of the multiperiod effects of firms' inventory decisions on firms' equilibrium values—assuming only tax-reporting issues are considered.

For simplicity, we shall also assume that FIFO is the only alternative to LIFO, unless otherwise indicated. This has no essential effect on the crux of our discussion.

We begin by specifying the basic model of the firm underlying our analysis. The application of our multiperiod evaluation tools is facilitated, as before, by first considering issues pertinent to the single-period evaluation of a cash flow to be observed at one point in time—time T. We shall then, as before, extend our results to a multiperiod evaluation of this same cash flow and, finally, to a multiperiod evaluation of a sequence of cash flows.

5.3.1 Basic Assumptions and Relationships

In order to highlight only central issues, we consider a finite horizon setting and a decision to use either LIFO or FIFO for all periods within this time horizon. As will be indicated, the basic aspects of the machinery developed here can be readily extended to

---

[2]Those interested in more details should see Sec. 1.471 of the U.S. Internal Revenue Code for Regulations pertaining to inventory accounting. Unless otherwise indicated, the compendium used for this chapter is Prentice-Hall [1963].

more complicated settings—at least in principle. With no loss of generality, we assume that all firms are all-equity firms.

Several macroconditions are also assumed to hold. They are essentially those used in much of the literature on tax incidence (see McClure and Thirsk [1975]). Specifically, we assume that the taxing authorities pursue "balanced budget" policies and that government expenditures are distributionally neutral. The latter condition implies that when private demand declines on account of income losses due to taxation, public demand for all goods exactly replaces the losses of private demand. Similar offsets are implied for tax-induced increases in private demand. For a discussion of the restrictiveness of this neutrality assumption, see McClure and Thirsk [1975, n. 12].

At the beginning of each period, the firm being analyzed acquires the services of factors of production needed to implement its selected production-investment activities. This firm is permitted to hold goods in inventory as a part of these activities. The firm finances its activities by selling fractional interests ("shares") in the distribution function of its future values—the realizations of which are available at the end of each period. For the final period, T, of our finite horizon, the value of the firm is equal to that period's net cash earnings plus the total value of whatever assets are still on hand.

As always, this firm is assumed to follow the "market value rule" in selecting its optimal production-investment decisions. That is, at the time these decisions are made, optimal decisions are those consistent with maximizing the total value of the firm's outstanding securities. A variety of issues pertinent to enforcing this rule are discussed by Fama [1978].

We focus first on the firm's net cash inflow at the end of period T. Let $\tilde{S}_T$ and $\tilde{C}_T$ denote the firm's gross operating inflows and outflows, respectively, for the period ending at time T (or "at time T" for short). Tilde (˜) again denotes a random variable. Let $\tilde{Y}_T$ denote this period's before-tax net cash earnings. Assuming, for convenience, that no assests with nonzero salvage values are still on hand, the before-tax value of the firm at time T is:

$$\tilde{Y}_T = \tilde{S}_T - \tilde{C}_T. \tag{5.19}$$

The firm's after-tax net operating inflows will depend on the inventory costing method used for tax purposes. The method selected determines the tax-deductible cost of goods sold. Only taxes levied against $\tilde{Y}_T$ are considered here. Moreover, for reasons given later, we shall ignore the lower-of-cost-or-market option available to a firm that chooses to use FIFO for tax reporting.[3] And cost-of-goods-sold is the only tax-deductible cost recognized here. This does not affect the crux of our analysis. (This is because many of our comparisons of LIFO and FIFO will presume that other things are held constant anyway.)

Let $\tilde{C}_t^L$ and $\tilde{C}_t^F$ denote the LIFO-determined and FIFO-determined cost of goods sold at time t, respectively. And let the constant rate of tax be denoted by τ. The firm's tax bill at time T is $\tau(\tilde{S}_T - \tilde{C}_T^L)$ if it opts to use LIFO, and it is $\tau(\tilde{S}_T - \tilde{C}_T^F)$ if it opts to use the FIFO method. Net operating after-tax profits under LIFO and FIFO are, respectively:

[3] Alternatively, one can assume that the cost-of-goods sold numbers recorded for tax purposes already incorporate the effects of this option, conditional on optimal use of the option at each point in time.

$$\begin{aligned}\tilde{\pi}_T^L &= (\tilde{S}_T - \tilde{C}_T) - \tau(\tilde{S}_T - \tilde{C}_T^L)\\ &= (\tilde{S}_T - \tilde{C}_T) - \tau(\tilde{S}_T - [\tilde{C}_T + \tilde{C}_T^L - \tilde{C}_T])\\ &= (1 - \tau)\tilde{Y}_T + \tau(\tilde{C}_T^L - \tilde{C}_T) \qquad (5.20)\end{aligned}$$

$$\tilde{\pi}_T^F = (1 - \tau)\tilde{Y}_T + \tau(\tilde{C}_T^F - \tilde{C}_T). \qquad (5.21)$$

Note that $\tilde{\pi}_T^L$ and $\tilde{\pi}_Y^F$ are equivalent to dollar returns on portfolios defined by the portfolio proportions $(1 - \tau)$ and τ, which, of course, sum to unity. Under the LIFO method, the total portfolio return consists of the two flows $\tilde{Y}_T$ and $(\tilde{C}_T^L - \tilde{C}_T)$. Under the FIFO method, it consists of $\tilde{Y}_T$ and $(\tilde{C}_T^F - \tilde{C}_T)$. Thus, not unexpectedly, the equilibrium value of the firm at time $T - 1$ will equal the weighted sum of the explicit or implicit equilibrium values of the flows corresponding to the firm's tax-reporting inventory method, where the weights for the flows are $(1 - \tau)$ and τ and where one of the flows, $\tilde{Y}_T$, is independent of that reporting method. In a complete, perfectly competitive capital market, there would be explicit equilibrium values for these flows.

The end-of-period values of the firm conditional on LIFO and FIFO are, respectively:

$$\tilde{V}_T^L = \tilde{V}_T + \tau(\tilde{C}_T^L - \tilde{C}_T) \qquad (5.22)$$

$$\tilde{V}_T^F = \tilde{V}_T + \tau(\tilde{C}_T^F - \tilde{C}_T), \qquad (5.23)$$

where $\tilde{V}_T \equiv (1 - \tau)\tilde{Y}_T$. Thus:

$$\tilde{V}_T^L - \tilde{V}_T^F = \tau(\tilde{C}_T^L - \tilde{C}_T^F). \qquad (5.24)$$

Expression (5.24) represents the difference between the terminal values of a LIFO and a FIFO firm, assuming that the inventory costing method is the only factor distinguishing one firm from the other. That is, the firm's production-investment decisions are identical; only their tax-reporting methods differ. This expression is, of course, reminiscent of the Modigliani and Miller [1958; 1963] result for the effects of tax-deductible interest payments on firms' equilibrium values, given fixed and identical production-investment decisions. But instead of the tax rate multiplied by a payment to debtholders at time T, we have in (5.24) the tax rate multiplied by the difference between the tax-deductible cost of goods sold under the LIFO and FIFO costing methods. Moreover, unlike the Modigliani/Miller result, the realized value of $\tilde{V}_T^L - \tilde{V}_T^F$ need not be non-negative. The probability that it will not be depends on the joint distribution function of $\tilde{C}_T^L$ and $\tilde{C}_T^F$—or, more directly, on the distribution function of the difference $\tilde{C}_T^L - \tilde{C}_T^F$.

When expression (5.24) is applied to different firms—one on LIFO and one on FIFO—it must be the case that these firms differ only with respect to their inventory costing methods used for tax reporting. In particular, the use of expression (5.24) for describing the equilibrium value of a switch to or from LIFO presumes that the production-investment decisions of the different firms are identical. In short, expression (5.24) takes firms' production-investment decisions as fixed and identical just as does the Modigliani/Miller result on the effects of debt financing on firms' equilibrium values. (We invoked the same sort of condition in Chapter 4 when we discussed the effects of financing decisions on firms' values.) In this regard, observe that a firm's production-investment decisions affect (for a given environment) the joint stochastic properties of $\tilde{C}_T^L$ and $\tilde{C}_T^F$. For given and identical decisions, all differences between the properties of $\tilde{C}_T^L$ and of $\tilde{C}_T^F$ turn on the fact that one variable is conditional on the LIFO method and the other is conditional on the FIFO method.

Expression (5.24) deals with the cash-flow effects of different tax-reporting methods at time T—which is the end of our finite time horizon. But similar expressions can be obtained for all of the cash-flow effects of the tax-reporting methods.

5.3.2 Multiperiod Valuation Conditions

Let τW_{ts} denote the equilibrium value as of time t of the difference between the cash flows induced by LIFO and those induced by FIFO at time s for fixed production investment decisions. Clearly, $\tau \tilde{W}_{TT} = \tau(\tilde{C}_T^L - \tilde{C}_T^F)$ and, as of time $T - 1$:

$$V_{T-1}^L - V_{T-1}^F = \tau(C_{T-1}^L - C_{T-1}^F) + \tau W_{T-1,T}. \tag{5.25}$$

As of time $T - 2$:

$$V_{T-2}^L - V_{T-2}^F = \tau(C_{T-2}^L - C_{T-2}^F) + \tau W_{T-2,T-1} + \tau W_{T-2,T}. \tag{5.26}$$

And, in general:

$$V_0^L - V_o^F = \tau\left(\sum_{i=1}^{T} W_{oi}\right), \tag{5.27}$$

where it is assumed that the inventory method is selected at time $t = 0$ and that it has its initial effects at time $t = 1$.

Consider a FIFO firm that opts for a switch to LIFO at time $t = 0$. (Arguments analogous to the following apply to a LIFO firm that opts for a switch to FIFO). Assume that this firm changes nothing else. In making this switch, it adds the stochastic scalar $\tau(\tilde{C}_t^L - \tilde{C}_t^F)$ to its net operating cash inflows at time t, $t = 1, 2, \ldots, T$. The equilibrium value of this sequence of additions, as of time $t = 0$, is equal to the difference between the time $t = 0$ equilibrium values of otherwise identical firms using the different inventory methods. In particular, these firms' production-investment decisions are identical. The equilibrium value of this sequence is also equal to the change in one firm's equilibrium value induced by a change, at $t = 0$, in inventory methods used for tax reporting. Given adherence to the "market value rule," this equilibrium value is necessarily nonnegative for a firm that actually switches. Quite trivially, no firm adhering to that rule would opt for LIFO over FIFO if doing so implies a decrease in the firm's equilibrium value.

In the next section, we discuss some means for enforcing the conditions given by (5.24) and (5.27). In Sec. 5.3.4, we briefly consider some forces that might lead to departures from these conditions. Such forces are given more attention in Sec. 5.3.9.

5.3.3 More on the Equilibrium Conditions

If firms' production-investment decisions, the number of firms, and firms' tax-reporting methods are all held fixed at time $t = 0$, and if there are both LIFO and FIFO firms making identical production-investment decisions, then expression (5.27) implies that a necessary condition for capital market equilibrium at time $t = 0$ is:

$$V_o^L = V_o^F + \tau\sum_{i=1}^{T} W_{oi}, \tag{5.28}$$

where V_o^L and V_o^F are the equilibrium values at $t = 0$ of firms that differ only with respect to tax-reporting methods—one using LIFO and one using FIFO, respectively—and where the value of $\tau\Sigma_{i=1}^{T} W_{oi}$ equals the equilibrium value, at $t = 0$, of a 100 percent ownership interest in the joint distribution function of the sequence $\{\tau(\tilde{C}_t^L - \tilde{C}_t^F); t = 1, 2, \ldots, T\}$ or some stochastically equivalent sequence.[4] This presumes, of course, that perfect substitutes for the ownership interests in $\{\tau(\tilde{C}_t^L - \tilde{C}_t^F); t = 1, 2, \ldots, T\}$ exist or can be created. This condition is satisfied in a perfect capital market, wherein there are perfect-substitute firms with respect to both production-investment decisions and tax-reporting methods. Equivalent ownership interests can be created by, for example, combining a long (short) position in a FIFO firm with both a long (short) position in an otherwise equivalent LIFO firm and an offsetting short (long) position in the same (or an otherwise equivalent) FIFO firm. Therefore, an inequality in (5.28) with respect to a LIFO and a FIFO firm that are, in all other respects, identical would represent an opportunity to get "pure profits" via portfolio transactions on personal account, which is inconsistent with equilibrium.

Condition (5.28) is a "short-run" condition, in the sense that the numbers of firms using different methods and firms' production-investment decisions are held fixed. If these things were not held fixed, then one would never actually observe different tax-reporting methods being used by firms pursuing identical production investment decisions, given adherence to the market value rule. Entry and exit by firms and entry and exit by management teams will ensure that, in equilibrium, the inventory method consistent with value maximization for given production-investment decisions will be the only method used for that set of decisions. Suppose, for example, that a FIFO firm with current value equal to V_o^F plans to pursue production-investment decisions requiring outlays with current value equal to I_0, where $V_o^F \geq I_o$. And suppose that $V_o^L > V_o^F$, conditional on the same decisions. Even without LIFO, new firms will enter until $V_o^F = I_o$ for a new entrant. Moreover, with the availability of LIFO, new firms will enter until $V_o^L = I_o$, given adherence to the market value rule. And every new entrant will opt for LIFO. Since $V_o^L > V_o^F$, then firms' values and the prices of factors of production will adjust so that $V_o^F < I_o$ in equilibrium. In short, for the given set of production-investment decisions, equilibrium prices of securities and factors of production will be such that use of FIFO method is inconsistent with general equilibrium.

Entry and exit of firms are not the only forces leading to this result. Pursuit of the market value rule by existing firms that plan to make identical production-investment decisions implies the same result. That is, if $V_o^L > V_o^F$ for a given set of decisions and prevailing equilibrium prices, then adherence to the market value rule implies that all firms pursuing this set of decisions will opt for LIFO. As a result, there will be no FIFO firms engaged in these decisions.

Switching from one inventory method to another at time $t = 0$ involves changing a stochastic component of the switching firm's net cash flow at time t, t = 1, 2, . . ., T. In the case of a switch from FIFO to LIFO, for example, the net cash flow component $\tau(\tilde{C}_t^F - \tilde{C}_t)$ is replaced by the component $\tau(\tilde{C}_t^L - \tilde{C}_t)$, for each t. In general, this alters the entire distribution function of the switching firm's period t net cash flow. Thus, it can alter the risk characteristics of the firm's periodic net cash flows. If it alters the type of risk for which investors demand compensation, then the altered risk properties will be one of the determinants of the difference between the equilibrium values V_o^L and V_o^F. In short,

[4]The random variable $\tilde{x}$ is said to be "stochastically equivalent" or just "equivalent" to the random variable $\tilde{y}$ if $Pr(\tilde{x} \neq \tilde{y}) = 0$, where $Pr(\cdot)$ denotes probability.

a switch from one inventory costing method to another (for tax reporting) involves both return and risk issues—of the sort that usually enter into the selection of optimal production-investment decisions via the market value rule. In equilibrium, further changes in either production-investment decisions or inventory costing methods should permit no increases in any firm's value at time $t = 0$.

This, of course, is why an analyst can infer that firms selecting the same production-investment decisions will end up selecting the same inventory methods. If a given firm's decisions were such that, say $V_o^L > V_o^F$ and if the firm were now on FIFO, then a mere shift of its inventory costing methods would have the same effect as adoption of an investment proposal with positive gross equilibrium value and with a required investment outlay equal to zero. That is, it would be equivalent to a "pure profit" opportunity—the existence of which is inconsistent with equilibrium.

Next suppose that all inventory-method switches consistent with value maximization are effected by existing firms. In order for the prevailing conditions to be consistent with general equilibrium, there must be no motivation for firms making different types of production-investment decisions to reallocate their resources, via revisions of their decisions, and there must be no motivation for entry into any activity by new firms (or new managerial teams—via, e.g., takeovers). This will be the case when stochastically equivalent cash-flow sequences induced by the same outlays have the same current equilibrium values. Consider, for example, a LIFO firm making production investment decisions of, say, type j and a FIFO firm making production-investment decisions of type i. Denote the prevailing values of these firms, at $t = 0$, by V_{jo}^L and V_{io}^F, respectively, and assume that the time $t = 0$ outlays required by these firms' decisions are equal to the same amount, I_o. From our earlier remarks, we know that $i \neq j$. If $i = j$, then either both firms would opt for LIFO or both would opt for FIFO.

The distribution functions of our illustrative firms' cash-flow sequences are defined by the two-tuples (j, LIFO) and (i, FIFO)—not just the different types of production investment decisions, i and j. This follows from the fact that the inventory costing method used for tax reporting affects the distribution function of firms' cash-flow sequences in a manner that is, in general, dependent upon firms' production-investment decisions. For the example at hand, we are assuming that the distribution function induced by (j, LIFO) is equivalent to the distribution function induced by (i, FIFO)—at least with respect to whatever factors are relevant in the determination of firms' equilibrium values. We are also assuming that both firms' current outlays are equal to the same amount, I_o.

In view of the above, we can state that equilibrium implies:

$$V_{jo}^L = V_{io}^F. \tag{5.29}$$

This condition implies, in turn, that firms' selected inventory reporting methods can be used to sort firms into mutually exclusive sets of *types* of production-investment decisions. In any event, if condition (5.29) is violated for $i \neq j$, then there will be profitable entry/exit opportunities and profitable arbitrage opportunities—all of which are inconsistent with equilibrium in both the capital market and the markets for goods and services (outputs and inputs).

5.3.4 Potential Complications: Frictions and Restrictions on Firms' Selections of Methods

In general, an analyst can infer that the equilibrium conditions discussed above need not hold if there are restrictions on entry and exit by firms regarding production-investment decisions or on firms' selections of tax-reporting methods. One obvious restriction of this sort is a tax-code regulation that precludes (or at least hinders) freely switching from, say, LIFO to FIFO by existing firms—in spite of changes in economic conditions or modifications in some aspect(s) of the firms' operating decisions. But, taken by itself, the existence of this sort of restriction need not be sufficient to invalidate the equilibrium conditions described above. If existing firms (or collections of real resources) can be converted into new organizational forms—via, e.g., reorganizations, corporate takeovers, mergers, etc.—and if the resulting new organizational forms can be paired with either the FIFO or the LIFO method for tax reporting, then the restrictions on existing firms' selections of tax-reporting methods are, other things being equal, of no consequence insofar as satisfying the equilibrium conditions discussed above.

Of course, conversion costs induced by effecting such new organizational forms may introduce frictions into the system. In addition, differences between the costs of implementing a LIFO system and the costs of implementing a FIFO system may be large enough to preclude full satisfaction of the conditions described above. In general, these types of costs can be recognized via adjustments to the cash-flow sequence $(\tau(\tilde{C}_t^L - \tilde{C}_t^F); t = 1, 2, \ldots, T)$. After they are recognized, the relevant equilibrium condition is still condition (5.28), applied to the adjusted cash-flow numbers, for a given set of production-investment decisions. As before, if $V_o^L > V_o^F$, no firm pursuing this set of decisions will opt for the use of FIFO.

5.3.5 Remarks on Empirical Work: First Pass

The framework developed above provides a basis for understanding why firms pursuing different production-investment decisions select different inventory costing methods for tax reporting.[5] As indicated, the stochastic attributes of the cash-flow sequence $\{\tau(\tilde{C}_t^L - \tilde{C}_t^F)\}$ are dependent on the substantive characteristics of these decisions, such as firms' inventory-management systems (which affect the quantities underlying the cost numbers used for tax reporting) and the stochastic properties of relative prices faced by firms in the markets for factors of production (such as raw materials and labor services). For some types of decisions, the equilibrium value of the potential LIFO sequence, $\{\tau\tilde{C}_t^L\}$, will be less than that of the potential FIFO sequence, $\{\tau\, \tilde{C}_t^F\}$. In this case, $(\Sigma_{i=1}^T W_{oi}) < 0$ in expression (5.28) and, for these decisions, LIFO will not be chosen. (This is equivalent to stating that assets with negative values will not be issued.) This mundane observation points to an approach for empirically "explaining" firms' LIFO/FIFO choices.

Suppose that these choices are made in a manner consistent with the above framework, that we have a model for specifying the time $t = 0$ equilibrium value of any cash-flow sequence, and that this model is expressed in terms of estimable parameters (so that empirical application is feasible). Under these conditions, the estimated values of those pa-

---

[5]Evidence consistent with a relationship between attributes of production-investment decisions and firms' inventory-method choices is provided by Biddle [1980] and Ricks [1980], in papers that appeared after earlier versions of this chapter. Indeed, in Ricks' work, systematic differences among the attributes of decisions made by firms pursuing different inventory-method choices were detected even though his pairs of firms pursuing different choices were supposedly "matched" so as to "hold other things constant" (see Ricks [1980, p. 118]). Unfortunately, neither Biddle nor Ricks exploited the theoretical connection between inventory-method choices and the risks of the cash-flow probability distributions induced by alternative methods. This connection is considered at length below.

rameters can be used to make inferences about firms' perceptions of the equilibrium value of the sequence $\{\tau(\tilde{C}_t^L - \tilde{C}_t^F)\}$, conditional on the firms' production-investment decisions. For firms pursuing different production-investment decisions, these inferred values should be consistent (across firms) with firms' actual LIFO/FIFO decisions, conditional on the framework developed above. Such empirical results provide a basis for an analyst's inferring whether firms' managements are behaving in a manner consistent with the market value rule. In any event, as far as empirical work is concerned, an important next step is to specify a model for establishing the equilibrium value of the sequence $\{\tau(\tilde{C}_t^L - \tilde{C}_t^F)\}$ and to identify the testable implications of this model. We shall use the multiperiod version of the two-parameter model that we developed earlier. But first we consider an additional aspect of the LIFO/FIFO decision—the Lower-of-Cost-or-Market option. Specifically, we indicate why it seems justifiable for an analyst to ignore this option.

5.3.6 The Lower-of-Cost-or-Market (LCOM) Rule and LIFO/FIFO Deductions

The variables $\tilde{C}_t^F$ and $\tilde{C}_t^L$ denote the tax-deductible cost-of-goods sold numbers for period t. Under the LIFO method, the value of this number is determined by the use of "historical cost" valuation procedures. Thus, in general, there are no "unrealized" amounts in the value of $\tilde{C}_t^L$. Under FIFO, however, the value of the tax-deductible cost-of-goods sold number may be based on "historical cost" valuation methods or methods based on market values, possibly incorporating "unrealized" amounts. The following excerpt from Sec. 1.471 of the U.S. Internal Revenue Code (IRC) regulations is pertinent here:

> The bases of valuation most commonly used by business concerns and which meet the requirements of [this section] are (1) cost and (2) cost or market, whichever is lower. . . . Any goods in an inventory which are unsalable at normal price or unusable in the normal way because of damage, imperfections, shop wear, changes of style, odd or broken lots, or other similar causes, including second hand goods taken in exchange, should be valued at bona fide selling prices less direct cost of disposition . . . or if such goods consist of raw materials or partly finished goods held for use or consumption, they shall be valued upon a reasonable basis, taking into consideration the usability and the condition of the goods, but in no case shall such value be less than the scrap value. Bona fide selling price means actual offering of goods during a period ending not later than 30 days after inventory date.

In later stipulations, the regulations elaborate on the notion of "market" to be used in implementing the LCOM rule. These stipulations cover both purchased and manufactured items. In addition, they indicate that under the LIFO costing method, "the inventory shall be taken at cost regardless of market value." That is, no LCOM option is granted to a LIFO firm. Moreover, the regulations indicate that once a taxpayer chooses between the cost and LCOM bases of valuation, his chosen method should be used consistently. In particular, once a taxpayer chooses to use the cost (LCOM) basis of valuation, permission from the Commissioner of the IRS must be secured to switch to the LCOM (cost) basis.

For precision, therefore, we should distinguish between two general FIFO methods—the one based on "historical cost" valuation methods and the one based on LCOM methods.[6] After this is done, all of our remarks and results apply to whatever FIFO method is selected for examination. But, given our objectives, there is really no need to distinguish between these two general FIFO methods. And we shall not do so. The reader can treat all results as applying to one or the other of these methods.

Some additional remarks on LIFO and LCOM are in order. As indicated above, the LCOM rule is not (as of today) available to those who opt to use LIFO for tax reporting. At first glance, this might seem to provide a basic valuation method to FIFO firms but not to LIFO firms. And, when "market" is below LIFO "cost," it seems to deny a tax deduction of the sort that can be obtained by a FIFO firm when FIFO cost exceeds "market." There are, however, devices for undoing this seemingly discriminatory regulation. For example, a LIFO firm can effectively obtain the results of the LCOM rule by actually liquidating the inventoried items whose "costs" exceed their "market" values—and then by repurchasing them if it is optimal to do so.[7] This route often seems to escape the attention of works on inventory methods. But recognition of it is not novel. It was recognized many years ago by, for example, Butters and Niland [1949] in some remarks on the implications of LCOM rules for LIFO firms. They noted the following [1949, pp. 118–119]:

> Most Lifo inventories are carried at prices well below current levels. If these inventories are reduced, as of the end of any taxable year for any category of goods, the difference between Lifo costs and current costs will be brought into income. With the pronounced price rises of recent years, the effects on income will be large; hence the tax incentive not to liquidate Lifo inventories and incur increased tax liabilities.
>
> Tax incentives also tend to discourage physical increments to Lifo inventories when prices are high. Since such increments must be carried permanently at their acquisition costs, regardless of future price declines, it is obviously desirable to build up physical inventories at as low prices as possible.

---

[6]It is worth noting that write-downs under LCOM (or equivalent loss recognitions secured via sales/repurchases) alter the *timing* of loss realizations for tax purposes. If, at time t, the market value of inventory is less than the inventory's "historical cost" by an amount equal to, say, X_t, then the use of LCOM induces a tax "saving" equal to τX_t at time t and an ending inventory valuation equal to an amount that is less than it would otherwise be by an amount equal to X_t. If inventory turnover exceeds unity, then the FIFO period $t + 1$ cost of goods sold (taxable income) will be less (greater) than it would otherwise be by an amount equal to X_t. Thus, taxes payable will be greater than they would otherwise be by an amount equal to τX_t. If there is no write-down at time t, then cost of goods sold (taxable income) at time $t + 1$ will be higher (lower) than it would otherwise be by an amount equal to X_t—resulting in taxes payable equal to an amount less than they would otherwise be by an amount equal to τX_t at time $t + 1$. In the end, the write-down at time t allows the firm to increase its wealth by an amount equal to whatever profits are expected on the additional investment of τX_t for the period from t to $t + 1$. Similar remarks apply to available write-downs at each point in time in a multiperiod setting. Of course, under the existing tax system, no firm will survive if sales of inventoried items constitute its sole source of profits and if it systematically acquires (produces) goods that are sold at less than acquisition (production) cost.

[7]There is no "wash sale" rule that precludes this. Of course, "arms-length" transactions must be used for both the sales and the repurchases.

> A Lifo company may, however, get out from under inventory increments acquired at high prices by liquidating them in later years; in this event, the liquidated goods will be charged against income at their high book valuations. Thus, the tax incentives to hold inventories down to beginning-year quantities are not so strong as those to build inventories up to this level. If Lifo inventories are expanded in periods of high costs, the inability to reduce income by writing down the high-cost increments during a period of future price decline can be overcome at the taxpayers' option by the actual liquidation of these increments as of the end of any year. If, however, Lifo inventories are partly liquidated when inventory costs are high, the income resulting from charging low-cost Lifo inventories against current sales must be taken into income immediately and taxes be paid on it with no opportunity for later offsetting adjustments. The special dispensation given to involuntary wartime liquidations constitutes the only exception to this last statement.

If a LIFO firm incorporates these (or similar) loss-recognition opportunities into its tax-reporting decision rules, then the definition of $\tilde{C}_t^L$ must recognize the effects of exploiting these opportunities. In the end, this simply leads to distinctions among methods of implementing LIFO. Our results must be understood to pertain to one such implementation strategy. As will be indicated, there are a variety of other reasons for treating the inventory-method choice problem as one involving a multidimensional decision variable (see Sec. 5.3.9). There is more involved here than just choosing LIFO over FIFO, because there are many acceptable ways of implementing these basic inventory valuation methods. (More on this later.)

5.3.7 Explicit Equilibrium Valuation of Alternative Inventory Methods

5.3.7.1 Preliminaries

The value of W_{oi}, $i = 1, 2, \ldots, T$, and thus the equilibrium value of $V_o^L - V_o^F$, can be expressed via whatever model characterizes the setting of cash-flow sequences' equilibrium values. We shall assume that a descriptively adequate characterization is provided by the multiperiod extension of the Sharpe/Lintner two-parameter asset-pricing model developed earlier. As was indicated, this assumption places some important restrictions on the sources of uncertainty that are permitted to exist. And some additional restrictions not required by the Sharpe/Lintner framework will be invoked for the sake of tractibility. In return, we shall get a framework that provides insights on the LIFO/FIFO choice problem and that leads to testable propositions on the extent to which firms' choices are consistent with value maximization.

We begin by establishing the equilibrium value of one of the cash-flow differences associated with switching from one inventory method to another—say from FIFO to LIFO. Consider the value of the difference $(\tilde{C}_T^L - \tilde{C}_T^F)$ as of time $T - 1$, i.e., the value of $W_{T-1,T}$. Conditional on the Sharpe/Lintner version of the two-parameter asset-pricing model, one gets:

$$W_{T-1,T} = (1 + R_{fT})^{-1}\left[E_{T-1}(\tilde{C}_T^L - \tilde{C}_T^F) - \lambda_T \frac{\mathrm{Cov}_{T-1}(\tilde{C}_T^L - \tilde{C}_T^F, \tilde{V}_{mT})}{\sigma_{T-1}(\tilde{V}_{mT})}\right], \tag{5.30}$$

where $E_{T-1}(\cdot)$, $\sigma_{T-1}(\cdot)$ and $\text{Cov}_{T-1}(\cdot,\cdot)$ denote, respectively, expectation, standard deviation, and covariance assessed at time $T - 1$; $\tilde{V}_{mT}$ is the value of the "market portfolio" (or aggregate wealth) at time T; R_{fT} is the value of the equilibrium zero variance ("risk-free") rate of return for the period $T - 1$ to T; $(1 + R_{fT})^{-1}$ is the time $T - 1$ equilibrium price per unit of expected dollar return (for a return that will be observed at time T); and $(1 + R_{fT})^{-1}\lambda_T$ is the time $T - 1$ equilibrium price per unit of risk (applied to the risk of a payoff to be observed at time T).[8] With risk-averse investors, $\lambda_T > 0$ (see Sharpe [1964] or Lintner [1965]). We shall again assume that the assessed variance of $\tilde{V}_{mt}$ is constant over time.

By imposing some additional restrictions, this expression and those to follow can be made substantially more tractable. The following restrictions are added:

(R.1) For every t, the quantity of output sold at time t, q_t^*, is less than or equal to the quantity produced during the period $t - 1$ to t.

(R.2) For every t, the quantity of output sold at time t exceeds or equals the quantity, q_t^B, in the beginning inventory of the period $t - 1$ to t. Thus, q_t^B equals the quantity of output available at time $t - 1$ and sold at time t. This restriction is equivalent to the assumption that inventory "turnover" (in terms of quantities) exceeds or equals unity.

Restriction (R.1) implies that there will never be any "LIFO liquidations" for the LIFO firm. Cost of goods sold for the LIFO firm will, therefore, be determined entirely by current period costs of acquisition and production. Restriction (R.2) implies that the FIFO firm will never have to consider more than two "cost layers"—the current period's production and acquisition costs and the previous period's costs.

By definition, for each t, the quantity sold is:

$$q_t^* \equiv q_t^B + (q_t^* - q_t^B), \tag{5.31}$$

where, from (R.2), $q_t^* \geq q_t^B$. At the end of each period t, conditional on information available at $t - 1$, the LIFO and FIFO costs of goods sold are, respectively:

$$\begin{aligned} \tilde{C}_T^L &= \tilde{p}_t \tilde{q}_t^* && \text{[from (R.1)]} \\ &= \tilde{p}_t q_t^B + \tilde{p}_t(\tilde{q}_t^* - q_t^B) && \text{[from (5.31)]} \end{aligned} \tag{5.32}$$

$$\tilde{C}_t^F = \tilde{p}_t(\tilde{q}_t^* - q_t^B) + p_{t-1}q_t^B \quad \text{[from (5.31) and (R.2)]} \tag{5.33}$$

where, for each t, $\tilde{p}_t$ is the per unit cost of production (or acquisition) incurred for a unit produced (or acquired) during the period from $t - 1$ to t. This is a "historical cost" number—except when the LCOM basis of valuation is adopted. When the LCOM basis is adopted and "market" is less than "cost," the total inventory write-down at time t is assumed to be allocated to units sold at time t—on a constant per unit basis. Thus, in the latter case, the per unit "historical costs" that would otherwise be used to determine costs of goods sold are reduced by an amount equal to the total write-down divided by q_t^*.

---

[8]In general, the distribution function of $\tilde{V}_{mt}$, for any t, depends on the private sector's choices of tax-reporting methods. But we are looking at things from the perspective of one firm in a perfect market setting—a setting in which each firm behaves as if it does not affect the distribution function of $\tilde{V}_{mt}$, for any t.

Using (5.32) and (5.33), one gets, for each t:

$$\begin{aligned}\tilde{C}_t^L - \tilde{C}_t^F &= p_t q_t^B - p_{t-1} q_t^B \\ &= (\tilde{p}_t - p_{t-1}) q_t^B \\ &= \Delta \tilde{p}_t q_t^B \end{aligned} \tag{5.34}$$

where $\Delta \tilde{p}_t = (\tilde{p}_t - p_{t-1})$. By using (5.34) in (5.30), one gets:

$$\begin{aligned} W_{T-1,T} &= (1 + R_{fT})^{-1} \left[E_{T-1}(\Delta \tilde{p}_t q_T^B) - \lambda_T \frac{\text{Cov}_{T-1}(\Delta \tilde{p}_T q_T^B, \tilde{V}_{mT})}{\sigma(\tilde{V}_{mT})} \right] \\ &= E_{T-1}(\Delta \tilde{p}_T q_T^B) \left[\frac{1 - \lambda_T^* \text{Cov}_{T-1}(\Delta \tilde{p}_T q_T^B, \tilde{R}_{mT}) / E_{T-1}(\Delta \tilde{p}_T q_T^B)}{1 + R_{fT}} \right] \end{aligned} \tag{5.35}$$

since $\tilde{V}_{mT} = (1 + \tilde{R}_{mT}) V_{mT-1}$, where $\tilde{R}_{mT}$ is the rate of return on the market portfolio from time $T - 1$ to T, and where $\lambda_T^* \equiv \lambda_T / \sigma(\tilde{R}_{mT})$.

Note that $\tilde{W}_{TT} = \Delta \tilde{p}_T q_T^B$. Also, by definition:

$$E_{T-1}(\tilde{W}_{TT}) = (1 + E_{T-1}(\tilde{R}_{TT})) W_{T-1,T} \tag{5.36}$$

where, in general, $\tilde{R}_{st}$ is the rate of return from time $s - 1$ to s on an asset whose sole cash payoff is $\tilde{C}_t^L - \tilde{C}_t^F$. Thus, using (5.35) and (5.36), one has:

$$[1 + E_{T-1}(\tilde{R}_{TT})]^1 = \left[\frac{1 - \lambda_T^* \text{Cov}_{T-1}(\Delta \tilde{p}_T q_T^B, \tilde{R}_{mT}) / E_{T-1}(\Delta \tilde{p}_T q_T^B)}{1 + R_{fT}} \right]. \tag{5.37}$$

Observe that the only cash-flow-specific quantity on the right-hand side of (5.37) is:

$$\begin{aligned} \frac{\text{Cov}_{T-1}(\Delta \tilde{p}_T q_T^B, \tilde{R}_{mT})}{E_{T-1}(\Delta \tilde{p}_T q_T^B)} &= \text{Cov}_{T-1} \left(\frac{\Delta \tilde{p}_T q_T^B}{E_{T-1}(\Delta \tilde{p}_T q_T^B)}, \tilde{R}_{mT} \right) \\ &= \text{Cov}_{T-1} \left(\frac{\tilde{E}_T(\Delta \tilde{p}_T q_T^B)}{E_{T-1}(\Delta \tilde{p}_T q_T)}, R_{mT} \right) \end{aligned} \tag{5.38}$$

where $\tilde{E}_T(\Delta \tilde{p}_T q_T^B) = \Delta \tilde{p}_T q_T^B$, from the calculus of probability. This is a specific instance of a general result encountered earlier. Conditional on our multiperiod model, the only source of cross-sectional variation in the time $T - 1$ equilibrium expected rates of return on different assets is the extent to which the percentage changes in the *expected* payoffs on the assets covary with the percentage changes in aggregate wealth. The values of λ_T^* and R_{ff} also affect the investment opportunity set facing investors at time $T - 1$. But these values do not vary across assets.

The previous expressions result from applying the Sharpe/Lintner version of the two-parameter model to a single-period setting—with the period extending from time $T - 1$ to time T. From Sec. 5.1, we know that additional conditions must, in general, be invoked in order to apply this model to a multiperiod setting—and thus to obtain values of W_{sT} for all $s < T$. Recall that we invoked a sufficient condition pertaining to the opportunity sets facing investors at different times. Specifically, we assumed that the opportunity set facing investors at each future point in time is known at all preceding points in time within the multiperiod horizon. Recall that this implies that expected rates of return on all assets from $t - 1$ to t, for any t, are known at all times $s \leq t - 1$. And this implies, in turn, that the values of λ_t^*, R_{ft}, and $\text{Cov}_{t-1}(\Delta\tilde{p}_t q_t^B, \tilde{R}_{mt})/E_{t-1}(\Delta\tilde{p}_t q_t^B)$, for each t, are nonstochastic.

Insofar as $\tilde{W}_{T-1,T}$, defined by (5.35), is concerned, a major consequence of these conditions is that the only admissable source of uncertainty is uncertainty about the value of $\tilde{E}_{T-1}(\Delta\tilde{p}_T q_T^B)$. From the calculus of probability, we can again infer that this random variable must evolve according to a martingale process, such as the following:

$$\tilde{E}_s(\Delta\tilde{p}_T\tilde{q}_T^B) = \tilde{E}_s(\tilde{C}_T^L - \tilde{C}_T^F) = E_{s-1}(\tilde{C}_T^L - \tilde{C}_T^F)(1 + \tilde{\eta}_{sT}), \tag{5.39}$$

where $E_{s-1}(\tilde{\eta}_{sT}) = 0.0$. The random variable $\tilde{\eta}_{sT}$ is the percentage change, from time $s - 1$ to s, in the expected value of $(\tilde{C}_T^L - \tilde{C}_T^F)$.

When the multiperiod evaluation mechanics developed in Sec. 5.1 are applied to the inventory-method differential flow $(\tilde{C}_T^L - \tilde{C}_T^F)$, one finds that as of time $t = 0$:

$$W_{0,T} = E_0(\tilde{C}_T^L - \tilde{C}_T^F)\prod_{i=0}^{T-1}[1 + E_i(\tilde{R}_{i+1,T})]^{-1}. \tag{5.40}$$

Thus, whether or not LIFO should be preferred to FIFO for given production investment decisions—i.e., whether or not $W_{o,T} > 0$—depends on the sign of $E_o(\tilde{C}_T^L - \tilde{C}_T^F)$ and the signs of the equilibrium expected values of the one-period rates of return $\tilde{R}_{i+1,T}$, $i = 0, 1, \ldots, T - 1$. Whether or not the latter are positive depends, in part, on the values of $\text{Cov}_i(\tilde{W}_{i+1,T}, \tilde{R}_{m,i+1})/E_i(\tilde{W}_{i+1,T})$, for $i = 0, 1, \ldots, T - 1$. From the results in Sec. 5.1, we know that the values of the latter covariances ultimately depend on the joint stochastic properties of $\tilde{E}_{i+1}(\tilde{C}_T^L - \tilde{C}_T^F)/E_i(\tilde{C}_T^L - \tilde{C}_T^F)$ and $\tilde{R}_{m,i+1}$, for $i = 0, 1, \ldots, T - 1$. Since $(\tilde{C}_T^L - \tilde{C}_T^F) = \Delta\tilde{p}_T\tilde{q}_T^B$, we can get some insights on the determinants of these values by considering the stochastic properties of $\Delta\tilde{p}_T\tilde{q}_T^B$, as seen at any time $i < T$. Since, in general, for $i < T$:

$$\begin{aligned}\tilde{E}_{i+1}(\tilde{C}_T^L - \tilde{C}_T^F) &= \tilde{E}_{i+1}(\Delta\tilde{p}_T\tilde{q}_T^B) \\ &= \tilde{E}_{i+1}(\Delta\tilde{p}_T)\tilde{E}_{i+1}(\tilde{q}_T^B) + \tilde{\text{Cov}}_{i+1}(\Delta\tilde{p}_T, \tilde{q}_T^B)\end{aligned} \tag{5.41}$$

attention must be given to both the expected values of $\Delta\tilde{p}_T$ and $\tilde{q}_T^B$ and the covariance between $\Delta\tilde{p}_T$ and $\tilde{q}_T^B$. We tackle this task in the next two sections. First we provide some general remarks. Then we make more specific assumptions about distribution functions and, as a result, we get specific results on the relative attractiveness of LIFO and FIFO in a multiperiod setting.

5.3.7.2 Remarks on the Determinants of Equilibrium Values

First note that $\Delta\tilde{p}_T$ need not be uncorrelated with $\Delta\tilde{q}_T^B$. Indeed, it is unlikely to be uncorrelated. Thus, one should probably not expect $\tilde{\text{Cov}}_{i+1}(\Delta\tilde{p}_T, \tilde{q}_T^B) = 0$ for any i. One reason for expecting (or at least not precluding) an association between $\Delta\tilde{p}_T$ and $\tilde{q}_T^B$ is that the latter variable is a result of a firm's production (or acquisition) and inventory management strategies. And it seems likely that the decisions made at any point in time—such as decisions about ending inventory levels—would be based on anticipated production costs relative to the current period's production costs. That is, it seems likely that the value of $\tilde{q}_T^B$ will be based on predictions of $\Delta\tilde{p}_T$. If the forecasting method used by a firm exploits some of the systematic features of the process generating values of $\Delta\tilde{p}_T$, then the forecasted values of $\Delta\tilde{p}_T$ will be correlated with $\Delta\tilde{p}_T$. And if $\tilde{q}_T^B$ is monotonically related to the forecasted value of $\Delta\tilde{p}_T$, then one can expect an induced correlation between $\tilde{q}_T^B$ and $\Delta\tilde{p}_T$ in this case. (Of course, this correlation may be nonlinear).

It seems worth noting that various "market structure" factors may influence the strength of the connection between $\tilde{q}_T^B$ and $\Delta\tilde{p}_T$. Presumably, the inaccuracy of a firm's cost-change forecasts (as measured by, e.g., mean-squared errors) will vary directly with the number and importance of exogenous sources of uncertainty (i.e., those beyond the firm's control)—for a given level of total variability of $\Delta\tilde{p}_T$. In other words, inaccuracy should vary inversely with the extent to which a given firm influences $\Delta\tilde{p}_T$. Thus, for given total variability of $\Delta\tilde{p}_T$, one should expect a lower absolute value of $\text{Cov}_{i+1}(\Delta\tilde{p}_T, \tilde{q}_T^B)$, for any i, in a perfectly competitive market than in an imperfectly competitive one, such as a perfect monopsony.[9]

The extent to which per unit costs reflect intertemporal cost allocations—which may be to a large extent in capital intensive industries—will also contribute to a relationship between $\Delta\tilde{p}_T$ and $\tilde{q}_T^B$ if those allocations are of amounts fixed in total but variable per unit, such as periodic depreciation charges on manufacturing equipment. In this case, if the observed level of $\tilde{q}_T^B$ is correlated with total output for period T or period $T - 1$, then this level will be inversely correlated with $\tilde{p}_T$ or $\tilde{p}_{T-1}$. This may induce a relationship between $\tilde{q}_T^B$ and $\Delta\tilde{p}_T = \tilde{p}_T - \tilde{p}_{T-1}$, depending on the joint stochastic properties of output in period $T - 1$ and output of period T. In the extreme case where per unit production costs reflect nothing but intertemporally allocated costs, there will be no exogenous sources of uncertainty affecting $\Delta\tilde{p}_T$ except for those affecting the levels of expenditures on "fixed factors" and those that directly affect utilization of these factors—such as uncertainties regarding demanded quantities, bottlenecks, strikes, and breakdowns. In line with our previous remarks, one should expect a strong association between $\Delta\tilde{p}_T$ and $\tilde{q}_T^B$ in this case, for a given total variability of $\Delta\tilde{p}_T$.

The above remarks provide some insights on the types of factors that will affect the periodic assessed values of $\tilde{\text{Cov}}_{i+1}(\Delta\tilde{p}_T, \tilde{q}_T^B)$ and thus the values of $\tilde{E}_{i+1}(\tilde{C}_T^L - \tilde{C}_T^F)$. Consequently, they provide insights on some of the determinants of the equilibrium value of $W_{o,T}$, as expressed in (5.40). Additional and more precise insights can be obtained by imposing seemingly reasonable restrictions on the joint distribution function of $\tilde{E}_{i+1}(\Delta\tilde{p}_T)$, $\tilde{E}_{i+1}(\tilde{q}_T)$, and $\tilde{R}_{mi+1}$, for each $i < T$. This is done in the next section, which imposes the condition of joint symmetry.

5.3.7.3 Determinants of Equilibrium Values Under Joint Symmetry

Applying the mechanics behind (5.14) to any i, $i = 0, 1, 2, \ldots, T - 1$, one gets, as of time i:

$$\text{Cov}_i\left(\frac{\tilde{E}_{i+1}(\tilde{C}_T^L - \tilde{C}_T^F)}{E_i(\tilde{C}_T^L - \tilde{C}_T^F)}, \tilde{R}_{m,i+1}\right) = [E_i(\Delta\tilde{p}_T\tilde{q}_T^B)]^{-1}\,\text{Cov}_i(\tilde{E}_{i+1}(\Delta\tilde{p}_T q_T^B), \tilde{R}_{mi+1}). \tag{5.42}$$

And from the discussion below (6.40):

---

[9]Monopsony rather than monopoly is relevant here because Δp_T is the change in the per unit *cost* of production, not the per unit price to purchasers of the produced output.

$$\text{Cov}_i(\tilde{E}_{i+1}(\Delta\tilde{p}_T\tilde{q}_T^B), \tilde{R}_{mi+1}) = \text{Cov}_i(\tilde{E}_{i+1}(\Delta\tilde{p}_T)\tilde{E}_{i+1}(\tilde{q}_T^B), \tilde{R}_{mi+1}) + \text{Cov}_i(\tilde{\text{Cov}}_{i+1}(\Delta\tilde{p}_T, q_T^B), \tilde{R}_{mi+1}). \tag{5.43}$$

We add the following restrictions:

(R.3) For each i, $\tilde{\text{Cov}}_{i+1}(\Delta\tilde{p}_T, \tilde{q}_T^B)$ is uncorrelated with $\tilde{R}_{mi+1}$.

(R.4) For each i, $\text{Cov}_o(\tilde{\eta}_{1T}, \tilde{R}_{ml}) = \text{Cov}_i(\tilde{\eta}_{i+1,T}, \tilde{R}_{mi+1})$.

(R.5) For each i, the random variables $\tilde{E}_i(\Delta\tilde{p}_T)$, $\tilde{E}_i(\tilde{q}_T^B)$, and $\tilde{R}_{mi}$ are jointly symmetric.[10]

Restriction (R.4) implies that, as of time $t = 0$:

$$\begin{aligned}\text{Cov}_o\left(\frac{\tilde{E}_1(\tilde{C}_T^L - \tilde{C}_T^F)}{E_o(\tilde{C}_T^L - \tilde{C}_T^F)}, \tilde{R}_{ml}\right) &= \text{Cov}_1\left(\frac{\tilde{E}_2(\tilde{C}_T^L - \tilde{C}_T^F)}{E_1(\tilde{C}_T^L - \tilde{C}_T^F)}, \tilde{R}_{m2}\right) \\ &= \ldots = \text{Cov}_{T-1}\left(\frac{\tilde{C}_T^L - \tilde{C}_T^F}{\tilde{E}_{T-1}(\tilde{C}_T^L - \tilde{C}_T^F)}, \tilde{R}_{mT}\right) \\ &= [E_o(\tilde{C}_T^L - \tilde{C}_T^F)]^{-1}\,\text{Cov}_o(\tilde{E}_1(\tilde{C}_T^L - \tilde{C}_T^F), \tilde{R}_{ml}).\end{aligned} \tag{5.44}$$

This restriction implies, therefore, that all temporal variation in the equilibrium expected one-period returns, $E_i(\tilde{R}_{i+1,T})$, $i = 0, 1, \ldots, T-1$, is due to temporal variation in the equilibrium prices of dollar return, $(1 + R_{fi})^{-1}$, $i = 1, 2, \ldots, T$, or in the equilibrium prices of risk $(1 + R_{fi})_i^{-1}\lambda^*$, $i = 1, 2, \ldots, T$.

Restriction (R.3) implies that the value of the last covariance term in expression (5.43) is equal to zero. Thus, a joint implication of restrictions (R.3) – (R.5) is:

$$\text{Cov}_i(\tilde{\eta}_{i+1,T}, \tilde{R}_{mi+1}) = [E_o(\tilde{C}_T^L - \tilde{C}_T^F)]^{-1}\,\text{Cov}_o(\tilde{E}_1(\Delta\tilde{p}_T)\tilde{E}_1(\tilde{q}_T^B), \tilde{R}_{ml,}) \tag{5.45}$$

for each i, where:[11]

$$\begin{aligned}E_o(\tilde{C}_T^L - \tilde{C}_T^F) &= E_o(\Delta\tilde{p}_T\tilde{q}_T^B) \\ &= E_o(\Delta\tilde{p}_T)E_o(\tilde{q}_T^B) + \text{Cov}_o(\Delta\tilde{p}_T, \tilde{Q}_T^B).\end{aligned} \tag{5.46}$$

---

[10]The implication of joint symmetry used below is as follows. Let $\tilde{x}$, $\tilde{y}$, and $\tilde{z}$ be jointly symmetric. Then:

$$E(\tilde{x} - \mu_y)(\tilde{y} - \mu_y)(\tilde{z} - \mu_z) = 0.0,$$

where μ_x, μ_y, and μ_z denote the expected values of $\tilde{x}$, $\tilde{y}$, and $\tilde{z}$, respectively.

[11]The general result underlying expression (5.47) is as follows. In general, for any random variables $\tilde{x}$, $\tilde{y}$, and $\tilde{z}$:

$$\text{Cov}(\tilde{x}\tilde{y}, \tilde{z}) = E(\tilde{x})\,\text{Cov}\,(\tilde{y}, \tilde{z}) + E(\tilde{y})\,\text{Cov}(\tilde{x}, \tilde{z}) + E(\tilde{x} - \mu_x)(\tilde{y} - \mu_y)(\tilde{z} - \mu_z),$$

where μ_x, μ_y, and μ_z denote the expected values of $\tilde{x}$, $\tilde{y}$, and $\tilde{z}$, respectively. If the joint distribution function of $\tilde{x}$, $\tilde{y}$, and $\tilde{z}$ is symmetric, then the last term in the above sum has a value equal to zero. A derivation of this result on covariances of products of random variables is given by Bohrnstedt and Goldberger [1969].

$$\text{Cov}_o(\tilde{E}_1(\Delta p_T)\tilde{E}_1(q_T^B), \tilde{R}_{ml}) = E_o[\tilde{E}_1(\Delta\tilde{p}_T)]\ \text{Cov}_o(\tilde{E}_1(\tilde{q}_T^B), \tilde{R}_{ml}) + E_o[\tilde{E}_1(\tilde{q}_T^B)]\ \text{Cov}_o(\tilde{E}_1(\Delta\tilde{p}_T), \tilde{R}_{ml}). \tag{5.47}$$

Since $E_o[\tilde{E}_1(\Delta\tilde{p}_T) = E_o(\Delta\tilde{p}_T)$ and $E_o[\tilde{E}_1(\tilde{q}_T^B)] = E_o(\tilde{q}_T^B)$, (5.47) can be rewritten as:

$$\text{Cov}_o(\tilde{E}_1(\Delta\tilde{p}_T)\tilde{E}_1(\tilde{q}_T^B), \tilde{R}_{ml}) = E_o(\Delta\tilde{p}_T)\ \text{Cov}_o(\tilde{E}_1(\tilde{q}_T^B), \tilde{R}_{ml}) + E_o(\tilde{q}_T^B)\ \text{Cov}_o(\tilde{E}_1(\Delta\tilde{p}_T), \tilde{R}_{ml}). \tag{5.48}$$

Under restrictions (R.1)–(R.5), expressions (5.46) and (5.48) give the only firm-specific parameters relevant to the choice of either LIFO or FIFO, at least insofar as one of the cash-flow differences, $\tau(\tilde{C}_T^L - \tilde{C}_T^F)$, induced by this choice is concerned. All other parameters that are determinants of the value of W_{oT}, in (6.40), are common to all firms. The next section provides some remarks on the firm-specific parameters.

5.3.7.4 Remarks on Equilibrium Values Under Joint Symmetry

From (5.40), (5.46), and (5.48), it is seen that the equilibrium value, τW_{oT}, of the LIFO-induced flow, $\tau\tilde{C}_T^L$, over the FIFO-induced flow, $\tau\tilde{C}_T^F$, for period T depends on the forecast of time $T - 1$ ending inventory $\tilde{q}_T^B$, the forecast of the change in per unit production (or acquisition) costs, $\Delta\tilde{p}_T$, from time $T - 1$ to time T, the covariation of future *forecasts* with percentage changes in aggregate wealth, $\text{Cov}_o(\tilde{E}_1(\Delta\tilde{p}_T),\tilde{R}_{ml})$ and $\text{Cov}_o(\tilde{E}_1(\tilde{q}_T^B), \tilde{R}_{ml})$, and the covariation, $\text{Cov}_o(\Delta\tilde{p}_T, \tilde{q}_T^B)$, of the time $T - 1$ ending inventory and the per unit cost change, $\Delta\tilde{p}_T$, from time $T - 1$ to time T. All of these forecasts and values of covariances are as of time $t = 0$, when the LIFO and FIFO methods are being compared.

Presumably, for a given level of output (and thus a given level of intertemporally allocated costs per unit of sales), the covariance between $\tilde{E}_1(\Delta\tilde{p}_T)$ and $\tilde{R}_{ml}$ will vary directly with the extent to which events at time $t = 1$ alter time $t = 1$ *forecasts* of prices for factors of production (e.g., raw materials) and the extent to which the input-price changes from $T - 1$ to T are expected to affect the per unit change in costs from $T - 1$ to T. Evidently, this covariance's absolute value will be lower the greater the extent to which per unit production costs consist of intertemporally allocated amounts (e.g., depreciation) and thus amounts that are less responsive to period-by-period variations in the economy, as reflected by the percentage changes in aggregate wealth.

Of course, the value of $\text{Cov}_o(\tilde{E}_1(\Delta\tilde{p}_T), \tilde{R}_{ml})$—and that of $E_0(\Delta\tilde{p}_T)$ and of $\text{Cov}_o(\Delta\tilde{p}_T, \tilde{q}_T^B)$—will, in general, depend on a firm's cost accounting system (e.g., standard cost system vs. actual cost system). This covariance's absolute value will be larger the greater the extent to which a firm's system allows the economic events of period T to be reflected in the per unit costs for period T and the greater the extent to which the value of $\tilde{R}_{ml}$ has implications for the cost-affecting events of period T.

Moreover, the value of $\text{Cov}_o(\tilde{E}_1(\Delta\tilde{p}_T), \tilde{R}_{ml})$—and of $E_0(\Delta\tilde{p}_T)$ and $\text{Cov}_o(\Delta\tilde{p}_T, \tilde{q}_T^B)$—will depend on technological features of the firm's production process—such as changes in optimal factor proportions along the firm's expansion path and changes in optimal factor proportions along an isoquant (in response to changes in relative input-prices).[12] It seems

[12]The latter changes in factor proportions could be summarized via elasticities of substitution, given perfectly competitive input markets.

reasonable to expect $\tilde{E}_1(\Delta\tilde{p}_T)$ to be more sensitive to "current" (time $t = 1$) economic developments if these developments have implications for the events of time T and if the firm's production process implies an important role for productive factors that will be purchased on a period-by-period basis at prevailing market prices. This is the type of setting in which the value of $\Delta\tilde{p}_T$ will be significantly affected by contemporaneous changes in input-prices, which are likely to be correlated with changes in the state of the economy (as reflected by variation in the market portfolio's returns). Of course, if firms within an industry (or some other specified grouping) are homogeneous regarding these attributes of their production processes, then one should expect to see industry concentrations of LIFO and FIFO use.

The elasticity of a firm's supply function is also likely to affect the firm's evaluation of alternative inventory methods. Presumably, at any point in time, a firm's quantity expectations—such as $E_o(\tilde{q}_T^B)$—will be consistent with the characteristics of its supply function. It seems unlikely, for example, that a firm's expected level of output and expected inventory balance will be substantially altered by current economic developments—as captured by $\tilde{R}_{ms}$, $s = 1, 2, \ldots, T$—if the firm knows that it will face an inelastic supply function at time T. There is, however, more to this story.

As indicated at several points, the expectations being considered here are as of each point in time $s < T$ and they are for random variables whose values will be observed at time T. Thus, the implications of $\tilde{R}_{ms}$ for *subsequent* events are relevant in evaluating the covariance terms involving $\tilde{R}_{ms}$ in (5.48). If such events are not among the arguments of the optimal decision rules that ultimately define output quantities, costs per unit of sales, and inventory levels, then there should be no correlation between $\tilde{R}_{ms}$ and the period s expectation of $\tilde{q}_T^B$ or of $\tilde{p}_T$. Moreover, there should be "internal consistency" regarding the assessed correlation between $\tilde{R}_{ms}$ and $\tilde{E}_s(\Delta\tilde{p}_T)$ and between $\tilde{R}_{ms}$ and $\tilde{E}_s(\tilde{q}_T^B)$, because, in general, $\tilde{q}_T^B$ and $\Delta\tilde{p}_T$ are not independently distributed random variables.

Of course, if the *expected* value of $(\tilde{C}_T^L - \tilde{C}_T^F)$, assessed as of time $s < T$, is uncorrelated with $\tilde{R}_{ms}$, then the single-period discount rates that determine the value of W_{oT} in (6.40) are the single-period zero-variance (or "risk-free") rates corresponding to the time periods $i = 1, 2, \ldots, T$, because (from 5.45) and (5.47)) the risk associated with $(\tilde{C}_T^L - \tilde{C}_T^F)$ would be zero for each i, $i = 1, 2, \ldots, T$. In this case, the only cash-flow-specific determinant of W_{oT} is $E_o(\tilde{C}_T^L - \tilde{C}_T^F) = E_o(\Delta\tilde{p}_T)E(\tilde{q}_T^B) + \text{Cov}_o(\Delta\tilde{p}_T, \tilde{q}_T^B)$.

In general, the value of W_{oT} increases with the extent to which the period T cost per unit, $\tilde{p}_T$, is expected to be greater than the period $T - 1$ cost per unit, $\tilde{p}_{T-1}$. If $E_o(\Delta\tilde{p}_T)$ is greater (less) than zero, then W_{oT} increases (decreases) with the importance of the firm's expected inventory position, as reflected in $E_o(\tilde{q}_T^B)$. Moreover, the value of W_{oT} varies directly with the extent to which the change in per unit costs and the importance of inventory position vary together, as reflected in the value of $\text{Cov}_o(\Delta\tilde{p}_T, \tilde{q}_T^B)$. The value of this covariance will depend on the types of uncertainty that a firm faces and the nature of competition. If, for example, a firm in a perfect output market faces long-run supply function uncertainty but no demand function uncertainty, then output levels and production costs per unit should be uncorrelated. That is, all pairs of per unit costs and output levels should lie along a fixed demand function—which is horizontal for a given firm in a perfectly competitive market. In any event, it is clear that the production technology and the production uncertainty facing a firm are among the determinants of a firm's optimal choice of tax-reporting methods.

5.3.7.5 The Equilibrium Value of All Cash-Flow Effects Induced by Alternative Reporting Methods

Expression (5.40) provides the equilibrium value of the cash-flow difference ($\tilde{C}_T^L - \tilde{C}_T^F$) for the last period of a multiperiod horizon, conditional on the Sharpe/Lintner version of the two-parameter asset-pricing model. From Secs. 5.1 and 5.2, we know that the mechanics leading to this result can also be used for the cash-flow difference induced at each point in time s, $s = 1, 2, \ldots, T - 1$. This provides an expression for the overall equilibrium value of LIFO over FIFO as of time $t = 0$, $V_o^L - V_o^F$, as given in (5.27). Specifically:

$$V_o^L - V_o^F = \tau \sum_{i=1}^{T} W_{oi}$$
$$= \tau \sum_{i=1}^{T} E_o(\tilde{C}_i^L - \tilde{C}_i^F) \prod_{s=o}^{i=1} [1 + E_s(\tilde{R}_{s+1,i})]^{-1}. \quad (5.49)$$

Note that the "discount factors" applied to a given expected cash-flow difference—$\tau E_o(\tilde{C}_i^L - \tilde{C}_i^F)$ for a fixed i—can vary over time. And the sequence of discount factors used for a given period's expected cash-flow difference may differ, in whole or in part, from the sequence used for a different period's expected cash-flow difference. From our previous analysis of W_{oT}—now applied to W_{oi} for each i—one can see that the temporal differences for a given period's expected cash-flow difference will depend on the temporal variation in the risk of *that period's* cash-flow difference. Also, quite naturally, the differences across different periods' cash-flow differences will depend on the risk variations across these cash-flow differences, which may be induced by temporal changes in the sorts of economic determinants discussed in Secs. 5.3.7.2–5.3.7.4. Of course, for the cash-flow difference, ($\tilde{C}_i^L - \tilde{C}_i^F$), of each period i, $i = 1, 2, \ldots, T$, the relevant measure of risk at each time $s < i$ is $\mathrm{Cov}_s(\tilde{\eta}_{s+1,i}, \tilde{R}_{ms+1})$, where $\tilde{\eta}_{s+1,i}$ denotes the percentage change from s to $s + 1$ in the expected value of ($\tilde{C}_i^L - \tilde{C}_i^F$). If the *forecasted* values of all cash-flow differences induced by switching from one inventory method to another are completely unaffected by contemporaneous events (as summarized in the value of $\tilde{R}_{ms}$, for each s), then all of these cash-flow differences are "riskless" payoffs, conditional on the Sharpe/Lintner model.

But this "riskless" case is a special case. And nothing unique to inventory-reporting methods implies that a firm should expect to be faced by that case. In general, therefore, a firm may rationally select FIFO even though the expected cost-of-goods-sold deduction for taxes under LIFO (i.e., $E_o(\tilde{C}_t^L)$) exceeds the expected value of this deduction under FIFO (i.e., $E_0(\tilde{C}_T^F)$) for each period t, $t = 1, 2, \ldots, T$. The relevant issue is whether each period's expected "tax savings" under LIFO is sufficient to compensate for the additional risk induced by a switch from FIFO to LIFO. As indicated earlier, selecting the optimal tax-reporting method is analogous to making optimal production-investment decisions in the sense that a balancing of "risk" and "return" is required. A firm that opts to use FIFO is not necessarily "sacrificing" a LIFO-induced "tax subsidy," as is often implied by discussions of LIFO's effects on cash flows and its effects on reported income numbers. In this regard, the following argument from Wallich and Wallich [1974, p. 128] is typical:

> In a period of inflation, FIFO has two great shortcomings. First, it overstates profits by including in them a sizable quantity of what are in essence capital gains on inventory. Second, by enlarging profits it also enlarges tax liabilities. This

happens because the government insists that identical methods of inventory accounting be used in reporting to stockholders and to the Internal Revenue Service. A corporation, to be sure, can put one part of its inventories on LIFO and another part on FIFO or some other accounting basis. But the same accounting method or methods must still be used for both stockholders and tax collectors. So when roughly three out of four companies vote against LIFO, they are in effect choosing to pay additional taxes.

Last year's surge of inventory profits confronts management with a serious question. Is it justifiable to forego a legitimate means of holding down tax liabilities—namely, LIFO—in order to show higher profits? To go one step further, is it justifiable to make this tax sacrifice in order to show low-grade profits that by their nature are transient and in some measure illusory? Inventory profits generate no direct cash flow for investment, dividends, or even taxes. They are already embodied in the costlier inventory that the company needs to stay in business. Inventory profits, in other words, do not contribute to what today is the foremost function of profits—to increase the supply of investable funds. On the contrary, they deplete that supply by requiring corporations to make unnecessarily large tax payments.

. . . .

Only one argument on the anti-LIFO side seems to have gained in strength as inflation has escalated. Corporate officers are well aware that in a time of rapid inflation a switch to LIFO will have a negative impact on reported profits. They may fear that this would drag down the price of the stock. Surely, they can argue, it is in the interest of stockholders to pay even a substantial tax premium in order to avoid a decline in the price of the stock.

That the generalizations in this excerpt are, as they stand, somewhat misguided should be clear from our analysis. Note, for example, that a firm may rationally opt to use LIFO even though its expected tax deductions under LIFO are less than its expected deductions under FIFO in each period, t, $t = 1, 2, \ldots, T$. If, to consider an extreme case, the risks of the cash-flow differences, $\tau(\tilde{C}_t^L - \tilde{C}_t^F$, $t = 1, 2, \ldots, T$, are such that a firm concludes that:

$$\prod_{i=0}^{t-1}[1 + E_i(\tilde{R}_{i+1,t})]^{-1} < 0, \tag{5.50}$$

for each t, then $V_o^L - V_o^F > 0$ in (5.49) when $E_o(\tilde{C}_t^L - \tilde{C}_t^F) < 0$ for each t.[13] The situation is even more complicated when some of the cash-flow differences induced by a switch to LIFO have positive time $t = 0$ equilibrium values and others have negative values. Whether LIFO is or is not optimal in this case depends, from (5.49), on the value of the sum $\tau\Sigma_{i=0}^{T} W_{oi}$, which may incorporate a variety of offsetting values. In any event, the framework developed here indicates that, in general, it is not necessary to assume—as was effectively done by Sunder [1973*b*] and Abdel-khalik and McKeown [1978], among oth-

---

[13]In a world with "limited liability," no outstanding asest will have $E_i(\tilde{R}_i + {}_{1,t}) < -1.0$ for any i, $i = 0, 1, \ldots, t - 1$, and any t. But this does not imply that a firm will never forecast such a value when contemplating alternative accounting techniques.

ers—that the expected tax deduction under LIFO exceeds the expected deduction under FIFO in order to infer the desirability of switching to LIFO.[14]

The literature on financial statement analysis is becoming increasingly concerned with possible empirical tests on the effects of accounting methods and with available empirical results. (This can be seen by examining the sorts of papers published in, e.g., the *Financial Analysts Journal* and the *Journal of Portfolio Management*.) Thus, it seems appropriate to consider the testable propositions identified by our framework. Also relevant are the identified "empirical problems" likely to be encountered in work on the effects of accounting techniques and changes in techniques on capital market equilibrium. These are among the topics considered in the next section.

5.3.8 Assessing the Effects of Accounting Techniques: Relative Risk Differences, Other Empirical Problems, and Some Testable Propositions

Several studies on accounting methods (or method changes) point to an empirical connection between relative risk (or risk changes) and accounting methods (or method changes). Evidence on this issue with respect to inventory method changes is provided by Sunder [1973b, table 6] and Ball [1972, table 4]. Both authors infer that, on average, firms switching to (or extending their use of) LIFO experience increases in relative risk. Various possible reasons for a relationship between changes in accounting methods and relative risk changes were offered by these authors, on grounds of plausibility. But they were, nevertheless, *ad hoc,* as in other studies of this type.[15] More specifically, it was not presumed at the outset that risk changes should be expected for firms that change the inventory methods used for tax reporting.

The framework developed in Secs. 5.3.1–5.3.7 clearly indicates, however, that, other things being equal, a change in relative risk should be regarded as "the rule" rather than "the exception" when there is a change in inventory costing methods. From expression (5.28), it is seen that, for given production-investment decisions, the single-period dollar payoff conditional on LIFO, $\tilde{V}_1^L$, is equivalent to the combined payoffs $\tilde{V}_1^F$ and $\tau\tilde{W}_{1i}$, $i = 1, 2, \ldots, T$. Thus, the relative risk of the dollar return conditional on LIFO, β_v^L, as of $t = 0$, can be written as:

$$\beta_v^L = \beta_v^F + \tau\sum_{i=1}^{T} \beta_w^i$$

where β_v^F is the time $t = 0$ relative risk conditional on FIFO and β_w^i is the time $t = 0$ relative risk of the asset with time $t = 1$ payoff $\tilde{W}_{1i}$, $i = 1, 2, \ldots, T$. (As before, we

---

[14]This assumption can be inferred from the discussion on pp. 854–855 of the Abdel-khalik/McKeown paper. In Sunder's paper, it is implied by his assumptions of an "inflationary" environment and nondecreasing inventory levels; see pp. 8 and 9 of his paper or pp. 27 and 28 of Sunder [1973a].

[15]Note that Sunder's attempted explanation of risk changes (see Sunder [1973a, sec. 5]) is conditional on his assumption that changes in accounting methods are independent of changes in the characteristics of production-investment decisions (see Sunder [1973a, p. 27]). The framework developed here makes it clear that changes in accounting methods and changes in the characteristics of production-investment decisions necessarily go together—given adherence to the market value rule. Also, contrary to Sunder's statements, neither the wage-lag hypothesis nor the debtor-creditor hypothesis plays any special role in linking the characteristics of production-investment decisions to accounting methods.

assume that the tax rate, τ, is constant over time.) It would seem somewhat coincidental to have $\Sigma_{i=1}^{T} \beta_w^i = 0$. Thus, rather than designing empirical tests on the assumption of constant relative risks—and thus exposing oneself to one of the internal validity deficiencies noted by Demski [1973, p. 49]—it appears that one should presume that relative risk changes are likely to be experienced by firms that change inventory-costing methods for tax reporting. This, in effect, involves a change in one of the maintained hypotheses underlying empirical work regarding the effects of accounting changes on capital market equilibrium.

The situation is a little different for analyses of firms that change both their production investment decisions and their inventory-reporting methods. It is also different for cross-sectional analyses wherein firms that may be pursuing different production-investment decisions end up being treated as homogeneous because they are pursuing the same inventory-costing method.

As indicated in Sec. 5.3.1, a given set of production-investment decisions implies the optimality of either LIFO or FIFO. Thus, all firms pursuing that set will, in equilibrium, pursue one or the other reporting method. But then not all firms pursuing the same reporting method will be pursuing the same set of production investment decisions if more than two sets of decisions are on the efficient frontier of feasible production-investment decisions. In this case, homogeneity with respect to inventory methods used for tax reporting necessarily implies, in general, *heterogeneity* with respect to substantive attributes of production-investment decisions—as does heterogeneity with respect to inventory methods. Unless one is willing to presume that differences among the risk attributes of $(\tilde{C}_t^L - \tilde{C}_t^F)$; $t = 1, 2, \ldots, T$ for firms pursuing a given reporting method offset risk differences among their different production-investment decisions, one should presume, it seems, that firms pursuing a given inventory method have different relative risks. In other words, risk inequality rather than risk equality should be the "working hypothesis" guiding one's design of experiments.

The above remarks point to a specific aspect of a more general problem identified by our framework: holding "other things" constant when attempting to assess empirically the effects of alternative accounting methods. If, for example, a given firm is adhering to the market value rule and if it now changes its tax-reporting methods, our framework implies that it did so because of previous or anticipated substantive changes in its production-investment decisions. If the latter changes are not taken into account, attempts to assess the effects of accounting methods using both prechange and postchange data seem likely to produce misleading results, even though one is conducting the analysis on a firm-by-firm basis (which might otherwise make the "other things being equal" presumption plausible). For the case at hand, there are solid theoretical reasons for assigning a low probability to the descriptive adequacy of the "other things being equal" assumption.

Similar remarks apply to cross-sectional analyses based on different firms' data for a given time period. Attempts to assess the effects of accounting methods (using the observed different methods of the different firms) without explicitly recognizing the effects of substantive differences among the firms will probably not satisfy the condition of holding "other things" constant. The fact that the different firms opted for different accounting methods implies that their production-investment decisions are different. Moreover, as indicated above, there are grounds for expecting this to be the case also for the different firms that opted for the same accounting method.

These sorts of issues are often considered after a study is designed and perhaps initiated—typically as a result of observing anomalies. The lack of a model or framework for characterizing firms' selections of accounting methods is probably one reason for this. The framework provided above supplies some basic ingredients for filling this gap. As it stands, it only applies to the LIFO/FIFO decision. But it can obviously be extended to other accounting method choices, at least when they have direct (or contractually induced) effects on firms' future values.[16]

In addition to identifying problems that are likely to be encountered in the design of experiments dealing with the effects of accounting techniques, the framework developed here points to some basic testable propositions on firms' selections of accounting methods. Suppose that managers' and investors' distributional assessments are dominated by the weight of available sample evidence and that these assessments are in agreement.[17] Further suppose that sampling distributions conditional on available evidence adequately represent investors' and managers' predictive distributions. Under these assumptions, sample values of the parameters that appear in the valuation expressions for W_{ot}, $t = 1, 2, \ldots, T$, can be used to test for firms' adherence to the optimality conditions for alternative inventory methods. Pursuing this line of attack would not lead to unusual data problems if firms routinely disclosed values of accounting numbers based on their selected methods and alternative ones. But this is usually not done, at least not on a regular basis. Thus, an analyst might have to resort to the use of approximations to what firms would have disclosed. Such approximations for inventory and cost-of-goods-sold numbers can be secured via available conversion methods, most of which are based upon some variant of the Dollar-Value-LIFO method (see, e.g., Derstine and Huefner [1974]).

Alternatively, an analyst might use sample evidence on variables that are, on theoretical or empirical grounds, taken to be determinants of the parameter values that appear in the valuation expressions for W_{ot}, $t = 1, 2, \ldots, T$. For example, if it is felt that demand function uncertainty directly affects the risk contribution of the cash-flow sequence $\{(\tilde{C}_t^L - \tilde{C}_t^F); t = 1, 2, \ldots, T\}$, then data on the determinants of demand for a firm's output (e.g., data on relative prices, new product introductions, competitor's advertising expenditures, etc.) could be used. Supply function uncertainty could be modeled in terms of data on net new entry into a firm's markets, technological changes (as measured by, e.g., patent applications), and the flexibility/adaptability of so-called fixed factors of production (which influences the extent to which resources can be shifted from one use to another,

---

[16]Debt-agreement convenants expressed in terms of accounting numbers may lead to contractually induced effects; see, e.g., Fogelson [1978]. Incentive-compensation plan terms expressed in terms of accounting numbers may have the same effect. When these sorts of contractually induced effects are recognized, there may be substantive economic reasons for the types of economic behavior often referred to (somewhat pejoratively) as "income smoothing" or "earnings management." In short, seemingly "cosmetic" changes in reported earnings numbers may be motivated by substantive economic reasons. The mere fact that an accounting-technique change does not have direct effects on cash flows—because, e.g., it does not affect tax reporting—is not a sufficient basis for claiming that the change has no substantive economic implications or that it is motivated only by managements' attempts to make their past performance "look better" by "managing" reported values of accounting numbers.

[17]Under a variety of conditions, this would be the case after repeated updating of prior distribution functions for the random variables that are determinants of firms' terminal values, conditional on firms' production-investment decisions and inventory methods.

as indicated by, e.g., Stigler [1939]). In any event, a variety of indirect approaches can be used to conduct tests of the implication of firms' adherence to value maximization in their selection of inventory methods, perhaps with the aid of simplifying restrictions such as (R.1)–(R.5) (see Sec. 5.3.7). Since the data needed for direct tests may not be available or adequate, these indirect tests may be more appealing than direct tests. At least they cannot, it appears, be declared to be dominated by the currently feasible direct tests.

Of course, "data problems" are not the only ones to be tackled. The framework developed here is based on a variety of simplifications that may adversely affect its descriptive adequacy. Some of these simplifications and their potential effects are discussed briefly in the next section.

5.3.9 Complications and Extensions

By design, the equilibrium conditions given here fail explicitly to recognize a variety of complicating factors, some of which are induced by the regulations of the U.S. Internal Revenue Code (IRC). Some of these complications and their potential influence are considered below. They point to possible extensions of our theoretical framework and to factors that will probably complicate data analyses based on this framework.

We assumed that any firm can freely switch from one inventory method to another at time $t = 0$ and that new "managerial teams" can—after, for example, a takeover or a reorganization—freely switch methods at time $t = 0$. This assumption is important in our characterization of the mechanism which leads to enforcement of the market value rule. In reality, the "reporting history" of a firm and the perspective of the Internal Revenue Service (IRS) commissioner may constrain a firm's choices. Strictly speaking, switches of methods used for tax reporting must be approved by the IRS commissioner. Various conditions (pertaining to, e.g., restated values of inventory numbers and their effects on values of income numbers) may be imposed on a firm as a condition of approval. Presumably, if the switch is to a method that the IRS deems to be "correct," given the firm's production investment decisions, then the switch will be approved.[18] The firm's "reporting history" may also play a role here: it appears that IRS gives nontrivial weight to "consistency." We infer this from Sec. 1.471-2(f) of the IRC regulations. It is there stated that:

> . . . inventory rules cannot be uniform, but must give effect to trade customs which come within the scope of the best accounting practice in the particular trade or business. In order clearly to reflect income, the inventory practice of a taxpayer should be consistent from year to year, and greater weight is to be given to consistency than to any particular method of inventorying or basis of valuation. . . .

In short, this (and other) IRS regulation(s) on accounting changes may introduce frictions into the value maximization process underlying our framework. As a result, one might observe $V_o^L > V_o^F$ for a FIFO firm or $V_o^F > V_o^L$ for a LIFO firm. Yet, these firms might not switch to the value-maximizing methods because of the IRS regulations pertaining to switches. For the same reason, the value maximization conditions may not be enforceable via takeovers, reorganizations, or other devices for introducing new managerial teams.

---

[18]Helpful remarks on the technicalities of switching inventory methods are given in Coopers & Lybrand [1974, pp. 23 and 46–47] and in Ernst & Ernst [1977].

Another potentially restrictive condition is our assuming that inventory method choices are irrevocably made at time $t = 0$. That is, after $t = 0$, there are no provisions for additional switches during the horizon ending at time T. On the one hand, this restriction is made palatable by the IRS's apparent emphasis on "consistency." On the other hand, the degree of inflexibility implied by this restriction seems somewhat extreme. It precludes not only switches after time $t = 0$, but also "extensions" of methods first selected at time $t = 0$—no matter how production-investment decisions change after time $t = 0$.

Perhaps of greater importance is our treating the inventory method choice problem as one that involves a dichotomous choice: LIFO or FIFO (or, more precisely, LIFO and non-LIFO). A firm may, in actuality, be using both methods concurrently. Moreover, for each method, a variety of other decisions must be made. In general, a firm must select the types of inventories to which each method will be applied (e.g., raw materials, work-in-process, finished goods, and various subclasses of the latter) and it must select the specific methods to be used in computing "cost" (e.g., actual acquisition costs, dollar-value LIFO, average acquisition costs computed over a specified time period, among others). These sorts of details increase the dimensionality of the decision variable associated with optimal selections of inventory methods. They do not, however, alter the basic aspects of our framework; they just add to the variety of ingredients defining an "optimal method." For example, these additional details do not alter our conclusions about the correspondence between optimal methods and the characteristics of firms' production-investment decisions. Nor do they eliminate the connection between firms' relative risks and their selected methods.

Finally, although our framework recognizes the dependence of optimal inventory methods on production-investment decisions, it does not deal explicitly with a potential dependence between optimal inventory methods and other accounting methods used for tax reporting. An obvious example of a potential connection of this sort is that between inventory methods and depreciation methods used for manufacturing equipment. Since the resulting values of depreciation charges affect the costs allocated to inventoriable goods, the depreciation methods can affect the stochastic characteristics of cost-of-goods-sold numbers and, therefore, the stochastic characteristics of the tax deductions attainable under alternative inventory methods. In short, developing a more descriptively adequate framework may involve using an explicitly *joint* optimization approach with respect to several accounting methods used for tax reporting.

5.3.10 Summary of Application

Our application of multiperiod valuation tools deals with the general topic of the effects of firms' accounting techniques and changes in techniques on firms' equilibrium values. The specific technique considered is the inventory-costing method adopted for tax reporting. But the general issues pertinent to this inventory-method choice problem are also pertinent to firms' selections of other techniques that have (direct or indirect) effects on the distribution functions of firms' future values. A general issue of particular interest here is the connection between the effects of accounting techniques on firms' equilibrium values and the substantive attributes of firms' production-investment decisions. A framework dealing with this issue provides a basis for obtaining theoretical insights into firms' selections of accounting techniques, for explaining some available empirical results that have heretofore been regarded as somewhat mysterious, and for improving the experimental designs used in empirical work on the effects of accounting techniques.

Our results indicate that a value-maximizing firm's optimal inventory method is inextricably bound to the characteristics of a firm's production-investment decisions and that the method selected affects the characteristics of the distribution function of a firm's future value as of the end of any period—and thus, in general, it affects the firm's current equilibrium value. Moreover, in equilibrium, all firms pursuing production-investment decisions of the same type will also pursue the same inventory-costing method. But the same method will, in general, be optimal for firms pursuing different types of production-investment decisions, so long as the number of production-investment decisions exceeds the number of different inventory methods. Loosely speaking, the value-maximizing mapping from types of decisions to optimal inventory methods is a many-to-one mapping.

Our results have a variety of implications for available empirical work on the effects of accounting techniques. For example, they imply that, in general, an analyst should expect to observe changes in the relative risks of firms that change inventory methods—assuming that multiperiod two-parameter asset-pricing adequately describes the setting of assets' equilibrium values. This connection between relative risks and changes in inventory methods is not an anomaly, a reflection of some systematic sample selection bias, or a quirk of available sample evidence—which seems to be the way it is usually treated in available empirical studies (see, e.g., Ball [1972] and Sunder [1973a; 1973b]). Nor is it something to be ignored in the design of one's analyses. Indeed, one should presume from the outset that relative risks change and, therefore, that it is not appropriate to use estimation methods that do not allow for such changes at the time inventory methods are changed.

CHAPTER SIX

Accounting Procedures

6.1 Introduction

The illustration used in Chapter 5 identifies a topic of numerous theoretical and empirical investigations: the effects of alternative accounting techniques on firms' equilibrium values. This topic will be the focus of our attention in this chapter. Two of our main objectives are (1) to introduce a variety of theoretical issues pertinent to an analysis of alternative accounting procedures' effects and (2) to provide an overview of some important empirical assessments of these effects (as well as the statistical problems that studies of these effects have encountered).

The framework that we use should now be familiar. We view accounting numbers as random variables that may constitute useful sources of sample evidence regarding the probability distributions of securities' future values. The framework developed in Chapters 4 and 5 identifies some attributes of accounting numbers' probability models that may be useful in making inferences about these values' distributions. Recall that the material in those chapters focused primarily on firms' production-investment and financing decisions.

But these decisions are not the only determinants of accounting numbers' probability models. Firm's accounting procedures can also determine accounting numbers' stochastic properties. These procedures' effects on accounting numbers may conflict with the effects of production-investment and financing decisions or they may intensify the latter decisions' effects. In either case, it seems useful to assess the effects of accounting procedures on accounting numbers' properties before using accounting numbers as sources of evidence regarding production-investment and financing decisions. This is part of the motivation for examining (1) the effects of accounting procedures, (2) the regulatory mechanism that impinges on firms' selections of accounting techniques, (3) the kinds of disclosures made about accounting techniques, and (4) the relationship between accounting procedures and firms' equilibrium values. As usual, the emphasis of our discussion is on external accounting.

Much of the material on the effects of accounting techniques deals with changes in such techniques. This seems like a natural approach. If changes in techniques are not important, then—all other things unchanged—neither the old nor the new techniques can be any more important than the other.

We shall not present or discuss the mechanics of alternative accounting techniques (e.g., alternative depreciation procedures, etc.). That task is adequately handled by most standard financial accounting texts. Our primary concern is with the implications of those alternative techniques for financial statement analysis and, more generally, for capital market equilibrium.

We present arguments based on various perspectives in order to provide a variety of insights on accounting techniques. Some of our arguments are based on the perspective of an individual agent involved in financial statement analysis, which is a type of information-production activity. Other arguments are based on the vantage point of one who chooses accounting procedures for a firm or one who regulates such choices. A question that might be asked by such a person is: "What are the probable effects of my choice of techniques on the equilibrium value of a particular firm or the equilibrium values of firms in general?" Such a question can be attacked by adopting a somewhat global perspective of the capital market and the market for information.

We shall deal with the accounting techniques that firms voluntarily adopt and the rules and regulations about techniques promulgated by, e.g., the SEC and the FASB. These rules and regulations pertain to selections of techniques as well as disclosures pertaining to firms' selected techniques. In our view, the decisions made by such regulatory bodies can be viewed simply as decisions imposed upon firms.

Parts of our discussions of available empirical work are somewhat technical. These discussions deal with results, methods, theoretical underpinnings, and problems encountered in empirical work. The subsections dealing with methods and theoretical underpinnings will probably be "rough going" for some. But the reader should at least skim through these sections so as to gain some familiarity with the material covered there. As always, the name of the game is "best efforts."

6.2 Some Perspective on Accounting Procedures: Review of Salient Points

Accounting numbers (e.g., "income," "sales," "depreciation") are viewed as random variables.[1] The observed values (or realizations) of these variables are the reported values found in, for example, published annual reports, filings with the SEC, filings with the IRS, and responses to the Department of Commerce's data requests (such as its questionnaires on inventories, sales, and plant and equipment expenditures). The stochastic properties of a given firm's accounting numbers—e.g., the numbers' expected values, variances, and autocorrelation functions—depend, in general, on the economic environment, the firm's production-investment and financing decisions, and the firms accounting techniques.[2] Since the economic environment is a determinant of the attributes of firms' decisions, we can simply say that the stochastic properties of a firm's accounting numbers are jointly determined by its accounting techniques and the attributes of its decisions.

We are interested in accounting numbers to the extent that their systematic properties provide bases for making inferences about the substantive economic attributes of firms' operations. Treating accounting numbers as if they do provide such bases presumes that

---

[1]Random variables with degenerate distribution functions (and thus "deterministic" variables) are not precluded.

[2]"Stochastic" properties, "time series" properties, and "systematic" properties will be used interchangeably. We shall use these descriptions when referring to aspects of the entire probability model that applies to a particular process. A "stationary first-order autoregressive process with a normally distributed disturbance" is an example of such a probability model. Note, in particular, that "systematic" properties, as that description is used herein, are not synonymous with the description "permanent" component, a description often encountered in empirical economics. The latter description is often used in, for example, work on consumer expenditures, where a distinction is often drawn between the "permanent" and "transitory" components of income.

The behavior of competitors, the constraints imposed by legislation, the rules enforced by regulatory agencies, and the constraints of "generally accepted accounting principles" are subsumed into "the economic environment."

Throughout, we assume that the disclosed observed values of accounting numbers are, in fact, the values defined by whatever accounting techniques were selected by or imposed upon firms' managements. That is, we assume that managements "honestly" disclose the results of applying these techniques—given that they decide (or are compelled) to make such disclosures.

there is some structural model connecting accounting numbers—viewed as observable indicators—to observable and unobservable attributes of firms' decisions.

The specific attributes of firms' decisions that are important for any given exercise in financial statement analysis depends on the exercise's objectives. But the specific objectives notwithstanding, a major assumption is that changes in the systematic properties of firms' accounting numbers are primarily induced by changes in the identified relevant attributes of firms' decisions. Similarly, differences among the systematic properties of different firms' numbers are assumed to be largely due to differences among those relevant attributes of firms' decisions.

However, accounting techniques (e.g., inventory-costing methods and depreciation procedures) provide the computational specifications of accounting numbers. Consequently, they also can affect accounting numbers systematic properties, just as the procedures used to compute the "Consumer Price Index" and "the money supply" are determinants of the latter series' systematic, or "time series," properties. As a result, some changes in the properties of individual firms' accounting numbers may be induced by changes in their accounting methods and not by changes in any relevant attributes of their decisions. Alternatively, some changes in those attributes may not produce detectable changes in the systematic properties of accounting numbers because of interactions between the effects of accounting techniques and the attributes of firms' decisions. The same may hold for differences among the systematic properties of different firms' accounting numbers. That is, some may not be due to differences among the attributes of the different firms' decisions, whereas some differences among those attributes may not produce detectable differences among the systematic properties of the different firms' accounting numbers.

The importance of accounting techniques is increased by the possibility of their actually influencing the attributes of firms' decisions, rather than just interacting or combining with attributes of independently made decisions in the determination of accounting numbers' properties. Several reasons for expecting such an influence are discussed below. By way of preview, we give one example here. First, assume that part of a management's total compensation is provided by a "profit-sharing" or "incentive" plan that links management's compensation to its firm's performance as measured by accounting numbers (e.g., income numbers). Second, assume that the accounting techniques used to compute the values of these numbers are fixed, so that the probability distribution of the plan's payoffs is fixed once the attributes of the firm's decisions are given. In this situation, management's decisions may differ from those it would make under a different specification of accounting techniques because of the given techniques' effects on accounting numbers' properties and, therefore, the given techniques' effects on the probability distribution of management's total compensation. If changes in accounting techniques are imposed on management, then it may—for the same reason—change its decisions.

Of course, connections between managements' decisions and accounting techniques may lead to managements' selecting techniques in ways that depend upon their decisions whenever they can exercise control over firms' accounting techniques. Thus, given a connection between accounting techniques and, say, the terms of pension/incentive plans and given the attributes of managements' operating and financing decisions, managements' selected accounting techniques may differ from what they would have been given different attributes of their operating and financing decisions. And if the latter attributes change, managements may be motivated to change their accounting techniques.

As will be seen, a wide variety of connections may prevail between accounting techniques and firms' decisions.[3] Some may seem quite complicated. But the basic point should be clear. Accounting techniques are, in general, among the determinants of accounting numbers' systematic properties both because these techniques constitute accounting numbers' computational specifications and because there may be connections between these techniques and managements' decisions.

Before we move on, two additional points are worth noting. First, much of what we shall say deals entirely with assessing the *effects* of accounting techniques. Assessing the *desirability* of alternative techniques is quite a different matter. And it is this latter assessment that is one of the major tasks facing regulatory agencies, like the SEC and the FASB. Desirability assessments are often based on assessments of effects. Nevertheless, the two types of assessments are different and the tools adequate for one type may be inadequate for the other.

Second, the complications introduced by the connections between accounting numbers' properties (e.g., information content) and accounting techniques are not eliminated by imposing "uniformity" on firms' selections of techniques or by observing that firms are already behaving as if uniformity were imposed. Evidently, uniformity simply results in most firms' using the same techniques—such as the expensing technique for Research and Development Costs (required by FASB *Statement No. 2*). For a given firm, this does not, by itself, imply that changes in the systematic properties of the firm's accounting numbers are primarily induced by changes in the substantive characteristics of the firm's decisions. Nor does it, by itself, imply that differences among the properties of different firms' numbers can be largely ascribed to any differences among the substantive attributes of firms' decisions. In the latter situation, the effects of interactions between accounting techniques and the attributes of firms' decisions may differ as a result of the different attributes.

Since accounting techniques affect the characteristics of sample evidence—via their effects on the properties of accounting numbers—we can treat selections of accounting techniques as types of information-production decisions. These decisions are made by or imposed upon firms. In any event, when viewed in this light, it is natural to ask questions similar to those asked about other kinds of production decisions. These questions include the following: (1) What costs are incurred in pursuing the adopted decision? (2) What motivated the final decision? (3) Are there any external effects (i.e., social costs and/or benefits) not incorporated into the private costs and benefits of the decision-making unit? (4) What are the output consequences of the adopted decision (e.g., what are the characteristics of the sample evidence made available as a result of the information-production decision)? (5) What guidelines are available for making optimal decisions? And (6) Are there perfect substitutes for the sources of information (i.e., the inferential bases) induced by a firm's decisions, or is the firm exploiting resources (tangible or intangible) unavailable to others on the same terms of trade?

The above questions are among those that we shall consider at various points in this chapter. Suffice it to note here that they point to a variety of substantive issues that may surround changes in accounting techniques. Contrary to what might be inferred from con-

[3]See Gonedes [1978] for examples not covered in this chapter and Watts and Zimmerman [1978] for some evidence and a perspective that have motivated a substantial amount of work. A valuable survey of work in this area is given by Holthausen and Leftwich [1983].

ventional accounting and "popular press" discussions, there is more involved here than the possibility of "ulterior" managerial motives—a theme most prevalent in the literature on "managing earnings" (or "income smoothing") and on discretionary changes of accounting techniques. Moreover, contrary to what might be inferred from the latter discussions, the mere fact that a firm does not alter its accounting techniques is no cause for comfort. As is the case with activities other than information-production activities, the mode of production currently in use need not be the best available one, however "best" is defined and from whomever's perspective it is defined (e.g., some individual's versus "society's" perspective).

6.3 Effects of Accounting Changes: First Pass

One question encountered in the economic theory of production is whether there is any discrimination regarding the costs of or the opportunities for production. Alternatively stated, are all opportunities for production equally available to each existing and potential producer on the same terms of trade? A situation in which there might be effective discrimination is where some mode of production is "protected," wholly or partially, by patent restrictions. In this case, agents other than the patent holder may be unable to replicate the patented mode of production. Therefore, the latter is not equally available to each producer on the same terms of trade; there is discrimination with respect to production opportunities. Analogous situations may arise with respect to information-production opportunities.

Suppose, for example, that a particular agent is attempting to assess the implications of a firm's operating decisions for the relative risk of its equity shares. From Chapter 4, we know that the firm's lines of business are determinants of this relative risk. Since the managers of a firm can, as a result of their own decisions, determine the firm's lines of business, one expects these managers to have access to important information about the latter and, thus, about the relative risk of the firm's equity shares. What opportunities does an individual ("outside") agent have for producing information on lines of business? Can those opportunities yield perfect substitutes for the information that can be produced by managers ("insiders"), in the sense that the same inferences are induced? Can those substitutes be produced at the same cost or must an outside agent incur a different cost?

There are a variety of ways of making inferences about a firm's lines of business and the associated implications for relative risk. Several possibilities were discussed in Chapter 4. Each one involved some form of statistical inference, based on sample evidence on accounting numbers or other kinds of random variables. None of these possibilities seems to be exactly equivalent to the information-production opportunities available to our hypothetical manager(s). Moreover, one expects the departure from equivalence to be greater when the firm's line-of-business profile has been or will be changing. Such structural changes make the task of statistical inference quite difficult. In short, this seems to be a type of situation where the information-production opportunities available to one group (insiders and perhaps those with whom they trade information) differ from the opportunities available to another group.

This difference among agents' opportunities implies that a firm's selection of accounting techniques may affect the firm's equilibrium value. Specifically, its choice of techniques dealing with signals pertaining to its lines of business may affect its equilibrium value. This potential exists because firms' equilibrium values are conditional on available information. In the setting considered above, the firm's managers—via their selections of accounting procedures—may affect the kinds of information that are available. Moreover, as was indicated earlier, there are several reasons for expecting managers to be motivated to exercise their control over available information (e.g., reasons that turn on issues of "moral hazard" and "adverse selection"). But this is not the only way that selections of accounting techniques can affect firms' equilibrium values.

As with other kinds of production activities, information-production involves the use of resources (e.g., labor and capital). Thus, if different information-production activities are not equally costly to a given firm, then the firm's information-production decisions will affect the resources consumed by its productive activities. In general, the kinds of information-production activities considered here (i.e., those associated with external accounting) do not yield outputs that induce an inflow of revenues (via sales of output). Thus, these activities' direct effects involve resource usage but not resource acquisition. This feature, taken by itself, induces a decrease in the firm's equilibrium value.[4]

Under some conditions, a firm's information-production decisions may affect the incidence of the aggregate information-production costs incurred by all information producers as well as the value of total costs. Suppose, for example, that the costs of collusion among agents, for the purpose of information-production, are sufficiently high so as to preclude unrestricted collusion. Suppose, in addition, that a signal inferentially equivalent to one that the firm can produce is now being produced by several agents or several distinct groups of colluding agents. Finally, suppose that each "outside" producer's costs are no less than those that the firm would incur if it produced an equivalent signal.

Clearly, if the signal being produced by the outsiders is equivalent to one that the firm can produce—by an appropriate selection of accounting procedures—then the two signals are perfect substitutes in the usual economic sense.[5] If the firm produces the equivalent signal, it will not be necessary for the outsiders to produce their signal.

For the reasons given above, a direct consequence of the firm's decision to produce the equivalent (costly) signal will be a decrease in the firm's equilibrium value, holding other things constant. This decrease implies a decrease in the wealths of the firm's current shareholders. If they were among those originally producing the signal on personal account, then the reduction in their portfolios' values—due to the information-production costs incurred by the firm—will be partially or wholly offset by the reduction in costs incurred on personal account for information-production activities. On the other hand, if some current shareholders are not among the original producers, then some of those experiencing wealth decreases—due to the firm's increased costs—will not be among those experiencing cost reductions on personal account. That is, some of the firm's current shareholders are "subsidizing" other shareholders' information-production activities. Of course, if all firms make decisions of this sort, then every agent may be being subsidized by and he may be subsidizing other agents. In any event, the basic point is unchanged: the firm's choice of accounting techniques may affect the incidence of information-production costs (and thus the distribution of wealth).

Cost incidence is, however, not the only thing that may be affected. First, if the firm's

---

[4]This is a partial effect. We are ignoring here the changes in equilibrium value induced by the information content of the signals produced and announced by the firm, i.e., we are considering only the costs of making those signals available, not the new inferences induced by the signal.

[5]Recall that the output of interest is a conditional distribution function; see Section 6.2.

cost function actually does differ from that of any single outside producer, then the total costs of producing the equivalent signal will be changed if the firm does the producing. Under the assumption made above, the total cost will be reduced.

Second, if—because of imperfect collusion—several outside producers were producing the same signal, then letting the firm do the producing will eliminate some avoidable (and costly) duplication. That is, information production via a firm may serve as a vehicle for more efficient collusion in the production of information. Rather than having each of several outside producers incur the costs of producing the signal, we end up with the firm's incurring those costs once and the agents' getting a signal equivalent to what they would have produced themselves. In short, the output is the same but the total cost of getting that output is reduced.

Of course, the consequences of letting the firm produce an equivalent signal may be the opposite of those indicated above. That is, (1) the firm may not be a more efficient producer of signals or (2) there may not be any avoidable duplication because, for example, the outside agents may not view the firm's signal as equivalent to theirs.[6] But that does not alter our basic point: firms' selections of accounting techniques may alter the total costs incurred for information production as well as the incidence of those costs.

The above scenario points to some reasons for expecting an association between the attributes of firms' information-production activities and firms' equilibrium values. Such an association can arise in yet another way. Specifically, if the signals produced by firms convey information pertinent to establishing firms' values, then revelations of those signals (e.g., realizations of accounting numbers) will be associated with changes in firms' values. In line with our earlier definitions, this is a situation wherein the signals produced by the firm have "information content," in the sense that they alter agents' assessed distributions of returns (because they induce new inferences). Of course, if the information content of a firm's signals is also provided, wholly or partially, via a different signal (produced by the firm or others), then the apparent effect of the firm's information-production decision cannot be ascribed to information uniquely provided as a result of that decision, which may be a decision to alter accounting techniques. One can still assert, however, that the signals produced by the firm have information content, in the sense that they convey information pertinent to establishing its equilibrium value.

Changes in firms' equilibrium values induced by the information content of signals produced by firms should not be confused with the value changes induced by the marginal costs of implementing those decisions. The latter types of changes arise because of the costs of the inputs used for information-production decisions. The first type of change can be ascribed to the outputs of those decisions, *viz.*, the assessed conditional distributions discussed in Chapter 2.

A basic point of the above (somewhat loose) discussion is that changes in accounting techniques—viewed as information-production decisions—can have a variety of substantive economic effects. Some of the potential effects turn on issues of private costs and

---

[6]Agents might, for example, believe that the "quality" of the firm's signal differs from the quality of their signal, in the sense that inferences based on the former are less reliable. Or they might believe that, even if the quality is the same now, it may be different (because of, say, moral hazard and adverse selection issues) if they stop producing their own signal. In order to detect such a quality change, agents might have to incur monitoring costs. The latter are really just information-production costs, where the information produced is about the signal produced by the firm.

benefits; others turn on issues of social costs and benefits. In short, changes in accounting techniques may involve more than cosmetic "bookkeeping" changes. This is easy to see when those changes are treated as types of production decisions.

In view of the above, it seems that a classification scheme for accounting changes would be useful, at least for structuring one's thinking. One such scheme is provided in the next subsection. Many of the basic points made above will reappear, albeit in a more structured way.

6.4 Types of Accounting Changes:[7] A Classification Scheme

A change in the accounting techniques used for external reporting purposes can have an effect on capital market equilibrium because (1) the change leads to the provision of accounting numbers that convey information pertinent to valuing a firm; (2) the change per se (or, more precisely, the act of making the change) has a substantive economic impact independent of the accounting numbers affected by the change in reporting techniques; or (3) the change per se signals other events that have economic importance.

A complete analysis of the second type of change leads naturally to issues of so-called signaling behavior. We shall devote considerable attention to this issue and its many ramifications in Chapter 8.

In order to deal with issues of immediate interest, one can use the following classification scheme for types of accounting changes.

(T.1) A change in the techniques used for external reporting (one result of a firm's information-production decisions) that does not affect the information-production costs incurred by the firm or the information-production decisions and/or costs of agents external to the firm.

(T.2) A change having the properties of (T.1) except that it does affect a firm's information-production costs.

(T.3) A change having the properties of (T.1) except that it does affect the information-production decisions and/or costs of agents external to the firm.

(T.4) A change in the techniques used for external reporting that is, for whatever reason, associated with a change in some other aspect of a firm's production-investment activities.

(T.5) A change in the accounting techniques used for tax reporting.

The above types are neither exhaustive nor mutually exclusive; e.g., a change of type (T.1) may also be of type (T.4). But this list of types will suffice for our purposes.

If a change is only of type (T.1), then the change per se will have no effect on equilibrium prices. But the accounting numbers produced by the new technique may affect those prices. They will (not) do so if the information conveyed by those numbers is (not) pertinent to valuing firms, insofar as capital market agents are concerned.[8] If this information is also being provided by a different source, then the apparent effect of the ac-

---

[7]See Gonedes and Dopuch [1974] for a further discussion and rationale for using this classification of accounting changes.

[8]As always, whenever we say that accounting numbers "convey information" or "have information content," we mean that some observed values of those numbers have implications (or induce inferences) that influence assessed distribution functions of securities' future values. The different ways in which signals can substitute for or complement each other—with respect to their implications—are discussed in Chapter 8.

counting change really cannot be ascribed to information uniquely associated with the numbers produced via the new reporting technique. One can still assert, however, that these numbers have information content, in the sense that they convey information pertinent to valuing a firm.

A change of type (T.2) also conveys information pertinent to valuing a firm. In this case, however, part or all of the change's information content is due to its implications about the resources required for implementation or the firm's information-production decisions, a subset of the firm's production-investment decisions.

A type (T.5) change is similar to a type (T.2) change in the sense that it conveys information on a firm's real resources and, thus, information pertinent to valuing the firm. In the case of a type (T.5) change, however, the information content of the change is attributable to its implications for tax purposes, rather than information-production costs or the accounting numbers produced by the new reporting technique. Of course, some changes can be simultaneously of, for example, type (T.1) and (T.5) or (T.2) and (T.5).

A change of type (T.3) can affect capital-market equilibrium because it affects the opportunities available to external agents for information-production on personal account or because it induces those agents to alter their information-production activities. We consider the second possibility first.

Suppose that a change in accounting techniques provides numbers that do convey information pertinent to valuing a firm and suppose that these numbers were previously being produced by agents on personal account. If the firm's provision of these numbers induces agents to cease producing them on personal account, then the accounting change will have induced a change in the incidence of information-production costs and thus the distribution of wealth. This redistribution of wealth can alter the details of capital market equilibrium, and perhaps equilibria in other markets.[9]

Similar consequences can characterize the first possibility. Suppose that some types of accounting numbers are inputs to capital market agents' decision models. Further suppose that (a) the currently used accounting techniques are such that accounting numbers can be converted to numbers based on any set of alternative techniques at a trivial cost; (b) each of the conversions noted in (a) is required by at least one capital market agent's decision model; and (c) the costs of converting to numbers conditional on current techniques from numbers conditional on any alternative set of techniques are quite sizable. Next, suppose that all firms switch their accounting techniques. In this case, and assuming (for simplicity) no changes in decision models, the firms' decisions affect the costs borne by, and thus the wealths of, some capital market agents. This is, of course, an extreme example, but it illustrates another change of type (T.3).

Note that our type (T.3) category does not preclude an effect by one firm on available information-production opportunities. This situation is consistent with capital market efficiency. To be sure, if one firm's actions do affect the opportunities available in a given market, then that market is not perfect. But we are talking about the market for information, not the capital market. The latter market can be fully perfect even though the former is not. See Chapter 3 for a detailed discussion of the market for information.

If the change is of type (T.4), it can have an effect even though (1) the numbers

---

[9]An extensive analysis of the relationship between private and public information-production decisions is given in Gonedes [1980].

produced by the change convey no information pertinent to valuing a firm and (2) the costs and decisions mentioned in (T.1) are unaffected. This can occur when the change provides signals about other events that are not devoid of economic substance. The "effect" of this type of accounting change is analogous to the "effect" of dividend policy changes in a perfect capital market. Within such a market, dividend policy changes per se have no effect on the equilibrium value of a firm. However, if dividend policy changes are used by management as a device for disseminating information about the firm's prospects, then such changes can affect the equilibrium value of the firm because of the new information indirectly provided via the changes, and not because of the changes themselves. With respect to accounting changes, this kind of situation can arise when, e.g., different accounting techniques are highly associated with different industries. In this case, a change in accounting technique can serve as an indication of a change in a firm's industry membership and the risk of that firm's ownership shares.

The distinguishing feature of a type (T.4) change is its association (perhaps coincidental) with some other aspect(s) of a firm's decisions or activities (e.g., a change in management's plans or forecasts or a change in industry membership). If such an association exists, then changes in accounting techniques may be associated with changes in securities' equilibrium prices because of the association between the changes in the techniques and the other aspects of a firm's activities. Whether agents use the changes in accounting techniques as their source of information (i.e., their "signal") about those other aspects is, of course, an entirely different matter—and an irrelevant one at this point. Also irrelevant is whether managements *intended* to have their decisions about accounting techniques used as sources of information.

6.5 Some Possible Substantive Reasons for Changes in Accounting Techniques

6.5.1 Preliminaries

In Sections 6.3 and 6.4 we focused on the potential effects of accounting changes. At this point, it seems worthwhile to consider some factors that might motivate changes in accounting techniques. One frequently mentioned factor is a desire to get investors to assign a higher value to the firm, even though there may be no substantive reasons for doing so. This has often been the reason given by, e.g., analysts and accountants when a firm switches to, say, the straight-line depreciation method from an accelerated method for only external reporting or when a firm switches from immediate expensing of the costs of intangibles to a method involving capitalization and amortization of those costs over several periods. Such reasoning is illustrated by the following excerpt, which relates to several steel firms' switches to straight-line depreciation (for external reporting) at a time (in the 1960s) when larger depreciation expense numbers would have been induced by an accelerated method:

> For steel executives, the next best thing to import quotas would be a surge in their companies' stock prices. Because of, relatively low prices and fat cash flows, all but a few of the giants in the industry are ripe for take-overs.
>
> To attract investors who have let steel rust for the last four years, companies are switching accounting methods. Instead of putting the depreciation of new equipment on the books the accelerated way, which lops more off reported earnings in early years, steel is finally following other industries in adopting the straight-line method.

> By averaging out depreciation costs on a straight yearly basis, per-share earnings get a quick boost—and it's perfectly legal, Washington concedes, because it doesn't affect tax liability.
>
> Though they may be just playing with numbers, steelmen hope all this will make their stocks more attractive to investors, and boost price/earnings ratios. Other companies not so worried about take-over attempts still want to compare favorably with the rest of the industry. So, they're going along with the accounting change.[10]

The same type of perspective seems to have motivated the following suggestions for analyzing firms' annual reports to stockholders:

> Glance through the financial footnotes for changes in accounting policies during the year. A switch from accelerated to straight-line depreciation or a change from the LIFO to the FIFO method of evaluating inventories will boost otherwise flat or falling earnings.
>
> ***
>
> Pore over the company's statement of accounting policies, now required in annual reports, and try to determine how big a chunk of a company's major costs—money spent for research and development, advertising, promotion, training or engineering—the company is capitalizing. A company can buy time by deferring these costs to future years. The current earnings will look more rosy, but essentially these items represent deferred costs rather than genuine assets.[11]

Note that the kinds of changes mentioned in the above excerpts have "bookkeeping" effects that can be rather easily assessed, at least in a qualitative way. Indeed, the articles excerpted above purport to provide such assessments and these articles seem to suggest that the implications of some changes are unambiguous. Moreover, the fact that a firm switched its accounting techniques is disclosed—in the footnotes to its financial statements and/or in the auditor's report on those statements.[12]

In short, the above excerpts—which are not atypical—seem to be dealing with public data and announcements that are performed to have unambiguous implications. Conditional on this presumption, it is difficult to accept the argument that the purely mechanical (or "bookkeeping") effects of accounting changes will, *taken by themselves,* induce changes in firms' equilibrium values. This is a scenario for which one can expect publicly available data to be fully and correctly used—which includes ignoring irrelevant data.

The evidence provided by Leftwich [1983] is consistent with our view, at least insofar as the capital market is concerned. His evidence deals with borrowers and lenders engaged in private placements. This evidence is consistent with the claim that at least this group of capital market agents (which includes firms' managements) understand existing accounting rules and the substantive effects of changes in those rules. Indeed, his results indicate that these agents often devised and used modified versions of external accounting

---

[10] "Shining up Steel Stocks," *Business Week* (November 2, 1968).

[11] "The Quality of Earnings Is Under Attack," *Business Week* (December 23, 1972), p. 76.

[12] Recently adopted disclosure rules dealing with accounting changes will be discussed later. These rules require more than just footnote disclosures.

As always, "materiality" issues may affect the nature of the disclosures.

rules (i.e., Generally Accepted Accounting Principles) when formulating the terms of debt coverants. And, Leftwich argues that there seems to be substantive economic justifications for the modifications that he observed. It is difficult to believe that agents who are sufficiently sophisticated to alter existing external accounting rules to accommodate lending arguments are not also sophisticated enough to understand the substantive implications of accounting changes made by firms for the preparation of general purpose financial reports.

Conditional on our arguments (and our interpretations), it is difficult to accept (or even understand) the view that managements really expect purely cosmetic accounting changes, by themselves, to induce changes in firms' equilibrium values.[13] In this regard, it is, of course, important to distinguish between (1) what managements really expect and their actual reasons for making accounting changes and (2) what managements say they expect (or expected) and what they advertise as their reasons.

In any event, we are still left with the question: what motivates changes in accounting techniques? Several (of the many possible) reasons are discussed in the next section. Before getting to that, however, we note that this general area of "accounting choice" has been the subject of substantial research effort within the past few years. The primary objective of this recent work is to examine voluntary and mandatory choices of accounting procedures from the perspective of rational economic behavior. To date, the available theoretical analyses in this area seem somewhat limited. Yet, it appears to be one of the more fruitful areas of research on external accounting. A timely and extensive review of this work is provided by Holthausen and Leftwich [1983].

6.5.2 Consistency with SEC Disclosure Rules and Preferences

One obvious and mundane reason for making accounting changes is to attain consistency with the Securities and Exchange Commission's (SEC's) disclosure rules and tastes. One of the SEC's rules requires that filings with the SEC and published statements be prepared in accordance with "generally accepted accounting principles."

Both the Securities Act of 1933 and the Securities Exchange Act of 1934 give the SEC ultimate authority over the accounting procedures used to prepare filings with the SEC. For example, Section 13-2(b) of the 1934 Act states the following with respect to reports required by the SEC:

> The Commission may prescribe . . . the form or forms in which the required information shall be set forth, the item or details to be shown in the balance sheet and the earnings statement, and the methods to be followed in the preparation of reports, in the appraisal or valuation of assets and liabilities, in the determination of depreciation and depletion, in the differentiation of investment and operating income, and in the preparation, where the Commission deems it necessary or desirable, of separate and/or consolidated balance sheets or income accounts of any person directly or indirectly controlling or controlled by the issuer, or any person under direct or indirect common control with the issuer. . . .

For the most part, the SEC has relied upon "generally accepted accounting principles" (GAAP), rather than prescribing its own set of acceptable accounting procedures. In this

---

[13]This is the type of reasoning often used in the literature on so-called income smoothing. An analysis of this activity—including its feasibility—is given in Gonedes [1972].

regard, the importance of GAAP was concisely emphasized in an SEC release entitled "Administrative Policy on Financial Statements" (issued on April 25, 1938):

> In all cases where financial statements filed with this Commission pursuant to its rules and regulations under the Securities Act of 1933 or the Securities Exchange Act of 1934 are prepared in accordance with accounting principles for which there is no substantial authoritative support, such financial statements will be presumed to be misleading or inaccurate despite disclosures contained in the certificate of the accountant or in footnotes to the statements provided the matters involved are material. In cases where there is a difference of opinion between the Commission and the registrant as to the proper principles of accounting to be filed, disclosure will be accepted in lieu of corrections of the financial statements themselves only if the points involved are such that there is substantial authoritative support for the practices followed by the registrant and the position of the Commission has not previously been expressed in rules, regulations, or other official releases of the Commission, including the published opinions of its chief accountant.

This release provided no definition of "substantial authoritative support." At and after the time of this release's issuance, it was widely recognized that the SEC chose to rely heavily on the accounting profession for the development of accounting principles having such support.[14] It appears, however, that pronouncements of official accounting bodies were not the only sources of "substantial authoritative support" (see Rappaport [1972, pp. 2.8–2.9]).

In its *Accounting Series Release No. 150* (issued on December 20, 1973), the SEC specifically stated that the FASB's Statements and Interpretations will be considered "substantial authoritative support" for accounting procedures used in filings with the SEC. As indicated in Chapter 4 there may be differences between filings with the SEC and accounting reports to shareholders, which are heavily influenced by the pronouncements of the Accounting Principles Board and the FASB. Any important differences are supposed to be explained by management.

It is well to note, however, that the SEC's current program for an "integrated disclosure system" may reduce the extent to which such differences prevail. As indicated in one analysis of this program:

> . . . The SEC has now mandated that the primary financial statements in the annual report to shareholders must conform to Regulation S-X. Previously, differences in the form and content between the financials in the annual report to shareholders and those in the 10-K were allowed, provided the differences were disclosed in a note to the financials in the shareholders report and provided the differences were not substantive.[15]

Of course, even if a firm uses a "generally accepted accounting procedure," the SEC may find its filings unacceptable. The SEC may argue that a particular procedure used by

---

[14]See, e.g., Sommer [1974] and Loomis [1974]. Sommer and Loomis are currently Commissioners of the SEC.

[15]Touche Ross & Co. [1980, p. 8]. Regulation S-X mandates the form and content of the audited primary financial statements included in documents filed with the SEC under the Securities Act of 1933 and the Securities Exchange Act of 1934.

a specific firm induces "misleading" results because of the nature of the firm's activities.

The point of the above is this: if a firm wants to begin or continue to have its securities publicly traded, it must adopt accounting techniques acceptable to the SEC—or be prepared to defend any departures from what the SEC views as acceptable. Changes in what the SEC deems acceptable or in the departures that it will tolerate (for all firms or a specific firm) may induce a firm to change its accounting techniques, independent of any substantive changes in the firm's economic attributes.

The above discussion points to a reason for accounting changes that is tied to an aspect of the contemporary institutional framework. Some other relevant aspects of this framework pertain to profit-sharing or "incentive" plans, bond indentures, and exposure to antitrust actions (initiated by the Federal Trade Commission or the Department of Justice). These other aspects are discussed below.

6.5.3 Profit-Sharing and Incentive Plans

Part of the total compensation received by many corporate officers is dependent upon their firms' performance as measured by accounting numbers—particularly income numbers.[16] A somewhat typical footnote description of such a plan is as follows:[17]

> The Company has a Key Personnel Incentive Profit Sharing Plan under which compensation contingent upon consolidated income is provided for key personnel, including officers. A provision of $10,577,000 ($12,076,000 in 1972) has been charged against income in anticipation of the distribution of the profit sharing fund in cash and shares of Goodyear common stock.

In general, the provisions of these kinds of plans do not specify the accounting procedures to be used in computing the realizations of accounting numbers used as bases for compensation awards, except perhaps for a restriction to "generally accepted accounting procedures." This implies that there are at least two ways of changing the probability distributions of payoffs facing the plans' beneficiaries. First, the basic provisions of the plan can be altered; this involves renegotiating contract provisions. Such changes may require stockholder approval and a review by the Internal Revenue Service. Second, the firm can alter its accounting techniques. The specific route that a firm follows will depend on a variety of factors, such as the effects of accounting techniques on accounting numbers other than those used by compensation plans and the extent to which a compensation plan's beneficiaries are among those who influence a firm's selections of accounting techniques. It is still the case, however, that changes in accounting techniques are among the tools that can be used to alter the probability distributions of payoffs to corporate personnel. Thus, executive compensation plans' attributes may motivate some changes in accounting techniques. The increased use of "performance plans" during the past 15 years or so—which essentially involve common stock bonuses based entirely on accounting income (or related) numbers—seems to have given this possibility added importance.[18]

---

[16]See, e.g., Lewellen [1968; 1971]. (National Bureau of Economic Research, 1971).

[17]From the Goodyear Tire and Rubber Co. Annual Report for the year ended December 31, 1973 (p. 6). A more detailed description is provided on p. 36 of this report.

[18]A brief description of "performance plans" is given in "Performance Shares: Popular—But Under Fire," *Business Week* (May 5, 1973), p. 56.

The fact that a firm uses changes in accounting techniques rather than a route requiring stockholder approval does not imply an attempt to "fool" anybody. As is the case with all voting and negotiation procedures, obtaining stockholder approval is costly—for both the stockholder and the managers. Effecting changes in incentive plans' payoffs by changing techniques may be less costly and no less acceptable to all parties affected by the change.[19]

6.5.4 Exposure to Anti-Trust Actions

The arguments underlying anti-trust actions are often based on studies that use reported accounting numbers, for example, the various industry studies conducted by the staff of the Federal Trade Commission. Many of them deal with analyses of profitability—as measured by accounting numbers—and market structure variables, such as "concentration ratios." Presumably, the FTC believes that a case built on an analysis of actual data is stronger than one not based on an analysis of that sort.

The stochastic properties of accounting numbers are, however, dependent upon accounting techniques. Thus, the results of studies that use accounting numbers are affected by those techniques. This implies that a firm can affect an analysis based on its accounting numbers via its choice of accounting techniques. A group of firms (acting, for example, through a trade association) can affect analyses based on aggregations of their accounting numbers via its members' choices of accounting techniques. Of course, if these kinds of factors do motivate changes in accounting techniques, it is unlikely that the changes will be defined in terms of those factors.

To be sure, the fellows at the FTC and the Department of Justice are not oblivious to these possibilities. Suppose, however, that the firms' selections of accounting techniques—however justified—were deemed acceptable by the accounting profession (via its GAAP), by the SEC, and perhaps by the IRS, (if the techniques affect tax reporting). In this case, the *anti-trust-agencies* may have difficulty arguing in court that the firms' accounting techniques are "unacceptable" and, in particular, that those techniques disguise the effects of "anti-competitive behavior." Indeed, given the ambiguous nature of GAAP's underpinnings, there may be no rigorous grounds for declaring any set of techniques to be "unacceptable."

Nor is the effect of accounting techniques on profitability/market-structure studies ignored by academic researchers. It was, for example, identified as a potentially serious problem in the extensive survey of the literature on profitability and concentration provided by Weiss [1974]. The accounting methods used for research and development expenditures, advertising expenditures, and the effects of inflation are usually singled out as problem areas. For the most part, the proposed remedies involve recommended changes in GAAP, so as to constrain managements' selections of accounting techniques.

The debate over the FTC's now defunct "line-of-business" (LOB) reporting program illustrates the importance of accounting techniques in anti-trust matters. In effect, the FTC sought to impose accounting techniques on firms. These techniques were to be used in LOB reports submitted to the FTC. The FTC claimed that the techniques used by firms

---

[19]Additional remarks on connections between accounting numbers and management compensation plans can be found in Larcker [1983].

for other types of LOB reporting (in, e.g., SEC filings and annual reports) do not yield numbers useful to the FTC. Not unexpectedly, several large firms affected by the FTC's rules—and some prominent accounting firms—voiced loud opposition to the FTC's imposing accounting techniques for LOB reporting. In their view, the LOB numbers reported by firms in accordance with the techniques that they choose—subject to the SEC's somewhat mild rules—are adequate for the FTC's purposes.[20] The FTC and several large firms actually fought about this issue in court. The FTC's reporting program was ultimately upheld, though not in its original form. But this may turn out to be "beside the point." As of January 1982, the FTC suspended collecting LOB data for years after 1977. It will complete its work on the 1977 data and then determine whether its LOB program is "cost justified" and, therefore, worthy of being continued.[21]

6.5.5 Bond Indenture Provisions

The provisions of bond indentures may also induce changes in accounting techniques. Such provisions impose various restrictions on firms' production-investment and financing decisions. If these restrictions are violated, default is said to have occurred. Many indentures state that an event of default shall not occur for breach of any covenant until a specified time period has expired. Within this time period, amending the indenture provisions can be considered. Some amendments can be made by mutual agreement of the obligor and the bond trustee. Others require approval by a specified percentage of the securityholders (often 66 2/3 percent). Of course, if the debt was privately placed, there may be no trustee. In this case, the obligor and the securityholders bargain directly over such matters.[22]

Many indenture restrictions on firms' production-investment and financing decisions are expressed in terms of accounting numbers—e.g., current ratios, debt/equity ratios, and ratios involving fixed assets and total assets. The properties of these random variables are, in general, affected by firms' accounting techniques. For example, the properties of current ratios are, in general, affected by firms' inventory-accounting methods. Consequently, the probability of violating an indenture covenant—and thus being in default—is affected by firms' accounting techniques. A firm that is confident of violating a covenant dealing with, say, its current ratio might find a change in inventory-accounting techniques highly attractive.

To be sure, the holders of the securities covered by the indenture will probably not be ignorant of accounting techniques' effects. But they may not disapprove of an accounting change if they would have been willing to renegotiate the covenant whose violation is at issue. Not raising any "flak" about the firm's accounting change may be viewed as implying a de facto mutually acceptable amendment. This mode of behavior may not be less acceptable than engaging in the formalities of amending the bond indenture.

---

[20]A summary of the accounting profession's (i.e., the FASB's) proposals for LOB reporting and the FTC's program is provided in Arthur Anderson and Co. [1975]. An "easy-to-read" overview of issues is given in Benston [1975].

[21]See Ernst & Whinney [1982, item #3].

[22]An extensive discussion of bond indenture provisions is given in Kennedy and Landau [1975]. Also relevant is the discussion in Smith and Warner [1979].

As indicated above, there are various rules for amending indentures.[23] These are supposed to be spelled out in the indenture itself. Suppose that changes in the covenants pertaining to relationships among accounting numbers (e.g., current ratios) can only be approved by, say, a majority of the securityholders and suppose that getting this approval—which involves a political process—is costly (because of, e.g., the use of management's time). Also assume that these covenants do not specify the accounting techniques to be used in defining accounting numbers. Finally, assume that management acts so as to further the equityholders' interests. Under these conditions the incentive for management to use accounting techniques so as to avoid an event of default and costly negotiations with bondholders seem obvious. Moreover, the existence of these incentives does not imply that bondholders are irrational or that management is attempting to "fool" anybody.

Presumably, the specifics of indenture covenants arise from bargaining—via an impersonal pricing mechanism or direct negotiations (as with "private placements"). In either case, the final set of convenants must be acceptable to all parties when the securities are issued, conditional on the price being paid for the borrowed dollars and the information then available to each consenting person. If the indenture convenants permit (or at least do not preclude) managements' use of accounting techniques to avoid an event of default, then one can assume that such an arrangement was—at the time of the bonds' issuance—understood by and acceptable to the parties involved. Of course, if this type of arrangement leads to unforeseen outcomes, then the price of having such an arrangement in future indentures may change, other things being equal. Also, the obligor may find that the willingness of the trustee and/or the securityholders to grant amendments pertaining to other matters is affected by the obligor's use of accounting techniques.

6.5.6 Management Changes

The occurrence of management changes—via takeover, mergers, retirements, resignations, etc.—may also lead to accounting changes.[24] For example, when two or more entities are brought under common management via a merger, the managers of the new combined entity may decide that their objectives are best served when the combining entities' accounting numbers are defined by the same accounting techniques. Presumably, this decision will be conditional on the foreseen production-investment activities of the combined entity (e.g., the industry in which it will operate). Of course, these managers might also decide that—given their planned decisions—different accounting techniques are warranted for combining entities that previously used the same techniques. In any event, the business combination may lead to accounting changes motivated by the new common management's view of the world and not because of some "ulterior motive." Since selections of accounting techniques involve matters of taste and perspective rather than implementation of an unambiguous pristine theory, this possibility should not be surprising.

---

[23]One seemingly general rule is that any provision that does not affect a substantive right of the securityholders may be added by mutual agreement of the obligor and the trustee without the consent of the securityholders. See Kennedy and Landau [1975, p. 34].

[24]Some prior evidence on accounting changes and changes in management is provided by Eggleton, Penman, and Twombly [1975] and Moore [1973].

6.5.7 Remarks

The point of the above discussion is not to provide an actual explanation of any particular accounting change. Rather, its purpose is (1) to identify a variety of substantive factors that may motivate accounting changes and (2) to emphasize that those effecting accounting changes (i.e., management) need not be attempting to "fool" investors by using accounting acrobatics. Since accounting changes (and often their effects) are disclosed, one wonders whether the "attempt to fool" argument is taken very seriously. It might make sense if the issues involved turned on information over which management had monopolistic control and, thus, management's opportunities and incentives for producing distorted information. But those who seem to espouse the "attempt to fool" argument place no such restrictions on their arguments.

6.6 Disclosure Rules Dealing with Accounting Techniques

6.6.1 Preliminaries

This section briefly reviews several pronouncements that have an important effect on disclosures about accounting procedures. The objective of this review is to identify the kinds of data that one can expect to find in firms' published financial statements. For the most part, the review deals with three pronouncements: (1) *APB Opinion NO. 20* (issued July 1971), which deals with disclosures about *changes* in accounting techniques, among other things; (2) *APB Opinion No. 22* (issued April 1972), which deals with disclosures about the important accounting techniques selected by a firm; and (3) *FASB Statement No. 3* (issued December 1974), which deals with disclosures about accounting changes in interim reports.[25]

Before the issuance of these pronouncements, the SEC's filing requirements and the AICPA's auditing standards provided the important disclosure rules dealing with procedures. The disclosure rules induced by the latter were based on the auditing standard of "consistent application of generally accepted accounting principles." This standard is allegedly imposed "to give assurance that the comparability of financial statements as between periods has not been materially affected by changes in the accounting principles employed or in the method of their application . . ." (AICPA [1963, p. 42]). It was argued that "if comparability has been materially affected by such changes," then the firm must provide "a statement of the nature of the changes and their effects on the financial statements" (AICPA [1963, p. 42]).

Prior to the issuance of *APB Opinion No. 22*, the extent and nature of disclosures (in published financial reports) about firms' important accounting procedures varied considerably across firms. There were, however, some specific reporting requirements imposed by the SEC on filings with it—specifically, Rules 3-07 and 3-08 of Regulation S-X. For example, methods of inventory valuation and depreciation methods had to be disclosed in those filings.[26]

---

[25]Since the rules imposed by the pronouncements are now parts of GAAP, they affect firms' filings with the SEC as well as disclosures in published financial statements. The SEC's reliance on GAAP was discussed earlier.

[26]It is well to note that all filings with the SEC are available for use by the public unless the SEC makes a specific grant of confidentiality, which is rare.

The basic thrust of the three pronouncements identified above (as well as the corresponding changes in the requirements for SEC filings) is to reduce firms' flexibility in determining what has to be disclosed about procedures and how the disclosures are to be made. For example, *APB Opinion No. 20* requires that managements provide justification for changes in accounting techniques. They were not required to do this before *Opinion No. 20* took effect. Indeed, *SAP No. 33* explicitly stated that "the reason for [a] change [from one principle to another] need not be stated" (AICPA [1963, p. 43]).

6.6.2 APB Opinion No. 20: Accounting Changes (Effective for Fiscal Year Beginning after July 31, 1971)

In general an "accounting change" involves some alteration in reporting methods that is believed to affect the "comparability" of the financial statements issued by a firm for different time periods. In *Opinion No. 20*, an accounting change is defined to include a change in any of the following: (1) an accounting principle (or the method of applying it); (2) an accounting estimate; or (3) the reporting entity. The *Opinion* recognizes that the third type of change is one type of change of accounting principle. Also, the *Opinion* discusses corrections of errors that affected previously issued financial statements. Such corrections are not considered to be "accounting changes."

Some examples of a change in accounting principles are (1) a change in the method of inventory valuation from, say, FIFO to LIFO; (2) a change in the method used to compute depreciation expense, such as a change from the straight-line method to an accelerated method; and (3) a change from 100 percent expensing of advertising expenditures in the year of the expenditure to capitalization and subsequent amortization at a rate less than 100 percent.

Changes in accounting estimates include changes in the estimated service lives or salvage values of depreciable assets, changes in the estimated amounts of uncollectible receivables, and changes in the estimated costs of fulfilling warranty obligations.

The *Opinion* recognized that a change in an accounting estimate may not be easily distinguished from a change in an accounting principle.[27] It notes, as an example, that a firm might switch from capitalizing a cost and amortizing it over several periods to immediate expensing because of revised estimates of "future benefits." In this case, the new accounting method is adopted in recognition of the changed estimates. The APB concluded that:

> Changes of this type are often related to the continuing process of obtaining additional information and revising estimates and are therefore considered as changes in estimates for purposes of applying this Opinion. (*APB Opinion No. 20*, ¶ No. 11.)

A change of reporting entity occurs when, for example, consolidated financial statements are presented in lieu of statements for individual firms or when there is a change in the set of subsidiaries for which consolidated financial statements are provided. *Opinion No. 20* states that a business combination accounted for as a pooling of interests should also be considered as a change in the reporting entity.

---

[27]Nor is it clear that the distinction between "accounting errors" and "changes in accounting estimates" is unambiguous.

Corrections of errors involve factors that may seem similar to those underlying accounting changes—in particular, changes in accounting estimates. *Opinion No. 20* asserts the following distinction:

> Errors in financial statements result from mathematical mistakes, mistakes in the application of accounting principles, or oversight or misuse of facts that existed at the time financial statements were prepared. In contrast, a change in accounting estimate results from new information or subsequent developments and accordingly from better insight or improved judgment. . . . A change from an accounting principle that is not generally accepted to one that is generally accepted is a correction of an error for purposes of applying [Opinion No. 20]. (*APB Opinion No. 20*, ¶13.)

In general, *Opinion No. 20* requires a company to justify an accounting change and to disclose the nature and effects of a change in financial statements prepared for the period during which the change was made. The specific reporting requirements are summarized in Exhibit 6-1.

EXHIBIT 6-1

SUMMARY OF *APB OPINION NO. 20*'s REPORTING REQUIREMENTS

Types of Changes	Required Reporting	Paragraphs of APBO No. 20 that Indicate the Required Reporting
I. Change in accounting principle		
A. General changes	Cumulative effect of the change in accounting principle to the beginning of the period should be separately shown in the income statement following extraordinary items but before net income in the year of change.	15–28
B. Special changes 1. Change from LIFO to another inventory method 2. Change in accounting for long-term construction contracts 3. Change to or from "full cost" method of accounting in extractive industries	Retroactive restatement	27–28
C. Special exemption for initial public filing	Restatement is optional	30
II. Change in entities	Retroactive restatement	34–35
III. Change in estimate	Current and future periods only. (No restatement unless conditions are met for a "prior period adjustment" under APBO No. 9).	31–33
IV. Correction of an error	Restatement of financial statements (report as prior period adjustment under APBO No. 9)	36–37

Source: Goodman and McRae [1974, p. 3].

Note, using Exhibit 6-1, that three types of changes of principle are singled out for special treatment: (a) a change from LIFO to another inventory valuation method, (b) a change in the method of accounting for long-term construction contracts, and (c) a change to or from the "full cost" method of accounting, which is used in the extractive industries (e.g., the oil industry). The *Opinion* provides no justification for its special treatment of these changes. One can, however, speculate that these changes were singled out for essentially political reasons rather than theoretical niceties. Around the time that *Opinion No. 20* was being drafted, accounting in the extractive industries and accounting for long-term construction contracts received much attention—in the financial press and the accounting literature—because of alleged abuses and/or distortions. Also, it was around this time that Chrysler Corp. switched from the LIFO to the FIFO method of inventory valuation—for both external and tax reporting.[28] This switch, taken by itself, allowed Chrysler to report a profit rather than a loss, and could have potentially cost Chrysler a sizable tax subsidy.[29] As a result, it attracted considerable attention in the financial press.

As can be seen from Exhibit 6-1, *Opinion No. 20* prescribes that the direct cumulative effects and related income tax effects, computed retroactively, of most changes in principle be recognized in the income statement for the period of the change. These effects are to be reported as a separate item between the captions "extraordinary items" and "net income." (This treatment was modified in the Financial Accounting Standards Board's *Statement of Financial Concepts No. 5*.) If determinable, the pro forms effects of retroactive application on the following are to be presented: net income before extraordinary items; net income; and primary and fully-diluted earnings per share.

Opinion No. 20 contains an exemption that permits restatements of prior periods' financial statements for changes in accounting principles effected when a firm issues financial statements for (1) obtaining equity capital, (2) effecting a business combination, or (3) registering securities. This exemption is available only once—at the time a firm's financial statements are first used for any of the latter purposes. It is not available to firms whose securities are already widely held.

Exhibit 6-2 provides an illustration of applying *Opinion No. 20* to a change in principle for which previously issued statements are not to be restated. The illustration is based on Amerada Hess's 1972 annual report to stockholders. The reader is encouraged to examine this exhibit to gain familiarity with some of the disclosures induced by *Opinion No. 20*. Additional illustrative material is provided later.[30]

6.6.3 APB Opinion No. 22: Disclosure of Accounting Policies (Effective for Fiscal Years Beginning After December 31, 1971)

This pronouncement deals with disclosures of firms' "accounting policies" in published financial statements. Its reporting requirements complement those of *Opinion No. 20*, which deals with *changes* in accounting techniques. For purposes of applying *Opinion*

---

[28]This switch took effect in January 1970.

[29]Because of a special arrangement with the IRS, Chrysler was able to offset additional taxes from the charge against subsequent losses; hence the company escaped paying a substantial part of this liability.

[30]A compendium of illustrations is provided in Goodman and McRae [1974].

EXHIBIT 6-2

AMERADA HESS CORPORATION

	1972	1971
Income before extraordinary items and cumulative effect of a change in the method of accounting for costs of undeveloped oil and gas leases	$46,229,000	$133,249,000
Extraordinary items, net of income tax effect	1,187,000	—
Cumulative effect on years prior to 1972 of a change in the method of accounting for costs of undeveloped oil and gas leases, net of income tax effect (Note 2)	(21,415,000)	—
Net income	$26,001,000	$133,249,000
Earnings per share		
Income before extraordinary items and cumulative effect of a change in the method of accounting for costs of undeveloped oil and gas leases	$1.27	$3.66
Extraordinary items	.03	—
Cumulative effect on years prior to 1972 of a change in the method of accounting for costs of undeveloped oil and gas leases	(.58)	—
Net income	$.72	$3.66
Pro forma amounts under the new method of accounting for costs of undeveloped oil and gas leases (Note 2)		
Income before extraordinary items	$46,229,000	$127,029,000
Extraordinary items	1,187,000	—
Net income	$47,416,000	$127,029,000
Earnings per share		
Income before extraordinary items	$1.27	$3.49
Extraordinary items	.03	—
Net income	$1.30	$3.49

Note 2: Change in Accounting Method–Effective January 1, 1972, the Corporation changed its method of accounting for the costs of all undeveloped oil and gas leases. Undeveloped oil and gas leases were previously carried at cost and charged against income in full when properties were relinquished. Under the new method, costs of undeveloped oil and gas leases are amortized over the primary lease term with any unamortized costs charged against income at the time the properties are relinquished. As a result of the substantially higher cost of lease acquisitions in recent years, the newly adopted accounting method is more conservative and preferable in that it provides a systematic write-off of undeveloped oil and gas lease costs from date of acquisition. This accounting change decreased 1972 income before extraordinary items by $1,687,000 ($.05 per share). The cumulative effect of such accounting change on years prior to 1972 amounted to $21,415,000 ($.58 per share) after deducting the related deferred income tax effect of $19,758,000. The pro forma amounts shown in the Statement of Consolidated Income give effect to the retroactive application of this accounting change.

Source: AICPA [1973, p. 30].

No. 22, the term "accounting policies" is defined to include the accounting principles used to prepare financial statements and the methods of applying those principles.

The essential prescription of *Opinion No. 22* is this:

> When financial statements are issued purporting to present fairly financial position, changes in financial position, and results of operations in accordance with generally acepted acounting principles, a description of all significant accounting policies of the reporting entity should be included as an integral part of the financial statements. [APB Opinion No. 22, ¶8.]

> [This provision is] not intended to apply to unaudited financial statements issued as of a date between annual reporting dates (e.g., each quarter) if the reporting entity has not changed its accounting policies since the end of its preceding fiscal year. (APB Opinion No. 22, ¶ 10.)

Opinion No. 22 attempted to provide guidelines for satisfying its reporting requirements. It indicated that disclosures about accounting policies should include important judgments regarding the appropriateness of principles related to the recognition of revenue and the allocation of costs to current and future periods. Specifically, these disclosures should deal with (a) a selection from existing acceptable alternative principles and methods, (b) principles and methods peculiar to the industry in which the reporting entity operates, even if such principles and methods are commonly used in that industry, and (c) "unusual or innovative" applications of acceptable accounting principles and methods (whether or not they are peculiar to the reporting firm's industry).

Opinion No. 22 gives the following as examples of accounting policies covered by its reporting requirements: (1) those related to basis of consolidation, (2) depreciation methods, (3) amortization of intangibles, (4) inventory pricing, (5) translation of foreign currencies, (6) recognition of profit on long-term construction-type contracts, and (7) recognition of revenue from franchising and leasing operations. The *Opinion* provided no examples of "unusual or innovative" applications of acceptable principles and methods.

By way of background, it is probably of interest to note that this opinion was issued at a time of (and because of?) increased emphasis on disclosing accounting policies. In 1971, the Financial Executives Institute recommended such disclosures. During the same year the Institute of Chartered Accountants in England and Wales made a similar recommendation in one of its *Statements of Standard Accounting Practice*.[31] All of this should be interpreted within the context of our earlier remarks on the political aspects of disclosure rule formulation.

Exhibit 6-3 provides a lengthy illustration of the kinds of disclosures induced by both *Opinion No. 22* and *Opinion No. 20*, which was discussed earlier. The illustrative material is from the 1972 annual report of Swift and Company. Note that two of the accounting changes made by Swift (the change from LIFO and the change from the "full cost" method for its oil and gas exploration/development activities) are among those for which *Opinion No. 20* requires retroactive restatements of financial statements. Thus, the material from Swift's report illustrates disclosures that did not appear in Exhibit 6-2. The "Statement on Accounting Policies" provided by Swift discusses both procedures that were not changed and those that were. This kind of cross-referencing within the notes to financial statements is not uncommon. Thus, all of the notes should be read to grasp fully the effects of *Opinions 20* and *22* on Swift's disclosures.

6.6.4 FASB Statement No. 3: Reporting Accounting Changes in Interim Financial Statements, An Amendment of APB Opinion No. 28 (Effective for Fiscal Years Ending on or after December 31, 1974)

This Statement amends the reporting requirements of APB *Opinion No. 28,* which deals with interim reports (e.g., quarterly financial statements). One section of *Opinion No. 28* establishes disclosure rules for accounting changes, as defined by APB *Opinion*

---

[31] See Richter [1973, p. 27].

EXHIBIT 6-3

SWIFT & COMPANY

Consolidated Statement of Current and Accumulated Earnings

(Dollars in thousands, except per share data)

	Year ended	
	Oct. 28, 1972	Oct. 30, 1971 *(As restated)*
Revenues:		
Net sales	$3,240,931	$2,996,210
Other—net	4,872	4,096
Total revenues	3,245,803	3,000,306
Costs and expenses:		
Cost of goods sold	2,971,517	2,741,765
Selling, advertising and administrative	197,833	196,084
Interest charges	12,495	12,725
Total costs and expenses	3,181,845	2,950,574
Earnings before income taxes and other items shown below	63,958	49,732
Income taxes	26,383	23,814
Earnings before items shown below	37,575	25,918
Equity in earnings of nonconsolidated subsidiaries and affiliated companies	2,315	519
Minority interests in subsidiaries' earnings	(2,887)	(327)
Net earnings	37,003	26,110
Preferred stock dividends	(1,733)	(1,733)
Common stock dividends	(8,488)	(8,460)
Increase in accumulated earnings	26,782	15,917
Accumulated earnings at beginning of year	247,719	231,802
Accumulated earnings at end of year	$ 274,501	$ 247,719
Net earnings per common share:		
Primary	$2.90	$2.00
Fully diluted	2.77	1.96

The financial comments beginning on page 20 and the statement of accounting policies beginning on page 40 are an integral part of the consolidated financial statements.

Consolidated Statement of Financial Position

(Dollars in thousands)

	Oct. 28, 1972	Oct. 30, 1971 *(As restated)*
Current assets:		
Cash	$ 1,180	$ 618
Temporary investments	27,630	32,064
Receivables	202,692	189,781
Inventories	254,532	232,209
Prepayments and other current assets	8,729	7,948
Total current assets	494,813	462,620
Less current liabilities:		
Notes payable	16,272	9,079
Accounts payable and accrued liabilities	139,416	126,996
Income taxes	14,145	358
Current maturities of long-term debt	9,760	21,029
Total current liabilities	179,593	157,462
Net working capital	315,220	305,158
Investments and other assets	41,955	36,531

EXHIBIT 6-3 Cont.

SWIFT & COMPANY

Consolidated Statement of Current and Accumulated Earnings

(Dollars in thousands, except per share data)

	Year ended	
	Oct. 28, 1972	Oct. 30, 1971 *(As restated)*
Property and operating facilities	376,625	382,130
Excess of cost over net assets of purchased businesses	22,455	22,626
Total assets less current liabilities	756,255	746,455
Less:		
Direct costs of facility realignment program		13,639
Pensions and other noncurrent amounts	31,672	31,607
Deferred income taxes	42,064	37,247
Long-term debt	176,127	184,736
Minority interests in subsidiaries	52,340	49,473
Total	302,209	319,702
Net assets applicable to stockholders' equity	$ 454,046	$ 426,753
Stockholders' equity:		
Preferred stock	$ 36,485	$ 36,485
Common stock	12,601	12,592
Other paid-in capital	142,750	142,703
Accumulated earnings	274,501	247,719
Common stock in treasury, at cost	(12,291)	(12,746)
Total stockholders' equity	$ 454,046	$ 426,753
Total assets	$ 935,848	$ 903,917

The Financial Comments beginning on page 198 and the Statement of Accounting Policies beginning below are an integral part of the consolidated financial statements.

Statement of Accounting Policies

Inventories

Substantially all inventories are valued at the lower of current cost (determined on the first-in, first-out or average methods) or market. A substantial portion of the product inventories (43% at October 30, 1971) was previously valued at cost under the last-in, first-out (LIFO) method. The change in method of valuing these inventories has been applied retroactively pursuant to provisions of Accounting Principles Board Opinion No. 20. The effects of this change on the consolidated financial statements are summarized in the Financial Comments under "Changes in Accounting."

The change in valuation method was made to more fairly present the company's financial position and operating results. The change applies primarily to the material components of agricultural product inventories, of which available supplies and purchase costs are subject to substantial cyclical fluctuations. Use of the LIFO cost method for these inventories has magnified the effect of these cycles on the earnings of the company's businesses engaged in processing and selling these products and has reduced comparability of the company's earnings to those of most other corporations, the majority of which do not use the LIFO method of inventory valuation. Further, use of the LIFO method has resulted in the reporting of inventories at amounts substantially less than the current costs of such inventories, thereby affecting significant financial statement amounts and ratios and understating the stockholders' investment in the business. These unfavorable effects on the company's financial statements are eliminated by the accounting change.

Investments.

Investments in nonconsolidated subsidiaries are carried at cost plus equity in accumulated earnings. The nonconsolidated life insurance companies prepare their financial statements in accordance with practices prescribed or permitted by the state regulatory agencies to which they are subject, which practices differ in certain

EXHIBIT 6-3 Cont.

respects from generally accepted accounting principles. For purposes of determining Swift's equity in the net assets and net earnings of these companies, adjustments are made to conform certain statutory practices with generally accepted accounting principles. These adjustments include restating common stock investments from market value to cost, restoring "nonadmitted assets" to net assets, classifying the mandatory securities valuation reserve as an equity reserve, deferring commission expense on policies other than ordinary life policies, including realized gains and losses on investment dispositions in net earnings, and providing deferred income taxes on timing differences other than differences relating to amounts designated for federal income tax purposes as "policyholders' surplus."

Investments in affiliated (20% to 50% owned) companies are accounted for by the equity method. The company's equity in affiliates' net earnings is adjusted for income taxes which would be payable if the earnings were distributed. Other investments are carried at cost or less.

The investments in the affiliated companies were previously carried at cost less allowances for possible losses. The change in method of accounting was made to conform with provisions of Accounting Principles Board Opinions Nos. 13 and 24 and has been applied retroactively pursuant to these opinions. The effects of this change on the consolidated financial statements are summarized in the Financial Comments under "Changes in Accounting."

Property and operating facilities.

The company's subsidiaries, principally TransOcean Oil, Inc., engaged in oil and gas exploration and development activities use the field cost method of accounting.

Under this method, costs of exploratory dry holes are charged to expense as incurred. Other costs of acquisition, exploration and development, including lease costs, delay rentals and developmental dry holes identifiable with specific fields, are capitalized as oil and gas properties. Costs associated with a producing field are depleted on the unit-of-production method over the remaining proven developed reserves of the field as estimated by the company. Capitalized costs in excess of the estimated economic value of a field's estimated reserves are charged against operations by additional provisions for depreciation and depletion. Capitalized costs applicable to fields which prove to be nonproductive are written off when such determinations are made. Costs of lease and well equipment are depreciated on the straight line method.

Prior to 1972, the company used the total cost method of accounting. Under this method, all acquisition, exploration and development costs, including costs relating to surrendered or abandoned fields, exploratory dry holes and a portion of general and administrative expenses, were capitalized as oil and gas properties. These costs were identified with one of the broad geographic areas in which each of the company's subsidiaries operate and, together with costs of lease and well equipment, were depleted and depreciated on the unit-of-production method. Costs were written off when the properties in a broad geographic area were determined to be valueless or when such costs were determined to be in excess of net revenues expected to be realized from production in the area.

The change in method of accounting for these costs has been applied retroactively pursuant to provisions of Accounting Principles Board Opinion No. 20. The effects of this change on the consolidated financial statements are summarized in the Financial Comments under "Changes in Accounting." The change, which conforms the company's practices to those adopted by TransOcean Oil, Inc. at its March 31, 1972 fiscal year end, was made to place the company on a more conservative accounting basis and one which more closely approximates methods most commonly used in the petroleum industry.

Depletion provisions on agricultural chemical mining properties are determined on the unit-of-production method.

Depreciation provisions on all other property and operating facilities are determined primarily on the straight line method.

Provision was made in prior years for significant direct costs and losses to be incurred under the facility realignment program adopted in 1966, substantially expanded in 1968, and essentially concluded in 1972. During the period of the program, the allowances so established were charged as the costs and losses were incurred and credited as gains were realized. Gains and losses on unusual facility dispositions and closings, other than dispositions and closings under the facility realignment program, are reflected in the year of disposition for gains and in the year in which the decision is made to close for losses. Gains and losses on normal dispositions of facilities and equipment are included in accumulated depreciation except as to certain foreign subsidiaries which include such amounts in earnings.

EXHIBIT 6-3 Cont.

Pensions.

Pension expenses are accrued in amounts equal to the normal costs of the plans (including interest on the unfunded actuarial liabilities) and amortization of prior service costs under certain of the plans over periods of not more than forty years. Contributions to the pension trusts are made periodically in amounts authorized by the Board of Directors and, in addition, certain pension costs are paid directly by the company.

The unit credit actuarial cost method is used for the major plans. Revisions in pension cost determinations made in 1972 included (1) an updating of most of the actuarial assumptions used, including a revision in the earnings assumption as to the major plans from 6% to an average rate of approximately 6.75%, (2) a change from an adjusted cost basis of valuing pension fund assets to a market value basis (under which a portion of annual market appreciation is included in the value of fund assets over a ten-year period), and (3) a change from a cash method of accounting for the cost of pensioners' medical insurance to a method by which this cost is included in the actuarial computation of pension expense. The net effect on 1972 pension expense of these revisions, which have been applied prospectively pursuant to provisions of Accounting Principles Board Opinion No. 8, is discussed in the Financial Comments under "Changes in Accounting."

The change in accounting for the pension fund assets was made to more appropriately reflect changes in the market value of the pension funds' investments in the determination of the funds' financial status and earnings. Under the previously used method, changes in fund asset values and earnings were more responsive to the gain and loss effects of investment sales than to changes in the actual market value of the funds' investments.

The change in accounting for pensioners' medical insurance was made to reflect the cost of this element of the company's pension program, which has increased substantially over the past several years on the accrual basis.

Financial Comments

Accounting Changes.

During 1972, several changes were made in accounting method as discussed under the caption "Changes in Accounting." Certain of these changes required restatement of the financial statements for 1971 and prior years from the amounts previously reported. The effects of the significant changes were to increase 1972 net earnings from $27.7 million to $37.0 million (from $2.14 to $2.90 per common share) and to decrease 1971 net earnings from $34.1 million to $26.1 million (from $2.66 to $2.00 per common share). Comments on the significant changes follow.

Inventory Valuation.

To more fairly present the company's total financial position and operating results, the last-in, first-out (LIFO) cost method of inventory valuation, which had been utilized by the company since the early 1940's, was discontinued. The more commonly used lower of current cost or market method was adopted. The change applies primarily to agricultural products which are subject to substantial cyclical fluctuations in costs.

Petroleum Exploration and Development Costs.

The company adopted the field cost method of accounting for petroleum exploration and development costs. The total cost method was used previously. This change, which conforms the company's practices to those adopted earlier in 1972 by TransOcean Oil, Inc. (51% owned subsidiary), places the company on a more conservative accounting basis and one which more closely approximates methods most commonly used in the petroleum industry.

Investments in Affiliated Companies.

To conform to opinions of the Accounting Principles Board which become mandatory for the company in its 1973 fiscal year, the company adopted the equity method of accounting for investments in affiliated (20% to 50% owned) companies. Prior to 1972, the company used the cost method of accounting for these investments.

Pension Costs.

Completion of the facility realignment program placed the company in a position of having a stable level of employment for the first time in a number of years. Considering this, a study was made of the company's total pension program, including actuarial assumptions, cost computation practices, and benefit programs. This study resulted in increases in certain plan benefits and revisions in the actuarial assumptions and the method of

EXHIBIT 6-3 Cont.

computing expense, the latter changes primarily to reflect on a more current basis the market values of the pension fund assets and the earnings from such assets.

Changes in Accounting.

Significant revisions were made in 1972 in the accounting methods used by the company. Three of the newly adopted methods have been applied retroactively as required by generally accepted accounting principles. These are (1) the adoption of the lower of current cost or market method for valuing substantially all inventories previously valued under the last-in, first-out (LIFO) cost method, (2) the adoption of the field cost method of accounting for oil and gas exploration and development activities for which the total cost method was used previously, and (3) the adoption of the equity method of accounting for investments in affiliated (20% to 50% owned) companies which were previously accounted for under the cost method. The 1971 consolidated financial statements have been restated to reflect the application of these revised accounting methods.

The company also revised its method of computing pension expense. This revision, which includes an updating of actuarial assumptions and changes in accounting methods, is being applied prospectively as required by generally accepted accounting principles and, therefore, had no effect on the 1971 consolidated financial statements.

Each revision is discussed more fully in the Statement of Accounting Policies. The effects of the revisions on the consolidated financial statements are summarized below.

Effects on results of operations.

The retroactively applied revisions in accounting methods decreased 1971 net earnings from the previously reported amount by $8.0 million or $.66 per common share. If these changes had not been made, it is estimated that net earnings for 1972 would have been $6.7 million or $.55 per common share less than the amounts reported.

The revision in the assumptions used in the actuarial computation of pension expense reduced such expense for 1972 by approximately $1.5 million and the changes in accounting method reduced 1972 pension expense by approximately $3.5 million. As previously mentioned, these reductions in pension expense were partly offset by the cost of increased benefits.

The effects of each of the above changes on net earnings, in millions of dollars, and on net earnings per common share, are as follows:

	1972		1971	
	Net earnings	Per share	Net earnings	Per share
Increase (decrease) due to changes for:				
Inventories	$6.2	$.51	$ (.9)	$(.07)
Oil and gas	(.2)	(.02)	(5.2)	(.43)
Affiliated companies	.7	.06	(1.9)	(.16)
Pensions	2.6	.21		
Increase (decrease)	$9.3	$.76	$(8.0)	$(.65)

Other accounting changes were made in 1972 and 1971, none of which had a material effect on net earnings for those years or is expected to have a material effect on future earnings. The one-time effect of these changes was to increase net earnings by approximately $.4 million ($.03 per common share) in 1972 and $.6 million ($.05 per common share) in 1971.

Effects on financial position.

The retroactively applied revisions in accounting methods resulted in significant changes in several amounts in the consolidated statement of financial position at October 30, 1971, from the amounts previously reported. Increases were reflected in inventories ($49.8 million) and deferred income taxes ($25.0 million). Decreases were reflected in investments and other assets ($2.5 million), property and operating facilities ($12.7 million), current liabilities ($6.5 million), and minority interests ($6.6 million). Accumulated earnings were increased by $19.7 million at October 30, 1971 and $27.7 million at October 31, 1970. Working capital was increased $56.3 million at October 30, 1971 and $58.9 million at October 31, 1970.

EXHIBIT 6-3 Cont.

Auditor's Opinion

The Board of Directors and Stockholders—Swift & Company

We have examined the accompanying consolidated statement of financial position of Swift & Company at October 28, 1972 and October 30, 1971 and the related consolidated statements of current and accumulated earnings and changes in financial position for the years then ended. Our examinations were made in accordance with generally accepted auditing standards, and accordingly included such tests of the accounting records and such other auditing procedures as we considered necessary in the circumstances.

In our opinion, the statements mentioned above present fairly the consolidated financial position of Swift & Company at October 28, 1972 and October 30, 1971, and the consolidated results of operations and consolidated changes in financial position for the years then ended, in conformity with generally accepted accounting principles consistently applied during the period, except for the 1972 change in the method of determining pension expense, and after restatement for the changes in methods of accounting for (1) inventories, (2) exploration and development costs incurred in the oil and gas operations, and (3) investments in affiliated companies, all as described in the Financial Comments under the caption "Changes in Accounting." We concur with the above mentioned changes in accounting.

Summary of Significant Consolidated Financial Data

(Dollars in millions, except per share data)

	Revenues				Net earnings (b)			
	1972		1971 (a)		1972		1971 (a)	
Lines of Business	$	%	$	%	$	%	$	%
Foods	2,601.7	80.1	2,295.7	76.5	27.7	74.8	25.3	97.1
Chemicals and industrial products	492.1	15.2	572.9	19.1	6.3	17.0	1.1	4.2
Petroleum (c)	145.2	4.5	125.9	4.2	1.5	4.1	(2.6)	(10.2)
Insurance (d)	6.8	.2	5.8	.2	1.5	4.1	2.3	8.9
Consolidated	3,245.3	100.0	3,000.3	100.0	37.0	100.0	26.1	100.0

Notes:

(a) 1971 has been restated to give retroactive effect to the changes in methods of accounting described in the Financial Comments under the caption "Changes in Accounting."

(b) Interest and other indirect corporate expenses have been allocated generally on the basis of assets employed. Income taxes have been allocated generally on the basis of taxable income.

(c) Net earnings are after minority interests of $2.9 million in 1972 and $.3 million in 1971.

(d) Excludes revenues, principally premiums, of nonconsolidated life insurance companies of $41.4 million in 1972 and $28.8 million in 1971.

Results of Operations	1972	1971
Primary earnings per common share	$ 2.90	$ 2.00
Fully diluted earnings per common share	2.77	1.96
Cash dividends per common share	.70	.70
Per cent of earnings distributed as dividends	27.6%	39.0%
Return on total assets at year end	4.0%	2.9%
Return on stockholders' equity at year end	8.1%	6.1%
Financial Positions		
Working capital	$315.2	$305.2
Property and operating facilities—net	376.6	382.1
Total assets	935.8	903.9
Invested capital:		
Long-term debt	176.1	184.7
Stockholders' equity	451.0	426.8
Total invested capital	$630.1	$611.5
Ratio of current assets to current liabilities	2.76	2.94

EXHIBIT 6-3 Cont.

Results of Operations	1972	1971
Ratio of invested capital to total assets	.67	.68
Ratio of stockholders' equity to total assets	.49	.47
Ratio of long-term debt to invested capital	.28	.30
Net assets per common share outstanding at year end	$ 34.42	$ 32.24
Changes in Financial Position		
Working capital increase	$ 10.1	$ 6.6
Principal sources of working capital:		
Operations	75.2	80.6
Long-term borrowings	3.6	50.0
Principal uses of working capital:		
Property and operating facility additions	52.0	83.8
Long-term debt reductions	12.2	36.3
Dividend payments	10.2	10.2

5 Year Financial Summary
(Dollars in millions, except per share and per employe data)

Fiscal Years*	1972	1971	1970	1969	1968
Revenues and Earnings					
Net sales and other revenues	$ 3,245.8	3,000.3	3,082.8	3,111.3	2,936.8
Earnings before extraordinary charge	$ 37.0	26.1	28.0	25.6	15.1
Per common share**	$ 2.90	2.00	2.16	1.92	1.07
Per cent of common stockholders' equity at year end**	% 8.4	6.2	7.0	6.7	3.8
Extraordinary charge	$				57.0
Per common share	$				4.54
Net earnings (loss)	$ 37.0	26.1	28.0	25.6	(41.9)
Per common share**	$ 2.90	2.00	2.16	1.92	(3.47)
Common dividends	$ 8.5	8.5	7.3	7.3	11.0
Per common share	$ .70	.70	.60	.60	.90
Financial Position					
Working capital	$ 315.2	305.2	298.6	308.8	299.6
Current ratio	2.76	2.94	2.86	3.03	2.99
Total assets	$ 935.8	903.9	870.2	790.0	779.5
Property and operating facilities—net	$ 376.6	382.1	356.1	290.8	290.5
Long-term debt	$ 176.1	134.7	171.1	173.0	182.1
Common stockholders' equity	$ 417.6	390.3	373.3	336.7	351.0
Per common share	$ 34.42	32.24	30.94	29.39	27.98
Average number of stockholders	44,500	47,700	50,200	53,000	54,700
Average number of employees	33,600	34,900	38,900	42,700	46,600
Total employment costs	$ 332.5	332.2	349.7	377.3	381.2
Average per employee	$ 9,396	9,518	8,989	8,335	8,180

*Fiscal years 1971, 1970, 1969 and 1968 have been restated for accounting changes.
**After recognizing annual preferred stock dividend requirement.

No. 20. In general, those rules extended the applicability of *Opinion 20* to interim reports. According to *Opinion No. 28,* when interim reports for a period of a change and pre-change-period interim reports are both reissued after the change period (for comparison with post-change-periods' results), the pre-change and change periods' results are supposed to be retroactively restated. As indicated in *Statement No. 3,* that requirement would lead to several restatements of some interim period's reports when accounting changes occur in interim periods after the first one of a fiscal year. Moreover, the disclosures made for changes effected in the last interim period of a fiscal year would depend on whether a firm issued a separate interim report for that period.[32]

The two major conclusions of *Statement No. 3* are as follows. First, the effect of any change in accounting principle made in an interim period other than the first one should be reported as if the change were made during the first period. For reports on the interim period during which the change was made, the following rules apply:

1. In the operating results of that period, only include the change's effects on that period's results. The effects for previous periods should be included in "year to date" results.

2. The effects of the change on each previous interim period's results should be separately disclosed (in total and on a per share basis) and results for those periods should be restated whenever they are presented.

3. If there is any effect on amounts reported for previous fiscal years, it should be recognized as a "cumulative effect" adjustment in the restated results for the first interim period. (This refers to the "cumulative-effect" adjustments of retained earnings as described by *Opinion No. 20.*)

Second, if a firm makes a change in the last interim period of a fiscal year (e.g., in the last quarter) and if it does not issue a separate report on the operations of that period, then the effect of the change on *each* interim period of the fiscal year should be disclosed in a footnote to the annual statements. Here, the "effect" of the change is to be determined in accordance with the first conclusion (see above) of the *Statement*. That is, the change is treated as if it were made in the first interim period.

6.6.5 Remarks

The pronouncements described above are among those affecting disclosures about the effects of accounting techniques on accounting number realizations. Of course, they are not the only disclosure rules that lead to disclosures of accounting techniques and changes in techniques. Satisfaction of disclosure rules that do not deal specifically with accounting techniques may also require disclosures about techniques and their effects. For example, the SEC now requires the filing of various kinds of information when there are disagreements between a firm's management and its external auditors.[33] Fulfillment of these filing requirements may involve making disclosures about the firm's accounting techniques and the effects of alternative techniques on the firm's reported accounting numbers.

The fact that a particular accounting-number realization (e.g., observed net income) is altered by an accounting change or the fact that a sequence of realizations conditional

---

[32] Some firms do not issue such a report on the assumption that the last interim period's results can be inferred from results for the entire fiscal year and the results for all interim periods other than the last one.

[33] Securities and Exchange Commission [1974]. This release extends disclosure rules adopted in 1971 regarding management/auditor disagreements. The disclosures required by this release are made on the SEC's Form 8-K.

on one set of (unchanged) techniques differs from what it would have been conditional on a different set does not imply that there are any substantive economic differences in the firm's operations. Nor do these factors imply that the probability model that best describes the accounting number is different because of the procedural differences. The next few sections deal with approaches for assessing the extent to which accounting techniques affect the probability models that describe accounting numbers. In addition, they describe approaches for assessing the relationship (if any) between accounting changes and substantive changes in the economic characteristics of firms, as assessed by capital market agents.

6.7 Assessing the Effects of Alternative Accounting Techniques: A Time Series Approach

6.7.1 Discussion

Suppose that agents make inferences on the basis of accounting numbers. Then, in accordance with the Theory of Rational Expectations (Muth [1961]), one expects agents to exploit the (detectable) systematic properties of those numbers by inquiring into their underlying generating processes—i.e., the probability models from which the observed values of the numbers were drawn. In different words, one should expect agents to use accounting numbers in a way that depends on the structure of the stochastic system generating those numbers. If that were not done, agents would not be fully utilizing available information—i.e., the systematic properties of the numbers. Of course, if the cost of using that information is too large—relative to the foreseen "benefits"—then incomplete utilization can be justified.

Exploiting the systematic properties of accounting numbers is one aspect of using such numbers to make inferences about the distributions of returns on firms' securities. Using accounting numbers for that purpose assumes, of course, that their properties can be connected, in one way or another, to the substantive economic attributes of firms' operations, along the lines suggested in, for example, Chapter 4. There, we identified the attributes of firms' decisions that are important in determining firms' equilibrium values, conditional on the two-parameter asset-pricing model. We also suggested how the systematic properties of accounting numbers can be used in making inferences about the relevant attributes of firms' decisions. Those suggestions assume that changes in the systematic properties of firms' accounting numbers are induced by changes in the relevant attributes of firms' decisions (i.e., the attributes important in determining firms' equilibrium values). Moreover, they assume that differences among the systematic properties of different firms' numbers can be ascribed to differences among the relevant attributes of the firms' decisions.

According to the framework used herein, however, accounting techniques constitute determinants of accounting numbers' systematic properties. Thus, some changes in those properties may not have been induced by changes in the determinants of firms' equilibrium values. Also, some changes in those determinants may not induce changes in the detectable systematic properties of accounting numbers; this will depend on the effects of accounting techniques. In short, the systematic properties of accounting numbers are jointly determined by the attributes of firms' decisions and the accounting techniques selected by firms. That is, those systematic properties are induced by "joint inputs."

The above remarks provide some motivation for assessing the extent to which accounting techniques; taken by themselves, affect the detectable systematic properties of accounting numbers. The ultimate objective is to make inferences about the extent to which the techniques alter those properties independently of the attributes of firms' decisions. This is best explained via the results of a specific application. We shall use the empirical results provided by Lopuch and Watts [1972]. Use of this work as a basis for explanation should help clarify the explanation and will provide several illustrations of the kinds of problems encountered in empirical work. The specific inferences made by Dopuch and Watts are of secondary importance.

6.7.2 The Dopuch/Watts Study

During the 1950s several firms in the steel industry switched from the straight-line to an accelerated method of computing depreciation expense. For each firm that switched there are, therefore, two sets of sample evidence: (1) accounting numbers based on straight-line depreciation (observed prior to the switch) and (2) accounting numbers based on an accelerated depreciation method (observed after the switch). The Dopuch/Watts [1972] study deals with two types of numbers: net income for common stockholders and a rate of return on common equity (net income for common stockholders divided by common equity). Their major question, with respect to each type of number, is this: can the generating processes of the numbers before and after the change of depreciation methods be described by the same stochastic model? In asking this question, they assumed that the attributes of the switching firms' production-investment and financing decisions were the same after the change as they were before the change in accounting techniques. Thus, a negative answer to their question would lead them to ascribe the changes in the inferred time series models to the influence of the changes in depreciation methods. Their assumption about the attributes of firms' decisions will be reconsidered below.

The sample of firms used by Dopuch and Watts is a subset of that used by Watts in his work on income numbers; see Chapter 7. The firms in their sample are identified in Table 6-1, which also identifies the time intervals of the pre- and post-change data available for each firm. For each firm, at least 30 years of data are available before the depreciation switch, whereas only about 11 years of data are available after the switch. Data for years after the late 1960s were not used—even when available—because the firms switched back to the straight-line method during the late 1960s.

Dopuch and Watts used the kinds of procedures described in Chapter 7 in order to identify and estimate time series models. The details of their procedures are given in Box and Jenkins [1970]. They are reviewed in Chapter 7.

For each firm, the first step of the Dopuch/Watts procedures involved identifying and estimating the parameters of the time series model that best described each number series, conditional on the *pre-change* data. The model identified in the first step was then re-estimated using the post-change sample evidence and then all of the sample evidence (consisting of both the pre- and post-change observations).[34] The crux of their formal tests

[34]For example, if a first-order autoregressive model was identified in the first step, then that model's parameters were simply re-estimated using (1) the post-change data and then (2) both the pre- and post-change-data. No attempt to re-identify the appropriate model was made. This approach assumes that the depreciation-method change will affect only the values of the appropriate model's parameters, if it affects anything, rather than the type of model (e.g., first-order autoregressive versus first-order moving average) that is appropriate.

TABLE 6-1

SAMPLE OF COMPANIES USED BY DOPUCH AND WATTS

	Time Interval Prior to Change	Time Interval After Change
Armco	1923–1954	1955–1967
Bethlehem Steel	1914–1953	1954–1967
Crucible Steel	1914–1955	1956–1966
Eastern Stainless Steel	1920–1956	1957–1967
Inland Steel	1915–1953	1954–1967
Jones and Laughlin	1922–1953	1954–1967
Pittsburgh Steel	1914–1955	1956–1967
Republic Steel	1914–1953	1954–1964
U.S. Pipe and Foundry	1916–1954	1955–1967
U.S. Steel	1915–1946	1947–1967
Youngstown	1921–1954	1955–1967

Source: Dopuch and Watts [1972, table 1).

deals with the importance of the changes in the values of the identified model's parameters (one model for each firm). If, conditional on the sample evidence, those values were inferred to have undergone important changes, then Dopuch and Watts inferred that the depreciation change did affect the accounting number's time series properties.

The class of models underlying their results can be represented as follows:

$$\phi_p(B)\Delta^d\tilde{Z}_t = \theta_0 + \theta_q(B)\tilde{\epsilon}_t \tag{6.1}$$

where, as always, tilde (˜) denotes random variable and:

$\tilde{Z}_t$ is the random variable under examination (net income or rate of return on common equity),

$\phi(B) = 1 - \phi_1 B - \phi_2 B^2 - \ldots - \phi_p B^p$,

B is the backshift operator, $B^k Z_t = Z_t - Z_{t-k}$,

$\Delta^d = (1 - B)^d$ is the differencing operator, $\Delta Z_t = Z_t - Z_{t-1}$, $\Delta^2 Z_t = \Delta(\Delta Z_t) = \Delta(Z_t - Z_{t-1}) = Z_t - Z_{t-1} - Z_{t-1} + Z_{t-2} = Z_t - 2Z_{t-1} + Z_{t-2}$, etc.,

θ_0 is a constant

$\tilde{\epsilon}_t$ is the disturbance at time t, which is assumed to be an independent identically distributed (over time) normal random variable with $E(\tilde{\epsilon}_t) = 0$ and $\mathrm{Var}(\tilde{\epsilon}_t) = \sigma^2_{\tilde{\epsilon}}$, and

$\theta_q(B) = 1 - \theta_2 B - \theta_2 B^2 - \ldots - \theta_q B^q$.

Identifying a model from this class involves inferring appropriate values of p, d, and q in (6.1). The resultant model is, in technical terms, an Autoregressive Integrated Moving Average (ARIMA) model of type, or "order," (p, d, q).

Given an estimated model of this sort, one can compute the corresponding value of the "sum of squared residuals," SSE $= \Sigma_t \hat{\epsilon}_t^2$, where $\hat{\epsilon}_t$ is the estimated realisation of $\tilde{\epsilon}_t$.[35] Let SSE_B, SSE_A, and SSE_O denote the sums of squared residuals conditional on, respec-

[35]Why is the residual for t an *estimate* of the realization of $\tilde{\epsilon}_t$?

tively, (1) the before-change data, (2) the after-change data, and (3) both the before- and after-change data. Let N_B and N_A be the numbers of observations in the pre- and post-change periods, respectively, and let $N_O = N_B + N_A$. Finally, let k denote the number of parameters to be estimated (including the constant term) for a given identified model. That is, $k = p + q + 1$ if θ_0 is estimated and $k = p + q$ if it is not.

Consider the ratio:

$$F = \left[\frac{\text{SSE}_B + \text{SSE}_A - \text{SSE}_O}{\text{SSE}_B + \text{SSE}_A}\right] \Big/ \left[\frac{N_A + N_B - 2k}{k}\right]. \tag{6.2}$$

Under the assumption that $\tilde{\epsilon}_t$ is an independent identically distributed normal random variable over the *entire* time period (i.e., over the pre- and post-change periods), the statistic defined by (6.2) has the distribution function of $\tilde{F}(k, N_O - 2k)$, a central "F" random variable with k and $N_O - 2k$ degrees of freedom, conditional on the hypothesis of no change in the identified model's parameters' values.[36] The observed value of $\tilde{F}(k, N_O - 2k)$—defined by (6.2)—can be used to assess the consistency of the sample evidence with this hypothesis.

TABLE 6-2

IDENTIFICATION AND ESTIMATION RESULTS FOR NET INCOME. RESULTS BASED UPON VALUES OBSERVED PRIOR TO DEPRECIATION SWITCHES

Company	Model $p\ d\ q$	ϕ_1	σ_{ϕ_1}	ϕ_2	σ_{ϕ_2}	θ_1	σ_{θ_1}	θ_0^a	σ_{θ_0}
Armco	010							1,214	923
Bethelehem Steel	200	.69	.18	.24	.18			6,150	5,570
Crucible Steel	100	.53	.14					2,418	866
Eastern Stainless Steel	011					.47	.16	51	50
Inland Steel	200	.72	.18	.21				1,500	1,487
Jones and Laughlin	100	.81	.12		.18			2,875	189
Pittsburgh Steel	100	.65	.13					844	414
Republic Steel	100	.96	.08					1,962	1,699
U.S. Pipe and Foundry	200	1.18	.17	−.40	.18			669	361
U.S. Steel	200	.74	.14	−.23	.14			32,140	12,903
Youngstown	100	.79	.11					3,089	1,847

[a]In $000's.
Source: Dopuch and Watts [1972, table 2].

Tables 6-2–6-7 contain the results of the Dopuch/Watts model identification and estimation efforts. Tables 6-8 and 6-9 provide the observed values of $\tilde{F}(k, N_O - 2k)$ for net income and rate of return on common equity, respectively.

Taken at face value, and conditional on the Dopuch/Watts assumptions, the results in Tables 6-8 and 6-9 are consistent with the depreciation switches' having had an effect on the generating process for income but not for the return on equity. This result is not implausible. Since the depreciation method used by a firm for external reporting affects

[36]And, of course, conditional on the maintained hypothesis that the identified model is still appropriate after the depreciation switch.

TABLE 6-3

IDENTIFICATION AND ESTIMATION RESULTS FOR RATE OF RETURN ON COMMON EQUITY. RESULTS BASED UPON VALUES OBSERVED PRIOR TO DEPRECIATION SWITCHES

Company	Model *p d q*	ϕ_1	$\sigma_{\phi 1}$	ϕ_2	$\sigma_{\phi 2}$	θ_1	$\sigma_{\theta 1}$	θ_0	$\sigma_{\theta 0}$
Armco	200	1.15	.18	−.37	.18			.02	.01
Bethlehem Steel	201	1.07	.18	−.3454	.15	.50	.25	.02	.01
Crucible Steel	100	.59	.13					.03	.01
Eastern Stainless Steel	200	.44	.17	.06	.17			.03	.02
Inland Steel	200	.78	.13	−.30	.12			.06	.01
Jones and Laughlin	200	.80	.19	−.11	.19			.02	.01
Pittsburgh Steel	200	.83	.16	−.25	.16			.02	.01
Republic Steel	100	.63	.13					.02	.01
U.S. Pipe and Foundry	200	.90	.17	−.30	.17			.03	.01
U.S. Steel	200	.71	.13	−.18	.13			.02	.01
Youngstown	200	.87	.18	−.29	.18			.03	.01

Source: Dopuch and Watts [1972, table 3].

both its net income and common equity numbers (in the same direction), the end result of a switch may be "no important affect" on the properties of the return on equity ratio, depending on the importance of depreciation expense relative to sales and other expenses.

One should not, however, place undue reliance on the formalities of tests of "statistical significance." Such tests' performance can be adversely affected by model inadequacies (e.g., a seriously nonnormal distribution for $\tilde{\epsilon}_t$, nonstationarity of the variance of $\tilde{\epsilon}_t$, etc.). The situation here, as in most hypothesis-testing exercises, is such that the sharp null hypothesis of "no change in the parameters' values" is really a (devilish) strawman. The

TABLE 6-4

ESTIMATION RESULTS FOR NET INCOME. BASED ON VALUES OBSERVED AFTER DEPRECIATION SWITCHES AND MODELS INDENTIFIED USING PRE-SWITCH OBSERVATIONS

Company	Model *p d q*	ϕ_1	$\sigma_{\phi 1}$	ϕ_2	$\sigma_{\phi 2}$	σ_1	$\sigma_{\theta 1}$	θ_0^a	$\sigma_{\theta 0}$
Armco	010							525	3,824
Bethlehem Steel	200	.52	.30	−.07	.32			73,660	48,715
Crucible Steel	100	.58	.28					2,800	2,160
Eastern Stainless Steel	011					1.63	.79	249	271
Inland Steel	200	.60	.36	−.06	.36			25,700	16,516
Jones and Laughlin	100	.32	.27					28,450	11,544
Pittsburgh Steel	100	.49	.25					936	900
Republic Steel	100	.51	.30					33,000	19,556
U.S. Pipe and Foundry	200	.16	.28	.23	.28			3,912	2,234
U.S. Steel	200	.53	.26	.04	.24			106,100	52,768
Youngstown	100	.59	.25					15,230	9,788

[a]In $000's.

Source: Dopuch and Watts [1972, table 4].

TABLE 6-5

ESTIMATION RESULTS FOR RATE OF RETURN ON COMMON EQUITY. BASED ON VALUES OBSERVED AFTER DEPRECIATION SWITCHES AND MODELS IDENTIFIED USING PRE-SWITCH OBSERVATIONS

Company	Model *p d q*	ϕ_1	$\sigma_{\phi 1}$	ϕ_2	$\sigma_{\phi 2}$	θ_1	$\sigma_{\theta 1}$	θ_0	$\sigma_{\theta 0}$
Armco	200	.54	.28	−.30	.22			.07	.04
Bethlehem Steel	201	1.10	.09	−.48	.11	1.67	.58	.03	.01
Crucible Steel	100	.44	.24					.03	.01
Eastern Stainless Steel	200	.38	.35	−.12	.36			.06	.03
Inland Steel	200	.62	.31	.10	.30			.02	.02
Jones and Laughlin	200	.47	.28	−.19	.28			.05	.02
Pittsburgh Steel	200	.62	.34	−.37	.30			.01	.01
Republic Steel	100	.71	.25					.03	.02
U.S. Pipe and Foundry	200	.19	.27	.29	.23			.03	.02
U.S. Steel	200	.51	.25	.14	.25			.03	.02
Youngstown	200	.49	.33	−.18	.28			.05	.02

Source: Dopuch and Watts [1972, table 5].

important issue is this: does a perspective assuming no change in those values lead to a model whose descriptive validity is poor—relative to alternative models—and will use of such a model (for explanations and actions) induce serious, avoidable errors? Resolving that issue involves a more searching analysis of the data than is called for by mechanically relying on statistical tests.

For example, one might want to subject the estimated identified models to various diagnostic checks, relative to (1) the post-change sample evidence and (2) the pooled pre-change and post-change evidence. And one might want to consider the implications of the

TABLE 6-6

ESTIMATION RESULTS FOR NET INCOME. BASED ON VALUES OBSERVED BEFORE AND AFTER DEPRECIATION SWITCHES AND MODELS IDENTIFIED USING PRE-SWITCH OBSERVATIONS

Company	Model *p d q*	ϕ_1	$\sigma_{\phi 1}$	ϕ_2	$\sigma_{\phi 2}$	θ_1	$\sigma_{\theta 1}$	θ_0^a	$\sigma_{\theta 0}$
Armco	010							1,527	1,302
Bethlehem Steel	200	.72	.14	.22	.15			6,901	5,168
Crucible Steel	100	.58	.28					2,800	2,160
Eastern Stainless Steel	011					.54	.13	4,466	38
Inland Steel	200	.86	.15	.12	.16			1,428	1,336
Jones and Laughlin	100	.84	.08					3,898	2,234
Pittsburgh Steel	100	.62	.11					851	367
Republic Steel	100	.95	.05					2,569	1,963
U.S. Pipe and Foundry	200	.92	.15	−.06	.15			638	364
U.S. Steel	200	.83	.13	.00	.13			21,580	13,771
Youngstown	100	.86	.08					3,535	1,936

[a]In $000's.

Source: Dopuch and Watts [1972, table 6].

TABLE 6-7

ESTIMATION RESULTS FOR RATE OF RETURN ON COMMON EQUITY. BASED ON VALUES OBSERVED BEFORE AND AFTER DEPRECIATION SWITCHES AND MODELS IDENTIFIED USING PRE-SWITCH OBSERVATIONS

Company	Model $p\ d\ q$	ϕ_1	$\sigma_{\phi 1}$	ϕ_2	$\sigma_{\phi 2}$	θ_1	$\sigma_{\theta 1}$	θ_0	$\sigma_{\theta 0}$
Armco	200	1.13	.15	−.36	.15			.02	.01
Bethlehem Steel	201	1.05	.16	−.33	.13	.45	.21	.02	.01
Crucible Steel	100	.58	.11					.02	.01
Eastern Stainless Steel	200	.44	.14	.06	.14			.03	.02
Inland Steel	200	.79	.11	−.30	.10				
Jones and Laughlin	200	.74	.16	−.06	.16			.02	.01
Pittsburgh Steel	200	.83	.14	−.24	.14			.02	.01
Republic Steel	100	.65	.11					.02	.01
U.S. Pipe and Foundry	200	.88	.14	−.26	.14			.03	.01
U.S. Steel	200	.73	.14	−.09	.13			.02	.01
Youngstown	200	.84	.15	−.26	.15			.03	.01

Source: Dopuch and Watts [1972, table 7].

point estimates of the model's parameters, relative to the estimated standard errors of the estimators. In this regard, one should note that the Dopuch/Watts post-change estimation results are based on numbers of observations equal to about one-third of their pre-change counterparts. Thus, the post-change parameter estimates are characterized by substantially greater sampling error (i.e., less precision).

It is not clear, however, that a more searching analysis of the Dopuch/Watts results will really be fruitful. Their specific application of the "time series approach" (though not the general approach itself) seems to suffer from some fundamental problems.

TABLE 6-8

OBSERVED VALUES OF $\tilde{F}$ FOR EVIDENCE ON NET INCOME

Company	Model	Degrees of Freedom		$F(k, N_A + N_B - 2k)$
		k	$N_A + N_B - 2k$	
Armco	010	1	43	7.65[a]
Bethlehem Steel	200	3	48	2.72
Crucible Steel	100	2	49	.50
Eastern Stainless Steel	011	2	44	3.98[b]
Inland Steel	200	3	47	3.48[b]
Jones and Laughlin	100	2	42	5.42[a]
Pittsburgh Steel	100	2	50	.33
Republic Steel	100	2	47	3.15[b]
U.S. Pipe and Foundry	200	3	46	5.35[a]
U.S. Steel	200	3	47	5.08[a]
Youngstown	100	2	53	5.37[a]

[a]Significant at the .01 probability level.
[b]Significant at the .05 probability level.
Source: Dopuch and Watts [1972, table 7].

TABLE 6-9

OBSERVED VALUES OF $\tilde{F}$ FOR EVIDENCE ON RATE OF RETURN ON COMMON EQUITY

Company	Model $p\ d\ q$	Degrees of Freedom k	$N_A + N_B - 2k$	$F(k, N_A + N_B - 2k)$
Armco	200	3	49	1.63
Bethlehem Steel	201	4	46	.98
Crucible Steel	100	2	49	.20
Eastern Stainless Steel	200	3	42	.04
Inland Steel	200	3	47	.37
Jones and Laughlin	200	3	40	.18
Pittsburgh Steel	200	3	48	.45
Republic Steel	100	2	47	.23
U.S. Pipe and Foundry	200	3	46	1.34
U.S. Steel	200	3	47	2.94[a]
Youngstown	200	3	51	.86

[a]Significant at the .05 probability level.
Source: Dopuch and Watts [1972, table 9].

The first problem turns on cross-sectional correlation. A variety of reasons leads one to expect different firms' accounting numbers to be influenced by common factors. Consequently, estimation results for different firms are unlikely to represent independently drawn sets of results—particularly when the firms examined are all members of a fairly homogeneous industry.[37] In short, the eleven sets of results (one set per firm) used by Dopuch and Watts are probably not eleven independent "pieces of information." To some extent, each set probably reflects factors already reflected in the other sets. In a loose sense, this leads to a kind of "multiple counting" of a factor's effects. Thus, the inconsistency of the Dopuch/Watts evidence with unchanged values of parameters is, as it stands, less forceful than one might think after being told that the inconsistency was inferred for "8 out of 11 firms." An appropriate multivariate test—which would explicitly recognize the influence of cross-sectional correlation—would probably lead one to infer fewer inconsistencies.[38]

Suppose that the Dopuch/Watts results are free of shear statistical problems. Can one then say that their results deal with the effects of the depreciation-method switches, taken by themselves? That could probably be said if Dopuch and Watts successfully held "all other factors" constant, i.e., if the oft-invoked "ceteris paribus" assumption has descriptive validity. Of course, it is rarely possible to guarantee that. Insofar as the Dopuch/Watts results are concerned, there are strong reasons to suspect that "other things" were not held constant.

Because of their study's design, one thing was certainly not held constant—time. That is, in comparing estimation results conditional on straight-line and accelerated depreciation

[37]Recent evidence on the importance of industry-wide commonalities is provided by Magee [1974].
[38]A multivariate test would not lead one to infer an inconsistency where a univariate test has already led one to infer consistency with the "null hypothesis." Some important attributes of multivariate tests are described by Morrison [1976].

methods, they were necessarily comparing results that were also conditional on different time periods—because of their use of pre- and post-change data. If, over the entire period covered by the Dopuch/Watts study, the attributes of firms' production-investment and financing decisions changed in any way, then the effects (if any) of these attributes' changes will be confounded with the effects (if any) of the depreciation switches. Since the time period covered by the Dopuch/Watts study is so lengthly (and includes the World War II period), one suspects that the attributes of firms' decisions did undergo some changes. The effects (if any) of the latter changes on the systematic properties of accounting numbers may lead one to infer important effects for the depreciation switches when, in fact, the switches may have had no effect whatsoever.[39] Or the effects of changes in the attributes of firms' decisions may offset—wholly or partially—the effects (if any) of the depreciation switches.

Within the context of the Dopuch/Watts study, an obvious way of dealing with this "other factors" problem is to use sets of observed accounting numbers based on different accounting techniques but computed, for each firm, over the same time period. One might examine, for example, the properties of observed values of net income for the period 1925–1967 conditional on each of several depreciation methods, rather than vary both the depreciation methods and the time period underlying the observations.[40]

The above critique of the Dopuch/Watts paper is not intended to detract from their basic approach. It merely serves to indicate some implications of conventional assumptions and some important problems likely to arise in assessing the effects of accounting techniques. The basic approach used by Dopuch and Watts and the perspective underlying it are important and quite consistent with the view of accounting numbers developed herein.

Another interesting set of results on the effects of accounting techniques is provided by Derstine and Huefner [1974]. A brief discussion of those results is provided next.

6.7.3 The Derstine/Huefner Study

This study deals with the effects of inventory-costing methods on several financial ratios, among other things. Specifically, it deals with the First-In-First-Out (FIFO) and Last-In-Last-Out (LIFO) costing methods. The empirical results discussed below are based on annual accounting data for 24 firms that reported *both* a LIFO and a FIFO inventory number for at least one year from the period 1951–1960. These firms were selected on the basis of information provided in the 1952–1961 editions of *Accounting Trends and Techniques*, published by the American Institute of Certified Public Accountants. The inventory balances (under both FIFO and LIFO) disclosed by a firm had to constitute at least 70 percent of its total inventory balance in order for a firm to be included in the sample.[41] Of the 24 firms ultimately selected, 3 made the dual disclosure of LIFO and FIFO amounts during the year that they switched from LIFO to FIFO; 10 did so when

---

[39]Dopuch and Watts reported some results consistent with the presence of this problem in their study (see Dopuch and Watts [1972, p. 191, footnote 19]).

[40]This might require the use of approximation methods designed to approximate the values that firms would have reported if they used accounting methods other than those actually adopted. The Derstine and Huefner study reviewed below employed this approach.

[41]Some firms do not disclose inventory methods for all categories of inventoried items. And some firms do not use one inventory method for all categories of inventoried items.

they switched from FIFO to LIFO; and 11 firms that used LIFO throughout the period 1951–1960 made the dual disclosure in some year of the latter period. A list of the 24 sample firms is provided in Table 6-10.

The accounting numbers provided by the 24 firms' dual disclosures were used to provide benchmarks and "starting conditions" for approximation procedures. Such procedures were used to convert FIFO- (LIFO-) based accounting numbers to LIFO- (FIFO-) based numbers. In the end, Derstine and Huefner obtained both a LIFO- and a FIFO-based set of numbers for each of the 24 firms for the entire ten-year period, 1951–1960. The so-called Dollar Value LIFO approach was used to convert LIFO- (FIFO-) based numbers to FIFO- (LIFO-) based numbers (see Derstine and Huefner [1974, pp. 218–219] for details). All required financial statement data were obtained from issues of *Moody's Industrial Manual*.

The effects of the inventory costing methods on attributes of four financial ratios were examined. The attributes examined are as follows:

(R.1) *Weighted Average Dividend Payout Ratio*

$$\sum_{t=1}^{T} \left(\frac{E_t}{\sum_t E_t} \right) \left(\frac{D_t}{E_t} \right).$$

(R.2) *Average Leverage Ratio*

$$\frac{1}{T} \sum_{t=1}^{T} \left(\frac{B_t + S_t}{A_t} \right).$$

(R.3) *Standard Deviation of Rate of Return on Equity (Net Income Available for Common Stockholders Divided by Book Value of Net Worth)*

$$\left[\frac{1}{T} \sum_{t=1}^{T} \left(\frac{E_t}{W_{t-1}} - \overline{\left(\frac{E}{W} \right)} \right)^2 \right]^{1/2},$$

where:

$$\overline{\left(\frac{E}{W} \right)} = \frac{1}{T} \sum_t \left(\frac{E_t}{W_{t-1}} \right).$$

(R.4) *Scaled Covariance of Return on Net Worth and a Market-Wide (Average) Return on Net Worth*[42]

$$\frac{\sum_{t=1}^{T} \left[\frac{E_t}{W_{t-1}} - \overline{\left(\frac{E}{W} \right)} \right] [M_t - \overline{M}]}{\sum_{t=1}^{T} (M_t - \overline{M})^2},$$

where:

[42]This is simply the estimated value of the slope parameter in a regression model wherein the value E_t/W_{t-1} is regressed on M_t, for $t = 1, 2, \ldots, T$.

TABLE 6-10

COMPANIES USED IN LIFO-FIFO COMPARISON, CLASSIFIED BY INDUSTRY

Industry	Company
Furniture and Other Household Durables:	Allied Stores Corporation
	Associated Dry Goods
	City Stores Company
	Gimbel Brothers, Inc.
	Maytag Company
Machinery and Motive Products:	Chrysler Corporation
	Deere and Company
	Gar Wood Industries, Inc.
	General Electric Company
	Hercules Motors Corporation
	Oliver Corporation
	Reliance Electric and Engineering Co.
	Safety Car Heating and Lighting Co. Inc.
	Square D Company
	Stewart Warner Corporation
Metals and Metal Products:	Acme Steel Company
	Colorado Fuel and Iron Company
	Reynolds Metal Company
Nonmetallic Mineral Products:	Penn-Dixie Cement Corporation
Processed Foods:	Beech-Nut Packing Company
	First National Stores, Inc.
	Holly Sugar Corporation
	Hunt Foods and Industries, Inc.
	A. E. Staley Manufacturing Company

Source: Derstine and Huefner [1974, appendix B].

$$\overline{M} = \frac{1}{T} \sum_{t} M_t.$$

The following notations apply to the above:

A_t = total assets at the end of year t.
B_t = current liabilities plus long-term debt at the end of year t.
D_t = cash dividends paid to common stockholders during year t.
E_t = income available for common stockholders in year t.
M_t = an equally weighted average of the values of E_t/W_{t-1} observed for all New York Stock Exchange listed firms on the COMPUTSTAT Industrial Tape with all necessary data.
S_t = preferred stock outstanding at the end of year t.[43]
T = number of years' data included in study (= 10).
W_t = book value of net worth at end of year t.

[43] Derstine and Huefner do not indicate whether they used "Preferred Stock at Redemption Value" or "Preferred Stock at Liquidation Value."

The values of (R.1)–(R.4) were computed for each of the 24 firms conditionally on both the FIFO- and the LIFO-based accounting numbers. Thus, there are two values of each statistic for each firm. Each value is based upon annual data from the ten-year period 1951–1960.

Derstine and Huefner ranked their 24 firms according to the observed values of each of (R.1)–(R.4), conditionally on both the FIFO- and LIFO-based accounting numbers. For each statistic, they used an estimate of the Spearman Rank Correlation Coefficient to assess the association between the rankings based on different inventory methods. They also created rankings based on mixed LIFO-FIFO numbers by randomly determining whether a firm (from their original set of 24 firms) would be represented in terms of its FIFO- or LIFO-based numbers. Results based on the data for this "mixture" sample are supposed to provide insights into situations wherein different firms use different accounting techniques.

The estimated rank correlation coefficients obtained by Derstine and Huefner are presented in Table 6-11. When these results are taken at face value, there appears to be a close correspondence between the values of (R.1)–(R.4) conditional on different inventory methods. Moreover, the estimated rank correlation coefficients for the mixed LIFO/FIFO-based numbers appear to be quite high. To be sure, these estimates are somewhat misleading to the extent that accounting numbers are cross-sectionally correlated. But given the values of the estimates reported in Table 6-11, one is still likely to infer that there is a high association between (R.1)–(R.4) conditional on the different inventory methods.

Of course, one can think of a variety of statistical problems (other than cross-sectional correlation) that may have affected the Derstine/Huefner results. For example, if the sto-

TABLE 6-11

ESTIMATION RESULTS FOR RANKINGS UNDER LIFO AND FIFO[a]

Ratio	Spearman Rank Correlation Coefficient
Dividend Payout Ratio:	
LIFO Sample vs. FIFO Sample	.971
LIFO Sample vs. Mixed Sample	.981
FIFO Sample vs. Mixed Sample	.980
Leverage Ratio:	
LIFO Sample vs. FIFO Sample	.997
LIFO Sample vs. Mixed Sample	1.000
FIFO Sample vs. Mixed Sample	.996
Standard Deviation of Earnings/Net Worth Ratio:	
LIFO Sample vs. FIFO Sample	.917
LIFO Sample vs. Mixed Sample	.988
FIFO Sample vs. Mixed Sample	.925
Covariance of Earnings/Net Worth Ratio with Overall Market Average Earnings/Net Worth Ratio:	
LIFO Sample vs. FIFO Sample	.988
LIFO Sample vs. Mixed Sample	.980
FIFO Sample vs. Mixed Sample	.971

[a]All results are "significant" at the .01 level.
Source: Derstine and Huefner [1974, table 1].

chastic processes applicable to their ratios (e.g., dividend payout, rate of return on equity, etc.) are nonstationary processes, then the statistics that they chose to use may be meaningless. If those stochastic processes imply that the ratios are serially correlated, then their estimated standard deviations and (scaled) covariances may be seriously misleading.

There is also an "internal consistency" problem. According to the regulations of the U.S. Internal Revenue Service, the LIFO method must be used for external reporting purposes if it is used for tax reporting purposes. If one is converting the numbers of a LIFO firm and if that firm uses LIFO for tax reporting and (as a result) for external reporting, one should adjust the firm's tax payments as well as all other numbers affected by the inventory method. This tax aspect of the conversion process would involve changing the firm's cash flows. One would then have to make some assumptions about the effects of this cash-flow change on the characteristics of the firm's production-investment and financing decisions. Nothing in the Derstine/Huefner paper indicates that this aspect of a change from LIFO was ever considered in their work.

However, for present purposes, the important aspect of the Derstine/Huefner paper is that it provides another illustration of applying the perspective developed herein. Specifically, it attempts to assess the effects of accounting techniques by inferring the extent to which the techniques, taken by themselves, alter the stochastic properties of reported accounting numbers. Derstine and Huefner attempted to abstract from the effects of "other factors" (e.g., changes in the characteristics of firms' decisions) by computing numbers over the same time period conditionally on each of the different inventory methods examined. The implicit assumption here is that those "other factors" are independent of the accounting techniques.[44] This implies that Derstine's and Huefner's numbers based on, say, LIFO for a firm that actually used FIFO would (except for approximation errors) have been the numbers actually reported by the firm had it, in fact, used LIFO for external reporting.

6.8 Assessing the Effects of Accounting Techniques on Capital Market Equilibrium

6.8.1 Preliminaries

The preceding section dealt with the effects of accounting techniques on the stochastic properties of accounting numbers. These numbers constitute one of the potential sources of information that capital market agents might use in assessing distributions of returns on firms' securities. We have not yet considered the extent to which agents' assessments are, in fact, altered by changes in accounting techniques. That is the issue considered in this section. The main question asked is this: from the perspective of capital market agents (in the aggregate), do changes in accounting techniques correspond to changes in the substantive economic factors that determine firms' equilibrium values or, more precisely, changes in the available information about those factors?

Suppose one infers—using, e.g., the kinds of tools described in Section 6.7—that a particular set of accounting techniques does not affect the stochastic properties of accounting numbers. That is, changing from one technique to another within the set does

---

[44]One situation where this assumption might be violated is when a firm changes from LIFO for both external and tax reporting. This issue is discussed in the previous paragraph of the text.

not, taken by itself, induce changes in the systematic properties of accounting numbers. This implies that changes in the systematic properties of accounting numbers can be ascribed to changes in the attributes of firms' production-investment or financing decisions.[45] Does it also imply that capital market agents' assessed distributions of returns on firms' securities will be unaffected by those changes in techniques? Evidently not. That is, the mere fact that a particular change, taken by itself, has no direct effect on the stochastic properties of accounting numbers does not, taken by itself, imply that agents' assessed distributions will be unaffected. Similarly, if the change does affect the stochastic properties of accounting numbers, agents' distributional assessments need not be affected.

As indicated earlier, agents' assessments will be altered by new information about the attributes of firms' production-investment decisions. Changes in the systematic properties of accounting numbers constitute one possible source of such new information, assuming that those changes can be ascribed to changes in the attributes of firms' decisions. As indicated in Sections 8.3 and 8.4, changes in accounting techniques may also have implications for the attributes of firms' decisions, even when those changes, taken by themselves, do not alter the stochastic properties of firms' accounting numbers.[46] Consider the following mundane example.

Suppose that a firm changes from the FIFO to the LIFO method of inventory accounting for external reporting. Taken by itself, this change may have no effect on the systematic properties of accounting numbers. If it is believed, however, that this change for external reporting will later be matched by the same change for tax reporting, then the external reporting change is a source of information about the probability distribution of the firm's cash outflows induced by tax obligations (hence the probability distribution of its net cash flow outflows). The latter distribution of the firm's net cash flow is, of course, an attribute of the firm's decisions.

The FIFO/LIFO change may have implications for things other than tax obligations. Such a change may convey information about managements' expectations regarding the prices of its inputs (e.g., raw materials) and, therefore, the firms' net cash flow. If so, then the change in technique constitutes a potential source of information about the substantive attributes of firms' decisions. This potentiality is independent of any direct effects of the change on the systematic properties of accounting numbers.

Another way that changes in techniques can have substantive implications turns on their implications for a firm's information-production costs. Depending on the nature of a firm's accounting system (e.g., the kinds of data retained and the techniques used for internal accounting), a switch from one method to another may imply a change in the costs borne by the firm because of "set-up" costs or recurring costs. For example, a switch from one method of defining a group of assets for group depreciation to another method may require an initial restructuring of a firm's internal data. That implies a nonzero "set-up" (or "changeover") cost and, therefore, a change (perhaps insignificant) in the probability distribution of the firm's net cash earnings. In this case, the change in techniques has implications for the firm's equilibrium value, whether or not the change, taken by

---

[45]Those attributes may change because of changes in the decisions themselves or changes in the economic environment (e.g., the "state" of the economy, governmental policies, etc.).

[46]Additional reasons for this will be given in Chapter 8, where we consider "signaling" activities of firms' managements.

itself, alters the stochastic properties of accounting numbers. Moreover, those implications are independent of the change's direct effect on the properties of accounting numbers.

One can easily construct other scenarios wherein changes in accounting techniques may or may not convey information pertinent to valuing firms. In general, changes in techniques may convey such information whether they do or do not, taken by themselves, alter the stochastic properties of accounting numbers. Thus, one's inference about the effects of accounting techniques on the properties of reported accounting numbers may not have unambiguous implications about the effects of techniques on firms' equilibrium values.

6.8.2 Why Ask the Question?

There are a variety of reasons for being concerned with the effects of accounting techniques on capital market equilibrium. Many of them are similar to the reasons for being interested in the extent to which the capital market is efficient (see Chapter 3).

First, consider a manager contemplating a change in his firm's accounting techniques. Specifically, assume that he is considering a switch from FIFO to LIFO for tax reporting and, therefore, for external reporting.[47] Suppose that the possibility of altering the tax reporting method is motivated by the manager's belief that using LIFO will lead to lower expected tax payments because of his expectations about commodities' prices, among other things, but not to a change in the riskiness of his firms' net cash flows.[48] Given his expectations, he also recognizes that externally reported accounting income will be lower under LIFO than under FIFO.

In the above scenario, the switch to LIFO should be preferred because it will increase the firm's value (by reducing its expected cash outflows for tax payments). Yet, it is often alleged by some that the effect of the switch on reported earnings (in this case a downward effect, on average) should play a critical role in evaluations on such a switch. The usual justification for this turns on the perceived influence of reported accounting earnings on a firm's equilibrium value, which is established by the capital market. Such a justification implies something very fundamental about the way equilibrium values are established. In particular, it implies that there is a somewhat mechanical relationship between a firm's reported earnings and its equilibrium value. That implies, in turn, that agents' reaction to the FIFO/LIFO switch will be determined by the switch's effect on reported earnings rather than its effect on net cash flow. Another implication of this perspective, taken as it stands, is that a firm can change its equilibrium value by changing its accounting techniques, and the value change will be independent of the substantive economic implications for managers who are attempting to follow the market value rule (i.e., maximize the current shareholders' wealth). The descriptive validity of this perspective on accounting techniques can be assessed by dealing with the general issue of the effects of accounting techniques on capital market equilibrium.

The perspective just ascribed by some managements (and their advisors) is not unlike that often adopted by private and public accounting regulatory bodies such as the FASB

---

[47]Under the U.S. Internal Revenue Service's rules, LIFO must be used for external reporting if it is used for tax reporting.

[48]Recall, from Chapter 5, that the *riskiness* of a firm's cash flows is, in general, also affected by a switch to or from LIFO.

and the SEC. Moreover, the contents of those bodies' pronouncements (e.g., *Statements* of the FASB, *Opinions* of the Accounting Principles Board, and the SEC's *Accounting Series Releases*) seem to suggest that it has motivated some of those bodies' policy decisions. However, if the indicated perspective is not descriptively valid, then perhaps attention and resources are being diverted from more important issues—ones that might actually involve the information content of accounting numbers. This possibility provides additional motivation for assessing the effects of accounting techniques on capital market equilibrium.

6.8.3 The General Approach

6.8.3.1 Preliminaries

In Chapter 2, we described a mechanism for the evaluation of a source of information. A part of that machinery deals with assessing the implications of a particular source of information. Those implications are summarized by probability distributions of states conditional on each of the signals that can emanate from the source. These conditional distributions were then incorporated into an optimization model in order to determine the maximum amount that an agent would pay for the opportunity to receive and use such signals before optimal decisions are made.

For present purposes we are interested only in the information content of a source of information. As before, information content pertains to the effects of the source's signals on probability assessments.[49] Thus, our primary interest is in the assessed conditional distributions mentioned above. As a review, an illustration of the origin and role of these conditional distributions will be given.

6.8.3.2 The Origin and Role of Conditional Distribution Functions: An Illustration[50]

Suppose that we are dealing with an asset whose one-period rate of return, $\tilde{R}$, can have either of two values: $\tilde{R} = R_1$ or $\tilde{R} = R_2$. The probabilities of these two values are assumed to depend on the value of some parameter, $\tilde{S}$, which can also have either of two values: $\tilde{S} = S_1$ or $\tilde{S} = S_2$. If $\tilde{S} = S_1$, the probabilities of $\tilde{R} = R_1$ and $\tilde{R} = R_2$ are 0.5 and 0.5, respectively; if $\tilde{S} = S_2$, the probabilities are 0.25 and 0.75, respectively. In short, we have $Pr(R_1|S_1) = 0.5$, $Pr(R_2|S_1) = 0.5$, $Pr(R_1|S_2) = 0.25$, and $Pr(R_2|S_2) = 0.75$. A schematic representation of these conditions is given in Exhibit 6.4. Each node represents a point in time at which an observation on a random variable is made. Each line represents a particular realization.

Consider a decision maker interested in the distribution function of $\tilde{R}$. Suppose that the details given in Exhibit 6-4 represent his probability assessments. At the beginning of the period—and before any optimal decisions are made—he can contemplate the various gambles (i.e., distribution functions) on $\tilde{R}$ that he faces. Each gamble depends on a value of $\tilde{S}$. For example, $\tilde{S} = S_1$ might pertain to "prosperity" and thus $Pr(R_1|S_1)$ and $Pr(R_2|S_1)$ would define the gamble on $\tilde{R}$, if, in fact, prosperity obtains. If $\tilde{S} = S_2$ denotes the state

---

[49]More precisely, it depends on whether observed values of the potentially informative random variable induce implications not already impounded in investor's probability assessments (and relevant to distribution functions of assets' future values).

[50]See Chapter 2 for a rigorous discussion.

EXHIBIT 6-4

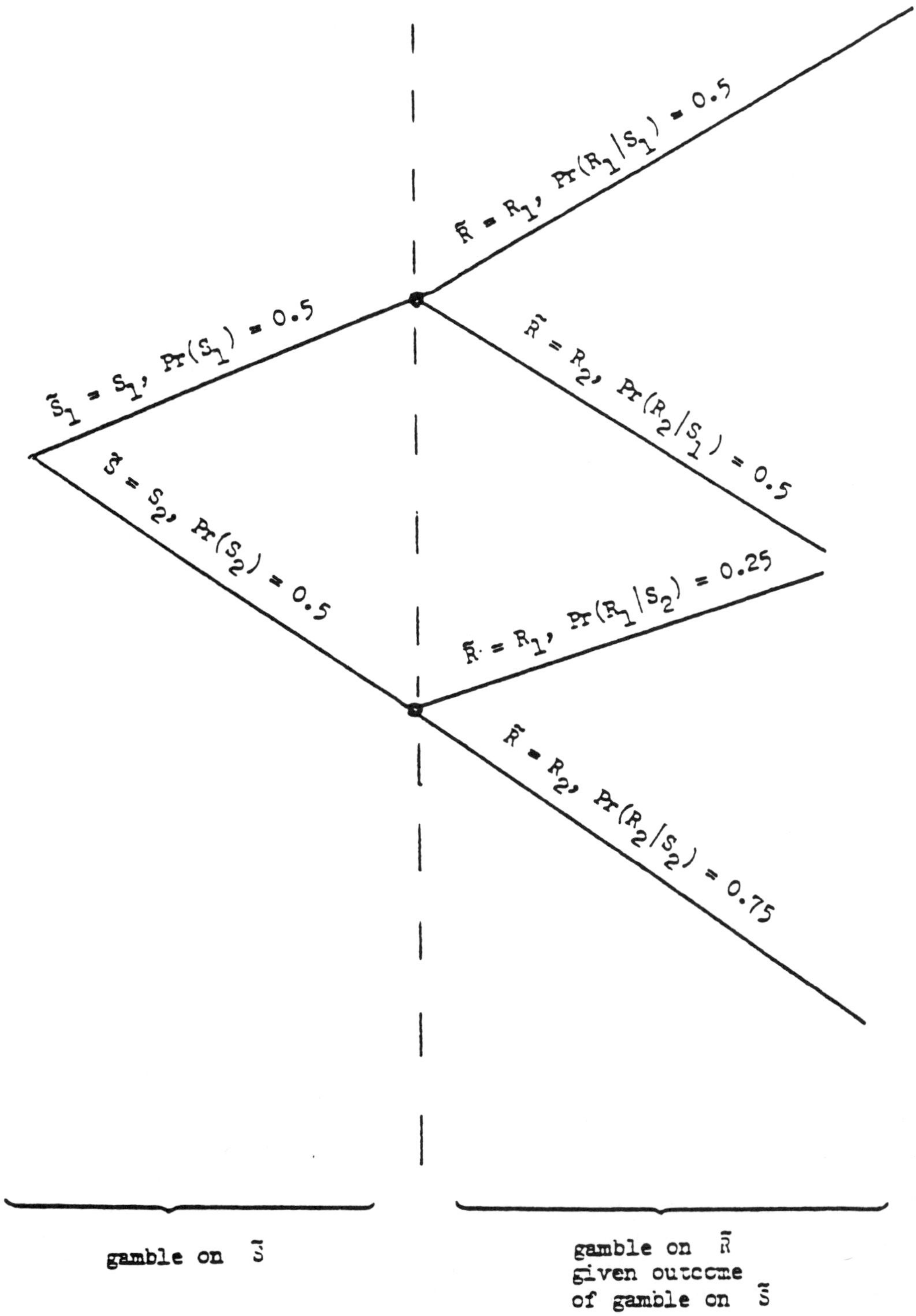
R̃ = R1, Pr(R1/S1) = 0.5
S̃1 = S1, Pr(S1) = 0.5
R̃ = R2, Pr(R2/S1) = 0.5
S̃ = S2, Pr(S2) = 0.5
R̃ = R1, Pr(R1/S2) = 0.25
R̃ = R2, Pr(R2/S2) = 0.75
gamble on S̃
gamble on R̃
given outcome
of gamble on S̃

"depression," then $Pr(R_1|S_2)$ and $Pr(R_2|S_2)$ define the gamble on $\tilde{R}$ if depression is the prevailing state.

In our example, the distribution function of $\tilde{R}$ conditional on $\tilde{S} = S_1$ (e.g., "prosperity") differs from the distribution function conditional on $\tilde{S} = S_2$ (e.g., "depression"). That is, when the decision maker contemplates the implications of $\tilde{S} = S_1$ for the distribution of $\tilde{R}$, he assesses a conditional probability distribution that is different from the one that he assesses conditionally on $\tilde{S} = S_2$. Thus, for this decision maker, we can say that $\tilde{S}$ has "information content" vis-à-vis the gamble on $\tilde{R}$, in the sense that realizations of $\tilde{S}$ affect the decision maker's probability assessments.

Suppose, however, that the realization of $\tilde{S}$ will be available after the beginning of the period and thus after the decision maker is supposed to make his optimal decision for the current period. If so, then his actual current-period decision cannot be made conditionally on any particular value of $\tilde{S}$. His decision must be made marginally with respect to $\tilde{S}$. That is, the decision maker's assessed joint distribution of $\tilde{S}$ and $\tilde{R}$—i.e., the values of $Pr(R_i, S_j)$ for all i and j—must be used (directly or indirectly) to derive probability information about $\tilde{R}$ that is not conditional on a specific value of $\tilde{S}$. This probability information is given by the marginal probability distribution of $\tilde{R}$: $Pr(R_i)$, $i = 1, 2$. It can be derived via the following:

$$Pr(R_i) = \sum_{j=1}^{2} Pr(R_i|S_j)Pr(S_j),$$

for $i = 1, 2$.

For the data given in Exhibit 6.4:

$$\begin{aligned} Pr(R_1) &= Pr(R_1|S_1)Pr(S_1) + Pr(R_1|S_2)Pr(S_2) \\ &= \left(\frac{1}{2}\right)\left(\frac{1}{2}\right) + \left(\frac{1}{4}\right)\left(\frac{1}{2}\right) \\ &= 3/8 \end{aligned}$$

and:

$$\begin{aligned} Pr(R_2) &= Pr(R_2|S_1)Pr(S_1) + Pr(R_2|S_2)Pr(S_2) \\ &= \left(\frac{1}{2}\right)\left(\frac{1}{2}\right) + \left(\frac{3}{4}\right)\left(\frac{1}{2}\right) \\ &= 5/8. \end{aligned}$$

Note that the marginal distribution of $\tilde{R}$ differs from the conditional distributions (i.e., the distribution conditional on $\tilde{S} = S_1$ and the one conditional on $\tilde{S} = S_2$). This is a reflection of our earlier observation: $\tilde{S}$ has information content vis-à-vis the gamble on $\tilde{R}$. We would conclude that it has no information content if the distributions of $\tilde{R}$ conditional on values of $\tilde{S}$ are identical to the marginal distribution of $\tilde{R}$, defined by $Pr(R_1)$ and $Pr(R_2)$. In the latter case, the decision maker's assessments are the same for all values of $\tilde{S}$. This is a different way of saying that the implications of one value of $\tilde{S}$ for the gamble on $\tilde{R}$ are the same as the implications of each other value of $\tilde{S}$. In our illustration, this would be indicated by $Pr(R_1|S_1) = Pr(R_1|S_2)$ and $Pr(R_2|S_1) = Pr(R_2|S_2)$. Since $Pr(S_1) + Pr(S_2) = 1$ from the mathematics of probability, we would have in this case:

$$
\begin{aligned}
Pr(R_1) &= Pr(R_1|S_1)Pr(S_1) + Pr(R_1|S_2)Pr(S_2) \\
&= Pr(R_1|S_1) \\
&= Pr(R_1|S_2)
\end{aligned}
$$

and:

$$
\begin{aligned}
Pr(R_2) &= Pr(R_2|S_1)Pr(S_1) + Pr(R_2|S_2)Pr(S_2) \\
&= Pr(R_2|S_1) \\
&= Pr(R_2|S_2).
\end{aligned}
$$

In short, each conditional probability distribution of $\tilde{R}$ is identical to the marginal distribution of $\tilde{R}$ when $\tilde{S}$ conveys no information about the probability distribution of (or the gamble on) $\tilde{R}$.[51]

Even though our decision maker is contrained to using the marginal probability distribution of $\tilde{R}$ in making decisions, we can always view his assessed marginal probabilities as having been derived from the joint distribution of $\tilde{R}$ and $\tilde{S}$. Thus, we can always view his behavior as having taken into account the information content of $\tilde{S}$. In short, the decision maker acts as if he "looks ahead" and determines what events (represented by realizations of random variables such as $\tilde{S}$) will affect his assessed distribution of $\tilde{R}$. He assesses the implications of those events for $\tilde{R}$ by assessing conditional probability distributions. He then assesses the probabilities of the events themselves. Finally, he combines all of his assessments in order to specify the implied marginal distribution of $\tilde{R}$—the probability distribution that he can in fact use in making his optimal decision at the beginning of the current period.

The above scenario provides a simplified illustration of a framework that can be used to assess the information content of any source of information for capital market agents. In using this approach, we shall be dealing with the "market's" assessed distributions. Under the homogeneous expectations assumption, these are the assessed distributions of each agent (see Chapter 4).[52] A general statement of the approach is provided next.

6.8.3.3 General Statement of the Approach

Let $\tilde{R}_{it}$, $i = 1, 2, \ldots, N$, denote the rate of return on asset i from t to $t + 1$, where N is the total number of assets. Let $\tilde{\theta}_{it}$ be a random variable that is thought to convey new information pertinent to valuing asset i at time t.

Suppose that the realization of $\tilde{\theta}_{it}$ becomes available after capital market equilibrium is established at time t. In line with the discussion in Chapter 3, the information content of $\tilde{\theta}_{it}$ can be assessed by comparing the distribution function of $\tilde{R}_{it}$ conditional on a value of $\tilde{\theta}_{it}$ to the unconditional distribution function of $\tilde{R}_{it}$. Alternatively, one can compare the distribution functions of $\tilde{R}_{it}$ conditional on different values of $\tilde{\theta}_{it}$. If either of these com-

[51]More precisely, in this case, $\tilde{S}$ conveys no *new* information (i.e., it induces no new implications) relative to the information (i.e., implications already reflected in the marginal distribution function of $\tilde{R}$).

[52]Under appropriate conditions, results that hold under "homogeneous expectations" (i.e., complete agreement) also hold under heterogeneous expectations. See, e.g., Gonedes [1976].

parisons indicates that the compared distributions are not equal, then one can infer that $\tilde{\theta}_{it}$ does have information content in the sense that some realizations of $\tilde{\theta}_{it}$ induce probability re-assessments.[53]

In formal terms, our approach involves the following. If $\tilde{\theta}_{it}$ does have information content, then there is at least one realization of $\tilde{\theta}_{it}$, say θ'_{it}, such that $G(R_{it}|Q'_{it}) \neq G(R_{it})$, where G is a generic symbol for a distribution function. Moreover, if $\tilde{\theta}_{it}$ does have information content, then one can find at least two realizations of $\tilde{\theta}_{it}$, say θ'_{it} and θ''_{it}, such that $G(R_{it}|\theta'_{it}) \neq G(R_{it}|\theta''_{it})$. If, however, $\tilde{\theta}_{it}$ does not have information content, then $G(R_{it}|\theta^{n}_{it}) = G(R_{it}|\theta^{m}_{it}) = E[G(R_{it}|\tilde{\theta}_{it})] = G(R_{it})$ for every pair of realizations, θ^{n}_{it} and θ^{m}_{it}.

Implementing the above approach involves testing for the inequality of distribution functions. That is a difficult task without some restrictions on the nature of those functions. Typically, it is assumed that all conditional and unconditional joint distributions are multivariate normal distributions.[54] This implies, of course, that the conditional and unconditional returns on a particular security are univariate normal. Thus, for a given asset's returns, the inequality of distribution functions can be tested by testing for the inequality of means and variances. That is, one can compare values of $E(\tilde{R}_{it}|\theta_{it})$ for different values of $\tilde{\theta}_{it}$ and values of $\text{Var}(\tilde{R}_{it}|\theta_{it})$ for different values of $\tilde{\theta}_{it}$.

For the most part, the available empirical work on information content is limited to tests based on means. In this regard, note that an inequality between $E(\tilde{R}_{it}|\theta'_{it})$ and $E(\tilde{R}_{it}|\theta''_{it})$ is a sufficient condition for the inequality $G(R_{it}|\theta'_{it}) \neq G(R_{it}|\theta''_{it})$—but it is not a necessary condition. That is, the conditional distributions may be different even though their conditional means are identical.

One can give an alternative explanation of our approach insofar as it relates to tests on means. Let I_t denote all available information at time t and, as usual, let $\tilde{R}_{it}$ denote the rate of return on asset i from t to $t + 1$ and $\tilde{\theta}_{it}$ a random variable that may convey information about the distribution of $\tilde{R}_{it}$. Assume that the realization of $\tilde{\theta}_{it}$ is known after time t, which is the time at which equilibrium prices are now being established in the market.

As was the case with the hypothetical decision maker of Chapter 2 capital market agents are viewed as contemplating the implications of different realizations of $\tilde{\theta}_{it}$ and then arriving at an assessment of the expected value of $\tilde{R}_{it}$. The latter expected value is marginal with respect to (i.e., unconditional on) $\tilde{\theta}_{it}$, but it is conditional on I_t. Thus, agents begin by assessing $E(\tilde{R}_{it}|I_t, \theta_{it})$ for all values, θ_{it}, of $\tilde{\theta}_{it}$. And they end up with the unconditional mean $E(\tilde{R}_{it}|I_t)$. From the mathematics of probability, we know that:

$$E\{\tilde{R}_{it}|I_t\} = E\{E(\tilde{R}_{it}|I_t, \tilde{\theta}_{it})\}, \tag{6.3}$$

where the first ("outside") expectation on the right-hand side (RHS) of (6.3) is with respect to the distribution of $\tilde{\theta}_{it}$ and the second ("inside") one is with respect to the distribution of $\tilde{R}_{it}$ conditional on a value of $\tilde{\theta}_{it}$. We can also write, conditional on information available at time t:

$$\tilde{R}_{it} = E(\tilde{R}_{it}|I_t) + \tilde{\epsilon}_{it}, \tag{6.4}$$

or:

---

[53]Or, more precisely, the implications of at least one value of $\tilde{\theta}_{it}$ induce probability re-assessments.
[54]Insofar as the unconditional distributions are concerned, this is the same distributional assumption usually made in deriving the two-parameter asset-pricing model.

$$\tilde{R}_{it} = E(\tilde{R}_{it}|I_t) + (\tilde{R}_{it} - E(\tilde{R}_{it}|I_t)), \tag{6.5}$$

where $\tilde{\epsilon}_{it} = \tilde{R}_{it} - E(\tilde{R}_{it}|I_t)$ is the so-called disturbance or stochastic error at time t, which is analogous to the disturbance of a conventional regression model.

As of time t, $E(\tilde{\epsilon}_{it}|I_t) = 0.0$ in a conventionally defined efficient capital market because I_t consists of all available information at time t (see Chapter 3).[55] Consider what happens, however, when the implications of various values of $\tilde{\theta}_{it}$ are contemplated. For each such value, the market assesses a value for $E(\tilde{R}_{it}|I_t, \theta_{it})$, where, from (6.5):

$$E(\tilde{R}_{it}|I_t, \theta_{it}) = E\{E(\tilde{R}_{it}|I_t)|I_t, \theta_{it}\}$$
$$+E\{(\tilde{R}_{it} - E(\tilde{R}_{it}|I_t)|I_t, \theta_{it}\}. \tag{6.6}$$

Since the value of $E(\tilde{R}_{it}|I_t)$ is deterministic, this value is equal to its expected value conditional on I_t and $\tilde{\theta}_{it} = \theta_{it}$. Thus, (6.6) can be restated as:

$$E(\tilde{R}_{it}|I_t, \theta_{it}) = E(\tilde{R}_{it}|I_t) + E\{(\tilde{R}_{it} - E(\tilde{R}_{it}|I_{it})|I_t, \theta_{it}\}$$
$$= E(\tilde{R}_{it}|I_t) + E\{\tilde{\epsilon}_{it}|I_t, \theta_{it}\}, \tag{6.7}$$

where $\tilde{\epsilon}_{it}$ is as defined for (6.4). When an examination of information content is restricted to using expected values, the values of $E\{\tilde{\epsilon}_{it}|I_t, \theta_{it}\}$ for various values of $\tilde{\theta}_{it}$ can be used to make inferences.

If $E\{\tilde{\epsilon}_{it}|I_t, \theta_{it}\} = 0$ for all values of $\tilde{\theta}_{it}$, then $E(\tilde{R}_{it}|I_t, \theta_{it}) = E(\tilde{R}_{it}|I_t)$ for all values of $\tilde{\theta}_{it}$. In line with our previous discussion, this is consistent with the statement that $\tilde{\theta}_{it}$ does not have information content vis-à-vis the distribution function of $\tilde{R}_{it}$.[56] On the other hand, if $E\{\tilde{\epsilon}_{it}|I_t, \theta_{it}\} \neq 0$ for at least one value of $\tilde{\theta}_{it}$, then one can infer that the distribution of $\tilde{R}_{it}$ conditional on some value of $\tilde{\theta}_{it}$ differs from the unconditional distribution of $\tilde{R}_{it}$—which has a mean equal to $E(\tilde{R}_{it}|I_t)$.[57] The implication of this is that $\tilde{\theta}_{it}$ does have information content vis-à-vis $\tilde{R}_{it}$, in the sense that some value of $\tilde{\theta}_{it}$ induces capital market agents to reassess the probability distribution based on only I_t.

In our scenario, the realization of $\tilde{\theta}_{it}$ will not be available until after time t—the time at which equilibrium prices are established. Thus, at time t, the only expected value of importance for decision making is the one taken marginally with respect to $\tilde{\theta}_{it}$, *viz.*, $E\{E(\tilde{\epsilon}_{it}|I_t, \tilde{\theta}_{it})\}$. For the latter expectation, the first ("outside") expectation is taken with respect to the distribution of $\tilde{\theta}_{it}$. The second ("inside") one is taken with respect to the distribution of $\tilde{\epsilon}_{it}$ conditional on I_t and a value of $\tilde{\theta}_{it}$. Since, at time t, $E\{E(\tilde{R}_{it}|I_t, \tilde{\theta}_{it})\} = E(\tilde{R}_{it}|I_t)$, it follows from (6.7) that $E\{E(\tilde{\epsilon}_{it}|I_t, \tilde{\theta}_{it})\} = E(\tilde{\epsilon}_{it}|I_t) = 0.0$ at time t. That is, whatever the various values of $\tilde{\theta}_{it}$ may imply about the probability distribution of $\tilde{R}_{it}$, the equilibrium prices established in the capital market at time t must be such that $E\{E(\tilde{\epsilon}_{it}|I_t, \tilde{\theta}_{it})\} = E(\tilde{\epsilon}_{it}|I_t)$ and, in a conventionally defined efficient capital market, $E(\tilde{\epsilon}_{it}|I_t) = 0.0$. The last equality holds because $\tilde{\epsilon}_{it}$ is the deviation of $\tilde{R}_{it}$ from its expected value conditional on all available information, I_t, as of time t.

In line with the above, one can make inferences about the information content of $\tilde{\theta}_{it}$—which is just a generic symbol for a random variable that may convey information—by

---

[55]Recall that this conventional definition incorporates aspects of both the capital market and the market for information.

[56]As indicated earlier, this is not a sufficient condition for the absence of information content.

[57]If $E(\tilde{\epsilon}_{it}/I_t, \theta'_{it}) \neq 0$ for one value, $\tilde{\theta}_{it} = \theta'_{it}$, then it must be different from zero for *at least* one other value of $\tilde{\theta}_{it}$ whose probability is nonzero, assuming $Pr(\theta'_{it}) \neq 0$.

estimating $E(\tilde{\epsilon}_{it}|I_t, \theta_{it})$ for various values of $\tilde{\theta}_{it}$. By comparing these values with $E(\tilde{\epsilon}_{it}|I_t) = 0.0$, one can make an inference about the descriptive validity of asserting that $\tilde{\theta}_{it}$ conveys information pertinent to assessing the distribution of $\tilde{R}_{it}$.[58] One has to generate observations on $\tilde{\epsilon}_{it} = \tilde{R}_{it} - E(\tilde{R}_{it}|I_t)$ in order to use this approach. That requires observations on $\tilde{R}_{it}$ and a value for $E(\tilde{R}_{it}|I_t)$. In actual empirical work, $E(\tilde{R}_{it}|I_t)$ will, of course, have to be estimated; its "true value" will rarely be known, for any i.

Since $E(\tilde{R}_{it}|I_t)$ is the equilibrium expected rate of return on asset i, estimating its value involves problems similar to those encountered in testing for capital market efficiency (see Chapter 3). Specifically, in order to test for the information content of $\tilde{\theta}_{it}$, we must be able to specify a model that characterizes equilibrium expected rates of return in terms of available information. Such a specification is also needed to get testable proportions on capital market efficiency. Much of the available empirical work uses some version of the two-parameter asset-pricing model as a basis for estimating $E(\tilde{R}_{it}|I_t)$. The underpinnings of that model were discussed in chapter 3; that discussion will not be repeated. Suffice it to note here that, under the assumptions given in Chapter 3, the two-parameter model implies (after omitting time subscripts for convenience):

$$E(\tilde{R}_i|I) = E(\tilde{R}_{zm}|I) + [E(\tilde{R}_m|I) - E(\tilde{R}_{zm}|I)]\beta_{im}(I), \tag{6.8}$$

where, as before, $\tilde{R}_i$ is the rate of return on asset i from t to $t + 1$; $\tilde{R}_m$ is the return on the market portfolio, m, from t to $t + 1$; $\beta_{im}(I) = \text{cov}(\tilde{R}_i, \tilde{R}_m|I)/\text{Var}(\tilde{R}_m|I)$ is the relative risk of asset i in the market portfolio; and $\tilde{R}_{zm}$ is the return from t to $t + 1$ on an asset z with $\beta_{zm} = 0.0$. Note that all of the parameters in this model of equilibrium are conditional on I because they are all parameters of the joint distribution of returns assessed conditionally on I. In much of the available empirical work, some or all of the parameters' values are assumed to be constant over time. That is equivalent to specifying that the value of each parameter is fixed and, in general, independent of the value of I.

Implementation of the above approach is best explained in terms of an actual study of the effects of changes in accounting techniques on capital market equilibrium. Sunder's [1973] paper on changes in inventory-costing methods will be used for this purpose.[59] Then, the findings of several other studies will be summarized.

The following discussion of Sunder's paper is intended to do more than illustrate an approach for assessing the information content of accounting changes. It is also intended (1) to convey the major message of some empirical results on accounting changes and (2) to point out some problems that usually arise in empirical work on accounting changes, and other topics. Parts of the discussion may be "rough going" for some readers. As always, the name of the game is "best efforts."

6.8.4 Assessments of the Effects of Changes in Inventory Methods on Capital Market Equilibrium

6.8.4.1 Study Purpose and Hypotheses

Sunder [1973] examined the effects of firms' decisions to extend or reduce their use of the LIFO inventory method. The following cases were examined:

---

[58] An alternative is to conduct tests directly on the conditional and unconditional expected values of $\tilde{R}_{it}$, along the lines proposed by, for example, Gonedes [1975] and Gonedes, Dopuch, and Penman [1976]. That approach will be considered in a later section.

[59] A more recent empirical study of inventory-costing methods is provided by Biddle [1980].

Case 1: Adopting or extending the use of LIFO for external reporting only.

Case 2: Adopting or extending the use of LIFO for both tax and external reporting.

Case 3: Wholly or partially abandoning the use of LIFO, which had been used only for external reporting.

Case 4: Wholly or partially abandoning the use of LIFO, which had been used for both tax and external reporting.

Sunder hypothesized that changing inventory methods for only external reporting has, taken by itself, no substantive economic implications. A change for tax purposes was recognized as one that does have such implications because it affects the probability distribution of a firm's cash flows. Sunder hypothesized that a change for tax reporting would have effects on a firm's value that turn on only the change's implications for expected values of future cash flows.[60] In terms of the classification scheme given in Section 6.4. this assumption restricts such a change to class (T.5). In other words, his assumption is that the tax-reporting changes would have had no implications for a firm's equilibrium value if, in fact, it had no implications for the expected values of future cash flows, conditional on the economic setting that actually prevailed.[61]

Recall that the conditional expected values, $E(\tilde{\epsilon}_{it}|I_t,\ \theta_{it})$ for different values of $\tilde{\theta}_{it}$, can be used to assess the information content of $\tilde{\theta}_{it}$. Also recall that $\tilde{\theta}_{it}$ is simply a generic symbol for a random variable that may convey information. In Sunder's study, $\tilde{\theta}_{it}$ refers to the ith firm's decisions regarding inventory-costing methods.

Let $\tilde{\theta}_{it} = 1$ if the ith firm switches to LIFO for tax reporting and $\tilde{\theta}_{it} = 0$ if it switches from LIFO for tax reporting. Conditional on Sunder's aforementioned assumptions, plus his assumption that use of LIFO has favorable cash-flow implications, one has $E(\tilde{\epsilon}_{it}|I_t,\ \tilde{\theta}_{it} = 1) > 0$ and $E(\tilde{\epsilon}_{it}|I_t,\ \tilde{\theta}_{it} = 0) < 0$.[62] That is, other things being equal, a switch to (from) LIFO for tax reporting is expected to increase (decrease) the ith firm's equilibrium value. This is not the result one expects if agents ignore LIFO's cash-flow implications (assumed to be favorable by Sunder) and react to LIFO's implications for reported income numbers. Under Sunder's assumptions, the switch to (from) LIFO for tax reporting induces a negative (positive) change in reported income. Hence, if LIFO's cash-flow implications are ignored, one would expect the signs of the conditional expected values of $\tilde{\epsilon}_{it}$ to be the opposite of those specified above.[63] One of Sunder's major objectives was to determine whether the information content of a change in inventory-costing methods turns on that change's implications for reported income or its implications for cash flows—in situations where income and cash flows are affected in different directions and where risk effects are presumed to be nonexistent.

Only the second and fourth of Sunder's cases involve tax effects. Cases 1 and 3 deal

---

[60]Sunder completely ignored the theoretical reasons for presuming that such changes for tax reporting will also have risk implications. See Chapter 5.

[61]Observe also that the "internal consistency" problem exhibited by the Derstine/Huefner treatment of LIFO is also present in Sunder's study.

[62]The anticipated effects of a LIFO switch on a firm's taxable income, and thus its net cash flow, depend on one's expectations about the behavior of input prices and tax rates, among other things. All of these conditioning arguments are subsumed into the "prevailing economic setting."

[63]The implicit assumption here is that a firm's equilibrium value and its income number are positively associated, which is a relationship for which one can find consistent empirical results. Most of the available results deal, however, with total income, not the components of income traceable to specific sources (e.g., changes in accounting techniques).

only with external reporting. Given Sunder's assumptions, the conditional expected values of $\tilde{\epsilon}_{it}$ for these cases should equal zero if the effect of an accounting change, taken by itself, turns on only its presumed cash-flow implications. The conditional expected values for Case 2 (4) should be positive (negative). He could not discriminate, however, between firms described by each case. The available data allowed him to classify a given firm as being a member of either of the following groups:

Group A: Firms described either by case 1 or by case 2.

Group B: Firms described either by case 3 or by case 4.

Redefine $\tilde{\theta}_{it}$ so that $\tilde{\theta}_{it}$ = A when the ith firm is in Group A and $\tilde{\theta}_{it}$ = B when the ith firm is in Group B. In view of the previous discussion, $E(\tilde{\epsilon}_{it}|I_t, \tilde{\theta}_{it} = \text{A}) \geq 0$ and $E(\tilde{\epsilon}_{it}|I_t, \tilde{\theta}_{it} = \text{B}) \leq 0$ if the effect of a change in inventory-costing techniques turns on the change's presumed cash-flows implications.

6.8.4.2 Sample of Firms

Sunder's sample consists of firms identified as being in Group A or Group B from the information given in the 1947–1967 editions of *Accounting Trends and Techniques* (published by the American Institute of Certified Public Accountants). These editions cover the fiscal years 1946–1966. Firms ultimately accepted for use had to satisfy various data availability criteria, pertaining to, among other things, the availability of monthly common stock price data from the data files of the Center for Research on Security Prices (CRSP) located at the University of Chicago. The sample underlying his major results consists of 113 firms. Some firms made more than one accounting change; hence the number of *changes* in Sunder's sample exceeds the number of distinct firms. Note that some of the multiple-change firms made changes of different types. There are 141 changes in his sample—119 in Group A and 22 in Group B.

Tables 6-12–6-14 provide some descriptive details on Sunder's sample. Table 6-12 is based on 129 (26) Group A (B) changes, rather than 119 (22). The additional changes are for firms ultimately dropped from Sunder's sample because they failed to satisfy his data-availability criteria.

Table 6-12 describes the industrial composition of Sunder's sample. Table 6-13 deals with the extent to which there is multiple counting of distinct firms, due to an individual firm's making more than one accounting change. Table 6-14 describes the time distribution of changes covered by his sample.

From Table 6-12, it is seen that 18 percent of the A changes were made by steel firms; 18 percent and 27 percent of the B changes were made by firms in the textile and retail-store industries, respectively. This apparent clustering of changes within particular industries leads one to wonder whether any inferences about the effects of accounting changes using Sunder's sample will be overly affected by other events occurring within specific industries rather than the effects of the changes per se. Moreover, one wonders whether the inferences about changes will be overly affected by any effects of changes for firms within specific industries. Since the importance of inventories is not the same for all industries, the second possibility must not be ignored. (More on this later.)

Some firms made more than one change of a given type (A vs. B), and some firms made both a type A and a type B change. As a result, a given firm may be counted more than once in either Group A or Group B and it may be counted at least once in A and at least once in B. Table 6-13 provides details on this multiple counting of distinct firms. On balance, the multiple counting within each group does not seem dramatic. The im-

TABLE 6-12

INDUSTRY PROFILE OF THE SAMPLE OF CHANGES IN INVENTORY METHODS

SIC Code	Industry	Number of A Changes	Number of B Changes	Total Number of Changes
100	Mining	3		3
200	Food Products	13	3	16
211	Tobacco	1		1
220	Textiles	3	7	10
260	Paper	9		9
270	Printing and Publishing	3		3
280	Chemicals	5	1	6
291	Petroleum	7		7
301	Rubber and Plastics	4	2	6
314	Leather and Shoe	1		1
320	Clay, Glass and Roofing Materials	7	1	8
331	Steel and Iron	23	1	24
333	Non-Ferrous Metals	5	1	6
340	Fabricated Metal Products	8	2	10
350	Machinery except Electrical	9	1	10
360	Electrical Equipment	8	1	9
370	Transportation Equipment	4		4
380	Instruments	3	1	4
390	Jewelry	3		3
500	Retail Stores	10	5	15
	TOTAL	129	26	155

Source: Sunder [1973, table 2a].

TABLE 6-13

MULTIPLE COUNTS PROFILE OF THE SAMPLE OF CHANGES IN INVENTORY METHODS*

	No. of Distinct Firms	No. of Changes in	
		Group A	Group B
Single change in Group A	81	81	
Single change in Group B	9		9
Two changes (both in Group A)	10	20	
Two changes (both in Group B)	1		2
Two changes (one in each group)	7	7	7
Three changes (all in Group A)	2	6	
Three changes (2 in Group A, 1 in Group B)	2	4	2
Three changes (1 in Group A, 2 in Group B)	1	1	2
TOTAL	113	119	22

*Some firms changed their accounting method more than once during the period 1946–1966. This table gives details of such occurrences.

Source: Sunder [1973, table 2.b].

TABLE 6-14

DISTRIBUTION OF DATES OF ACCOUNTING CHANGES*

Group	10%	20%	30%	40%	50%	60%	70%	80%	90%	100%
A	Dec. 48	Jan. 48	Dec. 50	Dec. 50	Oct. 51	Dec. 51	Dec. 52	Dec. 55	Dec. 57	Dec. 63

*Dates before which the given percentage of firms in the sample made the accounting change.
Source: Sunder [1973, table 2.c].

portance of overlaps due to firms' having made at least one change of each type is relatively more important for Group B because of its smaller total size. If the overlaps somehow induce misleading results on the effects of changes, one expects the impact to be greater for results pertaining to Group B. This and the small size of Group B do not make one optimistic about getting reliable results on the effects of the B changes. For that reason, the remainder of this discussion of Sunder's work deals with only the Group A changes.

Table 6-14 provides details on the timing of the changes in Group A. As can be seen, the changes are not uniformly distributed over the 1946–1966 period. Indeed, 70 percent of all of the changes occurred before January 1953. In other words, 70 percent of the changes occurred after the passage of about 30 percent of the time covered by Sunder's sample (1946–1966). This may have been due to a variety of reasons. The year 1946 represents the beginning of the post-World War II return to an "uncontrolled" economy and a period of observed and expected inflation. Corporate profits reflected and were probably expected to reflect the so-called inventory profits resulting from the sale of goods having replacement costs in excess of book values. Other things being equal, this provides motivation for a switch to LIFO for tax reporting and, given the Internal Revenue Service's rules, for external reporting. The outbreak of the Korean conflict in 1950 may have reinforced inflationary expectations and the motivation for using LIFO for tax reporting. Finally, the decision of the U.S. Tax Court in the 1947 *Hutzler* case—which permitted retail stores to use LIFO for tax reporting—may have stimulated the changes by firms in the retail stores industry. The historical overview provided by Eggleton, Penman, and Twombly [1975] does not point to any post-1946 and pre-1966 events that seem, a priori, to be as important as those just mentioned. In any event, it seems clear that an assessment of effects conditional on the changes in Sunder's Group A will probably be heavily affected by pre-1953 data, and thus any unusual or singular events of the pre-1953 time period.

6.8.4.3 Estimation Procedures

The rates of return used by Sunder are monthly rates of return adjusted for dividends and capitalization changes (e.g., stock splits). Observed returns were taken from the CRSP data files.

In order to get estimates of the expected values of $\tilde{\epsilon}_{it}$ for different i and t, Ordinary Least Squares (OLS) procedures were applied to the so-called market model. This model was used along with the Sharpe/Lintner version of the two-parameter asset-pricing model. The basic approach is as follows. The market model stipulates:

$$\tilde{R}_{it} = \alpha_{im} + \tilde{R}_{mt}\beta_{im} + \tilde{e}_{it}. \tag{6.9}$$

According to the Sharpe/Lintner version of the two-parameter asset-pricing model:

$$E(\tilde{R}_{it}|I_t) = R_{ft}(1 - \beta_{im}) + E(\tilde{R}_{mt})\beta_{im}, \tag{6.10}$$

where R_{ft} is the one-period rate of return on a "riskless" asset, f. This asset is riskless in the sense that $\mathrm{Var}(\tilde{R}_{ft}) = 0$ and, therefore, $\beta_{ft} = 0$.[64]

The conditioning argument I_t is omitted from the parameters on the RHS of (6.10) for convenience. In Sunder's work, the value of $R_{ft}(1 - \beta_{im})$ is assumed to be the same for all t. Thus, $\alpha_{im} = R_{ft}(1 - \beta_{im})$, the intercept from the market model. Thus, from our previous discussion and expressions (6.9) and (6.10):

$$\begin{aligned}\tilde{\epsilon}_{it} &= \tilde{R}_{it} - E(\tilde{R}_{it}|I_t)\\ &= (\tilde{R}_{mt} - E(\tilde{R}_{mt}))\beta_{im} + \tilde{\epsilon}_{it}.\end{aligned} \tag{6.11}$$

Note that $\tilde{\epsilon}_{it}$ consists of two random components. The first one involves the deviation of $\tilde{R}_{mt}$ from $E(\tilde{R}_{mt}|I_t)$. The second is $\tilde{e}_{it} = \tilde{R}_{it} - E(\tilde{R}_{it}|I_t, \tilde{R}_{mt} = R_{mt}) = \tilde{R}_{it} - [R_{ft}(1 - \beta_{im}) + R_{mt}\beta_{im}]$. But the deviations of $\tilde{R}_{mt}$ from $E(\tilde{R}_{mt})$ will appear as a component of $\tilde{\epsilon}_{it}$ for every i; it is not specific to any one firm. Therefore, if β_{im} is constant (and thus not affected by accounting changes), the first component of $\tilde{\epsilon}_{it}$ conveys no informations about the effects of the ith firm's accounting change on the equilibrium value of the ith firm. So, one might as well abstract from the variability in $\tilde{\epsilon}_{it}$ induced by $(\tilde{R}_{mt} - E(\tilde{R}_{mt}|I_t))$ by using $\tilde{e}_{it}$ wherever $\tilde{\epsilon}_{it}$ would otherwise be used. This is the approach used for Sunder's results, which are based on the assumption that β_{im} is stationary. That is, the value of β_{im} is assumed to be the same for all t. We shall return to this point later.

The values of α_{im} and β_{im} were estimated by OLS procedures. The time period from which observed returns were taken for the ith firm depended on the times at which its accounting changes occurred, i.e., the times at which the realizations of $\tilde{\theta}_{it}$ were available for the firms in Sunder's sample.

The exact dates at which the realized values of $\tilde{\theta}_{it}$ were announced, for each firm i and each of the fiscal years 1946–1966, were not known. For each firm and each accounting change, Sunder assumed that the change was announced on the last date of the fiscal year during which the change occurred. These assumed "change dates" were then used to define the time periods from which observed returns were taken in order to estimate α_{im} and β_{im}, for each i.

For each fiscal year during which a change occurred for firm i, the 12 monthly returns preceding the change-date and the 12 returns succeeding the change-date were excluded from the data used for estimation. This is a conventional procedure used to avoid biasing the empirical results against finding that accounting changes affect firms' values (see Sunder [1973, p. 16]).

For each *change* in Sunder's sample, the number of observations used to estimate α_{im} and β_{im} for the changing firm varied from a minimum of 24 to a maximum of 120 monthly returns from within the six-year period preceding and the six-year period succeeding the change date—after the exclusion of data mentioned above. Some firms changed procedures more than once; thus, estimates of α_{im} and β_{im} had to be obtained more than once for these firms.

The estimation procedure provides estimates of α_{im} and β_{im} denoted by $\hat{\alpha}_{im}$ and $\hat{\beta}_{im}$, respectively. These estimates can be used to get estimators, $\tilde{u}_{it}$, of the realizations of $\tilde{e}_{it}$.

---

[64]Why is $\beta_{ft} = 0$?

We can only get estimates of these realizations because we are using estimated values of α_{im} and β_{im}, rather than their "true" values. $\tilde{u}_{it}$ is defined by:

$$\tilde{u}_{it} = \tilde{R}_{it} - \hat{\alpha}_{im} - R_{mt}\hat{\beta}_{im}, \tag{6.12}$$

where R_{mt} is the value of $\tilde{R}_{mt}$ actually observed for time t. $\tilde{u}_{it}$ is simply the error from predicting $\tilde{R}_{it}$ with the estimates $\hat{\alpha}_{im}$ and $\hat{\beta}_{im}$ and the realization of $\tilde{R}_{mt}$. Since $\tilde{\hat{\alpha}}_{im}$ and $\tilde{\hat{\beta}}_{im}$ are unbiased estimators of α_{im} and β_{im}, $\tilde{u}_{it}$ is an unbiased estimator of ϵ_{it}.[65] That is, $E(\tilde{u}_{it}|R_{it}, R_{mt}) = \epsilon_{it}$, where, for simplicity, I_t is omitted from the conditioning arguments. Therefore,

$$E\{E(\tilde{u}_{it}|\tilde{R}_{it},\tilde{R}_{mt})\} = E(\tilde{\epsilon}_{it}) = 0. \tag{6.13}$$

This implies that we can use realizations of $\tilde{u}_{it}$ to estimate ϵ_{it} and, thus, the expected value of $\tilde{\epsilon}_{it}$, in a manner that does not involve bias.

The observed values of $\tilde{u}_{it}$ for the 12 months preceding the (assumed) change date are used to estimate the conditional expected values of $\tilde{\epsilon}_{it}$, one estimate for each of the 12 months. This procedure is consistent with the framework described earlier. Specifically, it is consistent with letting $\tilde{\theta}_{it}$ represent a random variable whose realized value is known after equilibrium is established at time t. Here time t is the beginning of a one-month interval, of which there are 12, and the value of $\tilde{\theta}_{it}$ becomes known after the beginning of each of the 12 intervals.

From the above discussion, it should be clear that identifying the actual "announcement date" of the potentially informative random variable $\tilde{\theta}_{it}$ is an important aspect of Sunder's approach. Identification errors with respect to these dates will induce imprecise, and perhaps biased, estimates of the conditional and unconditional expected values pertinent to Sunder's analysis. Note also that Sunder's approach presumes that there is, in fact, *one* well-defined announcement date for each accounting change. His framework does not allow for "partial" or "noisy" information on accounting changes.

If the conditional distribution of $\tilde{\epsilon}_{it}$ is stationary over time, then $E(\tilde{\epsilon}_{it}|\theta_{it})$ is the same for every t. Let T_2 be the interval at the end of which the value of $\tilde{\theta}_{it}$ is actually announced and change the subscripting on $\tilde{\theta}_{it}$ so that the time subscript pertains to the announcement date rather than the calendar date of the equilibrium prices being considered. That is, use the notation $\tilde{\theta}_{iT_2}$ rather than $\tilde{\theta}_{it}$ for months $t \leq T_2$ and an actual announcement date at the end of month T_2. Under the stationarity assumption, $E(\tilde{\epsilon}_{it}|\theta_{iT_2})$, which corresponds to the return from the beginning to the end of month t, is the same for all $t \leq T_2$. Thus, invoking the same stationarity assumption for $\tilde{u}_{it}$ and recalling the discussion immediately above expression (6.13), we have:

$$\begin{aligned} E(\tilde{\epsilon}_{it}|\theta_{iT_2}) &= \frac{1}{T_2 - T_1} \sum_{\tau=T_1}^{T_2} E\{E(\tilde{u}_{i\tau}|\tilde{R}_{i\tau}, \tilde{R}_{m\tau}, \theta_{iT_2})\} \\ &= \frac{1}{T_2 - T_1} \sum_{\tau=T_1}^{T_2} E(\tilde{\epsilon}_{i\tau}|\theta_{iT_2}) \\ &= \mu_{\epsilon}(\theta_{iT_2}) \end{aligned} \tag{6.14}$$

[65]What is the difference between an estimate and an estimator? Why do tildes appear on $\tilde{\alpha}_{im}$ and $\tilde{\beta}_{im}$ in this sentence? Why is there no tilde on ϵ_{it} in this sentence?

for all $t \leq T_2$, where $\mu_\epsilon(\theta_{iT_2})$ is the time invariant value of the conditional expected value of $\tilde{\epsilon}_{it}$. That is, $E(\tilde{\epsilon}_{it}|\theta_{iT_2}) = \mu_\epsilon(\theta_{iT_2})$ for all $t \leq T_2$.[66]

Under the above stationarity assumptions, one estimator of $\mu_\epsilon(\theta_{iT_2})$ is:

$$\tilde{\hat{\mu}}_\epsilon(\theta_{iT_2}) = \frac{1}{T_2 - T_1} \sum_{\tau=T_1}^{T_2} \tilde{u}_{i\tau}, \tag{6.15}$$

because $\tilde{u}_{i\tau}$ is an estimator of $\epsilon_{i\tau}$, the realization of $\tilde{\epsilon}_{i\tau}$ for time τ. A specific estimate or value of $\hat{\mu}_\epsilon(\theta_{iT_2})$ is obtained by applying (6.15) to a specific set of observations on $\tilde{u}_{i\tau}$.

The stationary assumptions used above seem overly restrictive. They rule out, for example, a situation in which the change in a firm's equilibrium value due to a new and certain tax subsidy is dependent on the date at which the new subsidy will take effect. Presumably, an unanticipated subsidy that is scheduled to take effect 60 months hence will induce a value change different from a subsidy of the same sort but which is scheduled to take effect 100 months hence. The subsidy that begins sooner is, one would expect, of greater value. Fortunately, we can dispense with most stationarity conditions without seriously affecting the tests for information content.

Recall that Sunder's hypothesis turns on the sign of the conditional expected values of $\tilde{\epsilon}_{it}$, not the values of those conditional expectations. Thus, it is sufficient to assume that the conditional distribution of $\tilde{\epsilon}_{it}$ is stationary at least insofar as the sign of its mean's value is concerned. The same degree of stationarity will suffice for the conditional distribution of $\tilde{u}_{it}$. Under this stationarity condition, inferences can be based on estimates of the Cumulative Average Error, CAE_{T_1,T_2}, where:

$$\text{CAE}_{T_1,T_2} = \sum_{\tau=T_1}^{T_2} E(\tilde{\epsilon}_{i\tau}|\theta_{iT_2}), \tag{6.16}$$

rather than estimates of (6.14). Clearly, if $E(\tilde{\epsilon}_{i\tau}|\theta_{iT_2}) \geq 0$ (≤ 0) for all τ such that $T_1 \leq \tau \leq T_2$, then $\text{CAE}_{T_1,T_2} \geq 0$ (≤ 0). One estimator of CAE_{T_1,T_2} is, under the given stationarity assumptions:

$$\widetilde{\widehat{\text{CAE}}}_{T_1,T_2} = \sum_{\tau=T_1}^{T_2} \tilde{u}_{i\tau}, \tag{6.17}$$

because $\tilde{u}_{i\tau}$ is an estimator of $\epsilon_{i\tau}$—which is, in turn, an estimate of $E(\tilde{\epsilon}_{i\tau}|\theta_{iT_2})$ based on a sample of size one. But an estimate based on a sample of size one is likely to exhibit a substantial amount of sampling error. Fortunately, there is a way out of this problem too—if an additional assumption is made.

Suppose we assume that the sign of the conditional expected value of $\tilde{u}_{i\tau}$ is the same for all i as of a given τ. Then, since we are interested in only the sign of CAE_{T_1,T_2}, we might as well estimate $\epsilon_{i\tau}$ for a portfolio of firms rather than one firm. Consider a portfolio, p, with a proportional investment of $x_{i\tau}$ in asset i at the beginning of τ, $\Sigma_i\, x_{i\tau} = 1$. The error, $\tilde{u}_{p\tau}$, for the portfolio, p, is given by:

---

[66]Note that none of our assumptions implies that $\mu_\epsilon(\theta_{iT_2})$ will have the same value for all i (i.e., for different firms).

$$\tilde{u}_{p\tau} = \sum_{i=1}^{N} \tilde{u}_{i\tau} x_{i\tau}, \tag{6.18}$$

where N is the number of securities in the portfolio. Clearly, if the conditional expected value of $\tilde{u}_{i\tau}$ for each i is positive (negative), then the conditional expected value of $\tilde{u}_{p\tau}$ is positive (negative). Here, we are assuming that the conditioning argument is the same for each security—either $\tilde{\theta}_{iT_2} = \text{A}$ or $\tilde{\theta}_{iT_2} = \text{B}$ for each firm, i, in the portfolio. An estimate of CAE_{T_1,T_2} that is adequate for our purposes is:

$$\widehat{\text{CAE}}_{T_1,T_2} = \sum_{\tau=T_1}^{T_2} u_{p\tau}. \tag{6.19}$$

Note that so long as $\tilde{u}_{it}$ and $\tilde{u}_{jt}$, $i \neq j$, are not perfectly positively correlated, the standard deviation of $\tilde{u}_{pt}$, $\sigma(\tilde{u}_{pt})$, will be less than $\Sigma_i\ \sigma(\tilde{u}_{it})x_{it}$, the average of the portfolio's components' standard deviations. That is, there will be a diversification effect. If, for example, $\sigma(\tilde{u}_{it}) = \sigma_t$, for all i, then $\sigma(\tilde{u}_{pt}) < \Sigma_i\ \sigma_t x_{it} = \sigma_t$. The last equality follows from the restriction, $\Sigma_i\ x_{it} = 1$. In this case, we can guarantee an increase in the precision of our estimator of $\tilde{\epsilon}_{it}$'s value, and thus an increase in the power of our test for information content. If $\tilde{u}_{it}$ and $\tilde{u}_{jt}$, $i \neq j$, are uncorrelated or negatively correlated, then—no matter what the values of the components' standard deviations are—the value of $\sigma(\tilde{u}_{pt})$ will converge to zero as more and more securities are added to portfolio p (with positive weights). Since the correlations between different firms' errors are typically close to zero, this provides strong motivation for using the portfolio estimator of ϵ_{it}.

The estimator used by Sunder is essentially that defined by (6.19). As is conventional, he set x_{it} in (6.18) equal to $1/N$. He dealt with two portfolios: one for firms in his Group A, for which $\tilde{\theta}_{iT_2} = \text{A}$ for each firm i in the group, and one for Group B, for which $\tilde{\theta}_{jT_2} = \text{B}$ for each firm j in the group. It is well to repeat that this procedure assumes that the effect of the inventory change is the same for each firm in a given group, at least in terms of the sign of $E(\tilde{\epsilon}_{it}|\theta_{iT_2})$, for $t \leq T_2$. Moreover, multiple counting of firms—due to multiple inventory method changes—is not precluded.

The above discussion of Sunder's sample and estimation procedures seems adequate for present purposes. A look at some of his results is now in order—at last! For the reasons given earlier, we discuss only the results for Sunder's Group A.

6.8.4.4 Results (for Group A)

Sunder obtained estimates of CAE_{T_1,T_2} in terms of months defined relative to his (assumed) change dates, rather than calendar time. This approach involves estimating $E(\tilde{\epsilon}_{pt}/\theta_{pT_2})$, for portfolio p, conditional on a specified interval of time between the evaluation of $E(\tilde{\epsilon}_{pt}/\theta_{pT_2})$ and the accounting change. Henceforth, all time subscripts will denote a month relative to the change date T_2 and we shall set $T_2 = 0$. Thus, for example, $t = -11$ represents the eleventh month prior to the month of change; $t = +1$ refers to the first month after the change month.

Values of $\tilde{u}_{p\tau}$, each of which is an estimate of an $\tilde{\epsilon}_{p\tau}$'s realization, and the corresponding values of $\text{CAE}_{-11,\tau}$, for $\tau = -11, -10, \ldots, 0, +1, \ldots, +12$ are presented in Table 6-15. A plot of $\text{CAE}_{-11,\tau}$ for the same values of τ is provided in Exhibit 6-5. Conditional on the conventional motion of capital market efficiency (which is the motion used by Sunder), $\text{CAE}_{s,t} = 0$ for $0 < s < t$. Since, for $t > -11$, $\text{CAE}_{-11,t} = \text{CAE}_{-11,s} + \text{CAE}_{s+1,t}$,

TABLE 6-15

ESTIMATED ERRORS AND ESTIMATED CUMULATIVE AVERAGE ERRORS FOR 24 MONTHS SURROUNDING THE DATES OF ACCOUNTING CHANGES TOWARD LIFO

	GROUP A; 119 CHANGES		GROUP A WITHOUT STEEL FIRMS; 97 CHANGES		STEEL FIRMS CF GROUP A ONLY; 22 CHANGES	
Month (τ) (1)	$U_{p\tau}$ (2)	$\widehat{\text{CAE}}_{-11,\tau}$ (3)	$U_{p\tau}$ (4)	$\widehat{\text{CAE}}_{-11,\tau}$ (5)	$U_{p\tau}$ (6)	$\widehat{\text{CAE}}_{-11,\tau}$ (7)
−11	0.000	0.000	−0.003	−0.003	0.012	0.012
−10	0.005	0.005	0.008	0.005	−0.004	0.008
−9	0.006	0.011	0.006	0.010	0.009	0.017
−8	0.005	0.016	0.001	0.011	0.020	0.037
−7	0.002	0.019	0.003	0.014	0.001	0.038
−6	0.006	0.025	0.004	0.018	0.018	0.055
−5	0.007	0.032	−0.002	0.016	0.047	0.102
−4	0.007	0.039	0.003	0.019	0.023	0.126
−3	0.000	0.039	−0.003	0.015	0.017	0.142
−2	0.007	0.047	0.003	0.018	0.026	0.168
−1	0.006	0.052	0.004	0.022	0.013	0.181
0	0.001	0.053	0.000	0.023	0.004	0.185
1	−0.008	0.045	−0.010	0.012	0.000	0.186
2	−0.002	0.044	0.004	0.017	−0.027	0.159
3	0.011	0.055	0.011	0.027	0.014	0.173
4	−0.004	0.051	−0.002	0.025	−0.010	0.163
5	−0.001	0.051	0.001	0.027	−0.009	0.154
6	0.004	0.054	−0.001	0.026	0.024	0.178
7	−0.006	0.049	−0.008	0.018	0.003	0.181
8	0.001	0.050	0.000	0.018	0.008	0.188
9	0.001	0.051	0.001	0.019	0.001	0.189
10	−0.008	0.043	−0.011	0.008	0.006	0.195
11	−0.000	0.043	0.004	0.012	−0.018	0.177
12	−0.001	0.042	0.002	0.014	−0.015	0.161

Source: Sunder [1973, table 3].

where $-11 \leq s < t$, we can infer capital market efficiency if, sampling error aside, the estimated values of $\text{CAE}_{-11,\tau}$ seem to "level off" for $\tau > 0$. That would imply $\text{CAE}_{1,t}$, $1 \leq t$, is zero, sampling error aside. Results consistent with the joint hypothesis of capital market efficiency and accounting changes' having an effect are given by results consistent with $\text{CAE}_{-11,\tau} \neq 0$ for $\tau \leq 0$. Results consistent with the accounting changes' effect turning on the implications for firms' cash flows are given by consistency with $\text{CAE}_{-11,\tau} \geq 0$ for $\tau \leq 0$, since the Group A changes involve changes toward LIFO (for tax reporting, external reporting, or both).

Taken at face value, Sunder's estimation results for $\tau \geq 0$ appear to be consistent with capital market efficiency (conventionally defined). This is most evident from the plot in Exhibit 6-5. Also, his results for $\tau \leq 0$ appear to be consistent with inventory changes' having some effect on firms' values.

Moreover, the results appear to be consistent with changes' effects turning on the

EXHIBIT 6-5

ESTIMATED CUMULATIVE AVERAGE ERROR FOR 119 CHANGES TOWARD LIFO

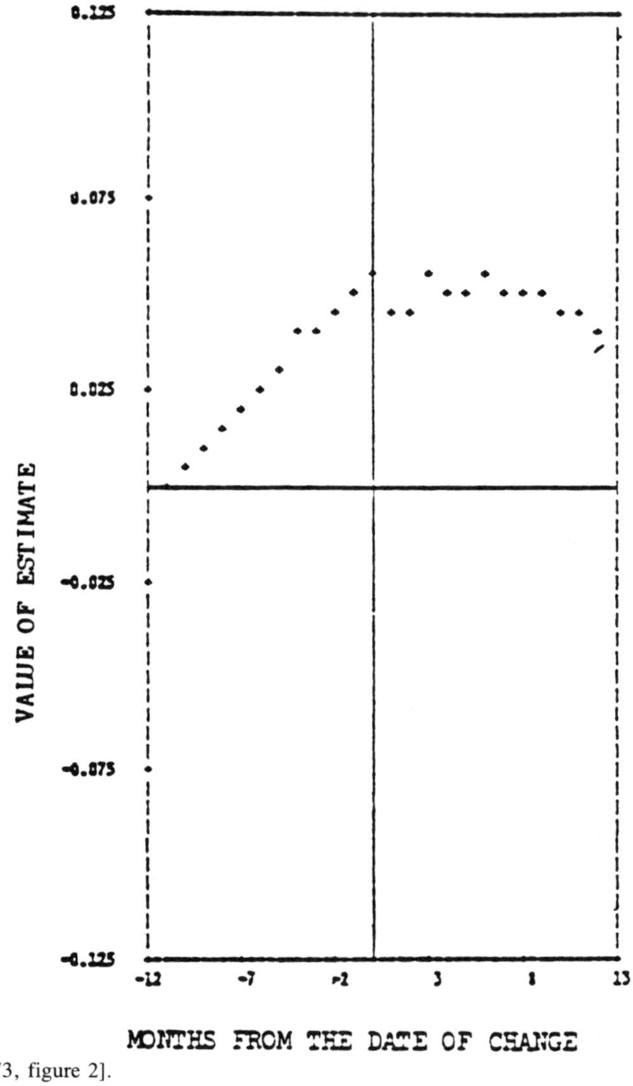

Source: Sunder [1973, figure 2].

presumed cash-flow implications of a switch toward LIFO for tax reporting, the implications for reported income notwithstanding.

An apparent clustering of changes within particular industries was discussed in Section 6.8.4.2. For Group A changes, steel firms seemed to provide a relatively large number of the changes. From Table 6-15, it seems clear that these firms did have an important influence on the overall results for Group A. Yet, if the results are taken at face value again, it does not appear that removing the steel firms from the sample leads to results that tell a very different story. The story just seems a little less dramatic.

The extent to which the overall results can be entirely or primarily ascribed to the steel firms is part of a broader question—the homogeneity of the overall sample with respect to the accounting changes' effects. One way of attacking this question is to examine results for nonoverlapping subsamples. That is the approach used by Sunder. He constructed five nonoverlapping samples using a procedure that would not, a priori, lead to one sample's being systematically different from another—in terms of industry composition, firms' sizes, etc. Each of the first four subsamples contains 24 changes; the fifth has 23. The estimated values of the Cumulative Average Errors for the subsamples are plotted in Exhibit 6-6. On balance, the results for the subsamples are consistent with the results for the entire sample. The major exception is provided by the first subsample. But that can be plausibly ascribed to sampling error.

Of course, consistency of sample evidence with one proposition does not preclude consistency with another proposition, perhaps a conflicting one. For example, the results in Table 6-15 are also consistent with the hypothesis that firms which perform well ex post are those that switch to LIFO—because they have sufficient accounting earnings to "absorb" the immediate depressing effects of such a switch on reported earning. If this is the correct interpretation, then there is no basis for ascribing any importance to the LIFO switch. Instead, the results can be explained in terms of an ex post sample selection bias—the selection of firms that were, for whatever reason, "good performers." The evidence reported by Sunder does not permit us to rule out this possibility.

Another possibility is that the results merely reflect the effects of sampling error. That is, there may be a high probability of observing such results for a randomly selected group of firms. If so, then the results may say little about Group A firms—and thus a LIFO switch—that cannot also be said for firms in general, whether or not the firms switched to a greater use of LIFO. One way of attacking this problem is to construct actual groups of randomly selected firms and to determine whether results on Cumulative Average Errors for those groups are similar to the corresponding results for Group A. This is essentially what Sunder did. He selected firms from the CRSP data file as follows (Sunder [1973, p. 21, footnote 20]):

1. Look for the first stock for which at least 48 months of data are available. Include it in the sample.
2. Skip 3 stocks.
3. Stop if 120 stocks have been selected. Otherwise go to Step 1.

For each firm in the resulting sample of 120 firms, the month at the midpoint of its available observed monthly rate-of-return series was assumed to be the hypothetical date of the accounting change (i.e., the date $t = 0$). The estimated Cumulative Average Errors for this "control" sample are plotted in Exhibit 6-7 (first plot). Also plotted there are the estimates for nonoverlapping successive subsamples of 24 firms. The estimates themselves are given in Table 6-16. The subsample results in Exhibit 6-7 are provided for comparison with the subsample results in Exhibit 6-6, which are based on subsamples of changes from the Group A changes.

On balance, the results for the entire control sample and its subsamples seem to be quite different from the results for Group A and the subsamples drawn from it. Specifically, the results for the control sample and four of its five subsamples seem to exhibit no systematic pattern like that exhibited by the results for Group A and four of its five subsamples. The major exception seems to be for the subsample underlying the last plot in Exhibit 6-7. That can, however, easily be ascribed to sampling error—as were the results for the "exceptional" sample in Group A's subsamples.

EXHIBIT 6-6

ESTIMATED CUMULATIVE AVERAGE ERRORS FOR SUBSAMPLES OF SAMPLE OF 119 CHANGES TOWARDS LIPO

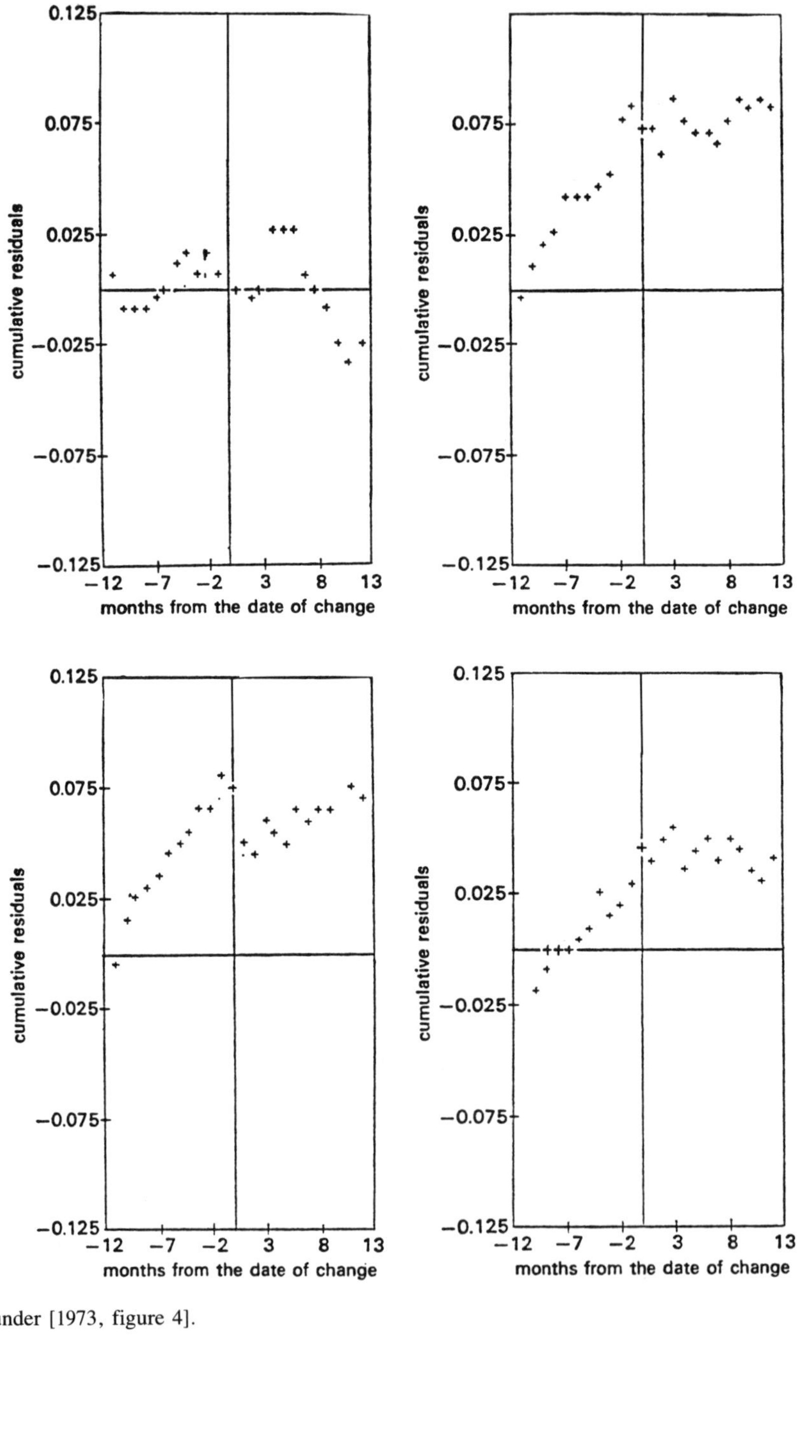

Source: Sunder [1973, figure 4].

EXHIBIT 6-6 Cont.

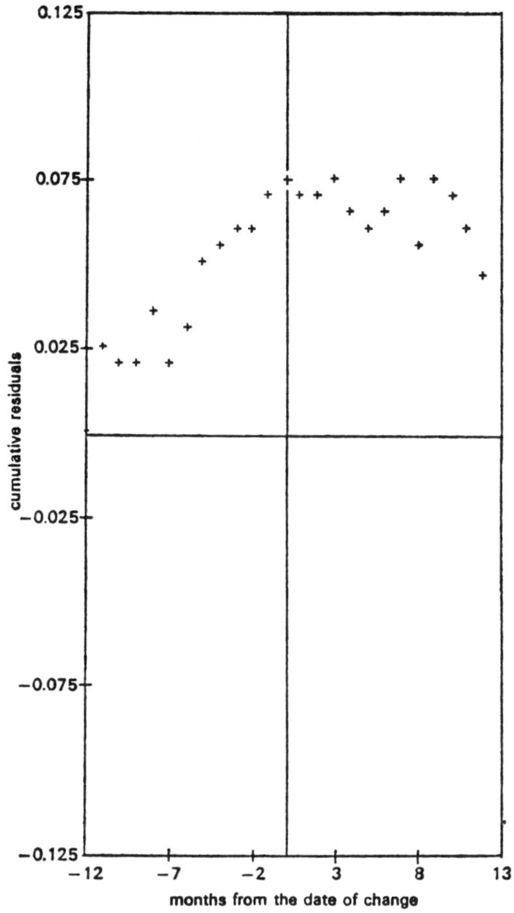

In short, if one is confident that the alleged control sample is really a valid control sample vis-à-vis the Group A firms, then one can, it appears, infer that the systematic patterns observed in Group A's results are probably not "due to chance." But the alleged control sample may not really provide evidence for making this inference.

Recall that the firms in Group A seemed to consist of a disproportionately large number of steel firms. Also, most of the Group A changes were made prior to 1953. Presumably one should want a control sample to have roughly the same industry composition as does Group A. Moreover, one should want the bulk of the hypothetical change dates selected for the control-sample firms to be pre-1953 dates. These are types of "other things" that one should want to hold constant, in order to invoke the usual ceteris paribus assumption. It does not appear that Sunder's control-sample selection procedures were specifically designed to hold these "other things" constant, so that the Group A and control samples would differ with respect to only the information on accounting changes. Nor

EXHIBIT 6-7

ESTIMATED CUMULATIVE AVERAGE ERRORS FOR CONTROL SAMPLE OF 120 HYPOTHETICAL ACCOUNTING CHANGES AND FIVE SUBSAMPLES OF 24 HYPOTHETICAL CHANGES FROM THE CONTROL SAMPLE

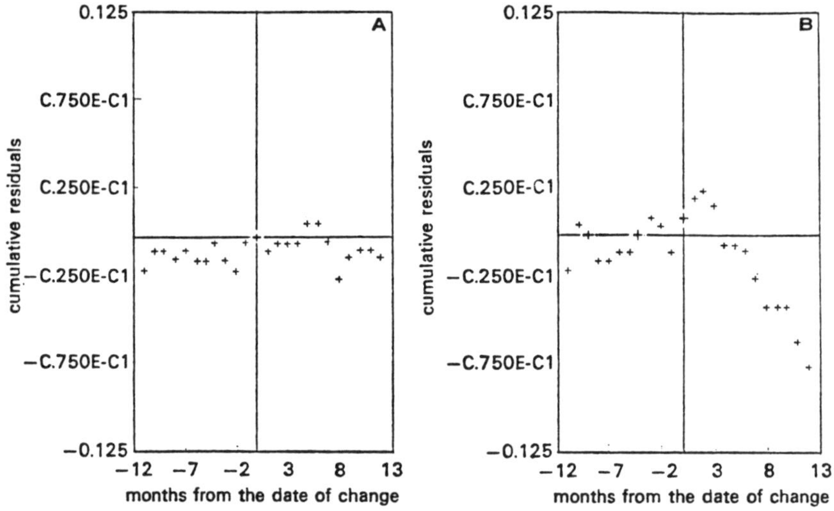

Source: Sunder [1973, figure 5].

does it seem likely that they were accidentally held constant.[67] In short, while the sample evidence conditional on the control sample is consistent with the inferences made earlier, they may also be consistent with alternative (and possibly conflicting) propositions—perhaps because of a test-design deficiency.

To sum up, Sunder's results, taken at face value, are consistent with the joint hypothesis of capital market efficiency (conventionally defined) and agents' reacting to LIFO in terms of its presumed cash-flow implications, rather than in terms of LIFO's bookkeeping effects on reported income numbers. It is also true, however, that his results are consistent with alternative hypotheses which cannot be ruled out using his evidence. The way in which one reacts to his sample evidence will, therefore, depend, as usual, on one's priors regarding the descriptive validity of the alternative hypotheses and the importance of the various deficiencies in the design of Sunder's test.

---

[67]There are plausible reasons for not expecting such a fortuitous accident. If most of the firms selected for the control sample had return data for all, or most, of the 1946–1966 period, then Sunder would have assigned a hypothetical change-date from within 1960 to most of his control-sample firms. Hence, the control sample's change dates would exhibit severe clustering around 1960's months. But the bulk of the actual changes for Group A had pre-January 1953 dates. Thus, the kinds of sheer "time-period" factors reflected in the results for Group A are probably quite different from those reflected in the control sample's results.

EXHIBIT 6-7 Cont.

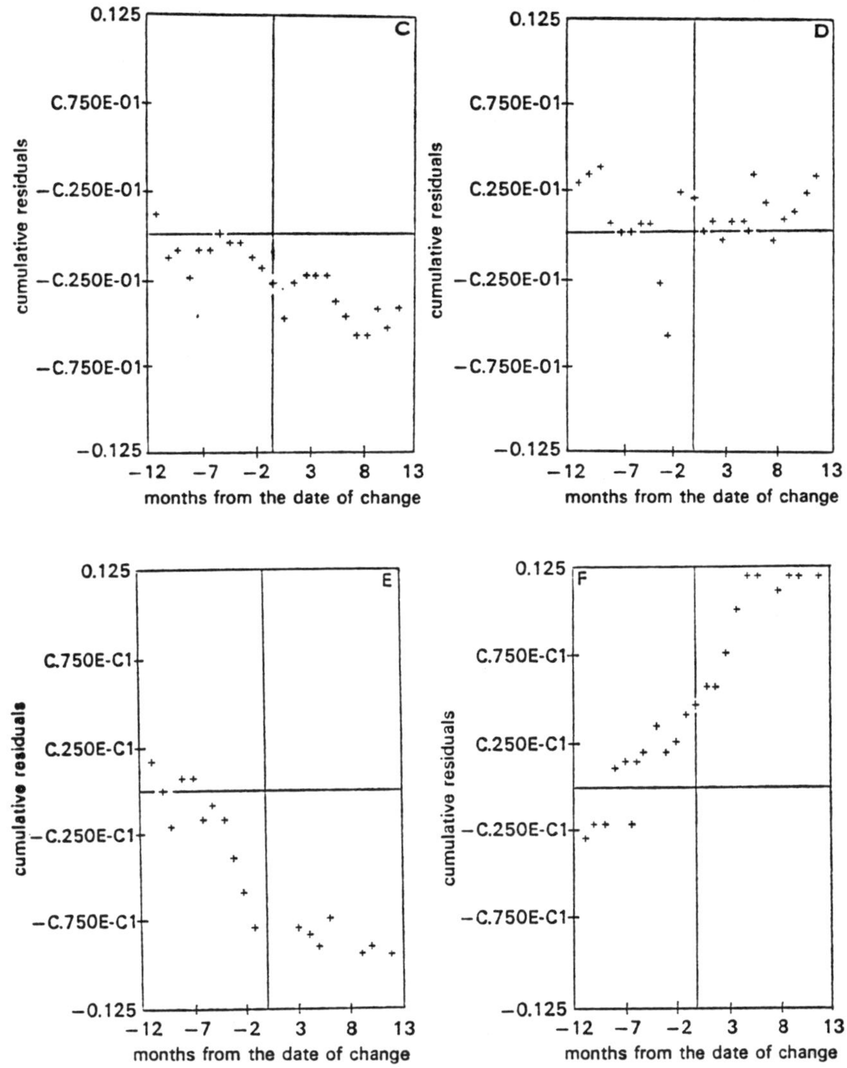

6.8.4.5 Chances in Relative Risk

Much of the early work based on the two-parameter asset-pricing model assumed that firms' relative risks (the values of β_{im} for different i) are constant over time. The evidence reported by Gonedes [1973], among others, is not, however, consistent with that assumption. Moreover, as indicated earlier, there are basic theoretical reasons for presuming that risk changes are, in general, associated with LIFO/FIFO switches made for tax reporting. Sunder, among others, chose to assume that he was dealing with a special case wherein no risk changes occurred. But we can still ask whether Sunder's results were affected by relative risk changes. This is an important question because such changes may lead to the conventional OLS estimators' being biased estimators of relative risks, de-

TABLE 6-16

ESTIMATED ERRORS AND ESTIMATED CUMULATIVE AVERAGE ERRORS FOR 24 MONTHS SURROUNDING HYPOTHETICAL ACCOUNTING CHANGES FOR CONTROL SAMPLE

	ENTIRE SAMPLE 120 CHANGES		SUBGROUP 1 24 CHANGES		SUBGROUP 2 24 CHANGES		SUBGROUP 3 24 CHANGES		SUBGROUP 4 24 CHANGES		SUBGROUP 5 24 CHANGES	
Month, τ (1)	$U_{p\tau}$ (2)	$\widehat{CAE}_{-11,\tau}$ (3)	$U_{p\tau}$ (4)	$\widehat{CAE}_{-11,\tau}$ (5)	$U_{p\tau}$ (6)	$\widehat{CAE}_{-11,\tau}$ (7)	$U_{p\tau}$ (8)	$\widehat{CAE}_{-11,\tau}$ (9)	$U_{p\tau}$ (10)	$\widehat{CAE}_{-11,\tau}$ (11)	$U_{p\tau}$ (12)	$\widehat{CAE}_{-11,\tau}$ (13)
−11	0.005	0.005	0.008	0.008	0.009	0.009	0.006	0.006	−0.010	−0.010	−0.006	−0.006
−10	0.009	0.014	0.023	0.031	−0.026	−0.017	0.003	0.009	−0.015	−0.025	0.012	0.006
−9	0.000	0.014	−0.004	0.027	0.004	−0.013	0.008	0.017	−0.024	−0.049	−0.002	0.004
−8	−0.008	0.006	−0.017	0.010	−0.012	−0.025	−0.034	−0.017	0.031	−0.019	0.032	0.036
−7	0.006	0.012	0.003	0.013	0.013	−0.012	−0.006	−0.023	0.001	−0.018	0.003	0.039
−6	−0.005	0.007	0.005	0.018	0.002	−0.010	−0.000	−0.023	−0.028	−0.046	0.000	0.039
−5	0.003	0.010	−0.001	0.017	0.008	−0.002	0.003	−0.020	0.001	−0.035	0.004	0.043
−4	0.008	0.018	0.010	0.027	−0.002	−0.004	0.002	−0.018	−0.011	−0.047	0.017	0.060
−3	−0.008	0.010	0.008	0.035	−0.004	−0.008	−0.034	−0.052	−0.021	−0.067	−0.014	−0.046
−2	−0.009	0.001	−0.007	0.028	−0.008	−0.016	−0.024	−0.076	−0.019	−0.086	0.003	0.049
−1	0.017	0.018	−0.012	0.016	−0.006	−0.022	0.079	0.003	−0.018	−0.014	0.016	0.065
0	0.005	0.023	0.019	0.035	−0.008	−0.030	−0.006	−0.003	−0.042	−0.146	0.005	0.070
1	−0.008	0.015	0.009	0.044	−0.018	−0.048	−0.022	0.025	0.002	−0.144	0.009	0.079
2	0.003	0.018	0.005	0.049	0.017	−0.31	0.009	−0.016	0.007	−0.137	0.002	0.081
3	−0.001	0.017	−0.007	0.042	0.003	−0.028	−0.010	−0.026	0.033	−0.104	0.017	0.098
4	0.003	0.020	−0.021	0.021	−0.000	−0.025	0.006	−0.020	−0.005	−0.110	0.027	0.125
5	0.008	0.028	0.001	0.022	0.000	−0.028	0.003	−0.017	−0.008	−0.117	0.022	0.147
6	0.000	0.028	−0.005	0.017	−0.014	−0.042	0.030	0.013	0.019	−0.098	−0.001	0.146
7	−0.009	0.019	−0.020	−0.003	−0.007	−0.049	−0.017	−0.004	−0.034	−0.132	0.014	0.160
8	−0.019	0.000	−0.014	−0.017	−0.012	−0.061	−0.022	−0.026	0.002	−0.130	−0.024	0.136
9	0.009	0.009	0.001	−0.016	0.000	−0.061	0.010	−0.016	0.012	−0.118	0.008	0.144
10	0.006	0.015	−0.001	−0.017	0.015	−0.046	0.005	−0.011	0.005	−0.113	0.002	0.146
11	−0.003	0.012	−0.020	−0.037	−0.010	−0.056	0.014	0.003	−0.011	−0.124	0.004	0.150
12	−0.002	0.010	−0.014	−0.050	0.010	−0.046	0.010	0.013	0.006	−0.118	−0.003	0.147

Source: Sunder [1973, table 5].

pending on the process determining risk changes. Biased estimators of relative risks will, in turn, induce biased estimators of Cumulative Average Errors, on whose values assessments of accounting changes' effects are based in our framework. Sunder attempted to gain some insights into this issue by examining alternative estimates of firms' relative risks.

In this stage of his work, Sunder worked with the changes of only those firms for which he had 60 consecutive monthly returns on either side of the month(s) of the firms' accounting changes—excluding, as before, the 12 observed returns immediately preceding the change date and the 12 immediately succeeding the change date. (Recall that some firms made more than one change.) This data requirement led to a reduction in the size of Group A—from 119 changes to 115 changes. He then obtained estimates of his firms' relative risks based on (1) pre-change observations (60 observed returns per firm), (2) post-change observations (60 observed returns per firm), (3) the pooled pre- and post-change observations (120 observations per firm). The same kinds of results were obtained for the 120 firms in his "control" sample, using the hypothetical change dates assigned to those firms.

Cross-sectional summary statistics are provided in Table 6-17. The results in the last panel for Group A relative to the control group seem to be consistent with the statement that, on average, the firms that increased their use of LIFO experienced increases in their relative risks. Such increases, if they did occur, could be ascribed to changes in the attributes of the firms' production-investment or financing decisions. The changes in those attributes might be induced by the cash-flow changes associated with increased usage of LIFO for tax reporting or the price expectations that presumably motivated the increased use of LIFO. If price expectations were the critical factor, however, then presumably the Group A firms would have experienced relative risk changes even if they did not switch to greater use of LIFO, other things being equal. This assumes that there is a positive relationship between expected prices of inputs and outputs, or the "replacement costs" of firms' inventoried items and their selling prices. Under this assumption, some of the motivation for using LIFO (i.e., increases in expected replacement costs) implies increases in expected selling prices. Expression (4.21) of Section 4 indicates that relative risk should increase if output prices are expected to increase, holding other things equal.[68]

The same expression exhibits the relationship between the relative risk of a firm and other attributes of its production-investment decisions. The relevant attributes of financing decisions appear in expression (4.63) in Section 4. Changes in any of those sets of attributes could have induced the risk changes that seem to be suggested by Sunder's results, when taken at face value.

Formal statistical tests of the "significance" of relative risk changes are difficult to conduct using the cross-sectional results provided by Sunder. This is because the risk estimates for different firms are not cross-sectionally independent, or even uncorrelated. Since the bulk of the changes underlying his sample were "clustered" in time, this problem's importance seems to be nontrivial, at least on a priori grounds. Thus, the "*t*-statis-

---

[68]Recall that expression 4.21 of Section 4 deals with *relative* prices of goods and services. Hence, a higher expected value for the rate of overall inflation will not suffice for this result. Higher expected values for the prices of the firms' outputs relative to other prices are needed, given no "money illusion."

TABLE 6-17

RESULTS ON CHANGES IN RISK COEFFICIENTS

	Regression 1[a]			Regression 2[b]			Regression 3[c]			Difference between regressions 2 and 3				
	$\bar{\bar{\beta}}$	$\hat{\sigma}_{\bar{\beta}}$	$\hat{\beta}_m$	$\bar{\bar{\beta}}$	$\hat{\sigma}_{\bar{\beta}}$	$\hat{\beta}_m$	$\bar{\bar{\beta}}$	$\hat{\sigma}_{\bar{\beta}}$	$\hat{\beta}_m$	$\Delta\bar{\bar{\beta}}$	$\hat{\sigma}_{\Delta\bar{\beta}}$	T	$\Delta\hat{\beta}_m$	$(\Delta\hat{\beta})_m$
Group A	1.030	.0017	1.05	1.012	.015	0.99	1.114	.020	1.12	+.102	.025	4.1	+.13	+.11
Control Group	.987	.019	.99	.959	.034	.92	.99	.026	.93	+.03	.043	0.7	+.01	−.01

[a]Regression 1: Based on 120 months of data (60 months on either side of change date excluding 24 months surrounding change date).
[b]Regression 2: Based on 60 months of data before the 12th month prior to change.
[c]Regression 3: Based on 60 months of data after the 12th month following the change.

$\bar{\bar{\beta}}$ = cross sectional mean of 12th month following the estimated $\hat{\beta}$'s

$$\hat{\sigma}_{\bar{\beta}} = \frac{1}{N}\left[\sum_{\substack{\text{Group}\\ \text{A or B}}} (\hat{\sigma}^2_{\hat{\beta}_j})\right]^{1/2}, \; N = \text{number of changes in the group}$$

$\hat{\beta}_m$ = median of estimated $\hat{\beta}$'s

$\Delta\bar{\bar{\beta}} = (\bar{\ })_2 - (\bar{\bar{\beta}})_1$

$\hat{\sigma}_{\Delta\bar{\beta}} = \hat{\sigma}^2_{\bar{\beta}1} + \hat{\sigma}^2_{\bar{\beta}2}$

$T = \Delta\bar{\bar{\beta}}/\hat{\sigma}_{\Delta\bar{\beta}}$

$\Delta\hat{\beta}_m = (\hat{\beta}_m)_2 - (\hat{\beta}_m)_1$ = change in median of $\hat{\beta}$

$(\Delta\hat{\beta})_m$ = median of changes in risk coefficients of individual stocks.

Source: Sunder [1973, table 6].

tics" reported by Sunder—which assume independent estimates—may be seriously misleading.[69] They should probably be used as rough descriptive guides rather than as bases for formal tests. (This is probably the way the results of most formal tests should be used anyway.)

Some insights into the potential influence of relative risk changes on assessments of accounting changes' effects can be obtained from Table 6-18. This table provides estimates of $CAE_{-11,0}$ and $CAE_{-11,+12}$ conditional on different estimates of firms' relative risks. Taken at face value, none of these results seems to alter the qualitative aspects of our earlier inferences about the accounting changes' effects. It does seem, however, that point estimates of the effects are somewhat sensitive to one's assumption about risk changes. That provides, of course, some motivation for wondering whether more is going on than just accounting changes and whether other events might have induced the observed results even without any accounting changes. If so, then the effects that one might ascribe to the accounting changes, using the results in, e.g., Table 6-15, may really be attributable to something else. See, for example, the discussion of type (T.4) accounting changes given in Section 6.4, above.

6.8.4.6 Summary

The above discussion of Sunder's work is intended to achieve several objectives: (1) to convey the major message of some empirical results on the information content of changes in accounting techniques; (2) to illustrate an approach for assessing the information content of accounting changes; and (3) to point out some problems that usually arise in empirical work on accounting changes' information content, as well as work on other topics.

Taken at face value, Sunder's results are consistent with the statement that capital market agents in the aggregate distinguish between (1) changes that appear to be external reporting changes having no substantive economic implications and (2) changes that do have such implications (e.g., implications about the probability distributions of firms' cash

TABLE 6-18

ESTIMATED CUMULATIVE AVERAGE ERRORS BASED ON DIFFERENT ESTIMATES OF RELATIVE RISK

Results for Changes Toward Use of LIFO (Group A)

Observations Used to Estimate Risk	$\widehat{CAE}_{-11,0}$	$\widehat{CAE}_{-11,+12}$
(1) Pre- and Post-Change Observations	0.053	0.042
(2) Pre-Change Observations	0.075	0.082
(3) Post-Change Observations	0.033	0.010
Pre-Change Observations Used to Estimate Risk for Pre-Change Months; Post-Change Observations Used to Estimate Risk for Post-Change Months	0.075	0.052

Source: Sunder [1973, table 8].

[69]From the notes to Table 6-17 it can be seen that Sunder's computations of standard deviations assume uncorrelated observations.

outflows for tax obligations). A variety of problems—e.g., ex post sample selection biases and a failure to hold "other things" constant—were discussed. These problems should be considered when interpreting his results. Whether any qualifications induced by these problems are sufficient to alter the crux of our inference depends on the strength of one's prior convictions, economic theory, and other sources of relevant empirical evidence—to which we now turn.

6.8.5 Additional Sources of Evidence

Insofar as other relevant evidence is concerned, it appears to be consistent with our major inference based on Sunder's results. One body of such evidence is provided by Kaplan and Roll [1972]. Their work deals with switches to the flow-through method of accounting for the investment tax credit in external reports and with switches from an accelerated method of depreciation to the straight-line method for external reporting. Another is the evidence provided by Ball [1972] on the effects of a variety of different types of accounting changes. The results recently provided by Foster [1975] on the accounting techniques used to compute the "income" numbers of insurance companies for external reports are also consistent with our interpretations of Sunder's results. A detailed review of work on the effects of alternative accounting techniques is provided by Gonedes and Dopuch [1974, section 8].

Our interpretation of the available evidence on accounting techniques motivates the view that selections of accounting techniques and predictions about the effects of alternative techniques should not be based on the belief that agents may be "confused" by accounting changes or accounting numbers based on different techniques. One is hard pressed to find any reliable evidence consistent with this belief.

6.9 Assessing the Desirability of Alternative Accounting Procedures Used for External Reporting: Brief Historical Perspective and Remarks on Basic Problems

6.9.1 Preliminaries

For the most part, the preceding sections deal with the information content of alternative accounting procedures. Recall that the "information content" of accounting techniques pertains to their effects on agents' assessed distribution functions of returns on firms' shares.

The information content of accounting techniques is not, however, the only thing of interest to those concerned with external reporting. For a variety of purposes, the desirability of alternative techniques is also of interest. This is the case when, for example, regulatory bodies—such as the Financial Accounting Standards Board, the Cost Accounting Standards Board, and the Securities and Exchange Commission—face the task of choosing one of several alternative procedures. That is what they do when they impose disclosure rules on firms. Such choices are so-called social choices as opposed to private choices (i.e., choices made by individual agents on personal account).

A discussion of the desirability of alternative accounting techniques from society's perspective requires some notion of social preference. We continue to use the notion of Pareto optimality, which is a unanimity rule. From a given individual's perspective, desirability is determined by that individual's preference ordering.

The remainder of this section provides some historical perspective on approaches for assessing the desirability of alternative techniques from a social perspective, on some seemingly basic changes in the kinds of desirability assessments made by regulatory bodies such as the SEC and FASB, and on some of the problems encountered in making desirability assessments. As always, our interest is in external accounting.

6.9.2 Some Historical Perspective and Remarks on Basic Problems

We begin by reviewing the basic connection between the equilibrium prices of firms' securities and information-production decisions or, more generally, resource allocation decisions and information-production.

Equilibrium prices of firms' securities are dependent on capital market agents' assessed distribution functions of returns to holders of those securities. Such distribution functions are dependent on the available information about firms' production-investment decisions. The nature of this available information is determined by the results of private and public decisions on investing in information production.[70] The latter decisions are simply additional types of production-investment decisions. An example of such a decision is one which generates accounting numbers via a particular set of accounting procedures. The selected procedures are parts of the prevailing technology used in the production of these numbers. In other words, the selected accounting procedures define, in part, an experiment. The resulting accounting numbers comprise the sample evidence produced by that experiment. A change in the accounting procedures is equivalent to a change in the underlying experiment. Just as the scheme used to produce, say, automobiles results from a production-investment decision, the experiment used to produce accounting numbers results from a production-investment decision.

What criteria should be used for optimally selecting accounting techniques by those who produce or regulate the production of accounting numbers? During recent years this question has become increasingly important for a variety of reasons. One is that the bodies charged with regulating disclosures have been placing greater emphasis on prescribing specific techniques rather than simply requiring firms' disclosure of whatever techniques the firms selected. This reflects a change from the prevailing philosophy of, say, the 1930s, when disclosure was something of a "hot topic." The crux of that philosophy is well expressed in statements made by George O. May, who had an important influence on disclosure developments of the 1930s. He argued that an "official" specification of accounting techniques was undesirable and that firms' managements are in the best position to select the most appropriate techniques for their reports, conditional on the nature of the firms' activities. He further argued that firms should simply be required to disclose the techniques selected for their external reports. Specifically, his argument was that:

> . . . every corporation should adopt a method of accounting described in considerable detail. The method should be certified by its auditors as being in accordance with reasonable standards of business practice, and should be freely described. The officers should then be guilty of falsification of accounts if they knowingly put forward any accounts not in conformity with the methods of ac-

---

[70]These decisions can interact with each other in a variety of ways depending on the complimentarily and substitution relationships that exist among the outputs of public and private information production activities. See Gonedes [1980] for a detailed analysis of this issue.

> counting so adopted, and the auditors would be required to certify that the accounts were prepared in accordance with the corporation's official method. . . .
>
> The trouble with an "official" system of accounting is that while it is possible to lay down broad principles, wide variations are possible within the limits of such principles and which variation should be adopted is a question on which one cannot be rightly dogmatic.[71]

The pervasiveness of this perspective decreased, especially after the 1940s. Currently, there appears to be an emphasis on requiring that firms follow a particular procedure under most or all conditions (e.g., requiring that firms always expense Research and Development costs). Consequently, the criteria used for selecting accounting techniques are of particular importance.

Prior to the mid-1960s, most attempts to deal with the issue of appropriate criteria for selecting techniques essentially used "a priori" models. The theoretical underpinnings and rigor of these models were, however, not always apparent. A review of these types of models is provided by Nelson [1973]. In general, they all purported to give criteria for identifying the "best" or "most appropriate" accounting techniques, conditional on stated (and unstated) assumptions about those who use and/or produce accounting numbers.

Well-known works that use the "a priori" model approach include Paton and Littleton [1940], Chambers [1966], Edwards and Bell [1965], and Sterling [1970]. One reason these works are theoretically deficient involves their treatment of information-production activities. Since each of them deals with selections of accounting techniques, each deals with such activities. And each provides conclusions about what "should" be produced via the external accounting mechanism. Yet, none formally incorporates uncertainty into its underlying framework—although each mentions it in some way. Also, none derived its conclusions from an explicit resource allocation model that encompasses information-production activities—a model incorporating the kinds of factors identified in Chapters 2 and 3. Instead, these works' conclusions are essentially based on their authors' "value judgments" and exhortations about what information is "essential," "needed," or "required." In short, the authors' conclusions are not uniquely implied by what they provided in the way of theoretical underpinnings.

Given the situation just described, one can conclude that the cited works are (for at least the indicated reasons) theoretically deficient. Moreover, since the conclusions of those works are not uniquely implied by their underpinnings and since those underpinnings provide incomplete characterizations of information-production activities, it is obvious that an alternative set of conclusions can—via exhortations and value judgments—be justified using the same underpinnings. That is, the same "a priori" model can be used to support conflicting conclusions. Thus, the apparent failure of such works to resolve disputes over the desirability (or effects) of alternative accounting techniques should come as no surprise. Additional perspective on this failure is provided by Sterling [1975] and Dopuch [1975].

In recent years the "a priori" approach—albeit still much used—has come under heavy criticism because of (1) the theoretical deficiencies of works that advocated or used it and

---

[71]Letter dated June 13, 1932. Cited in Zeff [1972, pp. 122–123].

(2) the fact that it has seemed possible, using that approach, to declare the superiority of just about any set of accounting techniques, depending on the particular a priori model adopted. Among other things, such criticism led to an increased emphasis on using empirical analyses in attempts to assess the desirability and effects of alternative techniques. Apparently, it was believed that an empirical approach would resolve issues that could not be (or at least had not been) resolved via the "a priori" approach. Alas, that outcome's attainment proved to be more difficult than expected.

Many of the available empirical studies dealing with accounting techniques were equally incapable of resolving the indicated assessment problems. This can be ascribed, in part, to the fact that the theoretical underpinnings used in, and available for, these efforts were underdeveloped (see, e.g., the review by Hakansson [1973]). Since serious empirical work in accounting was, as of the 1960s, a recent phenomenon, that situation should not have been entirely surprising.

Development in the theory of, and evidence on, capital market efficiency appears to have provided substantial impetus to the refinement of empirical work in accounting.[72] Capital market efficiency played an important role in available assessments of announcements of accounting numbers (Ball and Brown [1968] and Gonedes [1974]); dividend announcements (Watts [1973]); announcements of changes in accounting techniques (Kaplan and Roll [1972], Ball [1972], and Sunder [1973]) and stock-split announcements (Fama, Fisher, Jensen, and Roll [1969]), among others.

Capital market efficiency also played a critical role in several attempts to assess the desirability of alternative accounting procedures and regulations pertaining to selections of accounting procedures. This can be seen in the work of Beaver [1972, p. 409], Beaver and Dukes [1972 and 1973], Benston [1973], Friend [1972], Stigler [1964], and others.

There are two critical underpinnings of the arguments advanced in the papers that rely on capital market efficiency in dealing with alternative accounting procedures. We shall briefly remark on the logical validity of these underpinnings, which may be expressed as follows:

(A.1) Capital market efficiency, taken by itself, provides sufficient justification for using prices of (or rates of return on) firms' shares in assessing the *desirability* of alternative accounting procedures or regulations.

(A.2) Capital market efficiency, taken by itself, provides sufficient justification for using prices of (or rates of return on) firms' shares in assessing the *effects* of alternative accounting procedures or regulations.

Not all of the studies that deal with alternative accounting procedures invoke both of these arguments. And in some cases (e.g., Beaver and Dukes [1972]), the position expressed in (A.1) is qualified on the grounds of incomplete information about the available opportunities for, and the costs of, information-production. This qualification is not included in (A.1) because, as was indicated by Gonedes and Dopuch [1974], it is not a central factor in determining the logical validity of (A.1). That is, our remarks on the logical validity of (A.1) apply even if one has complete information on the available opportunities for and costs of information-production.

If assertion (A.1) is accepted, then one can proceed as if the prices of (or rates of

---

[72]The notion of capital market efficiency is discussed primarily in Section 3.

return on) firms' shares provide signals regarding capital market agents' preferences for the results of alternative information-production decisions involving accounting procedures. This seems to point the way around a fundamental deficiency of the other approaches described above—namely, their inability to provide unambiguous means of ranking procedures in terms of capital market agents' preferences, rather than, for example, some researcher's preferences.

An extensive analysis of the logical validity of both (A.1) and (A.2) is provided in Gonedes and Dopuch [1974]. The key factors leading to their conclusions involve (1) the rule of excluding nonpurchasers; (2) the relationship between production-investment decisions (e.g., information-production decisions), the market value rule, and the prices of firms' shares; and (3) the implications of capital market efficiency. Specifically, they conclude that when the rule of excluding nonpurchasers is not enforced, then the prices of firms' shares cannot be used to assess the desirability of the information-production decisions made by (or imposed on) these firms. They also conclude, however, that those prices can, under the same conditions, be used to assess the effects of the indicated information-production decisions.

Under the contemporary institutional setting, "exclusion of nonpurchasers" is not enforced vis-à-vis information produced via the external accounting mechanism (perhaps because of enforcement costs). Thus, Gonedes' and Dopuch's analysis implies that assertion (A.1) is logically invalid. In short, the works that relied on the logical validity of (A.1) cannot be given the theoretical justification and interpretations that their authors propounded.

The Gonedes/Dopuch theoretical results do not imply that there are no conditions which, when added to the assumption of capital market efficiency, will yield a special case wherein desirability issues can be (wholly or partially) resolved via empirical analyses of firms' share prices. Such special cases might be obtained by, for example, making special assumptions about information-production opportunities or capital market agents' preference orderings. Some illustrative special cases are developed in Gonedes and Dopuch [1974, Section 10].

Gonedes' and Dopuch's analysis implies that assertion (A.2) is logically valid. Thus, we obviously have in hand a justifiable approach for assessing the effects of alternative accounting procedures and regulations (at least insofar as the presence or absence of effects is concerned). Indeed, the framework and studies discussed in Section 6.8 attempt to exploit precisely that approach. Yet, one might ask whether assessments of effects are important, or at least as important as desirability assessments.

Perhaps the easiest way to appreciate assessments of effects is to recognize that recommendations and prescriptions regarding accounting procedures are often justified (rationalized?) in terms of the effects of the recommended or prescribed procedures and the available alternatives. As indicated in Section 6.8.2, such assertions can be found in a variety of APS *Opinions*, SEC *Accounting Series Releases*, and FASB *Statements*. However, they are rarely supported by references to available theory or empirical results.

Since assertions about effects are important parts of the justifications offered for recommendations and prescriptions, we can assess the strength of these justifications by evaluating the theoretical or empirical support for the assertions about effects. And one expects the perceived strength of the justifications to vary directly with the perceived support for the underlying assertions. In short, assessments of the effects of alternative accounting procedures and regulations can be useful to accounting policy-making bodies in making their decisions and to their constituencies in evaluating those decisions.

6.9.3 Back to Desirability Assessments

Where does all of this leave desirability assessments? Gonedes and Dopuch [1974, Section 10] discuss several possibilities for dealing with such assessments. Some of them involve altering the current institutional setting so that the market mechanism can be used to resolve such issues. Barring such alterations, one is left with essentially political schemes. That they suggest a political approach may seem surprising given accountants' frequent (and often emotional) objections to governmental influence on accounting, because that kind of influence "involves politics" (see, for example, Armstrong [1975, p. 30]). These kinds of objections ignore the essentially political nature of, for example, the FASB and the AICPA.[73] More important, they do not seem to recognize (or at least admit) that a political process is precisely what has long been used.[74] Pretending that existing disclosure rules and regulations resulted from attempts to operationalize and implement an accounting theory in some pure and pristine manner is probably a quick route to self-deception.

We conclude this section with a somewhat lengthy excerpt from a paper by Horngren [1973]. The excerpt provides and illustration of the political factors involved in the selection of disclosure rules and regulations. Accounting for marketable securities is the specific issue covered by the excerpt. By way of background, we note the following features of the debate on this issue.

An intensive study of accounting for marketable securities was launched by the (now defunct) Accounting Principles Board in 1968. The crux of the problem pertained to the recognition of portfolio gains and losses. One view asserted that only *realized* gains and losses should be included in the income of a period. Another asserted that *all* gains and losses of a period should be spread over several periods via some kind of averaging device. A third view asserted that *all* gains and losses should be accounted for on a flow-through basis, whereby all gains and losses of a period are included in that period's income. Another part of the debate focused on whether such gains and losses should be included in the income statement in the first place, as opposed to some separate statement.

What was the outcome of this debate? How were the issues resolved—by theoretical reasoning, by political actions, or by some other route? Horngren [1973, pp. 63–64] provides the following story.

> An intensive study of this topic was begun in September 1968. Heavy interaction persisted between the APB and all interested parties, particularly representatives of the insurance industry whose income statements would be dramatically affected by any new accounting standards. In May 1971, there was a two-day public hearing on the issues.
>
> After about three years of spasmodic deliberations, the APB was ready to issue an exposure draft of an Opinion. The Board had narrowed its preferences to two

[73]The importance of political forces is, of course, not unique to the accounting profession. Nor is it unique to professions identified with the "social sciences." Such forces are, for example, evident in the setting of rules for experimentation in the biological sciences; see, for example, Wade [1975].

[74]Note that "political" does not necessarily mean "governmental."

methods using one income statement: either flow-through or spreading. In September 1971, the Board approved a draft favoring flow-through. The draft was to be "mini-exposed" to the SEC, the insurance industry and others who had been actively involved. The intention of the Board was to have full public exposure of the Opinion after the October APB meeting.

The insurance companies were bitterly opposed to flow-through. They blitzkrieged Washington. The SEC, armed with its own preferences and buttressed by industry reactions, informed the APB that it could not support flow-through. At this point, flow-through was a dead duck because higher management (the SEC) had, in effect, overruled the APB.

At its October meeting, the APB again discussed the topic. Because flow-through was no longer an acceptable alternative, the Board changed its preferences to either spreading or a two-statement approach. The Board voted in favor of a two-statement approach, although strong voices were raised in support of spreading. In November, these alternatives were explored with the SEC and the insurance industry. At its December meeting, the Board was informed that the fire and casualty companies had also strongly objected to the spreading method. One potent spokesman for the SEC found some merit in the spreading method, but he informed the Board that the SEC would not *impose* it or any solution on an industry that was adamantly opposed to it. So spreading was dead.

The Board then discussed two alternatives: (1) some version of a two-statement method and (2) a modification of predominant current practice whereby all companies in all industries would show marketable securities at market value in the balance sheet, unrealized gains and losses in stockholders' equity, and only realized gains and losses in the income statement. However, the fire and casualty companies also vigorously opposed the two-statement method.

Note how the feasible alternatives changed in response to the likelihood of acceptability. The constraints became more binding as the months wore on:

1 September—flow-through or spreading.
2 October—spreading or two-statement.
3 December—two-statement or slight modification of status quo.

Discussions of various versions of the December alternatives were renewed in early 1972. But the Board could not resolve the issues and the SEC was noncommittal on anything except "no flow-through." During the course of the discussions, the top managements of 15 or 20 large insurance companies met together about the issue more than once and also with the SEC commissioners at least once.

An observer of a visit of Institute representatives to the SEC wrote to me that an SEC commissioner "asked the APB for the summary of the alternative methods together with the pros and cons of each. He also said that, once the SEC received this report, the SEC would tell the APB the parameters in which the APB could consider the subject. Presumably any method selected by the APB within these parameters would be acceptable to the SEC. . . . This event is perhaps the clearest demonstration of an SEC order to the APB that I can recall."

> The marketable securities scenario was concluded by an APB report to the SEC in March 1972 that summarized the APB deliberations and the alternatives. However, the report offered no preferred solution.

That does not seem to be a very cheery ending for those who persist in viewing the development of GAAP as the result of a disinterested search for "truth."

CHAPTER SEVEN

Empirical Properties of Accounting Numbers

7.1 Preliminaries

The framework provided thus far identifies several ways in which accounting numbers can serve as useful sources of sample evidence. In general, they are one of the available sources that can be used to make inferences about the attributes of firms' decisions that are pertinent to establishing firms' values. Of course, as with any source of sample evidence, there are a variety of tools (e.g., estimators of parameters) available for making inferences based on accounting numbers. This implies yet another choice problem, *viz.*, selecting inferential tools. Selecting from among alternative estimators of parameters (e.g., means, variances, and correlation coefficients) is a specific choice problem usually encountered in work with economic data. But, strictly speaking, the appropriateness of an estimator depends on the probability model that generated the sample evidence. Some estimators are inappropriate (on theoretical grounds) if, for example, the probability model changes over time—that is, if the model is nonstationary. If, say, the mean or the variance of net income changes over time, then that accounting number evolves according to a so-called nonstationary process. Thus, if we choose to use values of accounting numbers for some estimation task, we shall usually want to know (or have to assume) something about their empirical properties (e.g., stationarity vs. nonstationarity) in order to avoid getting potentially misleading empirical results. In short, we shall usually want to know (or have to assume) something about the consistency between the nature of whatever sample evidence we propose to use and the assumptions used to derive and define the properties of estimators that we consider using.

Knowing something about the model generating one's sample evidence is just one part of the task at hand. Another involves specifying (on empirical or a priori grounds) something about the "information content" of that source of sample evidence (i.e., that random variable or vector whose values make up the evidence at hand). Recall that a random variable is said to have information content if the probability distribution assessed conditionally on at least one of its possible values differs from the distribution that would be assessed without knowing anything about the random variable's value. For present purposes, the probability distributions of interest are the distributions of firms' future values. If sample evidence on some accounting number will never affect our assessments of these distributions in any way, then the accounting number has, by definition, no information content. Such a case may arise because the accounting number reflects no information beyond what is reflected in sample evidence already in hand (i.e., a perfect substitute for whatever information is reflected in the accounting number under examination). Of course, the latter sample evidence may consist of values of other accounting numbers.

This chapter deals primarily with various aspects of the first issue identified above. We begin by reviewing our perspective of accounting numbers, by reviewing some areas wherein accounting numbers are used as sources of sample evidence, and by comparing our perspective to the one that seems to be employed in the latter areas. The purpose of this is to further clarify our basic view on the role of accounting numbers in financial statement analysis and other types of economic analyses. The connection between our perspective and the "Theory of Rational Expectations" is also briefly considered.

We then focus on specific statistical models for accounting numbers. For the most part, we deal with annual income numbers—mainly because of the substantial amount of available evidence on income numbers' properties. But the basic issues that arise in modeling annual income numbers also arise in modeling other numbers. Thus, insofar as basics are concerned, our emphasis on annual income numbers seems to involve little loss of generality. And it has the advantage of dealing with a specific number with which most readers probably have some familiarity. Our discussion of annual income numbers points to some basic steps in statistical modeling and it provides a review of some available evidence on the time series properties of income numbers. We also identify some additional problems encountered in modeling interim (e.g., quarterly) income numbers, and we briefly review some available evidence on those numbers' properties too.

Our emphasis on time series analysis in this chapter is due primarily to two factors. First, the problem and tools associated with time series analysis are likely to be less familiar to most readers—relative to those associated with cross-sectional analyses (e.g., running regressions on data for different firms as of a particular time period, such as one year). Second, results from some type of time series analysis are likely to be among the most useful and most frequently encountered in work on financial statement analysis.

Our discussion of the methods of time series analysis is largely "tutorial." Those familiar with these methods should probably just skim through this part of the chapter.

7.2 Inferences and Accounting Numbers: A General Perspective

7.2.1 Accounting Numbers as Sources of Sample Evidence

Various types of economic analyses attempt to exploit the systematic properties of firms' accounting numbers, such as income numbers, sales, inventory, and plant and equipment numbers. These economic analyses include (1) research on industrial organization, generally involving market structure and market performance issues, and on the effects of governmental policies pertaining to industrial organization; (2) research on the effects of the Securities and Exchange Commission's disclosure rules on the functioning of the capital market; (3) macroeconometric modeling and analyses of the effects of governmental policies, such as economic stabilization and income redistribution policies; (4) analyses of the economy's dynamic properties (e.g., analyses of the implications of capital expenditure and inventory accumulation decisions for economic stability and resource use); (5) the economic aspects of environmental policies (e.g., the effects of pollution abatement programs on firms' profitability and capital expenditure decisions); and (6) financial statement analyses dealing with individual firms and groups of firms (e.g., firms in a particular industry). These types of economic analyses have, in general, an important common attribute. For these types of analyses, firms' reported accounting numbers are among the data used (or useful) in satisfying the demands of empirical work for these analyses. In each case, a basic assumption is that the systematic properties of firms' accounting numbers reflect (perhaps after some transformation) substantive economic attributes of firms' decisions regarding resource allocation and financing. In other words, it is assumed that sample evidence consisting of observed values of accounting numbers can serve as a basis for making inferences about the unobservable characteristics of firms' decisions—such as the probability of distribution of a firm's real resource inflows induced by the firm's production decisions and the characteristics of its input and output markets. Of course, the specific attributes of firms' decisions that are important for a given analysis depend on the objectives of the analysis. These attributes may be identified by available theory or by available evidence (via, e.g., exploratory data analysis).

The use of evidence on accounting numbers to make inferences about substantive economic issues is illustrated by work in the area of industrial organization. As indicated in Chapter 4, some of the issues and evidence encountered in this area are pertinent to the area of financial statement analysis. Moreover, as will be indicated in Section 7.4, it identifies an area of work that can be exploited when contemplating alternative probability models for accounting numbers. Thus, this illustration serves to illustrate a use of accounting numbers and to provide an overview of a type of research pertinent to analyses of indiviual firms.

A concise general view of work on industrial organization is provided by McKie [1972, p. 1]:

> Its mission is to apply to the facts the apparatus of microeconomic theory developed by model builders and systematic theoreticians. It is concerned with policy, at least to the extent of providing the best thought and analysis of economists to those who make policy. In its widest focus it is concerned with the efficiency of the arrangements, organizations, and institutions that men rely on to guide the production of what they need.

Two broad topics of traditional interest in this area are (1) the structure of the market environment and (2) the performance of the market mechanism. Several factors pertaining to the structure of the market environment are (a) the conditions of entry into and exit from an industry, (b) the number and size distributions of firms within an industry, (c) cost conditions and technology, (d) the influence of locational factors, and (e) the characteristics of firms' products (e.g., "differentiated" vs. "homogeneous"). Factors pertaining to performance of the market mechanism include (a) rates of profit, relative to some "norm," (b) the flexibility of prices relative to costs, (c) the propensity to innovate and to use technological improvements, and (d) the responsiveness of resource flows to profit opportunities. Research results on these types of issues often influence, and are motivated by, governmental policies, such as antitrust policies and policies dealing with externalities (e.g., air pollution), among other things.

The indicated basic assumption underlying this use of accounting numbers as sources of sample evidence can be exposed by considering the following scenario. Suppose that you face the task of making an inference about the extent to which a firm's (or an industry's) net real resource inflows differ from those that are consistent with a perfect market setting. Consider your position (1) before acquiring any additional sample evidence and (2) after acquiring evidence consisting of observed values of accounting numbers. Finally, suppose that you "package" your inferences in the form of a probability distribution for a dichotomous indicator random variable, $\tilde{h}$, where $\tilde{h} = 1$ denotes "inconsistency with perfect market setting" and $\tilde{h} = 0$ denotes "consistency with perfect market setting." One might be interested in making this sort of an inference when evaluating, say, the "better than average" profitability or "the growth opportunities" of a particular firm, which is not an unusual exercise in the area of financial statement analysis.

Before using the additional sample evidence consisting of accounting numbers, one can exploit evidence already available and existing economic theory in order to assess the probability distribution of $\tilde{h}$. Any evidence and any theoretical results pertinent to net real resource inflows and the given firm's operations can be used toward this end. One's assessments at this point are, say, $Pr(\tilde{h} = 1)$ and $Pr(\tilde{h} = 0) = 1 - Pr(\tilde{h} = 1)$. That is, $Pr(\cdot)$ is the presample evidence or "prior" probability distribution assessed for $\tilde{h}$.

Let $Pr(\tilde{h} = 1|E, M)$ and $Pr(\tilde{h} = 0|E, M) = 1 - Pr(\tilde{h} = 1|E, M)$ denote the postsample or "posterior" probability distribution of $\tilde{h}$. This distribution is assessed conditionally on the sample evidence, E, consisting of observed values of accounting numbers and the application of a particular model, M, to this evidence. Under what conditions would your assessment $Pr(\tilde{h} = 1)$ differ from your assessment $Pr(\tilde{h} = 1|E, M)$? These assessments will differ when, via the application of some model, M, it is possible to extract some "new" information on net real resource inflows from the evidence. They will not be different if, for any M, the evidence, E, does not reflect any information on those inflows that is not already reflected in the theory and evidence underlying the prior assessment $Pr(\tilde{h} = 1)$. Equivalently, the prior and posterior assessments will differ if there is a model, M, such that application of that model to E yields information pertinent to the substantive economic issues of interest, *viz.*, the characteristics of a given firm's net real resource inflows. That it does yield such information is a basic assumption underlying the use of E by an individual in this situation. This is a basic assumption made in work on industrial organization—to the extent that the latter involves empirical work based on values of accounting numbers. And it is an assumption made in the other types of economic analyses mentioned above.

But there is more to this story. Sample evidence does not literally "give" information to an analyst. Information pertinent to some issue is "extracted" from the evidence via the application of a model, M. This model may be an ad hoc model motivated by, say, intuitive reasoning and perhaps some empirical results based on other sample evidence. Or it may be the result of pure and pristine theoretical derivations. In any event, one's posterior assessments depend on both the sample evidence, E, and the model, M, applied to that evidence. It is, therefore, quite possible for the prior assessment $Pr(\tilde{h} = 1)$ to be the same as (different from) the posterior assessment $Pr(\tilde{h} = 1|E, M)$ because of M; a different M might (might not) induce a difference.

Moreover, the predictive performance of inferences made conditionally on E will depend on the particular model applied to E. One can always proceed as if there is some "correct" or "true" distribution of the random variable of interest, such as $\tilde{h}$, and as if one's assessments are intended to be as "close" to the correct distribution as is possible when the only sources of information are the sources underlying the prior assessment and the additional sample evidence E. By presumption, one's assessment would be the correct distribution—i.e., there would be no prediction error regarding the distribution of $\tilde{h}$—if one had complete specifications for all unobservables, such as the actual resource commitments of the firm under review, the actual decisions of its competitors, and the demand and supply functions for all markets in which the firm transacts. One faces an inference task precisely because such complete specifications are not available. In this situation, the best that one can do is to avoid making *systematic* errors and to attain as much precision as can be attained by fully exploiting whatever information is available—such as E—in a manner consistent with balancing gains and costs. This implies, in turn, that one will want to avoid selecting an M that is knowingly inconsistent with the systematic properties of the source of sample evidence whenever it is no more costly to apply a more adequately specified M or whenever, for given costs, a more adequately specified M is more beneficial (e.g., can provide better predictive performance). This is simply an attribute of rational behavior. (More on this later.) At this point, it seems best to illustrate the role of M. We do so by resuming our discussion of work on industrial organization, for which we already have discussed the role of sample evidence, E, consisting of accounting numbers' values.

Specifically, consider empirical work on the strength and prevalence of monopolistic conditions. One procedure used to assess this strength involves an examination of the "persistence" of differences among different industries' expected rates of return. A high degree of persistence is believed by some to be indicative of monopolistic conditions or, more generally, departures from the conditions for perfectly competitive markets. An early application of this approach was provided by Stigler [1963, chap. 3]. Subsequent applications include those by Brozen [1971] and Ellert [1974], among others. In empirical work, "persistence" is usually assessed by using estimated autocorrelation functions of firms' income numbers or rates of return (computed using observed values of accounting numbers). Since differences among the properties of different firms' income numbers or rates of return may reflect factors such as risk differences, rather than the strength of competitive forces, some adjustments are made so as to hold such "other things" constant. This is consistent with the principal aim of this approach: to make inferences about the extent to which decisions made by some firms can be replicated by others—on the same terms of trade—so as to eliminate "abnormal" profits and attain the resource allocation consequences of fully competitive conditions.

The above description serves as one illustration of how the information-content assumption on accounting numbers and the necessity of using some model (however informal) to extract information enter into empirical work based on sample evidence consisting of accounting numbers' values. In the work described above, it is obviously assumed that this sort of evidence reflects information on some substantive economic issues—in particular, the consistency between the attributes of firms' net real resource inflows and the attributes implied by perfectly competitive markets. Second, the above description indicates that some attempts to extract this information are based on a model incorporating the notions of persistence and autocorrelation functions of accounting numbers, all of which leads to the use of specific time series analysis tools in the empirical work described above. Making inferences on the basis of results from applying those tools assumes consistency between the assumptions underlying the tools—assumptions which pertain to the properties of the random variables analyzed—and the systematic properties of the specific sources of sample evidence used. Thus, in order to make statements about the tools' appropriateness, one must specify, on a priori or empirical grounds, something about the characteristics of the accounting numbers used as sources of evidence. This brings us back to our other major (and yet mundane) point: given the model used to extract information from sample evidence consisting of accounting numbers' values, the systematic properties of accounting numbers are determinants of the extent to which one finds that such evidence is informative; i.e., information on the source of sample evidence is useful in extracting information from the sample evidence—in a way that is consistent with the objective of making accurate inferences.

The same point applies to the kinds of inferential tasks discussed in Chapter 4. There, we identified the attributes of firms' decisions that are relevant for making inferences about the risks of the claims issued by a firm and, thus, for the equilibrium expected returns on those claims. The resulting theoretical relationships between those attributes and the risk of a claim provided a structure for financial statement analysis by identifying the relevant objects of analysis. That structure also provided a framework for identifying what kinds of inferences are potentially useful (e.g., parameters for which estimated values might be useful) and what kinds of data are potentially useful. Making any of the indicated inferences on the basis of any sort of evidence involves the application of some model (e.g., some type of estimator) to the evidence. Thus, inferences about risk will, in general, be affected by the consistency between the systematic properties of the source of evidence (e.g., are the random variables characterized by stationary probability models) and the assumptions of the models employed. This provides motivation for inquiring into the systematic properties of accounting numbers if those numbers will be used as sources of sample evidence.

7.2.2 "True Values" and Accounting Numbers

Our perspective on accounting numbers differs from one that seems to underlie much of the available literature on statement analysis and many empirical studies on topics such as those mentioned above. The alternative perspective seems to underlie, for example, the following assertion by a stockbroker:[1]

> . . . a corporation can disclose in a more complete manner their earnings, debt structure, etc. It is very difficult to get a true financial statement.

The same perspective seems to underlie the following assertion from the industrial organization literature:

> It is possible, even likely, that drug firm accounting rates of return are significantly biased upwards by standard accounting procedures that treat ARD [advertising, research, and development] expenditures as current expenses. In the case of drug firms, which spend heavily for ARD, this bias can be very large. The key to the bias is the fact that ARD expenditures are in reality investments that yield revenues to the firm over a number of years. These expenditures are investments in an intangible asset: knowledge. This knowledge is comprised of consumers' knowledge of the firm's products, that is, its reputation or goodwill, and the firm's knowledge of technological processes. When these investments are written off as current expenses, a very distorted picture of the firm's rate of return can result. If such a distortion is to be avoided, one must depreciate these investments over their actual lives, just as must be done in the case of tangible assets. (Ayanian [1975*a*, p. 82].)

Both of these statements implicitly assume that the informativeness of reported values of accounting numbers depends on the correspondence between those values and "true values" of accounting numbers. It is as if there were some exogenous values that can serve as benchmarks in any assessment of accounting numbers' information content. Of course, if such values did exist, one might ask why they are not provided as reported values. But there is more to this story. This perspective motivates attempts to "correct" reported values of accounting numbers so as to get values that are alleged to be "true values." A close examination of what is usually involved here suggests, however, that this approach really has no special theoretical virtue—in spite of appearances to the contrary. In the end, reliance on this perspective leads to an arbitrary substitution of one set of accounting techniques and values of accounting numbers for another. Thus, taken by itself, it provides

---

[1]Cited in Opinion Research Corporation [1974].

no exogenous benchmarks for determining which set of values is more informative. All of this can be clarified by considering a study that pursued the "true value" approach. We shall use Ayanian's [1975b] study of advertising. This study was selected because it is an unusually good representative study, not because it is unusually deficient.

Ayanian's work seems to have been motivated by the argument that advertising expenditures constitute investments in a long-lived asset called "advertising capital." In line with this argument, he suggests that studies claiming that advertising expenditures can lead to barriers to entry and, as a result, "above-normal" profitability may be misleading because of the accounting techniques underlying their data. Specifically, he states:

> Accounting practices, which treat advertising as a current expense, systematically exclude this intangible asset from the firm's assets thereby understating the firm's equity and, in general, misstate the firm's net revenue by substituting current advertising outlays for actual depreciation of the firm's advertising capital. If this is the case, accounting rate of return is generally biased; and further, it is possible it is biased upward by an amount which is positively related to the firm's advertising intensity. In this situation part, or all, of the positive relation between accounting profit rates and advertising intensity is spurious (Ayanian [1975b, p. 480]).

Ayanian attempted to "correct" reported values of accounting numbers by using estimation results for a rate-of-return model based on assumptions about the behavior of advertising expenditures over time, the relationship between sales and advertising, and the nature of advertising depreciation, among other things. His model is entirely deterministic. A firm's "true" rate of return is (implicitly) assumed to be constant, as is a firm's "accounting rate of return."[2]

It should be clear that the problem attacked by Ayanian arises only in a world of uncertainty. Strictly speaking, there would be no advertising in a world of certainty. And, for other worlds, all the real resource implications of advertising expenditures are, in general, not known with certainty. Moreover, the accounting problems of interest to Ayanian do not arise in a world of certainty. If, for example, advertising-expenditure growth rates, advertising depreciation rates, and the functional relationships among sales, advertising, and all other factors of production were known (which is what Ayanian assumes), conventional accounting would have no difficulty in recognizing advertising capital. The fact that they are not known provides much of the explanation for what accountants actually do with advertising expenditures (and similar items, such as R & D expenditures). Ayanian seems to ignore this. And there is more to this story.

Ayanian's main objective is to provide a measure of "true" income or "true" profitability. In a world of certainty and perfect markets, this notion can be defined unambiguously using standard characterizations of consumers' behavior and production activities carried out by firms on behalf of their securityholders. Evidently, Ayanian's results are not supposed to be limited to such a world. But in a world of uncertainty with po-

---

[2]For some parts of his model, Ayanian used available evidence from aggregate production function studies. Reported values of accounting numbers are among the sources of sample evidence used in these studies. Given Ayanian's assertions about the "biases" and "deficiencies" of conventionally defined accounting numbers, his reliance on the results of these studies is somewhat surprising.

tentially heterogeneous agents, imperfect markets, and multiperiod horizons, the notion of "income" has no generally applicable unambiguous meaning.[3] Thus, Ayanian's approach for dealing with accounting techniques is faulty for at least two reasons. First, since it does not recognize uncertainty, it does not even attack the problem with which contemporary accounting techniques must cope. Second, the notion of "true income" that it tries to use as a benchmark for evaluating and adjusting the results of these techniques has no unambiguous meaning in a world of uncertainty, for which market imperfections and multiperiod/multiperson elements induce further complications.

The point of the above is not that no income model can be derived for a world of uncertainty (under special assumptions). It is that Ayanian provided none. Thus, he provided nothing that can be used to assess or enhance accounting numbers' information content and nothing whose properties are any more or less appealing than those of contemporary accounting numbers and techniques. In the end, he provides just another set of computing procedures. His set, taken by itself, has no special virtue. It is just as arbitrary as many other conventional accounting techniques—in particular, those used for advertising expenditures. In short, Ayanian's "true" profitability numbers are true by fiat. This hardly provides either motivation or criteria for assessing the information content of accounting techniques. Moreover, it hardly provides grounds for claiming that accounting numbers are deficient, biased, misleading, etc.

One can find a variety of other shortcomings in Ayanian's work (and similar studies). For example, what should be subsumed into "advertising expenditures" is not entirely clear. A variety of a firm's activities may affect the type of productive factor identified as "advertising capital" by Ayanian. Participation in civic activities may, for example, enhance it; lobbying efforts directed toward protective legislation may decrease it. There are formal accounting procedures for classifying these things. And, presumably, a place can be found for them in Ayanian's computing procedures too. Nevertheless, both sets of procedures are arbitrary (which is not the same as useless). Since there is no exogenous benchmark against which the effects of either set of rules can be assessed, one can hardly claim that one set induces "true" values and the other does not.

Compare Ayanian's approach to ours. Our basic argument is that accounting numbers are potentially useful sources of sample evidence and, as a result, the stochastic properties of accounting numbers are pertinent to attempts to extract information from evidence consisting of accounting numbers' values. The last observation follows from the fact that the appropriateness of alternative estimators of parameters' values and the productivity of alternative methods of extracting information (e.g., linear regression models) depend, in general, on the stochastic properties (or "the probability model") of the random variable whose values constitute the sample evidence. According to our perspective, the information content of accounting numbers turns on the extent to which assessed distributions of random variables under analysis are altered by whatever information can be extracted from accounting numbers—which depends on the methods applied to sample evidence

[3] Actually, uncertainty per se is not the most basic problem. Market imperfections and incompleteness are the really basic problems, as is evidenced by, for example, Debreu's [1959] analysis of uncertainty. But the many reasons for imperfections and incompleteness are connected in one way or another with attributes of an uncertain world. So, our emphasis on uncertainty does not seem to be misplaced.

consisting of accounting numbers' values. Methods that are statistically inappropriate may induce unwarranted inferences, in the sense that they contribute to systematic errors. Moreover, methods that do not fully exploit the stochastic properties of the numbers to which they are applied will lead to imprecise inferences even if those inferences are not *systematically* "erroneous" or "off the mark."

Viewing accounting numbers as sources of sample evidence and recognizing the costliness of making avoidable unwarranted or imprecise inferences provide sufficient grounds for being interested in the properties of accounting numbers. There is, however, no basis for asking whether the numbers' observed values are "true" or "false"—just as there are no grounds for doing this when dealing with other sources of sample evidence. Taken by themselves, such questions lead to no special insights into the information content of accounting numbers.

A substantial part of the accounting literature and the literature on financial statement analysis deals with accounting numbers in terms of a "true value" perspective. The preceding discussion applies to works in these areas too. To be sure, the "true value" approach may serve purposes other than those we are pursuing or it may serve the same purpose via a different route. In any event, we see no need to invoke any of the somewhat metaphysical notions of "true value" in an analysis of financial statements.

7.2.3 The Theory of Rational Expectations

Our concern with the stochastic properties of accounting numbers can also be motivated by invoking the so-called Theory of Rational Expectations. This concept is particularly important when statistical models are used to characterize the behavior of or the perspective of (e.g., the expectations of) economic agents—as is done when the two-parameter asset-pricing model is used to describe capital market equilibrium.

Loosely stated, the Theory of Rational Expectations characterizes agents as forming expectations as if they know the process that generates the actual outcomes of some stochastic process of interest. In other words, agents are treated as if their assessed distributions for such a process are, on average, identical to the "correct" distribution conditional on the correct model of the economy (e.g., correctly specified demand and supply functions). As was indicated by Muth [1961, p. 316], in his seminal paper, this hypothesis asserts that "(1) Information is scarce and the economic system generally does not waste it" and that "(2) The way expectations are formed depends specifically on the structure of the relevant system describing the economy."

Thus, the Theory of Rational Expectations encompasses a proposition on agents' use of available information and a proposition on the information available to agents.[4] With respect to use, it essentially states that, given optimizing behavior, agents will exploit available information until equality between its marginal cost and the value of its marginal product is attained. With respect to information availability, this theory states, in effect, that the information available (or the available means of producing information) is sufficient to permit agents to infer the distribution functions that are "correct," given the relevant economic theory.

This implies that agents' behavior will be consistent with their not deliberately making

---

[4]The implications of those two propositions are examined in detail in Friedman [1979].

systematic forecasting (or inferential) errors. But then their behavior will be consistent with their having fully exploited the systematic properties of any random variable that conveys information on something of ultimate interest. This implies, in turn, that the specification of the model used to extract that information will be consistent with the stochastic properties of the random variables to which the model is applied. Since the stochastic properties of all random variables exogenous to a given agent's behavior are ultimately determined by the structure of the economy, each agent will, therefore, behave as if he is applying a model equivalent to the "correct" model, conditional on the information (or information-production opportunities) available to him. All of this is consistent with our perspective on accounting numbers—viewed as sources of sample evidence—and with the importance we ascribed to the systematic properties of accounting numbers.

The actual probability model defining any accounting number—and thus the actual systematic properties of any accounting number—is usually not known. Typically, one faces the task of inferring the characteristics of this model on the basis of available sample evidence. Some basic aspects of this task are examined in the next section, which is primarily concerned with annual income numbers. The basic issues that arise in modeling annual income numbers also arise in modeling other accounting numbers. Thus, given the objectives of this book, we lose little by focusing on income numbers. We begin with some perspective on empirical work.

7.3 Some Perspective on Empirical Work

Suppose that, for whatever reason, you face the task of forecasting annual income numbers. What kind of forecasting model would you use; i.e., how would you model the process in terms of its temporal behavior?

Modeling a stochastic process essentially involves exploiting the features of that process that are systematic (with respect to time). For example, if we specify the following model for income, $\tilde{y}(t)$, at time t:

$$\tilde{y}(t) = \mu + \tilde{\epsilon}(t), \tag{7.1}$$

with $E(\tilde{\epsilon}(t)) = 0$ and $\text{cov}(\tilde{\epsilon}(t), \tilde{\epsilon}(t-s)) = 0$, for all t and $s \neq 0$, then we are asserting that the income process has several recurring features. First, the expected value, $E(\tilde{y}(t))$, is the same in every period and equal to μ. Second, for every period t, the current deviation $\tilde{y}(t) - \mu$, from the mean is uncorrelated with each previous and every future deviation from the mean, i.e., $\text{cov}(\tilde{\epsilon}(t), \tilde{\epsilon}(t-s)) = 0$ for all t and $s \neq 0$. That is, the current and past values of the disturbance, $\tilde{\epsilon}(t-s)$, $s \geq 0$, convey no information about the expected value of any specific future period's income, $\tilde{y}(t+s)$, $s > 0$. This implies that a forecast of income for any period *conditional* on previously observed income numbers is identical to a forecast of income that is unconditional on those observed values; i.e., as of time $t - 1$, $E(\tilde{y}(t+s)|y(t-1), y(t-2), \ldots, y(t-n)) = E(\tilde{y}(t+s))$, for all $s \geq 0$ and $n \geq 1$. These are systematic features in the sense that they characterize what is known about the income process as of any period.

Of course, the "true" or "correct" model underlying a given process is unsually not known. Thus, we usually postulate some alternative plausible models and try to determine which model's implications are consistent with the available sample evidence. From among the alternatives considered, we should like to select the model with the most descriptive validity. This process is adequately characterized in the following figure:

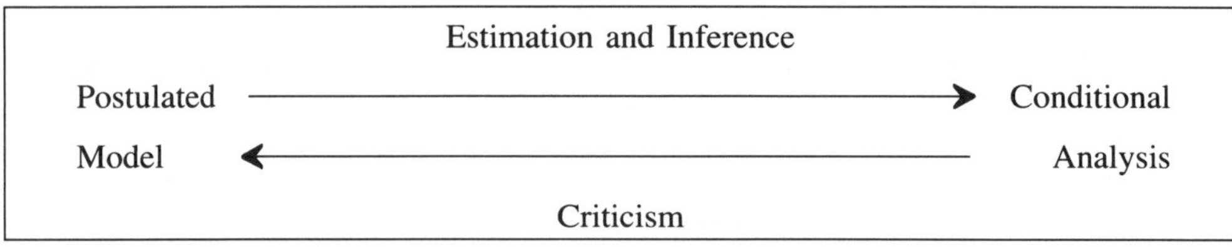

The process begins with a postulated model that incorporates (to the extent possible) whatever insights into the process can be provided by the analyst. These insights may be based on theoretical considerations (e.g., micro- and macroeconomic theory) or available empirical results. Usually, the model has unknown parameters, such as μ in model (7.1). These parameters are estimated using available sample evidence. Given these estimates, and conditional on the validity of the model, one can make inferences about the parameters. For example, one might want to infer whether μ, in model (7.1), differs from a specified value, say zero. Moreover, conditional on the model's validity, one can contemplate the implications of one's inferences relative to the objectives that are supposed to be served by the entire analysis. For example, one implication of model (7.1) when applied to income is that the expected value of the income number is a constant, μ. There is no "growth" or "trend" component in this number, conditional on model (7.1).

But the postulated model may not be the correct one for the process under examination. In order to deal with this issue, the analyst can alter his position from that of a tentative "believer" in the model to that of a critic. Various analyses can then be performed which would be unnecessary if the model were correct but which are capable of indicating inadequacies of the model if they exist. Those who are familiar with regression analysis should recognize that analyzing the residuals from an estimated regression model is one type of analysis that can point to model inadequacies. This process of criticism provides the basis for model modification. Then, the whole process is repeated—preferably with new data (or "a holdout sample"). This continues until one is satisfied that he has found a model that is a reasonably adequate model for the series being investigated, relative to the available alternatives.

Note that there will always appear to be some inconsistencies between the sample evidence and a postulated model. No model will ever be perfect. But that is, we believe, beside the point. The important issue is whether one has a model that appears to provide a reliable characterization of the process, *relative to the available competing models*. Since the set of competing models may change (because of new theoretical or empirical results), one should always be prepared to reassess the descriptive validity of a model.

The above perspective underlies the remaining sections of this chapter, which deal with time series analyses of accounting numbers. Univariate time series models constitute our first specific topic.

7.4 Models for Annual Income and Related Numbers

7.4.1 Univariate Time Series Models

7.4.1.1 Motivation and Specification

Univariate time series models are among those frequently used to model annual income and related numbers. A univariate time series model for the process $\tilde{y}(t)$, $t = 1, 2,$

..., is a representation of the current value of the process, $\tilde{y}(t)$, in terms of past values, $\tilde{y}(t - s)$, $s = 1, 2, \ldots$, plus a disturbance, $\tilde{\epsilon}(t)$. The current value of the disturbance may also be modeled in terms of its past values, along lines discussed below.

Such time series models may seem appealing ("plausible") for a variety of reasons. For example, they may be attractive solely because of their empirical properties when applied to accounting numbers—relative to alternative models. Some of the alternatives, of course, may attempt to model $\tilde{y}(t)$ successfully in terms of other random variables, say $\tilde{w}(t)$ and $\tilde{x}(t)$, which may be other accounting numbers (e.g., variable costs, total assets, etc.). In addition, they may have appeal because they appear (at least intuitively) to be consistent with some general conceptions about the evolution of accounting numbers. A common conception encountered in the literature on industrial organization (and elsewhere) will be used for illustrative purposes.

As indicated earlier, one view of an accounting income number asserts that there is a relationship between the autocorrelation functions of firms' income numbers and the market-structure/market-conduct attributes of a firm's operations. The general argument was concisely expressed by Stigler [1963, p. 70]:

> Competitive industries will have a volatile pattern of rates of return, for the movements into high-profit industries and out of low-profit industries will—together with the flow of new disturbances of equilibrium—lead to a constantly changing hierarchy of rates of return. In the monopolistic industries, on the other hand, the unusually profitable industries will be able to preserve their preferential position for considerable periods of time.

In line with this hypothesis, Stigler examined correlation coefficients for $\tilde{y}(t)$ and $\tilde{y}(t + s)$ for various values of s, where $\tilde{y}(t)$ is the rate of return on total assets. Rates of return for various industries were examined. Stigler inferred [1963, p. 70] that "On the whole, the pattern of coefficients agrees remarkably well with the hypothesis."

In general, this view of income and related numbers (e.g., rates of return) postulates a form of persistence: a tendency for firms with above-average rates of return in one period to have, on average, above-average rates of return in the subsequent period. The strength of this persistence is taken to be dependent on the extent to which firms' market-structure/market-conduct characteristics depart from those of a perfect market. And, presumably, if there are barriers to exit from some types of economic activities, this perspective would lead one to expect negative persistence rather than positive persistence; i.e., a tendency for the affected firms with below-average rates of return in one period to have, on average, below-average rates of return in the subsequent period. Indeed, this is the major prediction of Caves' and Porter's [1976] characterization of barriers to exit:

> Exit barriers influence the behavior of firms through their power to inflict persistently subnormal profits. Their source is inputs that can become attached to the firm and then command persistently low earnings because they are *durable* and *specific* to an activity of the company. Such durable and specific assets . . . may be specific to the particular business or productive activity, to the company employing them, to the physical location, or to any combination of these. (Caves and Porter [1976, p. 40].)

As indicated earlier, "persistence" is usually assessed by using estimated autocorrelation functions of income numbers or rates of return (computed using observed values of accounting numbers).

Of course, one can justifiably question the extent to which there is any necessary connection between accounting income or related numbers' autocorrelation structures and the strength of monopolistic forces. We are not aware of any rigorous theoretical model of resource allocation under uncertainty that uniquely implies such a connection. Thus, the motivation for modeling accounting income and related numbers in terms of such a connection seems to be ad hoc. But resolving this issue is not our immediate objective. For our purposes, it is sufficient to note that this approach provides intuitive grounds for considering the descriptive validity of univariate time series models for income and related numbers.

Another argument providing similar intuitive grounds turns on managements' alleged use of accounting techniques for the purpose of "managing earnings."[5] The crux of this story is that managements select or use accounting techniques in order to "smooth" an income or rate-of-return series so as to give the appearance of an "acceptable" and "not very erratic" rate-of-return or income series. It has been alleged that this can be achieved by, for example, managements' exercising control over the *timing* of transactions that have immediate effects on income numbers or by varying the capitalization vs. expensing treatment of certain types of expenditures (e.g., maintenance expenditures, training program expenditures, and research and development expenditures). The following declaration on "income smoothing" seems typical:

> There are many . . . monopolistic situations that could induce persistence in earnings progress, but the same results could follow from accounting practices designed at "managing earnings." A clear example exists when provisions such as pension fund reserves are varied specifically to achieve a smooth earnings progression. A less blatant case arises when the profit from one effective economic transaction is taken into the income statement over several years. (Brealey [1969, p. 80].)

Whether managements actually behave as if they are "managing" earnings is a complex issue not yet resolved on the basis of available evidence. (See, e.g., Gonedes [1972] and Gonedes and Schneller [1986] for elaboration.) Nevertheless, this is another type of hypothesis that provides some intuitive motivation for univariate time series models, in particular, those consistent with "smooth" sample paths of income (or related) numbers. Models consistent with strong positive autocorrelation—a notion explained below—and models consistent with "trends" in expected values of income numbers are often viewed as being consistent with the essence of the "income-smoothing" hypothesis.

The above remarks simply illustrate the kinds of arguments that identify the potential usefulness of univariate time series models for accounting income (and related) numbers, mainly by providing intuitive underpinnings. We know of no general rigorously derived theoretical propositions that identify a particular type of model as being "appropriate." Thus, it appears that intuitive underpinnings are the most that one can get out of these sorts of arguments. The next step will usually involve specifying particular models and

---

[5]The role of accounting techniques is examined in detail in Chapter 6.

evaluating their descriptive validity on the basis of actual sample evidence (e.g., observed values of income numbers).

Before we proceed to this use of sample evidence, an important aspect of specifying models should be noted. Each entertained model will—because of its specifications—imply certain attributes of the stochastic process being modeled. For example, one specification might imply that the process is nonstationary while the other implies stationarity. Or one might imply a deterministic trend and the other might imply a stochastic trend. Clearly, some of these implications may seem inconsistent with one's prior beliefs—formed on the basis of intuition, theory, or empirical results. That is, a particular model may seem consistent with one's perspective at first glance; but it may seem inconsistent after a deeper analysis of what that model really implies. In this type of situation, it is not entirely clear that one should even bother assessing the model on the basis of sample evidence—an exercise that is, of course, affected by sampling error, among other things. If the model's implications are "absurd" or somehow nonsensical, sample evidence cannot make them less so. In short, a useful step prior to work with sample evidence is to consider the purely theoretical implications of one's alternative models. We illustrate this sort of exercise in the next subsection. Then we provide an illustrative application involving actual observations on one firm's earnings-per-share.

7.4.1.2 The First-Order Autoregressive Model

One model that seems consistent with the crux of the various arguments given above is:

$$\tilde{y}(t) = \beta_1 + \beta_2 \tilde{y}(t - 1) + \tilde{\epsilon}(t), \tag{7.2}$$

where $\tilde{y}(t)$ is, say, a firm's income number for period t (or "at time t") and $\tilde{\epsilon}(t)$ is the period t disturbance, which is assumed to be independent and identically distributed (over time) with $E[\tilde{\epsilon}(t)] = 0.0$ and $\text{Var}(\tilde{\epsilon}(t)) = \sigma_\epsilon^2$. Model (7.2) is simply a first-order autoregressive univariate time, series model. For technical reasons, we assume $|\beta_2| < 1$.[6]

It is not unusual to encounter work wherein model (7.2) is postulated for income (or related) numbers. The arguments given above are often used to motivate this specification. An important question to ask is: are the theoretical implications of model (7.2) consistent with what one had in mind when (7.2) was offered as an adequate model? Or does it imply some things that are "hard to swallow" insofar as income numbers are concerned? These are among the questions that can be addressed using the results provided below. Our derivations of results are presented to provide the reader with some exercise in the mechanics of time series models. Do not be put off by the mechanics—which may seem frightening to some. They are all simple manipulations.

First, write $\tilde{y}(t)$ in terms of past values of the disturbance by substituting for $\tilde{y}(t - 1)$, $\tilde{y}(t - 2)$, etc. That is, from (7.2) we have:

$$\tilde{y}(t - 1) = \beta_1 + \beta_2 \tilde{y}(t - 2) + \tilde{\epsilon}(t - 1). \tag{7.3}$$

Using (7.3) in (7.2) yields:

---

[6]If $|\beta_2| \geq 1$, then $\tilde{y}(t)$, $t = 1, 2, \ldots$, is a so-called nonstationary process. (More on this later.)

$$\begin{aligned}\tilde{y}(t) &= \beta_1 + \beta_2[\beta_1 + \beta_2\tilde{y}(t-2) + \tilde{\epsilon}(t-1)] + \tilde{\epsilon}(t)\\ &= \beta_1 + \beta_2\beta_1 + \beta_2^2\tilde{y}(t-2) + \beta_2\tilde{\epsilon}(t-1) + \tilde{\epsilon}(t).\end{aligned} \tag{7.4}$$

Moreover, since, from (7.2):

$$\tilde{y}(t-2) = \beta_1 + \beta_2\tilde{y}(t-3) + \tilde{\epsilon}(t-2), \tag{7.5}$$

we can rewrite (7.4) as:

$$\begin{aligned}\tilde{y}(t) &= \beta_1 + \beta_1\beta_2 + \beta_2^2[\beta_1 + \beta_2\tilde{y}(t-3) + \tilde{\epsilon}(t-2)]\\ &\quad + \beta_2\tilde{\epsilon}(t-1) + \tilde{\epsilon}(t)\\ &= \beta_1 + \beta_1\beta_2 + \beta_2^2\beta_1 + \beta_2^3\tilde{y}(t-3) + \beta_2^2\tilde{\epsilon}(t-2)\\ &\quad + \beta_2\tilde{\epsilon}(t-1) + \tilde{\epsilon}(t).\end{aligned} \tag{7.6}$$

Continuing with the substitution, we find that:

$$\tilde{y}(t) = \beta_1 \sum_{i=0}^{\infty} \beta_2^i + \sum_{i=0}^{\infty} \beta_2^i\,\tilde{\epsilon}(t-i). \tag{7.7}$$

Note that no past value of $\tilde{y}(t)$ appears on the right-hand side (RHS) of (7.7) because, since $|\beta_2| < 1$, $\beta_2^n \to 0$ as $n \to \infty$. Moreover, since $|\beta_2| < 1$, $\Sigma_{i=0}^{\infty} \beta_2^i = (1 - \beta_2)^{-1}$. Thus, (7.7) can be rewritten as:[7]

$$\tilde{y}(t) = \beta_1(1-\beta_2)^{-1} + \sum_{i=0}^{\infty} \beta_2^i\,\tilde{\epsilon}(t-i). \tag{7.8}$$

From (7.8), we see that:

$$E(\tilde{y}(t)) = \beta_1(1-\beta_2)^{-1}. \tag{7.9}$$

This is the unconditional mean of the process. Note that it is a constant, independent of time, t.

The result in (7.9) is implied by the specification of model (7.2). If the attribute of a constant mean seems, on a priori or empirical grounds, to be inconsistent with one's perspective on the process generating income numbers, then the specification of model (7.2)—with $|\beta_2| < 1$—as a description of the income number, $\tilde{y}(t)$, should be discarded. In short, the result in (7.9) is implied by (7.2). If (7.9) is not what one had in mind, then one should rethink the original specification of (7.2), which is where the problem really lies.

Next, consider the unconditional variance of the process:

$$\text{Var}(\tilde{y}(t)) = \text{Var}\left(\sum_{i=0}^{\infty} \beta_2^i\,\tilde{\epsilon}(t-i)\right). \tag{7.10}$$

Since the successive disturbances are (by assumption) serially uncorrelated, we can write:[8]

---

[7]Some will recognize that model (7.3), which is equivalent to (7.2), is simply an infinite-order moving average model with a constant term, $\beta_1(1-\beta_2)^{-1}$.

[8]As an exercise, convince yourself that (7.11) is correct (or incorrect). In doing so, recall the general formula for the variance of a sum of random variables.

$$\mathrm{Var}(\tilde{y}(t)) = \sum_{i=0}^{\infty} (\beta_2^i)^2 \,\mathrm{Var}(\tilde{\epsilon}(t-i)). \tag{7.11}$$

Since $\mathrm{Var}(\tilde{\epsilon}(t)) = \sigma_\epsilon^2$, a constant:

$$\mathrm{Var}(\tilde{y}(t)) = \sigma_\epsilon^2 \left(\sum_{i=0}^{\infty} (\beta_2^2)^i \right), \tag{7.12}$$

and since $|\beta_2^2| < 1$, we have $\Sigma_{i=0}^{\infty} (\beta_2^2)^i = (1 - \beta_2^2)^{-1}$, and thus:

$$\mathrm{Var}(\tilde{y}(t)) = \sigma_\epsilon^2/(1 - \beta_2^2). \tag{7.13}$$

As with the unconditional mean, $E(\tilde{y}(t))$, of the process, the unconditional variance, $\mathrm{Var}(\tilde{y}(t))$, is a constant. This too is automatically implied by the specification of model (7.2). And, as with the result in (7.9), it seems important for one to ask whether a constant value of $\mathrm{Var}(\tilde{y}(t))$ is consistent with one's perspective on the process generating $\tilde{y}(t)$. Note, for example, that this feature of model (7.2) rules out any effects of institutional changes on the variability of firms' operations—to the extent revealed by income numbers. Yet, it is frequently argued that post-1930 changes in the tools and conduct of both fiscal policy and monetary policy, among other things, have altered the variability of economic activity, as measured by various macroeconomic time series (e.g., Gross National Product, Employment, Disposable Income, Investment Expenditures, etc.). In view of this type of argument—as well as information dealing specifically with a firm under analysis—the result given in (7.13) may be assigned a low probability insofar as descriptive adequacy is concerned. There are some additional implications that might warrant the same response. In particular, consider the covariance of $\tilde{y}(t)$ and $\tilde{y}(t-j)$, for $j = 1, 2, \ldots$, i.e., the value of the covariance function $\mathrm{Cov}(\tilde{y}(t), \tilde{y}(t-j))$ at lag j, for $j = 1, 2, \ldots$.[9]

Using expression (7.2) for $\tilde{y}(t)$ and $\tilde{y}(t-1)$, we get:

$$\begin{aligned}\mathrm{Cov}(\tilde{y}(t), \tilde{y}(t-1)) &= \mathrm{Cov}(\beta_1 + \beta_2 \tilde{y}(t-1) + \tilde{\epsilon}(t), \tilde{y}(t-1)) \\ &= \beta_2 \,\mathrm{Cov}(\tilde{y}(t-1), \tilde{y}(t-1)) + \mathrm{Cov}(\tilde{\epsilon}(t), \tilde{y}(t-1)).\end{aligned} \tag{7.14}$$

But $\tilde{y}(t-1)$ involves disturbances before and up to period $t-1$, not disturbances after $t-1$. Thus, $\mathrm{Cov}(\tilde{\epsilon}(t), \tilde{y}(t-1)) = 0$ and:

$$\begin{aligned}\mathrm{Cov}(\tilde{y}(t), \tilde{y}(t-1)) &= \beta_2 \,\mathrm{Cov}(\tilde{y}(t-1), \tilde{y}(t-1)) \\ &= \beta \,\mathrm{Var}(\tilde{y}(t-1)) \\ &= \beta_2[\sigma_\epsilon^2/(1 - \beta_2^2)].\end{aligned} \tag{7.15}$$

It will be helpful to have some additional notation now. Let c_j be the value of the autocovariance function at lag j; e.g., $c_0 = \mathrm{Var}(\tilde{y}(t))$, $c_1 = \mathrm{Cov}(\tilde{y}(t), \tilde{y}(t-1))$, etc. Expression (7.15) can be reexpressed as:

$$c_1 = \beta_2 c_0. \tag{7.16}$$

Values of the autocovariance function at other lags can be evaluated from the relationship:

---

[9]Note that expression (7.13) gives the autocovariance function at lag zero because $\mathrm{Cov}(\tilde{y}(t), \tilde{y}(t)) = \mathrm{Var}(\tilde{y}(t))$.

$$
\begin{aligned}
c_j &= \mathrm{Cov}(\tilde{y}(t), \tilde{y}(t-j)) \\
&= \mathrm{Cov}(\beta_1 + \beta_2 \tilde{y}(t-1) + \tilde{\epsilon}(t), \tilde{y}(t-j)) \\
&= \mathrm{Cov}(\tilde{y}(t-1), \tilde{y}(t-j))\beta_2 + \mathrm{Cov}(\tilde{\epsilon}(t), \tilde{y}(t-j)) \\
&= \beta_2 \mathrm{Cov}(\tilde{y}(t-1), \tilde{y}(t-j)) \\
&= \beta_2 c_{j-1} \qquad (7.17)
\end{aligned}
$$

Expression (7.17) implies:

$$c_j = (\beta_2)^j c_0, \qquad (7.18)$$

where, by assumption, $|\beta_2| < 1$. That is, for the $\tilde{y}(t)$ modeled according to model (7.2), the value of the covariance function declines exponentially with the length of the lag j from an initial value (at $j = 0$) equal to $c_0 = \mathrm{Var}(\tilde{y}(t))$.

The result in (7.18) allows the autocovariance function to have nonzero values, which is consistent with the "persistence" arguments briefly reviewed above. But it does more. It places a special structure on that function. Specifically, it specifies that the linear relationship between $\tilde{y}(t)$ and $\tilde{y}(t - j)$, for any j, "dies out" exponentially. Thus, e.g., if one specified model (7.2) because of, say, the market-structure arguments reviewed above, then one is saying, in effect, that the "abnormally high" income or rate of return on assets allegedly permitted by market imperfections should not be predicted over an arbitrarily long future period. Rather, one should behave as if these alleged effects will gradually be dissipated—perhaps by market forces. That is, forecasts of performance ("profitability") made as of time t for periods $t + s$, $s = 1, 2, \ldots$, should exhibit convergence to $E(\tilde{y}(t))$, no matter what the observed performance for periods prior to t happened to be. If this is not what one has in mind as a result of market-structure considerations, then model (7.2) does not embody one's prior perspective and beliefs.

The implied structure of the relationship between $\tilde{y}(t)$ and $\tilde{y}(t - j)$, $j = 1, 2, \ldots$, can also be represented via the autocorrelation function, which defines values of correlation coefficients, rather than values of covariances, for various lags. Recall that the correlation coefficient between two random variables, say $\tilde{w}$ and $\tilde{x}$, equals $\mathrm{Cov}(\tilde{w}, \tilde{x})/(\sqrt{\mathrm{Var}(\tilde{w})}\sqrt{\mathrm{Var}(\tilde{x})})$. Thus, for any j, we can say that the correlation coefficient between $\tilde{y}(t)$ and $\tilde{y}(t - j)$ is:

$$\rho_j = \frac{\mathrm{Cov}(\tilde{y}(t), \tilde{y}(t-j))}{\sqrt{\mathrm{Var}(\tilde{y}(t))}\sqrt{\mathrm{Var}(\tilde{y}(t-j))}}. \qquad (7.19)$$

From (7.13) and the definition of c_0, we have that $\mathrm{Var}(\tilde{y}(t)) = \mathrm{Var}(\tilde{y}(t - j)) = c_0$, for all j. The numerator of (7.19) is c_j. Hence, using (7.18) and (7.19), we get:

$$\rho_j = \frac{c_j}{c_0} = \frac{(\beta_2)^j c_0}{c_0} = \beta_2^j. \qquad (7.20)$$

The result in (7.20) says that the coefficient of correlation between, say, income for period t, $\tilde{y}(t)$, and income for period $t - j$, $\tilde{y}(t - j)$, declines exponentially with the length of the lag, j (which is simply the number of periods separating the income numbers). Note that this correlation coefficient depends only on j; its value is not affected by t. Moreover, only the absolute value of the number of periods, $t - (t - j)$, matters; i.e., the coefficient of correlation between $\tilde{y}(t)$ and $\tilde{y}(t - j)$ has the same value as the coefficient of correlation between $\tilde{y}(t)$ and $\tilde{y}(t + j)$.

Thus, for example, if one specified model (7.2) because it seems consistent with one's beliefs about, say, managements' "income-smoothing" actions, then one is necessarily specifying that the resulting correlation between different periods' income numbers is independent of the particular periods that are involved (i.e., the values of t)—even though one also believes that particular periods' events are what induced managements' attempts and possibly the specific "smoothing" actions adopted (if any). Moreover, one is necessarily specifying that the resulting correlation between different periods' income numbers depends only on the number of periods separating the numbers, no matter what smoothing actions one might believe were adopted in particular periods. In short, depending on why (7.2) was specified in the first place, the implications of (7.2) for the relationships between different periods' numbers may not be what one had in mind when (7.2) was proposed as a potentially descriptively adequate model. Nevertheless, the result in (7.20) is what one is implicitly stipulating when adopting model (7.2).

Two other implications of model (7.2) are worth noting. They are:

$$E[\tilde{y}(t)|y(t - 1)] = \beta_1 + \beta_2 y(t - 1), \tag{7.21}$$

and

$$\begin{aligned} \text{Var}(\tilde{y}(t)|y(t - 1)) &= \text{Var}(\beta_1 + \beta_2 y(t - 1) + \tilde{\epsilon}(t)) \\ &= \text{Var}(\tilde{\epsilon}(t)) \\ &= \sigma_\epsilon^2. \end{aligned} \tag{7.22}$$

Expressions (7.21) and (7.22) provide expressions for the conditional mean and variance, respectively, of $\tilde{y}(t)$, where the conditioning argument is the realized value of $\tilde{y}(t - 1)$.

Expression (7.19) provides, in effect, a forecast of $\tilde{y}(\tau)$ for $\tau = t$ conditional on the observed values of $\tilde{y}(\tau - s)$, $s = 1, 2, \ldots$. Indeed, since this forecast is the expected value formed conditionally on those past values, it is the minimum mean square forecast of $\tilde{y}(\tau)$ for $\tau = t$ in the family of extrapolative forecasts (i.e., the family of forecasts based only on past values of the random variable being forecasted).[10] We are assuming here, of course, that model (7.2)—which is what led to (7.19)—is the correct univariate time series

[10]In different words, no other extrapolative forecast gives a smaller value of the expectation of the squared forecast error. The general result behind this observation is that the expectation of any random variable conditional on a specified set of information is a minimum mean-squared error forecaster relative to all other forecasters based only on that same set of information. That is, relative to a set of information, ϕ_t, available at time t, the forecaster $E[\tilde{y}(t + k)|\phi_t]$ of $\tilde{y}(t + k)$, $k > 0$, gives the smallest value of the expected squared forecast error conditional on ϕ_t, *viz.*, $E[(\tilde{y}(t + k) - f(t + k))^2|\phi_t]$, where $f(t + k)$ is a forecast of $\tilde{y}(t + k)$. To see this, let $f^*(t + k) = E[\tilde{y}(t + k)|\phi_t]$ and represent any other forecaster, $f(t + k)$, by $f(t + k) = f^*(t + k) + g$, where the value of g depends on $f(t + k)$. The expected value of the squared forecast error conditional on ϕ_t is then $E[(\tilde{y}(t + k) - f(t + k))^2|\phi_t] = E[(\tilde{y}(t + k) - f^*)^2|\phi_t] + g^2 + (2g)E[(\tilde{y}(t + k) - f^*)|\phi_t]$. Since $f^* = E[\tilde{y}(t + k)|\phi_t]$, the last quantity on the RHS of the equality equals zero no matter what the value of g is. But then $E[(\tilde{y}(t + k) - f)^2|\phi_t] = E[(\tilde{y}(t + k) - f^*)^2|\phi_t] + g^2$, which is minimized by setting $g = 0$, i.e., by setting $f(t + k) = f^*(t + k) = E[\tilde{y}(t + k)|\phi_t]$, the expected value of $\tilde{y}(t + k)$ conditional on the information available at time t, ϕ_t.

model for the stochastic process $\{\tilde{y}(\tau)\}$ and that the values of the parameters β_1 and β_2 used to compute the forecast are the "true" values.

With (7.19) in hand, we can derive the entire "forecast function" for $\tilde{y}(\tau)$. Let $E_t[\tilde{y}(t + k)|y(t), y(t-1), \ldots]$ denote the expectation of $\tilde{y}(t+k)$ evaluated at time t conditionally on the observed values of $\tilde{y}(\tau)$ for $\tau = t, t-1, \ldots$. This expectation is clearly a function of k for a given forecasting date, $\tau = t$ in our case. For a given value of k, the value of this function is the so-called k-step-ahead prediction of $\tilde{y}(\tau)$ as of time t. That is, it is the forecasted value of $\tilde{y}(\tau)$ for the kth period beyond the forecasting date and taken conditionally on information available at the forecasting date. In our case, this information consists of the observed values of $\tilde{y}(\tau)$ for periods $\tau = t, t-1, \ldots$. Of course, given model (7.2), only the value of $\tilde{y}(t)$ is needed to evaluate the forecast function at $\tau = t + 1$, as is implied by (7.19). That is, for any forecasting date t, only the value of $\tilde{y}(t)$ is needed to provide the one-step-ahead prediction of $\tilde{y}(\tau)$; i.e., $E_t[\tilde{y}(t+1)|y(t), y(t-1), \ldots] = E_t[\tilde{y}(t+1)|y(t)]$.

For period $\tau = t + k$, we have:

$$\tilde{y}(t+k) = \beta_1 + \beta_2\, \tilde{y}(t+k-1) + \tilde{\epsilon}(t+k). \tag{7.23}$$

Thus, the value of the forecast function at $\tau = t + k$ computed as of time t equals the value of:

$$\begin{aligned} &E_t[\tilde{y}(t+k)|y(t), y(t-1), \ldots] \\ &\quad = \beta_1 + \beta_2 E_t[\tilde{y}(t+k-1)|y(t), y(t-1), \ldots] \end{aligned} \tag{7.24}$$

since $E[\tilde{\epsilon}(t+k)|y(t), y(t-1), \ldots] = E[\tilde{\epsilon}(t+k)] = 0.0$, for all $k > 0$; i.e., the disturbance for any period t is independent of $\tilde{y}(\tau)$ for $\tau = t-1, t-2, \ldots$. This is a consequence of our original assumptions on the serial independence of $\tilde{\epsilon}(t)$, $t = 1, 2, \ldots$.

Looking at the RHS of (7.24), one finds that we now face the task of evaluating $E_t[\tilde{y}(t + k - 1)|y(t), y(t-1), \ldots]$. Using model (7.2) and taking expectations, we get:

$$\begin{aligned} &E_t[\tilde{y}(t+k-1)|y(t), y(t-1), \ldots] \\ &\quad = \beta_1 + \beta_2 E_t[\tilde{y}(t+k-2)|y(t), y(t-1), \ldots]. \end{aligned} \tag{7.25}$$

Using (7.25) in (7.24) gives:

$$\begin{aligned} &E_t[\tilde{y}(t+k)|y(t), y(t-1), \ldots] \\ &\quad = \beta_1 + \beta_2\{\beta_1 + \beta_2 E_t[\tilde{y}(t+k-2)|y(t), y(t-1), \ldots]\} \\ &\quad = \beta_1 + \beta_2\beta_1 + \beta_2^2 E_t[\tilde{y}(t+k-2)|y(t), y(t-1), \ldots]. \end{aligned} \tag{7.26}$$

Continuing along these lines, one finds that, in general, for any $k > 0$:

$$\begin{aligned} E_t[\tilde{y}(t+k)|y(t), y(t-1), \ldots] &= \sum_{i=0}^{l=1} \beta_2^i \beta_1 \\ &\quad + \beta_2^l E_t[\tilde{y}(t+k-l)|y(t), y(t-1), \ldots], \end{aligned} \tag{7.27}$$

where for all $l < k$, the RHS of this forecast function for $\tilde{y}(t+k)$ will involve the forecast function for $\tilde{y}(t+k-l)$. Clearly, both of these functions can be evaluated, as of time t, by setting $l = k$, in which case we get:

$$E_t[\tilde{y}(t+k)|y(t), y(t-1), \ldots] = \left[\sum_{i=0}^{k-1} \beta_2^i\right] \beta_1 + (\beta_2^k)\, y(t), \tag{7.28}$$

since $E_t[\tilde{y}(t+k-k)|y(t), y(t-1), \ldots] = y(t)$. In short, the value of the forecast function for $\tilde{y}(t+k)$ conditional on the values of $\tilde{y}(\tau)$ observed as of time $\tau = t$ is linear in the value of $\tilde{y}(t)$ for a given k. And for increasing k, the influence of $\tilde{y}(t) = y(t)$ on the forecast of $\tilde{y}(t+k)$ declines exponentially. Indeed, if we let the forecast horizon, k, become arbitrarily large and still keep $l = k$, we find that $\beta_2^k y(t) \to 0$, because $|\beta_2| < 1$, and $(\Sigma_{i=0}^{k-1} \beta_2^i)\, \beta_1 \to (\Sigma_{i=0}^{\infty} \beta_2^i)\, \beta_1 = (1 - \beta_2)^{-1}\, \beta_1$. Thus, using (7.9), we find that:

$$\lim_{k\to\infty} E_t[\tilde{y}(t+k)|y(t), y(t-1), \ldots] = \beta_1(1-\beta_2)^{-1}$$

$$= E[\tilde{y}(t+k)], \tag{7.29}$$

which is the unconditional expected value of $\tilde{y}(t+k)$. In short, no matter what the value of $\tilde{y}(t)$ is, as one's forecasting horizon increases in length, the influence of the value of $\tilde{y}(t)$ on one's forecast of $\tilde{y}(t+k)$ converges to zero—and one's forecast converges to the unconditional expected value of $\tilde{y}(t+k)$, $\beta_1(1-\beta_2)^{-1}$, which is a constant. As with all of our other results, this is a direct implication of the specification of model (7.2).

Along with the other implications of model (7.2), the result in (7.29) provides another basis for determining whether this model is really consistent with one's beliefs, which presumably motivated interest in (7.2) in the first place. If, for example, one's beliefs imply that the current value, $\tilde{y}(t) = y(t)$, should have a "permanent" influence on future values of the process, then the result in (7.29) implies that, strictly speaking, model (7.2) is inconsistent with one's beliefs. If this is the case, and if one's beliefs are strongly held, then applying model (7.2) to actual sample evidence (in order to estimate its parameters, etc.) would seem to serve no purpose.

To sum up, we have the following implications of model (7.2), for all t:

$$E[\tilde{y}(t)] = \beta_1(1-\beta_2)^{-1}, \tag{7.30}$$

$$\mathrm{Var}[\tilde{y}(t)] = \sigma_\epsilon^2(1-\beta_2^2)^{-1}, \tag{7.31}$$

$$c_j = \beta_2 c_{j-1} = (\beta_2)^j c_0, \qquad j = 1, 2, \ldots, \tag{7.32}$$

where c_j is the autocovariance function at lag j:

$$\rho_j = \beta_2 \rho_{j-1} = (\beta_2)^j, \qquad j = 1, 2, \ldots, \tag{7.33}$$

where ρ_j is the autocorrelation function at lag j:

$$E[\tilde{y}(t)|y(t-1)] = \beta_1 + \beta_2 y(t-1), \tag{7.34}$$

and:

$$\mathrm{Var}[\tilde{y}(t)|y(t-1)] = \sigma_\epsilon^2. \tag{7.35}$$

Expressions of (7.30) and (7.31) indicate that the first two moments, $E(\tilde{y}(t))$ and $\mathrm{Var}(\tilde{y}(t))$, of $\tilde{y}(t)$ are constants. This is equivalent to saying that the process $\{\tilde{y}(t)\}$ is a second-order stationary process. As can be seen from the derivations of expressions (7.30) and (7.31), the specification $|\beta_2| < 1$ plays an important role. The factors $(1-\beta_2)^{-1}$ and $(1-\beta_2^2)^{-1}$ that appear in (7.30) and (7.31), respectively, are obtained as the limits of the series $\Sigma_{i=0}^{\infty} \beta_2^i$ and $\Sigma_{i=0}^{\infty} (\beta_2^2)^i$, respectively. These series do not converge to any finite values when $|\beta_1| \geq 1$. In short, if $|\beta_2| \geq 1$, the two marginal moments $E(\tilde{y}(t))$ and $\text{Var}(\tilde{y}(t))$ are not defined.[11] In this case, it makes no sense to treat $\{\tilde{y}(t)\}$ as a process characterized by a "normal" or "average" value. As will be indicated below, when model (7.2) is applied to firms' annual income numbers, one usually observes results consistent with the specifications $|\beta_2| \approx 1$ or $|\beta_2| > 1$. Thus, for the most part, assertions such as the following appear to reflect an erroneous characterization of income processes:

> *Average earnings* over periods, such as 5 to 10 years, smooth out erratic and even extraordinary factors as well as cyclical influences, thus presenting a better and more reliable measure of "earning power" of an enterprise. (Bernstein [1974, p. 497].)

If the probability model that describes a firm's income number is nonstationary—as is implied by $|\beta_2| \geq 1$—then such a "smoothed out" value is not an estimate of any aspect of that probability model. Consequently, it is not clear that analyses based on such a value will yield precise insights into the process generating that income number.

7.4.1.3 Transformations to Attain Stationarity

Inferring that a process is nonstationary need not lead to a "dead end." Various transformations, such as differencing or taking logarithms, are available for converting nonstationary processes into stationary ones. As will be seen, such transformations are widely used in empirical analyses of income numbers.

Suppose, for example, that a particular firm's income number, $\tilde{y}(t)$, is believed to be adequately described by the condition $E[\tilde{y}(t)|\phi_{t-1}] = t\mu$, where ϕ_{t-1} denotes the available information being used to assess the expected value of $\tilde{y}(t)$ at time $t - 1$; i.e., conditional on this information, the process $\{\tilde{y}(t)\}$ is specified to have a deterministic linear time-trend in the mean. Insofar as the mean of this process is concerned, the process can be made stationary by taking first differences, as is indicated below.

Suppose that:

$$\tilde{y}(t) = t\mu + \tilde{\epsilon}(t), \tag{7.36}$$

where $E[\tilde{\epsilon}(t)] = 0.0$ and $\text{Var}[\tilde{\epsilon}(t)] = \sigma_\epsilon^2$. Then:

$$\begin{aligned} E[\Delta\tilde{y}(t)] &= E[\tilde{y}(t) - \tilde{y}(t-1)] \\ &= E[t\mu + \tilde{\epsilon}(t) - (t-1)\mu - \tilde{\epsilon}(t-1)] \\ &= E[\mu + \tilde{\epsilon}(t) - \tilde{\epsilon}(t-1)] \\ &= \mu, \end{aligned} \tag{7.37}$$

where $\Delta\tilde{y}(t) \equiv \tilde{y}(t) - \tilde{y}(t-1)$; i.e., Δ denotes the "first difference" operator. Since μ is a constant, the process $\{\Delta\tilde{y}(t))\}$ is stationary, insofar as its mean (or first moment) is concerned. This implies that a mean-stationary process is given by:

$$\Delta\tilde{y}(t) = \mu + \tilde{\eta}(t), \tag{7.38}$$

where $\tilde{\eta}(t) = \Delta\tilde{\epsilon}(t) = \tilde{\epsilon}(t) - \tilde{\epsilon}(t-1)$. Note, however, that if $\{\tilde{\epsilon}(t)\}$ was specified to be a

---

[11]This does not mean that the conditional moments $E[\tilde{y}(t)|y(t-1), y(t-2), \ldots]$ and $\text{Var}[\tilde{y}(t)|$ $y(t-1), y(t-2), \ldots]$ are not defined.

serially independent process when model (7.36) was proposed, then $\{\tilde{\eta}(t)\}$ cannot be a serially independent process. To see this, note that:

$$\begin{aligned}
\text{Cov}(\tilde{\eta}(t), \tilde{\eta}(t-1)) &= \text{Cov}[(\tilde{\epsilon}(t) - \tilde{\epsilon}(t-1)), (\tilde{\epsilon}(t-1) - (\tilde{\epsilon}(t-2))] \\
&= \text{Cov}[\tilde{\epsilon}(t), (\tilde{\epsilon}(t-1) - \tilde{\epsilon}(t-2))] \\
&\quad - \text{Cov}[\tilde{\epsilon}(t-1), (\tilde{\epsilon}(t-1) - \tilde{\epsilon}(t-2))] \\
&= \text{Cov}[\tilde{\epsilon}(t), \tilde{\epsilon}(t-1)] - \text{Cov}[\tilde{\epsilon}(t), \tilde{\epsilon}(t-2)] \\
&\quad - \text{Cov}[\tilde{\epsilon}(t-1), \tilde{\epsilon}(t-1)] + \text{Cov}[\tilde{\epsilon}(t-1), \tilde{\epsilon}(t-2)] \\
&= -\text{Cov}[\tilde{\epsilon}(t-1), \tilde{\epsilon}(t-1)] \\
&= -\text{Var}[\tilde{\epsilon}(t-1)] = -\sigma_\epsilon^2,
\end{aligned} \tag{7.39}$$

where σ_ϵ^2 is a constant, independent of t, if $\{\tilde{\epsilon}(t)\}$ is a stationary process, at least with respect to its variance. The covariance between $\tilde{\eta}(t)$ and $\tilde{\eta}(t-s)$ is zero for $s > 1$.[12] The correlation coefficient between $\tilde{\eta}(t)$ and $\tilde{\eta}(t-1)$ is as follows:[13]

$$\begin{aligned}
\rho_1 &= \frac{\text{Cov}[\tilde{\eta}(t), \tilde{\eta}(t-1)]}{\sqrt{\text{Var}(\tilde{\eta}(t))}\sqrt{\text{Var}(\tilde{\eta}(t-1))}} \\
&= \frac{\text{Cov}[\tilde{\eta}(t), \tilde{\eta}(t-1)]}{\text{Var}(\tilde{\eta}(t))} = \frac{-\sigma_\epsilon^2}{2\sigma_\epsilon^2} = -\frac{1}{2}.
\end{aligned} \tag{7.40}$$

As indicated above, first differencing eliminates a linear time-trend in the mean of a process. Similarly, a second differencing eliminates a quadratic time-trend in the mean, whereby $E[\tilde{y}(t)|\phi_{t-1}] = \mu_0 + \mu_1 t + \mu_2 t^2$. In general, if the mean of $\{\tilde{y}(t)\}$ is given by a deterministic dth order polynomial in t, then differencing $\tilde{y}(t)$ d times will eliminate the trend (i.e., the dependence of $E[\tilde{y}(t)]$ on time, t).

Differencing can also be used to remove stochastic trends in the mean of $\tilde{y}(t)$. Suppose, for example, that model (7.2) holds with $\beta_1 = 0.0$ and $\beta_2 = 1.0$, giving the model:

$$\tilde{y}(t) = \tilde{y}(t-1) + \tilde{\epsilon}(t), \tag{7.41}$$

where $\{\tilde{\epsilon}(t)\}$ is a serially independent process with $E[\tilde{\epsilon}(t)] = 0.0$ and $\text{Var}[\tilde{\epsilon}(t)] = \sigma_\epsilon^2$. Clearly, $E[\tilde{y}(t)|y(t-1), y(t-2), \ldots] = E[\tilde{y}(t)|y(t-1)] = y(t-1)$, which is not, in general, constant over time. Nor does it converge to any finite constant value, as did model (7.2) with $|\beta_2| < 1.0$. That is, for all $k \geq 0$, $E[\tilde{y}(t+k)|y(t-1), y(t-2), \ldots] = y(t-1)$, conditional on model (7.41). This is consistent with the fact that the unconditional mean

---

[12] Convince yourself that this statement is correct.

Those familiar with time series analysis will recognize that the model for $\{\Delta\tilde{y}(t)\}$ given in (7.38) is simply a first-order moving average model, where the moving average component, $\tilde{\epsilon}(t) - \tilde{\epsilon}(t-1)$, is noninvertible. The first-order moving average model is discussed below. The results given in the text constitute an application of the following general fact: if an autoregressive moving average process of order (p, q) is differenced d times, the result is an autoregressive moving average process of order $(p, q + d)$, where the moving average component is noninvertible. The invertibility condition is discussed in, e.g., Box and Jenkins [1976].

[13] Observe that $\text{Var}(\tilde{\eta}(t)) = \text{Var}(\tilde{\epsilon}(t) - \tilde{\epsilon}(t-1)) = \sigma_\epsilon^2 + \sigma_\epsilon^2$ if $\{\tilde{\epsilon}(t)\}$ is a serially independent process.

of $\tilde{y}(t)$ is undefined when model (7.41) prevails; thus, there is no defined constant value to which $E[\tilde{y}(t + k)|y(t - 1), y(t - 2), \ldots]$ can converge. The value of this expectation changes every time we observe a new value of $\tilde{y}(s)$, for all periods up to $s = t + k - 1$. In short, model (7.41) defines a process that is nonstationary with respect to its mean.

Applying the first-difference operator to model (7.41) yields:

$$\Delta\tilde{y}(t) = \tilde{y}(t) - \tilde{y}(t - 1) = \tilde{\epsilon}(t), \tag{7.42}$$

which is a stationary process, with $E[\Delta\tilde{y}(t)|\Delta y(t - 1), \Delta y(t - 2), \ldots] = E[\Delta\tilde{y}(t)] = E[\tilde{\epsilon}(t)] = 0.0$ and $\text{Var}[\Delta\tilde{y}(t)|\Delta y(t - 1), \Delta y(t - 2), \ldots] = \text{Var}[\Delta\tilde{y}(t)] = \text{Var}[\tilde{\epsilon}(t)] = \sigma_\epsilon^2$. For some processes, more than one round of differencing may be needed to eliminate stochastic trends. As will be indicated below, however, one round of differencing is usually adequate for work involving firms' annual income numbers.

7.4.1.4 The First-Order Moving Average Model

The autoregressive model given by expression (7.2) is, of course, not the only univariate model that might be applied to income (and related) numbers as a result of the sorts of arguments reviewed in Section 7.4.1.1. An alternative is the so-called first-order moving average model:

$$\tilde{y}(t) = \sigma + \tilde{\epsilon}(t) - \theta_1\tilde{\epsilon}(t - 1), \tag{7.43}$$

where $|\theta_1| < 1.0$ is assumed to hold.[14] It is also assumed that $\{\tilde{\epsilon}(t)\}$ is a serially independent stationary process, with $E[\tilde{\epsilon}(t)] = 0.0$ and $\text{Var}[\tilde{\epsilon}(t)] = \sigma_\epsilon^2$. σ is simply a constant, whose value may be zero. The first two unconditional moments of this process are, respectively:

$$\begin{aligned} E[\tilde{y}(t)] &= E[\sigma] + \text{E}[\tilde{\epsilon}(t) - \theta_1\tilde{\epsilon}(t - 1)] \\ &= \sigma, \end{aligned} \tag{7.44}$$

[14]The technical reason for this is to ensure "invertibility," i.e., that the weight given to past observations decreases as the elapsed time since the occurrence of those observations increases. This can be appreciated by successively substituting for $\tilde{\epsilon}(t - 1)$, $\tilde{\epsilon}(t - 2)$, etc. For example, (7.43) implies $\tilde{\epsilon}(t - 1) = \tilde{y}(t - 1) + \theta_1\tilde{\epsilon}(t - 2)$, and $\tilde{\epsilon}(t - 2) = \tilde{y}(t - 2) + \theta_1\tilde{\epsilon}(t - 3)$. Substituting for $\tilde{\epsilon}(t - 1)$ yields:

$$\tilde{y}(t) = -\theta_1\tilde{y}(t - 1) + \tilde{\epsilon}(t) - \theta_1^2\tilde{\epsilon}(t - 2).$$

Substituting for $\tilde{\epsilon}(t - 2)$ yields:

$$\tilde{y}(t) = -\theta_1\tilde{y}(t - 1) - \theta_1^2\tilde{y}(t - 2) + \tilde{\epsilon}(t) - \theta_1^3\tilde{\epsilon}(t - 3).$$

By continuing this process, one finds that:

$$\tilde{y}(t) = \tilde{\epsilon}(t) - \sum_{i=1}^{\infty} \theta_1^i\tilde{y}(t - i).$$

Clearly, if $|\theta_1| > 1$, then the weight attached to $\tilde{y}(t - i)$ increases—in absolute value—as i increases. This is usually considered to be a somewhat implausible situation. Finally, observe that so long as a moving average representation involves a finite number of disturbances, no conditions on the θ's are needed to ensure stationarity.

$$\begin{aligned}\mathrm{Var}[\tilde{y}(t)] &= \mathrm{Var}[\tilde{\epsilon}(t) - \theta_1\tilde{\epsilon}(t-1)] \\ &= \mathrm{Var}[\tilde{\epsilon}(t)] + \theta_1^2\,\mathrm{Var}[\tilde{\epsilon}(t-1)] \\ &\quad - 2\theta_1\,\mathrm{Cov}[\tilde{\epsilon}(t), \tilde{\epsilon}(t-1)] \\ &= \sigma_\epsilon^2 + \theta_1^2\sigma_\epsilon^2 \\ &= (1 + \theta_1^2)\sigma_\epsilon^2,\end{aligned} \tag{7.45}$$

where $\mathrm{Cov}[\tilde{\epsilon}(t), \tilde{\epsilon}(t-1)] = 0.0$ follows from the serial independence of the process $\{\tilde{\epsilon}(t)\}$. Clearly, the first two moments conditional on the observed values available as of time t are, respectively:[15]

$$\begin{aligned}E[\tilde{y}(t)|y(t-1), y(t-2), \ldots] &= E[\sigma + \tilde{\epsilon}(t) - \theta_1\tilde{\epsilon}(t-1)|\sigma \\ &\quad + \epsilon(t-1) - \theta_1\epsilon(t-2), \sigma + \epsilon(t-2) \\ &\quad - \theta_1\epsilon(t-3), \ldots] \\ &= E[\sigma + \tilde{\epsilon}(t) - \theta_1\tilde{\epsilon}(t-1)|\sigma, \\ &\quad \epsilon(t-1), \epsilon(t-2), \ldots] \\ &= \sigma + E[\tilde{\epsilon}(t)|\sigma, \epsilon(t-1), \\ &\quad \epsilon(t-2), \ldots] - \theta_1\epsilon(t-1) \\ &= \sigma + 0.0 - \theta_1\epsilon(t-1) \\ &= \sigma - \theta_1\epsilon(t-1)\end{aligned} \tag{7.46}$$

$$\mathrm{Var}[\tilde{y}(t)|y(t-1), y(t-2), \ldots] = \mathrm{Var}[\tilde{\epsilon}(t)] = \sigma_\epsilon^2. \tag{7.47}$$

As was the case with model (7.2) the specification given in (7.43) implies that the unconditional moments, (7.44) and (7.45), are constants and that the influence of past values of $\tilde{y}(t)$ on forecasts of future values is not the same for all future periods. Indeed, for model (7.43), the forecasts for periods $t + k$, $k \geq 2$, are actually independent of the value of $\tilde{y}(\tau)$ at $\tau = t$. The forecast of $\tilde{y}(t+1)$ conditional on $\epsilon(t)$, $\epsilon(t-1)$, ..., is, from (7.46), given by:

$$E[\tilde{y}(t+1)|\epsilon(t), \epsilon(t-1), \ldots] = \sigma - \theta_1\epsilon(t). \tag{7.48}$$

For $k \geq 2$, the forecasts are given by:

$$\begin{aligned}E[\tilde{y}(t+k)|\epsilon(t), \epsilon(t-1), \ldots] &= E[\sigma + \tilde{\epsilon}(t+k) \\ &\quad - \theta_1\tilde{\epsilon}(t+k-1)|\epsilon(t), \epsilon(t-1), \ldots] \\ &= \sigma + E[\tilde{\epsilon}(t+k)|\epsilon(t), \epsilon(t-1), \ldots] \\ &\quad - \theta_1 E[\tilde{\epsilon}(t+k-1)|\epsilon(t), \epsilon(t-1), \ldots].\end{aligned} \tag{7.49}$$

---

[15]Expressions (7.46) and (7.47) are based on the assumption that a "starting value" for the error process $\{\tilde{\epsilon}(t)\}$ is available, or that the error's values are directly observed.

Since $\{\tilde{\epsilon}(t)\}$ is characterized by serial independence, the conditional expected values on the RHS of (7.49) are identical to the corresponding unconditional expected values for $k > 1$. Thus:

$$E[\tilde{y}(t + k)|\epsilon(t), \epsilon(t - 1), \ldots] = \sigma + E[\tilde{\epsilon}(t + k)] - \theta_1 E[\tilde{\epsilon}(t + k - 1)] = \sigma. \quad (7.50)$$

This is quite different from the corresponding result in (7.29) for model (7.2). When the latter model prevails, the influence of $\tilde{y}(\tau)$ at $\tau = t$ on forecasts of $\tilde{y}(\tau)$ for $\tau \geq t + 1$ dies out exponentially. In short, the influence of $\tilde{y}(t)$ on forecasts for periods beyond t is monotonically decreasing and continuous in time. This general characteristic, although not necessarily the exact functional form, does not seem grossly inconsistent with the crux of the arguments reviewed in Section 7.4.1.1. For model (7.43), the influence of currently available values on forecasts for future periods does not last for more than one future period. Thus, if one was led to model (7.43) because of, e.g., market-structure issues or income-smoothing issues (see Section 7.4.1.1), then one is necessarily specifying a very short-lived form of persistence and, thus, a very short-lived form of "income smoothing" or market imperfection. If this is not what one had in mind, then the original specifications of (7.43) should probably be reconsidered—because (7.48)–(7.50) are direct implications of (7.43).

The structure of the dependence between $\tilde{y}(t)$ and $\tilde{y}(t + k)$, for any k, can also be investigated via the autocovariance function. Of course, for $k = 0$, $\text{Cov}(\tilde{y}(t), \tilde{y}(t + k)) = \text{Cov}(\tilde{y}(t), \tilde{y}(t) = \text{Var}(\tilde{y}(t))$. For $k = 1$, we have:

$$\begin{aligned} c_1 &\equiv \text{Cov}(\tilde{y}(t), \tilde{y}(t - 1)) \\ &= \text{Cov}[\delta + \tilde{\epsilon}(t) - \theta_1\tilde{\epsilon}(t - 1), \delta + \epsilon(t - 1) \\ &\quad - \theta_1\, \epsilon(t - 2)] \\ &= -\theta_1\, \text{Cov}[\tilde{\epsilon}(t - 1), \tilde{\epsilon}(t - 1)] \\ &= -\theta_1\sigma_\epsilon^2 \cdot \end{aligned} \quad (7.51)$$

For $k = 2$, one gets:

$$\begin{aligned} c_2 &\equiv \text{Cov}(\tilde{y}(t), \tilde{y}(t - 2)) \\ &= \text{Cov}[\delta + \tilde{\epsilon}(t) - \theta_1\tilde{\epsilon}(t - 1), \\ &\quad \delta + \tilde{\epsilon}(t - 2) - \theta_1\tilde{\epsilon}(t - 3)] \\ &= 0.0 \end{aligned} \quad (7.52)$$

and, in general, $c_j = 0.0$ for $j > 1$. The value of the autocorrelation function at lag one is:

$$\rho_1 = c_1/c_0 = -\theta_1\sigma_\epsilon^2/(1 + \theta_1^2)\sigma_\epsilon^2 = -\theta_1/(1 + \theta_1^2) \quad (7.53)$$

and $\rho_j = (c_j/c_0) = 0.0$ for $j > 1$. In short, if model (7.43) is applied to income numbers, then it follows that income numbers for periods separated by more than one intervening period are necessarily uncorrelated.

To sum up, the first-order moving average model (7.43) implies:

$$E(\tilde{y}(t)) = \delta, \tag{7.54}$$

$$\text{Var}(\tilde{y}(t)) = (1 + \theta_1^2)\sigma_\epsilon^2, \tag{7.55}$$

$$c_j = \begin{cases} -\theta_1\sigma_\epsilon^2, & \text{for } j = 1 \\ 0, & \text{for } j > 1 \end{cases} \tag{7.56}$$

$$\rho_j = \begin{cases} -\theta_1/(1 + \theta_1^2), & \text{for } j = 1 \\ 0, & \text{for } j > 1 \end{cases} \tag{7.57}$$

$$E[\tilde{y}(t + k) | \delta, \epsilon(t), \epsilon(t - 1), \ldots] = \begin{matrix} \delta - \theta_1\epsilon(t), & \text{for } k = 1 \\ \delta, & \text{for } k > 1 \end{matrix} \tag{7.58}$$

$$\text{Var}[\tilde{y}(t + k) | \delta, \epsilon(t), \epsilon(t - 1), \ldots] = \sigma_\epsilon^2, \quad \text{all } k \geq 1 \tag{7.59}$$

7.4.1.5 The Autoregressive Integrated Moving Average Model (Nonseasonal)

The first-order autoregressive model specified in (7.2) is a special case of the general p*th* order autoregressive model:

$$\tilde{z}(t) = \phi_0 + \phi_1\tilde{z}(t - 1) + \phi_2\tilde{z}(t - 2)$$
$$+ \ldots + \phi_p\tilde{z}(t - p) + \tilde{\epsilon}(t), \tag{7.60}$$

where $\{\tilde{z}(t)\}$ is the process under analysis, ϕ_0 is a constant, ϕ_1, $i = 1, 2, \ldots, p$ are parameters applied to the lagged values of $\tilde{z}(t)$, and $\tilde{\epsilon}(t)$ is the serially independent disturbance with $E[\tilde{\epsilon}(t)] = 0.0$ and $\text{Var}[\tilde{\epsilon}(t)] = \sigma_\epsilon^2$, for all t. The first-order moving average model specified in (7.43) is a special case of the general q*th* order moving average model:

$$\tilde{v}(t) = \theta_0 - \theta_1\tilde{\epsilon}(t) - \theta_2\tilde{\epsilon}(t - 1) - \ldots - \theta_q\tilde{\epsilon}(t - q), \tag{7.61}$$

where $\{\tilde{v}(t)\}$ is the process under analysis, θ_0 is a constant, θ_i, $i = 1, 2, \ldots, q$, are the parameters applied to the current and lagged values of the disturbance, $\tilde{\epsilon}(t)$, which is assumed to be, as before, a serially independent random variable with $E[\tilde{\epsilon}(t)] = 0.0$ and $\text{Var}[\tilde{\epsilon}(t)] = \sigma_\epsilon^2$.

Note that $\tilde{z}(t)$ in (7.60) and $\tilde{v}(t)$ in (7.61) may denote the original random variable of interest, say, $\tilde{y}(t)$. Or either may refer to differences of that random variable. Thus, we might have $\tilde{z}(t) \equiv \Delta^d\tilde{y}(t)$, the d*th* difference of $\tilde{y}(t)$, or we might have $\tilde{v}(t) = \Delta^d\tilde{y}(t)$. That is, either the general autoregressive model or the moving average model can be applied to $\Delta^d\tilde{y}(t) = \Delta(\Delta^{d-1}\tilde{y}(t)) = \Delta(\Delta(\Delta^{d-2}\tilde{y}(t)))$. Thus, if $d = 3$ is the level of differencing needed to attain stationarity (see Section 7.4.1.3), then the model selected is applied to:

$$\begin{aligned}
\Delta^3\tilde{y}(t) &= \Delta(\Delta(\Delta\tilde{y}(t))) = \Delta(\Delta(\tilde{y}(t) - \tilde{y}(t - 1))) \\
&= \Delta(\tilde{y}(t) - \tilde{y}(t - 1) - \tilde{y}(t - 1) + \tilde{y}(t - 2)) \\
&= [\tilde{y}(t) - \tilde{y}(t - 1)] - 2[\tilde{y}(t - 1) - \tilde{y}(t - 2)] + [\tilde{y}(t - 2) - \tilde{y}(t - 3)] \\
&= \tilde{y}(t) - 3\tilde{y}(t - 1) + 3\tilde{y}(t - 2) - \tilde{y}(t - 3) \\
&= \tilde{y}(t) - \tilde{y}(t - 3) - 3[\tilde{y}(t - 1) - \tilde{y}(t - 2)].
\end{aligned}$$

Also note that differencing, the autoregressive model, and the moving average model can all be used simultaneously, if necessary, to describe the behavior of some accounting number, $\tilde{y}(t)$. Suppose that $\tilde{y}(t)$ must be differenced d times to attain stationarity and that the d*th* difference of $\tilde{y}(t)$ is characterized by a p*th* order autoregressive model whose disturbance, denoted $\tilde{a}(t)$, is characterized by a q*th* order moving average model. That is, letting $\tilde{z}(t) \equiv \delta^d\tilde{y}(t)$:

$$\phi_p(B)\tilde{z}(t) = \delta + \tilde{a}(t), \tag{7.62}$$

$$\tilde{a}(t) = \theta_q(B)\tilde{\epsilon}(t), \tag{7.63}$$

where B denotes the backshift operator, $B^k\tilde{z}(t) = \tilde{z}(t - k)$, $\phi_p(B) = 1 - \phi_1 B - \phi_2 B^2 - \ldots - \phi_p B^p$, $\theta_q(B) = 1 - \theta_1 B - \theta_2 B^2 - \ldots - \theta_q B^q$, and δ is a constant. Taken together, (7.62) and (7.63) indicate that the process $\{\tilde{y}(t)\}$ can be characterized by an Autoregressive Integrated Moving Average (ARIMA) model of order (p, d, q), *viz.*:

$$\phi_p(B)\Delta^d\tilde{y}(t) = \delta + \theta_q(B)\tilde{\epsilon}(t), \tag{7.64}$$

which is commonly referenced as an ARIMA(p, d, q) model. The term "integrated" in the labeling refers to the operation that would be applied to the variable actually modeled, $\Delta^d\tilde{y}(t)$, in order to obtain the original variable, $\tilde{y}(t)$. The original variable is obtained via a d*th* order summation (or "integration") of the d-differenced variable.

Note that expression (7.64) defines an entire family of models, with each member distinguished by the value of the triple (p, d, q). In principle, the value of this triple must be identified before a model from this family can be estimated.[16]

Methods for identifying the value of (p, d, q) and for estimating the parameters of an ARIMA(p, d, q) model are discussed in readily available sources.[17] An elaborate discussion of those methods is beyond the scope of this book. We shall, however, provide an illustrative application of the ARIMA family to a firm's earnings-per-share in the text section. That illustration will indicate some of the steps and methods available for applications to actual sample evidence. It will also point to some pitfalls and problems.

The ARIMA family is a family of so-called univariate models. That is, it consists of models that deal with one random variable, such as $\tilde{y}(t)$. As of the time t, the "independent" variables used to model $\tilde{y}(t)$ consist only of past values of $\tilde{y}(t)$. Thus, for example, when an ARIMA(p, d, q) model, as defined in (7.64), is applied to a firm's income number, no use is made of sample evidence on such series as Gross National Product, the firm's industry's income number, Industrial Capacity Utilization, Expenditures on Producers' Durable Goods, Capital Expenditure Anticipations, etc. Time series models incorporating random variables such as the latter can be incorporated into the framework of ARIMA models, leading to so-called transfer function models.[18] Except for one special case of this expanded family—*viz.*, the index models discussed in Section 7.4.2—we shall have nothing to say about these additional models. Detailed discussions are given in, e.g., Box and Jenkins [1976], Granger and Newbold [1977], and Dhrymes [1971].

---

[16]Of course, estimation results may induce one to go back and reevaluate (p, d, q) and then estimate a different model. In short, model identification and estimation may proceed interactively.

[17]See, e.g., Anderson [1971], Jenkins and Watts [1968], Kendall [1973], Kendall and Stuart [1968], Box and Jenkins [1976], Nelson [1973], Fuller [1976], and Granger and Newbold [1977], among others.

[18]Or multi-equation models in some cases.

Members of the ARIMA family were used in several studies of accounting numbers' stochastic properties, particularly income numbers' properties. The evidence provided by several of these studies is reviewed in Section 7.4.1.7. Before getting to that, however, we provide a lengthy illustrative application of time series analysis tools to one firm's earnings-per-share number. The main purpose of the illustration is to indicate some of the methods and mechanics involved in applying the ARIMA family to actual sample evidence and to indicate some of the major problems that arise in applications of ARIMA models.

7.4.1.6. An Illustration of Univariate Time Series Analysis—Caterpillar Tractor's Earnings-per-Share

The sample evidence used here consists of observations on Caterpillar Tractor's Annual Earnings-per-Share (EPS). The sample consists of 52 observations, one for each of the years 1925–1976. The observations are adjusted for stock splits and stock dividends and computed using a weighted average of the number of common shares outstanding. All data are from Caterpillar Tractor's 1976 Annual Report. The raw data are presented in the third column of Exhibit 7-1. In the column labeled "Year," 25 refers to 1925, 26 to 1926, etc. The observations in columns 4 and 5 should be ignored for now. For purposes of this illustration, we shall mainly entertain the first-order autoregressive model, without and with differencing.

A sequence plot of the standardized values of EPS appears in Exhibit 7-2, along with estimation results based on several diagnostic tools.[19] Selected summary statistics—to be used by the reader as we proceed—are given in Table 7-1. We begin with Exhibit 7-2. On balance, these data appear to be consistent with substantial persistence, rather than an absence of correlation between consecutive periods' EPS. Further, note that all observed values up to the 38th one (the year 1962) are at or below the sample mean (which has a standardized value equal to zero). Beyond the 37th observation, all observations are above the sample mean. This sequence plot and the entertained first-order autoregressive model:

$$\tilde{y}(t) = \beta_1 + \beta_2\tilde{y}(t-1) + \tilde{\epsilon}(t) \tag{7.65}$$

seem to suggest a value of β_2 very close to +1.0, and perhaps even a nonstationary process (i.e., $|\beta_2| > 1.0$).

The characteristics of the sample evidence pre-1960 and post-1960 may have resulted from an essentially discrete shift in the level (or "process mean") of the EPS process as well as a shift in the variability of this process. Recall that (7.65) with $|\beta_2| < 1.0$ implies a constant unconditional mean, $E[\tilde{y}(t)]$, and a constant unconditional variance, $\mathrm{Var}[\tilde{y}(t))]$. The fact that all of the pre-1960 (post-1960) observations are below (above) or at the overall sample mean might be taken as evidence consistent with an upward shift in the mean's value around 1960. And the increased sample dispersion of the post-1960 observations might be taken as evidence consistent with a similar shift in the value of $\mathrm{Var}[\tilde{y}(t)]$. A complete analysis would address these possibilities by considering the firm's history, institutional changes, changes in the objectives and conduct of governmental policies (e.g., fiscal policy), changes in market structure, and the potential effects of changes in accounting techniques on the systematic properties of annual income numbers, among other

---

[19]The standardized value of the observed value, $y(t)$, for year t is given by $(y(t) - \bar{y})/\hat{\sigma}$, where $\bar{y}$ is the sample mean and $\hat{\sigma}$ is the sample standard deviation.

EXHIBIT 7-1

OBSERVED VALUES OF CATERPILLAR TRACTOR'S ANNUAL EARNINGS-PER-SHARE (EPS) FOR THE YEARS 1925–1976 AND SIMULATED DRAWINGS ON FIRST-ORDER AUTOREGRESSIVE MODEL, $\tilde{y}(t) = \beta_1 + \beta_2 \tilde{y}(t - 1) + \tilde{\epsilon}(t)$, FOR TWO VALUES OF β_2: $\beta_2 = 0.99$ (AR99) and $\beta_2 = 0.50$ (AR50). $\beta_1 = 0.0$, $\text{Var}(\tilde{\epsilon}(t)) = 1.0$, $E(\tilde{\epsilon}(t)) = 0.0$, AND $\epsilon(t)$ IS NORMALLY DISTRIBUTED FOR BOTH VALUES OF β_2.

(1) ROW	(2) YEAR	(3) EPS	(4) AR99	(5) AR50
* 1 *	25.00000	0.05100	0.05100	0.05100
* 2 *	26.00000	0.06800	0.48277	1.93363
* 3 *	27.00000	0.09100	1.24044	2.02521
* 4 *	28,00000	0.15100	1.57826	0.96898
* 5 *	29.00000	0.16900	2.08464	2.20969
* 6 *	30.00000	0.12400	2.86326	0.86022
* 7 *	31.00000	0.02100	3.32416	2.37835
* 8 *	32.00000	−0.02200	4.11151	2.20818
* 9 *	33.00000	0.00500	5.00662	1.90436
* 10 *	34.00000	0.05200	5.79052	1.48911
* 11 *	35.00000	0.08500	6.37002	1.45428
* 12 *	36.00000	0.13900	7.22908	2.24185
* 13 *	37.00000	0.14000	8.10234	2.08550
* 14 *	38.00000	0.03600	8.80539	2.11333
* 15 *	39.00000	0.07400	9.51969	1.14438
* 16 *	40.00000	0.10700	10.24777	2.33866
* 17 *	41.00000	0.10600	10.90814	2.12915
* 18 *	42.00000	0.09500	11.56707	1.94179
* 19 *	43.00000	0.10300	12.43163	2.23962
* 20 *	44.00000	0.10000	13.21518	0.78791
* 21 *	45.00000	0.08900	13.57016	1.61219
* 22 *	46.00000	0.08300	14.33204	1.85251
* 23 *	47.00000	0.18400	15.09981	2.62155
* 24 *	48.00000	0.23800	15.89364	1.52745
* 25 *	49.00000	0.22900	16.54870	2.08986
* 26 *	50.00000	0.38500	17.23435	3.28758
* 27 *	51.00000	0.19900	17.59449	3.44012
* 28 *	52.00000	0.29100	18.47794	4.25229
* 29 *	53.00000	0.26400	19.32965	2.02300
* 30 *	54.00000	0.33500	19.86561	2.93729
* 31 *	55.00000	0.46600	20.47615	2.48089
* 32 *	56.00000	0.67700	20.95556	1.84944
* 33 *	57.00000	0.48300	21.47560	2.17653
* 34 *	58.00000	0.38700	22.08327	1.28856
* 35 *	59.00000	0.56100	22.49223	1.82173
* 36 *	60.00000	0.51300	22.72707	2.79271
* 37 *	61.00000	0.67500	23.18649	2.04251
* 38 *	62.00000	0.74900	23.70330	2.37747
* 39 *	63.00000	0.94400	24.55791	2.44200
* 40 *	64.00000	1.52000	24.83432	2.14466
* 41 *	65.00000	1.86400	25.15404	1.56312
* 42 *	66.00000	1.76200	25.66059	2.68497
* 43 *	67.00000	1.24800	26.31902	3.89027
* 44 *	68.00000	1.42600	26.86406	3.54890

EXHIBIT 7-1 Cont.

(1) ROW	(2) YEAR	(3) EPS	(4) AR99	(5) AR50
* 45 *	69.00000	1.67000	27.27264	2.39792
* 46 *	70.00000	1.68500	27.58450	−0.36751
* 47 *	71.00000	1.50200	28.02948	1.09049
* 48 *	72.00000	2.41500	28.39392	1.33351
* 49 *	73.00000	2.88100	28.92836	−0.27353
* 50 *	74.00000	2.67100	29.34061	−0.06965
* 51 *	75.00000	4.64400	29.75275	0.96675
* 52 *	76.00000	4.45200	30.12470	0.72726

MEANS VARIABLE	MEAN	STD. DEV.
YEAR	5.0500E+01	1.51548E+01
EPS	7.53211E−01	1.06313E+00
AR99	1.63999E+01	9.32340E+00
AR50	1.90496E+00	9.60586E−01

things. This will not be done here because our main objective is to illustrate uses of methods to identify oft-encountered problems.

Estimates pertaining to the autocorrelation structure of EPS are also provided in Exhibit 7-2, in the form of estimated "serial correlation" coefficients, estimated "autocorrelation" coefficients, and the observed value of the runs statistic.

In general, the linear association between $\tilde{y}(t)$ and $\tilde{y}(t-j)$, for any j, is given by the correlation coefficient; $\rho(\tilde{y}(t), \tilde{y}(t-j)) = \mathrm{Cov}[\tilde{y}(t), \tilde{y}(t-j)]/(\sigma(\tilde{y}(t))\ \sigma(\tilde{y}(t-j)))$. One estimator of this parameter of the joint distribution of $\tilde{y}(t)$ and $\tilde{y}(t-j)$ is the "serial correlation coefficient" at lag j:

$$r_j = r(\tilde{y}(t), y(t-j))$$

$$= \frac{\sum_{t=j+1}^{N} (y(t) - \bar{y}_2)(y(t-j) - \bar{y}_1)}{\sqrt{\sum_{t=j+1}^{N} (y(t) - \bar{y}_2)^2 \sum_{t=j+1}^{N} (y(t-j) - \bar{y}_1)^2}}$$

where:

$$\bar{y}_2 = \frac{1}{N-j} \sum_{t=j+1}^{N} y(t)$$

$$\bar{y}_1 = \frac{1}{N-j} \sum_{t=j+1}^{N} y(t-j).$$

This estimator conforms to the usual estimator of a coefficient of correlation between two random variables. Since, however, $\tilde{y}(t)$ and $\tilde{y}(t-j)$ are the same random variable—only the dating differs—some authors introduce simplifications. First, rather than estimate two means, as is done above, only one estimate is used, and this is the estimate based on

EXHIBIT 7-2

SELECTED DIAGNOSTIC RESULTS FOR CATERPILLAR TRACTOR'S ANNUAL EARNINGS-PER-SHARE (EPS) FOR THE YEARS 1925–1976 (52 OBSERVATIONS)

```
PLTS
* VARIABLE : EPS

PLOT ALL ROWS ?Y

SEQUENCE PLOT  OF STANDARDIZED VALUES OF 'EPS
```

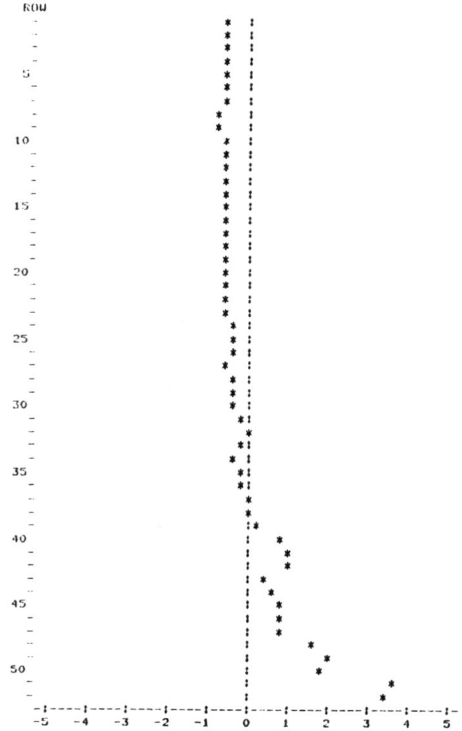

ORDER	SERIAL CORRELATION
1	+0.951
2	+0.938
3	+0.933
4	+0.885
5	+0.855
6	+0.875
7	+0.887
8	+0.887
9	+0.924
10	+0.959
11	+0.950
12	+0.922

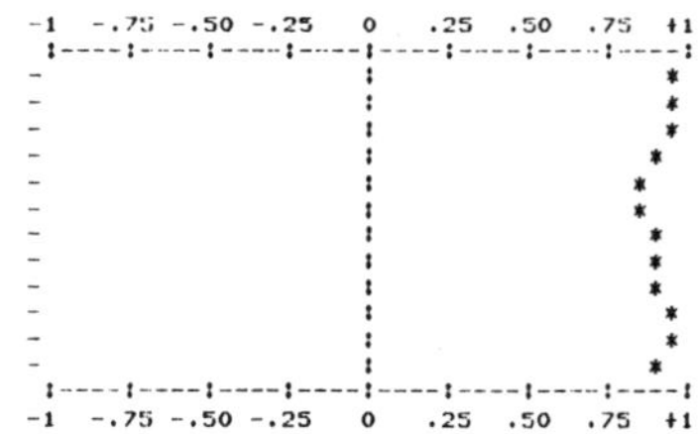

```
SERIES: EPS
BASED ON  52     ACTIVE OBSERVATIONS
```

ORDER	AUTO-CORRELATION
1	+0.824
2	+0.642
3	+0.580
4	+0.474
5	+0.400
6	+0.387
7	+0.359
8	+0.322
9	+0.307
10	+0.294
11	+0.234
12	+0.150

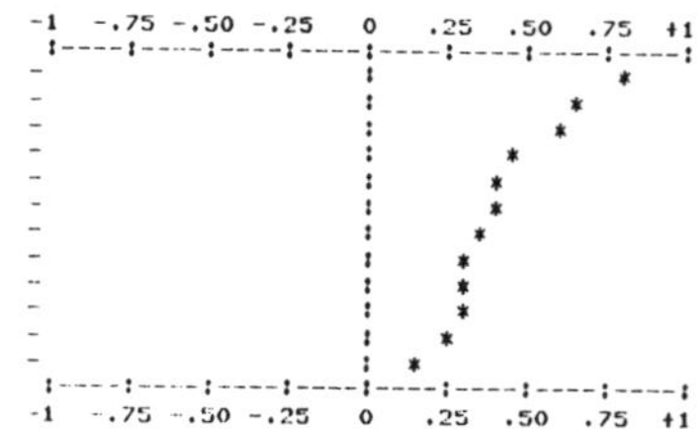

```
SERIES: EPS
BASED ON  52     ACTIVE OBSERVATIONS

S.E. OF EACH COEF. GIVEN RANDOM MODEL=0.139

BOX-PIERCE STATISTIC= 127.573
EXPECTATION GIVEN RANDOM MODEL= 12
        (OBS.-EXP.)/(STD.DEV.)= 8.94567

       OBSERVED NUMBER OF RUNS =  2
       EXPECTED NUMBER OF RUNS =  21.4615
   STANDARD DEVIATION OF RUNS =  2.7943
      (OBS.-EXP.)/(STD.DEV.) = -6.96473

SERIES: EPS

---------------------------------------+++++++++++++

+ = value > mean
- = value < = mean
Mean =  .753211
```

TABLE 7-1

SELECTED SUMMARY STATISTICS FOR LEVELS AND FIRST DIFFERENCES OF CATERPILLAR TRACTOR'S ANNUAL EPS FOR THE 52-YEAR PERIOD 1925–1976

Series	Number of Obser- vations	Time Period	Mean $\hat{\mu}$	Standard Deviation $\hat{\sigma}$	Runs Statistic z	Estimated Serial Correlation Coefficients r_1	r_2	r_3	r_4	r_5	r_6	Coefficient of Variation $\hat{\sigma}/\hat{\mu}$	t statistic $t(\hat{\mu})$
EPS	52	1925–1976	.753	1.065	−6.964	.951	.938	.933	.885	.855	.875	1.414	5.098
	26	1925–1950	.113	.084	−2.901	.752	.425	.086	−.198	−.043	.182	.743	6.859
	26	1951–1976	1.395	1.204	−3.997	.921	.896	.884	.788	.716	.752	.863	5.907
ΔEPS	51	1926–1976	.086	.341	−.402	−.135	.047	.436	−.088	−.121	−.025	3.965	1.801
	25	1926–1950	.013	.055	−1.834	.189	−.155	−.001	−.240	−.218	.098	4.230	1.182
	26	1951–1976	.156	.469	.534	−.203	−.002	.418	−.145	−.171	−.081	3.006	1.696

all N observations: $\bar{y} = \Sigma_{t=1}^{N} y(t)/N$. Second, for the same reason, the separate sample standard deviations used above are replaced by one, *viz.*, the sample standard deviation based on *all* N observations, $S^2 = \Sigma_{t=1}^{N} y(t) - \bar{y})^2/N$. The estimator used is the "autocorrelation coefficient" at lag j:

$$r_j^* = r^*(\bar{y}(t), \bar{y}(t-j)) = \frac{\sum_{t=j+1}^{N} (y(t) - \bar{y})(y(t-j) - \bar{y})}{\sum_{t=1}^{N} (y(t) - \bar{y})^2}$$

In some cases, this estimator is multiplied by the factor $N/(N - j)$ in recognition of the fact that the numerator is based on $N - j$ terms whereas the denominator is based on N terms. The multiplicative factor $N/(N - j)$ results from dividing the numerator by $N - j$ and the denominator by N.

Our objective in raising this issue is to broach the issue of finite-sample characteristics of estimators that are proposed and used because of their "large sample" (or asymptotic) characteristics. Both estimators, $\tilde{r}_j$ and $\tilde{r}_j^*$, of ρ_j have the same asymptotic properties. That is, speaking somewhat loosely, they are the same for samples that are sufficiently large. The first and second "large sample" (or asymptotic) moments are, respectively, $-(N - j)^{-1}$ and $(N - j)/N(N + 2)$ (see Box and Pierce [1970, p. 1510]), conditional on $\rho_j = 0.0$ for all $j \geq 1$. But there is no theoretical reason for expecting the estimators' values to be the same for any particular finite-sample size. And the sample results presented in Exhibit 7.2 should be sufficient to convince one that there is no empirical reason for expecting this. Since $\tilde{r}_j^*$ is usually proposed as an estimator that "approximates" the estimator $\tilde{r}_j$ (see, e.g., Kendall [1973]), it appears that $\tilde{r}_j$ should be used directly when the adequacy of the approximation is in doubt, *viz.*, when the sample size is "too small." The approximation of $\tilde{r}_j$ given by $\tilde{r}_j^*$ is also poor when the sample serial correlation is large. To see this, consider the key differences between observed values of $\tilde{r}_j$ and $\tilde{r}_j^*$, conditional on the same sample evidence.

For any given sample, the sum of squared deviations $\Sigma(y(t) - c)^2$ is minimized when c is set equal to the sample mean. Thus:

$$\sum_{t=j+1}^{N} (y(t) - \bar{y}_2)^2 \leq \sum_{t=j+1}^{N} (y(t) - \bar{y})^2 \tag{7.66}$$

and:

$$\sum_{t=j+1}^{N} (y(t-j) - \bar{y}_1)^2 \leq \sum_{t=j+1}^{N} (y(t-j) - \bar{y})^2 \tag{7.67}$$

where $\bar{y}_2$, $\bar{y}_1$, and $\bar{y}$ are as defined above. In addition, the sum of squared deviations from $\bar{y}$ taken over the entire sample of N observations is at least equal to any sum taken over a subsample, because all summands are nonnegative. Thus:

$$\sum_{t=j+1}^{N} (y(t) - \bar{y})^2 \leq \sum_{t=1}^{N} (y(t) - \bar{y})^2 \tag{7.68}$$

$$\sum_{t=j+1}^{N} (y(t-j) - \bar{y})^2 \leq \sum_{t=1}^{N} (y(t) - \bar{y})^2. \tag{7.69}$$

The results in (7.66)–(7.69) imply that the denominator of $\tilde{r}_j^*$ will always be greater than or equal to the denominator of $\tilde{r}_j$. Taken by itself, this implies $|\tilde{r}_j^*| \leq |\tilde{r}_j|$. But the numerators also differ. The observed effect of the latter difference depends on the observed drift in the sample, as is indicated below.

By adding and subtracting $\bar{y}$ to each of the two deviations, $(y(t) - \bar{y}_2)$ and $(y(t - j) - \bar{y}_1)$, of each summand in the numerator of r_j, and then rearranging the result, one gets:

$$\sum_{t=j+1}^{N} (y(t) - \bar{y}_2)(y(t - j) - \bar{y}_1 = \sum_{t=j+1}^{N} (y(t) - \bar{y})(t - j) - \bar{y})$$

$$- \sum_{t=j+1}^{N} (y(t) - \bar{y}) \sum_{t=j+1}^{N} (y(t - j) - \bar{y})$$

$$= \sum_{j+1}^{N} (y(t) - \bar{y})(y(t - j) - \bar{y})$$

$$- (N - j)^2[\bar{y}_2 - \bar{y}][\bar{y}_1 - \bar{y}]. \tag{7.70}$$

If the sampled observations exhibit, on balance, an upward drift, then $\bar{y}_2 > \bar{y} > \bar{y}_1$. If they exhibit a downward drift, then $\bar{y}_2 < \bar{y} < \bar{y}_1$. On average, when β_2 is strongly positive (e.g., β_2 near or above 0.70), smooth upward or downward drifts will be observed—as is observed in the sequence plot for EPS given in Exhibit 7-2.[20] For these cases, the differences among $\bar{y}_2$, $\bar{y}$, and $\bar{y}_1$ can be quite large, relative to the standard error of, say, $\bar{y}$. In any event, when the observed drift is, on balance, either upward or downward, $\bar{y}$ will overestimate one of the subsample means and underestimate the other. Thus, the last term on the RHS of (7.70) will be less than zero—except when $\bar{y}$ is equal to either $\bar{y}_2$ or $\bar{y}_1$.[21] But this implies that:

$$\sum_{t=j+1}^{N} (y(t) - \bar{y}_2)(y(t - j) - \bar{y}_1) \geq \sum_{t=j+1}^{N} (y(t) - \bar{y})(y(t - j) - \bar{y})$$

in such cases. Therefore, in these situations (i.e., high positive β_2) the numerator of $\tilde{r}_j^*$ will—if exceptional equality cases are ignored—be less than the numerator of $\tilde{r}_j$. This effect reinforces the effect of the differences between these estimators' denominators. Thus, it provides further support for the inequality $\tilde{r}_j^*| < |\tilde{r}_j|$.

Values of $\bar{y}_2$ and $\bar{y}_1$ for various lags (denoted by j in the expressions above) are provided below, along with values of the corresponding sample standard deviations. Taken at face value, the observed differences among $\bar{y}_2$, $\bar{y}_1$, and $\bar{y}$ seem nontrivial. (The results for $j = 0$ pertain to $\bar{y}$ and s.) Of course, in view of the post-1960 observations, the value of $\bar{y}$ is heavily influenced by the more recent values of $\bar{y}(t)$. Thus, the differences between $\bar{y}_1$ and $\bar{y}$ appear to be more dramatic than the differences between $\bar{y}$ and $\bar{y}_2$, since the latter

---

[20] Relevant statistical theory behind this result is considered by Gonedes and Roberts [1977*a*; 1977*b*; 1977*c*].

[21] The sum of the sample deviations about the sample mean is, of course, zero. Thus, if $\bar{y} = \bar{y}_2$, $\Sigma_{t=j+1}^{N} (y(t) - \bar{y}) = 0.0$. If $\bar{y} = \bar{y}_1$, then $\Sigma_{t=j+1}^{N} (y(t - j) - \bar{y}) = 0.0$. In either case, the value of the product $\Sigma_{t=j+1}^{N} (y(t) - \bar{y}) \Sigma_{t=j+1}^{N} (y(t - j) - \bar{y})$ will be zero.

is always based on the more recent observations. This is also why the difference between $\bar{y}_2$ and $\bar{y}_1$—and thus the observed values of $\tilde{r}_j$ and $\tilde{r}_j^*$—increases with j.

	Sample Means		Sample Standard Deviations	
Lag	$\bar{y}_2$	$\bar{y}_1$	S_2	S_1
0	.753	.753	1.065	1.065
1	.767	.681	1.071	.937
2	.781	.601	1.077	.754
3	.795	.559	1.084	.700

Notes

(1) For a given j, $\bar{y}_2 = \Sigma_{t=j+1}^{N} y(t)/(N - j)$ and $\bar{y}_1 = \Sigma_{t=j+1}^{N} y(t - j)/(N - j)$.

(2) For a given j, $S_2 = \sqrt{\sum_{t=j+1}^{N} (y(t) - \bar{y}_2)^2/(N - j - 1)}$ and $S_1 = \sqrt{\sum_{t=j+1}^{N} (y(t - j) - y_1{}^2/(N - j - 1)}$.

(3) Original number of observations = N = 52.

In short, for time series that happened to evolve in a more or less unidirectional fashion over finite time intervals, approximating $\tilde{r}_j$ with $\tilde{r}_j^*$ may seriously increase the frequency of a so-called Type II error: failure to reject the null hypothesis (of no serial correlation) when that hypothesis is false.[22] And, as indicated above, the reasons for this consequence turn on "small" or "finite" sample issues. Precisely what sample size is "too small" is, unfortunately, not known. More important, the size at hand now (52 observations) is not uncommon in empirical economics. If anything, it is larger than what is usually encountered (in, e.g., work with data from the post-World War II period). Moreover, for many economic time series (before application of any transformations), smooth unidirectional observed drifts are not unusual. Thus, the issues identified above are certainly not unique to our EPS series, to which we now return.

The estimated serial correlation function exhibits seemingly large values of $\tilde{r}_j$ for all j, $j = 1, 2, \ldots, 12$, as does the estimated auto-correlation function. Neither estimator of ρ_j appears strongly consistent with an exponentially declining function, which is what we earlier derived for a stationary first-order autoregressive model. Results based on both estimators provide motivation to consider a nonstationary autoregressive process (i.e., $|\beta_2| > 1.0$) or, at least, one that is nearly nonstationary (e.g., $\beta_2 > 0.95$). On the other hand, one can justifiably ask whether these sorts of estimation results can really facilitate distinguishing one type of process from another. The simulation results described in Exhibits 7-3 and 7-4 are supposed to provide insights into this issue. Before getting to that, however, we briefly comment on the Box-Pierce and Runs statistics, the values of which also appear in Exhibit 7-2. These statistics are often used in tests for serial correlation.

The Box-Pierce and Runs statistics are additional tools that can be used for diagnostic purposes. Conditional on the estimator $\tilde{r}_j^*$, the Box-Pierce statistic for the first m values $\tilde{r}_j^*$ $j = 1, 2, \ldots, m$, is defined by $\tilde{Q}(m) = n \; \Sigma_{j=1}^{m} (\tilde{r}_j^*)^2$, where n is the size of the original sample adjusted for differencing (if any). If this statistic is evaluated for the residuals from a fitted ARIMA(p, d, q) model, then the asymptotic distribution of $\tilde{Q}(m)$ is that of $\tilde{\chi}^2(m - p - q)$, a (central) chi-squared random variable with $(m - p - q)$ degrees of freedom,

[22]Rejecting the null hypothesis when it is true is a so-called Type I error.

EXHIBIT 7-3

SELECTED DIAGNOSTIC RESULTS FOR SIMULATED DRAWINGS ON FIRST-ORDER AUTOREGRESSIVE MODEL, $\tilde{y}(t) = \beta_1 + \beta_2 \tilde{y}(t-1) + \tilde{\epsilon}(t)$, WITH $\beta_1 = 0.0$ AND $\beta_2 = 0.99$. $\tilde{\epsilon}(t)$ IS NORMALLY DISTRIBUTED WITH $E(\tilde{\epsilon}(t)) = 0.0$ AND $\text{VAR}(\tilde{\epsilon}(t)) = 1.0$ SAMPLE SIZE = 52.

WANT TO PLOT ALL ROWS OF ACTIVE DATA MATRIX ?Y

SEQUENCE PLOT OF STANDARDIZED VALUES OF 'AR99

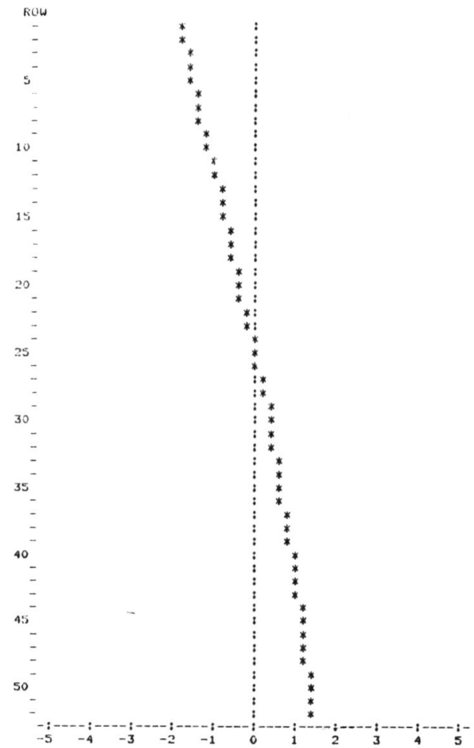

ORDER	SERIAL CORRELATION
1	+1.000
2	+1.000
3	+0.999
4	+0.999
5	+0.999
6	+0.999
7	+0.998
8	+0.998
9	+0.998
10	+0.998
11	+0.998
12	+0.997

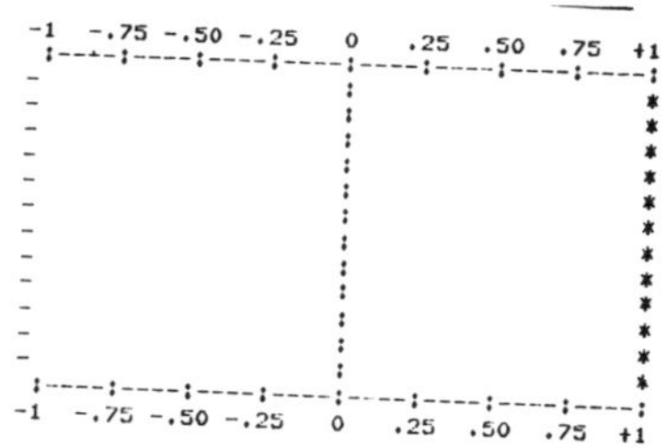

SERIES: AR99
BASED ON 52 ACTIVE OBSERVATIONS

ORDER	AUTO-CORRELATION
1	+0.946
2	+0.891
3	+0.837
4	+0.780
5	+0.724
6	+0.667
7	+0.610
8	+0.552
9	+0.496
10	+0.441
11	+0.387
12	+0.334

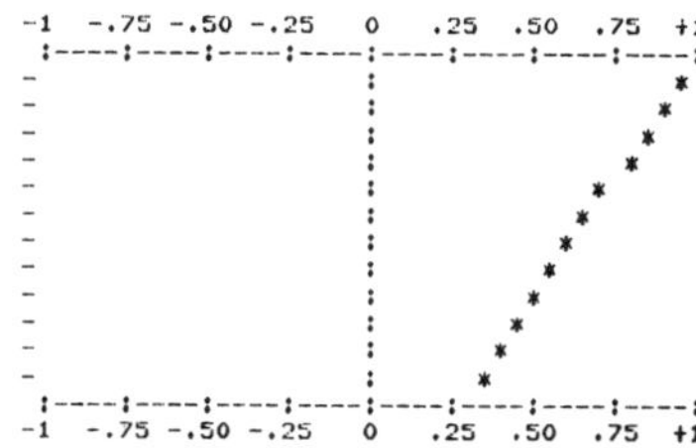

SERIES: AR99
BASED ON 52 ACTIVE OBSERVATIONS

S.E. OF EACH COEF. GIVEN RANDOM MODEL=0.139

BOX-PIERCE STATISTIC= 277.987
EXPECTATION GIVEN RANDOM MODEL= 12
(OBS.-EXP.)/(STD.DEV.)= 13.7357

OBSERVED NUMBER OF RUNS = 2
EXPECTED NUMBER OF RUNS = 26.8462
STANDARD DEVIATION OF RUNS = 3.54848
(OBS.-EXP.)/(STD.DEV.) = -7.00191

SERIES: AR99

```
-------------------------++++++++++++++++++++++++++
```

+ = value > mean
- = value < = mean
Mean = 16.3999

EXHIBIT 7-4

SELECTED DIAGNOSTIC RESULTS FOR SIMULATED DRAWINGS ON FIRST-ORDER AUTOREGRESSIVE MODEL, $\tilde{y}(t) = \beta_1 + \beta_2\,\tilde{y}(t-1) + \tilde{\epsilon}(t)$, WITH $\beta_1 = 0.0$ and $\beta_2 = 0.50$. $\tilde{\epsilon}(t)$ IS NORMALLY DISTRIBUTED WITH $E(\tilde{\epsilon}(t)) = 0.0$ and $VAR(\tilde{\epsilon}(t)) = 1.0$. SAMPLE SIZE = 52.

```
* GIVE NAME OR COLUMN NUMBER FOR THE VARIABLE TO BE PLOTTED : AR50
WANT TO PLOT ALL ROWS OF ACTIVE DATA MATRIX ?Y
SEQUENCE PLOT  OF STANDARDIZED VALUES OF 'AR50
```

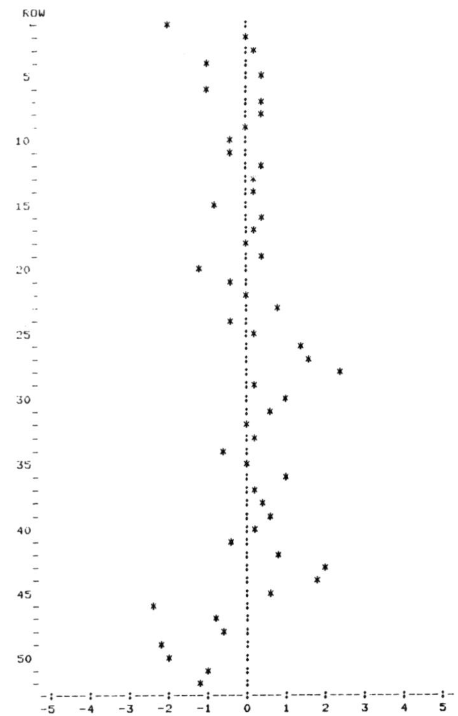

ORDER	SERIAL CORRELATION
1	+0.459
2	+0.260
3	+0.195
4	+0.080
5	+0.129
6	-0.212
7	-0.274
8	-0.232
9	+0.006
10	-0.073
11	-0.018
12	+0.040

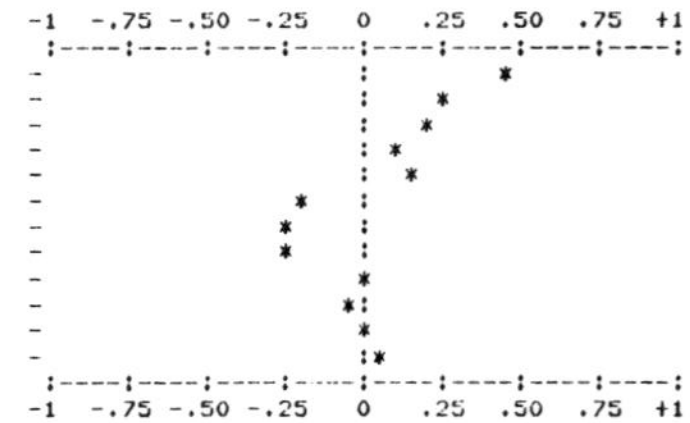

```
SERIES: AR50
BASED ON  52     ACTIVE OBSERVATIONS
```

ORDER	AUTO-CORRELATION
1	+0.436
2	+0.253
3	+0.177
4	+0.073
5	+0.113
6	-0.156
7	-0.184
8	-0.154
9	+0.014
10	-0.038
11	-0.002
12	+0.034

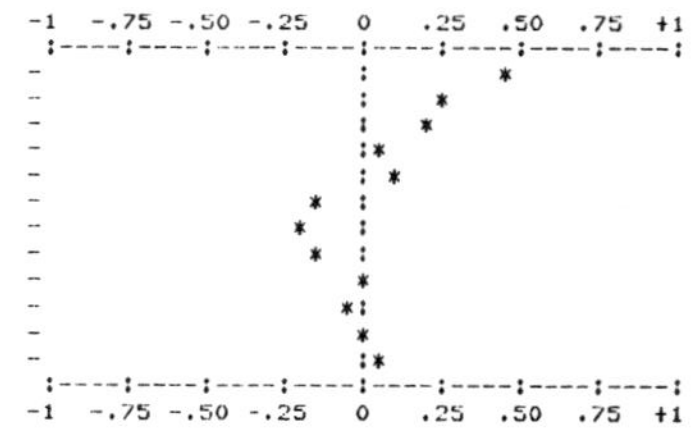

```
SERIES: AR50
BASED ON  52     ACTIVE OBSERVATIONS

S.E. OF EACH COEF. GIVEN RANDOM MODEL=0.139

BOX-PIERCE STATISTIC= 20.201
EXPECTATION GIVEN RANDOM MODEL= 12
        (OBS.-EXP.)/(STD.DEV.)= 1.52927

   OBSERVED NUMBER OF RUNS =  21
   EXPECTED NUMBER OF RUNS =  26.3846
STANDARD DEVIATION OF RUNS =  3.48384
    (OBS.-EXP.)/(STD.DEV.) = -1.5456

SERIES: AR50

-++-+-++---+++-++++---+-+++++++-+--+++++-++++-------

+ = value > mean
- = value < = mean
Mean =  1.90496
```

conditional on the hypothesis that the data are drawings on a serially uncorrelated process (i.e., $\rho_j = 0$ for all $j > 0$). The results in Exhibit 7-2 are, in effect, for the model ARIMA(0, 0, 0) with a constant term, i.e., $\tilde{y}(t) = \delta + \tilde{\epsilon}(t)$. And the value of $\tilde{Q}(m)$ given is for $m = 12$. The expected value and variance of the asymptotic distribution of $\tilde{Q}(12)$ are $E[\chi^2(12)] = 12$ and $\text{Var}[\chi^2(12)] = 24$, respectively.[23] The large sample distribution of $[\tilde{Q}(12) - E[\tilde{Q}(12)]]/\sigma[\tilde{Q}(12)]$ is that of a standardized normal random variable. The fractiles of that distribution can be used, for sufficiently large sample sizes, to test for the "statistical significance" of the observed value of $\tilde{Q}(12)$. If these formalities are used for the results given in Exhibit 7-2, one can reject the null hypothesis of no serial correlation in the EPS series at a level of significance far beyond the 0.01 level (or, in conventional jargon, beyond the level of significance $\alpha = 0.01$).[24]

The Runs statistic, $\tilde{z}$, for the observations on $\tilde{y}(t)$ is defined as follows. Let n_1 denote the number of observations above the sample mean, $\bar{y}$, and let n_2 be the number of observations below or equal to the sample mean. One "run" is one consecutive string of observations either (1) above or (2) below or equal to the sample mean. In the case of EPS, all observations up to and including the 37th observations are below $\bar{y} = 0.753$; all the succeeding observations are above $\bar{y}$. Thus, this series exhibits two runs, as is indicated in Exhibit 7-2. The expected number of runs conditional on stationarity and no serial correlation is:

$$\mu = [2n_1n_2/(n_1 + n_2)] + 1, \tag{7.71}$$

and the variance of the number of runs is:

$$\sigma^2 = \frac{2n_1n_2(2n_1n_2 - n_1 - n_2)}{(n_1 + n_2)^2(n_1 + n_2 - 1)}. \tag{7.72}$$

For large $n = n_1 + n_2$, the random variable:

$$\tilde{z} = \frac{\tilde{u} - \mu + \dfrac{1}{2}}{\sigma} \tag{7.73}$$

is approximately normally distributed, with $E(\tilde{z} = 0$ and $\text{Var}(\tilde{z}) = 1$, where $\tilde{u}$ is the observed number of runs.[25] (See Draper and Smith [1966, p. 97].) The observed value of $\tilde{z}$ can be used to test the null hypothesis of no serial correlation. For EPS, $\tilde{z} = -6.965$. This value is inconsistent with the null hypothesis at a level of significance substantially beyond the 0.01 level. There appears to be a significant deficiency of runs, which points to positive serial correlation. Values above the mean are followed by values above the mean more frequently than expected.

Given the sequence plot provided in Exhibit 7-2, the observed values of $\tilde{Q}(12)$ and $\tilde{z}$ seem pretty uninformative, in the sense that they are not surprising. Nor were they dis-

---

[23]In general, $E[\tilde{\chi}^2(m)] = m$ and $\text{Var}[\tilde{\chi}^2(m)] = 2m$, where $\tilde{\chi}^2(m)$ is a central "chi-squared" random variable with m degrees of freedom.

[24]The 0.90, 0.95, and 0.99 fractiles of the standardized normal distribution are approximately 1.282, 1.645, and 2.326, respectively. In this and all other exhibits, the value of the Box-Pierce statistic is based on the estimated values of the autocorrelation coefficients at lags 1 through 12.

[25]The addition of 1/2 in the numerator of $\tilde{z}$ is due to a so-called continuity correction.

cussed because they would be surprising. They were discussed here because they will be routinely reported in much of what follows and it seemed best to dispose of the related definitional and notational issues at the outset of our illustration.

The results in Exhibits 7-3 and 7-4 are based on simulated drawings from two stationary first-order autoregressive models. Recall that this model, ARIMA(1, 0, 0) is given by:

$$\tilde{y}(t) = \beta_1 + \beta_2 y(t-1) + \tilde{\epsilon}(t), \tag{7.74}$$

where $|\beta_2| < 1.0$ for stationarity and $\{\tilde{\epsilon}(t)\}$ is a disturbance process exhibiting serial independence; also, $E[\tilde{\epsilon}(t)] = 0.0$ and $\text{Var}[\tilde{\epsilon}(t)] = \sigma_\epsilon^2$.

Our objective is to get simulation results that will aid in analyzing Caterpillar's EPS process. We specified values of the parameters of (7.74) with this in mind. We specified values of the mean and variance of $\tilde{y}(t)$ equal to the sample mean and sample variance, respectively, of EPS, conditional on the annual data described in Exhibit 7.2. For these data, $\bar{y} = 0.753$ and $S^2 = 1.1345$. In order to get results that would provide insights into the characteristics of nearly nonstationary processes, we specified $\beta_2 = 0.99$ for one simulation and, for comparative purposes, $\beta_2 = 0.50$ for the other. The model with $\beta_2 = 0.50$ is well within the region of stationarity, defined by $\beta_2 \in (-1.0, 1.0)$. Thus, we expected its properties to be visibly different, on balance, from those of the process with $\beta_2 = 0.99$. The appropriate value of σ_ϵ^2 for each case is implied by the specified values of $\text{Var}[\tilde{y}(t)]$ and β_2. As indicated in expression (7.31), $\sigma_\epsilon^2 = (1 - \beta_2^2)\ \text{Var}[\tilde{y}(t)]$. Thus, for the case $\beta_2 = 0.99$, we specified $\sigma_\epsilon = 0.1502$; we specified $\sigma_\epsilon = 0.9222$ for the case $\beta_2 = 0.50$. The appropriate value of β_1 for each case is implied by the specified values for $E[\tilde{y}(t)]$ and β_2. As indicated in expression (7.30), $\beta_1 = E[\tilde{y}(t)](1 - \beta_2)$. Thus, for the case $\beta_2 = 0.99$, we specified $\beta_1 = 0.00753$; for the case $\beta_2 = 0.50$, we specified $\beta_1 = 0.3765$. For both cases, $\tilde{\epsilon}(t)$ is specified to be an independent, identically distributed normal random variable, with $E[\tilde{\epsilon}(t)] = 0.0$. The sample size for each set of simulated observations—one for each value of β_2—is set equal to $N = 52$, which is the number of observations on EPS. The "starting value," or the value of $\tilde{y}(1)$, is specified to be 0.051, which is the observed value of the first year's EPS.

The resulting simulated observations for the case $\beta_2 = 0.99$ are described in Exhibit 7-3; Exhibit 7-4 deals with the case $\beta_2 = 0.50$. These exhibits provide the same sorts of plots and values of the same statistics displayed for EPS. The actual simulated values are given in columns (4) and (5) of Exhibit 7-1. AR99 (AR50) refers to the case $\beta_2 = 0.99$ ($\beta_2 = 0.50$).

The similarity of EPS's properties and those of the simulated process with $\beta_2 = 0.99$ seems quite vivid. The sequence plot for the simulated drawings displays the same smooth upward evolution observed for EPS. No such pattern is observed for the simulated drawings on the process with $\beta_2 = 0.50$. In addition, both the estimated serial correlation function and the estimated autocorrelation function for EPS bear a closer resemblance to the counterpart results for the simulated data with $\beta_2 = 0.99$ than to the simulated data with $\beta_2 = 0.50$. And, not unexpectedly, the results of the values of the Box-Pierce and Runs statistics are similar for EPS and the simulated data conditional on $\beta_2 = 0.99$; such a similarity is not evident with respect to EPS and the simulated data for $\beta_2 = 0.50$.

In short, the simulation results reinforce our "first pass" reaction: Caterpillar's EPS seems to behave in a manner consistent with a first-order model having β_2 close to (and perhaps above) unity. This is, of course, a tentative inference. If we want to work conditionally on it, then we are led to consider differencing EPS in order to attain stationarity if, in fact, $\beta_2 \approx 1.0$. Recall that differencing is a transformation that can eliminate stochastic nonstationarities of the sort implied by $\beta_2 = 1.0$. But before pursuing that approach, we shall provide estimation results for our originally proposed first-order autoregressive, or ARIMA(1, 0, 0), model. Results for EPS and our simulated observations will be presented.

Selected estimation results for EPS and the two series of simulated observations are given in Table 7-2. The general model estimated is:

$$\tilde{y}(t) = \beta_1 + \beta_2 y(t - 1) + \beta_3 t + \tilde{e}(t), \tag{7.75}$$

where $\tilde{e}(t)$ is the disturbance term, with the usual properties. The time variable, t, was added to the ARIMA(1, 0, 0) model for diagnostic purposes. If the latter model is, in fact, well specified, then the disturbance, $\tilde{\epsilon}(t) = \tilde{y}(t) - \beta_1 - \beta_2\tilde{y}(t - 1)$, should be an independent and identically distributed random variable, with $E[\tilde{\epsilon}(t)] = 0.0$ and $\text{Var}[\tilde{\epsilon}(t)] = \sigma_\epsilon^2$ for all t. These properties of $\{\tilde{\epsilon}(t)\}$ would not be consistent with the sample evidence if the time variable, t, turns out to be an important explanatory variable. If it is important, then $\tilde{\epsilon}(t) = \tilde{y}(t) - \beta_1 - \beta_2\tilde{y}(t - 1) = \beta_3 t + \tilde{e}(t)$, with $\beta_3 \neq 0.0$. Thus, if the time variable is important, $E[\tilde{\epsilon}(t)] = \beta_3 t$, which is not equal to zero (except for $t = 0$) and which is not constant over time. In short, addition of the time variable to the ARIMA(1, 0, 0) model provides one basis for evaluating the extent to which that model is well specified, conditional on the available sample evidence.

The estimation results in Table 7-2 are based on applying Ordinary Least Squares (OLS) procedures to model (7.75). The results reported there include the point estimates of β_1, β_2, and β_3—$\hat{\beta}_1$, $\hat{\beta}_2$, and $\hat{\beta}_3$, respectively—the observed values of the t-statistics corresponding to these estimates, with each measured relative to the "null hypothesis" value of zero, the estimated standard deviation of the disturbance, $\hat{\sigma}_\epsilon$, the estimated standard errors of the intercept's and slope-coefficients' estimators, $S(\hat{\tilde{\beta}}_1)$, $S(\hat{\tilde{\beta}}_2)$, and $S(\hat{\tilde{\beta}}_3)$, and the coefficient of multiple determination adjusted for degrees of freedom, $\bar{R}^2$.[26] Estimated values, $\hat{\rho}_j(\tilde{e}(t))$, $j = 1, 2, \ldots, 12$, of the lag-j serial correlation coefficients of the disturbance, $\tilde{e}(t)$, are given in Exhibit 7-5 for EPS.

One indication of EPS's being nearly nonstationary is the estimated value of β_2, which equals 0.996 for the model that allows for $\beta_3 \neq 0$ and which equals 1.087 when the constraint $\beta_3 = 0.0$ is invoked (i.e., when time, t, is not included among the independent variables). For the model allowing $\beta_3 \neq 0$, the estimated standard error of $\hat{\tilde{\beta}}_2$, $S(\hat{\tilde{\beta}}_2)$, equals 0.081; it equals 0.051 when the constraint $\beta_3 = 0.0$ is invoked. Thus, conditional on both models, the estimated value of β_2 is consistent with $\beta_2 = 1.0$, or at least a value near unity, at (better than) conventional levels of significance (e.g., levels of significance equal to 0.05 or 0.01).

Results pertinent to the specification of model 7.75 are given in Exhibit 7-5. All of these results pertain to the residuals from the estimated model. The estimated serial correlation function does not point to any gross departures from the specification that $\{\tilde{e}(t)\}$

---

[26]Specifically, $\bar{R}^2 = R^2 - [(k - 1)/(N - k)](1 - R^2)$, where R^2 is the coefficient of multiple determination, N is the number of observations used for estimation, and k is the number of "independent variables" (including the intercept) in the regression model. This adjustment "penalizes" models in a way varying directly with k. See Goldberger [1964, p. 217].

TABLE 7-2

ESTIMATION RESULTS FOR CATERPILLAR TRACTOR'S ANNUAL EPS FOR THE 52-YEAR PERIOD 1925–1976 AND FOR SIMULATED DATA[a] THE MODEL ESTIMATED IS $\tilde{y}(t) = \beta_1 + \beta_2 y(t-1) + \beta_3 t + \tilde{\epsilon}(t)$, WHERE $t = 1$ FOR 1925

Constraint	Data Series	$\hat{\beta}_1$	$S(\hat{\tilde{\beta}}_1)$	$t(\hat{\tilde{\beta}}_1)$	$\hat{\beta}_2$	$S(\hat{\tilde{\beta}}_2)$	$t(\hat{\tilde{\beta}}_2)$	$\hat{\beta}_3$	$S(\hat{\tilde{\beta}}_3)$	$t(\hat{\tilde{\beta}}_3)$	$\hat{\sigma}_\epsilon$	$\bar{R}^2$
None	EPS	−.099	.106	−.931	.996	.081	12.280	.007	.005	1.412	.332	.904
	AR99	.748	.048	15.648	1.026	.027	37.234	−.022	.017	−1.286	.168	.999
	AR50	1.272	.339	3.752	.447	.124	3.605	−.007	.008	−.935	.839	.193
$\beta_3 = 0.0$	EPS	.027	.058	.469	1.087	.051	21.493				.335	.902
	AR99	.746	.048	15.515	.990	.003	381.585				.169	.999
	AR50	1.076	.266	4.043	.449	.124	3.619				.837	.195
$\beta_2 = 0.0$	EPS	−.706	.190	−3.720				.057	.006	8.916	.668	.611
	AR99	.844	.258	3.269				.611	.008	70.662	.908	.990
	AR50	2.142	.266	8.056				−.008	.008	−.868	.936	.000

[a]The simulated series AR99 (AR50) consists of simulated drawings on $\tilde{y}(t) = \beta_1 + \beta_2 y(t-1) + \tilde{\epsilon}(t)$ with $\beta_2 = 0.90$ (0.50). See text for complete details. Each simulated series contains 52 observations.

EXHIBIT 7-5

SELECTED DIAGNOSTICS FOR RESIDUALS FROM THE ESTIMATED MODEL $\tilde{y}(t) = \beta_1 + \beta_2\tilde{y}(t-1) + \beta_3 t + \tilde{e}(t)$ BASED ON CATERPILLAR TRACTOR'S ANNUAL EARNINGS-PER-SHARE FOR THE 52 YEARS 1925–1976

RESIDU

WANT TO PLOT ALL ROWS OF ACTIVE DATA MATRIX ?Y

SEQUENCE PLOT OF STANDARDIZED VALUES OF 'RESIDU'

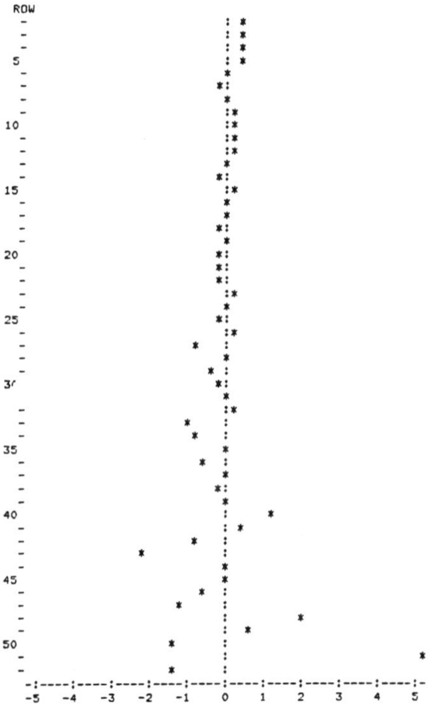

HISTOGRAM

ABS. FREQ.

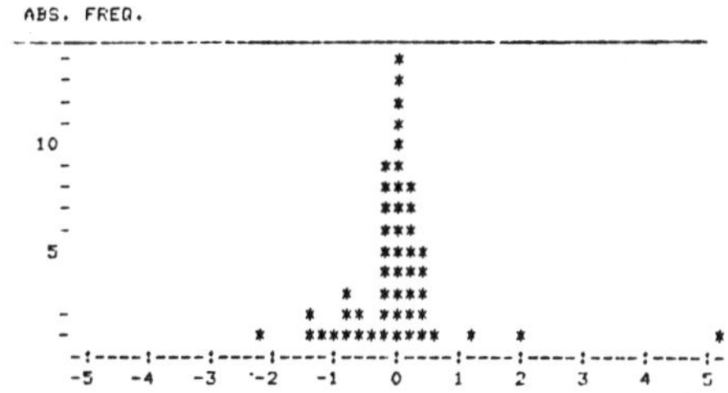

MEAN = 0
STD. DEV. = .331693
SAMPLE SIZE = 51

ORDER	SERIAL CORRELATION
1	-0.266
2	-0.040
3	+0.362
4	-0.196
5	-0.187
6	-0.109
7	+0.082
8	-0.284
9	+0.097
10	+0.193
11	+0.329
12	-0.141

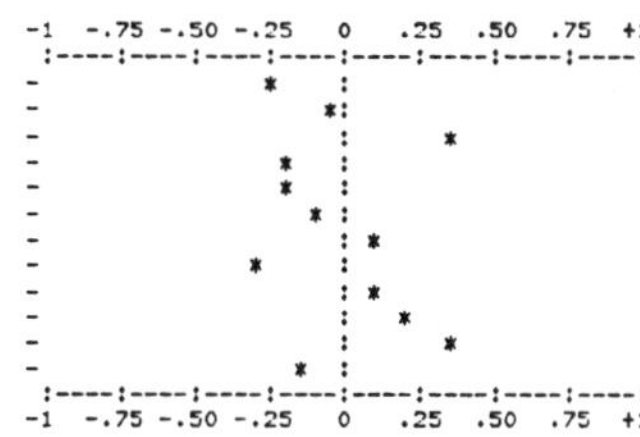

SERIES: RESIDU
BASED ON 51 ACTIVE OBSERVATIONS
(FIRST ACTIVE ROW = 2 , LAST ACTIVE ROW = 52)

ORDER	AUTO-CORRELATION
1	-0.250
2	-0.023
3	+0.209
4	-0.109
5	-0.087
6	-0.047
7	+0.039
8	-0.125
9	+0.046
10	+0.067
11	+0.106
12	-0.043

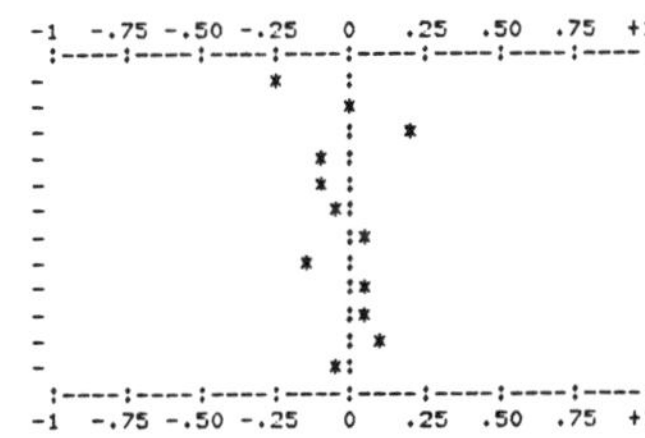

SERIES: RESIDU
BASED ON 51 ACTIVE OBSERVATIONS
(FIRST ACTIVE ROW = 2 , LAST ACTIVE ROW = 52)

S.E. OF EACH COEF. GIVEN RANDOM MODEL=0.140

BOX-PIERCE STATISTIC= 8.42693
EXPECTATION GIVEN RANDOM MODEL= 12
(OBS.-EXP.)/(STD.DEV.)=-.680685

is a serially uncorrelated process. The estimated serial correlation coefficients are reasonably consistent with the condition $\rho_j = 0$ for all $j \neq 0$. But there are some hints at potential inadequacies. In particular, the estimates at values of j equal to 3, 8, and 11 are somewhat large, relative to the theoretical standard error of about $1.0/\sqrt{n} \approx 0.140$, where n is the number of observations used for estimation.[27] The sequence plot given in Exhibit 7-5 identifies some sets of consecutive observations above and below the sample mean. These observations may have contributed to the signs of inadequacy that seem to appear in the estimated serial correlation function. Nevertheless, the extent to which these results are consistent with the specifications on the disturbance at least suggests we are "moving in the right direction."

For hypothesis-testing purposes, it is usually desired that $\tilde{e}(t)$ have a normal distribution, or at least a distribution adequately approximated by a normal distribution. The histogram given in Exhibit 7-5 is one conventional tool used to deal with this issue. The basic shape of the displayed sample frequency distribution seems acceptable. There are, however, signs of inadequacy here too; in particular, the distribution seems skewed to the right. But this seems due to only one observation (observed EPS for 1975), which may best be treated as an outlier.

Finally, note that the apparent change in the variability of EPS is exhibited by the residuals too. At least for this sample, there is a seemingly dramatic increase in variability and, thus, an inconsistency with the specified constancy of $\mathrm{Var}[\tilde{\epsilon}(t)]$.

Results of the sort given in Exhibit 7-5 were also obtained for model (7.75) with the constraint $\beta_3 = 0.0$. There were no striking differences between them and what is given in Exhibit 7-5. The reason for this should be clear: the time variable does not provide much additional "explanatory power" to begin with. So, imposing the constraint $\beta_3 = 0.0$ when the value of β_2 is unconstrained does not change much, relative to the unconstrained case.

Estimation results for the simulated observations are also given in Table 7-2. A key question to ask is this: if one is dealing with a nearly nonstationary ARIMA(1, 0, 0) model, will the estimation results lead one to infer near nonstationarity? And if one is dealing with an ARIMA(1, 0, 0) model whose autoregressive parameter's value is well within the region of stationarity, $\beta_2 \in (-1, 1)$, will the estimation results lead one to infer that? Moreover, given a well-specified stationary ARIMA(1, 0, 0) model, will estimation results for the generalized model (7.75) be consistent with the correct value $\beta_3 = 0.0$?

Taken at face value, the estimation results presented in Table 7-2 seem to provide a support for affirmative responses to those questions. For both correct models, $\beta_2 = 0.50$ and $\beta_2 = 0.99$, the estimated values of β_2 are well within one standard error of the true values of β_2, whether or not one allows for $\beta_3 \neq 0.0$. For the generalized model—where $\beta_3 \neq 0.0$ is allowed—the estimate of β_3 for the case $\beta_2 = 0.99$ is within two standard errors of the correct value, $\beta_3 = 0.0$. For the case $\beta_2 = 0.50$, the estimate of β_3 is within one standard error of the correct value, $\beta_3 = 0.0$. Finally, results from applying the sorts of diagnostic tools underlying Exhibit 7-5 did not point to any serious inconsistencies between the specification of the ARIMA(1, 0, 0) models and the simulated sample evidence, for either value of β_2. In short, the benchmarks for estimation results supplied by

---

[27]The original number was 52. But one observation is "lost" because a lagged value of $\tilde{y}(t)$ is included as an independent variable. Thus, $n = 51$.

the simulated data reinforce our tentative inference about EPS's being a nonstationary ARIMA(1, 0, 0) process or something close to it.

Conditional on the ARIMA(1, 0, 0) model, it appears that EPS is characterized by $\beta_2 \approx 1.0$. This provides motivation for analyzing the first differences of observed EPS. If $\beta_2 = 1.0$, then the first difference of EPS is a stationary process, at least as far as $E[\tilde{y}(t)]$ is concerned. Before getting to that, however, we digress to consider results based on model (7.75) with the constraint $\beta_2 = 0.0$.

If we add this constraint to model (7.75), we get the pure linear trend model:

$$\tilde{y}(t) = \beta_0 + \beta_3 t + \tilde{e}(t). \tag{7.76}$$

This model and variants of it are among the most widely used models for income numbers within the context of financial statement analysis and many areas of empirical economics.[28] Estimation results based on (7.76) are given in Table 7-2. If one evaluated this model solely in terms of the adjusted coefficient of determination, $\bar{R}^2$—which is a measure of the proportion of variation in $\tilde{y}(t)$ that can be accounted for by variation in t—one might conclude that (7.76) provides a decent characterization of EPS and a somewhat spectacular description of the simulated process having $\beta_2 = 0.99$. But this is where we run into a well-known "trap." Specifically, the seemingly good description provided by the time-trend model can, for the case at hand, be attributed to the high autocorrelation of the original series. A process that has high positive autocorrelation will, on average, exhibit a smooth observed evolution over a finite number of periods. As a result, it will often appear that the underlying processes can be described in terms of deterministic time trends, conditional on small- or moderate-sized samples. This phenomenon is related to the time series analysis problems recognized many years ago by Yule [1926] in a paper entitled, "Why Do We Sometimes Get Nonsense Correlations Between Time Series?—A Study in Sampling and the Nature of Time Series."[29] For the case at hand, the two time series under analysis are $\{\tilde{y}(t)\}$ and $\{t\}$. The fact that model (7.76)'s performance can "look good" even though it is incorrect is illustrated by the estimation results for the simulated process with $\beta_2 = 0.99$. We know that the model underlying this process has $\beta_3 = 0.0$. Yet, the observed value of $\bar{R}^2$ for model (7.76) applied to this process is 0.99, which is pretty sobering!

The inadequacy of (7.76)—and other misspecified models—can often be detected via conventional diagnostic checks on the consistency between the model's specifications and the sample evidence. Results from applying some of the checks used earlier for Exhibit 7-5 are displayed in Exhibits 7-6, 7-7, and 7-8 for the residuals from model (7.76) applied to, respectively, EPS, the simulated observations for the case $\beta_2 = 0.99$, and the simulated observations for the case $\beta_2 = 0.50$.

If model (7.76) with $\beta_3 \neq 0.0$ were a well-specified model, then the disturbance, $\tilde{e}(t)$, would be an independent, identically distributed random variable with constant variance (over time) and constant mean, equal to $E[\tilde{e}(t)] = 0.0$. Using Exhibit 7-6, it seems clear that the sample evidence on EPS is not consistent with the absence of serial correlation. This inconsistency seems clear from the estimated serial correlation function. (The stan-

[28] See, for example, Mendelson and Robbins [1976, pp. 355 ff.], Fischer and Jordan [1975, chap. 10], Feldstein and Summers [1977], and Fisher and Hall [1969].

[29] See also Gonedes and Roberts [1977*a*; 1977*b*; 1977*c*] for additional material relevant to this issue.

EXHIBIT 7-6

SELECTED DIAGNOSTICS FOR RESIDUALS FROM THE ESTIMATED MODEL $\tilde{y}(t) = \beta_1 + \beta_3 t + \tilde{e}(t)$ BASED ON CATERPILLAR TRACTOR'S ANNUAL EARNINGS-PER-SHARE FOR THE 52 YEARS 1925–1976.

RESIDU

WANT TO PLOT ALL ROWS OF ACTIVE DATA MATRIX ?Y

SEQUENCE PLOT OF STANDARDIZED VALUES OF 'RESIDU'

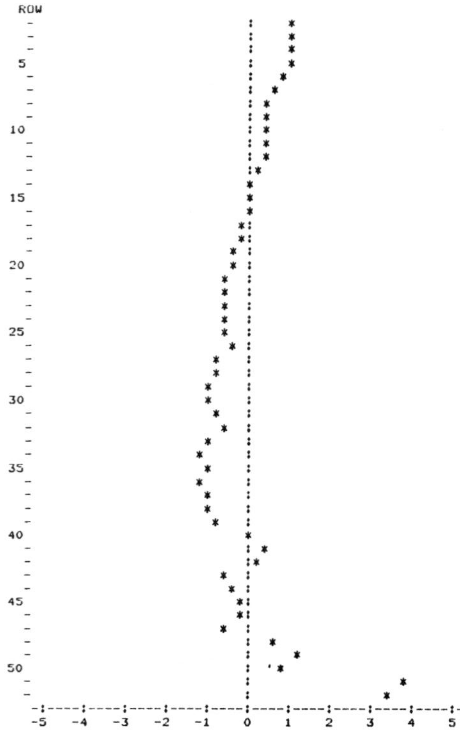

ORDER	SERIAL CORRELATION
1	+0.853
2	+0.722
3	+0.644
4	+0.410
5	+0.240
6	+0.259
7	+0.247
8	+0.197
9	+0.230
10	+0.259
11	+0.126
12	-0.111

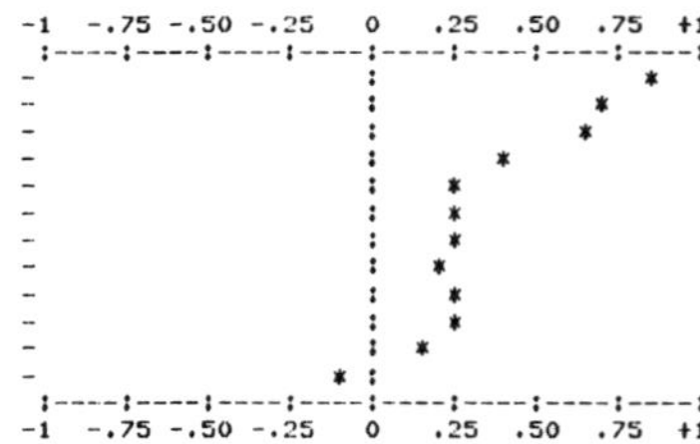

SERIES: RESIDU
BASED ON 51 ACTIVE OBSERVATIONS
(FIRST ACTIVE ROW = 2 , LAST ACTIVE ROW = 52)

> CHGP
* LEVEL = 3

Note: The time trend model was estimated after the data were arranged for estimation of the model with the lagged value of $\tilde{y}(t)$ as an "independent" variable. Hence, one observation was lost due to the lagging operation.

EXHIBIT 7-7

SELECTED DIAGNOSTICS FOR RESIDUALS FROM THE ESTIMATED MODEL $\tilde{y}(t) = \beta_1 + \beta_3 t + \tilde{e}(t)$ BASED ON THE 52 SIMULATED DRAWINGS FROM THE ARIMA(1, 0, 0) PROCESS WITH $\beta_2 = 0.99$. (SEE TEXT FOR DETAILS ON SIMULATION.)

SEQUENCE PLOT OF STANDARDIZED VALUES OF 'RESIDU'

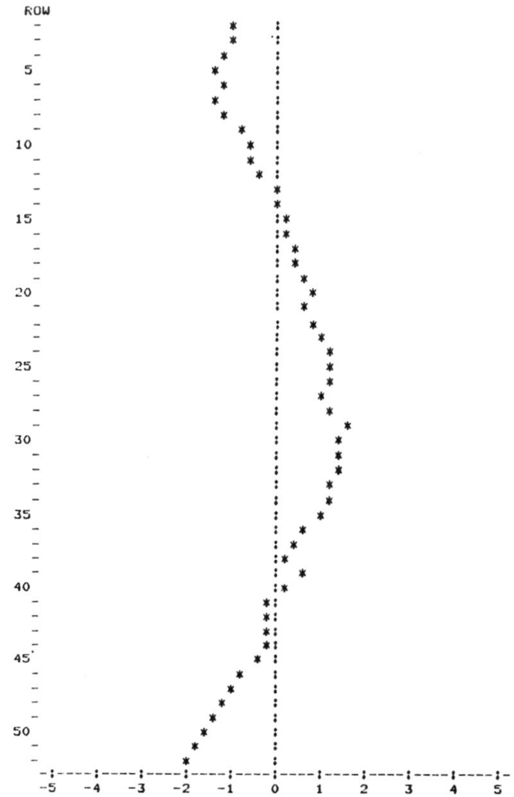

ORDER	SERIAL CORRELATION
1	+0.977
2	+0.939
3	+0.889
4	+0.821
5	+0.728
6	+0.610
7	+0.469
8	+0.339
9	+0.222
10	+0.093
11	-0.057
12	-0.202

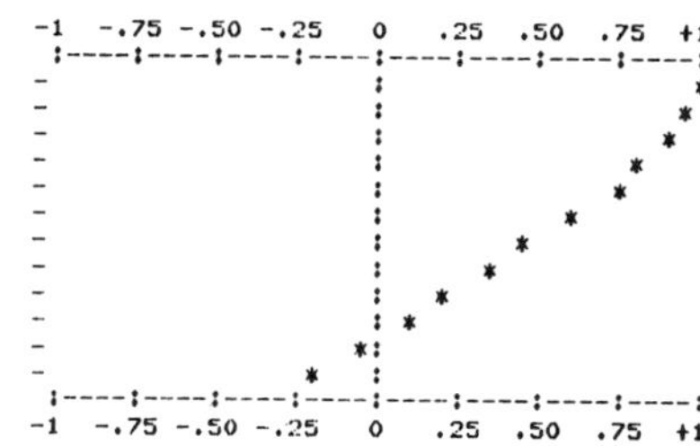

SERIES: RESIDU
BASED ON 51 ACTIVE OBSERVATIONS
(FIRST ACTIVE ROW = 2 , LAST ACTIVE ROW = 52)

Note: The time trend model was estimated after the data were arranged for estimation of the model having the lagged value of $\tilde{y}(t)$ as an "independent" variable. Hence, one observation was lost due to the lagging operation.

EXHIBIT 7-8

SEQUENCE PLOT FOR RESIDUALS FROM THE ESTIMATED MODEL $\tilde{y}(t) = \beta_1 + \beta_3 t + \tilde{e}(t)$ BASED ON THE 52 SIMULATED DRAWINGS FROM THE ARIMA(1, 0, 0) PROCESS WITH $\beta_2 = 0.50$. (SEE TEXT FOR DETAILS ON SIMULATION.)

```
> PLTS
* VARIABLE : RESIDU

PLOT ALL ROWS ?Y

SEQUENCE PLOT  OF STANDARDIZED VALUES OF  RESIDU
```

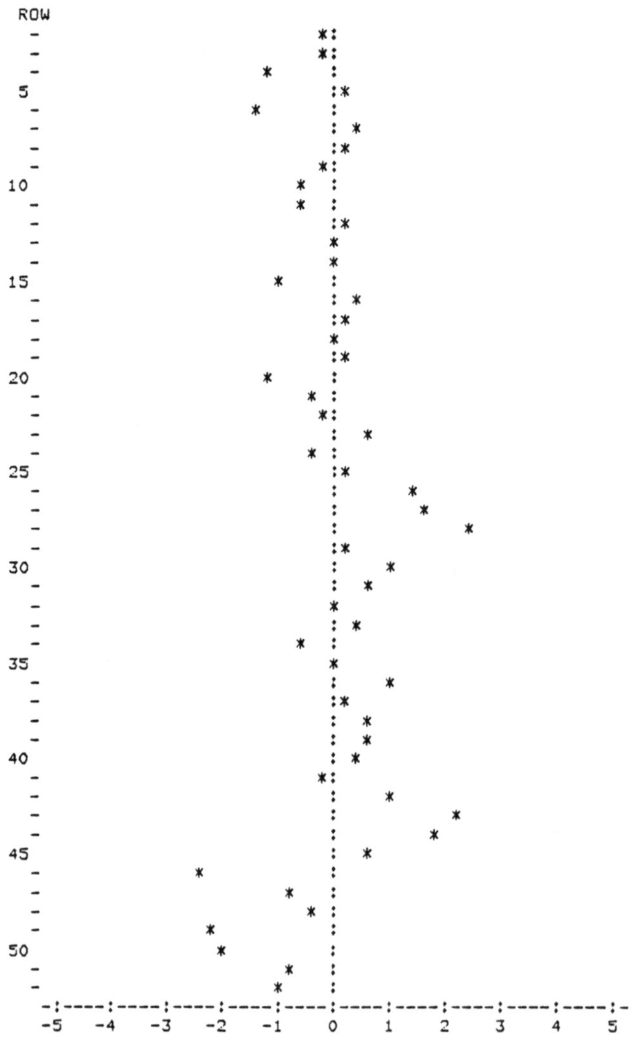


```
HISTOGRAM

ABS. FREQ.
```

EXHIBIT 7-8a

SELECTED DIAGNOSTIC RESULTS FOR FIRST DIFFERENCES OF CATERPILLAR TRACTOR'S ANNUAL EARNINGS-PER-SHARE (DEPS) FOR 52 YEARS 1925–1976.

```
OBS. IN ROW  51 AN OUTLIER; PLOTTED AS 5.2

SEQUENCE PLOT OF STANDARDIZED VALUES OF 'DEPS
```

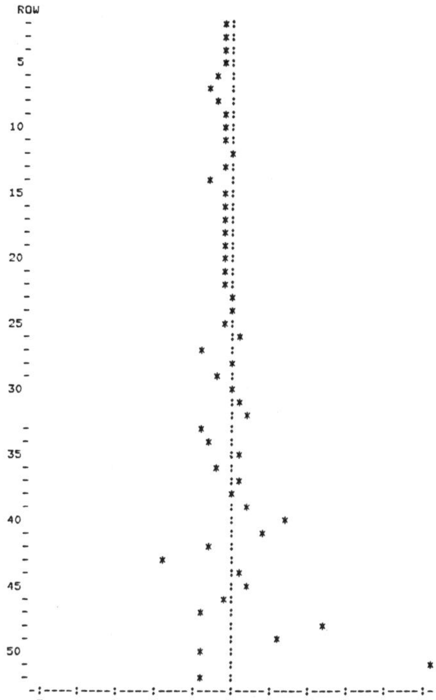

```
HISTOGRAM

ABS. FREQ.
```

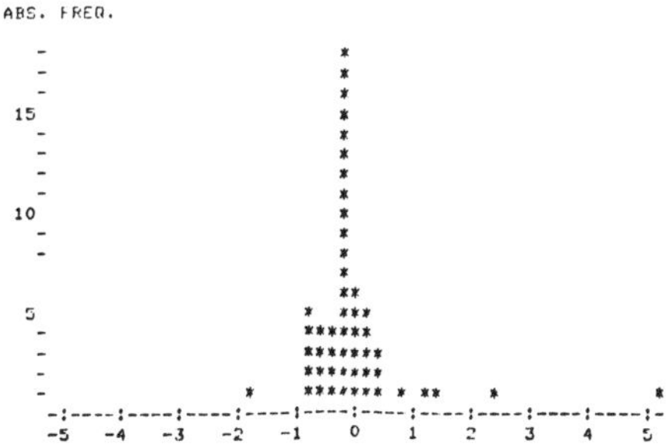

```
MEAN =  8.62941E-02     STD. DEV. =  .341482     FOR SAMPLE OF 51
```

```
RUNS
* VARIABLE ? DEPS

    OBSERVED NUMBER OF RUNS =  21
    EXPECTED NUMBER OF RUNS =  22.1765
 STANDARD DEVIATION OF RUNS =  2.92324
      (OBS.-EXP.)/(STD.DEV.) = -.402456

SERIES: DEPS

---------------------+--+-+--++--+-+-+++--++--++-+-

+ = value > mean
- = value < = mean
Mean =  8.62941E-02

FIRST ACTIVE ROW IS 2        LAST ACTIVE ROW IS 52

> SERC
* VARIABLE ? DEPS
* MAX. ORDER : 12
```

ORDER	SERIAL CORRELATION
1	-0.135
2	+0.047
3	+0.436
4	-0.088
5	-0.121
6	-0.025
7	+0.168
8	-0.206
9	+0.178
10	+0.315
11	+0.445
12	+0.016

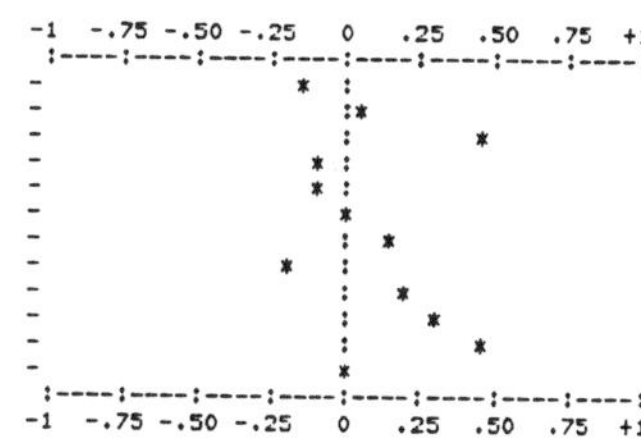

```
SERIES: DEPS
BASED ON  51      ACTIVE OBSERVATIONS
(FIRST ACTIVE ROW =  2      , LAST ACTIVE ROW =  52    )

> AUTO
* VARIABLE ? DEPS
* MAX. ORDER : 12
```

ORDER	AUTO-CORRELATION
1	-0.134
2	+0.028
3	+0.258
4	-0.052
5	-0.057
6	-0.015
7	+0.066
8	-0.093
9	+0.066
10	+0.104
11	+0.147
12	-0.003

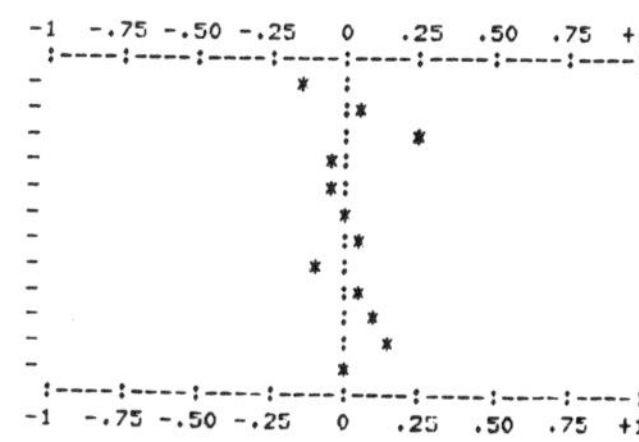

```
SERIES: DEPS
BASED ON  51      ACTIVE OBSERVATIONS
(FIRST ACTIVE ROW =  2      , LAST ACTIVE ROW =  52    )

S.E. OF EACH COEFF. GIVEN RANDOM MODEL=0.140

BOX-PIERCE STATISTIC= 7.21963
EXPECTATION GIVEN RANDOM MODEL= 12
          (OBS.-EXP.)/(STD.DEV.)=-1.00882
```

dard error for each estimated serial correlation coefficient, conditional on $\rho_j = 0$ for all $j \geq 1$, is roughly $1.01/\sqrt{51} \approx 0.14$.) And it seems vivid in the sequence plot of residuals. Similar remarks apply to the residuals from model (7.76) applied to the simulated data for the case $\beta_2 = 0.99$, for which results are given in Exhibit 7-7.

The estimation results (see Table 7-2) based on applying model (7.76) to the simulated data for the case $\beta_2 = 0.50$ are consistent with the condition $\beta_3 = 0.0$, which is the correct value of β_3. In view of this, the residuals from applying model (7.76) to these data do not point to the deficiencies inferred for EPS and the simulated process with $\beta_2 = 0.99$. In short, these residuals exhibit the same characteristics as the original data for the case $\beta_2 = 0.50$, because model (7.76) becomes $\tilde{y}(t) = E[\tilde{y}(t)] + \tilde{e}(t)$ when $\beta_3 = 0.0$. Thus, the crux of the results displayed in Exhibit 7-4—which pertains to the simulated values of $\tilde{y}(t)$ when $\beta_2 = 0.50$—applies to these residuals too. This can be seen by comparing the sequence plot based on the residuals, which is given in Exhibit 7-8, with the sequence plot based on the original simulated observations on $\tilde{y}(t)$, which is given in Exhibit 7-4.

The differences between the results on model (7.76) when applied to the simulated data for $\beta_2 = 0.99$ and the simulated data for $\beta_2 = 0.50$ are not difficult to explain. Since the process with $\beta_2 = 0.50$ is less autocorrelated, one is less likely to observe data that appear to have evolved in a smooth evolutionary manner; compare the sequence plots in Exhibits 7-4 and 7-5. As a result, application of model (7.76) to the simulated data based on $\beta_2 = 0.50$ is less likely to lead to, e.g., the misleadingly high sample values of $\bar{R}^2$.

In short, we are still left with the tentative inference that EPS behaves according to a nearly nonstationary ARIMA(1, 0, 0) process. The near nonstationarity of the type given by $\beta_2 \approx 1.0$ provides motivation for an analysis of first differences, to which we now turn.

The ARIMA(1, 0, 0) model under analysis is:

$$\tilde{y}(t) = \beta_1 + \beta_2 y(t - 1) + \tilde{\epsilon}(t), \tag{7.77}$$

where $|\beta_2| < 1.0$ is specified for stationarity. It should be clear that if this model is well specified for $\tilde{y}(t)$, then the same model is *not* well specified for $\Delta\tilde{y}(t)$. In fact, it can be shown that the appropriate model for a first-differenced stationary ARIMA(1, 0, 0) process is a stationary ARIMA(1, 1, 1) process.[30] If, however, $\beta_2 = 1.0$, then first differencing $\tilde{y}(t)$ leads directly to the simple model $\Delta\tilde{y}(t) = \beta_1 + \tilde{\epsilon}(t)$, or an ARIMA(0, 1, 0) model for $\tilde{y}(t)$. Thus, the results from applying the AR(1, 0, 0) model to the *first difference* of $\tilde{y}(t)$ can be used for diagnostic purposes. If the results are substantially consistent with an ARIMA(0, 1, 0) model for $\tilde{y}(t)$—which is equivalent to an ARIMA(0, 0, 0) model for $\Delta\tilde{y}(t)$—then we have results consistent with $\beta_2 = 1.0$ in model (7.77). The crux of what is involved here can be seen from the following.

Lag model (7.77) and subtract the result from (7.77), to get:

$$\begin{aligned}\Delta\tilde{y}(t) = \tilde{y}(t) - y(t - 1) = \beta_2[y(t - 1) - y(t - 2)]& \\ + \tilde{\epsilon}(t) - \epsilon(t - 1).&\end{aligned} \tag{7.78}$$

But $\epsilon(t - 1) = y(t - 1) - \beta_1 - \beta_2 y(t - 2)$. Using this in (7.78) and rearranging the resulting expression gives:

$$\begin{aligned}\Delta\tilde{y}(t) &= \beta_2[y(t - 1) - y(t - 2)] + \tilde{\epsilon}(t) \\ &\quad + \beta_1 + \beta_2 y(t - 2) - y(t - 1) \\ &= \beta_2[y(t - 1) - y(t - 2)] + \tilde{v}(t),\end{aligned} \tag{7.79}$$

---

[30]In general, a well-specified ARIMA(p, O, q) process becomes a well-specified ARIMA(p, d, $q + d$) process after d levels of differencing, with a moving average component that is noninvertible.

where $\tilde{v}(t) \equiv \tilde{\epsilon}(t) + \beta_1 + \beta_2 y(t-2) - y(t-1)$. The last equality in (7.79) is in the form of a first-order autoregressive model applied to $\{\Delta\tilde{y}(t)\}$. Note, however, that if $\beta_2 \neq 1.0$, then $\tilde{v}(t)$ does not satisfy the standard specifications of the disturbance for that model. For example, $\tilde{v}(t)$ is correlated with $\Delta\tilde{y}(t-1)$, which appears on the right hand side of (7.79). In addition, $\tilde{v}(t)$ is not independently distributed (over time). On the other hand, if $\beta_2 =$ 1.0, then (7.79) becomes:

$$\Delta\tilde{y}(t) = \beta_1 + \tilde{\epsilon}(t), \tag{7.80}$$

which is well specified if the original model for $\tilde{y}(t)$—$\tilde{y}(t) = y(t-1) + \beta_1 + \tilde{\epsilon}(t)$—is well specified.

In addition to pursuing the above analysis of $\Delta\tilde{y}(t)$, we shall, as before, add time, t, to our model for diagnostic purposes. In summary, the general model to be considered now is:

$$\Delta\tilde{y}(t) = \beta_1' + \beta_2'\Delta y(t-1) + \beta_3' t + \tilde{v}(t). \tag{7.81}$$

Before presenting estimation results for model (9.79), we provide, in Exhibit 7-8a, results from applying some standard diagnostic checks to the sample evidence on $\Delta\tilde{y}(t)$. The sequence plot in Exhibit 7-8a seems consistent with a shift in Var$[\Delta\tilde{y}(t)]$, just as the sequence plot for the evidence on $\tilde{y}(t)$ seemed consistent with a shift in Var$[\tilde{y}(t)]$. Moreover, a comparison of the first 23 standardized values with the value of the mean of the standardized data—*viz.*, zero—and a comparison of the remaining values with that mean's value seem to suggest a shift in the value of $E[\Delta\tilde{y}(t)]$. All of the first 23 standardized values are less than or equal to zero. The remaining values seem consistent with random drawings on a process with a mean equal to zero. Since this shift, if it occurred, is positively correlated with time, t, it may induce signs of serial correlation. The estimated serial correlation coefficients seem consistent with this. The estimates for lags 3, 10, and 11 are suspiciously large. Yet, any induced correlation appears to be too small to give an observed runs statistic seriously inconsistent with the absence of serial correlation. Nor does the observed value of the Box-Pierce statistic—which is based on the estimated autocorrelation coefficients—seem particularly bothersome. Nevertheless, we should probably be prepared to see evidence consistent with a weak nonstationarity in $E[\Delta\tilde{y}(t)]$, at least within the sample at hand.

Estimation results from applying (7.81) to EPS are given in Table 7-3. The first row of results is for the unconstrained model. The second row is for (7.81) with the constraint $\beta_3' = 0.0$. The third row is for the constraint $\beta_2' = 0.0$.

These estimation results for EPS are not solidly consistent with $\beta_2' = 0.0$, which is implied by $\beta_2 = 1.0$. The estimated value of β_2', -0.278, is almost twice the estimated standard error of $\hat{\tilde{\beta}}_2'$, 0.143. Moreover, the estimate of β_3, 0.009, is close to three times the estimated standard error of $\hat{\tilde{\beta}}_3$. The time variable may be picking up serial correlation in $\tilde{v}(t)$ which is due to $\beta_2 \neq 1.0$; see the development surrounding expression (7.79), above.

If $\beta_2 \neq 1.0$ for EPS, then the first differences of EPS are serially correlated. Thus, part of the explanation for the estimation results for (7.81) applied to EPS may turn on nonzero sample correlations between the "independent" variables $\Delta\tilde{y}(t-1)$ and t, which is due to both variables' being correlated over time. If so, then improved results should obtain when (7.81) is estimated with the constraint $\beta_3 = 0.0$. The results presented in the middle row of Table 7-3 seem to be consistent with this. Conditional on the constrained

TABLE 7-3

ESTIMATION RESULTS FOR FIRST DIFFERENCES OF CATERPILLAR TRACTOR'S ANNUAL EPS FOR THE 52-YEAR PERIOD 1925–1976
THE MODEL APPLIED IS $\Delta\tilde{y}(t) = \beta_1' + \beta_2'\Delta y(t-1) + \beta_3' t + \tilde{e}(t)$, WHERE $t = 1$ FOR 1925

Constraint	$\hat{\beta}_1'$	$S(\hat{\beta}_1')$	$t(\hat{\beta}_1')$	$\hat{\beta}_2'$	$S(\hat{\beta}_2')$	$t(\hat{\beta}_2')$	$\hat{\beta}_3'$	$S(\hat{\beta}_3')$	$t(\hat{\beta}_3')$	$\hat{\sigma}_e$	$\bar{R}^2$	$\hat{\rho}_1(\tilde{e}(t))$[1]
None	−.141	.097	−1.451	−.278	.143	−1.939	.009	.003	2.845	.322	.127	−.020
$\beta_3' = 0.0$	.100	.051	1.981	−.136	.144	−.946				.345	.000	.002
$\beta_2' = 0.0$	−.106	.098	−1.083				.007	.003	2.252	.331	.077	−.275

[1]This column provides estimated values of the lag-1 serial correlation coefficients. Values at other lags for the results in rows 1 and 2 are given in Exhibits 7-10 and 7-9, respectively.

model (7.81), these results are consistent with $\beta_2' = 0.0$, which implies, in turn, that they are consistent with $\beta_2 = 1.0$, or at least a value of β_2 near 1.0. The results in the last row of Table 7-3 are consistent with nonzero correlation between "time" and $\Delta\tilde{y}(t)$, and thus they are consistent with the reasoning that led to the constrained version (i.e., $\beta_3' = 0.0$) of (7.81) for EPS. The results in this last row are based on (7.81) with the constraint $\beta_2' = 0.0$.

As before, it is important to apply some diagnostic checks to the estimated model's results. Results from analyses of residuals for (7.81) applied to EPS are given in Exhibits 7-9 and 7-10. Exhibit 7-9 is for model (7.81) with the constraint $\beta_3' = 0.0$. Exhibit 7-10 is for that model without any constraints.

That there are inconsistencies between the sample evidence and the model's specifications seems clear from these exhibits. For example, there are signs in Exhibit 7-9 of serial correlation in the constrained model's disturbance, conditional on the evidence at hand. Note, for example, that all of the first 24 residuals are below zero. Also note the seemingly large estimated serial correlation coefficients at lags 3, 10, and 11, relative to the theoretical "large sample" standard error of roughly $(N)^{-1/2} \approx 0.14$. Inclusion of the time variable seems to induce smaller estimates at these and other lags, as is indicated in Exhibit 7-10. But the observed value of the Runs statistic (-1.992) is just as bothersome here as in the constrained case (-1.211). These results are, on balance, consistent with the view that β_2 is not exactly 1.0 and, therefore, with the view that model (7.81) is not well specified, especially insofar as the characteristics of its disturbance, $\tilde{v}(t)$, are concerned. And, of course, a shift in the variability of $\tilde{v}(t)$ seems just as evident as did a shift in the variability of EPS itself and $\tilde{\epsilon}(t)$ in the ARIMA(1, 0, 0) model given in (7.77) for EPS.

It is important to remember, however, that our tentative inference is that EPS is nearly nonstationary (i.e., $\beta_2 \approx 1.0$ in (7.77)). Thus, it should come as no surprise that results based on (7.77) are not wholly consistent with $\beta_2 = 1.0$. Perhaps we should be more excited about this model's doing as well as it does.

Additional support for modeling EPS as if $\beta_2 = 1.0$ is correct is provided by the extensive simulation results presented by Gonedes and Roberts [1977c] in their paper on the nearly nonstationary first-order autoregressive model. They note that the traditional rationale for first differencing is to attain stationarity. This is what underlay our analysis of EPS's first differences. But Gonedes' and Roberts' work point to a complementary rationale: if one suspects near nonstationarity of the AR(1, 0, 0) process, if one's sample size is not too large, and if good one-step-ahead prediction performance is the goal, then it seems wise to difference one's observations and to treat these differences as observations on a stationary AR(1, 0, 0) process. And their finite-sample results suggest that Ordinary Least Squares estimators of the AR(1, 0, 0) model applied to the differenced data perform quite satisfactorily. Gonedes and Roberts also note that differencing an already stationary (but "nearly" nonstationary) process can be motivated by Bayesian concepts: differencing can be viewed as an easy way to incorporate nondiffuse prior judgment—that the process is nearly nonstationary—into one's analysis. For the kinds of data often encountered in empirical economics, such as accounting income numbers, this is a compelling argument. In any event, the observed inconsistencies between model (7.81) applied to EPS and the sample evidence, by themselves, should not be taken as sufficient reason to reject the model. As indicated earlier in Section 7.3, some inconsistencies between a model and

EXHIBIT 7-9

SELECTED DIAGNOSTICS FOR RESIDUALS FROM THE ESTIMATED MODEL $\Delta\tilde{y}(t) = \beta_1' + \beta_2'\Delta\tilde{y}(t-1) + \tilde{\epsilon}(t)$ BASED ON FIRST DIFFERENCES OF CATERPILLAR TRACTOR'S ANNUAL EARNINGS-PER-SHARE FOR THE 52 YEARS 1925–1976.

OBS. IN ROW 51 AN OUTLIER; PLOTTED AS 5.2

SEQUENCE PLOT OF STANDARDIZED VALUES OF 'RESIDU'

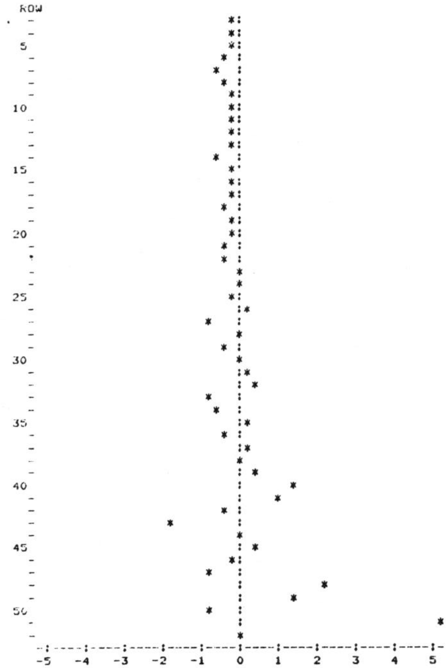

ORDER	SERIAL CORRELATION
1	+0.002
2	+0.094
3	+0.426
4	-0.036
5	-0.128
6	-0.023
7	+0.137
8	-0.156
9	+0.185
10	+0.387
11	+0.478
12	+0.099

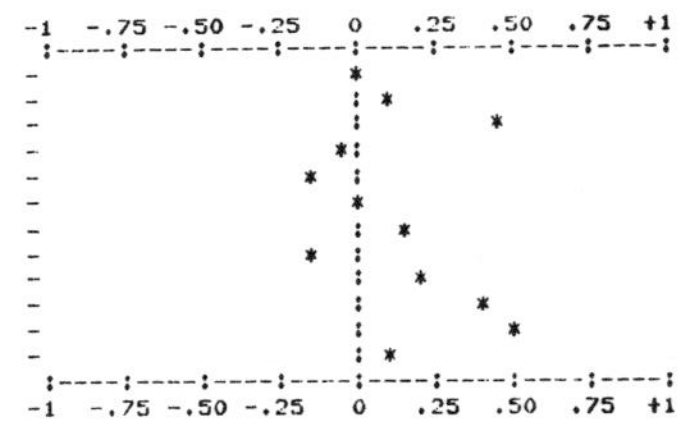

```
SERIES: RESIDU
BASED ON  50     ACTIVE OBSERVATIONS
(FIRST ACTIVE ROW =  3      , LAST ACTIVE ROW =  52   )

   OBSERVED NUMBER OF RUNS =  17
   EXPECTED NUMBER OF RUNS =  20.24
 STANDARD DEVIATION OF RUNS =  2.67619
     (OBS.-EXP.)/(STD.DEV.) = -1.21068

SERIES: RESIDU

----------------------+-----++--+-+-+++--++--++-+-

+ = value > mean
- = value < = mean
Mean =  0
```

HISTOGRAM

ABS. FREQ.

15

EXHIBIT 7-10

SELECTED DIAGNOSTICS FOR RESIDUALS FROM THE ESTIMATED MODEL $\Delta\tilde{y}(t) = \beta_1' + \beta_2'\Delta\tilde{y}(t-1) + \beta_3't + \tilde{\epsilon}(t)$ BASED ON FIRST DIFFERENCES OF CATERPILLAR TRACTOR'S ANNUAL EARNINGS-PER-SHARE FOR THE 52 YEARS 1925–1976.

```
> RUNS
* VARIABLE ? RESIDU

   OBSERVED NUMBER OF RUNS =  19
   EXPECTED NUMBER OF RUNS =  25.96
STANDARD DEVIATION OF RUNS =  3.49356
    (OBS.-EXP.)/(STD.DEV.) = -1.99224

SERIES: RESIDU

++++-++++++-++-------++-+----++-------++---+--++-++

+ = value > mean
- = value < = mean
Mean =  0

FIRST ACTIVE ROW IS 3        LAST ACTIVE ROW IS 52


> SERC
* VARIABLE ? 12
NO DATA IN COL(S). 12   THROUGH 19
ISSUE 'NAME' FOR VARIABLE LIST
ISSUE 'SERC' AT FIRST PROMPT LEVEL FOR EXPLANATION.

> SERC
* VARIABLE ? RESIDU
* MAX. ORDER : 12


         SERIAL
ORDER  CORRELATION    -1   -.75 -.50 -.25   0    .25  .50  .75  +1
                       :----:----:----:----:----:----:----:----:
  1      -0.020       -                    *
  2      -0.008       -                    *
  3      +0.295       -                    :     *
  4      -0.136       -                 *  :
  5      -0.240       -               *    :
  6      -0.156       -                 *  :
  7      -0.028       -                   *:
  8      -0.241       -               *    :
  9      +0.052       -                    :*
 10      +0.262       -                    :    *
 11      +0.332       -                    :      *
 12      -0.043       -                   *:
                       :----:----:----:----:----:----:----:----:
                      -1   -.75 -.50 -.25   0    .25  .50  .75  +1

SERIES: RESIDU
BASED ON  50    ACTIVE OBSERVATIONS
(FIRST ACTIVE ROW =  3     , LAST ACTIVE ROW =   52    )
```

available evidence are always to be expected. The critical question is: how well does the model do relative to available alternatives?

All of the above results are based on the first-order autoregressive model—applied to both undifferenced and first-differenced EPS. That is, they are based on the ARIMA models with (p, d, q) equal to (1, 0, 0) and (1, 1, 0). It is, of course, possible that a different specification of values for p, d, and q will lead to an improved characterization of EPS. In view of this, several alternative specifications were considered. Table 7-4 provides estimation results based on several of these. As can be seen, the ARIMA(2, 1, 2) and the ARIMA(0, 1, 2) models provide characterizations that have about as much explanatory power as the first-order model applied to EPS. This judgment is based on the estimated standard deviation of the models' disturbances. An analysis of residuals for each of these alternatives suggested that these alternatives are about as well specified as the first-order model applied to EPS. Selected results based on the residuals for the ARIMA(2, 1, 2) model are given in Exhibit 7-11. By now, the reader should be able to interpret these types of results.

In summary, it appears that the ARIMA(1, 0, 0) model—or something close to it—leads to a characterization of EPS that performs reasonably well relative to a variety of alternatives. It also appears that EPS is a nearly nonstationary process. There are some inconsistencies between the sample evidence and the nearly nonstationary ARIMA(1, 0, 0) model applied to EPS. But they are not so strong that they lead to dominance by the alternatives considered here.

As indicated earlier, there is evidence of a shift in the mean and the variability of EPS. We did little to deal with this, since doing so seems beyond the scope of this illustrative exercise. The purpose of this exercise is to give the reader some feel for some basics of time series analysis, particularly the kinds of problems that one is likely to encounter; it is not to find the "best" model for Caterpillar's EPS. Indeed, there may be no one model that is appropriate for EPS over the time period examined here—which includes both pre- and post-World War II years. A complete analysis would involve exploring this and other plausible alternatives—by exploiting, for example, firm-specific and industry background material as well as material dealing with the economy as a whole. Such an analysis might lead one to analyze separately the first and second halves of the observations on EPS, on the assumption that important structural changes had occurred.

If our nearly nonstationary first-order model is adopted as a descriptive model for

TABLE 7-4

SELECTED ESTIMATION RESULTS FOR ALTERNATIVE ARIMA (p, d, q) MODELS APPLIED TO CATERPILLAR TRACTOR'S ANNUAL EPS FOR THE 52-YEAR PERIOD 1925–1976

Model (p, d, q)	$\hat{\delta}$	$\hat{\phi}_1$	$\hat{\phi}_2$	$\hat{\theta}_1$	$\hat{\theta}_2$	$\hat{\sigma}_e$
2, 1, 2	.082	.293	−.155	.509	−.546	.338
1, 1, 1	.089	−.031		.102		.345
0, 1, 2	.097			.307	−.364	.338
1, 1, 0[1]	.099	−.136				.342
2, 1, 0	.097	−.132	.056			.345

[1]Additional results for ARIMA(1, 1, 0) are given in Table 7-3.

EXHIBIT 7-11

SELECTED DIAGNOSTICS FOR RESIDUALS FROM ESTIMATED ARIMA(2, 1, 2) MODEL BASED ON CATERPILLAR TRACTOR'S ANNUAL EARNINGS-PER-SHARE FOR THE 52 YEARS 1925–1976.

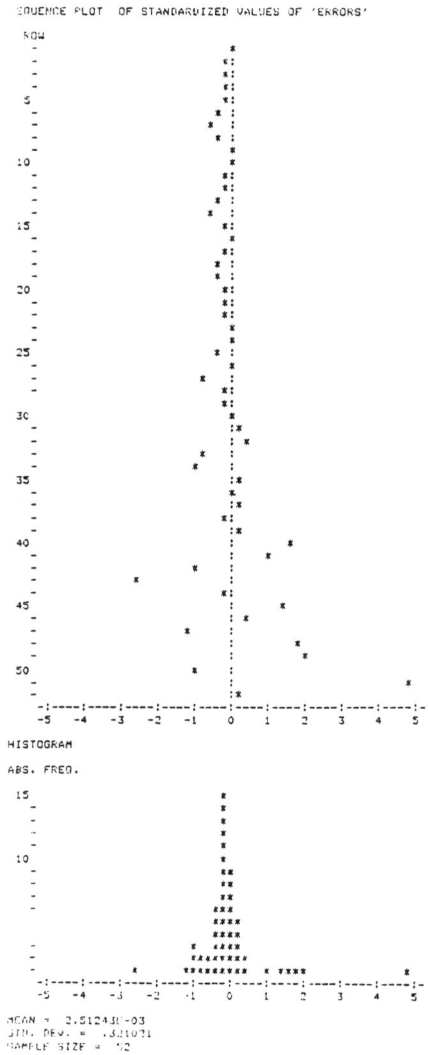

ORDER	SERIAL CORRELATION
1	+0.024
2	-0.099
3	+0.215
4	+0.049
5	+0.046
6	+0.013
7	-0.013
8	-0.208
9	+0.123
10	+0.338
11	+0.322
12	-0.004

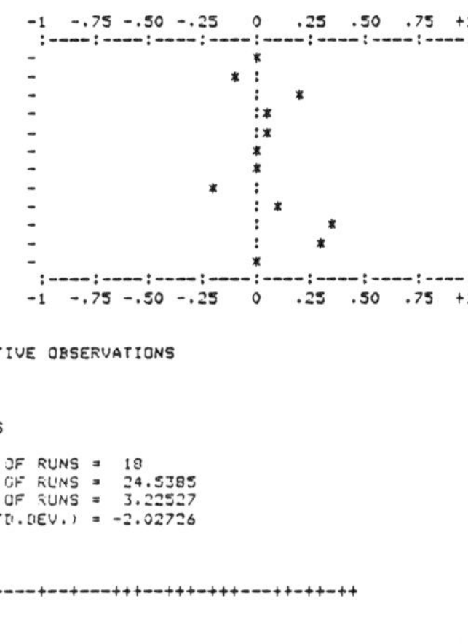

```
SERIES: ERRORS
BASED ON  52    ACTIVE OBSERVATIONS

> RUNS
* VARIABLE ? ERRORS

   OBSERVED NUMBER OF RUNS =  18
   EXPECTED NUMBER OF RUNS =  24.5385
STANDARD DEVIATION OF RUNS =  3.22527
    (OBS.-EXP.)/(STD.DEV.) = -2.02726

SERIES: ERRORS

---------+-------------+--+----++--+++-+++----+-++-++

+ = value > mean
- = value < = mean
Mean =  2.51243E-03
```

EPS—with full recognition of its limitations—then an appropriate forecaster of EPS is given by the model:

$$\tilde{y}(t) = \tilde{y}(t-1) + \tilde{\eta}(t), \tag{7.82}$$

where $\tilde{\eta}(t)$ is a disturbance. The forecast of EPS conditional on its past values for the periods up to and including period $t - 1$ is then:

$$E[\tilde{y}(t + k)|y(t - 1), y(t - 2), \ldots] = y(t - 1)$$

for all $k \geq 0$. Conditional on the evidence at hand, discrepancies between this model and EPS appear to turn on a seemingly slight drift in $\Delta\tilde{y}(t)$ or a discrete shift in the value of $E[\tilde{y}(t)]$ for the stationary first-order model—with β_2 close to unity but still $|\beta_2| < 1.0$. It will be seen that much of the available evidence on firms' annual income numbers points to essentially the same type of model, or something close to it. Our next task is to survey this evidence.

Before proceeding to that survey, we must introduce some frequently encountered jargon. If, in model (7.82), $E[\tilde{\eta}(t)|y(t - 1)] = 0.0$, then, as indicated, $E[\tilde{y}(t)|y(t - 1)] = y(t - 1)$. This is known as the strict *martingale* model. If $E[\tilde{\eta}(t)|y(t - 1)] \geq 0$ ($<$ 0), then $E\tilde{\eta}(t)|y(t - 1)] \geq y(t - 1)$ ($< y(t - 1)$. This is known as a (lower) *semimartingale*.[31] If $\{\tilde{\eta}(t)\}$ is a sequence of independent and identically distributed random variables with $E[\tilde{\eta}(t)] = 0.0$, then $\{\tilde{y}(t)\}$ is said to follow a *random walk*. If the latter conditions hold with $E[\tilde{\eta}(t)] = \delta$, a constant, then $\{\tilde{y}(t)\}$ is said to follow a *random walk with drift,* with a drift factor equal to δ. Thus, each random walk model is a special version of a martingale model. To obtain the random walk model, distributional conditions are specified for $\{\tilde{\eta}(t)\}$.

7.4.1.7 Some Evidence on the Time Series Properties of Annual Income Numbers

This section provides a review of some available evidence on annual accounting income (and related) numbers. Our review is not intended to cover all available studies. Moreover, it covers only studies that modeled accounting numbers in terms of past values of those numbers. Studies that used "explanatory" variables other than past values of the numbers being modeled will be discussed at a later point. The studies covered are considered to be "classics" in this area.

The first study to be reviewed was conducted by Watts [1970]. His main interest was in the informational content of dividends. An examination of income numbers was one part of his work.

Watts attempted to model income numbers by using the class of models defined by expression (7.64); i.e., the class of autoregressive integrated moving average models. For given values of p, d, and q, he estimated the parameters of his models by using the estimation procedures described by Box and Jenkins [1976]. His objective was to identify the most adequate model for each firm in his sample.

Watts' sample contained 32 firms from the sample used by King [1966] in his examination of market and industry effects on common stocks' rates of return. The income number examined for each firm was Available for Common.[32] For each firm, Watts had 38 observations on its annual income number. These observations were for the years 1927–1964, inclusive.

Watts' sample is by no means a representative one. It includes firms from only three industries (railroads, petroleum companies, and companies in the metals industry, primarily steel companies). Moreover, his sample consists of firms that managed to survive over a fairly long period of time.

---

[31]When $E[\tilde{y}(t)|y(t - 1)] \geq y(t - 1)$ holds, the process is often called a submartingale.

[32]Available for Common is essentially Net Income minus dividends paid on preferred stock. On the annual Industrial COMPUSTAT data file, it is "date item" no. 20.

The models identified and estimated by Watts, for the firms in his sample, are given in Table 7-5. His estimate of the models' parameters and the estimated standard errors of the autoregressive and moving average parameters are also given there. Recall that the class of models in use is defined by:[33]

$$\tilde{z}_t = \phi_1\tilde{z}_{t-1} + \phi_2\tilde{z}_{t-2} + \ldots + \phi_p\tilde{z}_{t-p} + \tilde{\epsilon}_t + \theta_0$$
$$- \theta_1\tilde{\epsilon}_{t-1} - \theta\,\tilde{\epsilon}_{t-2} - \ldots - \theta_q\tilde{\epsilon}_{t-q} \,, \tag{7.83}$$

where θ_0 denotes a constant term and $\tilde{z}_t \equiv \Delta^d\tilde{y}_t$. In Table 7-5, σ_{ϕ_1} denotes the standard error of the estimate of ϕ_1, σ_{ϕ_2} denotes the standard error of the estimate of ϕ_2, etc. A summary of the types of models identified and estimated by Watts is provided in Table 7-6.

There appears to be an industry effect, at least for the railroad and petroleum firms. Of the 10 railroad firms, only one does not have an identified model that is of the type $(p, d, q) = (1, 0, 0)$. And of the 11 petroleums, only three do not have identified models that are of the type (0, 1, 1), i.e., a first-order moving average model in the first differences. For the metals industry, eight firms have stationary autoregressive models (of the first or second order) and three firms have (0, 1, 1) models.

Consider the estimated values of the autoregressive parameters, wherever included (i.e., wherever $p > 0$). For the most part, the estimates (viewed relative to their estimated standard errors) are pretty close to unity. This suggests that these income processes are not violently different from nonstationary series. Of course, for the ARIMA(1, 0, 0) model this implies that the processes are not very different from martingale models, for which:

$$E[\tilde{y}_t|y_{t-1}] = y_{t-1} \,. \tag{7.84}$$

In some cases, the numbers did, in fact, have to be differenced. This occurred for the models of type (0, 1, 1) and (0, 1, 2). Since these models contain moving average terms, expression (7.84) does not apply to them. And note that, for the most part, the estimates of the moving average parameters (especially θ_1) do not appear to be trivial, relative to their estimated standard errors. This may be due to some slight drift in the unconditional mean of each process, as appeared to be the case for Caterpillar Tractor's earnings-per-share series. If so, we could say that the models are misspecified because the series to which they were applied are nonstationary series, at least with respect to their expected values. On the other hand, it may be that the series is stationary and that the moving average terms really do induce more descriptively valid models.

Some insights on the importance of the moving average terms can be obtained by estimating the following model for each firm:

$$\Delta\tilde{y}_t = \theta_0 + \epsilon_t - \theta_1\epsilon_{t-1} \,. \tag{7.85}$$

That is, we can assume at the outset that each firm's numbers are drawings from a first-order moving average process in the first differences. The estimates of θ_1 obtained by Watts for (7.85) are presented in Table 7-7. For the railroads, the moving average parameter appears to be of little importance; this is consistent with the results presented in Table

---

[33]The notations $\tilde{z}(t)$ and $\tilde{z}_t$ will be used interchangeably. The same convention applies to other stochastic processes.

TABLE 7-5

MODELS IDENTIFIED FOR AVAILABLE FOR COMMON FOR 32 FIRMS 1927–1964

Firm No.	Name	Model *pdq*	Parameters									
			ϕ_1	$\sigma_{\phi 1}$	ϕ_2	$\sigma_{\phi 2}$	θ_1	σ_{θ_1}	θ_2	σ_{θ_2}	θ_2	$\sigma_{\theta 0}$
1	Chesapeake & Ohio Railroad	100	.70	.12							142.7	58.7
2	Southern Pacific	100	.92	.09							120.1	107.2
3	Atchison, Topeka Santa Fe	100	.87	.09							240.3	172.7
4	Louisville & Nashville Railroad	100	.77	.11							147.3	77.2
5	Kansas City, Southern Ind.	100	.94	.06							61.5	50.2
6	Missouri, Kansas, Texas Railroad	100	.74	.13							−96.7	58.2
7	Northern Pacific	100	.82	.10							94.1	170.9
8	Union Pacific Railroad	100	.93	.08							198.6	60.6
9	New York Central Railroad	201	1.24	.17	−.62	.13	.57	.21			82.9	28.1
10	Reading Co.	100	.86	.10							5.6	49.3
11	Conoco	011					.39	.17			53.1	18.2

12	Standard Oil Co. of New Jersey	011					−.14	.17			110.1	56.2
13	Texaco	011					−.26	.17			151.4	185.6
14	Atlantic Refining	011					.60	.14			112.8	61.6
15	Pure Oil	200	.67	.17	.27	.17					178.0	150.2
16	Shell Oil	011					.19	.20			49.6	21.6
17	Skelly Oil	100	.93	.06							174.5	120.0
18	Mobil Oil Corp.	012					−.20	.17	.25	.16	7.1	3.7
19	Sun Oil	011					.57	.14			171.1	50.2
20	Tidewater	011					.62	.14			8.2	5.5
21	Union Oil	011					−.11	.17			15.7	10.9
22	Republic Steel	100	.92	.08							32.7	31.7
23	American Smelting & Refining Co.	100	.79	.12							412.3	234.9
24	Amsted Ind.	011					.71	.12			15.9	12.8
25	Bethlehem Steel Corp.	100	.94	.07							73.7	54.5
26	Calumet & Hecla, Inc.	200	.77	.17	−.17	.17					52.3	32.3
27	Inland Steel Co.	011					.11	.18			171.1	101.9
28	Inspiration Consolidated Copper	100	.78	.11							77.8	42.3
29	Interlake Steel Co.	011					.53	.17			22.8	17.2
30	Magma Copper Co.	200	.70	.19	.29	.21					52.1	63.4
31	U.S. Steel Corp.	100	.86	.09							193.2	142.1
32	Vanadium	100	.69	.12							28.6	24.4

Source: Watts [1970, table 3-1].

TABLE 7-6

SUMMARY OF TABLE 7-2: NUMBER OF TIMES EACH MODEL TYPE WAS IDENTIFIED AND ESTIMATED

Group	Total # of Firms in Group	Model Type (p, d, q)				
		(1, 0, 0)	(0, 1, 1)	(0, 1, 2)	(2, 0, 1)	(2, 0, 0)
Railroads	10	9	0	0	1	0
Petroleums	11	1	8	1	0	1
Metals	11	6	3	0	0	2
All Firms	32	16	11	1	1	3

TABLE 7-7

DISTRIBUTION OF θ_1 WHEN FIRST-ORDER MOVING AVERAGE PROCESSES IN THE FIRST DIFFERENCES WERE ESTIMATED FOR 32 FIRMS OVER THE YEARS 1927–1964

Industry	No. of Firms	Mean	t-Value					
			Mean	Fractile				
				.1	.25	.50	.75	.9
Railroad	10	.01	.09	−1.29	−.59	.17	.71	1.24
Petroleum	11	.18	1.27	−2.61	−.10	.95	4.11	4.48
Metal	11	.22	1.46	−.48	.19	.78	2.61	5.64
Total	32	.14	.97	−1.20	−.18	.71	1.72	4.24

Source: Watts [1970, table 3-3].

7-5. For several firms in the petroleum and metals group, the estimates of θ_1 appear to be important, relative to the estimates of their standard errors.

The results in Table 7-7 are based on (7.85), which includes the constant term. Watts inferred that the models' constant terms were, for the most part, insignificantly different from zero. So, he also estimated (7.85) without the constant term. That led to a reduction in the number of estimates of θ_1 that were significantly different from zero. But the general picture was much the same as that presented in Table 7-7.

At this point, the major message consistent with Watts' results seems to be that the income numbers of the firms examined appear to be drawings from a process close to one for which:

$$E(\tilde{y}_t | y_{t-1}) = \delta + y_{t-1} , \tag{7.86}$$

that is, a martingale ($\delta = 0$), semimartingale ($\delta > 0$), or lower semimartingale ($\delta < 0$) model. The major observed departure from the implications of this model revolves around the importance of moving average terms.

Our examination of Caterpillar Tractor's EPS series led to two observations: (a) there appeared to be some indication of nonstationarity in the mean of the differenced series, and (b) there was a strong indication of a change in the variability of the series. As indicated earlier, if the first observation applies to the firms in Watts' sample, it can explain the role of the moving average term. Thus far we have not discussed the applicability or importance of the second observation. As for importance, we shall not go into technical details here. Suffice it to say that if the second observation applied to Watts' sample, then the estimated standard errors reported in Table 7-5 would not be very meaningful, because their computation assumes constant variances.

In order to deal with the second issue, Watts examined some aspects of residuals computed with the identified models given in Table 7-5. For each firm, he divided the series of residuals into two parts, each with about the same number of observations. He then conducted an F-test for equality of the variances estimated with the two subsets of residuals. He also conducted a t-test for equality of the means estimated conditionally on each subset of residuals. The results from these tests are reported in Table 7-8.[34]

For the first ten firms (the railroads), the results of the F-test appear to be consistent with the assumption of variance stationarity. The results for the 11th through the 32nd firms are less comforting. Relative to the critical value (approximately 3.25) of $\tilde{F}$ at the .01 level of significance, the observed values of $\tilde{F}$ are often somewhat large. On balance, it seems difficult to infer that these results are consistent with variance stationarity.

For the first ten firms, the results of the t-test do not appear to be inconsistent with the postulated equality of means. The results for the remaining firms are more difficult to interpret, because the test assumes variance stationarity.

The final stage of Watts' investigation involved an examination of prediction performance over the four-year period, 1965–1968. This examination was based on all firms with at least one observation for that period; 31 firms from the original sample of 32 firms had one such observation.[35]

For each firm in the analysis, annual forecasts for the period 1965–1968 were obtained using the identified model for that firm (see Table 7-5). The lead time for each forecast was one year; e.g., the 1965 forecast was made conditional on all available data on "independent" variables for 1964 and years prior to 1964. The parameters of the identified model were not reestimated, however. The properties of the forecasts from the identified models were compared to those from the following two "naive" models:

$$\hat{y}_{t+1} = y_t + \frac{y_t - y_l}{t} \tag{7.87}$$

$$\hat{y}_{t+1} = y_t \, , \tag{7.88}$$

for $t = 38, 39, \ldots, 42$. (Note that $t = 1$ refers to 1927, $t = 2$ to 1928, etc.) $\hat{y}_{t+1}$ denotes the forecast of $\tilde{y}_{t+1}$ conditional on the past values of $\tilde{y}$. That is, $\hat{y}_{t+1} = E(\tilde{y}_{t+1} | y_t, y_{t-1}, \ldots)$. Model 7.88 corresponds to a martingale model. Model (7.87) corresponds to a martingale

---

[34]Observe that the results in this table are for univariate tests. In principle, a multivariate test should have been used here, if one wants to make a joint inference for all firms in the sample. Such a test might lead to different inferences in those cases where one rejects the null hypothesis via a univariate test. In order to avoid too many unwarranted inferences, we shall use a significance level of .01, the higher of the two conventional levels (.05 and .01).

[35]The firm for which no observations were available, for 1965–1968, was Pure Oil, which was taken over in early 1965. Tidewater had one observation before it was taken over. New York Central and Calumet & Hecla each had three available observations. Complete data were available for the other firms.

TABLE 7-8

F-TEST PARAMETERS FOR VARIANCES OF THE RESIDUALS AND *T*-TEST PARAMETERS FOR THE MEANS OF THE RESIDUALS FROM THE ESTIMATION OF THE PROCESSES IDENTIFIED IN TABLE 7-5 WHEN THE RESIDUALS FOR EACH FIRM ARE SEPARATED INTO TWO APPROXIMATELY EQUAL SAMPLES

Firm No.	F $\sigma_1^2 < \sigma_2^2$	Degrees of Freedom Period 1	Degrees of Freedom Period 2	t $u_1 - u_2$
1	1.82	17	18	−1.61
2	.29	17	18	−1.19
3	.53	17	18	−1.76
4	2.16	17	18	−1.22
5	1.22	17	18	−.45
6	1.37	17	18	−.12
7	.55	17	18	−1.48
8	.85	17	18	−1.63
9	1.05	17	17	−.99
10	1.20	17	18	.85
11	1.44	17	18	−1.70
12	5.76	17	18	−1.41
13	1.56	17	18	−2.97
14	2.89	17	18	−1.25
15	4.29	17	17	−1.15
16	2.45	17	18	−1.77
17	7.60	17	18	−1.37
18	1.97	17	18	−1.59
19	6.60	17	18	−1.97
20	3.58	17	18	−.10
21	5.32	17	18	−1.43
22	1.29	17	18	−1.91
23	3.33	17	18	−1.94
24	1.22	17	18	−.85
25	2.86	17	18	−1.41
26	1.03	17	18	−1.83
27	4.05	17	18	−1.39
28	1.56	17	18	−1.84
29	2.70	17	18	−1.45
30	26.40	17	18	−1.12
31	1.36	17	18	−1.64
32	5.47	17	18	−1.20

Note: Probability $(F_{18,17} \geq 2.26 | \sigma_1^2 = \sigma_2^2) = .05$
Probability $(F_{17,17} \geq 2.28 | \sigma_1^2 = \sigma_2^2) = .05$
Probability $(F_{18,17} \geq 3.22 | \sigma_1^2 = \sigma_1^2) = .01$
Probability $(F_{17,17} \geq 3.25 | \sigma_1^2 = \sigma_2^2) = .01$
Probability $(t_{35} \geq 1.68 | u_1 = u_2, \sigma_1^2 = \sigma_2^2) = .05$
Probability $(t_{34} \geq 1.69 | u_1 = u_2, \sigma_1^2 = \sigma_2^2) = .05$
Probability $(t_{35} \geq 2.43 | u_1 = u_2, \sigma_1^2 = \sigma_2^2) = .01$
Probability $(t_{34} \geq 2.43 | u_1 = u_2, \sigma_1^2 = \sigma_2^2) = .01$.

Source: Watts [1970, table 3-2].

model with a constant. In model (7.87), $(y_t - y_l)/t$ represents an estimate of the expected value of the first difference, $\tilde{y}_{t+1} - y_t$, conditional on the first observation, y_l and on y_t.

For each firm, the annual prediction errors, $\tilde{y}_t - \hat{y}_t$, $t = 39, 40, \ldots, 42$, were squared and summed. The sums of squared errors were used in assessing the alternative models—i.e., the identified models and models (7.87) and (7.88). The results are summarized in Tables 7-9, 7-10, and 7-11.

Using Table 7-9, it can be seen that the identified models are not dramatically better than models (7.87) or (7.88), in terms of the total rankings of the models. In terms of the number of times each model was assigned a rank of 1—indicating that the model had the minimum sum of squared errors—the identified models seem to do better than the alternatives. But the results presented in Table 7-10 suggest that this does not reflect a situation in which the magnitudes of the differences among the models' performance are very large. In short, these results provide additional support for the proposition that income numbers are generated by models that are similar to the martingale model, perhaps with a constant term.

The results in Table 7-11 pertain to the firms having identified models of type (0, 1,

TABLE 7-9

MODELS IDENTIFIED OVER THE PERIOD 1927–1964 FOR AVAILABLE FOR COMMON FOR 31 FIRMS COMPARED WITH NAIVE MODELS FOR PREDICTION, 1965–1968

(A) By Industry

	Identified Models		Martingale		Martingale + Average Charge	
	Sum of Ranks[a]	1st[b]	Sum of Ranks	1st	Sum of Ranks	1st
Railroads	18	6	18	2	24	2
Petroleum	20	4	26	0	14	6
Metals	21	6	20	3	25	2
Total	59	16	64	5	63	10

(B) By Model

	Identified Models		Martingale		Martingale + Average Charge	
	Sum of Ranks[a]	1st[b]	Sum of Ranks	1st	Sum of Ranks	1st
100	30	9	30	3	36	4
011	22	5	25	2	19	4
200	4	1	4	0	4	1
012	2	0	3	0	1	1
201	1	1	2	0	3	0
	59	16	64	5	63	10

[a]Each prediction model (identified, martingale, martingale + change) was placed 1, 2, or 3 for each firm, depending on which had the minimum sum of squared errors over the years 1965–68. Then the ranks were summed across firms.

[b]The number of 1sts is the number of firms for which the particular prediction model ranked 1st under the minimum sums of squares as described above.

Source: Watts [1970, table 3-4].

TABLE 7-10

COMPARISON OF IDENTIFIED MODELS AND NAIVE MODELS ON THE BASIS OF WEIGHTED SUMS OF SQUARED ERROR

	Weighted by Square Mean[a]	Weighted by Total Sum of Squares[b]
Identified Models	92.53	.135
Martingale	97.78	.159
Martingale plus Trend	98.89	.162

[a]Calculated as follows: $\sum_{i=1}^{31} \frac{\sum_{t=1}^{4} e_{it}^2}{(\bar{x}_i)^2}$

[b]Calculated as follows: $\sum_{i=1}^{31} \frac{\frac{\sum_{t=1}^{4} e_{it}^2}{\sum_{t=1}^{4} x_{it}^2}}{31}$

e_{it} forecast error for firm i in year t.
x_{it} earnings for firm i in year t.

Source: Watts [1970, table 3-5].

1) with an estimated value of θ_1 that was at least twice its estimated standard error. Recall that the moving average term, θ_1, seemed to be at the heart of the more important inadequacies of the martingale models in Watts' study.

The results in Table 7-11 suggest, once again, that the martingale models provide reasonably good descriptions of the processes generating annual income numbers.

But we probably should not make too much of the evidence provided by Watts when making generalizations about the processes that appear to have descriptive validity vis-à-vis annual income numbers. After all, this evidence is based on a small number of firms from each of only three industries. Moreover, it is based on firms that were required to have data for the entire period 1927–1968. This requirement introduces a "survival" bias.

TABLE 7-11

COMPARISON OF IDENTIFIED MODELS OF FIRMS, WHICH HAD θ_1 PARAMETERS MORE THAN TWO STANDARD ERRORS FROM ZERO IN 011 MODELS, WITH NAIVE MODELS FOR THOSE FIRMS

	Sum of Ranks	No. of 1sts	Weighted Sum of Squared Error[a]
Identified Models	19	2	.080
Martingale	16	2	.070
Martingale plus Trend	13	4	.067

[a]The basis of calculation is as per note b in table 7-10.
Source: Watts [1970, table 3-6].

We can, however, use evidence from studies that appear to be based on more representative studies. Two of these studies are reviewed below.[36]

If annual income (or related) numbers are drawings from a process close to a martingale:

$$\tilde{y}(t) = y(t-1) + \tilde{\epsilon}(t), \tag{7.89}$$

or a semimartingale:

$$\tilde{y}(t) = \theta_0 + y(t-1) + \tilde{\epsilon}(t), \tag{7.90}$$

where θ_0 is a constant, then the disturbance, $\tilde{\epsilon}(t)$, should be an independently distributed random variable. Thus, one way of assessing the descriptive validity of (7.89) or (7.90) is to examine the correlation structure of first differences of income numbers. Evidence on this issue was provided by Ball and Watts [1972].

The Ball and Watts study is an extensive examination of the time series properties of income and related numbers. Four number series were examined: (i) Net income after taxes, (ii) Earnings per share, (iii) Net income divided by total assets, and (iv) Net sales.

In order to be included in the Ball/Watts sample, a firm must have been included in Standard and Poor's Annual Industrial CØMPUSTAT file and the firm must have had annual data in this file for the entire period 1947–1966. This data requirement was applied separately for each number series examined. In general, their results are based on 600–700 firms, with the exact number of firms depending on the number series.

Ball and Watts conducted a variety of tests for serial correlation of the first differences of net income (after taxes) and earnings-per-share. On balance, their results were consistent with the serial independence of changes in each of the examined series.

Ball and Watts also examined the extent to which the expected values of the numbers could be described by deterministic functions of time; they allowed for linear and quadratic dependencies on time. In addition, they considered simple partial adjustment models which do not incorporate deterministic time dependencies.

On balance, the results of their tests are consistent with the statement that the three income series are generated by processes close to martingales, perhaps with a constant drift.[37] The sale series behaved in a similar way, with the drift term being of somewhat greater importance.

We find, therefore, that the main thrust of the evidence presented in Watts' study is also the main thrust of the Ball/Watts study, which is based on a larger sample and a larger number of industrial groupings. It appears that the semimartingale and the martingale, which is a special case of the former, are models with a relatively high degree of descriptive validity vis-à-vis annual income (and related) accounting numbers. It is, however, not obvious that the more demanding distributional requirements of the random walk model are satisfied by these numbers.

Additional evidence on the time series properties of annual income numbers is provided by Watts and Leftwich [1977] in an extension and updating of the evidence provided

---

[36]Other studies that provide results on annual income (or related) numbers include Fama and Babiak [1968], Brealey [1967], Lintner and Glauber [1967], Beaver [1970], and Albrecht, Lookabill, and McKeown [1976], among others.

[37]The model would be of the form: $\tilde{y}_t = \theta_0 + y_{t-1} + \tilde{\epsilon}_t$, where θ_0 is a constant and $\tilde{\epsilon}_t$ is a disturbance having the usually specified properties.

by Watts [1970]. The Watts/Leftwich sample consists of the same 32 firms included in Watts' sample; the same income number, Available for Common, is the number examined. The data used by Watts were for the years 1927–1964. The data used in the Watts/Leftwich paper consist of all available observations, for each firm, for years prior to 1927 and after 1964 (up to and including 1974) using *Moody's Transportation* and *Moody's Industrial Manuals* as sources of data. The first and last years of data for each firm are given in Table 7-12. The minimum number of observations for a firm is 47; the maximum is 67. The Watts/Leftwich inferences are conditional on four sets of estimation/prediction results, based on four sets of observations for overlapping time periods: the first 38, 50, 55, and 60 observations for each firm. For these estimation periods, prediction results

TABLE 7-12

THE SAMPLE OF FIRMS AND THE YEARS AVAILABLE FOR ESTIMATION

Firm #	Firm Name (Most Recent)	Years Available	
		Start	End
1	Chesapeake & Ohio R'Road	1908	1974
2	Southern Pacific R'Road	1908	1974
3	Atchison, Topeka & Santa Fe R'Road	1908	1974
4	Louisville & Nashville R'Road	1908	1970
5	Kansas City, Southern Inds.	1908	1974
6	Missouri, Kansas & Texas R'Road	1908	1974
7	Northern Pacific R'Road	1908	1969
8	Union Pacific R'Road	1908	1974
9	New York Central R'Road	1908	1967
10	Reading Co.	1908	1974
11	Continental Oil	1919	1974
12	Exxon	1918	1974
13	Texaco Inc.	1910	1974
14	Atlantic Richfield	1912	1974
15	Pure Oil	1915	1964
16	Shell Oil	1922	1974
17	Skelly Oil	1920	1974
18	Mobil Oil Corp	1913	1974
19	Sun Oil	1921	1974
20	Tidewater	1910	1965
21	Union Oil	1910	1974
22	Republic Steel	1909	1974
23	Asarco	1911	1974
24	Amsted Industries	1908	1974
25	Bethlehem Steel Corp.	1908	1974
26	Calumet & Hecla Inc.	1917	1967
27	Inland Steel Co.	1910	1974
28	Inspiration Consolidated Copper	1916	1974
29	Interlake Inc.	1910	1974
30	Magma Copper Co.	1915	1968
31	U.S. Steel Corp.	1908	1974
32	Vanadium Corp.	1920	1966

Source: Watts and Leftwich [1976, table 1].

were obtained for the next 6, 5, 5, and 5 years, respectively. As in the Watts paper, the identification and estimation procedures for ARIMA models discussed by Box and Jenkins [1976] were used. Results based on estimated ARIMA models were compared to results based on the martingale model, with and without drift. The kinds of criteria used by Watts to evaluate relative predictive performance were also used by Watts and Leftwich. The three criteria used are based on squared values of forecast errors and absolute values of forecast errors. Finally, Watts and Leftwich attempted to determine whether the inferences that one might make for firms in general (on the basis of, e.g., cross-sectional summary results) would also be made on a firm-by-firm basis.

Some of their important inferences are as follows.

(I1) There are important inconsistencies between their sample evidence and two key specifications on the disturbance of the ARIMA class of models, *viz.*, that the values of the disturbance's ($\tilde{\epsilon}(t)$'s) mean and variance are constant over time. In view of this, Watts and Leftwich choose to weigh heavily the relative prediction performance—rather than the estimation results—of their identified ARIMA models.

(I2) On the basis of two of the three criteria used to evaluate relative prediction performance, a martingale model seems, on balance, to outperform the estimated ARIMA models. Moreover, the estimated ARIMA models—which yielded the minimum of squared residuals over the estimation periods—did not always provide forecasts with minimum squared errors. The cases for which this discrepancy is systematic constitute evidence inconsistent with stationarity of the estimated ARIMA models' parameters' values, and, thus, evidence consistent with structural changes in the stochastic processes examined. These inferences were further supported by additional prediction-performance analyses of ARIMA models that were "significantly" different from a martingale model on the basis of hypothesis tests applied to estimation results. Indeed, Watts and Leftwich observe that "the relative performance of the identified [ARIMA] models is 'worse' the higher the probability level at which the [martingale model] could be rejected. The result is very reminiscent of the 'regression fallacy'" [1976, p. 31].

(I3) For firms in general and on a firm-by-firm basis, it appears that the martingale model adequately characterizes the processes generating annual income numbers, relative to the alternatives considered—which consisted of the broad class of ARIMA models defined by expression (7.83), above.

In summary, this updated and more extensive version of Watts' [1970] investigation provides added support for viewing the martingale model as a descriptively adequate model of firms' income numbers. The various signs of changes in expected values and variances of disturbances suggest that the more specialized random walk model is not adequate.

7.4.2 Index Models of Annual Income Numbers

The time series models described above "explain" the behavior of income in period t in terms of income in periods $t - 1$, $t - 2$, etc. That is, the data set used to model income in period t consists only of past values of income. Of course, this is not the only data set available for use. There are a variety of other "independent" variables that can be used in modeling income numbers. But, as always, one should want to select variables—and a functional form—on the basis of the extent to which the resulting model represents a plausible depiction of the series being investigated; i.e., there is more involved here than simply grasping for independent variables. One class of models that seems to provide plausible depictions of accounting numbers is the class of so-called index models.

Index models represent attempts to describe firms' accounting numbers (e.g., income numbers, sales number, rates of return, etc.) by capitalizing on the effects of cross-sectional dependencies among the results of firms' operations (as represented by accounting numbers). Such cross-sectional dependencies can be expected for a variety of substantive economic reasons. For example, one might expect them because of macroeconomic events that operate within and across markets. Some specific (macroeconomic) sources of cross-sectional dependencies include changes in the economy's production technology, the effects of economic stabilization policies, and the resource flows and relative price changes associated with general equilibrium forces.

Observe that general economic forces need not affect all firms in the same way. The effect on any particular firm's operating results will depend on the nature of the firm's production/investment activities. For example, some aspects of stabilization policy changes may have a rapid and somewhat dramatic effect on some types of firms but not on others. The alleged sensitivity of the housing construction industry to changes in monetary policy is a pertinent example of this phenomenon. All of this provides some motivation for thinking in terms of industry factors as well as economy-wide factors, where an industry grouping is intended to represent firms with similar kinds of production/investment activities. Of course, if firms in a given industry are not identical in all respects, then one does not expect industry factors to have the same effect on each member firm's operations.

There are at least three related reasons for exploiting cross-sectional dependence with respect to firms' operations. First, this approach provides a basis for specifying statistical models for accounting numbers. If the resulting models exhibit stationary relationships over time and if economy-wide and industry factors can be predicted with sufficiently small prediction errors, then those models may serve as useful forecasting devices.

Another reason for recognizing cross-sectional dependencies is so that one can attempt to remove (or at least appreciate) the effects of these dependencies on cross-sectional distributions of estimation results. For example, one common procedure used in time series analyses of individual firms' accounting numbers involves estimating a time series model using each firm's data and then examining, or performing tests on, *cross-sectional* distributions of estimates (e.g., parameter estimates or estimates of disturbances). And these examinations and tests are usually conducted as if the cross-sectional observations were observations on independent random variables. If, however, there are cross-sectional dependencies among firms' accounting numbers, then such examinations and tests on these numbers (before adjustments for the dependencies) are, strictly speaking, inappropriate because the independence assumption is not satisfied.

A third reason for recognizing the effects of economy-wide and industry factors is because of the perspective that it provides *vis-à-vis* the results of firms' operations. These models lead one to recognize explicitly that the results of a firm's operations (as represented by accounting numbers) will reflect factors common to all firms as well as factors uniquely associated with the firm under investigation. If several firms are under investigation—which is the usual case in financial statement analysis—and if the effects of the commonalities are identified, then one can attempt to identify and explain the unique aspects of the results of a firm's operations. Such aspects may be attributable to managerial talent, special technological opportunities, special marketiing campaigns, and—of course—the accounting procedures which define that firm's accounting numbers, among other things.

Moreover, by identifying the effects of economy-wide and industry-wide factors on the results of a firm's operations, one can assess the extent to which forecasts and interpretations of that firm's operating results should be based on general economic and industry forces, rather than firm-specific forces. If, for example, a particular company's results appear to be heavily dependent on macroeconomic stabilization policy and if one is attempting to forecast that firm's net income, then it seems reasonable to consider devoting resources to (1) forecasting stabilization policy and then (2) making an income forecast, for the firm, that is conditional on the forecasted effects of stabilization policy.

Adoption of the above perspective of firms' accounting number series raises issues of representation. How can, and how should, one represent economy-wide and industry factors? Also, given some scheme for representing these factors, how can, and how should, one represent the relationship between these factors and a given firm's accounting numbers? This problem might be attacked via factor analytic tools, as was done by King [1966] in his work on the rates of return on common stocks. Alternatively, one could use linear models and prespecified indices in order to represent the economy and industry factors. To date, the latter approach has been used most frequently. An extensive empirical analysis of the resultant models' performance is provided in a study by Gonedes [1973], which is reviewed below. His results pertain to sales, cost, and income numbers. Only results for income numbers are considered in our review.

7.4.2.1 Index Models: Specification

We shall consider index models that include only "market-wide" indices, rather than both market-wide and industry indices or just industry indices. This is sufficient for our immediate objectives.

As before, let $\tilde{y}_i(t)$ denote the ith firm's income or income-related number (e.g., its "rate of return on common equity") and let $\tilde{M}(t)$ denote a market-wide (or aggregate) number of the same type. Then a linear index model for $\tilde{y}_i(t)$ is:

$$\tilde{y}_i(t) = \gamma_i + \delta_i \tilde{M}(t) + \epsilon_i(t), \tag{7.91}$$

where the intercept term, γ_i, and slope coefficient, δ_i, are parameters to be estimated and $\tilde{\epsilon}_i(t)$ is a disturbance. For reasons given below, the index model applied to first differences is also important:

$$\Delta\tilde{y}_i(t) = \omega_i + \pi_i \Delta\tilde{M}(t) + \tilde{u}_i(t), \tag{7.92}$$

where ω_i and π_i are parameters to be estimated and $\tilde{u}_i(t)$ is a disturbance.

The following specifications apply to models (7.90) and (7.91).

$$E[\tilde{\epsilon}_i(t)] = E[\tilde{u}_i(t)] = 0.0, \qquad \text{for all } i \text{ and } t. \tag{7.93}$$

$$E[\tilde{\epsilon}_i(t) \cdot \tilde{\epsilon}_j(s)] = \begin{cases} 0, & \text{if } i \neq j \text{ or } t \neq s \\ \sigma_\epsilon^2, & \text{if } i = j \text{ and } t = s. \end{cases} \tag{7.94}$$

$$E[\tilde{u}_i(t) \cdot \tilde{u}_j(s)] = \begin{cases} 0, & \text{if } i \neq j \text{ or } t \neq s \\ \sigma_\epsilon^2, & \text{if } i = j \text{ and } t = s. \end{cases} \tag{7.95}$$

$$E[\tilde{M}(t) \cdot \tilde{\epsilon}_i(t)] = E[\Delta\tilde{M}(t) \cdot \tilde{u}_i(t)] = 0, \qquad \text{for all } i \text{ and } t. \tag{7.96}$$

Restriction (7.96) ensures that the conventional estimators of the models' parameters will have a variety of seemingly desirable statistical properties that we shall not discuss here. (See Goldberger [1964, chap. 6] for a discussion of this restriction.) Restrictions (7.94) and (7.95) are more important for our present purposes.

Restrictions (7.94) and (7.95) for $i \neq j$ stipulate that the linear relationships among firms' income numbers are fully determined by the comovements of these numbers with the index of market income, $\tilde{M}(t)$ for (7.91) and $\Delta\tilde{M}(t)$ for (7.92). That is, after the effects of the index are accounted for, there are no remaining *cross-sectional* linear dependencies among different firms' income numbers. This is equivalent to asserting that for each t and for a given number of firms, say, $\tilde{N}$, the $\tilde{N}$-by-$\tilde{N}$ variance-covariance matrices with typical elements $((\text{Cov}[\tilde{\epsilon}_i(t), \tilde{\epsilon}_j(t)]))$ for (7.91) and $((\text{Cov}[\tilde{u}_i(t), \tilde{u}_j(t)]))$ for (7.92) are *diagonal* matrices (i.e., each "off diagonal" element of these matrices has a value equal to zero).

Conditional on (7.91) or (7.92), the variability of each firm's income number, or first-differenced income number, may be decomposed into two components: an "individualistic" component and a "systematic" component. Consider model (7.91). For this model, the so-called systematic component is that part of the total variability, $\text{Var}[\tilde{y}_i(t)]$, that is associated with the variability of income for the entire economy, as represented by $\text{Var}[\tilde{M}(t)]$. Since the total variability is given by:

$$\text{Var}[\tilde{y}_i(t)] = \delta_i^2\, \text{Var}[\tilde{M}(t)] + \text{Var}[\tilde{\epsilon}_i(t)], \tag{7.97}$$

the systematic component is defined by $\delta_i^2\, \text{Var}[\tilde{M}(t)]$. No component involving $\text{Cov}[\tilde{M}(t), \tilde{\epsilon}_1(t)]$ appears in (7.97) because of condition (7.98). Note that $\tilde{M}(t)$ appears in model (7.91) for every firm. That is, it is a *commonality* or *common factor*.

The individualistic component is that part of the total variability associated with the unique attributes of the ith firm. It is defined by $\text{Var}[\tilde{\epsilon}_i(t)]$.

7.4.2.2 Evidence on Index Models

Models (7.91) and (7.92) are among the models for which empirical results are provided by Gonedes [1973]. In his report, $\tilde{y}_i(t)$ is the ith firm's rate of return on common equity and $\tilde{M}(t)$ is an index of firms' rates of return on common equity. Some pertinent aspects of his report are reviewed in this section.

Gonedes' results, which include estimation results and assessments of prediction performance, are based on a sample of 316 firms selected from an Annual Industrial COMPUSTAT tape—one that contained data for 1,014 firms for (at most) 1946–1969. In order to be included in his study, a firm had to have a variety of accounting data for at least 1947–1968. The years 1953, 1960, and 1968 were not used for estimation results; they were used for prediction tests. (See Gonedes [1973, pp. 217–218] for the additional criteria used for sample selection.) Table 7-13 gives a profile of the 316 firms selected and all of the firms on the COMPUSTAT tape from which they were selected in terms of data availability, existence over the entire period 1947–1968, and industry membership.

The rate of return used in Gonedes' study for each firm is:

$$\tilde{y}_i(t) \equiv \frac{\text{Firm } i\text{'s Net Income for Year } t}{\text{Firm } i\text{'s Common Equity as of the Beginning of Year } t}.$$

The net income number is "Available for Common," the same number used in the Watts and Watts/Leftwich studies described above.

The corresponding "market-wide" number is an average taken across firms:

$$\tilde{M}(t) = \sum_{j=1}^{\tilde{N}(t)} x_j(t)\tilde{y}_j(t),$$

TABLE 7-13

INDUSTRIAL PROFILES OF SAMPLES OF FIRMS AND ALL COMPUSTAT FIRMS

"Two-Digit" COMPU-STAT Industry Code	Sample of Firms		All Firms on COMPUSTAT Tape		Firms Not on COMPUSTAT Tape For All Years 1947–68	
	Number	Proportion	Number	Proportion	Number	Proportion
0100	—	—	2	.0019	1	.0052
0800	1	.0031	8	.0078	1	.0052
1000	8	.0253	25	.0246	4	.0208
1200	2	.0063	8	.0078	4	.0208
1300	—	—	10	.0098	4	.0208
1400	1	.0031	4	.0039	1	.0052
2000	39	.1234	103	.1015	18	.0937
2100	6	.0189	9	.0088	1	.0052
2200	6	.0189	20	.0197	4	.0208
2300	6	.0189	19	.0187	6	.0312
2500	4	.0126	12	.0113	5	.0250
2600	11	.0348	28	.0276	5	.0260
2700	4	.0126	35	.0345	9	.0468
2800	39	.1234	109	.1074	16	.0833
2900	14	.0443	41	.0404	8	.0416
3000	5	.0158	13	.0128	2	.0104
3100	2	.0063	7	.0069	—	—
3200	15	.0474	26	.0258	3	.0156
3300	21	.0664	45	.0443	4	.0208
3400	10	.0316	40	.0394	9	.0468
3500	30	.0949	99	.0976	25	.1302
3600	17	.0537	69	.0680	8	.0416
3700	28	.0886	70	.0690	14	.0729
3800	8	.0253	22	.0216	3	.0156
3900	3	.0094	16	.0157	5	.0260
4200	2	.0063	11	.0108	2	.0104
4400	1	.0031	5	.0049	1	.0052
4500	11	.0348	14	.0128	—	—
4800	1	.0031	14	.0138	5	.0260
4900	1	.0031	6	.0059	2	.0104
5000	2	.0063	9	.0088	1	.0052
5300	8	.0253	32	.0315	1	.0052
5400	7	.0221	24	.0236	3	.0156
5600	—	—	5	.0049	1	.0052
5800	—	—	7	.0069	2	.0104
5900	—	—	2	.0019	1	.0052
6100	—	—	17	.0167	5	.0250
7000	1	.0031	3	.0029	1	.0052
7200	—	—	1	.0009	—	—
7300	—	—	1	.0009	1	.0052
7800	2	.0063	9	.0088	4	.0208
9900	—	—	14	.0138	2	.0104
TOTALS*	316	1.00 (approx.)	1014	1.00 (approx.)	192	1.00 (approx.)

*Proportions may not sum to 1.00 because of truncations.

Source: Gonedes [1973, table 1].

where $\bar{N}(t)$ is the total number of firms used to define "the market" in year t and $x_j(t)$ is the weight applied to the jth firm's rate of return for year t. The sample of 316 firms constituted the "market" in Gonedes' study. This provided much of the justification for not including industry indices along with the market index in models (7.91) and (7.92). In order to construct "representative" industry indices, one usually requires the availability of data for a prespecified minimum number (e.g., 10 or 15) of firms in each industry category. Examination of the profile in Table 7-13 suggests that the likely candidates for industry groups are already adequately represented within the sample (at least in terms of numbers) and, therefore, in the market index (as defined above). Thus, industry indices will probably not provide additional important sources of cross-sectional correlation for the sample firms. Gonedes tested the descriptive adequacy of this view by using estimation results on the cross-sectional correlation that remains after the effects of the market index are recognized. He inferred that the remaining cross-sectional correlation is small for model (7.92), which is the better-specified model.

Indeed, one recurring inference is that model (7.91) is not a well-specified model. There appeared to be inconsistencies between the sample evidence and the specifications on the disturbance, $\tilde{\epsilon}_i(t)$. In addition, there appeared to be inconsistencies between the sample evidence and various implied conditions that should be met by the parameters γ_i and δ_i if model (7.91) has descriptive validity.[38]

Some of Gonedes' estimation results are summarized in Table 7-14. Results for both model (7.91) and model (7.92) are summarized. The estimates of the serial correlation coefficients of the index models' disturbances are among the results used to assess model adequacy. The estimates for model (7.91) are, on balance, inconsistent with the absence of serial correlation. Conditional on the null hypothesis of $\rho_j = 0.0$, $j > 0$, the theoretical mean and standard deviation of β_1 are approximately equal to -0.05 and 0.22, respectively. On balance, the results for model (7.91) seem inconsistent with these theoretical values; the results for model (7.92) seem consistent with those values.[39]

The estimation results described by Table 7-14 are based on an equity-weighted market index of firms' rates of return. Specifically, the value of $x_j(t)$ used to define $M(t)$ in terms of $y_j(t)$, $j = 1, 2, \ldots, \bar{N}(t)$, is defined to be the value of $C_j(t - 1)/\bar{C}(t - 1)$, where $\bar{C}(t - 1) = \Sigma_{i=1}^{\bar{N}(t)} C_i(t - 1)$ and $C_j(t - 1)$ is the value of the jth firm's common equity number as of the end of year $t - 1$, i.e., as of the beginning of year t. For comparative purposes, Gonedes obtained estimation and prediction results for an equally weighted index too. The latter index's value for year t is defined by the weights $x_j(t) = 1/\bar{N}(t)$, for all j. An equally weighted index is the type most frequently used in work based on index models of accounting numbers. Gonedes inferred, however, that his index models based on equally

---

[38]The specifications of models (7.91) and (7.92) and the definition of $\tilde{M}(t)$ have implications for cross-sectional averages of γ_i, δ_i, ω_i, and π_i, where the averaging is done using the weights, $x_i(t)$, $i = 1, 2, \ldots, \bar{N}(t)$, that define $\tilde{M}(t)$—in particular, the common equity weights described below. Note that the sample means and sample standard deviations reported in Table 7.14 are not computed with common equity weights. The values provided in that Table are intended to be used as descriptive devices, rather than as bases for specification tests.

[39]That taking first differences induces negative estimated serial correlation coefficients is not unexpected. See the discussion surrounding expression (7.39), where it is indicated that the first difference of a serially uncorrelated random variable defines a random variable that is negatively serially correlated.

TABLE 7-14

CROSS-SECTIONAL SUMMARY STATISTICS FOR ESTIMATES OF ACCOUNTING NUMBER INDEX MODEL (BASED ON 316 FIRMS)[a]

		Estimated Intercept	Absolute Value of t-Statistic for Intercept	Slope Coefficient	Absolute Value of t-Statistic for Slope Coefficient	$\bar{R}^2$	$\beta_1 b$
First Differences	Mean	−.0025	1.8365	.9573	2.6845	.2322	.4041
	Std. Dev.	.2593	1.3781	1.7707	2.0910	.2286	.2734
	Deciles 1	−.1876	.3856	−.3314	.3602	.0	.0395
	5	.0075	1.5617	.8671	2.3959	.1875	.4402
	9	.1682	3.7433	2.3864	5.3562	.5794	.6747
No Transformation	Mean	.0007	.6286	1.0783	2.345	.2020	−.0908
	Std. Dev.	.0321	.5017	3.494	1.6913	.2044	.2555
	Deciles 1	−.0110	.0691	−.2141	.4284	.0	−.4308
	5	−.0011	.5518	.8098	2.2215	.1648	−.0904
	9	.0080	1.2318	2.2234	4.7529	.5249	.2150

[a]Data are annual data from the period 1946–1969, excluding 1953, 1960, and 1968. The latter years were used for prediction tests; see Gonedes [1973, esp. tables 2 and 3].

[b]Estimated first-order serial correlation coefficient for estimated disturbances. $E(\beta_1) = -1/(n - 1)$ and $\text{Var}(\beta_1) = 1/(n - 1)$, where n is the number of observations used to estimate model (7.91) or (7.92) for a given firm. n varies between 19 and 21 for model (7.91) and 18 and 20 for model (7.92). For details, see Gonedes [1973].

weighted indices were somewhat less well specified than those based on the equity-weighted indices.

The prediction performance of the index models was compared to that of several models used in recent work on the time series properties of annual accounting numbers. The specific alternatives considered were special cases of the following:

$$\tilde{y}_i(t) = \beta_i(t)y_i(t-1) + \alpha_i(t) + \tilde{e}_i(t), \tag{7.98}$$

where $\tilde{\epsilon}_i(t)$ is a disturbance. In some of the models considered, the parameters $\beta_i(t)$ and $\alpha_i(t)$ were specified to be constants. For example, one of the alternatives considered is defined by $\beta_i(t) = 1.0$ and $\alpha_i(t) = 0.0$, for all i and t. These specifications on (7.98) define a strict martingale. Prediction performance was evaluated in terms of average squared prediction errors, average absolute values of prediction errors, and average prediction errors. All prediction results pertain to the "levels," $\tilde{y}_i(t)$, for all i. When a model applied to differences was used for forecasts, the implied forecast of the level, $\tilde{y}_i(t)$, was given by $E(\tilde{y}_i(t)) = y_i(t-1) + E(\Delta\tilde{y}_i(t))$. As indicated earlier, predictions were obtained for each of three years: 1953, 1960, and 1968. Of the *alternative* models considered, the strict martingale model seemed to provide the best predictive performance. And the differences between the prediction performance of the index model in differenced form, (7.92), and the prediction performance of the strict martingale model appeared to be trivial. Not unexpectedly, the less well specified model (7.91) exhibited poorer prediction performance than the index model applied to first differences.

Some additional remarks on the prediction performance of the martingale model and model (7.92) are in order. The prediction results underlying Gonedes' inferences pertain to prediction error distributions for individual firms. Suppose, however, that one were interested in the prediction error distribution for a portfolio of firms. The error distribution for the portfolio will be affected by any cross-sectional correlation among prediction errors for individual firms. Consider, for example, the expected value of the squared prediction error for, say, year t. Let θ_i denote the weight given to firm i in the portfolio. Thus, the portfolio accounting rate of return on equity for year t is $\Sigma_j\ \theta_j\tilde{y}_j(t)$, where the summation is over the firms in the portfolio. Let $\tilde{\eta}_i(t)$ denote the prediction error for firm i. The expected value of the prediction error is $E[\Sigma_i\theta_i\tilde{\eta}_i(t)] = 0.0$, if whatever model is used gives unbiased forecasts, i.e., if $E[\tilde{\eta}_i(t)] = 0.0$, for all i and every t. The expected squared prediction error is:

$$E\left[\sum_i \theta_i\tilde{\eta}_i(t)]^2 = \sum_i \theta_i^2 \operatorname{Var}[\tilde{\eta}_i(t)\right]$$
$$+ \sum_i \sum_{i\neq j} \theta_i\theta_j \operatorname{Cov}[\tilde{\eta}_i(t), \tilde{\eta}_j(t)].$$

The results presented by Gonedes suggest that the value of the first summation on the RHS will be about the same for the strict martingale model and for model (7.92), for the same set of portfolio weights. Thus any difference between the values of $E[\Sigma\ \theta_i\tilde{\eta}_i(t)]^2$ induced by these models will turn on the covariance terms, $\operatorname{Cov}[\tilde{\eta}_i(t), \tilde{\eta}_j(t)]$, for all $i \neq j$. But this is the term that accounts for the cross-sectional correlation in the models' disturbances. Gonedes' results are consistent with the statement that these terms are, on balance, positive and higher for the martingale model than for model (7.92). This implies, in turn, that the expected value of the squared prediction error for a portfolio should be lower if predictions are based on model (7.92) rather than the strict martingale model. In short, even though these models' performance is "about the same" for a given firm, they need not be—and seem not to be—about the same for portfolio.

7.4.2.3 Summary

To sum up, Gonedes' estimation results, specification tests, and prediction results suggest that (1) "market-wide" factors are statistically important determinants of firms' operating results, as represented by rates of return on common equity and (2) relative to the variants of the market index model examined, the index model in first-difference form and defined in terms of an equity-weighted index is the more descriptively adequate model. The prediction performance of this model was about the same as, or superior to, that of the alternative models considered—insofar as predictions for individual firms are concerned. For portfolios, the prediction performance of the alternative models would be less favorable than model (7.92) because of the larger cross-sectional correlation among the prediction errors conditional on each alternative model.

As indicated earlier, index models are among the alternatives to univariate time series models. But the basic motivation for interest in index models is the same: to characterize the systematic characteristics of accounting numbers. The importance of information on these characteristics is discussed in Section 7.2.1.

All of the models and evidence discussed up to this point pertain to annual accounting numbers. Nothing specific has been said about interim (e.g., quarterly) accounting numbers. Many of the basic issues that arise with respect to annual numbers also arise with respect to interim numbers. But there are some additional issues. Perhaps the major one is the issue of seasonalities. We discuss this in the next section, which deals with univariate time series models and evidence pertinent to quarterly accounting numbers. We begin with a discussion on how such numbers fit into the modeling framework set forth earlier in this chapter.

7.5 Univariate Time Series Models for Interim Accounting Numbers

7.5.1 Seasonalities

The stationarity assumption used in our discussion of annual accounting numbers is a type of homogeneity condition. Loosely speaking, it says that the marginal stochastic properties of a given year's number are the same as the marginal stochastic properties of any other year's number. In short, the *marginal* distribution of, say, income, $\tilde{y}(\tau)$, does not change when the value of τ changes. Similarly, the stationarity condition says that the relationship between two consecutive year's numbers is the same for all pairs of consecutive years. That is, the specific years (i.e., the values of t and $t - 1$) are irrelevant vis-à-vis the joint distribution of, say, $\tilde{y}(t)$ and $\tilde{y}(t - 1)$—and therefore $\tilde{y}(t + 1)$ and $\tilde{y}(t)$. The fact that the years are consecutive is, in general, relevant. This last condition generalizes to pairs of years separated by 1, 2, 3, 4, or any other number of years; it is not limited to consecutive years' numbers. For example, for pairs of years separated by one year, we would be dealing with the joint distribution of the numbers $\tilde{y}(t)$ and $\tilde{y}(t - 2)$ and, therefore, $\tilde{y}(t + 2)$ and $\tilde{y}(t)$. The stationarity condition says that this joint distribution is the same for all values of t.

A similar homogeneity condition applies to the numbers of years taken three at a time, four at a time, etc., if full stationarity is assumed.[40] Thus, the stationarity assumption says that the *joint* distribution function of, for example, $\tilde{y}(t)$, $\tilde{y}(t + s)$, $\tilde{y}(t + r)$ is the same for all values of t, given the values of s and r. That is, the specific years involved do not matter; only the numbers of years separating all combinations of at least two of the random variables examined are important (i.e., the values of r and s).

A formal definition of (strict) stationarity is now in order. Let $T = \{1, 2, 3, \ldots\}$ denote an index set for the discrete-time stochastic process $\tilde{y}(t)$, $t \in T$. And let $t_1, t_2, \ldots, t_n$ be a collection of n elements from this set. The indices $t_1, t_2, \ldots, t_n$ need not be consecutive. The stochastic process $\{\tilde{y}(t); t \in T\}$ is defined to be a *strictly stationary* stochastic process if the joint distribution function of $(\tilde{y}(t_1), \tilde{y}(t_2), \ldots, \tilde{y}(t_n))$ is identical to the joint distribution function of $(\tilde{y}(t_1 + k), \tilde{y}(t_2 + k), \ldots, \tilde{y}(t_n + k))$ for any value of $n \geq 1$ and all sets of indices $t_1 + k$, $i = 1, 2, \ldots, n$ in the index set T. That is, the process is stationary if $F(y(t_1), y(t_2), \ldots, y(t_n)) = F(y(t_1 + k), y(t_2 + k), \ldots, y(t_n + k))$ for all values of $n \geq 1$ and all values of k such that the values $\tilde{y}(t_1) = y(t_1) = y(t_1 + k)$, $\tilde{y}(t_2) = y(t_2) = y(t_2 + k)$, $\ldots$, $\tilde{y}(t_n) = y(t_n) = y(t_n + k)$ are within the range of the random variable $\tilde{y}(t)$, and the values of the indices t_i and $t_i + k$, $i = 1, 2, \ldots, n$ are within the index set T. Thus, if a process is strictly stationary, the joint distribution function, $F(\ldots)$, only depends on the distances between the indices, not on the indices' actual values, for every N-tuple of indices, $N \geq 1$.

Consider the case of $N = 1$. If strict stationarity holds, then the distribution function $F(y(t_1))$ is the same for all values of t_1. Thus, the moments of this distribution—e.g., the mean, $E(\tilde{y}(t))$, and the variance, $\text{Var}(\tilde{y}(t))$—are constants (i.e., the same for all values of t_1). For $N = 2$, strict stationarity implies that the joint moments of $(\tilde{y}(t_1), \tilde{y}(t_2))$ are independent of the values of t_1 and t_2. Only the difference $|t_1 - t_2|$ matters, where $|x|$ denotes the absolute value of x. Thus, for example, $\text{Cov}[\tilde{y}(t_1), \tilde{y}(t_2)]$ is only a function of $|t_1 - t_2|$.

Weaker forms of stationarity are also encountered in works on time series analysis. For example, a "wide sense" or "second-order" stationary process is one for which the above definition holds for $N = 2$ but not necessarily for $N > 2$. In this regard, note that a pth-order stationary process is stationary for all orders $N \leq p$. Thus, for $N = 2$, $\text{Cov}[\tilde{y}(t_1), \tilde{y}(t_2)]$ does not depend on the specific values of t_1 and t_2 but only on the difference $|t_2 - t_1|$. Moreover, the *marginal* moments of $\tilde{y}(t_1)$ and $\tilde{y}(t_2)$ are identical (because they are independent of the values of the indices, t_1 and t_2).

With the above discussion of stationarity in hand, it should be easier to intuit some of the problems encountered when applying time series analysis methods to interim accounting numbers—such as quarterly income numbers. Unless otherwise indicated, the following discussion will focus on the latter. This is done for concreteness and because the available evidence on interim numbers is mainly for quarterly income numbers (or income-related numbers, such as rates of return on total assets or on common equity).

---

[40]Different degrees of stationarity are often specified in the literature on stochastic processes. For example, stationarity is often specified only for the mean and variance of a process; this corresponds to the notion of "second-order" or "covariance" stationarity. The label "strict" stationarity is often used when stationarity of all features of the probability model corresponding to a process is covered by the stationarity specification. This is what we mean by "full" stationarity. Unless otherwise indicated, we shall use this stationarity condition. Formal definitions of various degrees of stationarity are provided by, e.g., Cramér and Leadbetter [1967, Chap. 7].

Are quarterly numbers likely to satisfy stationarity conditions? What are your "priors"? For a first pass, consider the marginal distribution functions of different quarters' income numbers. Now, the elements of the index set $T = \{1, 2, \ldots\}$ pertain to different quarters. In this regard, note that, say, quarter 1 of a given year is viewed as different from quarter 1 of a different year. Indeed, one way to index quarterly numbers so as to relate them to annual numbers is to use a double index, (t, s), $t = 1, 2, \ldots$, and $s = 1, 2, 3$, or 4, where t denotes the year of interest and s denotes the quarter of interest. Conditional on this specification of the index set, we shall use the notation $\tilde{y}(t, s)$ for income of quarter s in year t. The corresponding index set is $\bar{T} = \{(1, 1), (1, 2), (1, 3), (1, 4), \ldots, (k, 1), (k, 2), (k, 3), (k, 4), \ldots\}$. A different specification of the index set will be introduced later; this one will suffice for now. Let us return to our original question.

If we adopt the stationarity assumption, we shall be treating the stochastic process $\{\tilde{y}(t, s); (t, s) \in \bar{T}\}$ as if the distribution functions of, say, $\tilde{y}(t, 2)$ and $\tilde{y}(t, 4)$ are identical univariate distribution functions, for any t. Thus, we shall be behaving as if, e.g., $E[\tilde{y}(t, 2)] = E[\tilde{y}(t, 4)]$ and $\text{Var}[\tilde{y}(t, 2)] = \text{Var}[\tilde{y}(t, 4)]$. More generally, we shall be behaving as if the values of $E[\tilde{y}(t, s)]$ and $\text{Var}[\tilde{y}(t, s)]$ are constants—and thus independent of *both* t and s. But there are often reasons for doubting the descriptive adequacy of this view—some of them quite mundane.

Consider, for example, a firm whose product is purchased mainly for holiday use—around, e.g., Easter or Christmas. A substantial amount of design and production work may take place throughout the year. Yet, actual sales will usually be "bunched" in the second and fourth quarters. Moreover, these characteristics may be recurring ones, in the sense that they apply, on balance, to all years. In short, some basic characteristics (e.g., production, selling, and distribution activities) of the firm's operations may vary across quarters within a year and repeat themselves across years for a given quarter. But this suggests that there may be *systematic* differences among the distribution functions of different quarters' accounting numbers for a given year (i.e., $s = 1, 2, 3$, and 4 for a given t) and homogeneity of a given quarter's numbers for different years (i.e., a given quarter s for years $t = 1, 2, 3, \ldots$). The most extreme case is where the distribution function is different for each quarter. That is, the distribution function of $\tilde{y}(t, s)$ is independent of t for a given s. But for a given t, the distribution function varies with s—so that there are really four different distribution functions applicable to each year's four quarterly numbers. This is what is known as a *seasonality*.

In formal terms, the stochastic process $\{\tilde{y}(t, s)\}$ exhibits seasonalities—and thus non-stationarity—if any of the marginal or joint distribution functions associated with it are periodic functions. In general, a function $g(j)$ with domain J is *periodic* if there exists an $H > 0$ such that for all j and $j + H$ in J, $g(j) = g(j + H)$. The parameter H is known as the *period* of the function. In effect, the function $g(j)$ takes on all of its possible values in an interval of length H or, for discrete index processes, over a number of points equal to H. Note that if H is the period of $g(j)$, then $g(j) = g(j + kH)$ for any positive integer k.

To see how this applies to quarterly accounting numbers, recode the index set $\bar{T} = \{(t, s); t = 1, 2, \ldots, s = 1, 2, 3, 4\}$ by replacing (t, s) with the scaler $\tau = (t - 1)(4) + s$, thus getting the respecified index set $T^* = \{1, 2, 3, 4, 5, \ldots\}$. In this scheme the index value, say, $\tau = 5$ pertains to the fifth quarterly number in a sequence of consecutive quarterly numbers; this number is also the first-quarter ($s = 1$) number of the second year ($t = 2$)—i.e., for $(t, s) = (2, 1)$, we have $\tau = (t - 1)(4) + s = (1)(4) + 1 = 5$. To each value of τ, we can associate a marginal distribution function, *viz*., that of $\tilde{y}(\tau)$, denoted $F(y(\tau))$. For a given value of $\tilde{y}(\tau)$, this function is, in general, a function of τ. It is a periodic function if there exists an $H > 0$ such that $F(y(\tau)) = F(y(\tau + H))$ for τ, $\tau + H$ in T^*. For a quarterly series with a quarterly seasonal, $H = 4$. That is, the probability distribution "repeats itself" every four time slots—i.e., every four quarters. This implies, of course, that the marginal moments of the quarterly income numbers are such that $E[\tilde{y}(\tau)] = E[\tilde{y}(t + 4)]$ and $\text{Var}[\tilde{y}(\tau)] = \text{Var}[\tilde{y}(\tau + 4)]$, for all values of $\tau \in T^*$.

What about joint distribution functions and joint moments—such as covariances of pairs of quarters' income numbers? The notion of a periodic function still applies—but this time to the joint distribution function of pairs of quarters' income numbers. For any two values, τ_1 and τ_2, the joint distribution function of $\tilde{y}(\tau_1)$ and $\tilde{y}(\tau_2)$, denoted $F[y(\tau_1), y(\tau_2)]$, is periodic if there is an $H > 0$ such that $F[y(\tau_1), y(\tau_2)] = F[y(\tau_1 + H), y(\tau_2 + H)]$ for all τ_1, τ_2, $\tau_1 + H$, and $\tau_2 + H$ in the index set T^*. This implies, of course, that $\text{Cov}[\tilde{y}(\tau_1), \tilde{y}(\tau_2)] = \text{Cov}[\tilde{y}(\tau_1 + H), \tilde{y}(\tau_2 + H)]$, i.e., that the covariance function takes on all of its possible values over a number of points equal to H. Also implied by periodicity is $\text{Cov}[\tilde{y}(\tau_1), \tilde{y}(\tau_2)] = \text{Cov}[\tilde{y}(\tau_1 + kH), \tilde{y}(\tau_2 + kH)]$ for all positive integers k.

Observe that the preceding remarks assume that the nature of the periodicity itself is stationary (i.e., the value of H is constant over time) and that the periodicity is the only source of nonstationarity in the process $\{\tilde{y}(\tau)\}$. Nothing rules out nonstationarities due to both periodicities and other nonperiodic changes in distribution functions. That is, several sources of nonstationarity may be superimposed on each other. For example, the distribution function of each quarter's income number may, for every year, differ from that of each of the other three quarter's numbers and, in addition, it may be changing from one year to the next. For example, in terms of our new index set, T^*, the distribution of $\tilde{y}(\tau = 1)$ may differ from that of $\tilde{y}(\tau = 5)$, even though both $\tilde{y}(1)$ and $\tilde{y}(5)$ are quarter-1 income numbers. In this situation, the above characterization of seasonality in terms of periodic functions is appropriate after *each quarter's* number is transformed so as to attain stationarity of that quarter's number. This may involve applying a different transformation to each quarter's number. The end result consists of, in general, four distribution functions of income—one for each quarter—which may be characterized, for each value of income, as one periodic function. That is, for each value of $\tilde{y}(\tau)$, $\tau \in T^*$, $F(y(\tau)) = F(y(\tau + H))$, for a period equal to H and $\tau + H \in T^*$.

Since, in general, each quarter's number is characterized by a different distribution function and successive drawings of a *given quarter's* income number are drawings from the same distribution function (after stationarity transformations, if needed), one possibility is to apply time series analysis tools to consecutive observations on each quarter's number. In general, this leads to four time series models—one for each quarter. This is no different from applying time series analysis tools to four *different* random variables, such as four different accounting numbers (e.g., sales, cost of goods sold, advertising costs, and administration costs). Indeed, since we are distinguishing between the income numbers corresponding to different quarters in terms of the numbers' distribution functions, we are really behaving as if the income numbers of different quarters are different random variables. It just turns out that between drawings on one of these numbers, we must have one drawing on each of the other three. We cannot *simultaneously* draw from the four distributions.

As indicated, the time series models that best describe different quarters' income numbers may differ from each other. One might infer, for example, that the quarter-1 income number is best described by an ARIMA(1, 1, 0) model, the quarter-2 number by an AR-

IMA(0, 1, 0) model, the quarter-3 number by an ARIMA(0, 0, 1) model, and the quarter-4 model by an ARIMA(1, 0, 0) model. The relevant models are, therefore, as follows, for $(t, s) \in \bar{T}$:

Quarter 1: $$\tilde{y}(t, 1) - \tilde{y}(t-1, 1) = \delta + \phi_1(\tilde{y}(t-1, 1) - \tilde{y}(t-2, 1)) + \tilde{\epsilon}(t, 1)$$

$$\text{or } \Delta\tilde{y}(t, 1) = \delta + \phi_1\Delta\tilde{y}(t-1, 1) + \tilde{\epsilon}(t, 1)$$

$$\text{or } \tilde{y}(t, 1) = \delta + (1 + \phi_1)\tilde{y}(t-1, 1) - \phi_1\tilde{y}(t-2, 1) + \tilde{\epsilon}(t, 1).$$

Quarter 2: $$\tilde{y}(t, 2) - \tilde{y}(t-1, 2) = \delta_0 + \tilde{\epsilon}(t, 2)$$

$$\text{or } \Delta\tilde{y}(t, 2) = \delta + \tilde{\epsilon}(t, 2)$$

$$\text{or } \tilde{y}(t, 2) = \delta + \tilde{y}(t-1, 2) + \tilde{\epsilon}(t, 2).$$

Quarter 3: $$\tilde{y}(t, 3) = \delta + \tilde{\epsilon}(t, 3) - \theta_1\tilde{\epsilon}(t-1, 3).$$

Quarter 4: $$\tilde{y}(t, 4) = \delta + \phi_1\tilde{y}(t-1, 4) + \tilde{\epsilon}(t, 4).$$

Note that the first-difference operator, Δ, applies to the index t, which refers to year t. In the statement of each quarter's model, the index s, which refers to quarter s, $s = 1, 2, 3, 4$, is fixed for $\tilde{y}(t, s)$. In short, the operator Δ is an annual differencing operator in the above expressions.

If each quarter's number is analyzed separately, then the same tools and potential problems encountered when dealing with annual numbers are, in general encountered when dealing with quarterly numbers. There is no theoretical difference between analysis of an annual number and analysis of any one of the quarterly numbers. And if no quarter's income number reflects information about any other quarter's number, then nothing is lost by separate analyses of the four quarters' numbers. On the other hand, if the income numbers of consecutive quarters are related to each other, then, in principle, a joint analysis can be justified. In short, in the latter situation, we can justify superimposing one model on the four separate quarterly models so as to account for the *inter-quarter* relationships of quarterly income numbers. (The models specified above account for the *inter-year* behavior of each quarter's number.)

Conditional on the stationarity assumption for each quarter's number (perhaps after a transformation), the time series model applied to each quarter's number is dependent of t. Thus, in the above illustration, the ARIMA(1, 1, 0) model selected for the quarter-1 number is selected for all t and the values of this model's parameters are the same for all t.

What are the implications of stationarity for modeling the inter-quarter relationships of quarterly numbers? This modeling exercise for $\tilde{y}(t, s)$ involves changes in s for a given t. And stationarity implies that the model characterizing inter-quarter relationships is the same for all s. Thus, for example, strict stationarity implies that the covariance between *consecutive* quarters' income numbers—the numbers of quarters 2 and 1 or quarters 3 and 2 or quarters 4 and 3 or quarter 1 and the preceding 4th quarter—is independent of the particular quarters specified.

With respect to inter-quarter relationships, the stationarity condition says that the observed disturbances from the quarterly models can be treated as observations on the same stochastic process, $\{\tilde{\epsilon}(\tau);\ \tau \in T^*\}$, at the values of the index, τ, *corresponding to a given year* and that this process is stationary, perhaps after a stationarity-inducing transformation—such as differencing. Of course if one model is going to be used for the entire process $\{\tilde{\epsilon}(\tau);\ \tau \in T^*\}$, even for τ covering different years, then some kind of homogeneity restriction must be placed on different years' inter-quarter relationships. A commonly used restriction is that one model can be used to describe all years' inter-quarter relationships.

Suppose that this condition is invoked for, say, the dth differences of the disturbances from consecutive quarters' models. That is, suppose that the stationarity condition is satisfied by the sequence $\{(1 - B)^d\tilde{\epsilon}(\tau);\ \tau \in T^*\}$ where, for $d = 1$ and $\tau > 1$, $\tau \in T^*$:

$$\begin{aligned}
\Delta\tilde{\epsilon}(2) &= \tilde{\epsilon}(2) - \tilde{\epsilon}(1) \equiv \tilde{\epsilon}(1, 2) - \tilde{\epsilon}(1, 1)\\
\Delta\tilde{\epsilon}(3) &= \tilde{\epsilon}(3) - \tilde{\epsilon}(2) \equiv \tilde{\epsilon}(1, 3) - \tilde{\epsilon}(1, 2)\\
\Delta\tilde{\epsilon}(4) &= \tilde{\epsilon}(4) - \tilde{\epsilon}(3) \equiv \tilde{\epsilon}(1, 4) - \tilde{\epsilon}(1, 3)\\
\Delta\tilde{\epsilon}(5) &= \tilde{\epsilon}(5) - \tilde{\epsilon}(4) \equiv \tilde{\epsilon}(2, 1) - \tilde{\epsilon}(1, 4)\\
\vdots \quad & \quad\ \vdots \qquad\qquad\qquad \vdots
\end{aligned}$$

Note that $\Delta\tilde{\epsilon}(5)$ is defined in terms of quarterly disturbances for *two different years*. This is justified by the just-stated assumption that inter-quarter relationships are independent of year. Thus, the appropriate stationarity-inducing transformation for two consecutive quarters within a year is applicable to consecutive quarters from different years.

Next, suppose that an ARIMA(1, d, 1) model best characterizes the inter-quarter relationships. Then our final model for quarterly income is, for $\tau \in T^*$:

$$\tilde{z}(\tau) = \delta + \phi_1\tilde{z}(\tau - 1) + \tilde{\alpha}(\tau),$$

where $\tilde{z}(\tau) \equiv (1 - B)^d\tilde{\epsilon}(\tau)$, as given above, and $\tilde{\alpha}(\tau)$ is the disturbance of our final model—an identically distributed serially uncorrelated random variable with $E[\tilde{\alpha}(\tau)] = 0.0$ and $\mathrm{Var}[\tilde{\alpha}(\tau)] = \sigma^2$.

The above discussion covers the most basic aspects of modeling quarterly number series. A fundamental point to keep in mind is that two types of relationships can be attacked: inter-year relationships and inter-quarter relationships. The tools usually used assume that the model that best characterizes the inter-year relationship for a given quarter is independent of any specific year; this is what is implied by assuming stationarity for the given quarter's number. These tools assume that the model that best characterizes inter-quarter relationships for any year is independent of specific quarters. This too is subsumed into the stationarity assumption. Successive quarters are simply treated as successive periods with respect to which a stationary stochastic process is under analysis. In the end, we could have a total of five models for $\{\tilde{y}(t, s)\}$: one for each quarter, to account for inter-year relationships, and another to account for all inter-quarter relationships.

Of course, by imposing additional assumptions (and thus additional structure) on this modeling exercise, one can considerably simplify one's ultimate description of quarterly numbers. One frequently used approach is to assume that the four quarterly models that account for inter-year relationships are identical models. In short, under this assumption the same ARIMA(p, d, q) model is presumed to characterize the inter-year relationships of each quarter's number. Thus, rather than writing four different models for $\tilde{y}(t, s)$—one for each s, $s = 1$, 2, 3 and 4—one ends up specifying:

$$\phi(B)(1 - B)^d \tilde{y}(t, s) = \delta + \theta(B)\tilde{\epsilon}(t, s)$$

for every s. Note that $\phi(B)$, d, δ, and $\theta(B)$ are independent of s. Also note that the differencing and lagging implicit in this model pertain to the t argument. Thus, for example, $\Delta \tilde{y}(t, s) = \tilde{y}(t, s) - \tilde{y}(t - 1, s)$ *for a given* s when $d = 1$ in the above model.

Since, by assumption, the above model is independent of s, we can, using the respecified index set T^*, rewrite it as:

$$\phi(B^H)\nabla_H^D \tilde{y}(\tau) = \Theta(B^H)\tilde{\epsilon}(\tau),$$

where the B^H is the *seasonal* backshift operator, $B^H \tilde{y}(\tau) = \tilde{y}(\tau - H)$, and ∇_H is the seasonal differencing operator, $\nabla_H \tilde{y}(\tau) = \tilde{y}(\tau) - \tilde{y}(\tau - H)$. Thus, $\nabla_H \equiv 1 - B^H$). Note that H in the above defines the period of the seasonal series (see our previous discussion of periodic functions). $\phi(B^H)$ and $\Theta(B^H)$ are polynomials in B^H of orders P and Q, respectively. They define the autoregressive and moving average components of the model that describes the *inter-year* behavior of our quarterly series. In the conventional jargon, this is an ARIMA model of order $(P, D, Q)_H$, where the subscript parameter, H, is the period of the process. Suppose, for example, $\phi(B^H)$ has $P = 1$, $\Theta(B^H)$ has $Q = 1$, and $D = 1$. Then the model of *every* quarter's *inter-year* behavior is (assuming a zero intercept for convenience):

$$(1 - \phi_1 B^4)(1 - B^4)\,\tilde{y}(\tau) = (1 - \theta_1 B^4)\tilde{\epsilon}(\tau)$$

or:

$$(1 - \phi_1 B^4)(\,\tilde{y}(\tau) - \tilde{y}(\tau - 4)) = \tilde{\epsilon}(\tau) - \theta_1\tilde{\epsilon}(\tau - 4)$$

or:

$$\tilde{y}(\tau) - \tilde{y}(\tau - 4) = \phi_1(\,\tilde{y}(\tau - 4) - \tilde{y}(\tau - 8)) + \tilde{\epsilon}(\tau) - \theta_1\tilde{\epsilon}(\tau - 4)$$

or:

$$\nabla_4\,\tilde{y}(\tau) = \phi_1\nabla_4\,\tilde{y}(\tau - 4) + \tilde{\epsilon}(\tau) - \theta_1\tilde{\epsilon}(\tau - 4).$$

Note that the same values of ϕ_1 and θ_1 are used for all quarters' numbers. In short, the relationship between the current year's quarter-1 number and previous years' quarter-1 numbers is assumed to be identical to the relationship between the current year's quarter-2 number and previous years' quarter-2 numbers, and similarly for all other quarters' numbers.

The last model—used to characterize *inter-quarter* relationships—is applied to the disturbance process, $\{\tilde{\epsilon}(\tau);\ \tau \in T^*\}$. Let $\phi(B)$ and $\theta(B)$ denote the autoregressive and moving average components of this process. Also, let ∇ refer to the usual differencing operator, e.g., $\nabla\tilde{\epsilon}(\tau) = \tilde{\epsilon}(\tau) - \tilde{\epsilon}(\tau - 1)$. Let p and q denote the orders of the polynomials $\phi(B)$ and $\theta(B)$, respectively. As before, B denotes the backshift operator, $B\tilde{\epsilon}(\tau) = \tilde{\epsilon}(\tau - 1)$, and, in general, $B^k\tilde{\epsilon}(\tau) = \tilde{\epsilon}(\tau - k)$. Then the last model is:

$$\phi(B)(1 - B)^d\tilde{\epsilon}(\tau) = \theta(B)\tilde{\alpha}(\tau) \tag{7.99}$$

for $\tau \in T^*$. Using model (7.99) for $\tilde{\epsilon}(\tau) = [\Theta(B^H)]^{-1}\,\Phi(B^H)\nabla_H^D\tilde{y}(\tau)$, we can write:

$$\phi(B)(1 - B)^d[\Theta(B^H)]^{-1}\,\Phi(B^H)\nabla_H^D\,\tilde{y}(\tau) = \theta(B)\tilde{\alpha}(\tau)$$

or:

$$\phi(B)\Phi(B^H)(1 - B)^d\,\nabla_H^D\,\tilde{y}(\tau) = \theta(B)\Theta(B^H)\tilde{\alpha}(\tau). \tag{7.100}$$

This is the so-called general multiplicative model for a seasonal stochastic process, $\{\tilde{y}(\tau); \tau \in T^*\}$. Applying this approach to actual data involves the same basic steps encountered in fitting ARIMA models to nonseasonal series. One first identifies the orders of the autoregressive and moving average polynomials—both seasonal (P and Q) and nonseasonal (p and q)—after determining the degrees of seasonal (D) and nonseasonal (d) differencing needed to attain stationarity. Then one estimates the parameters of the identified $(p, d, q) \times (P, D, Q)_H$ model. As was the case with the nonseasonal models, the estimated autocorrelation function is used for identification purposes. Indeed, the multiplicative seasonal model is really just an ARIMA model with an autoregressive part of order $p + PH$ and a moving average part of order $q + QH$—with many coefficients of each constrained to equal zero. So one expects the identification methods for seasonal and nonseasonal models to be similar. In the case of seasonal models, "identification" involves selecting values for p, d, q, P, D, Q, and H.

But the behavior of the autocorrelation function of $\{\tilde{y}(\tau), \tau \in T^*\}$ is more complicated, in general, when $\tilde{y}(\tau)$ is a seasonal series. Clearly, when the numbers for different quarters are independently distributed, no new complexities arise. For then model (7.100) becomes

$$\Phi(B^H)(1 - B^H)^D \tilde{y}(\tau) = \Theta(B^H)\tilde{\epsilon}(\tau) \tag{7.101}$$

for which $\tilde{\epsilon}(\tau)$, $\tau \in T^*$, is a serially uncorrelated identically distributed disturbance. This is simply an ARIMA(PH, O, QH) model applied to the *seasonal differences* $(1 - B^H)^D \tilde{y}(\tau)$. If $Q = 0$ and $P \neq 0$, then the autocorrelation function is nonzero only at successive *seasonal* lags, O, H, $2H$, $3H$, ..., kH, ..., where k is a positive integer. Moreover, the autocorrelation function gradually converges to zero as the seasonal lag increases. This is similar to the behavior of the autocorrelation function of a seasonal autoregressive process.

If $P = 0$ and $Q \neq 0$, then the autocorrelation function of $(1 - B^H)^D \tilde{y}(\tau)$ has nonzero spikes only at the seasonal lags (i.e., only at positive integer multiplies of H) up to lag QH. Beyond lag QH, the value of the autocorrelation function is zero at all lags.

When both $P \neq 0$ and $Q \neq 0$, the autocorrelation function is, in general, nonzero only at seasonal lags. Across seasonal lags, the autocorrelation function for lags 0, H, $2H$, ..., QH will be affected by the moving average part of the process; beyond lag QH, it will follow the structure given by the autoregressive part. (For details, see Box and Jenkins [1976].)

When the income numbers from different quarters are not independently distributed, then $p \neq 0$ and/or $q \neq 0$ cannot be ruled out. That is, the full multiplicative model must be entertained. For these cases, the autocorrelation function's behavior is quite complicated. But results for some simple cases are available (see, e.g., Froeschle [1975] and Box and Jenkins [1976]). Results for several of these cases are recorded in Exhibit 7-12. In this exhibit, $\{\tilde{z}(\tau)\}$ is a stationary process and $\{\tilde{\alpha}(\tau)\}$ is a sequence of serially uncorrelated identically distributed random variables, with $E[\tilde{\alpha}(\tau)] = 0.0$. Also, ρ_j denotes the autocorrelation coefficient of $\{\tilde{z}(\tau)\}$ at lag j. That is, $\rho_j = \text{Corr}[\tilde{y}(\tau), \tilde{y}(\tau - j)]$. The cases described in Exhibit 7-12 are among those that are often useful in dealing with evidence on accounting numbers, such as evidence on quarterly income numbers—to which we now turn.

7.5.2 Empirical Results on Quarterly Income Numbers

The characteristics of quarterly income numbers are discussed in numerous papers. The studies of particular interest here are Foster [1977], Griffin [1977], Watts [1975], and

EXHIBIT 7-12

CHARACTERISTICS OF SELECTED SEASONAL MODELS' AUTOCORRELATION FUNCTIONS

Case 1 ARIMA $(0,0,1) \times (0,0,1)_H$

$$\tilde{z}(\tau) = (1 - \theta_1 B)(1 - \Theta_1 B^H)\tilde{\alpha}(\tau)$$

$$\rho_1 = -\theta_1/(1 + \theta_1^2)$$

$$\rho_j = 0,\ 2 \le j \le H - 1$$

$$\rho_{H-1} = \theta\Theta/(1 + \theta^2)(1 + \Theta^2)$$

$$\rho_H = -\Theta/(1 + \Theta^2)$$

$$\rho_{H+1} = \rho_{H-1}$$

$$\rho_j = 0,\ j > H + 1$$

Case 2 ARIMA $(0,0,1) \times (0,0,2)$

$$\tilde{z}(\tau) = (1 - \theta_1 B)(1 - \Theta_1 B^H - \Theta_2 B^{2H})\tilde{\alpha}(\tau)$$

$$\rho_1 = -\theta_1/(1 + \theta_1^2)$$

$$\rho_j = 0,\ 2 \le j \le H - 1$$

$$\rho_{H-1} = [\theta_1\Theta_1(1 - \Theta_2)]/(1 + \theta_1^2)(1 + \Theta_1^2 + \Theta_2^2)$$

$$\rho_H = -[\Theta_1(1 - \Theta_2)]/(1 + \Theta_1^2 + \Theta_2^2)$$

$$\rho_{H+1} = \rho_{H-1}$$

$$\rho_j = 0,\ H + 1 < j < 2H - 1$$

$$\rho_{2H-1} = [\theta_1\Theta_2]/(1 + \theta_1^2)(1 + \Theta_1^2 + \Theta_2^2)$$

$$\rho_{2H} = -\Theta_2/(1 + \Theta_1^2 + \Theta_2^2)$$

$$\rho_{2H+1} = \rho_{2H-1}$$

$$\rho_j = 0,\ j > 2H + 1$$

Case 3 ARIMA $(0,0,1) \times (1,0,0)_H$

$$(1 - \Phi_1 B^H)\tilde{z}(\tau) = (1 - \theta_1 B)\tilde{\alpha}(\tau)$$

$$\rho_1 = -\theta_1/(1 + \theta_1^2)$$

$$\rho_j = 0,\ 2 \le j \le H - 1$$

$$\rho_{H-1} = -\theta_1\Phi_1/(1 + \theta_1^2)$$

$$\rho_H = \Phi_1$$

$$\rho_{H+1} = \rho_{H-1}$$

$$\vdots$$

$$\rho_j = \Phi_1\rho_{j-H},\ j \ge H + 2$$

Case 4 ARIMA $(1,0,0) \times (0,0,1)_H$

$$(1 - \phi_1 B)\tilde{z}(\tau) = (1 - \Theta_1 B^H)\tilde{\alpha}(\tau)$$

Case 4 $$\rho_k = \begin{cases} \phi_1^k - \dfrac{\phi_1^{H-k}\Phi_1(1 - \phi_1^{2k})}{1 - \Phi_1^2 - 2\phi_1^H\Phi_1}, & k = 1, 2, \ldots, H \\ \phi_1\rho_{k-1}, & k \ge H + 1 \end{cases}$$

Source: Froeschle [1975, chap. 3].

Brown and Rozeff [1979]. Each of these studies provides detailed results on quarterly income numbers. The Foster study reports results on sales numbers and total cost numbers as well, where total costs are defined to be total sales minus total income for common stockholders (after taxes).

All of these authors used fairly restrictive criteria for purposes of sample selection. Thus, the results that they reported need not be "representative" vis-à-vis firms in general. Moreover, since there are overlaps in the time periods covered, samples of firms used, and statistical methods employed, these studies' findings are really not independent sources of evidence.

Since the major procedures and perspectives underlying these studies are similar, we shall focus mainly on one of them, *viz,* Foster's. Our remarks on the other studies are less detailed.

Foster's sample consists of 69 firms. These firms met the following criteria used by Foster to construct his sample: (1) Quarterly earnings (after tax but before dividends) and quarterly sales numbers had to be available for the period 1946–1974. Quarterly data for 1946–1961 were taken from various Moody's manuals. Data for 1962–1974 were taken from Standard and Poor's CØMPUSTAT data base. (2) Daily rates of return on common stock had to be available for the period June 1962 to June 1975. (3) Announcements of quarterly sales and earnings numbers for the 1962–1974 period had to be recorded in the *Wall Street Journal Index*.

The rate-of-return data and announcement dates demanded by criteria (2) and (3) were used in tests not described in this chapter. Only the empirical results based entirely on values of accounting numbers are described below.

An "industry profile" of Foster's sample is given in Table 7-15. As can be seen, the first four two-digit S.I.C. industry groups account for 43 percent of the sample. At first glance, this seems overly "lopsided." On the other hand, it may reflect the relative im-

TABLE 7-15

S.I.C. INDUSTRY BREAKDOWN OF FOSTER'S SAMPLE

S.I.C. Two-Digit Industry Code	Industry Title	Number of Firms
29	Petroleum and coal products	11
49	Electric, gas and sanitary seervices	9
28	Chemicals and allied produced	8
35	Machinery, except electrical	7
32	Stone, clay and glass products	5
33	Primary metal industries	5
37	Transportation equipment	4
20	Food and kindred products	3
26	Paper and allied products	3
10	Metal mining	2
36	Electrical equipment and supplies	2
59	Miscellaneous retail stores	2
	Other industries	8
		69

Source: Foster [1977, table 1].

portance of different industry groups in at least one of Foster's sources of data, *viz.*, the CØMPUSTAT data base. The latter source does not cover (by design) all of the firms represented in Foster's other source of data—Moody's manuals. This problem of potentially "nonrepresentative" samples is often encountered in empirical work of this sort—for which organized data bases and stringent data-availability criteria are "standard fare."

Foster's results consist of estimation results and prediction results. The period 1946–1961 was used for estimation; 1962–1974 was used for prediction results.

The following five quarterly models are among those considered by Foster:

(M1) $$\tilde{y}(\tau) = \tilde{y}(\tau - 4) + \tilde{\epsilon}(\tau)$$

(M2) $$\tilde{y}(\tau) = \delta + \tilde{y}(\tau - 4) + \tilde{\epsilon}(\tau)$$

(M3) $$\tilde{y}(\tau) = \tilde{y}(\tau - 1) + \tilde{\epsilon}(\tau)$$

(M4) $$\tilde{y}(\tau) = \delta + \tilde{y}(\tau - 1) + \tilde{\epsilon}(\tau)$$

(M5) $$\nabla_4\tilde{y}(\tau) = (1 - B^4)\tilde{y}(\tau) = \delta + \phi_1\nabla_4\tilde{y}(\tau - 1) + \tilde{\epsilon}(\tau)$$

or

$$\tilde{y}(\tau) - \tilde{y}(\tau - 4) = \delta + \phi_1(\tilde{y}(\tau - 1) - \tilde{y}(\tau - 5)) + \tilde{\epsilon}(\tau)$$

for $\tau \in T^*$. In all cases, $\tilde{\epsilon}(\tau)$ is, conditional on the model under analysis, specified to be serially uncorrelated and identically distributed, with $E[\tilde{\epsilon}(\tau)] = 0.0$. Note that (M2) is simply (M1) with δ not constrained to equal zero. And (M4) is (M3) with δ not constrained to equal zero. Models (M3) and (M4) are consistent with the hypothesis that there is no seasonality in the process $\{\tilde{y}(\tau)\}$. That is, they are consistent with the statement that inter-year relationships with respect to a particular quarter's number do not contribute to any dependence among quarterly numbers; only the inter-quarter relationships matter. Models (M1) and (M2) are consistent with the statement that only the inter-year relationships with respect to a particular quarter's number matter. For (M1) and (M2) there is no inter-quarter correlation. Therefore, each quarter's number may be analyzed independently of each other quarter's number. Model (M5) allows for inter-year and inter-quarter relationships. In terms of our ARIMA notation, the above five models can be described as follows:

(M1) $$\text{ARIMA}(0, 0, 0) \times (0, 1, 0)_4.$$

(M2) Same as (M1) with intercept not constrained to equal zero.

(M2) $$\text{ARIMA}(0, 1, 0) \times (0, 0, 0).$$

(M3) Same as (M2) with intercept not constrained to equal zero.

(M5) $$\text{ARIMA}(0, 1, 0) \times (0, 1, 0)_4.$$

Note that all of the above are special cases of the general multiplicative seasonal model defined earlier in expression (7.100). Also note that these models were specified by Foster in advance of any examination of his sample evidence. That is, the values of p, d, q, P, D, Q, and H defining a model in the class ARIMA$(p, d, q) \times (P, D, Q)_H$ were not selected after, say, estimated autocorrelation functions were examined. Such estimates were, of course, used to decide which model is most consistent with the available sample evidence.

As indicated, Foster's models are members of the class of models defined by (7.100). Therefore, his results are based on the assumption that the four stochastic models that account for the four quarterly numbers' inter-year behavior are identical models. There is, as a result, no provision for a difference between the probability model for, say, the quarter-1 number and the model for the quarter-4 number. Moreover, it is assumed that the appropriate probability model for any year's inter-quarter relationships is the same for all years and all quarters. In short, the disturbance in the ARIMA model identified for a given quarter's number is assumed to be drawn from the same process as that from which the disturbance for all other quarters' models is drawn. And this process is assumed to be the same for all years. These seemingly strong homogeneity conditions are often invoked in work on seasonal models. The same conditions were invoked in, for example, the papers by Watts [1975] and Griffin [1977] on quarterly accounting numbers—papers that are described later.

Prespecifying models as described above guarantees that those models will be actively entertained in all estimation and prediction stages of the analysis. No such guarantee is provided merely by specifying that a model belong to the class of multiplicative seasonal ARIMA models defined by expression (7.100). Foster was motivated to provide results for (M1)–(M4) because these models were used in other studies dealing with quarterly accounting numbers; model (M5) was considered because it appeared likely to overcome the inadequacies of (M1)–(M4) observed in the results of those other studies.

Previous use notwithstanding, some member other than (M1)–(M5) may provide a better characterization of a firm's earnings, sales, and cost numbers. In order to allow for this possibility, Foster used a "searching algorithm" that selects the "best fitting" model from this class.[41] He imposed some constraints on the models that this algorithm searched over—by imposing restrictions on the values of p, d, q, P, D, and Q. The value of H was specified to equal 4 for all models that allowed for a seasonality (i.e., all models for which $P \neq 0$, $Q \neq 0$, or $D \neq 0$).

Of course, the model that provides the "best fit" conditional on a given set of sample evidence (i.e., given observations on random variables) need not provide the most descriptively adequate model for the process (e.g., income numbers) under analysis. A model can, after all, provide the "best fit" by overemphasizing rare events and singularities unique to a given sample. This is hardly a reliable route to effectively modeling the systematic ("recurring") features of a process. One approach for assessing the general descriptive adequacy of a model that best fits a given sample of data is to evaluate the model's performance at predicting "new" data—i.e., observations not included in the sample used to identify and estimate the "best fitting" model. If the latter model also provides the best prediction performance, then one has stronger grounds for inferring descriptive adequacy *for the process* under analysis—and not just "best fit" for a *particular sample* of observations on that process.[42] Thus, in the end, Foster reported estimation and prediction results based on six models: (M1)–(M5), as defined above, and the "best fitting" model selected by a model search algorithm.

Table 7-16 gives some basic estimation results from his study. Provided there are the

---

[41]The searching algorithm incorporated the modeling procedures described by Box and Jenkins [1976].

[42]Providing just a "best fit" to the observed values of dependent and independent variables from a given sample is not, per se, an ultimate objective because new samples will contain different values and, from an ex ante perspective, the model cannot take those specific values into account in its "fit" to the sample at hand.

TABLE 7-16

CROSS-SECTIONAL SAMPLE AUTOCORRELATION: 1946–1974 (MEAN AND STD. DEVIATION)

		Logs											
d	*D*	*1*	*2*	*3*	*4*	*5*	*6*	*7*	*8*	*9*	*10*	*11*	*12*
		Panel A. Earnings Series											
0	0	.650	.521	.511	.618	.428	.349	.351	.452	.297	.238	.265	.377
		(.281)	(.347)	(.263)	(.210)	(.250)	(.305)	(.254)	(.248)	(.250)	(.287)	(.239)	(.224)
1	0	−.296	−.125	−.153	.408	−.162	−.076	−.139	.344	−.139	−.091	−.111	.304
		(.197)	(.310)	(.195)	(.281)	(.177)	(.284)	(.160)	(.258)	(.155)	(.257)	(.164)	(.251)
0	1	.445	.244	.128	−.121	.001	.019	−.017	−.034	−.026	−.032	−.008	−.005
		(.220)	(.205)	(.180)	(.233)	(.185)	(.179)	(.149)	(.145)	(.144)	(.143)	(.132)	(.133)
1	1	−.253	−.059	.106	−.335	.065	.052	−.014	−.019	.011	−.028	.020	.005
		(.172)	(.124)	(.154)	(.141)	(.140)	(.127)	(.115)	(.106)	(.090)	(.102)	(.097)	(.111)
		Panel B. Sales Series											
0	0	.890	.813	.772	.753	.682	.635	614	.608	.554	.516	.505	.507
		(.075)	(.117)	(.086)	(.098)	(.104)	(.122)	(.108)	(.115)	(.111)	(.123)	(.107)	(.110)
1	0	−.171	−.063	−.112	.428	−.137	−.050	−.126	.346	−.108	−.069	−.115	.322
		(.248)	(.341)	(.195)	(.253)	(.164)	(.297)	(.142)	(.247)	(.150)	(.266)	(.140)	(.217)
0	1	.617	.418	.274	.065	.108	.111	.095	.071	.073	.067	.055	.052
		(.224)	(.200)	(.173)	(.223)	(.162)	(.149)	(.141)	(.155)	(.138)	(.136)	(.129)	(.121)
1	1	−.144	−.027	.090	−.351	.039	.027	.009	−.038	.027	.004	−.012	.024
		(.245)	(.118)	(.149)	(.153)	(.138)	(.124)	(.098)	(.132)	(.102)	(.078)	(.086)	(.108)
		Panel C. Expense Series											
0	0	.893	.821	.777	.753	.689	.645	.621	.613	.564	.529	.515	.512
		(.070)	(.101)	(.084)	(.099)	(.101)	(.113)	(.105)	(.109)	(.105)	(.111)	(.099)	(.103)
1	0	−.165	−.055	−.094	.396	−.115	−.050	−.112	.317	−.089	−.072	−.093	.289
		(.249)	(.329)	(.188)	(.248)	(.161)	(.288)	(.138)	(.236)	(.140)	(.258)	(.141)	(.216)
0	1	.605	.414	.266	.047	.102	.104	.087	.069	.072	.066	.059	.056
		(.234)	(.202)	(.176)	(.233)	(.161)	(.147)	(.139)	(.148)	(.135)	(.131)	(.124)	(.117)
1	1	−.155	−.018	.096	−.359	.050	.030	.034	−.036	.027	.001	−.009	.020
		(.252)	(.109)	(.144)	(.148)	(.143)	(.117)	(.102)	(.124)	(.108)	(.071)	(.079)	(.112)

Source: Foster [1977, table 2].

estimated autocorrelation functions of $\tilde{z}(\tau)$ where:

$$\tilde{z}(\tau) = (1 - B)^d (1 - B^4)^D \tilde{y}(\tau)$$

and $\tilde{y}(\tau)$ is the number of ultimate interest: earnings in Panel A, sales in Panel B, and total costs in Panel C. For each number, results for four combinations of values of d and D are given. Other things being equal, the most appropriate combination is the one that induces a $\tilde{z}(\tau)$ process for which a lack of serial correlation can be inferred. Where this cannot be inferred, the estimation results provide information on what other values of d or D might be more appropriate and on the autoregressive and moving average characteristics of the processes. As always, the objective in differencing is to attain stationarity—which is contradicted by serial correlation functions that do not decay or cut off (see Section 7.4.1.3).

The estimates in Table 7-16 summarize the results for individual firms. For example, the estimate of 0.650 at lag 1 for earnings conditional on $d = 0$ and $D = 0$ is an average of the estimates obtained for individual firms. The number appearing below it in parentheses—0.281—is the sample standard deviation of the estimates for individual firms.

Consider the results for the sales number. The summarized point estimates for $d = 0$ and $D = 0$—when taken at face value—appear inconsistent with the absence of serial correlation. These results resemble those observed for Caterpillar's EPS (see Section 7.4.1.6). The autocorrelation function does not appear to die out fast enough; nor does it appear just to cut off. Specifying $d = 1$ and $D = 0$ seems to improve things except at lags 4, 8, and 12, i.e., at integer multiples of the period $H = 4$. And, taken at face value, the estimates at these seasonal lags—0.428, 0.346, and 0.322—do not appear to be consistent with an autocorrelation function that is nonzero only at seasonal lags and whose values at these lags decay or cut off. Seasonal nonstationarity is consistent with these results. The summarized point estimates for $d = 0$ and $D = 1$ appear consistent with an autocorrelated but stationary series. If only ρ_1 is inferred to be nonzero—conditional on the average estimate of 0.650—a first-order moving average model for the seasonally differenced series would be inferred, other things being equal. A low-order autoregressive model (with low values of autoregressive parameters) is another possibility. The results for $d = 1$ and $D = 1$, particularly at lag 4, suggest over-differencing; these results are, in turn, inconsistent with inter-quarter nonstationarity (of the sort requiring $d \neq 0$, conditional on $D > 0$).

Similar remarks apply to the other numbers—earnings and total costs. In general, the results for sales and these other results point to the existence of (1) seasonal nonstationarity—of the sort removed by $D = 1$—and inter-quarter serial correlation—of the sort that can be captured by a first-order moving average model applied to seasonal differences or (2) a low-order autoregressive model with autoregressive parameters having small positive values (also applied to seasonal first differences). In any event, these results seem consistent with seasonal components in the numbers and important inter-quarter correlation after accounting for seasonalities.

Additional analyses by Foster reinforced these initial (and tentative) inferences. His additional analyses incorporated examinations of the "best fitting" models determined by the searching algorithm mentioned above, analyses of his competing models' prediction performance with respect to observations not used for model identification and estimation, and simulation results designed to provide insights on the reliability of his model identification tools. On the basis of these analyses and examinations, it appears that a descriptively adequate model for the quarterly numbers examined is model (M5), a first-order autoregressive model applied to seasonal first differences. This is an ARIMA(1, 0, 0) × $(0, 1, 0)_4$ model. The most important competitors appear to be an ARIMA(0, *d*, 1) × $(0, D, 1)_4$ or an ARIMA(1, *d*, 0) × $(0, D, 1)_4$, with one or both of the scalers *d* and *D* equal to unity. Only values of unity and zero were considered for *d* and *D*. These two competitors were identified by the model search algorithms for the seasonal ARIMA models defined by (7.100). For sales and total costs, the differences between the models—in terms of observed adequacy—did not appear too marked. For income numbers, the results were inferred to favor (M5) for most firms.

Foster's inferences about income numbers are not radically different from what was inferred by either Griffin [1977] or Watts [1975] in their analyses of income numbers. Griffin's study is based on observed values of "earnings available for common" from the period 1958 (quarter 1)–1971 (quarter 4). His sample consists of 94 firms selected according to the following sample selection criteria: (1) values of quarterly earnings were available for the 56 consecutive quarters, 1958 (quarter 1) to 1971 (quarter 4); (2) values of quarterly cash dividends were available for the same 56 quarters; (3) the firm was listed on the New York Stock Exchange throughout the period 1958–1971; and (4) the realized value of the firm's net sales for the first quarter of 1964 exceeded $50 million. The fourth criterion reflects an attempt to select only "large" firms. These criteria were originally developed in conjunction with a different study (Griffin [1976]). Thus, some of them—e.g., (3) and (4)—demanded data irrelevant for our immediate interests. Nevertheless, they did affect the sample underlying Griffin's results on the time series properties of quarterly earnings. The data sources used by Griffin are the Quarterly Industrial CØMPUSTAT tape, for the period 1964–1971, and the *Wall Street Journal Index*, for 1958–1963.

Griffin entertained the following models for quarterly earnings, $\tilde{y}(\tau)$, $\tau \in T^*$:

(GM1) $\underline{\text{ARIMA}(0, 1, 0) \times (0, 1, 0)_4}$

$$(1 - B)(1 - B^4)\tilde{y}(\tau) = \tilde{\epsilon}(\tau)$$

(GM2) $\underline{\text{ARIMA}(0, 1, 1) \times (0, 1, 1)_4}$

$$(1 - B)(1 - B^4)\tilde{y}(\tau) = (1 - \theta_1 B)(1 - \theta_1 B^4)\tilde{\epsilon}(\tau)$$

(GM3) $\underline{\text{ARIMA}(1, 0, 0) \times (1, 0, 0)_4}$

$$(1 - \phi B(1 - \Phi_1 B^4)(\tilde{y}(\tau) - \mu) = \tilde{\epsilon}(\tau)$$

(GM4) $\underline{\text{ARIMA}(0, 0, 1) \times (0, 0, 1)_4}$

$$(\tilde{y}(\tau) - \mu) = (1 - \theta B)(1 - \theta_1 B^4)\tilde{\epsilon}(\tau)$$

where $\mu \equiv E(\tilde{y}(\tau))$, a constant.[43]

Unlike Foster's study, no model-search algorithm and no prediction performance evaluations were incorporated into Griffin's study. All inferences about model adequacy were

---

[43]In models (GM1) and (GM2), a nonzero process mean, μ, is not defined, as indicated by the appearance of differencing—which is used to attain stationarity.

based on estimation results for the above prespecified models, which are members of the class of ARIMA models defined by (7.100).

The estimates of autocorrelation functions obtained by Griffin were quite similar to those obtained by Foster. And their final inferences were similar. Griffin's results are consistent with the descriptive adequacy of model (GM2) or (GM3) with Φ_1 constrained to equal unity. The latter model is identical to Foster's model (M5). Griffin inferred that model (M5) did not account for the seasonality in income numbers as well as did model (GM2)—which is contrary to Foster's ultimate inference. Recall, however, that Foster's inference was based on more than estimation results (i.e., more than observed "fit" to sample evidence). He also used prediction and simulation results. In any event, the two studies are in agreement over the really serious contenders for the most adequate model, on average, for firms' quarterly income numbers. Consistent inferences were made by Watts, to the extent made feasible by the set of models that he prespecified.[44]

Watts' results on quarterly earnings numbers were obtained as part of a study dealing with broader issues. Thus, as with Griffin's study, some of his simple selection criteria were imposed to attain objectives other than those specific to his analysis of quarterly income numbers.

Watts' results are based on a sample of 175 firms drawn at random from all firms that satisfied the following criteria (of which there were around 350 firms): (1) values of quarterly and annual earnings per share were available for 1958–1962 from the *Wall Street Journal Index;* (2) daily rates of return on common stock were available from the Wells Fargo Bank daily returns file for the period July 2, 1962 to July 11, 1969; (3) listed on the New York Exchange for the entire period July 2, 1962 to September 27, 1968; (4) unchanged fiscal-year-ending month over the period January 1958 to December 1969.

As indicated, values of quarterly earnings for the period 1958 to 1969 were obtained from the *Wall Street Journal Index*. In addition, wherever data availability permitted, values of quarterly earnings for the selected firms for the period 1950 to 1957 were obtained from various Moody's manuals. For various reasons, only data from the period January 1950 to June 1962 were allowed to be used for estimation results. In the end, the number of quarterly observations used to estimate a firm's earnings model ranged from 18 to 50.

A profile of Watts' sample in terms of numbers of observations is given in Table 7-17. As can be seen, the sample frequency distribution has two modes: one at 18 observations and the other at 50 observations. Watts obtained separate sets of estimation results for the subsets of firms at each mode and for his entire sample of 175 firms. He inferred that the results for the two subsamples were essentially the same.

Watts' estimation results are for 15 prespecified models. Some of these models allow for seasonalities. The different models that allow for seasonalities do so in different ways. Other models simply imposed different relationships on the (nonseasonal) inter-quarter behavior of earnings numbers. One of the models entertained by Watts is the ARIMA $(0, 1, 1) \times (0, 1, 1)_4$ model, which was also entertained by both Griffin and Foster.

---

[44]There are some differences in the sets of models excluded by Griffin, Foster, and Watts. For example, the ARIMA$(1, 0, 0) \times (0, 1, 0)_4$ model considered by Foster was excluded from Watts' set of entertained models. Given these differences, differences in the authors' ultimate inferences need not be due to any actual conflicts in their results.

TABLE 7-17

FREQUENCY DISTRIBUTION FOR THE NUMBER OF OBSERVATIONS OF QUARTERLY EARNINGS FOR EACH FIRM, JANUARY 1950–JUNE 1962

Number of Observations	Frequency
18	79
34	9
38	1
42	5
43	1
46	6
48	1
50	73
	175

Source: Watts [1975, table 1].

The estimation tools used and problems encountered by Watts are similar to those encountered by both Griffin and Foster. So, we shall not go over these details. In the end, Watts inferred that the ARIMA(0, 1, 1) × $(0, 1, 1)_4$ model is, on balance, the most descriptively adequate model relative to the set of prespecified models entertained. At first glance, this may seem to be somewhat inconsistent with Foster's results (see above). Note, however, that the ARIMA(1, 0, 0) × $(0, 1, 0)_4$ model found to be almost equally (if not more) adequate by Foster was excluded from Watts' set of prespecified models. Thus, the fact that he did not ascribe as much importance to it as did Foster is not surprising. But this difference should not becloud the consistency between Watts' ultimate inferences and those of both Griffin and Foster. Specifically, both he and they inferred that the ARIMA (0, 1, 1) × $(0, 1, 1)_4$ model could not be discredited as a descriptively adequate model for quarterly income numbers.

Brown and Rozeff [1979] provide additional comparative results on the models favored by Foster, Watts, and Griffin and results on the model that Brown and Rozeff end up favoring, *viz.*, the ARIMA(1, 0, 0) × $(0, 1, 1)_4$ model. Note that the nonseasonal part of this model is identical to Foster's model, ARIMA(1, 0, 0) × $(0, 1, 0)_4$. The difference between the models turns on Brown's and Rozeff's inclusion of a first-order *seasonal* moving average term.

Brown and Rozeff obtained estimation and prediction results for each of the above models using a sample of 23 firms. Moreover, they also obtained, for each firm, estimation and prediction results for the univariate seasonal model that provided the "best fit" to that firm's historical data.[45]

Conditional on both their estimation and their prediction results, Brown and Rozeff infer that Foster's model is the least adequate of those examined. In terms of estimation results, the Brown-Rozeff model—ARIMA(1, 0, 0) × $(0, 1, 1)_4$—seemed to be about the same as the "best fitting" time series models and the ARIMA(0, 1, 1) × (0, 1, 1) model favored by Watts and Griffin. Similar inferences were made conditionally on their

[45]Recall that the models discussed in the preceding paragraph purport to be "good" models for firms in general, or for a "representative firm." None is necessarily the optimal model for any specific firm conditional on given sample evidence.

one-quarter-ahead prediction results. For longer prediction horizons (five-quarter and nine-quarter prediction horizons), they inferred that the ARIMA$(1, 0, 0) \times (0, 1, 1)_4$ model, on balance, did better that the others. Hence, they end up favoring this model. Additional results pertaining to this topic were supplied by Welch [1984], Lorek [1979], and Lorek, Icerman, and Abdulkader [1983]. Conditional on these additional results, the superiority of the Brown-Rozeff model is much less striking and sometimes nonexistent. Since the theoretical differences between this model and the others are not very dramatic, it is not surprising that samples of the sizes commonly used in these studies do not consistently favor one of the models.

Before we conclude, it seems appropriate to identify a basic limitation of all of these papers: cross-sectional correlation with respect to different firms' accounting numbers—an issue that arose in our discussion of index models. Given this, the income number of one firm is, on balance, not independently distributed vis-à-vis the income numbers of other firms. One should expect, therefore, some stochastic characteristics of different firms' income numbers—such as the numbers' autocorrelation functions—to exhibit sample commonalities. In this case, the conventional tests used to make inferences conditionally on results for different firms are not, in principle, wholly appropriate tests—because they do not take the effects of commonalities into account. The end result tends to be results whose statistical significance is somewhat overstated. Alternative formal tests are available, but a discussion of them—which would get us too deeply into the realm of multivariate statistics—is beyond the scope of this book. An excellent discussion of relevant issues is given in Miller [1966].

7.5.3 Summary

Seasonalities induce elements of periodic behavior in accounting numbers. As such, they are among the potential sources of nonstationarity exhibited by accounting numbers, such as income numbers. Our discussion focused on seasonalities due to quarterly influences. Other sources of seasonalities are, of course, possible. The tools available for attacking them are the same as those used for quarterly influences.

Seasonalities are of interest because, if they exist, they are among the systematic time series characteristics of ultimate interest to us. And the evidence reviewed above is consistent with the presence of seasonalities in accounting numbers—in particular, income, sales, and cost numbers. The consequences of ignoring seasonalities when dealing with quarterly accounting numbers are, insofar as statistical theory is concerned, the same as those caused by ignoring other systematic properties. We discussed the issue of exploiting accounting numbers' systematic properties in Section 7.2.1.

Why certain univariate time series models have more descriptive adequacy than others is, as yet, a largely unanswered question. Hence, we cannot "explain" why, for example, the serial correlation structure of quarterly income numbers (or annual income numbers) does (or should) adhere to any particular pattern. The explanations that are encountered in the available literature are, appearances notwithstanding, basically ad hoc (at best).

CHAPTER EIGHT

Signaling and Screening: Implications for Accounting Numbers and Capital Market Equilibrium

8.1 Introduction

Managements are assumed to make production-investment and financing decisions in accordance with the "market value rule." That is, we assume that these decisions are made so as to maximize the market values of firms' currently outstanding securities.[1] For each firm, this value is the aggregate current value of the probability distributions of its outstanding securities' future values. The characteristics of the decisions made by a firm's management are determinants of the attributes of these probability distributions. In general, variations in the details of those characteristics induce changes in firms' current equilibrium values via their effects on the probability distributions of securities' future values. The equilibrium values of securities ultimately set in the capital market are, therefore, conditional on the perceived characteristics of the decisions made by firms' managements.

In general, both the characteristics of firms' decisions and the resultant distributions of securities' values are "unobservables." Thus, in general, setting firms' equilibrium values involves (at least in an "as if" sense) making inferences about the characteristics of firms' decisions and then making consistent inferences about the distributions of securities' future values. This, in turn, involves using available sample evidence (or "observables") corresponding to values of random variables whose systematic properties are affected by (and thus "reflect") the characteristics of firms' decisions.[2] Consequently, in an indirect sense, the equilibrium values of firms' securities are conditional on available sources of sample evidence. Accounting numbers—the random variables of interest here—constitute one such source, because their systematic properties depend, in general, on the attributes of firms' decisions.[3]

But the systematic properties of accounting numbers do not depend only on the characteristics of firms' production-investment and financing decisions. They also depend on firms' accounting techniques and disclosure rules. Moreover, firms' managements have some (and in some cases a substantial) latitude of choice with respect to their firms' accounting techniques and disclosure rules. Thus, if managements perceive that (and if they behave as if) investors use the properties of accounting numbers as bases for inferring distributions of securities' future values and then for setting equilibrium prices, then managements may be motivated to behave as if they use accounting techniques and disclosure rules for the purpose of maximizing the equilibrium values of their currently outstanding securities. Specifically, they may behave as if they select and use such techniques and

---

[1]"Me first" rules (or equivalent compensatory/protective devices) of the sort discussed in Chapter 4 are assumed to be in force.

The "market value rule" is discussed by Fama [1972; 1976], Jensen and Long [1972], and Stiglitz [1972], among others.

[2]The details of the probability distributions (or "probability models") of these random variables constitute their systematic properties.

[3]Accounting numbers with degenerate distribution functions (and thus "deterministic" variables) are not precluded by our characterization of accounting numbers as random variables.

rules so as to affect investors' inferences about the characteristics of managements' decisions and, as a result, to affect investors' assessed distributions of securities' future values.[4] This sort of scenario leads to a so-called signaling perspective of external accounting, which explicitly recognizes that investors' inferential activities may affect managements' incentives with respect to selections of accounting techniques and disclosure rules, and perhaps other types of decisions as well.[5]

One of the major assumptions of the signaling perspective is that there are asymmetries among agents with respect to information-production opportunities or information-production costs. For present purposes, one appropriate characterization is that managements are believed to have access to information-production opportunities that are not available to "outsiders" or that are only available to outsiders on less favorable cost conditions (i.e., it is more costly for outsiders to pursue the same opportunities). Of particular interest here are opportunities to produce information pertinent to assessing the characteristics of managements' decisions and plans, such as the probability distributions of net cash earnings induced by managements' current decisions.[6] Another critical assumption is that the benefits of signaling (in the form of, e.g., a higher firm value) and the costs of signaling are such that "dishonest" signaling does not prevail in equilibrium. (More on this later.)

Given the assumed informational asymmetries, the signaling perspective can lead to a variety of insights into and tentative explanations of several external reporting phenomena. For example, this perspective can be used to explain why some firms voluntarily disclose the realized values of some accounting numbers and why they might submit external reports for an "independent audit" even in the absence of regulations (e.g., SEC filing rules) that require such audits. It can also be used to explain why investors behave as if the properties of some accounting numbers, taken by themselves, reflect no information pertinent to setting firms' equilibrium values, whereas those same properties are treated as if they reflect such information when they are jointly exploited with the prop-

---

[4]This mode of communication may be encouraged by regulation-induced disincentives to use more direct means. For example, until early 1973 the SEC did not, in general, allow firms to include earnings forecasts in filings with the SEC. Modifications of this general policy were announced in a "general statement on projections" on February 2, 1973 (SEC Release No. 33-5362) and embodied in a series of formal rule proposals announced on April 25, 1975 (SEC Release No. 33-5581). These proposals were withdrawn on April 23, 1976 (SEC Release No. 33-5699). But in the latter release, the SEC did amend its Rule 14a-9 (issued under the Securities and Exchange Act of 1934) to delete the reference to predictions of earnings as being possibly misleading. In the same release, it proposed "Guides" designed to encourage registrants to include projections of earnings in filings with the SEC. In any event, the SEC's announcements on earnings projections since 1973 seem consistent with the view that the SEC now recognizes that its own regulations may have impeded disclosures of potentially informative sources of sample evidence. And these impediments may have encouraged firms to use more indirect means of "communicating" with investors.

[5]That is, our characterization of managerial behavior does not preclude an influence of accounting techniques or disclosure rules on the substantive features of management's production-investment and financing decisions. See, for example, Gonedes and Dopuch [1979] and Chapter 6.

The general topic of signaling is discussed by Spence [1974], among others. Recent applications pertinent to the issues at hand are given by Ross [1977], Leland and Pyle [1976], Jaffee and Russell [1976], and Penman [1977].

[6]Recall our assumption that agents having the same information are in complete agreement with respect to their distributional assessments.

erties of other numbers. Third, it can be used to explain how (even in the absence of regulations) a substantial amount of information about some firms can be made available even though those firms voluntarily choose to disclose very little.[7] Finally, and at a more generl level, it can be used to identify some of the factors (including institutional factors) that are determinants of accounting numbers' information content.[8] As will be seen, much more is involved here than what is usually incorporated into statements of "accounting theory" (e.g., definitions of accounting notions, such as "assets," "liabilities," etc.) and into assertions about what is "needed" by users of financial statements.

The remainder of this chapter deals with various aspects of the signaling perspective, including a discussion of its essential features. This discussion begins in the next section, where we provide an overview (in "loose terms") of some key notions and relationships associated with signaling and screening phenomena. Following that, we provide a characterization of managerial decision making tied to the two-parameter asset-pricing model. This is used to identify the details of some key potential referents of signaling and screening activities. We then discuss potential substitution and complementary relationships among accounting numbers. As will be seen, a variety of debates over accounting numbers, accounting techniques, and disclosure rules turn on implicit assumptions about these sorts of relationships and the nature of managerial signaling activities. Some of the debates over the effects of extraordinary items and the effects of disclosures of dividend policy changes (viewed as sources of information about expected values of income numbers) fall into this category. Providing empirical evidence dealing specifically with these debates is the final major task of this chapter.

The remaining sections of this chapter are quite heterogeneous with respect to the demands placed on the reader. Some sections constitute "easy reading." Others may appear to be overly technical—because of an emphasis on formalities of modeling or on the technicalities of statistical tests. As always, the reader should not be "put off" by seemingly technical material. The reader should at least skim through such material to get at the main lines of development and the main results. Our calling for "best efforts" should, by now, be familiar.

Section 8.4 is a fairly detailed treatment of empirical evidence and statistical methods. It will probably be of greatest use to those involved (or planning to be involved) in empirical work. Others may want to just skim through this section, or go directly to Section 8.5.

8.2 Signaling and Screening

8.2.1 Some Fundamental Aspects of Signaling and Screening

Capital market agents, in the aggregate, face the task of setting firms' equilibrium values in a way that reflects agents' assessed distributions of securities' future values. So long as the characteristics of these distributions differ across different types of securities

---

[7]Under appropriate conditions, the fact that a firm chooses not to do something can be informative. Also, when there is cross-sectional correlation, signals supplied by one firm may alter inferences about another firm.

[8]Recall that the extent to which accounting numbers have information content depends on the extent to which assessed distribution functions of firms' future values are altered by values of accounting numbers.

or across securities of the same type (e.g., common stocks) issued by different firms, there are incentives to allocate real resources to activities that facilitate distinguishing one distribution from another in terms of whatever characteristics are relevant to setting equilibrium prices. This activity is a *screening* activity, which is simply a process that is supposed to permit *discrimination*. That is, it is supposed to facilitate discriminating among things that would otherwise be treated as homogeneous—at least insofar as allocations of real resources are concerned and notwithstanding any sources of heterogeneity. For example, investors might know that the values of firms' expected future values are different (cross-sectionally), conditional on firms' current decisions. But identifying the "true value" of each firm's expected future value by directly observing that value may be impossible. Any indirect means that can be used to discriminate among firms in terms of their expected future values can serve as a screening device in this scenario. It is as if the firms' distributions of future values are eggs of different grades and we are looking for an egg-sorting device. One obvious means of such discrimination involves using past data to get estimates of the values of firms' expected future values. This approach assumes, among other things, that the available past data are drawings from the distribution functions that now characterize firms' future values—and thus the distribution functions now induced by firms' given current decisions. If this stationarity condition does not hold, then estimation results based only on past data may not be too helpful in discriminating among firms in terms of the current value of their expected future values.[9] Nonstationarity may be induced by, for example, changes in the characteristics of firms' decisions. (Even if there is stationarity, one must still contend with specification and estimation errors.)

In summary, distinguishing among firms in terms of the distributions of their future values involves identifying the characteristics of these distributions. But these distributions, and thus their characteristics, (e.g., their expected values) are not, in general, directly observable. Thus, if distinctions are to be made, they must be based on "a priori" (or assumed) conditions or on "observables" that are deemed to be dependent (in some way) on the unobservables of interest. In the end, some set of surrogates or "proxies" must be employed.

But if the characteristics of these surrogates are subject to the influence of those with whom agents transact, then agents' inferences—or the implications about unobservables that they perceive—may be subject to that influence. In general, their inferences will be affected when the effects of that influence (assuming there are some) are not offset or somehow taken into account by agents' actions—perhaps because those effects are not identifiable on the basis of available means of information-production. In this case, the selection of observables for screening purposes may induce changes in the incentives of those with whom agents transact, such as the managements of firms that sell securities in the capital market to finance their production-investment decisions. This situation is, it appears, important when the properties of accounting numbers are used as bases for assessing distributions of securities' future values. In general, accounting techniques and disclosure rules are among the determinants of the information reflected in accounting numbers, or the properties of accounting numbers *qua* screening devices. The techniques and rules used by a firm are, to some extent, subject to the control of management. Thus, management's perceptions about how the properties of accounting numbers affect inves-

---

[9]The concept of stationarity is discussed in Chapter 7.

tors' inferences may alter management's selections of accounting techniques and disclosure rules—perhaps independently of whatever is alleged to provide "conceptual underpinnings" for external reporting.[10] And changes in management's perceptions about investors' screening behavior may lead to changes in management's selections and applications of accounting techniques and disclosure rules—even though management did not effect any changes in the substantive attributes of either their production-investment decisions or their financing decisions. This implies, of course, that investors can (knowingly or unknowingly) influence selections and applications of accounting techniques and disclosure rules via their screening and price-setting behavior—independently of the "principles of accounting." The extent to which this can be done depends, evidently, on management's latitude of choice with respect to those techniques and rules.

The prediction that management will behave as if they are using techniques and rules in this way presumes that management view investors as behaving as if the properties of accounting numbers reflect information about the characteristics of management's decisions and that management view themselves as having information not already available, or not available at the same (or lower) costs, to investors. If management believes that all the information-production opportunities available to themselves are also available (at the same time or sooner) to investors, they can hardly expect to exercise control over the information to which investors have access. At most, they might be able to affect the total costs of information production by producing once what otherwise might be produced several times by each of several agents producing on personal account. And if the costs of producing some information are incurred by firms (and thus their securityholders), the incidence of these production costs might be altered. This is, of course, a nontrivial matter, since it does pertain to the allocative efficiency of the economy's ultimate information-production activities. But this aspect of management's decisions should be distinguished from the extent to which their selections and applications of accounting techniques and disclosure rules "communicate" information to which management have "privileged" or "restricted" access—because it is *not feasible* for "outsiders" to produce this information.[11] (More on the cost issue later.)

Evidently, there is no fundamental reason to suppose that investors are unaware of the implications of their behavior for management's selections and uses of accounting techniques and disclosure rules. Indeed, if investors do not behave as if they want to conceal their use of accounting numbers' properties, one can presume that they are behaving *as if* they deliberately indicate that they will assess disitributions of firms' future values—and, thus, establish firms' current equilibrium values—conditionally on firms' revealed choices vis-à-vis accounting techniques and disclosure rules. In effect, they are behaving as if they offer firms the opportunity to sort themselves out via these revealed choices. Presumably, this is done on the assumption that (1) management has access to,

---

[10]The various statements of the "objectives of financial reporting" are among the sources of such alleged underpinnings. Discussions of some alternatives and problems pertinent to statements of such objectives are available in the Financial Accounting Standards Board's Discussion Memorandum on this topic, *Conceptual Framework for Financial Accounting and Reporting: Elements of Financial Statements and Their Measurement* (December 2, 1976).

[11]And note that what is of ultimate interest are the implications and inferences that are induced by data available to management, not the data themselves. The same inferences and implications may be induced by different sources of sample evidence.

and will exploit, some information-production opportunities to which investors do not have access, or to which they do have access but only on less favorable terms of trade; and (2) management's revealed choices with respect to accounting techniques and disclosure rules will be correlated, in some detectable way, with the results of management's information-production activities—in particular, those results relevant to assessing the characteristics of management's decisions. In effect, this scenario involves "self-selection" or "self-identification" by firms (in terms of the attributes of their decisions) via management's choices with respect to accounting techniques and disclosure rules. This is a critical feature of managerial signaling.[12]

If managerial signaling is to be a usable equilibrium phenomenon, investors must be confident that signals are not "dishonest" or they must be able to identify "dishonest" managerial signaling. Here, "dishonest" signaling refers to a setting where management signals in order to affect investors' inferences in a way not justified (in management's view) by the substantive implications of management's information. Note that the crux of this issue is not whether management attempts to alter investors' inferences. What is relevant is the consistency between the inferences induced by management and the substantive implications of information available to management but not to outsiders.

A standard assumption of the signaling literature is that, for a given signal, the signaling costs faced by a dishonest signaler exceed those faced by an honest signaler. If the honest signaler signals up to the point where marginal costs equal marginal gains (e.g., marginal change in firm value is zero), then a dishonest signaler who attempts to mimic this honest signaler will find that his marginal costs exceed his marginal benefits. (More on this later.)

8.2.2 Illustrations of Potential Managerial Signaling: Dividend Policy Changes and Extraordinary Items

This sort of reasoning has, in fact, been explicitly or implicitly used in several areas of finance and accounting. For example, it has been used as a basis for explaining the effects of firms' dividend policies on capital market equilibrium. For the kind of capital market setting used here, a major conclusion of Miller and Modigliani [1961] is that, in equilibrium, a firm's dividend policy does not affect the firm's value, given the firm's production-investment decisions. But it is often observed that securities' prices change after unexpected dividend policy changes. This led to the so-called information content of dividends hypothesis, about which Miller and Modigliani [1961, p. 430] wrote:

---

[12]Note that a signaling management need not think of itself as actually engaging in signaling. The critical issue is whether it ends up providing observables that are potentially useful in making inferences about unobservable characteristics of its production-investment and financing decisions.

In this scenario, signals can contribute to an efficient allocation of resources because of the relationship between agents' inferences on personal account and real resource allocation; see, e.g., Gonedes [1975*a*]. Thus, signaling can be a productive activity in this scenario. This situation corresponds to Spence's scenario wherein education signals are used to allocate people to jobs; see Spence [1974, appendix E].

Finally, note that the forms of signaling used by management may be affected by disclosure rules, accounting regulations, and management's exposure to statutory liability, among other things.

> . . . in the real world a change in the dividend rate is often followed by a change in the market price (sometimes spectacularly so). Such a phenomenon would not be incompatible with irrelevance to the extent that it was merely a reflection of what might be called the "informational content" of dividends, an attribute of particular dividend payments hitherto excluded by assumption from the discussion and proofs. That is, where a firm has adopted a policy of dividend stabilization with a long-established and generally appreciated "target payout ratio," investors are likely to (and have good reason to) interpret a change in the dividend rate as a change in management's views of future profit prospects for the firm. The dividend change, in other words, provides the occasion for the price change though not its cause, the price still being solely a reflection of future earnings and growth opportunities. In any particular instance, of course, the investors might well be mistaken in placing this interpretation on the dividend change, since the management might really only be changing its payout target or possibly even attempting to "manipulate" the price. But this would involve no particular conflict with the irrelevance proposition, unless, of course, the price changes in such cases were not reversed when the unfolding of events had made clear the true nature of the situation.

This perspective on dividend policy, which has spawned a substantial amount of research, is simply that managerial decisions about dividend policy—which are among a firm's financing decisions—may induce signals about managerial earnings expectations. Whether or not this is an intended effect is beside the point (see footnote number 12). The connection between dividend policy changes and investors' inferences about managerial earnings expectations depends on investors' views on the determinants of management's dividend policies and their views on management's information-production opportunities. According to the "information content" hypothesis, management is presumed to behave as if they select dividend changes according to a target payout ratio and their expectations about the future values of income numbers. If investors behave as if these expectations are conditional on information not yet available to "outsiders" and as if income numbers reflect information about the characteristics of firms' decisions, then investors will, other things equal, behave as if dividend changes reflect information beyond that currently available to "outsiders"; i.e., those changes will be used as effective signals when investors make inferences about the attributes of firms' decisions.[13]

Other examples of possible signaling behavior are management's decisions about classifying the effects of transactions as "extraordinary items," at least according to some perspectives on such items. The fact that "extra-ordinary," or "unusual" components of a period's total income number are often viewed as reflecting information pertinent to assessing firms' values is illustrated by the following remarks—which deal with both "unusual items," and items induced by so-called prior period adjustments:

---

[13] A recent analysis of this topic is provided by Miller and Rock [1985], for cases of symmetric and asymmetric information (regarding "directors" and "outsiders"). In the former case, dividends convey information, but not directly and not necessarily as a result of deliberate managerial policy. In the asymmetric information case, dividends can serve as "signals" in the sense defined by Spence [1974].

> . . . Once identified, unusual and prior-period items should not be pushed aside. They must be considered, since they indicate that past earnings figures are incorrect in the light of subsequent information. Also, they may indicate that a company's future income presentation will carry a higher degree of uncertainty than previously assumed, since experience suggests that those companies that have unusual and prior-period items are more likely to have them again in the future than companies that have never had these items. (Hawkins [1976, p. 5].)

Whether or not this characterization has descriptive validity is not relevant at this point. The fact that it views extraordinary (or unusual) items as potentially informative is the relevant point.

In general, viewing extraordinary items as potential signals stem from management's latitude of choice over disclosures about such items, management behaving as if they assume that investors view income numbers as reflecting information about the attributes of firms' decisions, and the assumption that investors do behave in this way. This will be discussed later. Suffice it to note here that this perspective and the potential for "misleading" or "distorted" management signaling via extraordinary items seem to have been among the factors that motivated the SEC's 1973 changes in the rules for Form 8-K reporting and some of the (now defunct) Accounting Principles Board's changes in income-reporting rules.[14] Moreover, the previously discussed "big bath" and "income-smoothing hypotheses," which pertain in part to managerial uses of extraordinary items, can really be viewed as hypotheses about the characteristics of managerial signaling. Both hypotheses involve propositions about managerial attempts to alter what investors infer by altering available sample evidence. The inferences of interest are those made conditionally on the systematic properties of accounting numbers. Both hypotheses propose that management will attempt to induce inferences different from those that would otherwise be made, given the characteristics of the production-investment and financing decisions that management plans to pursue and the accounting techniques in use before managerial attempts to alter inferences. According to the "income-smoothing" hypothesis, management will attempt to alter inferences by altering the *sample* variability of reported values of income numbers. According to the "big bath" hypothesis, those attempts to alter inferences involve altering the timing of loss recognitions.

8.2.3 Signaling and Managerial Choices

The above characterization of investors' inferential behavior and management's self-selecting responses implies that management choices *per se* may be informative—perhaps independently of the implications of their choices for the systematic properties of accounting numbers. The mere fact that a firm chooses, say, accounting technique A rather than the alternative accounting technique B may be just as important as the relative effects of A on the properties of the firm's accounting numbers. For example, a firm's selection of an accelerated method of depreciation rather than the straight-line method may be important because of what this selection is inferred to imply about the technology embodied in the capital services that management plans to use, given its current production-invest-

[14]See, e.g., Securities and Exchange Commission [1973] and APB *Opinions Nos. 9* and *30*. Unless otherwise indicated by the FASB (the APB's successor), APB *Opinions* still apply to external reporting.

ment decisions. The effects (if any) of this technique on the properties of, say, the firm's net income number constitute a distinct potential influence on investors' inferences. Whether or not management's selections are, by themselves, informative depends partially on whether investors infer a systematic connection between choices of techniques or disclosure rules and the attributes of firms' decisions. Also important, of course, is management's latitude of choice regarding accounting techniques—and thus the rules enforced by firms' "independent" auditors and other constraining bodies (such as the SEC and the IRS). Finally, note that the potential importance of management's selections of techniques and rules, *taken by themselves,* is one reason for expecting the effects ("information content") of accounting numbers, taken by themselves, to be rather indeterminant on an a priori level.[15] We shall return to this issue.

Consider this from a different angle. In general, managerial decisions are affected by managerial objectives, various constraints, and management's expectations—all of which are, of course, conditional on the information currently available to management. Management selections and uses of accounting techniques and disclosure rules are not exceptions—since they too constitute decisions. As a result, managerial changes in these techniques and rules may provide bases for making inferences about managerial objectives, constraints, and expectations, conditional on firms' production-investment and financing decisions. Specifically, if investors establish unambiguous links between (1) management selections and uses of accounting techniques and disclosure rules and (2) the individual or joint characteristics of managerial objectives, constraints, and expectations, then managerial changes in those techniques or rules may reflect pertinent information (with respect to establishing capital market equilibrium) independently of any information reflected in the properties of whatever accounting numbers are affected by those managerial changes. The nature of the links established between (1) and (2) is, of course, critical. The issues here are analogous to those that arise when determining whether one can solve a system of equations for its unknowns.[16] Loosely speaking, one must specify enough structure—in the form of relationships among variables and restrictions on variables' values—so that inferences about unknown unobservables can be made in terms of observables. If enough structure is not specified, then, in general, one may not be able to make reliable inferences about the separate roles of all or some changes in objectives, changes in constraints, and changes in expectations vis-à-vis known managerial decisions about accounting techniques and disclosure rules. That is, in this case, the observables would not serve as signals vis-à-vis some or all unobservables of interest.[17]

---

[15]For example, management's selections of techniques for tax reporting may serve as signals with respect to their goals—especially their adherence to the market value rule. The effects of these techniques on values of accounting numbers is a separate issue.

[16]Consider, for example, a system of linear equations, with n equations and m unknowns. Clearly, this system has no unique solution if $m > n$. Moreover, there is always the possibility that the equations are inconsistent. This points to the importance of specifying an internally consistent set of relationships and restrictions.

[17]In other words, the specifications and restrictions that characterize investors' behavior are among the determinants of an observable's status as an effective signal. Thus, whether some random variable is or is not a source of informative sample evidence depends on investors' behavior. This applies to accounting numbers too. And it implies that their information content is, in general, not determinate on a priori grounds independent of details on investors' behavior.

The importance of such specifications and restrictions is reinforced by the potential influence of accounting techniques on the attributes of firms' decisions and, thus, on the decisions themselves. As stated above, the potential signaling role of accounting techniques and disclosure rules is within the context of given production-investment and financing decisions. Taking these decisions as given constitutes a restriction of the sort we are now describing. Yet, as indicated in Chapter 6, there are settings in which one should expect accounting techniques and disclosure rules to affect the substantive features of such decisions and, therefore, management's selections of production-investment and financing decisions. Settings in which accounting numbers play important roles in determining the payoffs to management from incentive compensation plans, in determining the probability of default under various bond indentures, and in determining the probability of antitrust actions against a firm based on allegations of, say, "monopoly profits" are three examples. In these settings, selections and applications of accounting techniques and disclosure rules influence the attributes of management's decision (e.g., the probability distribution of profits, after taking into account the possibility of antitrust actions); they do not, in general, simply "reflect" the *given* attributes of *given* decisions. The nature of this influence may affect management's preferences for alternative techniques and rules. Thus, a descriptively valid set of restrictions and specifications—invoked to establish the implications of selections of techniques and rules—may involve explicitly recognizing that such techniques and rules and the attributes of management's decisions are, in general, *jointly determined*. This implies that using management's selections of techniques and rules as signals about the attributes of their decisions may be a truly complicated affiar.[18]

The fact that managerial selections and applications of accounting techniques and disclosure rules and the attributes of production-investment and financing decisions are, in general, jointly determined does not imply that those selections, by themselves, are ineffective signals. It does imply that they may reflect information about the attributes of *given* decisions or of induced *changes* in the attributes of managerial decisions (perhaps because of induced changes in the decisions themselves). So long as one can establish unambiguous links between the observable changes in techniques and rules and the unobservable beliefs, constraints, expectations, and attributes of decisions corresponding to those observable changes, it is possible to use those observables as effective signals. In short, the major burdens turn on the difficulties of providing a sufficient set of restrictions and specifications, along the lines discussed above.

8.2.4 Signaling, Information Asymmetries, and Accounting Techniques

According to our earlier discussion of the potential effects of accounting techniques on the systematic properties of accounting numbers (e.g., means, autocorrelation functions, etc.), it is appropriate to consider altering *reported* values (e.g., recomputing reported income numbers) of accounting numbers so as to abstract from the purely mechanical effects of accounting techniques on those properties. Now, we seem to be saying that such abstractions will not take place (or will be unsuccessful)—at least in management's view—and, as a result, management behaves as if their selections and applications of accounting techniques and disclosure rules will alter inferences made conditionally on

---

[18]The difficulties encountered here are probably obvious to those familiar with the econometric problems surrounding so-called simultaneous equations biases and related phenomena.

sample evidence consisting of accounting numbers' values—independently of the substantive attributes of firms' decisions. This is one perspective, but not the one we have in mind. We have in mind a scenario wherein "outsiders" face information-production opportunities or costs that differ from those faced by insiders and, as a result, a scenario where full abstraction from the effects of accounting techniques and full incorporation of any managerially planned changes in the properties of their decisions may be infeasible or too costly. In this setting, management choices and applications of accounting techniques and disclosure rules can—via their effects on accounting numbers' properties—influence inferences based on accounting numbers. In short, we are allowing for a situation where there is a persistent asymmetry between the information available to management and that available to outsiders. Moreover, the signaling perspective allows for the possibility that management in this situation will have incentives to communicate the essence of their information to outsiders via some sort of signaling apparatus. Of course, as indicated earlier, the consistency of this sort of "signaling" behavior with equilibrium presumes that the costs of signaling (including the penalties for dishonest signaling) will be such that dishonest signalers are dissuaded from attempting to mimic honest signalers.

Note that our perspective allows for the possibility that management choices and applications may, taken by themselves, affect inferences—independently of the choices' and applications' implications for the systematic properties of accounting numbers.[19] On the one hand, such choices and applications may—since they are decisions—be used to make inferences about management's tastes and beliefs, after taking into account the constraints implied by "generally accepted accounting principles," the SEC's disclosure regulations, etc. On the other hand, they may lead to inferences about changes in the substantive aspects of management's decisions because of any connections between external accounting techniques and the characteristics of either (1) production-investment decisions or (2) financing decisions. The type of connection in (1) may arise if, for example, accounting numbers based on external accounting techniques are inputs for management's internal performer-evaluation and control systems, the outputs of which can affect production-investment decisions. Type (2) may arise if, for example, such accounting numbers are incorporated into the specifications of bond indenture provisions, which are properties of financing decisions.

In short, a scenario that can induce signaling is one wherein there are asymmetries with respect to the opportunities for or costs of information-production. In such a setting, some agents (e.g., "outsiders") will find it infeasible or too costly to fully abstract from the effects of accounting techniques on accounting numbers. Thus, in the end, there will be an asymmetric distribution of information (between, e.g., insiders and outsiders) of the sort that motivates screening by investors and signaling by management.

Of course, one cannot expect management to have access to information having only favorable implications for the equilibrium values of their firms. Since the positive incentives for signaling turn on adherence to the market value rule, it is natural to wonder whether information having unfavorable implications will also be "revealed" (or detected) via managerial behavior consistent with signaling. There are several reasons for expecting this to be the case.

---

[19]This, of course, provides additional motivation for understanding the effects of accounting techniques—because that understanding may facilitate appreciation of the signaling implications of accounting techniques.

Presumably, investors recognize that a firm has positive incentives to signal when the attributes of its given decisions have implications that are, according to management's assessments, relatively more favorable than those of other firms' corresponding attributes and relatively more favorable than what investors would, in management's view, otherwise infer.[20] If the costs of "dishonest" signaling are such that only these firms provide signals consistent with these relatively more favorable implications, then the nonsignaling firms are automatically singled out as being the firms whose given decisions have relatively unfavorable implications for those firms' equilibrium values—relative to the values that would otherwise be established. This result is effected even though the "unfavorable implication" firms did not actively signal. Thus, under the indicated cost condition, both information having unfavorable implications and information having favorable implications are disclosed if a signaling mechanism prevails.

There is another reason for expecting the same result, under appropriate conditions. If the information available to management but not others is of the sort that will ultimately be revealed (because, for example, it pertains to values of random variables that will ultimately be observed by outsiders or because of prevailing disclosure regulations), then investors will recognize which firms seem to be deliberately concealing information pertinent to establishing firms' equilibrium values. Over time, these firms will tend to acquire reputations for being "dishonest" signalers—or at least sources of unreliable signals. As a result, when they actively signal nothing, outsiders will tend to assume that concealed information has unfavorable implications.[21] And when these firms do actively signal—which, by assumption, will be when insiders' information has favorable implications—their signals will be partially or wholly ignored (or interpreted in an unintended way) because they too will be treated as "dishonest," or at least unreliable. This will adversely affect the equilibrium value of the firm even though the favorable implications of the information to which management has restricted access would be enough to induce a higher equilibrium value if this information were "revealed" via signals not "tainted" by the inferred dishonesty (or unreliability) of the firm's signals. This implies that a firm has a definite stake in not acquiring a reputation for dishonest (or unreliable) signaling if it plans to continue using the capital market. In short, there is a type of "survivorship" mechanism at work which establishes incentives for honest signaling behavior on the part of firms that want to "stay in the market."

8.2.5 The Determinants of Equilibrium Values, Production-Investment Decisions, and Signaling

In this section, we provide a somewhat formal representation of the signaling setting discussed above. Our main objective in doing so is to further clarify our key arguments by presenting them in more concrete terms. Moreover, this discussion highlights the role of asset-pricing models in a signaling setting.

---

[20]There is an important almost hidden assumption here: that a firm's managers are able to accurately identify—via direct or indirect means—what investors would infer in the absence of managerial signaling and how investors "price out" securities.

[21]Of course, if outsiders are confident that management does not have access to any information not already available to outsiders, then there is no basis for presuming that anything is being concealed.

The single-period two-parameter asset-pricing model used in Chapter 4 to characterize production-investment decisions is used here too. Under the assumptions invoked in Chapter 4, a firm's financing decisions have no effect on the firm's equilibrium value, given its production-investment decisions. Thus, for convenience, we focus only on firms' production-investment decisions. This will suffice for our purposes.

Recall that the equilibrium value of the ith firm at the beginning of period 1, or "at time 1," is given by:

$$V_{i1} = (1 + E(\tilde{R}_z))^{-1}\left[E(\tilde{V}_{i2}) - \lambda_m^* \frac{\text{Cov}(\tilde{V}_{i2}, \tilde{V}_{m2})}{\sigma(\tilde{V}_{m2})}\right], \tag{8.1}$$

where, as in Chapter 4, $(1 + E(\tilde{R}_z))^{-1}$ is the equilibrium price of a unit of expected dollar return and $(1 + E(\tilde{R}_z))^{-1}\lambda_m^*$ is the equilibrium price of a unit of dollar risk. The value of $E(\tilde{V}_{i2})$ is the number of units of expected dollar return contributed by the ith firm to aggregate expected dollar return, $\Sigma_I\ E(\tilde{V}_{i2}) = E(\tilde{V}_{m2})$, given firms' production-investment decisions. Given these decisions, the ith firm's contribution to aggregate dollar risk, $\sigma(\tilde{V}_{m2})$, is equal to the value of $\text{Cov}(\tilde{V}_{i2}, \tilde{V}_{m2})/\sigma(\tilde{V}_{m2})$, since $\Sigma_I[\text{Cov}(\tilde{V}_{i2}, \tilde{V}_{m2})/\sigma(\tilde{V}_{m2})] = \sigma(\tilde{V}_{m2})$. Finally, recall that $\lambda_m^* = [E(\tilde{V}_{m2}) - (1 + E(\tilde{R}_z))\ V_{m1}]/\sigma(\tilde{V}_{m2})$. The value of λ_m^* may be interpreted as the period-2 payment for bearing a unit of risk now (i.e., at time 1). In a world of risk-averse investors, $\lambda_m^* > 0$.

As indicated in Chapter 4, expression (8.1) can be interpreted as saying that the equilibrium value of the ith firm is equal to the equilibrium value of a composite commodity consisting of an amount of expected dollar return, $E(\tilde{V}_{i2})$, and an amount of dollar risk, $\text{Cov}(\tilde{V}_{i2}, \tilde{V}_{m2})/\sigma(\tilde{V}_{m2})$. Insofar as establishing the equilibrium value of the ith firm is concerned, the values of $E(\tilde{V}_{i2})$ and $\text{Cov}(\tilde{V}_{i2}, \tilde{V}_{m2})/\sigma(\tilde{V}_{m2})$ are the "relevant properties" of the bivariate distribution of the vector random variable $(\tilde{V}_{i2}, \tilde{V}_{m2})$. When the ith firm makes its production-investment decisions, it establishes the values of these properties, conditional on the relationships between $\tilde{V}_{i2}$ and $\tilde{V}_{m2}$ and on the distribution function of $\tilde{V}_{m2}$—where the latter relationship and distribution affect the resulting value of $\text{Cov}(\tilde{V}_{i2}, \tilde{V}_{m2})/\sigma(\tilde{V}_{m2})$.

The ith firm's production-investment decisions are made in accordance with the production function $\tilde{q}_{ij} = h_{ij}(y_{i1}, y_{i2}, \ldots, y_{ik} | \tilde{\theta}_{ij})$, where $\tilde{q}_{ij}$ denotes the ith firm's output of product (or service) j conditional on the known inputs, $y_{i1}, y_{i2}, \ldots, y_{ik}$, and the random variable $\tilde{\theta}_{ij}$. The inputs include, for example, labor services, the services of nonhuman capital, etc. The random variable $\tilde{\theta}_{ij}$ captures uncertainty about the (maximum) output corresponding to the given inputs. The value of the ith firm at time 2 in our single-period framework is given by:

$$\tilde{V}_{i2} = \sum_j \tilde{p}_j \tilde{q}_{ij} - \sum_k \tilde{p}_k y_{ik} - F_i, \tag{8.2}$$

where F_i denotes fixed costs induced by the ith firm's decisions.

By assumption, the firm's objective is to maximize the value of its outstanding securities, which is given by the value of V_{i1}. This is to be attained by selecting a feasible combination of factors of production such that the equilibrium value of V_{i1} is made as large as is possible—where the equilibrium value of V_{i1} is given by expression (8.1); where the feasibility of a combination of factors of production for any of the firm's outputs (i.e., $\tilde{q}_{ij}$ for any j) is determined by the stochastic production function corresponding to each output ($h_{ij}(y_{i1}, y_{i2}, \ldots, y_{ik} | \tilde{\theta}_{ij})$ for $\tilde{q}_{ij}$) and the distribution function of $\tilde{\theta}_{ij}$ for the corresponding value of j;[22] and where the values of expected dollar return and dollar risk are given by, respectively:

$$E(\tilde{V}_{i2}) = \sum_j E(\tilde{p}_j\tilde{q}_{ij}) - \sum_k E(\tilde{p}_k)y_{ik} - F_i \tag{8.3}$$

$$\frac{\text{Cov}(\tilde{V}_{i2}, \tilde{V}_{m2})}{\sigma(\tilde{V}_{m2})} = \frac{\sum_j \text{Cov}(\tilde{p}_j\tilde{q}_{ij}, \tilde{V}_{m2}) - \sum_k \text{Cov}(\tilde{p}_k y_{ik}, \tilde{V}_{m2})}{\sigma(\tilde{V}_{m2})}. \tag{8.4}$$

If the joint distribution of prices for goods and services ($\tilde{p}_j$, all j) is independent of each of the firm's output decisions—as would be the case if markets for goods and services are perfect markets—then expression (8.4) becomes:

$$\frac{\text{Cov}(\tilde{V}_{i2}, \tilde{V}_{m2})}{\sigma(\tilde{V}_{m2})} = \frac{\sum_j E(\tilde{p}_j)\,\text{Cov}(\tilde{q}_{ij}, \tilde{V}_{m2})}{\sigma(\tilde{V}_{m2})}. \tag{8.5}$$

See the derivations given in Chapter 4. In this case, the values of $E(\tilde{p}_j)$, for all j, are exogenously given insofar as the ith firm's decisions are concerned. In the case of imperfections in the markets for goods and services, the joint distribution function of prices facing the ith firm ($\tilde{p}_j$, all j) is, in general, dependent on the ith firm's decisions—here represented by the values of the inputs (y_{ik}, all k) selected by the firm. (Technically, this situation warrants a subscript on prices—since each firm may face a different joint distribution function, depending on its decisions. For convenience, we shall omit such a subscript for every price.)

In the end, the ith firm's optimizing actions lead to optimal values for all the factors of production, y^*_{ik}, $k = 1, 2, \ldots, K$. This optimal solution is, of course, conditional on (1) management's assessed joint distribution function of the prices (the $\tilde{p}_j$'s) of all goods and services (both inputs and outputs), the sources of output uncertainty (the $\tilde{\theta}_{ij}$'s), aggregate real wealth at time 2 ($\tilde{V}_{m2}$), and the production functions for alternative outputs ($h_{ij}(\ldots|\,\tilde{\theta}_{ij})$, for all j), and on (2) the prevailing values of the market prices of expected dollar return and dollar risk, *viz.* $(1 + E(\tilde{R}_z))^{-1}$ and $\lambda^*_m(1 + E(\tilde{R}_z))^{-1}$, respectively. These conditioning factors are exogenous variables and functions vis-à-vis the ith firm's decisions, for each i.

The details of management's optimizing decisions are, in addition, conditional on management's objective function. In this regard, we are assuming that the management of each firm behaves as if it adheres to the market value rule. Inducing this sort of behavior may involve imposing various types of compliance devices on management and adopting various enforcement actions. Of course, the agents who pursue enforcement of the market value rule—such as the firm's current securityholders or agents prepared to initiate "take-over" bids—do so conditionally on both the results of their information-production activities and the information available from other sources, such as disclosures by management itself.

Suppose that all aspects of the ith firm's production-investment problem are known to

---

[22]By restricting attention to values of $\tilde{c}_{ij}$ equal to those given by $h_{ij}(\ldots|\tilde{\theta}_{ij})$ we are, of course, restricting attention to efficient allocations, ex ante.

all agents except for management's beliefs—i.e., its assessed distribution functions (or inferences). And suppose that all information underlying management's assessments is also produced by (or somehow made available to) outsiders. Given our assumption that agents with the same information perceive the same implications (i.e., make the same inferences) and arrive at the same distributional assessments, the only interesting disclosures by management are their selected values of the factors of production, y_{ik}, $k = 1, 2, \ldots, K$. Conditional on these values, "outsiders" can, on the basis of information available to them, determine the distribution function of $\tilde{V}_{i2}$ that management thinks it is (and, in this case, is in fact) offering to the market via its decisions. These "outsiders" can determine whether management's decisions are consistent with the market value rule. And, as a result, they can establish the theoretically appropriate equilibrium value for the firm conditionally on the firm's given decisions. This is, loosely speaking, equivalent to a situation wherein management "tells all" after it identifies the details of all relevant exogenous factors and after it arrives at its distributional assessments. In this scenario, results are equivalent to those obtained when there are no asymmetries with respect to the opportunities for or costs of information-production. And, therefore, all of the theoretically attractive properties of our (fictional) tatonnément-with-recontracting process are readily attained insofar as "pricing out" securities is concerned. In fact, everything seems pretty mechanical in this scenario.

Things are not so straightforward when some of the information about the relevant exogenous factors cannot be, or is too costly to be, produced by (or somehow made available to) outsiders and, in particular, when agents behave as if management's information is "superior" to their own—in the sense that they would use it rather than their own if they could get it. Actually, even if management's information is not believed to be superior, one would still probably be interested in their assessments of distribution functions and in their beliefs about the prevailing production technology in order to distinguish violations, if any, of the market value rule—conditional on outsiders' assessments and beliefs—from the effects of differences between insiders' and outsiders' assessments and beliefs (but no intentional departures by management from the market value rule). But unless otherwise indicated, we shall assume that management does behave as if they are adhering to the market value rule—perhaps because a substantial part of their total compensation is positively related to the final equilibrium value of the firm.

Even when adherence to the market value rule is taken as a given, the underpinnings of management's decisions will still be of interest to "outsiders" in the case of informational asymmetries because those underpinnings will affect the details of management's current actions and planned responses to subsequently observed values of random variables—such as the sources of uncertainty affecting output quantities. This sort of information seems relevant for anticipating managerial responses (in the form of variations in production-investment decisions) to such realizations en route to assessing distribution functions for outputs (which are, of course, conditional on managerial actions and planned responses) and, ultimately, the distribution function of $\tilde{V}_{i2}$. Note that no presumption about the "superiority" of management's information is needed here. What is involved is inferring the characteristics of management's decisions—which are necessarily conditional on management's assessments and beliefs—whether "superior" or not. In short, information on the characteristics of managerial actions and plans has, in general, a bearing on the distribution function of $\tilde{V}_{i2}$. Such information obviously pertains to "unobservables" relevant to establishing the equilibrium value of the ith firm at time 1.

The relevance of this type of information, given the assumed informational asymmetries, is due to the discrimination it permits. It permits distrinctions (among truly different distribution functions) that investors would not otherwise be able to make (due to feasibility) or would find too costly to make. In addition, of course, it facilitates recognition of homogeneity when homogeneity (regarding the attributes of firms' decisions) does, in fact, prevail. In terms of our earlier remarks (see Section 8.2.1), this type of information makes a positive contribution to more accurate "screening" with respect to attributes of distribution functions of firms' future values, conditional on their proposed production-investment decisions.

To be sure, the attributes of management's production-investment decisions may be only partially revealed by managerial disclosures. And when there are informational asymmetries, some relevant details of those decisions may, other things staying unchanged, remain unknown to outsiders because of the differences between insiders' and outsiders' opportunities for and costs of information-production. Such asymmetries obviously increase the difficulty of screening firms in terms of the characteristics of their production-investment decisions.

Will all informational asymmetries persist? Are there incentives for management to make "honest" voluntary disclosures—thus alleviating the asymmetries' effects—or for management to make "dishonest" voluntary disclosures—thus taking advantage of the asymmetries, perhaps for personal gains made at the expense of nonmanagement securityholders? Our immediate interest is in situations wherein the market value rule characterizes managerial behavior—because it is consistent with management's personal interests or because of explicitly introduced enforcement devices.

As indicated in Section 8.2.1, this is the sort of setting that leads to incentives for managerial signaling. That is, it induces incentives for management to voluntarily provide (at least in an "as if" sense) observables (signals) that will, in their judgment, be accepted by outsiders as reflecting information pertinent to establishing firms' equilibrium values, because of a perceived correlation (in the view of outsiders) with the unobservables that ultimately determine the distribution functions of firms' future values. It terms of the formalities introduced above, these include the details of firms' stochastic production functions ($h_{ij}(\ldots | \tilde{\theta}_{ij})$, for all i and j), the distribution functions of the random variables that capture the sources of uncertainty in these production functions ($\tilde{\theta}_{ij}$, all i and j), the distribution functions of all prices of outputs and inputs ($\tilde{p}_j$, for all j),[23] and management's proposed optimal production investment decisions (y^*_{ik}, for all i and k). In short, they include management's proposed optimal decisions and all aspects of the demand and supply factors that are associated with those decisions and that have a bearing on the distribution functions of firms' future values.

8.2.6 Things to Come

Whether or not investors behave as if any particular observable is an effective signal does not, of course, depend only on management's intentions and objectives. Indeed, this

---

[23]As indicated earlier, the joint distribution function of the prices facing firm i will generally be affected by that firm's decisions when markets for goods and services are imperfect. This implies that market-structure factors are, in general, pertinent to establishing individual firms' equilibrium values.

is, in the end, an empirical issue. The next few sections will lead up to an empirical analysis of this empirical side of signaling, by focusing on some numbers that are often alleged to serve as signals: *viz.*, dividends, income numbers, and extraordinary accounting items. The crux of the motivation behind such allegations was briefly reviewed in Section 8.2.2. We begin by identifying a few of the major factors that ultimately determine whether or not a particular observable is an effective signal. Much of this discussion restates ideas that have already been introduced in our previous remarks on signaling. This should serve as a useful review. The major new ideas appear in our discussion of complementary sources of signals and substitute sources. After discussing the complement/substitute issue, we discuss our empirical methods for characterizing the potentially informative attributes of signals on dividends, income numbers, and extraordinary items. After that, we discuss our specific tests for the information content of such signals and our empirical results.

The empirical results described below are from a study by Gonedes [1978]. Some unreported but discussed results appear in the April 1976 version of that report, which is available from the Center for Mathematical Studies in Business and Economics, University of Chicago.

8.3 Determinants of Investors' Responses to Corporate Signaling Actions

8.3.1 General Factors

Among the factors that will influence investors' responses to managerial signals are the signals' reliability, the relevance of the signals to assessments of probability distributions of securities' future values, the "honesty" of management's signals, and the availability and properties of other signals that are complements or substitutes. The complement/substitute factor is sufficiently important to justify separate and detailed treatment. This is provided in Section 8.3.2. The other factors are briefly reviewed in the remainder of this section.

Signals are important when they facilitate distinguishing between firms whose decisions have different unobservable characteristics, whether those signals are or are not supplied by management. The connection between those unobservables and the observable signals is what counts—because that connection affects inferences about the unobservables of interest. If a characteristic's presence or absence (or magnitude, if present) can be taken as certain conditional on a signal, then the signal is *perfectly reliable*. In general, and other things being equal, the private gross value of the right to receive and use a signal varies directly with its reliability (see Gonedes and Dopuch [1974, p. 57, fn. 5]).

Corporate signaling entails management behaving as if they are providing observables with which agents can make inferences about unobservables. As indicated earlier, there are a variety of reasons for which management might attempt to provide "distorted" or "dishonest" signals (see, e.g., Gonedes, Dopuch, and Penman [1976]). In this context, a "dishonest" or "distorted" signal is one that management expects to be interpreted in a manner inconsistent with their actual beliefs about the unobservable attributes of their decisions.[24] If, in fact, (1) firms whose decisions are, and firms whose decisions are not

---

[24]The attributes of "honesty" and "reliability" are not the same. First of all, a perfectly honest potential signal may be wholly unreliable relative to some set of unobservable attributes of firms' decisions. Second, *successful* dishonest signaling involves investors' behaving as if the signals exhibit some reliability relative to some set of unobservable attributes of firms' decisions.

characterized by a given set of attributes, can both issue the same signals on the same terms of trade, and (2) incentives for distortion exist, then those signals will be useless as far as agents' inferences are concerned. In this situation, the observable signals cannot be used to discriminate among firms in terms of the unobservable characteristics of their decisions. A dishonenst signaler imitates an honest signaler when it is advantageous to do so.[25] Here, "advantageous" is determined by management's objective—taken to be adherence to the market value rule.

There are a variety of reasons for not expecting dishonest signaling to persist and, if it does, for not expecting it to be successful. Suppose, for example, that systematic dishonest signaling would induce agents—if they relied on the signals—to commit detectable systematic errors in classifying firms. This implies that dishonest signalers are identifiable. But if a signaler intends to remain "in the market," he has a stake in not becoming known as a dishonest signaler. Thus, there is a force working against systematic dishonest signaling. Even if dishonest signaling did occur in this setting, it is not clear that it could be successful. Agents would simply disregard a potential signal that really provides (in their view) no reliable basis for discriminating among firms in terms of the attributes of firms' decisions. Other possibilities are suggested by Barzel [1976]. In general, the detectability of dishonest signaling depends on the nature of the market for information and the information-production decisions made by agents on private account (see Gonedes [1976b;1980]).

Agents' responses to a potential signal also depend on the relevance of the unobservables about which inferences are aided by using that signal. As indicated earlier, the specific unobservables that are important are the relevant characteristics of the probability distributions of securities' future values—as identified by whatever asset-pricing model characterizes equilibrium prices of securities. If a signal is not helpful in making inferences about a relevant characteristic, then it will not affect any of the assessments that ultimately underlie asset-pricing behavior.

8.3.2 Complementary and Substitute Signals

The above factors are among those that influence agents' responses to potential signals. Those factors pertain to properties of a particular signal viewed in isolation. Agents' responses to intentional and unintentional managerial signaling will also depend on relationships among different signals, such as substitution and complementarity relationships. The inference that one makes about the information content of a random variable—the realizations of which are potential signals—can be drastically altered when these relationships are recognized.

Some definitions are in order. Let I_t denote the implications of information available to agents at the time t before any time t signaling occurs. Let I_t^θ and I_t^ω denote the marginal implications of the (vector or scalar) signals θ and ω, respectively, and the initial information and let $I_t^{\theta\omega}$ denote the joint implications of the pair (θ,ω) and the initial information.[26] Since the information initially available at t is still available upon observing θ, ω, or (θ, ω), I_t is a subset of I_t^θ, I_t^ω, and $I_t^{\theta\omega}$.

---

[25]These types of situations are discussed in greater detail by Akerloff [1970] and Spence [1974, chap. 12].

[26]There is no need for any of the indicated sets of implications to be the same for all agents. For convenience, we omit notation that formally recognizes the possibility of differences across agents. Unless otherwise indicated, the same approach is used throughout this chapter. Also, the phrases "at time t" and "at the beginning of period t" will, as always, be used interchangeably.

The various "sets of implications" are simply collections of all inferences about the characteristics of firms' decisions, where the inferences are made conditionally on the signal associated with the set (i.e., θ or ω) and the initially available information. These inferences might be about, for example, prevailing demand functions and supply functions, the potential effects of technological changes, management's capabilities, financing plans, plans for investment and disinvestment in capital stock, product-line changes, levels of production activity, the effects of existing and proposed governmental regulations, and changes in real resources corresponding to feasible decisions. (This listing is not exhaustive and none of its components are necessarily independent of the others.) For a given t, some of the inferences in the set induced by a given signal may be revisions of inferences made at a previous value of t. Also, for a given signal and a given t, some of the induced inferences may be revisions of inferences induced by other signals as of the same t. Any revision may, of course, conflict with the initial inferences.

Whether any one of the implications induced by a signal is "favorable" or "unfavorable" and whether the entire set of implications is "favorable" or "unfavorable" depends on the nature of distributions of securities' values assessed conditionally on these implications and on the characteristics of distributions relevant to asset pricing. Also, given the set of implications induced by a signal, one can identify subsets specific to given firms. These subsets need not be independent. That is, the inferences made about one firm's decisions may be dependent on the inferences made about other firms' decisions. This type of situation can arise when, for example, inferences are being made about the implications of one firm's new product-introductions for the product-introduction decisions of competing firms.

The following definitions can now be provided:

Definition 1. Insofar as information content is concerned, the random variable $\tilde{\theta}$ is a *perfect substitute* for $\tilde{\omega}$ at time t if $I_t^{\theta} = I_t^{\omega} = I_t^{\theta\omega}$ for all signals (= realizations) $\tilde{\theta} = \theta$ and $\tilde{\omega} = \omega$. (Throughout, tilde ($\tilde{}$) denotes a random variable.)

Definition 2. Insofar as information content is concerned, the random variables $\tilde{\theta}$ and $\tilde{\omega}$ are *perfect (or "strict") complements* at time t if $I_t^{\theta} = I_t$, $I_t^{\omega} = I_t$, and $I_t \subset I_t^{\theta\omega}$ for all signals (= realizations) $\tilde{\theta} = \theta$ and $\tilde{\omega} = \omega$.

In the case of perfect substitutes, one of the two signals can be eliminated without affecting any inferences. In this situation it may appear that $\tilde{\theta}$ has no information content if no account is taken of the availability of perfect substitutes. This inferred lack of information content might erroneously be ascribed to, for example, irrelevance or unreliability. If the inferred lack of information content is, however, due to the prior availability of observations on $\tilde{\omega}$ rather than to the marginal properties of $\tilde{\theta}$, one gets a different picture of agents' responses to signals. If, for example, investors view both extraordinary income items and dividend changes as signals about management's assessments of distributions of future income, then it seems important to recognize substitution possibilities when attempting to characterize investors' assessments as a function of signals about dividend changes and extraordinary items.

If $\tilde{\theta}$ and $\tilde{\omega}$ are strict complements, then neither one affects inferences when used in isolation. It is only when observations on both $\tilde{\theta}$ and $\tilde{\omega}$ are available that inferences are affected, in the sense that I_t is a strict subset of $I_t^{\theta\omega}$. This kind of situation may arise when observations on $\tilde{\theta}$ lead to unambiguous implications only when observations on $\tilde{\omega}$ are available, and vice versa. The ambiguity may be due to the ease or "costlessness" of a firm's using either $\tilde{\theta}$ or $\tilde{\omega}$—but not both $\tilde{\theta}$ and $\tilde{\omega}$—as sources of dishonest signals. Alternatively, it may be due to management not adopting an unchanging (or "stationary") mode of signaling—one whose characteristics can be reliabily inferred by "outsiders" on the basis of information available to them. In a sense, investors may behave as if they are using the observations on $\tilde{\theta}(\tilde{\omega})$ as means of "guaranteeing" the implications of $\tilde{\omega}(\tilde{\theta})$.

Suppose, for example, that $\tilde{\omega}$ pertains to managerial announcements of intentions and $\tilde{\theta}$ pertains to contemporaneous managerial announcements of adopted actions (i.e., what is actually being done). Taken by itself, the implications of an observation on either $\tilde{\theta}$ or $\tilde{\omega}$ may be completely ambiguous, insofar as the characteristics of the firm's decisions (hence, the characteristics of the distribution of its securities' future values) are concerned. But taken together, the observations on $\tilde{\theta}$ and $\tilde{\omega}$ may have some concrete implications for those characteristics—perhaps because management's given actions would seem completely irrational if their announcements of intentions were inaccurate and, given the stated intentions, the implications of the actions appeared to be appropriate. In any event, an examination dealing with $\tilde{\theta}$ or $\tilde{\omega}$ in isolation would lead to the inference that $\tilde{\theta}$ or $\tilde{\omega}$ lacks information content, which would be misleading if $\tilde{\theta}$ and $\tilde{\omega}$ are strict complements.

Definitions 1 and 2 deal with extreme cases. A variety of intermediate ones can, of course, arise. For example, it may be that $I_t^{\theta} \subset I_t^{\theta} = I_t^{\theta\omega}$, $I_t^{\theta} \neq I_t$ for all realizations of $\tilde{\theta}$ and $\tilde{\omega}$. This implies $(I_t^{\theta} - I_t) \cap (I_t^{\omega} - I_t) = (I_t^{\theta}) - (I_t)$. In this case, $\tilde{\theta}$ has some substitution properties vis-à-vis $\tilde{\omega}$; but it is not a perfect substitute for $\tilde{\omega}$. However, $\tilde{\omega}$ provides a perfect substitute for $\tilde{\theta}$ and it induces implications beyond those induced by values of $\tilde{\theta}$.

A related intermediate case is one where $I_t^{\theta} \neq I_t$, $I_t^{\omega} \neq I_t$, $I_t^{\theta\omega} \neq I_t^{\omega}$, and $I_t^{\theta\omega} \neq I_t^{\theta}$. In this case, the degree of substitutability depends on the size of the intersection of I_t^{θ} and I_t^{ω}. If it is empty, there is no substitution.

Another intermediate case that is an alternative to strict complementarity is the case where, say, $\tilde{\omega}$ has information content when values of it are used alone but $\tilde{\theta}$ has information content only when its values are used along with values of $\tilde{\omega}$. That is, $I_t^{\omega} \neq I_t$, $I_t^{\omega} = I_t$, and $I_t^{\theta\omega} \neq I_t^{\theta}$, for all realizations of $\tilde{\theta}$ and $\tilde{\omega}$. This may arise when—to return to our earlier example—announcements of management's intentions ($\tilde{\theta}$) have no unambiguous implications for the characteristics of firms' decisions unless those announcements are interpreted along with statements about management's contemporaneous actions ($\tilde{\omega}$), and when the latter have some unambiguous implications even when interpreted in isolation. The same type of situation may arise with respect to extraordinary items and dividend changes. Taken by itself, an extraordinary-item signal may have ambiguous implications. For example, an extraordinary loss may have favorable implications if it is associated with disposal of an unprofitable division. It may have unfavorable implications if that division was acquired by a new entrant into the industry— that will subject the disposing firm to strong competitive pressures. Dividend changes may, however, be perceived to have unambiguous implications for the distribution of future earnings (a characteristic of the firm's decisions). Moreover, the joint implications of the two signals may be both unambiguous and different from the marginal implications of the dividend signal.

From the above, it seems that specifying a potential signal's effects on agents' assessments at time t is not straightforward. These effects depend on such things as the structure of the market for information, alternative signals made available at time t, the initially available information, and the ways in which agents interpret signals. In short, there may be a variety of joint effects. Insofar as accounting numbers are concerned, this suggests that the conventional treatments of accounting numbers may have few theoretical or empirical underpinnings. Those treatments usually deal with accounting numbers (e.g., net income, accounting ratios, etc.) as if they have unambiguous interpretations, at least insofar as changes are concerned.

8.3.3. Signals' Implications and Rate-of-Return Distributions

All of our empirical results pertain to one-period rates of return, from t to $t + 1$. The above characterizations of signals are easily restated into equivalent characterizations expressed in terms of rates of return.

Investors are viewed as behaving as if the implications of a given signal constitute conditioning arguments of their assessed joint distributions of securities' future values. A one-to-one relationship between sets of implications and assessed distributions is assumed. That is, a different set of implications is assumed to induce different assessments and different assessments are assumed to imply different implications. But there is no requirement that different (vector or scalar valued) sigmas induce different sets of implications, or the converse.

Given the time t prices of securities facing a given agent (presumed to be a price-taker), his assessed joint distribution of securities' values as of $t + 1$ induces an assessed joint distribution of rates of return from t to $t + 1$. Dropping time subscripts for convenience, let $\tilde{\underline{R}}$ denote the vector of these returns on all securities, let $F(\cdot)$ be a generic symbol for a distribution function, and let $F(\underline{R})$ denote the distribution assessed conditionally on I, the implications of information initially available at time t. By definition, a signal reflects information beyond that available at time t if it and the initial information have implications that induce an assessed distribution of returns different from $F(\underline{R})$; see Gonedes [1975*b*]. In terms of return distributions, the equivalent restatements of Definitions 1 and 2 are:

Definition 3. Insofar as information content is concerned, the random variable $\tilde{\theta}$ is a *perfect substitute* for $\tilde{\omega}$ at time t if $F(\underline{R}|\theta) = F(\underline{R}|\omega) = F(\underline{R}|\theta,\omega)$ for all realizations of $\tilde{\theta}$ and $\tilde{\omega}$.

Definition 4. Insofar as information content is concerned, the random variables $\tilde{\theta}$ and $\tilde{\omega}$ are *perfect (or "strict") complements* at time t if $F(\underline{R}|\theta) = F(\underline{R})$, $F(\underline{R}|\omega) = F(\underline{R})$, and $F(\underline{R}|\theta,\omega) \neq F(\underline{R})$ for all realizations of $\tilde{\theta}$ and $\tilde{\omega}$.

Restatement of the conditions for the other substitution/complementarity relationships proceeds along the same lines. The statements of these conditions in terms of return distributions underlie our empirical results on extraordinary items and dividend changes. The various propositions with which these results deal are discussed in the next section.

8.4 Tests for the Effects of Potential Managerial Signals: Dividends, Income, and Extraordinary Items

8.4.1 Extraordinary Items, Dividends, and Income Numbers

As with any other disaggregation or decomposition scheme, identifying extraordinary income items can be viewed as providing a basis for ferreting out the implications of available sample evidence— in this case, observations on income numbers. This specific type of disaggregation seems to be motivated by a belief that decomposing income numbers into their "ordinary" and "extraordinary" components induces implications beyond those induced by the aggregated income numbers (i.e., "income after extraordinary items") and—since both components are ultimately disclosed—beyond those induced by either component alone, particularly "income before extraordinary items."[27] A seemingly important empirical question is, therefore: do investors behave as if extraordinary income items reflect information beyond that reflected in the same period's "ordinary" income or beyond that reflected in the same period's aggregated income number? That is, do these management signals reflect information beyond that already reflected in available signals?

If agents behave as if the income numbers themselves reflect information, one can view agents behaving as if they assess distributions of returns by using predictive distributions of the events that directly affect firms' values or by using predictive distributions of functions of income numbers in their role as signals about those events. The specific functions used identify the attributes of income numbers that are deemed to be relevant in making inferences about the characteristics of firms' decisions and, thus, their future values. The tests discussed below require a specification of such attributes of income numbers. And our results are critically dependent on that specification. If irrelevant attributes are specified and if income numbers do have relevant attributes, then we face a high probability of inferring no "information content" when, in fact, we should infer the opposite.

Our specification exploits available evidence on annual income numbers. This evidence is consistent with the statement that a given firm's income, $\tilde{y}_t$, for period t does, on average, reflect information about the firm's value.[28] One attribute of $\tilde{y}_t$ that seems to reflect such information is the forecast error $\tilde{y}_{t+1} - E_t(\tilde{y}_{t+1})$, where $E_t(\tilde{y}_{t+1})$ denotes the expected value of $\tilde{y}_{t+1}$ as of the end of the period t—viewed as the time at which agents are assessing distributions of returns for the interval t to $t + 1$. The available evidence is consistent with a positive association between the forecast error for firm j and the contemporaneous change in the value of firm j's common stock.

We shall be interested in the extent to which various signals available at time $t + 1$ reflect information not already reflected in other signals available at time $t + 1$ and not already reflected in sample evidence available at time t. That is, do these time $t + 1$ signals reflect any of the new information that arose within the interval t to $t + 1$ and that was not already reflected in other $t + 1$ signals? With respect to income numbers, the time t sample evidence can be used in assessing a predictive distribution for $\tilde{y}_{t+1}$ and thus a value of $E(\tilde{y}_{t+1})$. Available empirical results are consistent with the statement that, conditional on only the past values, $Y_t = (y_t, y_{t-1}, \ldots,)$, of $\tilde{y}_{t+1}$, a descriptively valid model is $E_t(\tilde{y}_{t+1}|Y_t) = y_t + \delta$, where the scalar δ may equal zero.[29] This martingale model will be used to obtain proxies for investors' expectations. Note, however, that the previous discussion of signaling and the following discussion of testable hypotheses can accommodate any model of $\tilde{y}_t$. The role of the martingale model in time series analyses and empirical results from applications of it to accounting numbers were discussed in Chapter 7.

Given the martingale model and assuming $\delta = 0$ for simplicity, $\tilde{y}_{t+1} =$

---

[27] See, for example, the discussion in Accounting Principles Board [1966, sec. I] and Hendriksen [1970, pp. 190–192].

[28] See, for example, Ball and Brown [1968] and Gonedes [1974].

[29] See, e.g., Ball and Watts [1972], Watts [1970], and the references cited therein.

$E_{t+1}(\tilde{y}_{t+1+j}|\tilde{Y}_{t+1})$, for $j > 0$, is the forecast that will be made at time $t + 1$ of income for each period $t + 1 + j$, $j > 0$. Thus, the statement that $\tilde{y}_{t+1}$ has information content is equivalent to the statement that the (now unknown) value of the *mean*, $E_{t+1}(\tilde{y}_{t+1+j}|\tilde{Y}_{t+1})$, of income, $\tilde{y}_{t+1+j}$, for period $t + 1 + j$, $j > 0$, has information content. The value of $E_{t+1}(\tilde{y}_{t+1+j}|\tilde{Y}_{t+1})$, $j > 0$, is simply the value, as of time $t + 1$, of the mean of the predictive distribution of income for period $t + 1 + j$, $j > 0$.

The evidence cited above with respect to income numbers and common stock values is consistent with the statement that the random variable $\tilde{y}_{t+1} - E_t(\tilde{y}_{t+1}|Y_t) = E_{t+1}(\tilde{y}_{t+1+j}|\tilde{Y}_{t+1}) - E_t(\tilde{y}_{t+1}|\tilde{Y}_t)$ reflects information pertinent to assessing the probability distribution of returns from time t to time $t + 1$. This implies that some other signal that will be available at time $t + 1$—which is when the realization of $\tilde{y}_{t+1} = E_{t+1}(\tilde{y}_{t+1+j}|\tilde{Y}_{t+1})$, $j > 0$, will be available—will reflect information beyond that jointly reflected in the value of $\tilde{y}_{t+1}$ and the history of Y_t, if the other signal reflects information that alters the expected values of the predictive distributions of income for periods beyond $t + 1$. Since the values of these expectations (or forecasts) are, given the martingale model, simply values of future periods' income numbers, an equivalent statement is that the other signal reflects such information if it alters predictive distributions of income numbers for periods beyond period $t + 1$.

One can view disclosures about extraordinary items as forms of managerial signaling behavior that are intended to induce such alterations by altering the conditioning arguments of those predictive distributions. As with other forms of managerial signaling behavior, this type would be consistent with behaving as if it is intended to alter investors' inferences about the unobservable characteristics of firms' decisions. This treatment of extraordinary items seems natural given management's wide latitude of choice regarding the timing and nature of disclosures about extraordinary items—at least over the time period covered by our results (1946–1972).[30]

Suppose, for example, that a firm disposes of a division at a loss and assume that management behaves as if investors view (or at least behave as if they view) the martingale model as being appropriate for income. Other things being equal, the disposal at a loss induces (in management's assumed view) agents to forecast a lower value of income than would otherwise be forecasted for future periods. Assume, however, that the conditions surrounding the disposal really have (in management's view) favorable implications for the attributes of the firm's decisions.[31] One way of conveying this view is to disclose the

---

[30]One might argue that APB *Opinion No. 30* substantially reduced that latitude of choice. Since that opinion became effective for fiscal years beginning after December 31, 1973, its effect (if any) is not an issue considered herein. The same remark applies to the SEC's revisions in the rules for Form 8-K disclosures, which became effective for reports filed on or after February 28, 1973; see Securities and Exchange Commission [1973]. The extent to which the latter revisions really reduced management's latitude of choice has been questioned by Lurie and Pastena [1975]. Their descriptive data suggest a surprising degree of what can be interpreted as noncompliance and a seemingly wide latitude of choice.

An implicit assumption made here is that management's latitude of choice vis-à-vis reported income numbers is less than it is vis-à-vis changes in extraordinary-item numbers and dividend changes (discussed below). In this regard, some relevant constraints on income signaling are SEC requirements, GAAP, and auditor pressures.

[31]See the example given in Section 8.3.2.

loss separately, label it "extraordinary" or "nonrecurring," and—by implication—declare it to be something that should be ignored in assessing predictive distributions of income.

If management behaves as if such items will be ignored, what motivates their disclosing "extraordinary" gains? If the firm intends to remain in the market and if it plans on future signaling activities, then there are incentives for management to establish a favorable signaling reputation— or else who would "believe" its signals? If systematically distorted (or "dishonest") signals can be detected by investors, then management's signals would be uninformative and they might induce costs in addition to the direct costs of signaling—e.g., the costs of stockholder suits alleging "misleading" financial disclosures.[32] Detection of distorted signals might be due to information-production activities on agents' personal account, to the implications of other signals provided by management or resulting from management's actions, or to information-production activities imposed on firms by regulatory bodies (e.g., the SEC) or the firms' "independent" auditors.[33]

Consider another possible setting in which management might behave as if it uses extraordinary items as one means of altering agents' predictive distributions. First, suppose that management believes that agents behave as if "income after extraordinary items"—rather than "income before extraordinary items"—is the relevant income number. This implies that the decomposition of income into extraordinary and ordinary components should not affect agents' assessed predictive distributions. (I.e., only the final aggregated number counts.) Second, assume that management can effectively control the timing of some extraordinary item recognitions but not their ultimate classification as "extraordinary" items—perhaps due to the constraints of prevailing external reporting rules, pressure by the SEC, or pressure by the firm's auditors. Third, suppose that the distribution of opportunities to produce information is such that investors cannot detect management's influence over the timing of extraordinary item disclosures. In this scenario, management might be motivated to time such disclosures so as to convey a more favorable picture than would otherwise be conveyed by observed income—by, for example, recognizing extraordinary gains (losses) when the picture would otherwise look too unfavorable (favorable). This is the kind of setting covered by the so-called income smoothing hypothesis, which may be viewed as specifying the nature of managerial signaling.[34] Of course, management's signals can affect agents' assessments in this setting only so long as agents cannot identify "distortion." A variety of consequences may result from agents' ability to identify distorted signals. Agents may simply ignore the signals. Or the attempts to distort may induce unfavorable evaluations of management and perhaps the characteristics of their decisions.

---

[32]This statement assumes that the underlying states to which "distorted" signals pertain are unknown; only the fact of distortion is known. Clearly, if "distortion" simply means that a correct interpretation of a signal—insofar as management's actual beliefs and information are concerned—is simply the opposite of management's desired interpretation (or the "advertised" interpretation), then the signal is informative. The fact that management wanted investors to arrive at a different interpretation is irrelevant. Also note that detectable dishonest signaling constitutes a potentially useful source of information on the "quality" of management—and perhaps on the probability of takeover bids.

[33]Of course, if the imposed information-production activities eliminate management's latitude of choice with respect to disclosures of particular extraordinary items, then the signaling perspective is inapplicable insofar as these disclosures are concerned.

[34]An overview of available literature on this topic is provided by Gonedes and Dopuch [1974, sec. 9] and Gonedes [1972].

Even if agents ignore extraordinary items, management may not cease behaving as if it is exercising its control over the timing of extraordinary-item disclosures. Management may continue to do so because of nonsignaling objectives, such as avoiding technical violations of bond indentures expressed in terms of income numbers or affecting the payoffs of executive incentive schemes based on accounting income numbers. In short, there are conditions under which conscious signaling and nonsignaling behavior may be observationally equivalent. Obviously, this is one reason that specifying the reactions of investors to accounting numbers is not as straightforward as is sometimes believed. (See Section 8.3.2 for additional remarks on this issue.)

Management's influence over the classification of items as "extraordinary" and the timing of extraordinary-item disclosures are not the only sources of potential signals. Agents may behave as if other components of net income might also be used for signaling. Also, as indicated in Section 8.2.2, they may behave as if dividend policy changes may be used. The use of dividend policy changes for this purpose is predicted by the familiar information content hypothesis about dividends, which is discussed by Watts [1973] and Scholes [1973], among others. This hypothesis is adequately discussed in available literature. For our purposes, the discussion of this hypothesis given in Section 8.2.2 will suffice; it will not be developed further. Of greater importance here are the potential substitution/complementarity relationships among the period $t + 1$ net income signals, extraordinary item signals, and dividend signals.

Investors may behave as if each of these signals reflects information on the distribution functions of firms' income numbers for periods beyond $t + 1$, and thus on the characteristics of firms' decisions. Moreover, they may behave as if the implications of any one of these signals depends on one or more of the other signals. Such relationships among signals' implications are among those formally defined and discussed earlier (see Section 8.3.2). In short, a descriptively valid characterization of the way agents assess predictive distributions and the way signals influence those assessments may involve explicit recognition of the signals' joint implications. This would seem to be particularly important for those signals that do not have unambiguous marginal implications.

One possibility is that agents will behave as if the dividend signal is a means of "validating" the extent to which extraordinary-item signals reflect information. This validation may be sought because, as indicated earlier, a management may behave as if it uses an extraordinary-item signal to induce either warranted or unwarranted inferences about its actual earnings expectations. The use of a dividend signal as a validation device might be motivated by the fact that a substantive commitment is involved, *viz.*, a commitment to distribute assets.[35] In this scenario, the extraordinary-item signal's information content depends on the contemporaneous dividend signal. But the dividend signal itself may have marginal information content. The latter case is an example of the alternative to strict complementarity discussed in Section 8.3.2.

On the other hand, management may behave as if it uses a dividend signal to "override" the inferences that it thinks will be induced by an extraordinary item signal that it is forced to disclose, perhaps because of prevailing external reporting rules, pressure by

[35]Presumably, this commitment is not taken lightly by management. Also note that there are institutional factors that tie dividends to earnings expectations. For example, the indenture provisions of many debt issues require that dividends not exceed some fraction of periodic or cumulative earnings.

the SEC, or pressure by its auditors. Management may do this if it thinks the item will be treated as if it is a management signal in situations where it is not intended to be such a signal.[36]

The above discussion points to some of the dependencies that may prevail insofar as the signaling effects of accounting numbers are concerned. A variety of others are possible. The essential nature of each is, however, the same, namely, an empirical one. So, it seems best to head for some empirical results. Ultimately, we shall present results on both the joint and marginal implications of income signals, dividend signals, and extraordinary-item signals provided during period t. These results will be conditional on sample evidence already available at the beginning of period t.

The above discussion also points to the ambiguous nature of accounting signals' implications. This is contrary to, for example, many of the supporting arguments accompanying disclosure law specifications (e.g., *Statements of the FASB* and the SEC's *Accounting Series Releases*) as well as some recent research on the "information content" of accounting numbers (see Gonedes and Dopuch [1974] for a review of the latter work). In general, it is easy to specify plausible settings in which a given accounting signal has different (and possibly conflicting) implications, even if one is confident about the signals' relevant attributes.

8.4.2 More on Specifications of Signals' Relevant Attributes

The martingale model was adopted as a descriptively valid model of $\tilde{y}_t$, and the forecast error, $\tilde{y}_{t+1} - E_t(y_{t+1}|Y_t)$, was identified as a relevant attribute of the income signal at time $t + 1$. Conditional on this model, $E_t(\tilde{y}_{t+1}|Y_t) = \delta + y_t$ and $E_t(\Delta\tilde{y}_{t+1}|Y_t) = \delta$.

The distributional properties—and thus the potential information content—of the forecast error seems likely to be affected by a firm's size and the variability of its operations, among other things. Since our tests will involve comparisons of these errors across firms,

---

[36]One can apply this reasoning to any unwarranted potential signaling effects of adherence to specific accounting techniques. In such situations, management may also (or alternatively) overtly attempt to alter predicted interpretations of results induced by applications of some accounting techniques. For example, they might openly declare that such results are "distorted" because the underlying mandated accounting techniques are "inappropriate," given the nature of their firms' production-investment and financing decisions. This line of attack is illustrated by Royal Dutch/Shell Group's April 1978 announcements about the effects of the Financial Accounting Standards Board's *Opinion no. 8,* which pertains to foreign currency translations. As a result of this standard, Royal Dutch/Shell announced (in advance of the formal release of its first-quarter report) that there would be a "major charge" against its first-quarter earnings number. It then argued that FASB *No. 8* poses "unreasonable requirements which make reasonable interpretation of the group's performance unnecessarily difficult." It also stated that it was providing advance notice of the alleged effects of FASB *No. 8* because it felt ". . . that shareholders should, in this instance, be warned in advance of the likely distortion in reported results." It added that the alleged "distortion" does not affect "the underlying business reality or cash generation." And it argued that "Application of [FASB *No. 8*] creates major distortions on a short-term basis and is totally inappropriate to an international group such as the Royal Dutch/Shell Group . . .." See "Dutch/Shell Sets a Major Charge for First Period" (*Wall Street Journal* [April 18, 1978]: 2), from which all cited statements were drawn. This sort of advance managerial announcement may be viewed as a type of managerial signaling designed to mitigate the predicted and allegedly unwarranted effects of complying with external reporting rules imposed on firms.

some standardization seems appropriate. Throughout, the forecast error $\tilde{y}_{t+1} - E_t(\tilde{y}_{t+1}|Y_t) = \Delta\tilde{y}_{t+1} - \delta$ will be scaled by an estimate of $\sigma(\Delta\tilde{y}_{t+1})$, the standard deviation of $\Delta\tilde{y}_{t+1}$.

Similar specifications will be uscd for the relevant attributes of the dividend and extraordinary-item numbers. Let $\tilde{D}_t$ denote the annual cash dividend (including "extras") for period t. The forecast error for $\tilde{D}_t$ equals the forecast error for $\Delta\tilde{D}_t$, which is the error that we shall model using the Lintner model:

$$\Delta\tilde{D}_t = \pi_1 D_{t-1} + \pi_2 y_t + \tilde{\eta}_t.$$

The descriptive validity of this model has been examined in several studies (see, e.g., Fama and Babiak [1968], Fama [1974], Watts [1973], and Laub [1972]). Relative to competing models for annual cash dividends (regular plus extras), it performs quite well. According to the "information content" view of dividend changes, the forecast error $\tilde{\eta}_t = \Delta\tilde{D}_t - E_t(\Delta\tilde{D}_t|D_{t-1}, y_t)$ is positively correlated with changes in the mean of management's predictive distribution of income for periods beyond period t. As with $\Delta\tilde{y}_t$, the forecast error for $\Delta\tilde{D}_t$ will be standardized by an estimate of its conditional standard deviation, which is $\sigma(\tilde{\eta}_t)$.

The forecast of $\Delta\tilde{D}_t$ is conditional on the value of y_t and thus of $\Delta\tilde{y}_t$. This is consistent with our objective of assessing the extent to which the dividend signal reflects information in a way affected by or beyond that reflected in the contemporaneous income signal (as well as the contemporaneous extraordinary-item signal). In short, *our results do not deal with the information content of dividend changes per se*. They are, however, still pertinent to those versions of the dividend-information-content hypothesis asserting that dividend signals *reflect information beyond that reflected in contemporaneous income signals* (see Watts [1973] for a discussion of these versions). For other objectives, one might, of course, want to use the joint distribution of $\Delta\tilde{D}_t$, $\tilde{D}_{t-1}$, $\tilde{y}_t$) to obtain the conditional mean of $\tilde{y}_t$ and examine the implications of the associated forecast error for $\tilde{y}_t$.

Assume that $\tilde{y}_t$ refers to income after (or net of) extraordinary items and let $\tilde{y}_{Bt}$ and $\tilde{y}_{Et}$ denote the period t numbers for income before extraordinary items and total extraordinary items, respectively. By definition $\tilde{y}_t = \tilde{y}_{Bt} + \tilde{y}_{Et}$. Suppose that, conditional on $Y_{Bt} = (y_{Bt}, y_{Bt-1}, \ldots)$ and Y_t, both $\tilde{y}_t$ and $\tilde{y}_{Bt}$ can be adequately described by martingale models: $E_t(\tilde{y}_{t+1}|Y_t) = y_t + \delta$ and $E_t(\tilde{y}_{Bt+1}|Y_{Bt}) = y_{Bt} + \delta_B$. Then the implied forecast of $\Delta\tilde{y}_{Et}$, given Y_t and Y_{Bt}, is $\delta_E = \delta - \delta_B$.

Of course, an obvious alternative model for $\tilde{y}_{Et}$ is $E(\tilde{y}_{Et}) = 0$, which seems consistent with the arguments found in much of the accounting literature. But this alternative may not be consistent with the time series properties of $\tilde{y}_t$ and $\tilde{y}_{Bt}$. Our specifications of $E(\tilde{y}_{Et})$ is necessarily consistent with those properties, conditional on Y_{Bt} and Y_t.

The standard forecast error of $\Delta\tilde{y}_t$ is $(\Delta\tilde{y}_t - \delta)/\sigma(\Delta\tilde{y}_t) = [(\Delta\tilde{y}_{Bt} - \Delta_B)/\sigma(\Delta\tilde{y}_t)] + [(\Delta\tilde{y}_{Et} - \delta_E)/\sigma(\Delta\tilde{y}_t)]$. The first and second terms in this summation are specified to be the standardized forecast errors of $\Delta\tilde{y}_{Bt}$ and $\Delta\tilde{y}_{Et}$, respectively.

8.4.3 Data

All results are based on 1946–1972 annual accounting data for a sample of 285 firms. These firms were selected from the set of firms covered by Standard and Poor's Annual Industrial COMPUSTAT tape (dated September 1973) and by the common stock monthly rate of return files of the Center for Research in Security Prices (CRSP), University of Chicago. The criteria used in selecting firms are:

(C.1) Availability of consecutive observations (i.e., no "missing data") on selected annual numbers (listed below) for *at least* the period 1947–1970. If consecutive observations over a longer subinterval of the period 1946–1972 were available, the additional data were used. (The specific ways in which these and other data were used are discussed in Section 8.4.5.)[37]

(C.2) Availability of consecutive monthly rates of return on the firm's common stock over *at least* the period January 1947–December 1971. If consecutive returns for the period January 1972–March 1972 were available, they were used. (The available CRSP files with data for the post-1947 period covered only New York Stock Exchange firms.)

(C.3) A fiscal year ending during or after April of each year for which data are used. (The motivation for this restriction is given in Section 8.4.5.)

A "control" sample of firms was also drawn from the firms covered by the CRSP and COMPUSTAT files. No firm in the first sample of 285 firms was permitted to enter the control sample. Aside from this restriction, only criterion (C.2) was used in constructing the control sample, which ultimately included 208 firms. In order to distinguish one sample from the other, the sample of 285 firms will be called the "information sample" and the sample of 208 firms the "control sample" in the text and tables.

The following is a profile of the information sample in terms of the initial and terminal years for which consecutive observations on the desired annual COMPUSTAT numbers were available:

Initial Year	Terminal Year	Number of Firms
1946	1970	1
	1971	0
	1972	31
1947	1970	1
	1971	3
	1972	249
		285

Except for the two firms whose terminal years were 1970 for COMPUSTAT data, all firms in the information sample had consecutive observations on the CRSP files for the entire period January 1947–March 1972. The available CRSP data for each control sample firm covered the same period.

The required annual COMPUSTAT numbers are:

(N.1) Income Taxes

(N.2) Extraordinary Items (both those stated before and those stated after tax effects)

(N.3) Net Income

(N.4) Preferred Dividends

(N.5) Net Income for Common ("Available for Common")

(N.6) Common Dividends (Regular plus "Extra")

The Preferred Dividend numbers are used to compute several series of interest. The Lintner [1956] dividend model is not applied to those numbers.

[37] Firms whose dividends never changed and whose dividends were nonzero and firms whose dividends were never nonzero were treated in the same way. Note that paying a zero dividend in any year is just as much a form of signaling as is paying a nonzero dividend.

The Common Dividend numbers for a given year are the amounts firms *declared* (but did not necessarily pay out) during that year. Presumably, these declarations are the dividend numbers affected by the events of the year and, thus, the appropriate numbers to be compared to that year's net income numbers in our tests. Recall that our objective is to assess the extent to which dividend signals at time t reflect information *beyond that reflected in contemporaneous income signals and in the initially available sample evidence*.

The results presented below are based on Net Income minus Preferred Dividends. Corresponding results based on the Available for Common numbers were also obtained. There were no important differenes between these sets of results. (As computed by COMPUSTAT, these two number series may differ.)

Results were obtained for both before-tax and after-tax Net Income. And for each of the latter cases, results for Net Income stated both before and after Extraordinary Items were obtained. Similarly, results for both before-tax and after-tax Extraordinary-Item numbers were obtained. Once again, there were no essential differences among the results. The results presented below are for (1) Net Income Before Extraordinary Items and After Taxes (for both the income signal and dividend model) and (2) Extraordinary Items After Taxes.

COMPUSTAT's Net Income is stated (1) before Preferred Dividends, (2) after taxes, (3) before extraordinary items stated (by a firm) on a net-of-tax basis, and (4) after extraordinary items reported by a firm as not being net-of-taxes. For this study, Net Income after taxes, before extraordinary items and after preferred dividends was computed as: Net Income *plus* Extraordinary Items Not Stated Net of Taxes *minus* Preferred Dividends. Taxes on Extraordinary Items Not Stated Net of Taxes are included in COMPUSTAT's Income Taxes, which is used in its computation of Net Income. Taxes on Extraordinary Items Stated Net of Taxes are not included in COMPUSTAT's Income Taxes.

Total extraordinary items after taxes were computed as: Extraordinary Items Stated Net of Taxes *plus* (Extraordinary Items Not Stated Net of Taxes) × (estimated average tax rate). The estimate of the average tax rate for a given year is: (Income Taxes) ÷ (Net Income *plus* Income Taxes), where all numbers are as defined by COMPUSTAT.

The procedure used to estimate average tax rates is one of several crude ones. The results based on the before-tax data provide some insights into the sensitivity of our results to this procedure.[38] As indicated, there were no important differences between the results based on the before-tax numbers and those based on the after-tax numbers.

The next section provides summary statistics for the information-sample firms' accounting numbers.

8.4.4 Empirical Characteristics of the Income, Dividend, and Extraordinary-Items Numbers (Information Sample)

Table 8-1 provides cross-sectional summary statistics for the first differences of income after extraordinary items ($\Delta\tilde{y}_t$), income before extraordinary items ($\Delta\tilde{y}_{Bt}$), and extraordinary items ($\Delta\tilde{y}_{Et}$). These summaries are for the 285 firms in the information sample.

---

[38]The before-taxes equivalent of every after-taxes number of a given year (e.g., Preferred Dividends) was obtained by dividing the after-tax number by $(1 - \tau)$, where τ is the same year's estimated average tax rate.

As indicated above, all results presented here are for "after-tax" numbers. The sample means of the differenced series are standardized by the sample standard deviations, $\hat{\sigma}_A = \hat{\sigma}(\Delta\tilde{y}_t)$, in line with the discussion of Section 8.4.2.

One apparent message from the first three columns of Table 8-1 is that $\Delta\tilde{y}_{Et}$ contributes, on average, a small amount to the average drift, $\delta = E(\Delta\tilde{y}_t)$, of $\tilde{y}_t$, relative to the standard deviation of $\Delta\tilde{y}_t$. Similarly, the variability of $\Delta\tilde{y}_{Et}$ and its covariability with $\Delta\tilde{y}_{Bt}$ seem to contribute little to the variability of $\Delta\tilde{y}_t$, $\sigma(\Delta\tilde{y}_t)$, as can be seen using the results for $\hat{\sigma}^2(\Delta\tilde{y}_{Bt}/\hat{\sigma}^2(\Delta\tilde{y}_t)$ in Column 4. The median value of the latter is 0.97, which implies that, for the "typical" firm, $\sigma^2(\Delta\tilde{y}_{Et})$ and $\mathrm{Cov}(\Delta\tilde{y}_{Et}, \Delta\tilde{y}_{Bt})$ contribute roughly 3.0 percent to $\sigma^2(\Delta\tilde{y}_t)$. Upon regressing $\hat{\sigma}^2(\Delta\tilde{y}_t)$ on $\hat{\sigma}^2(\Delta\tilde{y}_{Bt})$, we found that the estimated linear relationship between these estimates has a slope coefficient of 0.994 and $\bar{R}^2$, the sample coefficient of multiple determination (adjusted for degrees of freedom), equal to 0.9946. In short, the drift and variability of $\tilde{y}_t$ seem, not unexpectedly, to be dominated by $\tilde{y}_{Bt}$.

The remaining columns of Table 8-1 deal with the serial correlation structure of $\Delta\tilde{y}_t$ and $\Delta\tilde{y}_{Bt}$. As indicated in Chapter 7, this is one of the important systematic properties of accounting numbers. Estimates of serial correlation play a large role in the available works on accounting numbers' time series properties.

The observed runs statistics, $z(\Delta\tilde{y}_t)$ and $z(\Delta\tilde{y}_{Bt})$, seem to be consistent with an absence of important serial correlation. For both series, the estimated first and second correlation coefficients, $\hat{\rho}_1$ and $\hat{\rho}_2$, respectively, seem to be quite small, on average, relative to their theoretical standard errors. On balance, the results are consistent with the statement that $\tilde{y}_t$ and $\tilde{y}_{Bt}$ behave as if they are martingales. This is consistent with the findings surveyed in Chapter 7.

Estimation results for the Lintner dividend-change model are summarized in Table 8-2. The results for $\hat{\pi}_1$ and $\hat{\pi}_2$ are consistent with the usual interpretation of this model. π_1 is the negative of the "speed of adjustment" coefficient, which is the fraction of $E(\Delta\tilde{D}_t)$ due to a difference between "target dividends" for period t and actual dividends for period $t - 1$. Target dividends are obtained by applying a target payout ratio to income for period t. π_2 is the target payout ratio multiplied by the speed of adjustment coefficient. Thus, for example, the values $\pi_1 = -0.23$ and $\pi_2 = 0.12$ imply a target payout ratio equal to $(0.12/0.23) \approx 0.52$. On balance, the results for $\hat{\pi}_1$, $\hat{\pi}_2$, $\bar{R}^2$, and the estimated first-order serial correlation coefficient, $\hat{\rho}_1(\tilde{\eta}_t)$, of the disturbance, $\tilde{\eta}_t$, seem consistent with the Lintner model's being an adequate model for $\delta\tilde{D}_t$.

The results reported in Table 8-2 are essentially the same as those reported by Fama and Babiak [1968] for the period 1946–1964 using a sample of 392 firms and by Fama [1974] for the period 1946–1966 using a sample of 298 firms. Those papers provide results from a variety of diagnostic checks of the adequacy of Lintner's model. On balance, this model seems to perform well relative to some leading competitors for annual cash dividends.[39]

8.4.5 Estimation of Conditional and Unconditional Return Distributions

Our tests for "information content" involve comparisons of return distributions, along the lines discussed in Section 8.3. The crux of the approach is the same as that described

---

[39]A variety of results for models of quarterly dividends are provided by Laub [1972], who proposes alternatives to the Lintner model.

TABLE 8-1

CROSS-SECTIONAL SUMMARY STATISTICS FOR INCOME NUMBER SERIES FOR INFORMATION SAMPLE OF 285 FIRMS

	$\overline{\Delta y_B}/\tilde{\sigma}_A$	$\overline{\Delta y_E}/\tilde{\sigma}_A$	$\Delta y/\tilde{\sigma}_A$	$\tilde{\sigma}_B^2/\tilde{\sigma}_A^2$	$\tilde{\rho}_1(\Delta\tilde{y})$	$\tilde{\rho}_2(\Delta\tilde{y})$	$z(\Delta\tilde{y})$	$\tilde{\rho}_1(\Delta\tilde{y}_B)$	$\tilde{\rho}_2(\Delta\tilde{y}_B)$	$z(\Delta\tilde{y}_B)$
Minimum	−.22	−.2714	−.27	.012	−.868	−.768	−4.371	−.698	−.715	−4.371
Deciles										
1	−.03	−.0329	−.02	.365	−.489	−.413	−1.857	−.356	−.424	−2.008
2	.03	−.0033	−.03	.625	−.357	−.321	−1.016	−.279	−.328	−1.043
3	.08	.0	.08	.800	−.280	−.248	−.526	−.195	−.265	−.626
4	.10	.0	.12	.910	−.208	−.181	−.175	−.123	−.214	−.209
5	.15	.0	.17	.972	−.142	−.101	.111	−.049	−.138	−.072
6	.23	.0	.22	.990	−.087	−.038	.358	.008	−.051	.209
7	.28	.0001	.29	1.000	.005	.063	.666	.080	.062	.592
8	.39	.0021	.42	1.020	.126	.149	.788	.193	.151	.727
9	.61	.0152	.61	1.105	.303	.344	1.086	.414	.317	1.086
Maximum	1.51	.0846	1.51	3.125	.914	.851	2.489	.920	.856	2.296
Mean	.23	−.0072	.23	.867	−.111	−.071	−.117	−.018	−.085	−.267
Standard Deviation	.26	.0421	.26	.349	.324	.298	1.275	.313	.298	1.298

Notes:

(1) *Notation:* Δ = first difference operator; y_B = Income Before Extraordinary Items and After Taxes; y_E = Extraordinary Items After Taxes (where a positive item is an increase in income); y_A = Income After Extraordinary Items and After Taxes; $\tilde{\sigma}_A$ = Estimated Standard Deviation of $\Delta\tilde{y}$; and $\tilde{\rho}_i(\Delta\tilde{y})$ = Estimated i^{th} Order Serial Correlation Coefficient. A bar above a variable denotes estimated mean of observed time series.

(2) For each number series and each firm in the sample, the number of observations is at least 24 (time period = 1947–1970) and at most 27 (time period = 1946–1972). In order to be included in the sample, observations on all series must have been available for at least the entire period 1947–1970. Differencing leads to a loss of one observation. Other data requirements are discussed in the text.

(3) For a series of length $n = 23$ (25), the approximate standard error of $\tilde{\rho}_1$ is $\sqrt{(n-1)/n(n+2)} \approx .196$ (.189), conditional on the hypothesis of no serial correlation; the approximate standard error of $\tilde{\rho}_2$ is $\sqrt{(n-2)/n(n+2)} \approx .191$ (.185). For $n = 23$ (25), the approximate expected value of $\tilde{\rho}_1$ is $-1/(n-1) \approx -.045$ ($-.042$); for $\tilde{\rho}_2$ it is $-1/(n-2) \approx -.048$ ($-.044$).

(4) $z(\tilde{x})$ is the observed standardized runs statistic for the random variable $\tilde{x}$. Its sampling distribution is, asymptotically, normal with mean equal to zero and standard deviation equal to unity.

TABLE 8-2

CROSS-SECTIONAL SUMMARY STATISTICS FOR DIVIDEND MODEL
$\Delta\tilde{D}_t = \pi_1 D_t - 1 + \pi_2 y_{Bt} + \tilde{\eta}_t$
y_{Bt} = Income Before Extraordinary Items and After Taxes

	$\hat{\pi}_1$	$\hat{\pi}_2$	$\bar{R}^2$	$\hat{\rho}_1(\tilde{\eta}_t)$	$\overline{\Delta D}_t/\hat{\sigma}(\Delta\tilde{D}_t)$
Minimum	−1.20	−.13	−.33	−.67	−.41
Deciles					
1	−.45	.05	.10	−.35	−.06
2	−.37	.08	.19	−.23	.02
3	−.31	.09	.26	−.15	.12
4	−.27	.10	.31	−.08	.21
5	−.23	.12	.37	−.01	.34
6	−.19	.15	.46	.05	.46
7	−.16	.18	.51	.12	.66
8	−.13	.22	.59	.21	.76
9	−.08	.27	.68	.33	.95
Maximum	.37	.56	.88	.59	1.60
Mean	−.25	.14	.38	−.02	.40
Std. Dev.	.16	.09	.22	.25	.41

Notes

(1) For each firm in the sample of 285 firms, the number of observations on $\tilde{D}_t$ and $\tilde{y}_{Bt}$ is at least 24 (time period = 1947–1970) and at most 27 (time period = 1946–1972). In order to be included in the sample, observations on both variables must have been available for at least the entire period 1947–1970. Differencing leads to a loss of one observation. See text for other data requirements.

(2) For a series of length n = 23 (25), the approximate standard error of $\hat{\rho}_1$ is $\sqrt{(n-1)/n(n+2)} \approx .196$ (.189), conditional on the hypothesis of no serial correlation; the approximate expected value is $-1/(n-1) \approx -.045$ (−.042).

(3) $\bar{R}^2$ is the sample coefficient of multiple determination adjusted for degrees of freedom.

in Chapter 6 with respect to tests of the effects of changes in accounting methods. Throughout, attention will be restricted to the means of return distributions. The testing approach used here is the one proposed by Gonedes [1975*b*] (see also Gonedes, Dopuch, and Penman [1976]. Only an overview of the approach is given here.

All analyses of return distributions are based on monthly returns of portfolios rather than individual shares. The primary reason for using returns on portfolios is to reduce sampling error, and thus increase the precision of our estimation results. If the firms included in a portfolio used to estimate a conditional distribution are homogeneous insofar as the implications of the conditioning signal are concerned, then the power of our tests is increased by using portfolios as the units of analysis.

Portfolios are formed at each of several portfolio formation dates. The observed returns on these portfolios between formation dates are used to estimate the means of the marginal and conditional distributions of interest.

The values of the standardized forecast errors (see Section 8.4.2) for changes in income, changes in cash dividends declared, and changes in extraordinary items are the bases for portfolio formation. For brevity, we denote these standardized errors by $\tilde{IE}$, $\tilde{DE}$, and $\tilde{EE}$, respectively, omitting time and firm subscripts for convenience.

The realizations of $\tilde{IE}$, $\tilde{DE}$, and $\tilde{EE}$, corresponding to the portfolio formation date of a given calendar year are assumed to be available anytime within the 12-month period following that date. No actual announcement dates were used. For each calendar year, the portfolio formation date is specified to be March of that year. The signals always pertain to accounting or dividend numbers for the fiscal year corresponding to that calendar year. Thus, for example, the portfolios formed at March 1960 are formed on the basis of the realized values of annual numbers pertaining to the fiscal year 1960 and, thus, all or part of the 12-month period beginning with April 1960. Firms with fiscal years ending on or before March 31 are excluded from our information sample (see Section 8.4.3, Criterion C.3). There is, therefore, at least one month between the portfolio formation month and the ending month of each firm's fiscal year corresponding to the calendar year of portfolio formation.[40] Thus, our assumption about the timing of signals' announcements seems "safe." In actuality, no more than one firm had a fiscal year that ended before May in any calendar year for which portfolios were formed (1952–1971). In each of these years, at least 216 firms' fiscal years ended in December. (On average, December fiscal year firms announce their annual accounting numbers in March of the next calendar year; see Ball and Brown [1968].)

Given the above procedures, our estimation results correspond to distributions conditional on signals announced after the time of portfolio formation and, thus, after the time at which capital market equilibrium is established (time t in Section 8.3.2). This is what is called for by the framework given in Gonedes [1975b] for the estimation of return distributions conditional in signals.

For a given portfolio formation date, one portfolio is formed for each of several percentile ranges of the estimated cross-sectional distributions of the standardized forecast errors $\tilde{IE}$, $\tilde{DE}$, and $\tilde{EE}$ associated with that date. For a given formation date, all firms in the information sample are ranked in terms of their observed values of $\tilde{IE}$. This ranked array is divided into three nonoverlapping groups with the top 33-1/3 percent of the firms in the first group, the next 33-1/3 percent of the firms in the second group, etc. All the firms in each of these three groups are then ranked in terms of their realized values of $\tilde{DE}$ corresponding to the formation date. For each of these three groups, all firms falling on either side of the median value of $\tilde{DE}$ are grouped together, thus yielding two nonoverlapping groups within each of the first three groups. At this point there are 6 groups: 3 IE-groups × 2 DE-groups. All the firms in each of the DE-groups are then ranked in terms of their realized values of $\tilde{EE}$. Two groups are formed for each of these ranked arrays: one for the top half and one for the bottom half. There are now 12 groups: 3 IE-groups × 2 DE-groups × 2 EE-groups. The firms in each of the 12 groups are ultimately combined into one portfolio; the end result is 12 portfolios.

The implications of the two-parameter asset-pricing model are exploited in forming portfolios. This is done in an attempt to hold "other things" constant, insofar as tests on means are concerned. Given the two-parameter model, which is discussed in Chapter 3 and in Chapter 4, "other things" can be held constant by comparing return distributions for assets whose relative risks are equal, as of the portfolio formation date. According to one version of that model:

$$E(\tilde{R}_{jt}) = E(\tilde{R}_{zt}) + [E(\tilde{R}_{mt}) - E(\tilde{R}_{zt})]\beta_{jt},$$

[40]The interval between the formation date and the release of the annual numbers will obviously exceed one month even if the fiscal year ends in April.

where $\tilde{R}_{jt}$ is the rate of return on asset j from t to $t + 1$; $\tilde{R}_{mt}$ is the rate of return on the market portfolio, m; $\beta_{jt} = \text{Cov}(\tilde{R}_{jt}, \tilde{R}_{mt})/\text{Var}(\tilde{R}_{mt})$ is the relative risk of asset j in portfolio m; and $\tilde{R}_{zt}$ is the return on an asset z such that $\beta_{zt} = 0.0$. A review of theory and evidence pertinent to this model is given by Jensen [1972]. (See also Roll [1977]).

Let $\tilde{\phi}_{pt} = \phi_{pt}$ be a (vector or scalar) signal announced by all firms in portfolio p after equilibrium is established at time t. Suppose that portfolio e consists of randomly selected assets. That is, portfolio e is not constructed conditionally on any value of a signal that will be announced after t. Finally, suppose that these portfolios are constructed so that $\beta_{pt} = \beta_{et}$.

If $\tilde{\phi}_{pt}$ reflects no information beyond that already available at time t, then $E(\tilde{R}_{pt}|\phi_{pt}) = E(\tilde{R}_{et})$ for all values, ϕ_{pt}, of $\tilde{\phi}_{pt}$ because $\beta_{pt} = \beta_{et}$. An inequality between these expected values can be ascribed to $\tilde{\phi}_{pt}$'s reflecting information beyond that available at time t. This is because all "other things" are held constant—insofar as equilibrium expected returns are concerned—by the condition $\beta_{pt} = \beta_{et}$.

The implications of relative risk are exploited in forming portfolios for each of the 12 groups constructed for both the information sample and the control sample. The 12 groups of the control sample were formed by randomly assigning the firms in that sample to 12 equal-sized groups. For each sample, every group is used to form a minimum variance portfolio with relative risk equal to unity. Since the original groups consisted of nonoverlapping sets of firms, the portfolios for both samples are constructed using nonoverlapping sets of firms. Details on the final portfolio formation/risk equalization procedures are given in Gonedes, [1975*b*].[41]

Estimates of relative risk were obtained by estimating the parameters of the "market model," $\tilde{R}_{it} = \alpha_1 + \beta_i\tilde{R}_{mt} + \tilde{\epsilon}_{it}$ for each firm, i, using Fisher's [1966] Arithmetic Index as a proxy for m. In order to allow for changes in firms' relative risks (see, e.g., Gonedes [1973]), relative risks were re-estimated at each portfolio formation month using returns from that month and the 59 preceding months. This involves, in effect, a simultaneous adding and dropping of 12 consecutive observed returns when the scheme moves from one formation month to the next one. The portfolio formation months underlying all of our results are the months of March for the 20 years 1952–1971.

Each control-sample portfolio is arbitrarily paired with one information-sample portfolio. The same pairs of portfolios underlie all results.

Note that our assignment of information-sample firms to portfolios corresponds to forming portfolios on the basis of observed signals that are realizations of vector indicator random variables. Let $\tilde{\underline{\theta}}_t^T = (\tilde{\theta}_{1t}, \tilde{\theta}_{2t}, \tilde{\theta}_{3t})$ denote a 3 × 1 vector indicator random variable, where $\tilde{\theta}_{1t}$, $\tilde{\theta}_{2t}$, and $\tilde{\theta}_{3t}$ pertain to $\tilde{IE}$, $\tilde{DE}$, and $\tilde{EE}$, respectively. The possible realizations of $\tilde{\theta}_{1t}$ are "high" (H), "middle" (M), and "low" (L), where $\tilde{\theta}_{1t}$ = H denotes an observed value of $\tilde{IE}$ above the .66-2/3 fractile of the estimated cross-sectional distribution of $\tilde{IE}$

[41]The procedure used to construct the minimum variance portfolios involves combining two equally weighted portfolios of securities ranked according to estimated relative risks. The weights assigned to these two portfolios were examined to determine whether there were any extreme weights. None was detected. The prespecified value of unity for relative risk never fell outside the range of values defined by the equally weighted portfolios' estimated relative risks. (Thus, there were never any short positions in these portfolios.) In general, the weights assigned to the two equally weighted portfolios fell within the internal range [.40, .60], with the weights summing to unity.

at portfolio formation date t, $\tilde{\theta}_{1t}$, $\tilde{\theta}_{1t} = M$ denotes an observed value of $\tilde{IE}$ between the .33-1/3 and .66-2/3 fractiles of that distribution, and $\tilde{\theta}_{1t} = L$ denotes an observed value below the .33-1/3 fractile. Similarly, $\tilde{\theta}_{2t} = H$ ($\tilde{\theta}_{3t} = H$) denotes an observed value of $\tilde{DE}$ ($\tilde{EE}$) above the median of the estimated cross-sectional distribution of $\tilde{DE}$ ($\tilde{EE}$) at portfolio formation date t. It is assumed that all firms with the same value of $\underline{\tilde{\theta}}_t$—and thus all firms in a given portfolio—are homogeneous insofar as this signal's implications for expected returns are concerned.

8.4.6 Relationships Among the Potential Signals

The weights defining the 12 minimum variance portfolios of the information sample were also used to compute the values of $\tilde{IE}$, $\tilde{DE}$, and $\tilde{EE}$ for these portfolios, for each of the portfolio formation dates. The resulting time series data were examined to determine whether there were any unambiguous relationships among these signals—interpreted relative to the framework of Section 2.[42] No such relationships were inferred to exist, even though there appeared to be systematic ("statistical") relationships among these potential signals. (Details appear in the April 1976 version of the report from which these results are drawn.) In short, the inferred systematic relationships are consistent with conflicting interpretations.

Given the discussion in Section 8.3, this result is not surprising. Moreover, it seems to make results on investors' assessments—conditional on the various potential signals—especially interesting. Do ambiguity surrounding a given mode of potential signaling and uncertainty regarding the mode adopted by a firm render the potential signals ineffective, management's objectives notwithstanding? That is, do investors behave as if the potential signals examined here reflect no information beyond that reflected in other sources about the attributes of firms' decisions—no matter what kinds of systematic relationships among the signals themselves might be inferred? We deal directly with this question in the next two sections. But before getting to that, we should note that ambiguity with respect to managerial signaling does not imply nonstationary or ill-defined managerial objectives or plans. The letter may be quite well defined and stationary. Yet, pursuing fixed objectives and plans may entail signaling behavior that is surrounded by ambiguity, insofar as outsiders are concerned. And asymmetries in the information endowments and information-production opportunities of insiders and outsiders may preclude precise elimination of this ambiguity.

8.4.7 Summary Statistics for Portfolios' Returns

Table 8-3 provides summary statistics for monthly rates of return on the information-sample and control-sample portfolios. The value of the indicator random variable, $\underline{\tilde{\theta}}^T = (\tilde{\theta}_1, \tilde{\theta}_2, \tilde{\theta}_3)$, corresponding to each portfolio is given in the column labeled "Information Class." The time series of monthly rates of return for each portfolio begins (ends) with the returns corresponding to the first (last) portfolio formation date, which is March 1952

---

[42]The same data were used to check for "extreme" values ("outliers") in the data used to compute the values of $\tilde{IE}$, $\tilde{DE}$, and $\tilde{EE}$ for each portfolio. Such extreme values might be consistent with the results for one (or a few) firms having an excessively large influence on results for a given portfolio. We identified no extreme values. Similar diagnostic checks were applied to the rate-of-return data for each portfolio.

TABLE 8-3

SUMMARY STATISTICS FOR MONTHLY RETURNS ($\tilde{R}$) ON INFORMATION-SAMPLE PORTFOLIOS AND ON CONTROL-SAMPLE PORTFOLIOS

Time Period of Observations: April 1952–March 1972
(240 Monthly Observations)

Port folio Number	Information Class	Information Sample: $10^2 \times$ Est. Mean $\hat{\mu}(\tilde{R})$	$10^2 \times$ Est. Std. Dev. $\hat{\sigma}(\tilde{R})$	$t(\hat{\mu})$	Studentized Range	$\hat{\rho}_1(\tilde{R})$	Control Sample: $10^2 \times$ Est. Mean $\hat{\mu}(\tilde{R})$	$10^2 \times$ Est. Std. Dev. $\hat{\sigma}(\tilde{R})$	$t(\hat{\mu})$	Studentized Range	$\hat{\rho}_1(\tilde{R})$
1	HHL	1.95	4.50	6.70	7.49	.097	1.25	4.51	4.27	5.97	.143
2	HHH	2.01	4.53	6.86	5.27	.121	1.04	4.66	3.47	6.30	.124
3	HLL	2.07	4.41	7.25	5.02	.077	1.00	4.38	3.53	5.91	.158
4	HLH	2.01	4.55	6.82	5.49	.085	1.17	5.07	3.55	6.26	.181
5	MHL	1.22	4.18	4.50	5.67	.102	1.21	4.51	4.14	5.99	.228
6	MHH	1.17	4.57	3.98	5.82	.114	1.08	4.61	3.63	6.44	.206
7	MLL	1.28	4.56	4.35	5.06	.161	1.33	4.82	4.28	5.69	.104
8	MLH	1.33	4.50	4.57	6.45	.139	1.13	4.49	3.90	6.10	.129
9	LHL	.31	4.70	1.02	6.59	.138	1.26	4.78	4.08	6.01	.187
10	LHH	.34	4.40	1.18	6.42	.184	1.40	4.93	4.38	6.80	.135
11	LLL	.43	4.67	1.44	6.45	.172	1.21	4.74	3.94	6.52	.101
12	LLH	.53	4.82	1.70	6.79	.130	1.14	4.82	3.67	6.73	.173
NYSE Equally Weighted Arithmetic Index							1.14	4.25	4.16	6.43	.175

Notes:

(1) Each portfolio is a minimum variance portfolio with estimated relative risk equal to unity; see text.

(2) Portfolios 4, 8, and 12 of the Information Sample contain 23 securities over the entire time period. Except for the last portfolio formation date (March 1971), all other portfolios of the Information Sample contain 24 securities over the entire period. For the last portfolio formation date, portfolios 6 and 10 of the Information Sample contain 23 securities. The two firms lost at the final portfolio-formation date are the firms whose terminal years were 1970 for COMPUSTAT data.

Portfolios 1, 3, 5, and 9 of the Control Sample contain 18 securities over the entire time period; all others contain 17 securities.

(3) The approximate values of $E(\hat{\rho}_1)$ and $\sigma(\hat{\rho}_1)$, conditional on no serial correlation and a sample of size n = 240, are $-1/(n-1) \approx -.004$ and

$$\sqrt{\frac{n-1}{n(n+2)}} \approx .064, \text{ respectively.}$$

(4) Values of fractiles of the distribution of the Studentized Range, conditional on normality, are:

Sample Size	Lower Percentage Points: 0.5	1.0	2.5	5.0	10.0	Upper Percentage Points: 10.0	5.0	2.5	1.0	0.5
200	4.50	4.56	4.67	4.78	4.90	6.15	6.38	6.59	6.85	7.03
500	5.06	5.13	5.25	5.37	5.49	6.72	6.94	7.15	7.42	7.60

(March 1971). For purposes of comparison, summary statistics for the returns on Fisher's Arithmetic Index (Fisher [1966]) are also provided. The returns on the various portfolios are not, of course, cross-sectionally independent. Thus, relationships among the results for different portfolios should not be overemphasized. It turns out, however, that some important hints provided by them are borne out by analyses dealing with that cross-sectional correlation, as will be seen in Section 8.4.8.

The point estimates of the standard deviation of portfolio return, $\hat{\sigma}(\tilde{R})$, the Studentized Range, and the first-order serial correlation coefficient, $\hat{\rho}_1(\tilde{R})$, do not seem to suggest any major differences among the portfolios within or between the two samples. Also, these point estimates for both samples' portfolios are quite similar to the corresponding estimates for Fisher's Index—which is our proxy for the market portfolio. Note, for example, that the reported values of $\hat{\sigma}(\tilde{R})$ are quite close to the estimate $\hat{\sigma}(\tilde{R}) = 0.0425$ for the return on Fisher's Index. This suggests that the portfolios are well diversified, insofar as eliminating so-called nonsystematic or diversifiable risk is concerned.

The values of the Studentized Range and $\hat{\rho}_1(\tilde{R})$ are similar to those usually observed for portfolios' returns, at least for the post-World War II period. On balance, the assumption of normally distributed serially uncorrelated returns seems to provide a sufficiently adequate description.

The point estimates, $\hat{\mu}(\tilde{R})$, of the expected rates of return, $\mu(\tilde{R})$, provide important clues to what will be discussed extensively in Section 8.4.8. First, consider the estimates for the control sample's portfolios. On balance, these estimates are similar to each other and to the estimate $\hat{\mu}(\tilde{R}) = 0.0114$ for Fisher's Index—before or after relating the point estimates to their standard errors by computing t-statistics, $t(\hat{\mu})$. These results appear to be consistent with the control sample's consisting of representative well-diversified portfolios with relative risks equal to unity.

Similar statements for the information sample's portfolios appear unwarranted. For these portfolios, the values of $\hat{\mu}(\tilde{R})$ for a given level of $\tilde{IE}$ (H, M, or L) seem similar. But there appear to be substantial inter-level differences. For example, the average $\hat{\mu}(\tilde{R})$ for portfolios 1–4 ($\tilde{IE}$ classified as H) is around 0.0201. The averages for portfolios 5–8 ($\tilde{IE}$ classified as M) a 9–12 ($\tilde{IE}$ classified as L) are around 0.0125 and 0.0040, respectively. In short, the estimates vary monotonically with the level of $\tilde{IE}$. A similar pattern is observed for the value of $t(\hat{\mu})$.

Moreover, with the possible exception of the portfolios corresponding to $\tilde{IE}$ classified as M, the values of $\hat{\mu}(\tilde{R})$ for the information sample's portfolios seem quite different from the corresponding portfolios in the control sample. And the differences seem quite reasonable. For the portfolios corresponding to $\tilde{IE}$ classified as H, M, and L, the values of $\hat{\mu}(\tilde{R})$ exceed, are about the same as, are less than, respectively, the values for their corresponding control-sample portfolios.

On balance, the point estimates given in Table 8-3 appear consistent with the statement that the return distributions conditional on some values of $\tilde{\theta}$ differ from the marginal distributions. The values of $\hat{\mu}(\tilde{R})$ and the other statistics seem consistent with the differences' turning on the means of the distributions rather than, for example, on their standard deviations or on their consistency with the normality assumption. Moreover, the differences between the conditional and marginal distributions seem to turn on the level of the income signal, $\tilde{IE}$. There are no hints of striking differences among the conditional means within any income signal class (H, M, or L).

The above remarks involve taking the point estimates at face value and ignoring cross-sectional correlation. In the next section, the sample evidence is analyzed in a more appropriate way. The material in the next section may seem overly technical to some readers. Suffice it to say that the reader should at least skim through this section to gain some familiarity with the major types of issues that arise in formal analyses of the types of data used here. Then he/she should go directly to Section 8.4.5, which provides a rather complete summary and discussion of our empirical work.

8.4.8 Results from Tests for Information Content

8.4.8.1 Procedures

Let $\tilde{\underset{\sim}{R}}_{1t}$ and $\tilde{\underset{\sim}{R}}_{2t}$ be the 12 × 1 vectors of returns from t to $t + 1$ on the information-sample and control-sample portfolios, respectively. By construction, each component of the vector of estimates of $E(\tilde{\underset{\sim}{R}}_{1t})$ is an estimated mean return conditional on a realization—e.g., (H, H, M)—of the vector indicator random variable $\tilde{\underset{\sim}{\theta}}_t$ and conditional on relative risk equal to unity. Each estimated component of $E(\tilde{\underset{\sim}{R}}_{2t})$ is an estimate of the mean of the marginal distribution of the return on an asset with risk equal to unity.

Formally, our "null hypothesis" is $E(\tilde{\underset{\sim}{R}}_{1t}) = E(\tilde{\underset{\sim}{R}}_{2t})$, which is equivalent to the null hypothesis:

$$\underset{\sim}{w}^T[E(\tilde{\underset{\sim}{R}}_{2t}) - E(\tilde{\underset{\sim}{R}}_{2t})] = 0 \tag{8.1}$$

for all values of the 12 × 1 vector $\underset{\sim}{w}$. Our alternative hypothesis is that equality does not hold for all (but it may hold for some) of the corresponding components of $E(\tilde{\underset{\sim}{R}}_{1t})$ and $E(\tilde{\underset{\sim}{R}}_{2t})$.[43] This is an appropriate specification of the alternative for our purposes because we do not insist that each realization of $\tilde{\underset{\sim}{\theta}}$ lead to a difference between the conditional and marginal distributions of returns in order to infer an inconsistency with the condition of "no information content." Conditional on this alternative and the multivariate normality of $(\tilde{\underset{\sim}{R}}_{1t}, \tilde{\underset{\sim}{R}}_{2t})$, an appropriate test of (8.1) is Hotelling's T^2 test (see Anderson [1958] or Morrison [1967]).[44] The statistic used for this test is defined by:

$$T^2 = \max_{\underset{\sim}{w}} t^2(\underset{\sim}{w}) = M(\hat{\underset{\sim}{\mu}}_1 - \hat{\underset{\sim}{\mu}}_2)^T \underset{\approx}{S}^{-1}(\hat{\underset{\sim}{\mu}}_1 - \hat{\underset{\sim}{\mu}}_2), \tag{8.2}$$

where

$$t(\underset{\sim}{w}) = \frac{\underset{\sim}{w}^T (\hat{\underset{\sim}{\mu}}_1 - \hat{\underset{\sim}{\mu}}_2)\sqrt{M}}{\sqrt{\underset{\sim}{w}^T \underset{\approx}{S} \underset{\sim}{w}}} \quad ; \tag{8.3}$$

$\hat{\underset{\sim}{\mu}}_1$ and $\hat{\underset{\sim}{\mu}}_2$ are the sample estimates of $E(\tilde{\underset{\sim}{R}}_{1t})$ and $E(\tilde{\underset{\sim}{R}}_{2t})$, respectively; $\underset{\approx}{S}$ is the sample variance/covariance matrix of $\tilde{\underset{\sim}{R}}_{1t} - \tilde{\underset{\sim}{R}}_{2t}$; and M is the number of observed return vectors in the sample. Condititonal on the null hypothesis, the distribution of $\tilde{T}^2$ is that of $\tilde{F}(N, M - N)$, a central "F" random variable with N and $M - N$ degrees of freedom. N is the dimensionality of $\tilde{\underset{\sim}{R}}_{1t} - \tilde{\underset{\sim}{R}}_{2t}$, which is 12 in our work.

Since we are using the differences between contemporaneous returns on equally risky

---

[43]See Gonedes [1975*b*] for a discussion of this alternative's implications and some motivation for its use in tests for information content.

[44]Of course, if a more specific alternative hypothesis is specified, then a more powerful test than the T^2 test can be constructed. An excellent discussion of some general issues involved in doing so is provided by Miller [1966, chap. 1].

portfolios, our results will not be systematically affected by peculiarities of the sample time period, to the extent that they affect equally risky assets' returns in the same way (in particular, by some affine transformation). Second, the above approach allows for a situation in which not all realizations of $\tilde{\theta}_t$ reflect information beyond that already available at time t. Third, the above test fully recognizes the implications of cross-sectional correlation among the differences between returns on the information-sample and control-sample portfolios.

Some evidence on this cross-sectional correlation is given in Table 8-4, which provides estimates of the correlation matrix of $\tilde{\underset{\sim}{R}}_{1t} - \tilde{\underset{\sim}{R}}_{2t}$. Observed values of a statistic for a likelihood ratio test of cross-sectional independence appear in the last column. Use of this statistic can be justified in terms of asymptotic results. Finite sample results reported by Aitkin, Nelson and Reinfurt [1968] suggest that the test performs well for the sample sizes underlying Table 8-7.

Overall, the results are not strongly consistent with independence. For the most part, the estimated correlation coefficients for portfolios within each income signal group are positive and they exhibit surprising stability across the subperiods April 1952–March 1962 and April 1962–March 1972. The estimates of many of the other coefficients appear to be unstable, which suggests that they may be consistent with coefficients equal to zero.

Even if the return differences are inferred to be independent, the T^2 test is still an appropriate test because we are still interested in a joint test of 12 propositions—one for each portfolio pair—against the alternative that includes all possible violations of (8.1).[45] The jointness should be considered in specifying the "rejection" region of one's test, at the level of formalities, and in any less formal treatment of the sample evidence's consistency with the no-information-content hypothesis against the alternative specified above.

8.4.8.2 Overall Test Results

The T^2 test results and a variety of summary statistics are provided in Table 8-5. All results given there pertain to differences between returns on paired portfolios, with each of the 12 pairs containing one portfolio from the information sample and one from the control sample. The information-sample portfolio in a particular pair is identified by the value of the indicator random vector given in the first column.

Given the observed value of $\tilde{T}^2$, it seems clear that the sample evidence shows little consistency with the no-information-content assertion. The nature of the inconsistency is, however, of greater interest.

As can be seen from the estimated mean return differences—and the corresponding values of $\tilde{t}(\hat{\mu})$ and $\tilde{F}(12, 228)$—the portfolio-by-portfolio inconsistency is systematically related to the observed level of $\tilde{IE}$ (H, M, or L). For portfolios conditional on $\tilde{IE}$ classified as H, the estimated conditional means exceed the corresponding estimates of the marginal mean. And the reported values of $\tilde{F}(12, 228)$ appear to be nontrivial. The direction of the differences is the opposite for portfolios conditional on $\tilde{IE}$ classified as L; the values of $\tilde{F}(12, 228)$ again seem nontrivial. The conditional means for the portfolios with $\tilde{IE}$ classified as M appear insignificantly different from the marginal mean.

The nature of the four estimates within each income-signal grouping is quite revealing.

[45]Specifically, the proposition $E(\tilde{R}_{i1t}) = E(\tilde{R}_{i2t})$, for each i, $i = 1, 2, \ldots, 12$, where $\tilde{R}_{i1t}(\tilde{R}_{i2t})$ is the ith component of $\tilde{R}_{1t}$ $(\tilde{R}_{2t})$.

TABLE 8-4

ESTIMATED CORRELATION MATRICES IN DIFFERENCES BETWEEN MONTHLY RETURNS ON INFORMATION-SAMPLE PORTFOLIOS AND MATCHING CONTROL-SAMPLE PORTFOLIOS
All Portfolios Are Minimum Variance Portfolios with Estimated Relative Risk Equal to Unity

Portfolio Formation Dates		Number of Monthly Observations	Information Class	Portfolio Pair	Portfolio Pair												Value of $\bar{x}^2(66)^a$
First	Last				1	2	3	4	5	6	7	8	9	10	11	12	
3/52	3/71	240	HHL	1	1.000												219.79
			HHH	2	.172	1.000											
			HLL	3	.169	.236	1.000										
			HHM	4	.106	.290	.326	1.000									
			HHL	5	.057	.192	.147	.184	1.000								
			HHL	6	.083	.211	.181	.163	.204	1.000							
			HHL	7	.052	0.80	.029	.035	.083	.146	1.000						
			HHL	8	−.045	0.89	.056	.136	.107	−.023	.062	1.000					
			HHL	9	.072	0.45	−.009	.090	.174	.019	−.089	.187	1.000				
			HHL	10	−.095	−.002	−.066	.007	.081	−.010	.189	.126	.109	1.000			
			HHL	11	−.020	.131	.116	.049	.241	.032	.045	−.007	.207	.072	1.000		
			HHL	12	.093	0.37	.070	0.96	0.48	.130	.115	.249	.105	.063	.184	1.000	
3/52	3/61	120	HHL	1	1.000												170.14
			HHL	2	.115	1.000											
			HHL	3	.165	.078	1.000										
			HHL	4	.120	.255	.338	1.000									
			HHL	5	.091	.166	.015	.139	1.000								
			HHL	6	.266	.165	.044	.233	.256	1.000							
			HHL	7	.108	.095	.014	.064	.033	192	1.000						
			HHL	8	−.052	.080	.085	.140	.071	−.055	.050	1.000					
			HHL	9	.085	.167	−.041	.223	.208	.046	−.063	.261	1.000				
			HHL	10	.002	−.021	−.107	.051	.064	−.060	.256	.191	.161	1.000			
			HHL	11	.178	.335	.220	.042	.276	.086	.060	.115	.173	.068	1.000		
			HHL	12	.318	.132	.206	.193	.195	.158	.151	.220	.100	−.027	.324	1.000	

3/62	3/71	120	HHL	1	1.000											121.47
			HHL	2	.212	1.000										
			HHL	3	.173	.326	1.000									
			HHL	4	.093	.315	.322	1.000								
			HHL	5	.033	.219	.234	.225	1.000							
			HHL	6	−.034	.231	.246	.114	.182	1.000						
			HHL	7	.014	.078	.044	.017	.115	.129	1.000					
			HHL	8	−.039	.105	.046	.110	.326	.006	.061	1.000				
			HHL	9	.068	−.022	.021	.900	.139	.024	−.130	.124	1.000			
			HHL	10	−.158	.023	−.036	−.018	.085	.034	.132	.075	.051	1.000		
			HHL	11	−.149	.007	.064	.057	.214	.008	.030	−.086	.222	.067	1.000	
			HHL	12	−.903	−.034	−.016	.013	−.084	.120	.081	.269	.100	.125	.079	1.000

[a]Let $\underset{=}{e}$ denote a correlation matrix for a multivariable normal random vector of dimension p. The likelihood ratio statistic for testing $\underset{=}{e} + \underset{=}{I}$, where $\underset{=}{I}$ is an identity matrix against the alternative $\underset{=}{e} \neq \underset{=}{I}$ is $|\hat{\underset{=}{e}}|^{N/2}$, where $\hat{\underset{=}{e}}$ is the maximum likelihood estimate of $\underset{=}{e}$ and N is the number of observations used for estimation. The asymptotic distribution of $-\ (W - 1 - (2p + 5)/6)\ (n|\hat{\underset{=}{e}}|$ is that of $X^2(r(p - 1)/2)$, a chi-squared random variable with $p(p - 1)/2)$ degrees of freedom. For the case at hand, $p = 12$ and $p(p - 1)/\epsilon = 66$. Values of selected fractions of the distributions of $\bar{x}^2(60)$ and $\bar{x}^2(70)$ are

Degrees of Freedom	Fractile .75	.900	.950	.975	.990	.995	.999
60	60.98	74.40	79.08	83.30	88.38	91.95	99.61
70	77.58	85.53	90.53	95.02	100.42	104.21	112.32

This test for independence is discussed in Press [1972, p. 180]. Some finite sample results are described in Aitken, Nelson, and Aelnfurt [1968].

TABLE 8-5

T^2 TEST RESULTS AND SUMMARY STATISTICS FOR DIFFERENCES ($\tilde{d}$) BETWEEN MONTHLY RETURNS ON INFORMATION-SAMPLE PORTFOLIOS AND MATCHED CONTROL-SAMPLE PORTFOLIOS
All Portfolios Are Minimum Variance Portfolios with Estimated Relative Risks Equal to Unity
Time Period of Observations: April 1952–March 1972 (240 Monthly Observations)

Information Class	Portfolio Pair	$10^3 \times Es$ Mean $\hat{\mu}(\tilde{d})$	$10^2 \times$ Est. Std. Dev. $\hat{\sigma}(\tilde{d})$	$t(\hat{\mu})$	$F(12,228)$[a]	Studentized Range[b]	$\hat{\rho}_1$[c]	Normalized Weights Implied by T^2[d]
HHL	1	7.05	2.78	3.92	1.22	7.73	−.034	−.985
HHH	2	9.68	2.95	5.08	2.05	6.03	−.063	−1.249
HLL	3	10.71	2.80	5.90	2.77	6.06	−.002	−1.466
HLH	4	8.40	3.01	4.32	1.48	5.93	.024	−.784
MHL	5	.09	2.52	.05	.00	5.78	−.064	−.138
MHH	6	.93	2.51	.58	.03	7.49	.023	.364
MLL	7	−.50	2.47	−.31	.01	6.35	−.137	.010
MLH	8	2.00	2.54	1.21	.12	6.07	−.023	−1.117
LHL	9	−9.50	2.61	−5.62	2.51	6.32	.057	1.962
LHH	10	−10.62	2.84	−5.79	2.66	6.10	−.011	1.637
LLL	11	−7.72	2.61	−4.57	1.66	6.85	−.007	1.376
LLH	12	−6.13	2.62	−3.61	1.04	7.21	−.100	1.390

Observed Value of $\tilde{T}^2 = 151.83$

Value of $\tilde{F}(12, 228)$ *Corresponding to* $T^2 = 12.07$

[a]Values of fractiles of the distributions of $\tilde{F}(12, 120)$ and $\tilde{F}(12, -)$ are:

Degrees of Freedom	Fractile .900	.950	.975	.990	.995
12, 120	1.60	1.83	2.05	2.34	2.54
12, –	1.55	1.75	1.94	2.18	2.36

$\tilde{F}(p, N-p) = (\tilde{t})^2 \cdot [(N-p)/p(N-1)]$, where N is the number of observations used for estimation and p is the number of portfolios. For $N = 240$ and $p = 12$, $[(N-p)/p(n-1)] \approx .0795$.

[b]See Note 4 of Table 8-3 for values of fractiles of Studentized Range's distribution.

[c]For a sample of size $n = 240$, the approximate mean and standard deviation of the estimated first-order serial correlation coefficient, $\hat{\rho}_1$, are $-1/(n-1) \approx -.004$ and $\sqrt{\frac{n-1}{n(n+2)}} \approx .064$, respectively, conditional on no serial correlation.

[d]The value of the normalization factor is −1,543.05.

Taken at face value, the estimates are consistent with roughly equal mean differences within each of these groupings. Moreover, the estimates for $\tilde{IE}$ classified as H are of roughly the same magnitude as the estimates for $\tilde{IE}$ classified as H are of roughly the same magnitude as the estimates for $\tilde{IE}$ classified as L; the signs are, not unexpectedly, different. For the portfolios with $\tilde{IE}$ observed to be H (L), the average of the sample mean differences is 8.96×10^{-3} (-8.49×10^{-3}). Taken at face value, one can infer from these results that the effects of the dividend and extraordinary-item signals are not strongly dependent on whether the contemporaneous income signal is classified as H or L. That could be due to those signals' reflecting little or no information beyond what is already reflected in the contemporaneous income signal and the sample evidence available at time t. The results presented below deal with this issue, among other things.

8.4.8.3 Results for Selected Linear Combinations: Marginal and Joint Effects of Signals

8.4.8.3.1 Preliminaries

The T^2 test results given in Table 8-5 are consistent with the existence such that condition (8.1) does not hold. A variety of interesting issues can be handled by specifying alternative values of $\underline{w}$, each of which is implied by a particular hypothesis, and by determining whether the evidence is consistent with (8.1) for these values. That exercise is pursued in this section. Since all of the tests considered are still conducted within the multivariate testing perspective described earlier, the appropriate value of $\tilde{F}$ corresponding to each observed value of $\tilde{t}(\underline{w})$—defined in (8.3)—is still given by an F distribution with 12 and 228 degrees of freedom, not the 1 and 228 degrees of freedom that would be used for a univariate test based on a specific $\underline{w}$.

Results for 7 values of $\underline{w}$ are given in Table 8-6. As with Table 8-5, these results pertain to the estimated expected values of $\underline{w}^T[\tilde{\underline{R}}_{1t} - \tilde{\underline{R}}_{2t}]$ for different values of $\underline{w}$.

8.4.8.3.2 A Consistency Check

The results given for the first volume of $\underline{w}$—equal weights—can be used to assess the extent to which factors other than the signals were, in fact, "held constant" (see Section 8.4.5). If our control sample is really a control sample, then the estimated mean return on each of its portfolios is an estimate of the marginal mean return, $E(\tilde{R}_t)$, on an asset with risk equal to unity. Since the risks on all information-sample portfolios equal unity, the same marginal mean return is given by $E(\tilde{R}_t) = E[E(\tilde{R}_t|\tilde{\underline{\theta}}_t)] = \Sigma_{i=1}^{12} E(\tilde{R}_t|\tilde{\underline{\theta}}_t = \underline{\theta}_t^i)\, Pr(\underline{\theta}_t^i)$, where $\underline{\theta}_t^i$ is the ith value of $\tilde{\underline{\theta}}_t$. We can estimate the latter expression by replacing $E(\tilde{R}_t|\theta_t^i)$ by the estimated mean for the ith information-sample portfolio and (since the values of $\tilde{\underline{\theta}}_t$ are equally likely) by letting $Pr(\underline{\theta}_t^i) = 1/12$ for all i. This implies that if the control sample is a control sample and if the information sample differs from it only because of conditioning by signals, then we should have $\underline{w}^T[E(\tilde{\underline{R}}_{1t}) - E(\tilde{\underline{R}}_{2t})] = 0.0$ when $\underline{w}^T = (1/12, 1/12, \ldots, 1/12)$. The results given in Table 8-6 are quite consistent with this condition and, therefore, with our having held "other things" constant.

8.4.8.3.3 Conditional Information Content of Extraordinary-Item and Dividend Signals

The second through the seventh sets of weights covered by Table 8-6 deal directly with the information content of the extraordinary-item signals—i.e., the value of $\tilde{\theta}_3$ (H or L)—conditional on both the income signal (the value of $\tilde{\theta}_1$) and the dividend signal (the value of $\tilde{\theta}_2$). These results are consistent with the condition: $E(\tilde{R}_t|\theta_1, \theta_2, \text{H}) - E(\tilde{R}_t|\theta_1, \theta_2, \text{L}) = 0$, for all values of $(\tilde{\theta}_1, \tilde{\theta}_2)$, and, thus, $E(\tilde{R}_t|\theta_1, \theta_2, \text{H}) = E(\tilde{R}_t|\theta_1, \theta_2, \text{L}) =$

TABLE 8-6

RESULTS FOR VARIOUS LINEAR COMBINATIONS (PORTFOLIOS) OF DIFFERENCES BETWEEN RETURNS ON PAIRED INFORMATION-SAMPLE AND CONTROL-SAMPLE PORTFOLIOS
Each Portfolio Is a Minimum Variance Portfolio with Estimated Relative Risks Equal to Unity
Time Period of Observations: April 1952–March 1972 (240 Monthly Observations)

		Vectors of Portfolio Weights Applied to Differences Between Returns on Paired Portfolios						
Portfolio Pair	Information Class	(1) Equal Weights	(2) HHL–HHH	(3) HLL–HLH	(4) MHL–MHH	(5) MLL–MLH	(6) LHL–LHH	(7) LLL–LLH
1	HHL	1/12	1					
2	HHH	1/12	−1					
3	HLL	1/12		1				
4	HLH	1/12		−1				
5	MHL	1/12			1			
6	MHH	1/12			−1			
7	MLL	1/12				1		
8	MLH	1/12				−1		
9	LHL	1/12					1	
10	LHH	1/12					−1	
11	LLL	1/12						1
12	LLH	1/12						−1
Estimated Mean of Differences Between Returns on Portfolios of Paired Portfolios		$.04 \times 10^{-2}$	$-.26 \times 10^{-2}$	$.23 \times 10^{-2}$	$-.08 \times 10^{-2}$	$-.25 \times 10^{-2}$	$.11 \times 10^{-2}$	$-.16 \times 10^{-2}$
Estimated Standard Deviation of Differences Between Returns on Portfolios of Paired Portfolios		1.12×10^{-2}	3.69×10^{-2}	3.38×10^{-2}	3.17×10^{-2}	3.43×10^{-2}	3.64×10^{-2}	3.34×10^{-2}
Value of $\tilde{t}$ for Estimated Mean		.505	−1.107	1.056	−.414	−1.126	.477	−.739
Value of $\tilde{F}(12,228)$ for Estimated Mean[a]		.020	.097	.089	.014	.101	.018	.004

[a]See Note a of Table 8-5 for defintion of $\tilde{F}(p, N - p)$ and values of its distribution's fractiles.

$E(\tilde{R}_t|\theta_1, \theta_2)$, for all values of $(\tilde{\theta}_1, \tilde{\theta}_2)$. The results are, therefore, consistent with the extraordinary-item signals' reflecting no information beyond that already *jointly* reflected in the dividend signal for period t, the income signal for period t, and whatever sample evidence was available at the beginning of period t. These results are, in turn, consistent with the dividend and income signals' being perfect substitutes for the extraordinary-item signals or with the latter signal's having no information content. Whether any extraordinary-item signal reflects information beyond that marginally reflected in either some dividend signal or some income signal is considered below.

Table 8-7 provides analogous results for the information reflected in the dividend signals, conditional on both the income and extraordinary-item signals. As can be seen, the evidence is consistent with the dividend signals' reflecting no information beyond that jointly reflected in the contemporaneous income and extraordinary-item signals and the evidence available at time t. That is, $E(\tilde{R}_t|\theta_1, \text{H}, \theta_3) = E(\tilde{R}_t|\theta_1, \text{L}, \theta_3) = E(\tilde{R}_t|\theta_1, \theta_3)$ for all values of $(\tilde{\theta}_1, \tilde{\theta}_3)$. These results are consistent with the "perfect substitute" interpretation given in the previous paragraph or with the dividend signal's having no information content.

8.4.8.3.4 Joint Information Content of (i) Extraordinary Items and Income and (ii) Dividends and Income

Results for the joint effects of extraordinary-item and income signals—i.e., values of $(\tilde{\theta}_1, \tilde{\theta}_3)$—are given in Table 8-8. The first six values of $\underline{w}$ deal with $E(\tilde{R}_t|\theta_1, \theta_3) - E(\tilde{R}_t)$ for all values of $(\tilde{\theta}_1, \tilde{\theta}_3)$. The letter "*A*" in a particular column refers to the indicator random variable that was averaged out. Equal-weight (or "simple") averaging was used throughout. For example, the first set of results, labeled HAL, refers to results after averaging over $\tilde{\theta}_2$ but conditional on $\tilde{\theta}_1 = \text{H}$ (the income class) and $\tilde{\theta}_3 = \text{L}$ (the extraordinary-item class). That is, it refers to $E[E(\tilde{R}_t|\tilde{\theta}_1 = \text{H}, \tilde{\theta}_2, \tilde{\theta}_3 = \text{L})] - E(\tilde{R}_t)$.

The first six sets of results are consistent with the joint income/extra-ordinary-item numbers' reflecting information beyond that already available at time t. That is, some realizations of $(\tilde{\theta}_1, \tilde{\theta}_3)$ induce revisions of return distributions.[46]

For a given value of $\tilde{\theta}_1$, say H, the contribution of the value of $\tilde{\theta}_3$ to the joint implications of $(\text{H}, \tilde{\theta}_3)$ can be assessed by examining results for $[E(\tilde{R}_t|\text{H}, \tilde{\theta}_3 = \text{H}) - E(\tilde{R}_t)] - [E(\tilde{R}_t|\text{H}, \tilde{\theta}_3 = \text{L}) - E(\tilde{R}_t)] = E(\tilde{R}_t|\text{H}, \tilde{\theta}_3 = \text{H}) - E(\tilde{R}_t|H, \tilde{\theta}_3 = \text{L})$. If this difference is inferred to be zero for all values of $\tilde{\theta}_1$, then we can infer: $E(\tilde{R}_t|\theta_1) = E(\tilde{R}_t|\theta_1, \tilde{\theta}_3 = \text{H}) = E(\tilde{R}_t|\theta_1, \tilde{\theta}_3 = \text{L})$, for all values, θ_1, of $\tilde{\theta}_1$. Therefore, we can infer that $\tilde{\theta}_3$ reflects no information beyond that already reflected in $\tilde{\theta}_1$ and sample evidence available at time t—at least insofar as information about expected returns is concerned. The results in Table 8-8 for vectors (7)–(9) are consistent with this proposition.

Corresponding results for the income-error and dividend-error numbers $\tilde{IE}$ and $\tilde{DE}$, respectively) appear in Table 8-9. As can be seen, the results are like those for the joint income/extraordinary-item signals. In short, the results are consistent with the dividend signals' reflecting no information beyond that jointly reflected in each possible contemporaneous income signal and sample evidence available at t.

---

[46]The results for the specific realizations defined by MAH and MAL are consistent with no differences between $E(\tilde{R}_t)$ and both $E(\tilde{R}_t|\tilde{\theta}_1 = M, \tilde{\theta}_3 = H)$ and $E(\tilde{R}_t|\tilde{\theta}_1 = M, \tilde{\theta}_3 = L)$. Strictly speaking, this does not imply that $(\tilde{\theta}_1 = M, \tilde{\theta}_3 = H)$ or $(\tilde{\theta}_1 = M, \tilde{\theta}_3 = L)$ induces no distributional reassessment. Either one may affect conditional variances rather than means. Our remarks deal only with means.

TABLE 8-7

RESULTS FOR VARIOUS LINEAR COMBINATIONS (PORTFOLIOS) OF DIFFERENCES BETWEEN RETURNS ON PAIRED INFORMATION-SAMPLE AND CONTROL-SAMPLE PORTFOLIOS

Each Portfolio Is a Minimum Variance Portfolio with Estimated Relative Risks Equal to Unity

Time Period of Observations: April 1952–March 1972 (240 Monthly Observations)

Portfolio Pair	Information Class	Vectors of Portfolio Weights Applied to Differences Between Returns on Paired Portfolios					
		(1) HHL–HLL	(2) HHH–HLH	(3) MHL–MLL	(4) MHH–MLH	(5) LHL–LLL	(6) LHH–LLH
1	HHL	1					
2	HHH		1				
3	HLL	−1					
4	HLH		−1				
5	MHL			1			
6	MHH				1		
7	MLL			−1			
8	MLH				−1		
9	LHL					1	
10	LHH						1
11	LLL					−1	
12	LLH						−1
Estimated mean of difference between returns on portfolios of paired portfolios.		$-.36 \times 10^{-3}$	1.27×10^{-3}	$.59 \times 10^{-3}$	-1.06×10^{-3}	-1.78×10^{-3}	-4.49×10^{-3}
Estimated standard deviation of difference between returns on portfolios of paired portfolios.		3.59×10^{-2}	3.54×10^{-2}	3.38×10^{-2}	3.61×10^{-2}	3.29×10^{-2}	3.74×10^{-2}
Value of $\tilde{t}$ for estimated mean.		−1.575	.558	.269	−.456	−.837	−1.860
Value of $\tilde{F}$ (12, 228) for estimated mean.[a]		.197	.025	.005	.016	.056	.275

[a]See Note a of Table 8-5 for definition of $\tilde{F}$ $(p, N - p)$ and values of its distribution's fractiles.

TABLE 8-8

RESULTS FOR INCOME/EXTRAORDINARY ITEMS CONTRASTS

Results Are for Selected Linear Combinations (Portfolios) of Differences Between Returns on Paired Information-Sample and Control-Sample Portfolios

Each Portfolio Is a Minimum Variance Portfolio with Estimated Relative Risk Equal to Unity

Time Period of Observations: April 1952–March 1972 (240 Monthly Observations)

		Vectors of Weights Applied to Differences Between Returns on Paired Portfolios								
Portfolio Pair	Information Class	(1) HAL	(2) HAH	(3) MAL	(4) MAH	(5) LAL	(6) LAH	(7) HAL–HAM	(8) MAL–MAH	(9) LAL–LAH
1	HHL	1/2						1/2		
2	HHH		1/2					−1/2		
3	HLL	1/2						1/2		
4	HLH		1/2					−1/2		
5	MHL			1/2					1/2	
6	MHH				1/2				−1/2	
7	MLL			1/2					1/2	
8	MLH				1/2				−1/2	
9	LHL					1/2				1/2
10	LHH						1/2			−1/2
11	LLL					1/2				1/2
12	LLH						1/2			−1/2
Estimated Mean of Differences Between Returns on Portfolios of Paired Portfolios		$.88 \times 10^{-2}$	$.90 \times 10^{-2}$	$-.02 \times 10^{-2}$	$.14 \times 10^{-2}$	$-.86 \times 10^{-2}$	$-.84 \times 10^{-2}$	$-.02 \times 10^{-2}$	$-.17 \times 10^{-2}$	$-.02 \times 10^{-2}$
Estimated Standard Deviation of Differences Between Returns on Portfolios of Paired Portfolios		2.13×10^{-2}	2.39×10^{-2}	1.84×10^{-2}	1.76×10^{-2}	2.03×10^{-2}	1.99×10^{-2}	2.60×10^{-2}	2.20×10^{-2}	2.53×10^{-2}
Value of $\tilde{t}$ for Estimated Mean		6.426	5.842	−.174	1.284	−6.560	−6.500	−.10	−1.176	−.145
Value of $\tilde{F}(12, 228)$ for Estimated Mean[a]		3.283	2.713	.002	.131	3.421	3.359	$.79 \times 10^{-3}$	.110	.002

[a]See note a of Table 8-5 for definition of $\tilde{F}(p, N - p)$ and values of the distribution's fractiles.

TABLE 8-9

RESULTS FOR DIVIDENDS/INCOME CONTRASTS

Results Are for Selected Linear Combinations (Portfolios) of Differences Between Returns on Paired Information-Sample and Control-Sample Portfolios

Each Portfolio Is a Minimum Variance Portfolio with Estimated Relative Risk Equal to Unity

Time Period of Observations: April 1952–March 1972 (240 Monthly Observations)

		Vectors of Weights applied to Differences Between Returns on Paired Portfolios								
Portfolio Pair	Information Class	(1) HHA	(2) HLA	(3) MHA	(4) MLA	(5) LHA	(6) LLA	(7) HHA–HLA	(8) MHA–MLA	(9) LHA–LLA
1	HHL	1/2						1/2		
2	HHH	1/2						1/2		
3	HLL		1/2					−1/2		
4	HLH		1/2					−1/2		
5	MHL			1/2					1/2	
6	MHH			1/2					1/2	
7	MLL				1/2				−1/2	
8	MLH				1/2				−1/2	
9	LHL					1/2				1/2
10	LHH					1/2				1/2
11	LLL						1/2			−1/2
12	LLH						1/2			−1/2
Estimated Mean of Differences Between Returns on Portfolios of Paired Portfolios		$.84 \times 10^{-2}$	$.95 \times 10^{-4}$	$.05 \times 10^{-2}$	$.07 \times 10^{-2}$	-1.0×10^{-2}	$-.69 \times 10^{-2}$	$-.12 \times 10^{-2}$	$-.02 \times 10^{-2}$	$-.31 \times 10^{-2}$
Estimated Standard Deviation of Differences Between Returns on Portfolios of Paired Portfolios		2.19×10^{-2}	2.37×10^{-2}	1.95×10^{-2}	1.8×10^{-2}	2.03×10^{-2}	2.01×10^{-2}	2.65×10^{-2}	2.48×10^{-2}	2.57×10^{-2}
Value of $\tilde{t}$ for Estimated Mean		5.896	6.237	.405	.633	−7.656	−5.317	−.695	−.148	−1.888
Value of $\tilde{F}(12,228)$ for Estimated Mean[a]		2.764	3.092	.013	.032	4.660	2.247	.038	.002	.283

[a] See Note a of Table 8-5 for definition of $\tilde{F}(p, N-p)$ and values of its distribution's fractiles.

8.4.8.3.5 Joint Information Content of Dividend and Extraordinary-Item Signal

Given any of the income signals, none of the dividend or extraordinary-item signals appears to reflect additional information pertinent to assessing expected returns. These signals may, however, reflect such information in the absence of the income signal. This is what one would expect if, for example, there is substitutability between (1) the income signals and (2) the dividend signals, the extraordinary-item signals, or the joint dividend/extraordinary-item signals.

Results conditional on values of $\tilde{\theta}_2$, $\tilde{\theta}_3$), $\tilde{\theta}_3$, and $\tilde{\theta}_2$ are given in Tables 8-10 and 8-11. As can be seen from Table 8-10, the results are consistent with the condition $E(\tilde{R}_t|\theta_2, \theta_3) = E(\tilde{R}_t)$ for each value of $(\tilde{\theta}_2, \tilde{\theta}_3)$. This implies the conditions: $E(\tilde{R}_t|\theta_2) = E[E[\tilde{R}_t|\theta_2, \tilde{\theta}_3]] = E(\tilde{R}_t)$ and $E(\tilde{R}_t|\theta_3) = E[E[\tilde{R}_t|\tilde{\theta}_2, \theta_3]] = E(\tilde{R}_t)$, for all values of $\tilde{\theta}_2$ and $\tilde{\theta}_3$. Since we are, however, using sample estimates rather than parameters' true values, it seems best to test these conditions directly.[47] The results appear in Table 8-11. They are consistent with the indicated conditions. To sum up, whether considered individually or jointly, the dividend and extraordinary-item signals appear to reflect no information beyond that available at time *t*.

8.4.8.3.6 Income Signals

In view of the T^2 test results and the results for the dividend and extraordinary-item signals, one expects that the inconsistency between the sample evidence and the initial null hypothesis—$E(\tilde{R}_{1t}) = E(\tilde{R}_{2t})$—is largely due to the income signals. Results dealing directly with this appear in Table 8-12. The evidence is consistent with the equality $E(\tilde{R}_t|\tilde{\theta}_1 = \text{M}) = E(\tilde{R}_t)$, but it is inconsistent with this equality for $\tilde{\theta}_1$ equal to H or L. Thus, it is inconsistent with the statement that income signals reflect no information beyond what is already available at time *t*.

8.4.8.3.7 Subperiod Results

The kinds of results presented above were also obtained for the first and second halves of the overall 20-year time period, April 1952–March 1972. These results are given in the April 1976 version of the report from which our results were taken. They are consistent with the results based on the overall time period. In short, it appears that the inferred marginal and joint properties of $(\tilde{\theta}_1, \tilde{\theta}_2, \tilde{\theta}_3)$ characterize the entire period rather than just some segment of it.

Given the increased interest and actions of the accounting profession and the SEC regarding extraordinary items, one might have expected to see some hint of nonstationarity in the signals' properties.[48] This period witnessed, for example, the adoption of Account-

---

[47]Analogous consistency checks were made for the results discussed earlier and those presented later. No contradictory results ever emerged.

[48]The SEC's concern over extraordinary items and, more generally, "unusual charges and credits" is motivated and summarized in its release on, the Form 8-K revisions proposed in 1972 and adopted in 1973 (see Securities and Exchange Commission [1973]). The accounting profession's perspective is summarized in Accounting Principles Board *Opinion No. 9*. In this regard, the SEC and the APB seem to have moved in somewhat different directions. Whereas *APBO No. 9* attempted to limit the kinds of items given special (i.e., separate) disclosure status under the label "extraordinary," the SEC opted for special disclosure treatment for items classifiable as "extraordinary" under generally accepted accounting principles and for a variety of other items. Evidently, the SEC was more interested in whether certain kinds of items should be separately disclosed rather than in the purely semantic issues surrounding the labeling of those items as being "extraordinary."

TABLE 8-10

RESULTS FOR DIVIDENDS/EXTRAORDINARY-ITEMS CONTRASTS
Results Are for Selected Linear Combinations (Portfolios) of Differences Between Returns on Paired Information-Sample and Control-Sample Portfolios
Each Portfolio Is a Minimum Variance Portfolio with Estimated Relative Risk Equal to Unity
Time Period of Observations: April 1952–March 1972 (240 Monthly Observations)

		Vectors of Portfolio Weights Applied to Differences Between Returns on Paired Portfolios			
Portfolio Pair	Information Class	(1) AHL	(2) AHH	(3) ALL	(4) ALH
1	HHL	1/3			
2	HHH		1/3		
3	HLL			1/3	
4	HLH				1/3
5	MHL	1/3			
6	MHH		1/3		
7	MLL			1/3	
8	MLH				1/3
9	LHL	1/3			
10	LHH		1/3		
11	LLL			1/3	
12	LLH				1/3
Estimated Mean of Differences Between Returns on Portfolios of Paired Portfolios		$-.79 \times 10^{-3}$	$-.16 \times 10^{-5}$	$.83 \times 10^{-3}$	$.14 \times 10^{-2}$
Estimated Standard Deviation of Differences Between Returns on Portfolios of Paired Portfolios		1.67×10^{-2}	1.70×10^{-2}	1.61×10^{-2}	1.80×10^{-2}
Value of $\tilde{t}$ for Estimated Mean		−.731	−.001	.792	1.220
Value of $\tilde{F}(12, 228)$ for Estimated Mean[a]		.042	$.79 \times 10^{-7}$	.050	.118

[a]See Note a of Table 8-5 for definition of $\tilde{F}(p, N-p)$ and values of its distribution's fractiles.

ing Principles Board *Opinion No. 9*, which altered the criteria for classifying items as extraordinary. Unreported results dealing directly with this *Opinion* are discussed below.

8.4.8.3.8 Accounting Principles Board Opinion (APBO) No. 9

APBO No. 9 was adopted in December 1966; it became effective for fiscal periods beginning after December 31, 1966. Since this date falls within the second subperiod considered above, a change in the properties of extraordinary-item signals may have been glossed over by our subperiod results. Thus, the kinds of results presented above were also obtained for two shorter five-year subperiods. The first one includes all of the 1962–1966 portfolio formation dates, this gives pre-*ABPO No. 9* results. The second covers the 1967–1971 portfolio formation dates. Each subperiod's results are, therefore, based on 60 observed vectors of portfolio returns. All results led to the same inferences made above. In short, the appearance of *APBO No. 9* seems to have had no effect on the marginal or joint properties of the income, dividend, and extraordinary-item signals.

TABLE 8-11

RESULTS FOR EXTRAORDINARY-ITEMS CONTRASTS AND DIVIDEND CONTRASTS
Results Are for Selected Linear Combinations (Portfolios) of Differences Between Returns on Paired Information-Sample and Control-Sample Portfolios
Each Portfolio Is a Minimum Variance Portfolio with Estimated Relative Risk Equal to Unity
Time Period of Observations: April 1952–March 1972 (240 Monthly Observations)

		Vectors of Portfolio Weights Applied to Differences Between Returns on Paired Portfolios					
		Extraordinary Item Contrasts			Dividend Contrasts		
Portfolio Pair	Information Class	(1) AAL	(2) AAH	(3) AAL–AAH	(4) AHA	(5) ALA	(6) AHA–ALA
1	HHL	1/6		1/6	1/6		1/6
2	HHH		1/6	−1/6	1/6		1/6
3	HLL	1/6		1/6		1/6	−1/6
4	HLH		1/6	−1/6		1/6	−1/6
5	MHL	1/6		1/6	1/6		1/6
6	MHH		1/6	−1/6	1/6		1/6
7	MLL	1/6		1/6		1/6	−1/6
8	MLH		1/6	−1/6		1/6	−1/6
9	LHL	1/6		1/6	1/6		1/6
10	LHH		1/6	−1/6	1/6		1/6
11	LLL	1/6		1/6		1/6	−1/6
12	LLH		1/6	−1/6		1/6	−1/6
Estimated Mean of Differences Between Returns on Portfolios of Paired Portfolios		$.19 \times 10^{-4}$	7.1×10^{-4}	$-.69 \times 10^{-4}$	-2.4×10^{-3}	6.7×10^{-3}	$-.91 \times 10^{-2}$
Estimated Standard Deviation of Differences Between Returns on Portfolios of Paired Portfolios		1.28×10^{-2}	1.39×10^{-2}	1.46×10^{-2}	7.92×10^{-2}	8.13×10^{-2}	8.77×10^{-2}
Value of $\tilde{t}$ for Estimated Mean		.023	.794	−.736	−.463	1.284	−1.612
Value of $\tilde{F}(12,228)$ for Estimated Mean[a]		$.042 \times 10^{-3}$	.050	.043	.017	.131	.207

[a]See Note a of Table 8-5 for definition of $\tilde{F}(p, N - p)$ and values of its distribution's fractiles.

TABLE 8-12

RESULTS FOR INCOME CONTRASTS

Results Are for Selected Linear Combinations (Portfolios) of Differences Between Returns on Paired Information-Sample and Control-Sample Portfolios

Each Portfolio Is a Minimum Variance Portfolio with Estimated Relative Risk Equal to Unity

Time Period of Observations: April 1952–March 1972 (240 Monthly Observations)

		Vectors of Portfolio Weights Applied to Differences Between Returns on Paired Portfolios					
Portfolio Pair	Information Class	(1) HAA	(2) MAA	(3) LAA	(4) HAA–MAA	(5) MAA–LAA	(6) HAA–LAA
1	HHL	1/4			1/4		1/4
2	HHH	1/4			1/4		1/4
3	HLL	1/4			1/4		1/4
4	HLH	1/4			1/4		1/4
5	MHL		1/4		−1/4	1/4	
6	MHH		1/4		−1/4	1/4	
7	MLL		1/4		−1/4		
8	MLH		1/4		−1/4		
9	LHL			1/4			−1/4
10	LHH			1/4			−1/4
11	LLL			1/4			−1/4
12	LLH			1/4		−1/4	−1/4
Estimated Mean of Differences Between Returns on Portfolios of Paired Portfolios		$.90 \times 10^{-2}$	$.06 \times 10^{-2}$	$-.85 \times 10^{-2}$	$.83 \times 10^{-2}$	$.91 \times 10^{-2}$	1.7×10^{-2}
Estimated Standard Deviation of Differences Between Returns on Portfolios of Paired Portfolios		1.86×10^{-2}	1.42×10^{-2}	1.56×10^{-2}	1.99×10^{-2}	1.78×10^{-2}	2.30×10^{-2}
Value of $\tilde{t}$ for Estimated Mean		7.460	.683	−8.411	6.479	7.924	11.736
Value of $\tilde{F}(12,228)$ for Estimated Mean[a]		4.424	.037	5.624	3.337	4.992	10.949

[a]See Note a of Table 8-5 for definition of $\tilde{F}(p, N - p)$ and values of its distribution's fractiles.

8.4.8.3.9 Some Additional Checks

The control sample used for the above results consists of portfolios containing randomly selected assets. The estimated relative risks of these control portfolios were set equal to unity, which is also—by defintion—the relative risk of the market portfolio (see Section 8.4.5). Therefore, a seemingly attractive alternative approach is to use returns on the market portfolio itself in order to estimate the expected return on an asset having relative risk equal to unity. Since there is no need to estimate (and, thus, no estimation error in) the value of the market portfolio's relative risk, one might expect this approach to lead to a more powerful test of our no-information-content hypothesis. Under certain conditions, this is the case, as is explained in the Appendix.[49] No tests were conducted in order to determine whether our portfolios satisfy such conditions. Rather, we proceeded directly to implementation of the alternative scheme involving use of the market portfolio in place of every original control-sample portfolio. As before, Fisher's Arithmetic Index was used to represent the market portfolio. The results led to the same inferences as those given above—fortunately.

The market portfolio was also used in a joint test on the means of the control-sample portfolios' return distributions. A T^2 test of the hypothesis that all of these means equal the expected return on the market portfolio was conducted. The results were consistent with this hypothesis and, thus, consistent with the control-sample's portfolios' having relative risks equal to unity and return distributions equal to the marginal return distributions on assets with risk equal to unity.

Finally, one might justifiably ask whether our portfolio formation procedures induced a bias in favor of our ultimate inference about the income signal's information content, because these procedures encompass a more refined partitioning of the range of income signals. Whereas three levels—high, medium, and low—of the income signal are used, only two levels (and thus more aggregation) of the dividend and extraordinary-item signals are exploited. There would be grounds for claiming such a bias if, for example, the results for the "medium" level of the income signal could somehow offset the results for either the "high" or "low" levels. Under this condition, grouping firms for only two levels of the income signal—using the same grouping method applied to the dividend and extraordinary-items signals—could lead to insignificant (or less significant) results for the income signal, relative to those actually obtained. Alternatively, using a higher degree of aggregation (e.g., two levels rather than three) might induce so much sampling error (because of heterogeneity *within* portfolios) in the results for income signals that inferring inconsistency with the no-information-content hypothesis would be less likely. Thus, we would be less likely to infer any differences among the properties of the three signals examined.

In order to gain some insights into this issue, results for two equal-sized portfolios of firms were examined. One portfolio consisted of all firms with an income signal above the median value of this signal. The other consisted of all the remaining firms. The results for these portfolios pertain to the marginal implications of the income signal, $\tilde{IE}$. These results are fully consistent with the results based on the three-level grouping. The estimated

---

[49]This issue is part of a broader more fundamental topic: incorporation of estimation risk into work on asset-pricing and capital market equilibrium and into portfolio optimization rules for individuals. Results from some beginning steps in this direction are provided by Brown [1976] and Klein and Bawa [1976].

mean (standard deviation) of the differences between the returns on the two information-sample portfolios is 1.16×10^{-2} (1.84×10^{-2}). The corresponding values of $\tilde{t}$ and $\tilde{F}(12{,}228)$ are 9.701 and 7.482, respectively. These results are solidly inconsistent with the income signals' reflecting no information beyond that already available to the capital market.

8.4.5 Summary and Discussion of Empirical Results

The extent to which three random variables reflect information pertinent to assessing firms' equilibrium values was investigated. The variables are income numbers, dividend numbers, and "extraordinary" income items. The conventional perspective is that income numbers reflect characteristics of firms' decisions. This implies that predictive distributions of income numbers can be used in making inferences about predictive distributions of the attributes of firms' decisions. It is frequently hypothesized that dividend numbers also reflect information pertinent to those inferences because of a connection with income numbers. The crux of this argument is that dividend-change announcements (which include announcements of no change) reflect information available to management (and perhaps other insiders) but not to investors in general, because of the way that management behaves in selecting dividend policy changes. Thus, dividend changes reflect information beyond what is already available from existing sample evidence or from other contemporaneous signals. Given this perspective, one expects a relationship between one or more attributes of dividend numbers and market agents' assessed predictive distributions of returns on firms' shares. Managements' latitude of choice regarding dividend changes provides much of the motivation for viewing dividend announcements as potential managerial signaling devices. Without some latitude of choice, it would be difficult to argue that announcements of dividend changes reflect aspects of management's predictive distributions and changes thereof. An overview of work on the information content hypothesis applied to dividends is given by Watts [1973], among others.

Similar arguments have been advanced about extraordinary items—often within the context of the "big bath" and "income-smoothing" hypotheses. The crux of these arguments is that the decomposition of income into its "ordinary" and "extraordinary" components can influence agents' assessed predictive distributions of events that affect the attributes of firms' decisions. This kind of argument appears to have motivated, to some extent, several of the SEC's disclosure regulations and the accounting profession's rules for income reporting.[50]

The evidence presented herein is uniformly inconsistent with the view that dividend or extraordinary-item signals reflect information beyond that reflected in contemporaneous income signals or other existing sample evidence. This inference applies to both the marginal and joint effects of the dividend and extraordinary-item signals: no substitutability or complementarity relationships could be inferred. Insofar as period t events are concerned, the income signal for period t appears to be the only one (of the three examined) that reflects information beyond that already available at the beginning of period t and pertinent to assessing return distributions.

A direct examination of relationships among the three potential signals themselves pointed to some systematic relationships. However, these relationships appeared to be

---

[50]See, e.g., Securities and Exchange Commission [1973] and Accounting Principles Board *Opinion No. 9* (esp. paragraph no. 9–paragraph no. 14).

consistent with various kinds of managerial signaling—both honest and "distorted" signaling. Insofar as period t events are concerned, investors seem to behave as if the *joint* period t dividend/extraordinary-item signal cannot be used as a reliable means of discriminating among firms in terms of the unobservable attributes of firms' decisions—and thus the factors affecting return distributions—to an extent beyond that already permitted by the period t income signal or the sample evidence available at the start of period t. This may be due to the ambiguity surrounding a particular mode of signaling via the joint use of dividend and extraordinary-item signals; i.e., a given mode of signaling can be interpreted as honest signaling or as dishonest signaling (see Section 8.3).

Given the debate surrounding several controversial disclosure rules, the inconsistency of our evidence with a complementarity relationship between income and extraordinary-item signals is quite interesting. For example, in Accounting Principles Board *Opinion No. 9* (adopted in December 1966) the Board identifies two major positions regarding extraordinary-item disclosures. Basically, one position opts for exclusion of extraordinary items from the income statement and direct adjustments to retained earnings. Advocates of this approach argue that inclusion in the income statement "might impair the significance of net income to such an extent that misleading inferences might be drawn from the amount so designated" (*APBO No. 9,* paragraph 10). The second position opts for inclusion of extraordinary items in the income statement, arguing that exclusion "increases the possibility that these items will be overlooked in a review of operating results for a period of years" (*APBO No. 9,* paragraph 9). Evidently, both positions assume that inferences based on net income numbers will be altered by extraordinary-item numbers. That is, both positions assume that agents behave as if there is a complementarity relationship between income and extraordinary-item signals. The positions differ in that the second (first) position asserts that extraordinary-item signals' influence on inferences may (may not) be justified and that inferences may (may not) be more reliable because of this influence. The second position seems to be the one adopted in *APBO Nos. 9* and *30* and in the SEC's 1973 changes in Form 8-K. The evidence presented here is inconsistent with both positions. Since results based on using "income *after* extraordinary items" in defining the income signal lead to the same inconsistency (see Section 8.4.3), our conclusions cannot be ascribed to our using "income *before* extraordinary items."

In one sense the results for extraordinary-item signals may not be surprising. Given rational expectations (see Muth [1961]), agents will attempt to exploit the systematic properties of stochastic processes, such as income numbers.[51] If, in fact, extraordinary-item signals (as defined by GAAP) are "infrequent and unusual" or if there is substantial ambiguity regarding the implications of these signals (for the reasons given earlier), then these signals may have few (if any) important implications for the systematic properties of income signals and thus the unobservables about which agents can make inferences using income signals. Therefore, one should not expect agents to behave as if the period t extraordinary-item signals reflect information about pertinent events of period t.

The results for the dividend signals are consistent with the statement that these signals do not reflect any special managerial information about predictive distributions of income numbers. These results are consistent with the findings of Watts [1973] but inconsistent

[51]The Theory of Rational Expectations is discussed in Chapter 7, in conjunction with our discussion of motivating probability models for accounting numbers.

with others, such as Scholes [1973] and Pettit [1972]. However, the Scholes study does not deal directly with the extent to which period *t* dividend signals reflect information beyond that reflected in period *t* income signals.[52] And Pettit's results seem to have been affected by a variety of statistical deficiencies (see Watts [1976] and Brown [1975]).

Our results do not necessarily imply that dividend and extraordinary-item numbers reflect no information whatsoever. In the case of the dividend number, an adjustment for the contemporaneous income number was effected via the Lintner model. Conditional on the Lintner model, one expects the preadjustment dividend number to reflect some of the information reflected in the contemporaneous income number. Even if this is ignored, it may still be the case that sample evidence consisting of past dividend and extraordinary-item signals is useful in assessing predictive distributions of income numbers and thus predictive distributions of the attributes of firms' decisions along the lines discussed below.

Given rational expectations, one expects agents to behave as if they are using sample evidence available at the beginning of period *t* if that evidence is informative with respect to the systematic features of firms' decisions. In this context, such evidence is informative if it supplies a basis for making or altering inferences about those systematic features. For example, available sample evidence may provide a basis for forecasting income numbers' values and for estimating the parameters of the Lintner model of dividend changes.

Additional sample evidence can, under appropriate stationarity conditions, increase the precision of one's inferences without altering the inferences themselves. For example, additional evidence may decrease the expected squared error of an income forecast without altering the forecast's value, or at least its implications. By at least this kind of route, additional dividend and extraordinary-item signals may be informative. If this additional evidence does not systematically induce changes in what is ultimately inferred about the characteristics of firms' decisions, then it will not be treated as reflecting information *beyond* the available information on those characteristics—which is not equivalent to saying it reflects no information whatsoever.[53] Of course, the descriptive validity of this kind of scenario for a given signal depends on the kinds of inferences investors attempt to make. Thus, it depends on what characteristics of firms' decisions are relevant for asset pricing (see Section 8.2.5).

Given the martingale model, one does not expect the above scenario to characterize income numbers' properties. Conditional on that model, each newly observed income number

---

[52]Scholes did subgroup firms according to whether they did or did not announce "other information." This is not, however, a direct means of testing for the information content of income signals or the extent to which dividend signals reflect pertinent information beyond that already reflected in contemporaneous income signals. Moreover, whatever things are in "other information" may have offsetting implications and thus no joint effect on investors' assessed distributions of securities' future values.

[53]Moreover, even though the dividend signal, $\tilde{DE}$, for a given year reflects no information beyond that reflected in the same year's income signal, $\tilde{IE}$, it may convey the information common to $\tilde{DE}$ and $\tilde{IE}$ at an earlier date *within* the given year if the realization of $\tilde{DE}$ is available before the realization of $\tilde{IE}$ is available. Our results say nothing about such intra-year timing issues—which might be attacked by conducting analyses for, e.g., interim external reports. Our results only deal with the extent to which the *annual* dividend and income signals reflect information associated with an entire year's events. Similar remarks apply to our results for extraordinary-item and income signals.

reflects new information about the systematic properties of future numbers. It does so by implying a change in expected income—for every future period. If agents view income numbers as reflecting substantive features of firms' decisions, then one expects period t income signals to alter the distributions of returns on firms' shares assessed at the beginning of period t. Our results are consistent with this characterization.

In any event, the crux of our inferences seems adequately consistent with the results presented here. These results are, on balance, inconsistent with the view that dividend or extraordinary-item signals systematically reflect information beyond that reflected in contemporaneous income signals or other existing sample evidence.

8.5 Summary

This chapter dealt with some of the basic assumptions and implications of screening and signaling. In addition, it presented empirical results on some numbers that are often (explicitly or implicitly) discussed within a signaling/screening perspective. As a part of this presentation, it described a general approach and statistical tools for conducting multivariate tests of the information content of potential managerial signals.

One of the key assumptions underlying the signaling perspective of external reporting is that there are asymmetries among agents with respect to information-production opportunities or information-production costs. The scenario emphasized here is one wherein management is believed to have access to information-production opportunities that are not available to "outsiders" or that are only available to "outsiders" under less favorable cost conditions. Of special interest were the opportunities to produce information pertinent to making inferences about the attributes of managements' production-investment and financing decisions—such as the probability distributions of net cash earnings induced by management's current decisions and plans.

We indicated that the signaling perspective can supply insights into a variety of issues bearing on disclosures made in, and accounting techniques used for, external reports. For example, it can be used to explain why some firms voluntarily disclose the realized values of some accounting numbers and why they might submit external reports for an "independent audit" even in the absence of regulations (e.g., SEC filing requirements) requiring that they do so. The crux of this explanation turns on managerial attempts to influence the inferences made by investors about the unobservable characteristics of management's decisions—in a manner consistent with the market value rule. But there is more to this story. The signaling perspective also explicitly recognizes that investors' inferential activities may alter management's incentives with respect to selections and uses of accounting techniques and disclosure rules. As a result, these selections and uses may be based on grounds other than what currently passes for "accounting theory."

Disclosures regarding income numbers, extraordinary items, and dividend policy changes were used to illustrate various aspects of managerial signaling. And we presented empirical evidence on the information content of these potential managerial signals. One major prevailing view of managerial decisions about dividend policy is that those decisions induce signals about management's earnings expectations. Management's decisions about classifying the effects of transactions as "extraordinary items" can be viewed along the same lines. Indeed, this is the sort of view implicit in many assertions about "income-smoothing" and "big bath" reporting—or, more generally, "managing" reported values of income numbers. The empirical evidence presented here seems, however, to be substantially inconsistent with the view that dividend or extraordinary-item signals systematically reflect information *beyond that* reflected in contemporaneous income signals or other existing sample evidence used by the capital market in setting the equilibrium prices of firms' securities. This does not imply—for the reasons specified earlier in the text—that dividend and extraordinary-item signals reflect no information whatsoever. Thus, it may still be the case that sample evidence consisting of past dividend and extraordinary-item signals is useful in assessing predictive distributions of the attributes of firms' decisions.

Our discussion of, and empirical work on managerial signaling highlighted a major unresolved problem of the signaling perspective: in general, a potential signal's effects on agents' assessments is not unambiguous. They depend on such things as the structure of the market for information, alternative contemporaneous signals, initially available information, and agents' ways of interpreting (or ferreting out the implications of) signals. This problem seems to be particularly important in analyses of accounting numbers' information content. This suggests that the conventional treatments of accounting numbers may have few solid theoretical or empirical underpinnings. Those treatments usually deal with accounting numbers (e.g., net income numbers, accounting ratios, etc.) as if they have unambiguous interpretations—at least insofar as changes in their realized values are concerned.

APPENDIX

Using The Market Portfolio as The Control Portfolio

Under some conditions, a more powerful test of the no-information-content hypothesis specified in Section 8.4.8.1 can be obtained by using the market portfolio as the control portfolio for each information-sample portfolio, rather than using a control portfolio consisting of randomly selected firms. This appendix identifies one set of conditions under which this additional power can be obtained. By doing so, it points to the types of general conditions under which additional power can be obtained by using the market portfolio as the control portfolio, when the relative risk of each information sample portfolio is set equal to unity.

As before, let $\tilde{R}_{zt}$ denote the return from t to $t + 1$ on the minimum-variance portfolio whose β-coefficient equals zero relative to the market portfolio, m, whose contemporaneous return is denoted $\tilde{R}_{mt}$. Also, let $\tilde{R}_{It}$ and $\tilde{R}_{ct}$ denote, respectively, the return on some information-sample portfolio, I, and the return on this portfolio's matching control-sample portfolio, c. Let β_I and β_c denote the β-coefficients of portfolios I and c, respectively.

Recall that all tests are conducted on time periods that follow the time periods used to get Ordinary Least Squares (OLS) estimates of β_I and β_c. Thus, given stationarity, joint serial independence of returns, and multivariate normality, we may write, for any such period, t, used for testing purposes:

$$\tilde{R}_{It} = \tilde{R}_{zt}(1 - \tilde{\hat{\beta}}_I) + \tilde{R}_{mt}\tilde{\hat{\beta}}_I + \tilde{e}_{It} \tag{A.1}$$

$$\tilde{R}_{ct} = \tilde{R}_{zt}(1 - \tilde{\hat{\beta}}_c) + \tilde{R}_{mt}\tilde{\hat{\beta}}_c + \tilde{e}_{ct}, \tag{A.2}$$

where $\tilde{e}_{It}$ and $\tilde{e}_{ct}$ are disturbances that are distributed independently of $\tilde{\hat{\beta}}_I$ and $\tilde{\hat{\beta}}_c$, respectively, because the latter OLS estimators are linear combinations of disturbances from previous periods (i.e., periods used for estimation) and because of the serial independence assumption on the vector $(\tilde{e}_{It}, \tilde{e}_{ct})$.

All test results are based on observed values of the difference between returns on I and c:

$$\tilde{R}_{It} - \tilde{R}_{ct} = (\tilde{R}_{mt} - \tilde{R}_{zt})(\tilde{\hat{\beta}}_I - \tilde{\hat{\beta}}_c) + (\tilde{e}_{It} - \tilde{e}_{ct}). \tag{A.3}$$

Conditional on the values $\tilde{R}_{mt} = R_{mt}$ and $\tilde{R}_{zt} = R_{zt}$, we have:

$$\begin{aligned}\text{Var}\,(\tilde{R}_{It} - \tilde{R}_{ct}|R_{mt}, R_{zt}) &= (R_{mt} - R_{zt})^2\text{Var}\,(\tilde{\hat{\beta}}_I - \tilde{\hat{\beta}}_c)\\ &\quad + \text{Var}\,(\tilde{e}_{It} - \tilde{e}_{ct}).\end{aligned} \tag{A.4}$$

And, since $E(\tilde{\hat{\beta}}_I) = E(\tilde{\hat{\beta}}_c) = \beta_I = \beta_c$ in our tests, $E[\tilde{R}_{It} - \tilde{R}_{ct}|R_{mt}, R_{zt}] = 0.0$ conditional on the "null hypothesis" of no information content.

In what follows, we assume that $\text{Var}\,(\tilde{e}_{It}) = \text{Var}\,(\tilde{e}_{ct}) = \sigma_e^2$, a parameter whose value is constant over time (given our stationarity assumption). Thus:

$$\begin{aligned}\text{Var}\,(\tilde{e}_{It} - \tilde{e}_{ct}) &= 2\sigma_e^2 - 2\,\text{Cov}\,(\tilde{e}_{It}, \tilde{e}_{ct})\\ &= 2\sigma_e^2 - 2\rho_e\sigma_e^2\\ &= 2\sigma_e^2(1 - \rho_e),\end{aligned} \tag{A.5}$$

where ρ_e is the coefficient of correlation between $\tilde{e}_{It}$ and $\tilde{e}_{ct}$, a parameter whose value is constant over time under our stationarity conditions.

Next, consider the parameter $\text{Cov}\,(\tilde{\hat{\beta}}_I, \tilde{\hat{\beta}}_c)$, which affects the value of $\text{Var}\,(\tilde{\hat{\beta}}_I - \tilde{\hat{\beta}}_c)$. Let $s \in S$ denote the time periods used to get the OLS estimates of β_I and β_c, where—as indicated above—$s < t$ for all $s \in S$. From the theory of OLS and conditional on the values of $\tilde{R}_{ms}$ for $s \in S$, we have:

$$\text{Cov}\,(\tilde{\hat{\beta}}_I, \tilde{\hat{\beta}}_c) = \left[\sum_{s\in S} R_{ms}^2\right]^{-2} E\left\{\sum_{s\in S}\sum_{q\in S} R_{ms}R_{mq}\tilde{e}_{Is}\tilde{e}_{cs}\right\}. \tag{A.6}$$

Since the disturbances, $\tilde{e}_{Is}$ and $\tilde{e}_{cs}$, are jointly serially independent, $E(\tilde{e}_{Is}\tilde{e}_{cq}) = 0.0$ for $s \neq q$. Thus:

$$\text{Cov}\,(\tilde{\hat{\beta}}_I, \tilde{\hat{\beta}}_c) = \left[\sum_{s\in S} R_{ms}^2\right]^{-2} \sum_{s\in S} R_{ms}^2\text{Cov}\,(\tilde{e}_{Is}, \tilde{e}_{cs}) \tag{A.7}$$

and, given the assumed equality of the disturbances' variances:

$$\begin{aligned}\text{Cov}\,(\tilde{\hat{\beta}}_I, \tilde{\hat{\beta}}_c) &= \left[\sum_{s\in S} R_{ms}^2\right]^{-2} \sum_{s\in S} R_{ms}^2\rho_e\sigma_e^2\\ &= \left[\sum_{s\in S} R_{ms}^2\right]^{-1} \rho_e\sigma_e^2.\end{aligned} \tag{A.8}$$

From the theory of OLS, we also have:

$$\text{Var}\,(\tilde{\hat{\beta}}_I) = \text{Var}\,(\tilde{e}_{Iq})\left[\sum_{s\in S} R_{ms}^2\right]^{-1} \tag{A.9}$$

$$\text{Var}\,(\tilde{\hat{\beta}}_c) = \text{Var}\,(\tilde{e}_{cq})\left[\sum_{s\in S} R_{ms}^2\right]^{-1}. \tag{A.10}$$

Thus, given our specifications:

$$\text{Var}(\tilde{\hat{\beta}}_I) = \text{Var}(\tilde{\hat{\beta}}_c) = \sigma_e^2\left[\sum_{s\in S} R_{ms}^2\right]^{-1}. \tag{A.11}$$

Therefore, the coefficient of correlation between $\tilde{\hat{\beta}}_I$ and $\tilde{\hat{\beta}}_c$ is given by:

$$\rho(\tilde{\hat{\beta}}_I, \tilde{\hat{\beta}}_c) = \frac{\left(\sum_{s\in S} R_{ms}^2\right)^{-1} \rho_e\sigma_e^2}{\left(\sum_{s\in S} R_{ms}^2\right)^{-1} \sigma_e^2} = \rho_e. \tag{A.12}$$

Using the above results, one gets:

$$\begin{aligned}\text{Var}(\tilde{\hat{\beta}}_I - \tilde{\hat{\beta}}_c) &= \text{Var}(\tilde{\hat{\beta}}_I) + \text{Var}(\tilde{\hat{\beta}}_c) - 2\,\text{Cov}(\tilde{\hat{\beta}}_I, \tilde{\hat{\beta}}_c)\\ &= (2\sigma_e^2 - 2\rho(\tilde{\hat{\beta}}_I, \tilde{\hat{\beta}}_c)\sigma_e^2)\left[\sum_{s\in S} R_{ms}^2\right]^{-1}\\ &= (2\sigma_e^2 - 2\rho_e\sigma_e^2)\left[\sum_{s\in S} R_{ms}^2\right]^{-1}.\end{aligned} \tag{A.13}$$

Using (A.13) and (A.5) in (A.4) yields:

$$\begin{aligned}\text{Var}(\tilde{R}_{It} - \tilde{R}_{ct}|R_{mt}, R_{zt}) &= (R_{mt} - R_{zt})^2[2\sigma_e^2(1 - \rho_e)]\left[\sum_{s\in S} R_{ms}^2\right]^{-1}\\ &\quad + 2\sigma_e^2(1 - \rho_e)\\ &= \left[\frac{(R_{mt} - R_{zt})^2}{\sum_{s\in S} R_{ms}^2} + 1\right]2\sigma_e^2(1 - \rho_e)\\ &= (K + 1)2\sigma_e^2(1 - \rho_e),\end{aligned} \tag{A.14}$$

where $K \equiv (R_{mt} - R_{zt}{}^2/(\Sigma_{s\in S}R_{ms}^2)$.

Clearly, if the value of the variance in (A.14) can be reduced, then we shall have a more powerful test of the null hypothesis $E(\tilde{R}_{It}) = E(\tilde{R}_{ct})$, conditional on the assumption that the information and control portfolios' relative risks, β_I and β_c, have the same value—specified to be unity in our tests. Suppose that the market portfolio, m, is used as the control portfolio. For the market portfolio, relative risk, β_m, is, by definition, equal to unity. In this case, there is no need to estimate relative risk for the control portfolio and $\text{Var}(\tilde{\hat{\beta}}_c) = \text{Var}(1.0) = 0.0$ when $c = m$. Moreover, $\tilde{e}_{mt} = 0.0$ in model (A.2) when $c = m$. Thus, when $c = m$, we get:

$$\begin{aligned}\text{Var}(\tilde{R}_{It} - \tilde{R}_{mt}|R_{mt}, R_{2t}) &= (R_{mt} - R_{zt})^2\text{Var}(\tilde{\hat{\beta}}_I)\\ &\quad + \text{Var}(\tilde{e}_{It})\\ &= \left[\frac{(R_{mt} - R_{zt})^2}{\sum_{s\in S} R_{ms}^2} + 1\right]\sigma_e^2\\ &= (K + 1)\sigma_e^2.\end{aligned} \tag{A.15}$$

The condition that makes the value of the variance in (A.15) less than the value of the variance in (A.14) applied to $c \neq m$ is as follows:

$$(K + 1)\sigma_e^2 < (K + 1)2\sigma_e^2(1 - \rho_e)$$

or:

$$\frac{1}{2} < (1 - \rho_e)$$

or:

$$\rho_e < \frac{1}{2}. \tag{A.16}$$

In short, when $\rho_e \equiv \text{Cov}\,(\tilde{e}_{It}, \tilde{e}_{ct})/\sigma_e^2 < 1/2$, then use of the market portfolio, m, as the control portfolio leads to a more powerful test of our no-information-content hypothesis. When $\rho_e > 1/2$ for a given $c \neq m$, the "diversification effect" of the covariance terms in Var $(\hat{\tilde{\beta}}_I - \hat{\tilde{\beta}}_c)$ is sufficiently great to make the test with this $c \neq m$ more powerful.

Note that the result in (A.16) is independent of t, independent of the values of $\tilde{R}_{mt}$ and $\tilde{R}_{zt}$, and independent of the sample size used to estimate portfolios' relative risks. In short, it is an unconditional result: it applies to Var $(\tilde{R}_{It} - \tilde{R}_{ct})$ independently of $\tilde{R}_{mt}$ and $\tilde{R}_{zt}$ and t.

REFERENCES

Abdel-khalik, A. Rashad, and J. C. McKeown, "Understanding Accounting Changes in an Efficient Market: Evidence of Differential Reactions," *Accounting Review* (October 1978): 851–868.

Accounting Principles Board *Opinion No. 9: Reporting the results of Operations* American Institute of Certified Public Accountants (December 1966).

———, *Opinion No. 30: Reporting the Results of Operations*. American Institute of Certified Public Accountants (June 1973).

Aitkin, M. A., W. C. Nelson, and K. E. Reinfurt, "Tests for Correlation Matrices." *Biometrika* (July 1968): 327–34.

Akerloff, G. A., "The Market for 'Lemons': Quality Uncertainty and the Market Mechanism." *Quarterly Journal of Economics* (August 1970): 488–500.

Albrecht, W. S., Larry Lookabill, and J. C. McKeown "The Time Series Properties of Annual Earnings: An Analysis of Individual Firms." *Journal of Accounting Research* (Autumn 1977): 226–244.

Altman, E. I. *Corporate Bankrupty in America* (Heath Lexington Book, 1971).

American Institute of Certified Public Accountants. *Statement on Auditing Procedures No. 33: Auditing Standards and Procedures* (AICPA, 1963).

———. *Accounting Trends and Techniques* (AICPA, 1973).

Anderson, T. W. *An Introduction to Multivariate Statistical Analysis* (John Wiley and Sons, Inc., 1958).

_____. *The Statistical Analysis of Time Series* (John Wiley & Sons, 1971).

Ang, James S. "Dividend Policy: Informational Content or Partial Adjustment." *Review of Economics and Statistics* (February 1975): 65–70.

Armstrong, Marshall S. "FASB Prospects." *Arthur Young Journal* (Spring 1975): 28–31.

Arrow, Kenneth "Limited Knowledge in Economic Analysis" *American Economic Review* (March 1974), 1–10.

Arthur Andersen & Co. *Executive News Briefs* (October 1975).

Ayanian, Robert. "The Profit Rates and Economic Performance of Drug Firms." In *Drug Developments and Marketing,* Edited by Robert B. Helms (American Enterprise Institute, 1975*a*).

_____. "Advertising and Rate of Return." *Journal of Law and Economics* (October 1975*b*): 479–506.

Ball, Raymond J., "Changes in Accounting Techniques and Stock Prices," *Empirical Research in Accounting: Selected Studies, 1972* Supplement to the *Journal of Accounting Research,* 10 (1972).

_____, and P. Brown, "An Empirical Evaluation of Accounting Income Numbers," *Journal of Accounting Research* (Autumn 1968): 159–177.

_____, and Watts, Ross "Some Time-Series Properties of Accounting Income," *Journal of Finance* (June 1972): 300–23.

Barlow, R. E., F. Proschen, and L. C. Hunter, *Mathematical Theory of Reliability* (John Wiley and Sons, 1965).

Barzel, Y. "Some Fallacies in the Interpretation of Information Cost." Discussion Paper No. 76-5, Institute for Economic Research (University of Washington, March 1976).

Basu, Joe. "Risk Information and Financial Lease Disclosures: Some Empirical Evidence." Working paper (McMaster University, April 1981).

Bawa, V. S., S. J. Brown, and R. W. Klein. *Estimation Risk and Optimal Portfolio Choice* (Amsterdam: North-Holland Publishing Co., 1979).

Beaver, W. H., "What Should Be the FASB's Objectives" *Journal of Accountancy* (August 1973), 49–56.

_____. "Financial Ratios as Predictors of Failure." *Empirical Research in Accounting: Selected Studies, 1966,* Supplement to *Journal of Accounting Research* (1966): 71–111.

_____."The Time Series Behavior of Earnings." *Empirical Research in Accounting: Selected Studies.* Supplement to *Journal of Accounting Research* (1970): 62–99.

_____, and R. E. Duker, "Interperiod Tax Allocation, Earnings Expectations, and the Behavior of Security Prices" *Accounting Review* (April 1972), 320–333.

_____, and _____. "Interperiod Tax Allocation and Delta Depreciation Methods: Some Empirical Results" *Accounting Review* (July 1973), 549–559.

Bellman, R. E., *Dynamic Programming* (Princeton University Press, 1957).

Benson, B. "Lawyers' Response to Audit Inquiries—A Continuing Controversy." *Journal of Accountancy* (July 1977): 72–78.

Benston, George J., "Required Disclosure and the Stock Market: An Evaluation of the

Securities Exchange Act of 1934" *American Economic Review* (March 1973), 132–155.

———. "The Baffling New Numbers Game of the FTC." *Fortune* (October 1975).

Bernstein, Leopold A. *Financial Statement Analysis: Theory, Application and Interpretation* (Richard D. Irwin, Inc., 1974).

———, "In Defense of Fundamental Investment Analysis" *Financial Analysts Journal* (Jan/Feb 1975), 57–61.

Berry, C. H. *Corporate Growth and Diversification* (Princeton University Press, 1975).

Bicksler, J. L., *ed, Handbook of Financial Economics* (North Holland, 1979).

Biddle, Gray. "Accounting Methods and Management Decisions: The Case of Inventory Costing and Inventory Policy." Ph.D. Dissertation (University of Chicago, 1980).

———, and R. K. Martin, "Inflation, Taxes, and Iptimal Inventory Policies," *Journal of Accounting Research* (Spring 1985): 57–83.

Bishop, Robert L. "Elasticities, Cross-Elasticities, and Market Relationships." *American Economic Review* (December 1952): 779–803.

Black, Fischer, "Implications of the Random Walk Hypothesis for Portfolio Management" *Financial Analysts Journal* (Mar/Apr 1971), 16–22.

Blattberg, Robert, and Nicholas J. Gonedes, "A Comparison of the Stable and Student Modles for Stock Prices." *Journal of Business* (April 1974): 244–80.

Blume, Marshall. "On the Assessment of Risk." *Journal of Finance* (March 1971): 1–10.

Bohrnstedt, G. W., and Arthur S. Golberger, "On the Exact Covariance of Products of Random Variables." *Journal of the American Statistical Association* (December 1969): 1439–1442.

Bookstaber, R. M. *Option Pricing and Strategies in Investing* (Addison-Wesley, 1981).

Boudreaux, K. J. "Competitive Rater, Market Efficiency, and the Economics of Security Analysis Financial Analysts Journal (Mar/Apr 1975), 18–24, 92.

Bowman, Ward S., Jr., *Patent and Antitrust Law* (University of Chicago Press, 1973).

Box, G. E. P., and G. M. Jenkins, *Time Series Analysis: Forecasting and Control* (Holden Day, 1976).

———, and ———. *Time Series Analysis: Forcasting and Control* (Holden-Day, Inc., 1976).

———, and D. A. Pierce, "Distribution of Residual Autocorrelations in Autoregressive Moving Average Time Series Models." *Journal of the American Statistical Association* (December 1970): 1509–26.

Brealey, R. A. "Statistical Properties of Successive Changes in Earnings." Manuscript (Keystone Custodian Funds, March 1967).

———. *An Introduction to Risk and Return on Common Stocks* (Press, 1969).

Bridge, J. I. *Applied Economics* (North-Holland, 1971).

Brooks, LeRoy D., and D. A. Buckmaster, "Further Evidence on the Time Series Properties of Accounting Income." *Journal of Finance* (December 1976): 1359–73.

Brown, L. D. and M. S. Rozeff, "Univariate Time Series Models of Quarterly Accounting Earnings Per Share: A Proposed Model." *Journal of Accounting Research* (Spring 1979): 179–189.

Brown, M., *On the Theory and Measurement of Technological Change* (Cambridge University Press, 1968).

Brown, Philip, "Dividend Policy and the Value of the Firm." Manuscript (Department of Accountancy, University of Western Australia, 1975).

Brown, Stephen H. "Optimal Portfolio Choice Under Uncertainty." Ph.D. Dissertation (University of Chicago, 1976).

Brozen, Yale. "The Persistence of High Rates of Return in High Stable Concentration Industries." *Journal of Law and Economics* (October 1971): 501–12.

Burstein, M. L., "The Economics of Tie—In Sales" *Review of Economics and Statistics* (Feb 1960), 68–73.

Butters, J. K., and P. Niland, *Inventory Accounting and Policies* (Division of Research, Graduate School of Business, Harvard University, 1949).

Caves, R. E., and M. E. Proter, "Barriers to Exit." In *Essays on Industrial Organization in Honor of Joe S. Bain,* edited by R. T. Masson and P. D. Qualls (Ballinger Publishing Co., 1976).

Chambers, R. J., "Stock Market Prices and Accounting Research" *Abachs* (June 1974), 39–54.

Coldwell, P. E., "Statement before the Committee on Banking, Housing, and Urban Affairs, U.S. Senate, July 16, 1975." *Federal Reserve Bulletin* (July 1975), 416–419.

Coopers & Lybrand. *LIFO: A Guide for Corporate Decision Makers* (New York: Coopers & Lybrand, 1974).

_____. *Interim Reporting A Program for Progress* (Coopers & Lybrand, 1975).

Copeland, T. E., and J. Fred Weston, *Financial Theory and Corporate Policy* (Addison-Wesley, 1979).

Cramer, H., and M. R. Leadbetter, *Stationary and related Stochastic Processes* (John Wiley & Sons, 1967).

Debreu, Gerard. *Theory of Value: An Axiomatic Analysis of Economic Equilibrium* (John Wiley & Sons, 1959).

Demsetz, Harold, "The Private Production of Public Goods" *Journal of Law and Economics* (1970), 293–306.

Davidson, Sidney. "Current Accounting Problems in Financial Analysis." Outline and Tables (August 15, 1977).

_____, and D. F. Drake, "Capital Budgeting and the 'Best' Tax Depreciation Method." *Journal of Business* (October 1961): 442–452.

_____, C. P. Stickney, and R. L. Weil, *Inflation Accounting* (McGraw-Hill, 1976).

Demski, Joel S. "Discussion of Relationship between Accounting Changes and Stock Prices: Problems of Measurement and Some Empirical Evidence by Sunder." *Empirical Re-*

search in Accounting: Selected Studies. 1973. Supplement to the *Journal of Accounting Research* (1973): 46–54.

Derstine, R. P., and R. J. Huefner, "LIFO-FIFO, Accounting Ratios and Market Risk." *Journal of Accounting Research* (Autumn 1974): 216–234.

Desai, M. *Applied Econometrics* (McGraw-Hill, 1976).

Dhrymes, Phoebus J. *Distributed Lags: Problems of Estimation and Formulation* (Holden-Day, Inc., 1971).

Diamond, L. H. "Funding Liability Under Union Pension Plans." *Journal of Accountancy* (September 1975): 74–79.

Doob, J. L., *Stochastic Processes* (John Wiley & Sons, 1953).

Dopuch, Nicholas. "Discussion of 'Toward a Science of Accounting' by Robert R. Sterling." *Stanford Lectures in Accounting: 1975*, pp. 15–18 (Graduate School of Business, Stanford University, 1715.

———, J. G. Birnberg and J. S. Demski, *Cost Accounting*, 3rd Ed. (Harcourt Brace Jovanovich, 1982).

———, and Ross Watts. "Using Time Series Models to Assess the Significance of Accounting Changes." *Journal of Accounting Research* (Spring 1972): 180–94.

Douglas, Edna. *Economics of Marketing* (Harper & Row, 1975).

Draper, N. R., and E. Smith, *Applied Regression Analysis* (John Wiley & Sons, 1966).

Dun & Bradstreet. *Business Failure Record, 1974* (Dun & Bradstreet, 1975).

Edwards, E. O., and P. W. Bell, *The Theory and Measurement of Business Income* (University of California Press, 1961).

Eggleton, Ian R. C., S. H. Penman, and J. R. Tombly, "Accounting Changes and Stock Prices: An Examination of Selected Uncontrolled Variables" *Journal of Accounting Research* (Spring 1976), 66–88.

Ellert, J. C. "Industrial Concentration and Rates of Return." Manuscript (Queen's University, Kingston, Canada, 1974).

Ernst & Ernst. *The 1974 Pension Reform Act* (Ernst & Ernst, 1974).

———, "Accounting for Leases." *Financial Reporting Developments* (March 1977*a*).

———, "Proposed SEC Rules on Reporting Business Segments." *Financial Reporting Developments* (July 1977*b*).

———, *Financial Reporting Developments* "Financial Reporting of Business Segments" (July 1977*c*).

———, National Tax Training Program. Level 1, Course Manual Part 2. Ernst & Ernst, 1977, Esp. Chap. 20: "Deductions: Inventories—General" and Chap. 21: "Deductions: Inventories—LIFO."

Ernst & Whinney. *Financial Reporting Briefs* (January 1972).

Eskew, Robert F., and W. F. Wright, "An Empirical Analysis of Differential Capital Market Reactions to Extraordinary Accounting Items." Research Paper No. 297 (Graduate School of Business, Stanford University. Revised version, February 1976).

Fama, Eugene F. "The Behavior of Stock Market Prices" *Journal of Business* (January 1965), 34–105.

_____, "Efficient Capital Markets: A Review of Theory and Empirical Work *"Journal of Finance* (May 1970), 383–417.

_____, *Foundations of Finance* (Basic Books, 1976).

_____, "Perfect Competition and Optimal Production Decisions Under Uncertainty." *Bell Journal of Economics and Management Science* (Autumn 1972): 509–30.

_____, "The Empirical Relationships Between the Dividend and Investment Decisions of Firms." *American Economic Review* (June 1974): 304–18.

_____, "The Effects of a Firm's Investment and Financing Decisions on the Welfare of Its Securityholders." Working Paper No. 75-43 (European Institute for Advanced Studies in Management, Brussels. Revised version, February 1976).

_____, "Multiperiod Consumption-Investment Decisions." *American Economic Review* (March 1970): 163–174.

_____"Risk-Adjusted Discount Rates and Capital Budgeting Under Uncertainty." *Journal of Financial Economics* (August 1977): 3–24.

_____, "The Effects of A Firm's Investment and Financing Decisions on the Welfare of Its Securityholders." *American Economic Review* (June 1978): 272–284.

_____, and H. Babiak, "Dividend Policy: An Empirical Analysis." *Journal of the American Statistical Association* (December 1968): 133–61.

_____, and M. Blume, "Filter Rules and Stock Market Trading Profits" *Journal of Business* (special supplement, January 1970), 226–241.

_____, Lawrence Fisher, M. Jensen, and R. Roll, "The Adjustment of Stock Prices to New Information" *International Economic Review* (February 1969), 1–21.

_____, and A. Laffer, "Information and Capital Markets" *Journal of Business* (July 1971), 289–298.

_____, and James MacBeth, "Tests of the Multiperiod Two Paramater Model." *Journal of Financial Economics* (1974): 43–66.

_____, and M. H. Miller, *The Theory of Finance* (Holt, Rinehart & Winston, 1972).

Feldstein, Martin, and L. Summers, "Is the Rate of Profit Falling?" *Brookings Papers on Economic Activity* 1 (1977): 211–28.

Ferguson, C. E. *The Neoclassical Theory of Production and Distribution* (Cambridge University Press, 1969).

Fiedler, Edgar R. *Measures of Credit Risk and Experience* (National Bureau of Economic Research, 1971).

Financial Accounting Standards Board. *Accounting for the Cost of Pension Plans Subject to the Employee Retirement Income Security Act of 1974: FASB Interpretation No. 3* (Financial Accounting Standards Board, December 1974).

Fischer, D. E., and R. J. Jordan, *Security Analysis and Portfolio Management* (Prentice-Hall, Inc, 1975).

Fisher, Franklin, and Karl Shell. *The Economic Theory of Price Indices* (Academic Press, 1972).

Fisher, I. N., and G. R. Hall, "Risk and Corporate Rates of Return." *Quarterly Journal of Economics* (February 1969): 79–92.

Fisher, L. "Some New Stock Market Indices." *Journal of Business* (Special Supplement, January 1966): 191–225.

———, and J. Kamin, "On the Nature and Estimation of Systematic Risk." Working paper (University of Chicago, February 1975).

Fogelson, James H. "The Impact of Changes in Accounting Principles on Restrictive Covenants in Credit Agreements and Indentures." *Business Lawyer* (January 1978): 769–787.

Foster, G., "Earnings and Stock Prices of Insurance Companies" *Accounting Review* (October 1975), 686–698.

———, "Quarterly Accounting Data: Time Series Properties and Predictive Ability Results." Report No. 7622, Center for Mathematical Studies in Business and Economics (University of Chicago, May 1976).

———, "Quarterly Accounting Data: Time Series Properties and Predictive Ability Results." *Accounting Review* (January 1977): 1–21.

Friedman, B. M. "Optimal Expectations and the Extreme Information Assumptions of 'Rational Expectations' Macro-models." *Journal of Monetary Economics* (1979): 23–41.

Friend, Irwin, "The Economic Consequences of the Stock Market" *American Economic Review* (May 1972), 211–219.

Froeschle, James R. "Analysis of Seasonal Time Series." Ph.D. Dissertation (University of Iowa, 1975).

Fuchs, V. R., ed. *Policy Issues and Research Opportunities in Industrial Organization* (National Bureau of Economic Research, 1972).

Fuller, Wayne A. *Introduction to Statistical Time Series* (John Wiley & Sons, 1976).

Fuss, Melvyn, and McFadden, eds., *Production Economics: A Dual Approach to Theory and Applications,* vols 1 and d (North Holland, 1978).

Goldberger, A. S., *Econometric Theory* (John Wiley, 1964).

Gonedes, N. J. "Capital Market Equilibrium and Annual Accounting Numbers: Empirical Evidence." *Journal of Accounting Research* (Spring 1974).

———. "Information-Production and Capital Market Equilibrium." *Journal of Finance* (June 1975*a*).

———. "Risk, Information, and the Effects of Special Accounting Items on Capital Market Equilibrium." *Journal of Accounting Research* (Autumn 1975*b*).

———. "Capital Market Equilibrium for a Class of Heterogeneous Expectations in a Two-Parameter World." *Journal of Finance* (March 1976).

———. "Evidence on the Information Content of Accounting Numbers: Accounting-Based and Market-Based Estimates of Systematic Risk." *Journal of Financial and Quantitative Analysis* (June 1973): 407–43.

———. "Income Smoothing Under Selected Stochastic Processes." *Journal of Business* (October 1972): 570–84.

_____. "The Capital Market, the Market for Information, and External Accounting." *Journal of Finance* (May 1976*b*): 611–630.

_____. "Corporate Signaling, External Accounting, and Capital Market Equilibrium: Evidence on Dividends' Income, and Extraordinary Items." *Journal of Accounting Research* (Spring 1978): 26–79. April 1976 version available from the Center for Mathematical Studies in Business and Economics, University of Chicago.

_____. "Public Disclosure Rules, Private Information-Production Decisions and Capital Market Equilibrium." *Journal of Accounting Research* (Autumn 1980): 441–76.

_____. "Properties of Accounting Numbers: Models and Tests." *Journal of Accounting Research* (Autumn 1973): 212–37.

_____ and Nicholas Dopuch, "Economic Analyses and Accounting Techniques: Perspective and Proposals." *Journal of Accounting Research* (Autumn 1979).

_____, and _____. "Capital Market Equilibrium, Information-Production and Selecting Accounting Techniques: Theoretical Framework and Review of Empirical Work." *Studies on Financial Accounting Objectives*. Supplement to the *Journal of Accounting Research* (1974): 48–169.

_____, Nicholas Dopuch, and Stephen H. Penman, "Disclosure Rules, Information-Production, and Capital Market Equilibrium: The Case of Forecast Disclosure Rules." *Journal of Accounting Research* (Spring 1976): 89–137.

_____, and Harry V. Roberts, "Autoregression versus Ordinary Regression: Lessons for Inference." Report No. 7531, Center for Mathematical Studies in Business and Economics (University of Chicago, May 1975).

_____, and _____. "Trends and Drifts?" Manuscript (University of Chicago, July 1977*a*.)

_____, and _____. "Gentle Trends and Gentle Drifts." Manuscript (University of Chicago, July 1977*b*).

_____, and _____. "Differencing of Random Walks and Near Random Walks." *Journal of Econometrics* (1977*c*): 289–308.

_____, and Meir Schneller, "Value Maximization and Earnings Management Via Accounting Techniques." Working paper (University of Pennsylvania, July 1986).

_____, and J. R. Twombly, "Aggregate Versus Disaggregate Models for Accounting Numbers: Empirical Results for Earnings Per Share." Working paper (University of Pennsylvania, 1981).

Goodman, H., and T. W. McRae. *Illustrations of Reporting Accounting Changes* (AICPA, 1974).

Gosman, M. L. "Characteristics of Firms Making Accounting Changes." *Accounting Review* (January 1973): 1–12.

Grady, Paul. *Inventory of Generally Accepted Accounting Principles for Business Enterprises* (American Institute of Certified Public Accountants, 1965).

Granger, C. W. J., and P. Newbold, *Forecasting Economic Time Series* (Academic Press Inc., 1977).

Griffin, P. A. "The Association Between Relative Risk and Risk Estimates Derived from Quarterly Earnings and Dividends." *Accounting Review* (July 1976): 499–515.

———. "The Time Series Behavior of Quarterly Earnings: Preliminary Evidence." *Journal of Accounting Research* (Spring 1977): 71–83.

Hagerman, R., and R. Richmond, "Random Walks, Martigales, and the OTC" *Journal of Finance* (Sept 1973), 897–909.

Hakansson, Nils, "Empirical Research in Accounting, 1960–1970: An Appraisal." *Accounting Research, 1960–1970: A Critical Evaluation*. Edited by Nicholas Dopuch and L. Revsine: Center International Education and Research in Accounting (University of Illinois, 1973), 137–173.

———, G. J. Kunkel, and J. Ohlson. 1979. "Sufficient and Necessary Conditions for Information to Have Value in Pure Exchange Manuscript (University of California, Berkeley, June 1979).

Harrison, T. "Different Market Reactions to Discretionary and Nondiscretionary Accounting Changes." *Journal of Accounting Research* (Spring 1977): 84–107.

Hawkins, David, *Accounting Bullentin No. 4: A Quick Update: Leases and Other Summer Happenings* (Drexel Burnhan and Co., September 1876).

Heckman, James J. "Sample Selection Bias as a Specification Error . . . " Report 7720, Center for Math Studies in Business and Economics (University of Chicago, February 1977).

Hemenway, D. *Industrywide Voluntary Product Standards* (Ballinger Publishing Co., 1975).

Hendriksen, Eldon S. *Accounting Theory*. Rev. ed. (Richard D. Irwin, Inc., 1970).

Hepworth, Samuel. "Smoothing Periodic Income." *Accounting Review* (January 1953): 32–39.

Herman, E. S., and C. F. Safanda, "Allocating Investment Information." *Financial Analysis Journal* (January, February 1973), 23–28, 188–90.

Hirshleifer, Jack, "The Private and Social Value of Information and the Reward to Inventive Activity." *American Economic Review* (September 1971), 561–574.

———, "Where Are We In the Theory of Information." *American Economic Review* (May 1973), 31–39.

Hite, G. L. "Leverage, Output Effects, and the M-M Theorems." *Journal of Financial Economics* 4 (1977): 177–202.

Holthausen, Robert W., and Richard W. Leftwich, "The Economic Consequences of Accounting Choice: Implications of Costly Contracting and Monitoring." *Journal of Accounting and Economics* 5 (1983): 11–117.

Jaffe, Jeffrey F., "Special Information and Insider Trading" *Journal of Business* (July 1974), 410–428.

Jaffee, D. M., and T. Russell, "Imperfect Information, Uncertainty, and Credit Rationing." *Quarterly Journal of Economics* (November 1976): 651–66.

Jenkins, G. M., and D. G. Watts, *Spectral Analysis and Its Applications* (Holden-Day, Inc., 1968).

Jensen, Michael, "Risk, the Pricing of Capital Assets and the Evaluation of Investment Portfolios" *Journal of Business* (April 1969), 167–247.

———. "Capital Markets: Theory and Evidence." *Bell Journal of Economics And Management Science* (Autumn 1972): 357–98.

———, and J. B. Long, Jr. "Corporate Investment Under Uncertainty and Pareto Optimality in the Capital Markets." *Bell Journal of Economics and Management Science* (Spring 1972): 151–74.

———, and W. H. Meckling "Theory of the Firm: Managerial Behavior, Agency costs, and Capital Structure" *Journal of Financial Economics* (October 1976), 305–360.

Johnson, N. L., and S. Kotz, *Distributions in Statistics*. Vol. 1: *Continuos Univariate Distributions* (Houghton Mifflin, 1970).

———, and ———. Distributions in Statistics. Vol. 4: *Continuous Multivariate Distributions* (Houghton Mifflin, 1972).

Johnston, J. *Statistical Cost Analysis* (McGraw Hill, 1960).

Kaplan, R. S., and R. Roll, "Investor Evaluation of Accounting Information: Some Empirical Evidence" *Journal of Business* (April 1972), 225–257.

Kelly, Paul V. "New Financing Techniques on Wall Street." *Financial Executive* (November 1974): 30–42.

Kendall, M. G. *Time-Series* (Hafner Publishing Co., Inc., 1973).

———, and Alan Stuart, *The Advanced Theory of Statistics*. Vol. 3. 2d ed (Haner Publishing Co., Inc., 1968).

Kennedy, J. C., and R. I. Landau, *Corporate Trust Administration and Management* (New York University Press, 1975).

King Benjamin F. "Market and Industry Factors in Stock Price Behavior." *Journal of Business* (January 1966, Special Supplement): 139–90.

Klein, R. W. and V. S. Bawa, "The Effect of Estimation Risk on Optimal Portfolio Choice." *Journal of Financial Economics* (June 1976): 215–232.

Kon, Stanley J., and W. P. Lau, "Tests of Stationarity for Common Stock Portfolio Regression Parameters and the Implications for Tests of the Two-Parameter Model and Market Efficiency." Working paper (University of Chicago, April 1977).

Kupiec, Paul H. "Microfoundations of Systematic Risk." Ph.D. Dissertation (University of Pennsylvania, 1985).

Krueger, Anne O., "The Political Economy of the Rent Seeking Society." *American Economic Review* (June 1974), 291–303.

Labys, W. C., and C. W. J. Granger, *Speculation, Hedging and Commodity Price Forecasts* (D. C. Heath & Co., 1970).

Larcker, D. F. "The Association Between Performance Plan Adoption and Corporate Capital Investment." *Journal of Accounting and Economics* (April 1983): 3–30.

Largay, J. A., III, and J. L. Livingstone, *Accounting for Changing Prices* (John Wiley and Sons, 1976).

Laub, P. Michael, "Some Aspects of the Aggregation Problem in the Dividend Earnings Relationship." *Journal of the American Statistical Association* (September 1972): 552–59.

LaValle, Irving H., *Introduction to Probability, Decision and Inference* (Holt Rinehart and Winston, 1970).

Leftwich, Richard. "Accounting Information in Private Markets: Evidence from Private Lending Agreements." *Accounting Review* (January 1983): 23–42.

Leland, H. E., and D. H. Pyle. "Informational Asymmetries, Financial Structure, and Financial Intermediation." Working paper No. 41, Research Program in Finance (University of California, Berkely, March 1976).

Levy, R. "On the Short Term Stationarity of Beta Coefficients." *Financial Analysts Journal* (November/December 1971): 55–62.

Lewellen, Wilbur G. *Executive Compensation in Large Industrial Corporations* (National Bureau of Economic Research, 1968).

——. *The Ownership Income of Management* (National Bureau of Economic Research, 1971).

Lintner, J., "The Aggregation of Investors Diverse Judgments and Preferences in Purely Competitive Securities Markets." *Journal of Financial and Quantitative Analysis* (December 1969), 347–400.

——. "The Valuation of Risk Assets and the Selection of Risky Investments in Stock Portfolios and Capital Budgets." *Review of Economics and Statistics* (February 1965): 13–37.

——. "Distribution of Incomes of Corporations Among Dividends, Retained Earnings, and Taxes." *American Economic Review* (May 1956): 97–113.

——, and R. Glauber. "Higgledy Piggledy Growth in America." Paper presented at the Seminar on the Analysis of Security Prices, Center for Research in Security Prices (University of Chicago, May 1967).

Lloyd-Davies, P., and M. Canes. 1978. "Stock Prices and the Publication of Second-Hand Information." *Journal of Business* (January 1978): 43–56.

Loomis, P. A., Jr. "The Independence of the Public Accountants." Address to the Seminar of the Florida Institute of Certified Public Accountants (Miami, December 1974).

Lorek, K. S. "Predicting Annual Net Earnings with Quarterly Earnings Time Series Model." *Journal of Accounting Research* (Spring 1979): 190–204.

——, J. D. Icerman, and A. A. Abdulkader. "Further Descriptive and Predictive Evidence on Alternative Time-Series Models for Quarterly Earnings." *Journal of Accounting Research* (Spring 1983): 317–28.

Luce, R. Duncan, and H. Raiffa, *Games and Decisions* (John Wiley, 1975).

Luenberger, D. G., *Optimization by Vector Space Methods* (John Wiley, 1969).

Lurie, Arlene J., and Victor S., Pastena. "How Promptly Do Corporations Disclose Their Problems?" *Financial Analysts Journal* (September/October 1975): 55–61.

Magee, R. P., "Industry-Wide Commonalities in Earnings." *Journal of Accounting* (Autumn 1974), 270–287.

Maisel, S. J., "Information and Financial Institutions." *National Bureau of Economic Research 55th Annual Report* (Sept 1975).

Mann, H. M., "The New York Stock Exchange: A Cartel At the End of Its Reign." *Promoting Competition in Regulated Markets,* Edited by Almarin Philips (The Brooking Institution, 1975) 301–28.

Marshall, John M. "Private Incentives and Public Information." *American Economic Review* (June 1974) 373–90.

Mendelson, Morris, and Sidney Robbins, *Investment Analysis and Securities Markets* (Basic Books, Inc., 1976).

Meyer, P. S. "The Bottom Line: New Disclosures Show Hot ITT Has Managed Steady Profit Growth." *Wall Street Journal* (January 10, 1974): 1, 12.

Miller, Merton H., and Franco Modigliani. "Dividend Policy, Growth, and the Valuation of Shares." *Journal of Business* (October 1961): 411–33.

_____, and Kevin Rock. "Dividend Policy Under Asymmetric Information." *Journal of Finance* (September 1985): 1031–52.

Miller, Rupert G., Jr. *Simultaneous Statistical Inference* (McGraw-Hill Book Co., 1966).

Modigliani, F., and M. Miller, "The Cost of Capital, Corporation Finance, and the Theory of Investment." *American Economic Review* (June 1963): 433–443.

Moore, M. L., "Management Changes and Discretionary Accounting Decisions." *Journal of Accounting Research* (Spring 1973), 100–07.

Morrison, D. F., *Multivariate Statistical Methods* (McGraw-Hill Book Co., 1967).

_____. *Multivariate Statistical Methods*. 2nd Edition (McGraw-Hill Book Co., 1976).

Moussa, H., and T. Murota. 1978. "Social Value of Public Information Re-examined." Manuscript, Department of Economics (Hitotsubashi University, Kunitachi, Tokyo, 1978).

Murota, T. 1976. "Public Information and Social Welfare Under Fine Alternative Market Mechanisms." Ph.D. Dissertation (University of Minnesota, 1976).

Muth, John F. "Rational Expectations and the Theory of Price Movements." *Econometrics* (July 1961): 315–35.

McClure, C. E., and W. R. Thirsk, "A Simplified Exposition of the Harberger Model I: Tax Incidence." *National Tax Journal* (March 1975): 1–27.

Namias, Jean. *Handbook of Selected Sample Surveys in the Federal Government* (St John's University Press, 1969).

Nelson, C. R. *Applies Time Series Analysis* (Holden-DAY, Inc., 1973).

Ng, David S. "Information Accuracy and Social Welfare Under Homogeneous Beliefs." *Journal of Financial Economics* (March 1975), 53–70.

Niederhoffer, Victor, "The Analysis of Wold Events and Stock Prices." *Journal of Business* (April 1971), 193–219.

Norby, William C. "Conceptual Framework for Financial Accounting and Reporting." *Financial Analysts Journal* (September/October 1977): 18ff. Opinion Research Corporation. *Public Accounting in Tranisito* (Arthur Andersen and Co., 1974).

_____. "Employers' Accounting for Pensions." *Financial Analysts Journal* (July/August 1981): 22ff.

Nurnberg, Hugo. "Some of the Essential Provisions of Opinion No. 8." *Accounting Review* (January 1974).

Owen, E. R., and Werner, L. *Accounting for Pension Costs* (Peat Marwick Mitchell & Co., 1967).

Parker, James E. "Impact of Price Level Accounting." *Accounting Review* (January 1977): 69–96.

Paton, W. A., and A. C. Littleton, *An Introduction to Corporate Accounting Standards* (American Accounting Association, 1940).

Penman, S. H. "Corporate Forecast Disclosure, Substitute Information, and the Market for Information." Ph.D. thesis (University of Chicago, 1977).

———, 1980. "InsiderTrading and the Dissemination of Firms' Forecast Information." Manuscript (University of California, Berkely, 1980).

Pettit, R. R. "Dividend Announcements, Security Performance, and Capital Market Efficiency." *Journal of Finance* (December 1972): 993–1008.

Philips, L. *Applied Consumption Analysis* (North-Holland, 1974).

Posner, R. A. "The Social Costs of Monopoly and Regulation." *Journal of Political Economy* (August 1975), 807–828.

Prentice-Hall. *Federal Income Tax Regulations*. Vol. 1 (Prentice-Hall, 1963).

Press, S. James, *Applied Multivariate Analysis* (Holt, Rinehart and Winston, 1972).

Raj, Des. *Sampling Theory* (McGraw-Hill, 1968).

Rappaport, L. H. *SEC Accounting Practice and Procedure*. 3rd ed (Ronald Press, 1972).

Ricks, William. "The Market's Response to the 1974 LIFO Switch," Ph.D. Dissertation (University of California, Berkely, 1980).

Rogalski, R. J. *Dynamic Call Option Models: Theory and Evidence*. Division of Research (University of Michigan, 1978).

Roll, Richard. "A Critique of the Asset Pricing Theory's Tests" *Journal of Financial Exonomics* (March 1977), 129–176.

Rosenberg, B., and J. Guy, "The Prediction of Systematic Risk." Working Paper NO. 33, Research Program in Finance, Graduate School of Business (University of California, Berkelcy, February 1975).

———, and V. Marathe, "Tests of Capital Asset Pricing Hypothesis." Working Paper No. 32, Research Program in Finance, Graduate School of Business (University of California, Berkeley, May 1975).

———, and W. McKibben, "The Prediction of Systematic and Specific Risk in Common Stocks." *Journal of Financial and Quantitative Analysis* (March 1973): 317–33.

Ross, S. A. "The Determination of Financial Structure: The Incentive-Signaling Approach." *Bell Journal of Economics* (Spring 1977): 23–40.

Samuelson, Paul A. "The Pure Theory of Public Expentiture." *Review of Economics and Statistics* (November 1954), 387–389.

———. "Diagrammatic Exposition of a Theory of Public Expenditure." *Review of Economics and Statistics* (November 1955) 350–356.

Scherer, F. M. *Industrial Market Structure and Economic Performance* (Rand McNally, 1970).

Scholes, Myron S. "The Market for Securities: Substitution Versus Price Pressure and the Effects of Information on Share Prices." *Journal of Business* (April 1972), 179–211.

______. "What Does the Dividend Freeze Really Mean and Why All the Fuss about Dividends?" Paper presented at the Seminar on the Analysis of Security Prices, Center for Research in Security Prices (University of Chicago, November 1973).

Securities and Exchange Commission. Release No. 4988 (Securities Act of 1933). Washington, D.C., (July 14, 1969).

______. Release No. 8650 (Securities Exchange Act of 1934). Washington, D.C., (July 14, 1969).

______. Release No. 9000 (Securities Exchange Act of 1934). Washington, D.C., (October 21, 1970).

______. *Accounting Series Release No. 138* (January 12, 1973).

______. Release No. 34-11079. Washington, D.C., (October 31, 1974).

______. *Accounting Series Release No. 165* (December 20, 1974).

______. Release No. 5581 (Securities Act of 1933), Release No. 11374 (Securities Exchange Act of 1934). Washington, D.C., (April 28, 1975).

Sharpe, William F. "Capital Asset Prices: A theory of Market Equilibrium Under Conditions of Risk," *Journal of Finance* (September 1964): 425–442.

Shephard, R. W., *Theory of Cost and Production Functions* (Princeton University Press, 1970).

Shoenthal, E. R., "Contingent Legal Liabilities." *The CPA* (New York Society of CPA's) (March 1976), 30–34.

Shoven, J. B., and J. Bulow, "Inflation Accounting and Nonfinancial Corporate Profits: Physical Assets." *Brooking Papers on Economic Activity* 3 (1975), 557–612.

______, and ______. "Inflation Accounting and Nonfinancial Corporate Profits: Financial Assets and Liabilities." *Brookings Papers on Economic Activity* 1 (1976), 15–66.

Singer, E. M., *Antitrust Economics* (Prentice Hall, 1968).

Smith, C. W., Jr., and J. B. Warner. "On Financial Contracting: An Analysis of Bond Covenants." *Journal of Financial Economics* (June 1979): 117–161.

Somer, A. A., Jr. "The American Experience with Accounting Principles." Paper delivered at a conference on International Business: Finance, Tax, and Accounting Problems (London, December 11, 1974).

Spacek, Leonard, "Business Success Requires an Understanding of Unsolved Problems of Accounting and Financial Reporting" (Arthur Andersen, Chicago, Ill, 1959).

Spence, A. Michael, *Market Signaling: Informational Transfer in Hiring and Related Screening Processes* (Harvard University Press, 1974).

Stanley, D. T., and M. Girth, *Bankruptcy: Problem, Process, Reform* (Brookings Institution, 1971).

Stapleton, R. C., and M. G. Subrahamanyam, "The Market Model and Capital Asset Pricing Theory: A Note." *Journal of Finance* (December 1983).

Sterling, Robert B., "On Theory Construction and Verification." *Accounting Reveiw* (July 1970), 444–457.

Stickel, S. "The Effect of Value Line Investment Survey Rank Changes on Common Stock Prices," *Journal of Financial Exonomics* (March 1985): 121–44.

Stigler, George J., "Public Regulation of the Securities Markets," *Journal of Business* (April 1964), 117–142.

———. "Production and Distribution in the Short Run," *Journal of Political Economy* (June 1939): 305–327.

———. *Capital and Rates of Return in Manufacturing Industries* (Princeton University Press, 1963).

Stiglitz, J. "On the Optimality of the Stock Market Allocation of Investment," *Quarterly Journal of Economics* (February 1972): 25–60.

Stillson, R. T. "An Analysis of Information and Transaction Services in Financial Institutions," *Journal of Money Credit and Banking* (November 1974), 517–535.

Subrahamanyam, M. G., and Stauros Thomadakis, "Systematic Risk and The Theory of the Firm," *Quarterly Journal of Economics* (May 1980).

Sunder, Shyam. "An Empirical Study of Stock Price and Risk as They relate to Accounting Changes in Inventory Valuation Methods," Ph.D. Dissertation (Carnegie-Mellon University, 1973a).

———. "Relationship Between Accounting Changes and Stock Prices: Problems of Measurement and Some Empirical Evidence." *Empirical Research in Accounting: Selected Studies, 1973*. Supplement to *Journal of Accounting Research* (1973b): 1–45.

———. "Optimal Choice between FIFO and LIFO." *Journal of Accounting Research* (Autumn 1976): 277–300.

———. "On the Stationarity of Market Risk of Common Stock." Working paper (University of Chicago, September 1976).

Swamy, P. A. V. B. *Statistical Inference in Random Coefficient Regression Models* (Springer-Verlag, 1971).

Swimmer, J. J., and Malca, E. *Pension and Institutional Portfolio Management* (Praeger Publishers, 1976).

Tennican, M. L. *Convertible Debentures and Related Securities* (Harvard University Press, 1975).

Theil, Henri. *Principles of Econometrics* (John WIley, 1971).

Thomadakis, Stavros, "A Model of Market Power and the Firm's Return" *Bell Journal of Economics and Management Science* (Spring 1976).

Tideman, T. N., and D. P. Tucker, "The Tax Treatment of Business Profits Under Inflationary Conditions." In *Inflation and the Income Tax,* edited by Henry J. Aaron, pp. 33–74 (The Brookings Institution, 1976).

Touche Ross & Co. *The Sec's Integrated Disclosure System* (Commerce Clearing House, Inc., 1980).

Treynor, Jack L. "Efficient Markets and Fundamental Analysis" *Financial Analysts Journal* (March/April 1974), 14.

_____, Regan, P. J., and W. W. Priest, Jr. *The Financial Reality of Pension Funding Under ERISA* (Dow-Jones Irwin, 1976).

Turc, N. B. *The Future of Private Pension Plans* (American Enterprise Institute, 1976).

Twombly, J. R. "The Information Content of Segment Reports." Ph.D. Dissertation (University of Chicago, 1980).

Van Frederikslust, R. A. I. *Predictability of Corporate Failure* (Martinus Nijhoff, 1978).

Wade, Nicholas. "Recombinant DNA: NIH Sets Strict Rules to Launch New Technology." *Science* (December 19, 1975): 1175–79.

Wallich, H. C., and M. Wallich, "Profits are not as Good at They Look," *Fortune* (March 1974): 126ff.

Watts, Ross. "The Informational Content of Dividends." Chapter 3, Ph.D. Dissertation (University of Chicago, June 1970).

_____. "The Information Content of Dividends." *Journal of Business* (April 1973), 191–211.

_____. "The Time Series Behavior of Quarterly Earnings." Manuscript (Department of Commerce, University of Newcastle, New South Wales, Australia, April 1975).

_____, and R. W. Leftwich, "The Time Series of Annual Accounting Earnings." *Journal of Accounting Research* (Spring 1977): 253–71.

_____, and J. Zimmerman, "Towards a Positive Theory of the Determination of Accounting Standards," *Accounting Review* (January 1978): 112–134.

Waud, R. N. "Public Interpretation of Discount Rate Changes: Evidence on the Announcement Effect," *Econometrica* (March 1970), 231–250.

Weiss, L. W. "The Concentration-Profits Relationship and Antitrust." In *Industrial Concentration: The New Learning,* edited H. J. Goldschmidetal., pp. 148–232 (Little, Brown and Co., 1974).

Welch, Paul R. "A Generalized Distributed Lag Model for Predicting Quarterly Earnings." *Journal of Accounting Research* (Autumn 1984): 744–757.

Wilcox, J. W. "A Prediction of Business Failure Using Accounting Data." *Empirical Research in Accounting: Selected Studies, 1973,* Supplement to *Journal of Accounting Research* (1973): 163–79.

Winn, D. N. *Industrial Market Structure and Performance 1960–1968* (Division of Research, Graduate School of Business, University of Michigan, 1975).

Young, Allan H. "Alternative Estimates of Corporate Depreciation and Profits: Part I." *Survey of Current Business* (April 1968a): 17 ff.

_____. "Alternative Estimates of Corporate Depreciation and Profits: Part II." *Survey of Current Business* (May 1968b): 16 ff.

_____. "New Estimates of Capital Consumption Allowances, Revision of GNP in the Benchmark." *Survey of Current Business* (October 1975): 14 ff.

Yule, G. U. "Why Do We Sometimes Get Nonsense Correlations Between Time Series?—

A Study in Sampling and the Nature of Time Series." *Journal of the Royal Statistical Society,* Series B (January 1926): 1–69.

Zeff, S. A., *Forging Accounting Principles in Five Countries: A History and Analysis of Trends*. Arthur Andersen Lecture Series (Champaign, Ill: Stipes, 1927), 110–268.

"Profits: The Big Bath." *Newsweek* (July 27, 1970).